Sat May 18 '57

Went to Guggenheim's for dinner. Sat beside Mrs
Fair-Benton, which I figured might be painful, because
I had written some scathing things about her father &
brother spending tax-payers money abroad & was just
getting ready to write some more. It's going to be difficult
to write in the future. She told me how she had
influenced her father to come out against Franco &
how this influences her husband to be against McCarthy.
George lost a couple of papers over McCarthy & the Bill
Hearsts, she said. didn't like his stuff. She surprised
me by saying that the country would be better off under
Nixon than Ike. "People do change", she said. "And I
really think Nixon has changed." She said she had
heard him speak before a Toledo group of
extreme reactionaries, yet he kept a liberal line.
This is the second time I've heard this from people
who have deep convictions — the other from Bill
Fullbright at the Square Dance last week, Maybe I
howled for out to dinner.

Jack yesterday told me reported that
Nixon paid $25,000 cash for his new house. I got a
0,000 Rloan from Riggs at 4½% on which he pays $300 a mo.
I had to pay 6% the other day & am paying $500 a
mo on the $40,000 I borrowed from Riggs. Nixon still
hasnt sold his first house, so where did he
get the $25,000 cash?

Drew Pearson
DIARIES

≫≫≫≫≫≫ · ≪≪≪≪≪≪

1949-1959

Drew Pearson

DIARIES

1949-1959

Edited by Tyler Abell

HOLT, RINEHART AND WINSTON

New York   Chicago   San Francisco

Copyright © 1974 by The Estate of Drew Pearson

All rights reserved, including the right to reproduce this book
or portions thereof in any form.

Published simultaneously in Canada by Holt, Rinehart and
Winston of Canada, Limited.

Library of Congress Cataloging in Publication Data

Pearson, Drew, 1897–1969.
Diaries, 1949–1959.

1. Pearson, Drew, 1897–1969. 2. United States—
Politics and government—1945–1953. 3. United States—
Politics and government—1953–1961. I. Abell, Tyler, ed.
PN4874.P38A3 1974   070.4'092'4   72–78142
ISBN 0–03–001426–3

FIRST EDITION

Designer: M. M. Ahern
Printed in the United States of America

CONTENTS

ACKNOWLEDGMENTS

In editing the diaries, I am in debt to many people.

First, to Drew himself; without his confidence in me I would never have had the temerity to tackle the job.

My mother, Luvie Pearson, I thank for her willingness to proceed with the publication of material she would as soon have forgotten about.

To my wife, Bess, I owe a special debt for her patience and understanding, but I am also indebted to her for the ready assistance she provided as a sounding board and for her constructive suggestions.

Thanks, too, to Aaron Asher, Editorial Director of the General Books Department of Holt, Rinehart and Winston, who understood the full importance of the diaries and whose wise decisions have enabled us to preserve the substance and the thrust of the diaries. To Marian Wood, Senior Editor at Holt, my thanks for her help and criticism. In seeing this first volume through to completion, she tended to each of the endless details, arguing with me when changes were necessary.

A special medal of commendation is reserved for my secretary, Macie Nicolson, who carved time from her own schedule to help in making the book a reality. It was she who typed all the notes, double-checked them for factual accuracy, and stood valiantly by the Xerox machine for days at a time, reproducing all twenty-seven volumes of the original manuscript.

Many, many others helped, providing information I did not have, patiently reading and checking the manuscript. I mention only a few: Drew's sisters, Barbara Lange and Ellen Fogg; David Karr, Jack Anderson, Bill Neel, Opal Ginn, and Kay Webb from Drew's staff; Joseph Borkin and Ernest Cuneo, both old friends and trustees of the Drew Pearson Foundation.

This diary is not just the story of a man's life, it is also a history of our times. Begun in 1949 when he was fifty-one, the diary was kept— sometimes in more detail, sometimes in less—until Drew Pearson's death in 1969. As such, it forms a unique record of the people and events that made headlines and history during the past two decades.

Drew Pearson was the ultimate reporter, forever observant, with photographic mind poised. His interest in political, economic, and social affairs was formed early in his life and reached far beyond the borders of the United States. It afforded him a perspective that spanned America's transition from rural isolationism to technological giant and major world power. Equally, his working life paralleled the terms of ten Presidents. Few working journalists—and Drew Pearson was working on the day he died—had such firsthand knowledge of the changes in Presidential power that began with Franklin D. Roosevelt; fewer still had so intimate an acquaintance with the men who held that power.

It was luck that his chosen career coincided with one of the most interesting periods in world history, but it was more than luck that made him an integral part of that history. From the beginning, he was an active participant, going far beyond the traditions of journalism established by Lincoln Steffens and Ida Tarbell. For him, it was not enough to reveal the facts, one had also to be involved in actual policy-making, and the influence he exerted far surpassed that of a sideline observer. As an activist, he regularly put himself on the line; yet, though he did battle throughout his career, he made few lifelong enemies, for his alliances were built on a strong and abiding concern for the issues, and today's antagonist could be tomorrow's ally.

The diaries, begun at the height of his career, offer ample evidence of his involvements in setting or redirecting policy. They also demonstrate his remarkable ability to uncover the truth. His success in this respect was in part the result of an extensive network of sources— people who, disturbed by corruption or incompetence, trusted him to do something, as well as people in positions of power who joined him in his fights. But it was also the result of his extensive knowledge of world affairs, which, when combined with his instinct for news, made him first in print with countless headline stories .

As some men live to paint and others to accumulate wealth, Drew Pearson lived to communicate. And concomitant with the range of his interests and the extent of his experience and knowledge was a ready and effortless ability to do so. Little he wrote would win a literary prize and he was seldom carried to flights of poetic fancy. Words for him were rarely used merely for the sake of using them. Words were for communicating ideas and facts.

The sheer volume of words was staggering. There were thirty-seven years of daily columns, twenty of weekly broadcasts; there were eight books, dozens of magazine articles, thousands of lectures. Even before the regular column was begun, thousands of column-inches of print existed. And amid all this, there were uncounted pounds of personal letters and business correspondence.

And then there were the diaries. Figured conservatively, they come to almost three million words.

Drew Pearson was a working journalist and almost everything he wrote—his columns, his broadcasts, his books—was done at the typewriter. (His handwriting would win no penmanship prizes.) A particular idiosyncrasy was his attachment to a Smith-Corona portable model that had been discontinued long before World War II; such were his feelings for this model that he stockpiled used machines whenever he could find them. But as much as the typewriter was an extension of his hands, when it came to the diaries he preferred to dictate entries into a tape recorder. These were then transcribed by a secretary. (Among his papers were found some longhand notes that clearly had been intended as diary entries but had never been transcribed.)

I suspect that he only rarely reread a diary entry after it had been transcribed. Interestingly, no one on his staff or in the family had ever read the whole diary before his death—not even the transcribing secretaries since, over the years, they changed. Few people even knew of the existence of the diaries, though occasionally he would give an excerpt to a staff member for use as background in a story. Such loans in part explain some of the gaps in the diaries, although others were undoubtedly due to personal and work-load pressures that kept him too busy to record daily events.

There were times when he feared someone might steal the diaries, which is likely why he did not want their existence widely known. Of course, the family knew about them since he would, on occasion, send excerpts off to various members; mostly, these concerned his foreign trips. And, although he feigned modesty about them, characterizing the excerpts as "boring prattle," at some point he clearly decided that he was writing for history. In the last of his many wills, dated December 1962, he wrote:

"I ask my stepson, Tyler Abell, to serve as executor of my estate and that he be the sole editor of my diaries. In the publication of these diaries, I ask him to bear in mind that they should be edited not from the viewpoint of what will hurt people, but what might hurt the public good."

In editing the diary, I have tried to follow this injunction. But I have also sought to edit it in such a way as to bring out a true picture of the man and his work. And, for practical purposes—reasons of length —I have had to cut a considerable amount of material. Projected as three volumes, the published diaries will nonetheless include only a third of the actual material.

The determination of what to cut was made only after several very close readings of the material. In cases where repetitions existed— anecdotes, reminiscences, and the like—the decision was relatively easy. Far more difficult were those cases in which the material had to be weighed for importance, freshness, or general interest. Once I had completed my evaluation of what could be cut, I compared notes with the publisher. Where we agreed, the cut was made; where we disagreed, discussions ensued. By using this approach, I hope the integrity of the text has been retained.

At no time were changes made to improve the style or alter the true substance. But because the diary was dictated, there were transcription errors. These have been corrected. Here and there, somewhat garbled sentences found their way into the diary—the result, no doubt, of the dictating process. These, too, have been corrected.

In a few cases, names occurred in the text that would be unfamiliar to younger readers. When these were of passing mention, I took the liberty of inserting an occasional subordinate clause to correct the situation without disturbing the reader by an excessive use of brackets. In some instances, it was necessary to annotate an entry either because the person or event, though of importance, had not been fully explained in the text or because, as is not uncommon to a diary kept over so long a time span, major changes in position or duties had occurred. Some readers may find the annotations too sketchy, but a more detailed job might well have insulted the intelligence of the more sophisticated and informed reader. For this reason, I tried to take a middle line, with the result that the footnotes will not appear consistent to the purist. As an additional aid, an index has been devised in such a way that the reader may use it to locate the entry in which a particular person is identified. The reader is referred to the explanatory note to that index.

Finally, in a very few instances, the language was questioned by the publisher's lawyers. Interestingly, Drew was never intentionally malicious in the diary, never gratuitously rude. The questioned material was always linked to important and ongoing stories. In order to preserve these stories and satisfy the lawyers, some modifications in wording were made. Future scholars will have the opportunity to go to the original; I think—and it is my hope—they will conclude that all of my changes were minimal and within the realm of acceptable editing.

Here then is volume one—the years 1949 to 1959—as my stepfather intended and, as I hope I have done, edited "not from the viewpoint of what will hurt people, but what might hurt the public good."

TYLER ABELL

Washington, D.C.
Autumn 1973

BIOGRAPHICAL NOTE

Born on December 13, 1897, in Evanston, Illinois, Andrew Russell Pearson was the first of four children of Paul M. and Edna Wolfe Pearson. In 1902, the family moved to Pennsylvania, where Paul Pearson had accepted a position as professor of public speaking at Swarthmore College.

It was a time in America, before the advent of the mass media, when the Chautauqua served as both education and entertainment—a kind of traveling intellectual circus—and during the summers Paul Pearson ran a Chautauqua circuit that toured the eastern seaboard. At fourteen, Drew began working with his father's Chautauqua; he would continue to do so throughout his summers until he graduated from college, eventually becoming a lantern-slide operator and lecturer himself. Showmanship and an appetite for hard work thus gained were never lost.

In the spring of 1915, Drew graduated from Exeter Academy and the following fall he entered Swarthmore. A Phi Beta Kappa, he also managed to find time during his college years to be on the swimming and lacrosse teams and to edit the campus paper, *The Phoenix*. In 1919, as Valedictorian, his concern with world affairs manifested itself as he spoke to his graduating class of the need "to make the world safe for democracy." The phrase was, for him, more than mere rhetoric; indeed, it was to be a guiding theme throughout his life.

Despite his Quaker background, Drew had been keen to get into the war, seeing it from a Wilsonian perspective. The same principles that made him want to fight led him, on graduation, to seek a way to put his beliefs into practice. Like idealistic youth of every generation, he found a great lack of demand for his services, but eventually Quaker friends put him in touch with the American Friends Service Committee. In the late summer of 1919, he left for Serbia to do relief work under the aegis of the Committee.

For two years, Drew labored in Serbia, rebuilding homes and villages that had been destroyed during the war. He also began a diary, which he sent back to the family. That diary, not included here, is filled with graphic descriptions of his work and of the Serbian countryside. It is also filled with complaints about bureaucratic slowness and muddling as well as about late trains and unventilated sleeping accommodations—concerns that would persist in irritating him throughout his lifetime.

After returning to America, Drew taught industrial geography at the University of Pennsylvania. Then, in 1923, he set out across the United States, traveling by train and stopping along the way to sell local newspapers on the idea of buying the articles he would produce from his travels. In Seattle, he signed on as a seaman on a ship going to Japan. From Japan, he went on to China and Siberia, then to Australia, New Zealand, and India, filing dispatches all the way. He was heading home when he received a wire from an American newspaper syndicate commissioning a set of interviews with "Europe's Twelve Greatest Men." His dispatches had begun to bring him recognition.

Recognition—but not much money. Arriving home with the same amount of money with which he had started, Drew returned briefly to the academic world, this time as a lecturer in commercial geography at Columbia University. Despite the security of a salaried position, he couldn't get used to the academic life and, by 1925, he was again roaming the globe: In 1925, he was reporting on the anti-foreigner strikes in China; in 1927, he covered the Geneva Naval Conference; in 1928, he reported on the Sixth Pan American Conference, held in Havana, and accompanied Secretary of State Kellogg to Paris to witness the signing of the Kellogg-Briand Pact; in 1930, he attended the London Naval Conference.

On one of his trips to Washington, he was invited to the home of Mrs. Eleanor "Cissy" Patterson. That same evening, he was introduced to Cissy Patterson's daughter, Felicia Gizycki. In 1925, Felicia and Drew were married. Two years later, Felicia gave birth to a daughter, Ellen Cameron Pearson, but despite this welcome event, the marriage was fast deteriorating and in 1928 the couple were divorced. Drew would remarry in 1936, and that marriage, to Luvie Moore Abell, would endure.

Drew was permanently settled in Washington when, in 1929, the *Baltimore Sun* hired him as its Washington correspondent. He would hold this position until August 3, 1932; on that date, his editors—having discovered that he was co-author with Robert S. Allen of *Washington Merry-Go-Round* and *More Merry-Go-Round* (published anonymously in 1931 and 1932 respectively)—summarily fired him.

The next step—which from hindsight, and especially given the enormous popularity of both books, seems obvious—was a Merry-Go-Round column. In the fall of 1932, Drew secured a contract for himself and Bob Allen with the Scripps-Howard syndicate, United Features. The first "Merry-Go-Round" column appeared on November 17, 1932, and one of the first papers to subscribe to the column was Cissy Patterson's *Washington Times-Herald.* Indeed, Drew and Cissy had remained friends despite the divorce, and she was to make "Merry-Go-Round" her paper's favorite column.

As the Roosevelt administration took hold, making Washington the focus of national attention and the column the focus for inside news, syndication increased. Equally, so did the controversy that surrounded the column and its authors who, as liberal journalists, actively supported the New Deal programs. Although many editors would have preferred not to run the column in their papers, its popularity was such that they had no choice—certainly not if they faced the possibility of a competing paper picking it up. Drew's love-hate relationship with editors (and publishers), begun during his days on the *Sun,* would continue unabated to his death. As the column began to urge U.S. involvement in the looming war in Europe, its authors found it increasingly blue-penciled out of the *Times-Herald.* Finally, in 1941, the "Merry-Go-Round" was switched to *The Washington Post.* An infuriated Cissy Patterson launched a series of vitriolic articles about her former son-in-law and continued her own personal war against him until her death in 1948.

On July 8, 1940, Drew took on a new channel of communications, for on that day he made his first radio broadcast. Here was a means of reaching a vast audience, far larger than that reached by the column. Although television, with its network control of news broadcasting, would ultimately undermine the power of the independent newscaster, radio in the forties was enjoying a golden age and Drew Pearson was one of its feature attractions. A radio audience intent on getting the very latest news of the war tuned him in almost religiously.

By the war's end, Drew, then forty-seven, was traveling again. This time he was off to San Francisco to cover the UN Conference; then, in 1946, it was off to Paris to report on the Peace Conference. His deep belief in world peace and in making the world safe for democracy led him, in 1947, to organize the Friendship Train, a project that was to give him his greatest satisfaction.

Originally planned as a single train of a few cars that would travel coast-to-coast collecting gifts of food for the hungry of France and Italy, the project snowballed to ten trainloads that filled two ships. Here was the true convergence of Drew's natural flair for showmanship and his deep desire for peace and democracy. Believing that governments always favor special interests and convinced that people-to-people friendship was the only way to assure the peace, Drew managed to organize the Friendship Train without official governmental involvement. Its reception was such that, two years later, the people of France would reciprocate with the Merci Train, and Drew would proudly accompany it across the country.

As the diaries open in January of 1949, Drew is fifty-one years old, an established and respected—though sometimes cussed at—professional. Though the next twenty years would see a diminishment of his overall impact as the television networks pushed him off the air, there would be no corresponding diminishment of his journalistic abilities and, indeed, the column would remain as vital as ever right to the end. The diaries that follow record the major events of those two decades. But they also record the man: battling with editors and publishers, pursuing world peace, attacking corruption and demagoguery, protecting the public interest against those in power who would abuse their trust.

1949

January 1: Mr. Karr [David Karr, chief leg man on the staff] insists that I keep a diary. I don't know how long it will last, but this is the beginning of my New Year's resolution.

The beginning of 1949 was uneventful other than that I saw the New Year in in bed. Luvie [Mrs. Pearson] was sick, and I came home early from a party given by Abe Spanel, who flattered me by hoping that my Lee Hat radio contract would be defaulted so that his International Latex could take over as sponsor of the program.

Dinner New Year's Day, 5 P.M., with the Jim Reynoldses. Cy Ching, the labor mediator, told of his fears of stopping the New York tugboat workers' strike. The day before he informed the strike leaders that if they didn't postpone: "I'll bring the full force of the federal government into play." "What will you do?" the strikers asked. "I'll tell you at 4 P.M.," replied Cy. The fact is, he confided, that he didn't know. He breathed a big sigh of relief when they postponed. All of which led to a discussion of democracy. Three hundred tugboat workers, plus one hundred tugboat companies, Cy pointed out, could penalize twelve million people living in and around New York—which is not democracy. During the war, Winston Churchill told Ching: "The most important thing we must do is not reveal how weak democracy is."

Jerry Doyle, former counsel for the National Labor Relations Board and one of the authors of the Taft-Hartley Act, pointed out that there was no power on earth to stop John L. Lewis and his United Mine Workers if Lewis wanted to buck the government. With the maritime strikes, he pointed out, the Navy could always unload ships or man ships, but you couldn't get 400,000 men to go into the mines.

"We are opposed to monopoly in this country," added Ching,

"but the real fact is that the coal operators and the miners' union have the power to tax the entire nation. Their levy of twenty cents a ton for a welfare fund is actually an excess tax for the benefit of one group. The railroads have the same welfare provision and the same tax. Social Security should be for the benefit of all, not for any one group or two groups. If John L. Lewis should thumb his nose at the government when an injunction is declared against him, then democracy would fall. The only solution may be nationalization of the mines—which is something neither John L. Lewis nor the rest of us want."

Jerry Doyle argued that compulsory arbitration might also be the solution. The Taft-Hartley Act provides no final solution—merely intermediary steps before final show-down strikes.

Cy thinks that John L. will probably call a strike this winter. The small coal mines are already beginning to close down because they can't stand the competition. During the war any kind of cheap-grade coal could be sold, but now consumers are getting choosy. John will probably call a strike in order to help out the small companies and even up production.

January 3:   Lunch with former Interior Secretary Ickes. His column contract expires March 31, and the *New York Post* isn't enthusiastic about renewing. He asked my advice about dropping the column. The old man seems a little discouraged that he hasn't turned out to be much of a columnist. I couldn't help telling him one reason was that he spurned my advice in the first place and went with *The Post.* It never pays for a liberal to work with a liberal organization. The Bell Syndicate, a conservative outfit, would have been better. Also he spread himself too thin. If I saved the best part of my material for books and magazines I wouldn't have much of a column either. I told him to give his best reminiscences and his best experiences from the Roosevelt days to his column and let the books and magazines take care of themselves.

Ickes also pulled out confidential hearings of the Ferguson Committee [Senate Committee on Expenditures in the Executive Departments] regarding his successor as Secretary of the Interior, Julius Krug. He had the expense account of a lobbyist for Howard Hughes, and the girls he had supplied for Krug and Governor Mon Wallgren of Washington. Ickes wasn't sure whether Krug rated the $200 girls or the $75 ones. When Krug was hauled up before the Ferguson Committee, he threw up his hands and said, "If you publish this, I'll have to resign."

Most interesting part to me was that while Krug was being supplied with the girls, he also supplied his wife with $10 nylons, also paid for by the Hughes lobbyist. Ickes isn't going to publish this.

However, he would like to publish something about Krug's textile rayon mill near Knoxville, Tennessee. Krug acquired 10 percent in the Brookside Mills in 1946 when he was out of the government. He found a new purchaser. His commission was supposed to be $100,000, but he took it out in 10-percent stock interest. Later the owners wanted to sell and Krug raised enough money to buy them out together with his partner, a New York lawyer named Epstein. Most interesting part of the deal was that Krug borrowed $700,000 under a contract by which he is not obligated to repay any part of the loan if it defaults (I'd like to borrow money this way myself). Krug's investment is practically nil. The mill is now worth about two million. I talked to Krug myself about this some months ago, and he had a fairly plausible excuse, though at that time I didn't know about the remarkable loan he had made. Chief factor in his favor is that the Ferguson Committee, if they could have got anything on him, undoubtedly would have brought it out. William Rogers, counsel for the Ferguson Committee, wants to be appointed to the Federal Trade Commission.

Talked to Fitzpatrick, the attorney for Miss Helen Campbell, regarding her indictment along with Parnell Thomas.* He is a reasonably smart lawyer though I think he is chiefly interested in making a grandstand jury plea for publicity reasons. I suggested that he plead *nolo contendere*, but he demurred.

Talked to District Attorney Morris Fay. Morrie says that this case was rushed through in record time so the FBI didn't get a chance to investigate everything. I gave them some new leads which they are following, particularly the case of a Negro politician in New Jersey who has helped to elect Thomas and who is employed on the Un-American Activities Committee with no apparent duties. Also a man who draws a salary of $8,000 from the Un-American Committee, lives in Lyndhurst, N.J., but apparently does no work. The suspicion is he is kicking back. The FBI has now looked over all of Thomas's bank accounts and finds he made about $7,500 from magazine articles since he became

---

*Helen Campbell was Congressman J. Parnell Thomas's (R-N.J.) confidential secretary. It was she who brought the story of the staff kickbacks to Drew Pearson. The columns that followed led to the Congressman's indictment.—ED.

chairman of the committee about three years ago. Also he received about $4,000 for expense vouchers. He was usually so hard up that he collected the money from the committee before he took a trip. Parnell also received approximately $7,000 in staff kickbacks. The Un-American Activities Committee refused to let the FBI see its files. Now that the Democrats have taken over, they may be available. Parnell asked Judge Schweinhaut for an indefinite delay on the ground the trial would mean his death. Schweinhaut agreed to get a report from Walter Reed Hospital. Apparently Thomas forgot that he called Harry Dexter White as a witness, despite warnings that it might mean White's death. One week afterward White died.

It developed that when Judge Schweinhaut was a baby he was pushed around in his carriage by Helen Campbell, who will now appear before him as a defendant.

January 4:   Carlos Davila,* together with the Chilean Ambassador, General and Mrs. Bob Ginsburgh, and several others came to dinner. Bob, who served under MacArthur, points out that the older MacArthur gets the more the Japs revere him, so MacArthur may never be removed as our Military Governor there.

Thousands of Japanese and GI's come down to his office to watch him leave every day at 2 P.M. I pointed out that whether MacArthur had done a good job or not couldn't be ascertained because of his heavy censorship. Also MacArthur, originally doing a good job of getting rid of the *Zaibatsu* (war corporations) has now relaxed. "The Army always tends to play with big business," remarked Bob. "The Army wants order and big business gives them order. That's the reason for the cooperation with the cartels in Germany."

Davila thinks one saving factor in Argentina is the rivalry between Perón and Evita. Evita is now almost more powerful than he. She controls the labor unions and has a tremendous following with the people. The strange thing about Perón is that, though a dictator, he has the masses with him—in fact is popular with the masses in other Latin American countries, largely because Argentine labor backs him.

*Davila, a former newspaperman and lawyer in Chile, had served briefly as that country's President. In 1949, he was a member of the U.N. Economic and Social Council. Davila's friendship with Drew Pearson was longstanding and had been cemented during his service as Chile's Ambassador to the United States.—ED.

Davila thinks we should have backed Chile in a war against Perón in 1944 and thus got rid of him. Now he is taking over the continent. Davila doesn't agree with my argument that war never cures anything —only leaves more headaches in its wake. The Ambassador feels war with Russia would be much better now than later. "We forget that Russia's operations are virtual acts of war," he claimed. "If Hitler had penetrated Hungary, Czechoslovakia, Rumania, Bulgaria, the way Russia has, Britain would have fought long ago. But Britain is weak now, while the United States vacillates." Davila has just written a book pointing to the way we have neglected Latin America while building up Europe—an area which is certain to fall to Russia. When that time comes Russia will reap rebuilt factories and all other advantages of the Marshall Plan. I remember that in 1936 I tried to sell Under Secretary of State Sumner Welles on the importance of a two-billion dollar lend-lease program to Latin America to develop South American re- sources and promote closer relations. The only man who favored the idea at that time was John L. Lewis, who actually talked to Roosevelt about it—without success.

A Colonel Woodall came in to see me about the way we are treating Korea as a puppet. Actually Moscow's broadcasts accusing us of making a puppet of Korea are correct. I can't help but wonder how we can keep on meddling with so many different parts of the world— or perhaps I am coming around to Senator Taft's view on isolation.

January 5:   Invited the 101 new Congressmen to a reception at the Carlton Hotel. Mrs. Pearson did not favor the idea. I also was skeptical but it turned out all right. They really had a good time and got acquainted. Senator Wherry, of Nebraska, whom I have ribbed unmer- cifully for a couple of years as the "Merry Mortician," arrived and seemed very human. Ex-Speaker Joe Martin came with the new Sena- tor from Maine, Margaret Chase Smith, who embraced Sam Rayburn. Sam came reasonably on time and stood in the receiving line despite many protestations in advance that he wasn't going to do any such thing. However, he seemed to enjoy it once he got there.

The new Congress looks good. There are dozens of youngsters, some a little timid, hardly knowing what it's all about, but who seem to be determined to avoid the pitfalls of the Eightieth Congress. It is a healthy cross-section of the U.S.A. Most of the new Senators also arrived, and they look, if anything, even better. Not since the early days of the New Deal has there been such a group of youngsters elected on a clear-cut liberal platform.

January 10:   Have fallen behind with Mr. Karr's diary.

Lunched with Harold Ickes, who saw Truman last week. Truman was cordial, but Ickes still thinks that he hasn't forgiven him for all the names Ickes once called him. Truman waited two months after the campaign to invite him in, meanwhile having seen every Tom, Dick, and Harry in the U.S.A.

Ickes is pleased over the Dean Acheson appointment as Secretary of State. He and Dean used to ride to work together during gasoline rationing. They got to know each other well. Ickes thinks Dean is a man of great ability, usually right ideas, but not a battler for his convictions.

Ickes was interested in the fact that Dean had once tried to get me indicted for criticism of the Supreme Court (at the instance of Justice Frankfurter), and asked me how Dean and I happened to cool off. Frankly, I don't know the answer. When I first came to Washington, Dean was one of my most intimate friends. I used to visit his farm almost every weekend and he spent part of the summers, when Alice was away, living in my house. I told Ickes that the answer probably was that when a man reaches high position, he always faces the choice of absorption in his duties or the retention of his friends. I have probably let some of my old friends drift by the wayside as a result of my increasing chores of late; and in Dean's case, having known him so well, I haven't liked to intrude on his time unless I was invited.

Had an interesting talk with Senator Elbert Thomas of Utah who is still a little hurt because people confuse him with Senator Elmer Thomas of Oklahoma. I assured him that people don't make that mistake, but he says *The New York Times* did only last Saturday. Thomas is irked over the helter-skelter leaders of the Democrats. Senate Majority Leader Scott Lucas only today announced that the Taft Labor Act would not be repealed, but a new "one-package" bill containing substitute provisions for Taft-Hartley would be passed. This is directly contrary to what Thomas, chairman of the labor committee, has already introduced. "Taft would never make a statement like that without consulting his committee chairman," said Thomas. "But our leaders wander all over the lot."

Thomas revealed what I always suspected but never knew definitely, that when he was chairman of the Military Affairs Committee during the war, all sorts of pressure were put on him to pass the bill creating five-star generals and admirals. "Here was the war not yet over," said Thomas, "yet these people demanded a new set of generals and admirals with permanent retirement of $17,500—more than a Cabinet officer. You have no idea of the pressure that was put on me at that time—far more important, it seemed, than winning the war."

January 13:   Louis Johnson,* believe it or not, took the bit in his teeth and went to see Truman regarding Secretary of Defense Forrestal. He told Truman that Marquis Childs had reported in his column that he, Johnson, was waging a vendetta against Forrestal, and he wanted Truman to know that this was not the case. This touched Truman off in a diatribe against Forrestal in which he resorted to Missouri mule-team language, calling him a "God-damn Wall Street bastard" and other names too foul to print. He said he wasn't going to tolerate Forrestal around very long, but that the "son of a bitch" came in and took "advantage of me and put me on the spot." I suspect this is partially true.

Truman hates to fire anyone, as witness the fact that he got Steve Early to call up Francis Biddle and fire Biddle as Attorney General.

As Louis was about to leave, Truman said, "Now, about this job of Secretary of Defense. . . ." Louis says that he held up his hand and said: "Mr. President. I don't want to talk about that or anything else. You don't owe me anything. I just want to tell you some time how Forrestal tried to cut your throat during the campaign."

Secretary of the Treasury John Snyder has been drinking heavily again. He would like to get out and away, but he doesn't want to retreat under fire. There's no fire on him now. Hope Winchell doesn't go after him before John can turn in his resignation. I told the Bank of America's Mario Giannini that I would write a laudatory story about the bank if he would just give John Snyder a job and get him out of the Treasury.

January 14:   Dined with the Cafritzes. I had a chance to look at the seating list while Luvie was putting away her wraps and knew we were in for a surprise. Luvie, however, didn't. When she saw Senator

*Johnson, cofounder of the law firm of Steptoe and Johnson, had briefly served under Roosevelt as Assistant Secretary for War. A major fund-raiser for Truman's 1948 campaign, Johnson felt he should be rewarded by being named Secretary of Defense. —Ed.

Brewster of Maine and Mrs. Brewster, her face dropped a mile long. As luck would have it, I got euchred off to one side of Mrs. Brewster. She was quite charming. So was the Senator.

Later when Mrs. Cafritz, as usual, called on her guests for speeches, the Senator, believe it or not, paid tribute to the Friendship Train and me.* Later on we had quite a talk, particularly about Forrestal. He recalled that the hearings he had held on Arabian Oil were damning regarding Forrestal and suggested that the New York lawsuit [against the Arabian American Oil Company] brought by Jim Moffett (formerly of Standard Oil of New Jersey) would go to trial in New York soon and reveal some more dynamite.

Only reference Brewster made to the many digs I have taken at him was that: "To say I was a pro-Dewey man was the unkindest cut of all." He is right. Brewster has always been a consistent and vigorous Taft man. How the pro-Dewey reference got into the column I haven't the vaguest idea. But it did.

January 16:   George Bowden† came for dinner. He doesn't like Dean Acheson's appointment; says Dean has a fine legal mind and is a great advocate, but doesn't know how to organize; is a sloppy executive; made sneering remarks in meetings about Latin Americans. Since the Latins, he said, were going to be with us anyway, why bother to help them? His jokes were repeated afterward at lunch. If the Latins had heard them, it would have been disastrous.

In 1944 Bowden was asked to review the proposed Winant agreement drawn up in London by our Ambassador John G. Winant whereby the British could resell lend-lease goods abroad. The British saw the war coming to an end and wanted to get some goods on hand to resume world trade. They asked us for permission to sell lend-lease goods, subject to a review by a three-man board. Bowden was supposed to head this board. However, when he reviewed the lend-lease situation, he declined. Acheson, then Assistant Secretary of State in charge of economic affairs, had let it get into a hopeless snarl. The British were already importing via lend-lease all sorts of purely peacetime goods for

---

*The Friendship Train, conceived and managed by Pearson in 1947, had collected contributions of food for war-ravaged France and Italy.—ED.

†A long-term friend of Drew Pearson, Bowden was a Chicago tax lawyer active in the Democratic Party. During World War II, he had been General Bill Donovan's deputy in OSS.—ED.

trade. Bowden wrote a memo to Roosevelt regarding the whole matter and later got word from the White House that the agreement would not be signed. It wasn't.

Relative to Truman and his elephant's mind regarding personalities: In 1944 at the Chicago convention, Democratic bosses Ed Flynn of the Bronx and Ed Kelly of Chicago came to CIO chief Phil Murray at the Blackstone Hotel to tell him Truman couldn't get the Vice Presidential nomination. It was the midnight after Senator Jackson of Indiana had gaveled the convention to adjournment, just as the Henry Wallace ranks (led by Dave Karr) were staging a tremendous demonstration. Flynn and Kelly said that while Truman could not win and they were ready to take Wallace, they did not want to break the news to Truman, so asked Phil Murray to do it. Murray telephoned Truman and asked him to come up to his room. Truman did so. As he came in the door, however, he said, "I know what you want me to do, and I'm not going to do it. There is no use talking about it. I am not going to withdraw."

After Truman became President, Murray called to pay his respects and the minute he entered the White House Truman said: "Do you remember that night at the Blackstone Hotel when you told me I couldn't win? You never expected me to be President, did you? But here I am. I made it in spite of you." Murray didn't go back to the White House for a couple of years. In fact, he never has asked to see Truman during the nearly four years since that time. Truman has sent for him occasionally. Whenever Truman has sent for him he always indirectly refers to the Chicago incident. Frequently he has said: "I know you are against me."

Truman's inability to forget a personal grudge is of course one of the reasons for some of his difficulty drafting good men.

Dean Acheson, according to George, got his job as Under Secretary wholly because of Ed Pauley. Truman wanted to appoint Ed Pauley as Under Secretary of State under Jimmie Byrnes. When Byrnes heard of this he got Acheson on the long-distance telephone at Saranac, New York, and demanded that he come back to take the Under Secretaryship.

I had a visit with Helen Duggan. She is convinced that Larry did not jump.* His back had not recovered from his recent operation and

---

*On December 20, 1948, shortly after preliminary FBI questioning on possible Communist activities, Laurence Duggan fell to his death.—ED.

he had been suffering from paroxysms of pain and semi-fainting spells. He was in remarkably good spirits—as everyone else has testified. She has borne up remarkably well.

January 18:   Air Secretary Symington's office called to say that Bob Ginsburgh's promotion to brigadier general had struck a snag—believe it or not from Clint Anderson. Anderson, who ran against Pat Hurley for the Senate in New Mexico, discovered that Ginsburgh had been Hurley's ghost-writer seventeen years ago. I called Anderson and got him to withdraw his objection. He told me that the new Senator from Illinois, Paul Douglas, was objecting to Ginsburgh because Ginsburgh had spearheaded the MacArthur for President Clubs.

Nothing could have been more preposterous. I didn't like to tell him how I knew Ginsburgh felt about the politics of both Hurley and MacArthur. Ginsburgh has been recommended for promotion five times but was always blocked by some of his brass-hat enemies. Now he was almost blocked by the new liberal members of the Senate.

Ginsburgh told me later that he had specifically asked that he not do any publicity work or ghost-writing for MacArthur. His wish was granted until the end of the war, following which he served for two weeks with MacArthur's publicity staff. Then Bob Patterson, Secretary of War, came through Japan and requisitioned him away from MacArthur. He has been in Washington ever since.

January 19:   Truman is boiling mad over my broadcast on Forrestal. He has told a friend: "Pearson and Winchell are too big for their breeches. We are going to have to have a showdown as to who is running this country—me or them—and the showdown had better come now than later."

Central Intelligence has been ordered to make a painstaking investigation of me, Winchell, Cuneo, and Karr. They have already turned up some amusing, alleged facts including one which will not amuse Walter—namely, that although his audience is much greater than mine, my influence is much greater than his. They have also dug up the claim and are reporting it as fact that I spent $250,000 a year to buy news, including large payments to certain Senators and Congressmen. They have requisitioned copies of my income tax, Winchell's, Cuneo's, Karr's, et al. It should be a nice report. Interesting thing is, if I can find out what Central Intelligence is doing, what can the Russians find out?*

January 20: Truman was inaugurated thirty-second President of the United States and enjoyed every minute of it. All the people who came to watch him did not enjoy it as much as he, though many of them did. His swearing-in ceremony lacked dignity and good taste. He was twenty minutes late appearing on the rostrum, then stood and smirked while waiting for various stage props to be brought in, Barkley to be sworn in as Vice President, two clergy to deliver prayers—one of them unforgivably long. (It sounded as if he was being inaugurated—not Truman.) A good actor—and the President has to be a good actor—times his exits and gets his stage-work done so that he doesn't play second fiddle to a lot of people who are supposed to do nothing but make sure that the inauguration runs smoothly. In a way, his swearing-in ceremony was like Truman's administration in the past and a portent of what it will be in the future—nice, mediocre, and bungling. Roosevelt, despite the fact that he couldn't walk, appeared with great dignity, took the oath of office, gave his speech, and left. There were no waits, no false moves, no bad timing.

The parade was similar, though this wasn't entirely Truman's fault. The military were the forefront, the Negro groups, the labor unions—which elected Truman—trailing along in the rear. Never have I seen such a show of military might in any Presidential inauguration ceremony. The three secretaries of Air, Army, and Navy, to say nothing of the Secretary of Defense himself, all had to have their troops trailing behind. Meanwhile thousands of other people shivered and waited. Secretary of the Army "Dumbo" Royall was smart. He brought Eisenhower along in the same car to make sure he got some applause, otherwise there might have been boos.

Alben Barkley seemed to have the best time of all. He clapped for

---

*On his January 16th broadcast, Drew Pearson said Forrestal would have been dropped from the Cabinet had not Walter Winchell forecast the step. He also retold an alleged incident charging Forrestal with cowardice during a jewel robbery involving Mrs. Forrestal. In response, Forrestal had his lawyers draw up a libel complaint. Ernest Cuneo, a New York lawyer with close White House ties during the New Deal, had for several years acted as ghost-writer and counsel for Winchell. Despite differences between the two columnists, Ernest Cuneo and Drew Pearson were life-long friends. —ED.

every little girl, every Indian, every float, everyone who took some effort to put on a good show as they passed. Truman clapped occasionally and smiled and doffed his hat affably. Only ones he cold-shouldered were Governor Strom Thurmond of South Carolina and Governor Talmadge of Georgia. When both passed, he deliberately looked the other way. General Vaughan, Truman's military aide, kept tugging at the President's coat sleeve trying to get him to go to the Mellon Art Gallery, but Truman stayed on until the last calliope trundled down the Avenue.

State Senator George Luckey of California supplied one important equestrian touch when he rode at the head of the California Sheriff's Posse, wearing a ten-gallon Lee hat. D. Karr scampered down the Avenue to meet him with another Lee hat, the same shape and size, which George proceeded to hand to the President. The photographers made the most of it. I am still wondering what Truman said when he saw the label inside.

Most comic figure at the inaugural—but a pathetic one—was Jim Farley, the Democrat's most famous Chairman, looking especially tall and especially out of place in a high silk topper. There was no place to go. There was no seat for him with the Senate, Cabinet, or other dignitaries. He had to sit down with the newspapermen, the Senators' wives, and other relative hoi polloi.

January 21:   Bob Hannegan [former Democratic National Committee Chairman] telephoned. He is much happier about Truman. Truman has now adopted all the things Hannegan used to argue for but which John Snyder opposed—social security, minimum wages, public housing, etc. Truman never believed in them then. Now he is 100 percent for them. Before, Hannegan says, Truman had Roosevelt men around him. Now he has adopted Roosevelt policies without the Roosevelt men. This may be one reason: he now feels that they are his policies, not Roosevelt's. And Bob is convinced he will try to carry them out.

The McGrath party wound up the inaugural with the wildest pandemonium of all. Drunken Democrats everywhere. Young men in corners relinquishing their food. Old ladies kissing youngsters. The Shoreham hastily changing the carpets to prepare for the Kentucky Society Dance. Too much liquor spilled on the floor.

Truman came in and made a speech which almost nobody heard because there was no loudspeaker. "Looks like some of the stiffs from

Battery D had been here," he said. Battery D [Truman's old World War I unit] didn't throw plates this time but Truman was probably right. Most of them faded away from their choice seats in the reviewing stand before the parade was over.

January 22: Town is practically empty of visiting Democrats—thank God!

January 23: Randolph Paul called up in high dudgeon right after the broadcast. Wanted to see me immediately. He said that at 6:15 the Patterson will squabble was settled when suddenly my broadcast came over the air reporting that the Justice Department would investigate and probably prosecute a Washington attorney (Louis Caldwell) for withholding early copies of the will. Louis was white and shaky. He said there could be no settlement now. People would think they had settled in order to get out of indictment. I told Randolph to cheer up, that the $400,000 had not yet slipped through his fingers.*

January 24: Mrs. Gifford Pinchot, her hair as red as ever, came to lunch. She had just come back from Greece, where things are going from bad to worse. The Peloponnesus, south of Athens, and 200 or more miles from the Yugoslav-Albanian borders, is now seething with revolt. Government gendarmes and post-office and telegraph service are all withdrawn. If the gendarmes had remained they would have been murdered. This is an area which was favorable to the government before the United States took over. In other words, American aid to Greece has been one prolonged miserable botch. Part of this is due to American personnel, part to our refusal to crack down on Greek officials. Officially we have given amnesty to political prisoners, but once they surrender they are charged with new crimes such as the murder of someone during the war. Actually many of them did kill collaborationists during the war. They were urged to do so by American and British radio and leaflets dropped over Greece, but now some of the

---

*Eleanor Medill (Cissy) Patterson, editor, publisher, and owner of the Washington *Times-Herald*, had died on July 24, 1948. Her daughter Felicia, who had been married to Drew in the 1920s, engaged Randolph Paul to break the will, which left the paper to its key employees and most of the remaining estate to charity. He had arrived at a tentative settlement of $400,000 outright payment. Louis G. Caldwell, chief counsel for the *Times-Herald*, represented the estate.—ED.

collaborators are in power and the guerrilla fighters are taking the rap.

Only remedy for Greece would be for Truman to send a special envoy to tell the King we are going to pull out. If he told the King in strict confidence it would go to the Cabinet members immediately. Then there might be a new election, a new parliament, and a change in Greece. Otherwise only hope for the United States is to leave.

Actually with new, modern, long-range planes, Greece has lost its strategic importance. We can fly over Greece from North Africa in a couple of hours. It was as usual the British who mousetrapped us into Greece. They scared Truman by threatening to withdraw. However, Roosevelt was never scared—though Churchill tried it several times.

January 25:   One stumbling block in the Patterson will case is that the twenty-one packing cases of Cissy's papers are supposed to go to Felicia and the *Times-Herald* bunch are afraid she will turn them over to me. They think I am going to expose Cissy—as if I didn't have enough to do exposing people who are alive.* Anyway they want the stipulation that they, not Felicia, will get her mother's papers. Her lawyers are willing to agree to burn them.

January 26:   Patterson will finally settled. Felicia finally gets about $400,000 tax free with no interest in the *Times-Herald* and no allowance of $25,000 a year. It is a bad deal for her but a good one considering the fact that she wasn't willing to go through with it anyway. The lawyers get $50,000. If she had stuck it out and continued the fight, she could have set the will aside completely. Some of the evidence was devastating. It looks more and more to me as if Porter, Cissy's bookkeeper, was either murdered or hounded into suicide. Most sensational deposition of all was given by Mrs. Campbell, the housekeeper, who admitted that, after putting Porter into a taxi to drive to West Virginia, she had gone to his apartment with a key and Eve Lindberg, Mrs. Patterson's maid. They ransacked the apartment and took out Porter's canceled checks and bank statements. This could only have been for one of two reasons: (1) Porter, a pansy, had been paying off to some young men around town; (2) and probably more important, Porter was

---

*Drew Pearson did not break with his former mother-in-law over his divorce from Felicia; in fact, she helped start his column. When he moved the "Merry-Go-Round" from her *Times-Herald* to *The Washington Post,* their feud began. It lasted until she died.—ED.

the only one who knew about Shelton's chicanery. He had been milking the tail for some time, including *Times-Herald* newsprint diverted to his own printing plant. Unquestionably, Mrs. Campbell persuaded Porter to leave town, then lifted the evidence out of his apartment. She admitted part of this in a sworn deposition.

Also important is the fact that the Washington *Times-Herald* editor, Mike Flynn, apparently was able to get his brother-in-law, D.C. Police Chief Barrett, to send two Washington police to Clarksburg, West Virginia, the same night that Porter fell out of the window—or was pushed. It was they who took over Porter's papers and arranged the story given out to the press by the West Virginia police. Harry Costello claims that when Porter hit the ground one side of his face—the side which did not strike the ground—was bruised from an apparent beating. Later Porter's body was cremated and his cousin who arrived to see the body was kept in Evie Robert's apartment at the Mayflower while the cremation was taking place. Apparently they were in an awful hurry to get the body out of the way.*

January 30:   Got a lot of kickbacks on my broadcast. Father Coughlin was up in arms over Dr. Gariepy, who claims he collected $68,000 from Coughlin for alienation of Mrs. Gariepy.†

January 31:   Saw Attorney General Tom Clark. Secretary Forrestal came in to see him two weeks ago about my broadcast on Mrs. Forrestal's jewelry robbery. "He was," to quote the Attorney General, "as nervous as a whore in church." "I told him," Clark said, "to forget about suing and to sit down and talk it over with you. Meanwhile, I said I would look over your broadcast. However, the girls in the office thought it was Winchell's broadcast, not yours, and they sent for it. Cuneo came in here all on fire, wanted to know what they were going to do to Walter. He didn't know it was your broadcast we really wanted.

---

*William C. Shelton, general manager, and Michael W. Flynn, managing editor, were two of seven *Times-Herald* executives who inherited the paper under the terms of the disputed will. Harry Costello occasionally did investigative work for Drew.—ED.

†In his broadcast, Drew Pearson had charged that Coughlin, the right-wing radio priest of the thirties, had given the money to Dr. Bernard F. Gariepy as a pay-off for the priest's attentions to Mrs. Gariepy. This entry marks the beginning of a long legal struggle that was to include both tax and libel actions. En route, considerable pressure would be brought to bear by Coughlin's supporters to get Drew Pearson off the radio. —ED.

Last Cabinet meeting I asked Forrestal: 'What did you decide about the Pearson matter?' He said Tom Corcoran had vetoed it, that it wouldn't do any good."

I knew Corcoran was running Forrestal's campaign to stay in office but I didn't know that he was handling every detail including how he should or should not treat the press.

February 2:   The SS *Magellan* arrived on time. Forty-nine "40 and 8" boxcars are home. Stuart Symington's airplanes carried out his promise with a terrific salute. We were worried about the jet planes, however. They only had fuel for thirty-five minutes, and the ship was a little late. None of them fell in the Bay, however. The French committee was a little irked that the cameramen concentrated on Grover Whalen and the French Consul. I don't blame them. After all, it's the French committee that has done all the work—not the French government. A certain amount of friction is developing inside the French committee.*

February 3:   We paraded up Broadway. This is only the second time I've gone up New York City's famous canyon in a parade tendered to distinguished visitors. Newsmen seemed to think it was one of the best. Grover Whalen pronounced it better than the reception given to Lindbergh. At any rate, our French friends were impressed; that is important.

Already some of the Frenchmen are saying they cannot visit the forty-eight states with the boxcars.

The ceremonies at City Hall were impressive. Mayor O'Dwyer made an excellent speech but nearly bowled me over by presenting me with a scroll from the City of New York for distinguished service. It was a most magnanimous gesture, but I couldn't help wish that the French, rather than I, had received the honor.

Mrs. Roosevelt was present at the luncheon given by the city in honor of the French committee. This was the highlight of their day. It touched them deeply to think she should take time out to attend a

---

*As a gesture of appreciation for the Friendship Train, a French citizens' committee organized the *Merci* Train—forty-nine boxcars containing gifts to the American people of every state plus the District of Columbia. From February 2 to 22, the train traveled across the country, and Drew Pearson was with it for most of the trip.—ED.

long and formal luncheon. She spoke briefly and in French. Afterward several Frenchmen showed me copies of her autograph as if it was the most sacred thing they owned. I couldn't help contrasting Mrs. Roosevelt's graciousness with General Eisenhower's refusal even to serve on the committee or to allow his name to be used. He took plenty of time to appear before Congressional committees urging more money for armament, but not five minutes to build friendship between peoples.

February 4: Back to Washington on the midnight sleeper. Carried out my threat to picket the Argentine Embassy in protest against General Vaughan's receiving a medal from President Perón of Argentina. Frankly, I couldn't recognize many of the guests, though some of them stopped to shake hands. A few, such as Brigadier General Wallace Graham, the special physician to Harry Truman, ducked in the door as if they were running from Satan. Most genial was the Yugoslav military attaché, who stopped to shake hands and even gave me his name. I spoke to him in Serbian.

February 5: I missed start of the first Gratitude Train. It's about the third train I have missed in my life.

Philadelphia had a tremendous reception, and I personally had a good time. Too many speeches, however, and the French delegation was a little tired. The Pennsylvania had trouble switching the boxcar just outside of Philadelphia.

February 6: Had special plane waiting for de la Vasselais to take him to the ceremony at Lancaster, Pennsylvania. My attorney, John Donovan, went up to his room at the Mayflower, but the Commandant refused to get out of bed. John flew alone to Lancaster where they corralled a visiting French bride and had a very nice ceremony.

Vice President Barkley, together with Senators Vandenberg and Tom Connally, came down to the Fourteenth Street Railroad Yards for the ceremony welcoming the French train. Tom Clark, Senator McGrath, and various others were also present. I was a very nervous master of ceremonies. I never like to speak in my home town. However, things went off fairly well. Barkley made a very touc ng impromptu address in which he so aptly said that in the French boxcars was the heart of France. Vandenberg was equally good. As Tom Connally cut the red, white, and blue ribbon on the door of the D.C. car, Vandenberg remarked to Barkley in a loud whisper: "I wonder if that's the first time Tom ever broke into a boxcar?"

M. Junot wanted to speak. I ruled him out and put in the French railway workers on the ground that Junot is merely a government man and the government came in to take the bows at the last minute.

There is something impressive about the way our elder statesmen cooperate in things of this kind. Barkley, Vandenberg, and Connally represent opposite sides of a lot of things. However, they are personally good friends and do a great job of representing their country on such occasions.

The Association of American Railroads gave a reception for the French after the ceremony. Very fine party. I got there after the broadcast. Nearly wore out my hand shaking hands.

Shouldn't have gone to the dinner at the French Embassy afterward, but I did. After the dinner, we had a meeting of the French committee, and I dropped a hint that since de la Vasselais wasn't able to go in the private plane we had arranged for him this morning, he wouldn't go anywhere else on the trip. I don't believe he fully appreciated this at the time, but the other Frenchmen did. They are all very cooperative now.

I learned by accident that Ambassador Bonnet is paying traveling expenses of some of the French people out of his own pocket. I hope he doesn't get stuck for as much as I am. Dave Karr figures I will be out about $5,000.

February 7:   Rain. Up at 6:30 to catch the special train to Richmond. Governor Tuck of Virginia was supposed to be aboard but didn't show. The Marines gave us a great welcome. Major General Lemuel Shepherd in command. I couldn't help wondering what I had written about him in the past. I have a sneaking suspicion I've taken him over the hurdles for airplane junketing.

The receptions get better at the smaller towns. A fine reception at Fredericksburg, Virginia, on the station platform, and at Ashland there was a terrific crowd, though the town has a population of only about a thousand. We had no loudspeaker. The folks jammed both sides of the train. We did our best, however, under our own lung power. Which reminds me that modern speakers have become effete. As a boy I remember William Jennings Bryan speaking at Belair, Maryland, and

I was able to hear him two blocks away. In my youth, I used to speak to a crowded Chautauqua tent of about a thousand people, in competition with streetcars, automobiles, and a dozen or so youngsters in the front row. Now I'm lazy and demand a loudspeaker system.

February 8: There is great excitement throughout the nation regarding the French train, but also an awful lot of headaches. Fort Worth wants the Texas car before Dallas. Oakland wants to stage a better celebration than San Francisco. The American Legion, which did almost nothing for the Friendship Train, now wants to get the "40 and 8" boxcar. The Junior Chamber of Commerce in Michigan is trying to take the ceremony away from Mayor Welsh of Grand Rapids. However, on the whole, things are going well.

Father Coughlin called up Mrs. Frank Lee, wife of my radio sponsor, demanding that I be taken off the air. We have received a deluge of mail from Detroit protesting my broadcast. People's memories are short. It's only a few months ago that certain Protestants were threatening to investigate me for the distribution of Friendship Train food in Italy because they thought I had favored the Catholics. People also seem to forget that Father Coughlin was a brazen speculator in silver at a time when he was trying to influence the silver market through Senator Thomas of Oklahoma; and that he was silenced by his own archbishop because of his word-for-word reproduction of Nazi propaganda in his own paper.

February 10: Ashtabula was cold but a good crowd. Cleveland was even colder. In fact, we stood on the gondola car with a terrific blizzard raging around us. Governor Lausche wore no hat. I am sending him a Lee. The crowd was thin but brave.

February 11: Got up early in Toledo and flew to Akron. After the ceremony I went through part of the Firestone Rubber Company's plant and saw a film telling the story of rubber. I went to sleep in the middle of it and nearly fell over on Harvey Firestone.

February 12: Picard, a Committee member, is in the tow of Frank Douglas, Secretary to A. F. Whitney of the Brotherhood of Railroad Trainmen. Douglas speaks French. At Akron, Picard finally insisted that he wanted to pay at least one bill so they told him he could pay for the breakfast. Douglas then whispered to the waitress to bring in a check for $25 for ham and eggs which the waitress did. Picard didn't appear to be fazed, though he did ask how much American workmen made per week. He has been flashing a $100 bill which he got exchanged in New York, though Douglas had warned him there were a lot of counterfeit big bills floating around. When Picard went to pay his bill the cashier, tipped off in advance, held the $100 up to the light and said: "Sorry, sir, this is counterfeit and I have to call the police."

February 13:   The stops at Topeka, Emporia, Newton were much like our earlier stops on the Friendship Train a year ago except the weather is colder and the crowds smaller, though more enthusiastic. People everywhere seemed to appreciate this reciprocal gesture from the French. I left the train at Newton and drove behind a very slow state trooper to Wichita for the broadcast. I wanted to broadcast from the train but union rules made it impossible. To broadcast from outside the Wichita radio station would have required a union engineer and none was any closer than Chicago. After the ceremony, Marcellus Murdoch, publisher of the *Eagle*, gave a reception while Governor Carlson made me an Admiral of the Kansas Navy.

I recall that when I was a very young newspaperman attending the Geneva Naval Conference I tried to sell Marcellus' brother, Victor, a series of articles on naval disarmament. Victor wrote back that the people of Kansas didn't know the difference between a mud-scow and a battleship. However, he bought the articles though he chiseled on the price. I had a brief visit with Harry and Henri Graber for whose successful marriage I always take all the credit, having helped them perform the ceremony in Pec, Serbia, in 1921. They still tell me that I rush around too much and I am too much of a showman—both of which are probably true.

February 16:   It seemed peaceful and quiet crossing the [New Mexico] desert late this afternoon, so peaceful that I didn't even write a column. I should have known that whenever there is a moment of peace the storm is brewing.

February 17:   About six feet of snow around the Grand Canyon. It has knocked the tourist trade into a cocked hat. I had never seen the Grand Canyon before, but I had heard so many descriptions of it that

I figured I would be disappointed. I wasn't. We spent the day driving around the Canyon and I even managed to get a haircut.

February 17: The storm broke just before we caught the train in the evening when Dave Karr called to say that the Coughlin thing was really getting hot and he was flying out to see me in Los Angeles. The heat has been put on the retail clothing stores in New York and Detroit.

February 18: Phoenix—the best weather of the entire trip. Governor Garvey staged quite a ceremony after which I addressed the Arizona legislature, supposed to be the most democratic legislature in the USA. Among its members are one Mexican, one Chinaman, one Philadelphian Mainliner, various cattlemen. This is the second state legislature I have addressed, the other having been the New Mexican. However, Monsieur D'Hugues, a railroad shop foreman, has been before not only these two but that of Vermont. I got [U.S. Supreme Court Justice] Frank Murphy on the telephone in Washington. He informs me that the Church is out to take me off the air. He says the Church has gone fascist and won't speak to him since he wrote a decision on the parochial schools case against the Church. The cardinals feel he should have followed the party line.

February 19: Breakfast at Bob Smith's of the Los Angeles *News*. Senator George Luckey was present, still beaming over the way he handed a Lee hat to Truman during the inaugural parade. The French weren't used to champagne for breakfast but took it in their stride.

Jack Beardwood of *Time* handed me a copy of *The Tidings*, the Catholic newspaper, which devoted about eight columns to raking me over the coals re Coughlin.

Governor Earl Warren came to Los Angeles for the ceremony. I still think the Republicans made a terrible mistake and that the country would be much better off had he been nominated. Perhaps I'm prejudiced. Mrs. Warren came with the Governor. She is a great lady.

February 20: Spent last night and today on the long-distance phone re the Coughlin matter. Weintraub* wants me to apologize on the air.

*Head of the ad agency for Lee Hats.—ED.

I told him I would much rather go off the air than apologize to Coughlin. I wrote various statements, but all of them probably would have incensed, so in the end I said nothing.

I remember two other brushes with the Church, one over Franco, which lasted a good many months in 1936 through 1938 and finally culminated in the Congressman Sweeney suit, which I discovered later to be financed by the Jesuits. Then there was the brush when I criticized Postmaster General Frank Walker for taking orders from the Church regarding censorship of the mails. Almost every Catholic paper in the United States denounced me at that time. The only difficulty is that I was not then selling a retail product on the air. The Church in several areas, particularly Boston, tried to cancel the column without success. But once you are selling a retail product you are really vulnerable.

February 21:   I went down to say good-bye to the last "40 and 8" boxcar we had to deliver—California's. It sat by itself alongside the freight yard. The band from Ft. Mather had just arrived. A loudspeaker sound truck had pulled up to one side. A few people were gathering. I stood among them. They didn't know who I was. These cars have really made an impression. This is the first time any foreign nation has taken any trouble to show its appreciation to the United States and as far as I can see, the American people are genuinely grateful. I shall be sorry to leave. We have traveled a long way together.

February 22:   Arrived in Washington in time for the events of Harry Truman's diatribe.*

*At a dinner honoring General Vaughan as "Minute Man of 1949," the President had made an impromptu speech in which he said: "I want you to distinctly understand that any s.o.b. who thinks he can cause any one of these people to be discharged by me, by some smart aleck statement over the air or in the paper, has another think coming." (The official transcript changed "any s.o.b." to "anyone.") Pearson proposed in his next broadcast (February 27) that "s.o.b." be given a new interpretation— "Servant of Brotherhood." In his March 3 column, he elaborated: "So, along with Harry Truman, I am familiar with mule-drivers' language. However, neither Harry nor I are mule-drivers any more. We have graduated, I hope, to bigger and better things. Therefore, I am getting up an engraved 'Servants of Brotherhood' membership certificate, and perhaps some other folks will join me in picking out people in their neighborhood or anyplace else who have really sacrificed for their fellow men."—ED.

February 24: By some odd coincidence, the Norwegian Parliament has recommended me among about twenty others for the Nobel Peace Prize. Mrs. Roosevelt was the other American. Mr. Truman at his press conference said I must have nominated myself.

February 25: Breakfast with Truman aide David Noyes, who has just spent several days off and on with the President. He reports that Truman is backsliding fast. Truman still stands by his program, but when some of his staff come in and suggest that they do something else instead of carrying out the program, Truman always agrees. His advisers vie with each other to tell funny stories. Their chief ambition is to make him feel good. When Noyes argued with Truman about the cronies around him, he replied: "When one of my boys comes in with a sad look and tells me of his troubles, I confess I try to do anything he wants." "And your boys are wise to your weakness," Noyes told him. "They take advantage of you. You can't build a good program without good workmen, and you have lousy workmen." Noyes says there is terrific jealousy inside the White House. Vaughan hates White House Counsel Clark Clifford and Press Secretary Charlie Ross doesn't love Vaughan. When Noyes told Truman that Clifford was using the White House as a means to an end, Truman replied: "Well, wouldn't you?" Clifford is described as a liberal by day and a conservative by night.

Forrestal is definitely out but is demanding that there be a face-saving arrangement whereby it won't look as if he were fired. He wanted Secretary Royall to act in his place for six months in order to ease the situation. Truman is quite aware that Royall is a nitwit but still tolerates him.

Noyes had a long talk with Snyder. "The trouble with you is that you have become the Taft of the Truman administration," he told him. "You think about bolts, nuts, and taxes, not about people. Our nation was founded to protect life, liberty and property, but property is not good unless you have life in it. The trouble with you is that you have forgotten about life." Several times before, Snyder has told Noyes: "If you tell me I'm bad for the administration, I'll get out. All you have to do is say the word." Snyder repeated this again last week and this time Noyes didn't discourage him. The reason Snyder won't get out, however, is that he hasn't had any really good offers.

February 26: The reaction to Truman's cussing seems to be overwhelming.

February 27: Weintraub didn't like my Servants of Brotherhood script answering Truman. I went ahead with it anyway. The reaction tonight, judging by the telephone and telegrams, has been excellent.

February 28: Wallach's [clothing store chain] have been getting more demands that I be taken off the air. Five Catholics closed their accounts and the priests in Brooklyn yesterday went after me again with petitions demanding that I be taken off the air.

March 1: Called on former Secretary of State Jimmie Byrnes to try to get him to head up the Servants of Brotherhood foundation. Jimmie was much interested in the idea but wouldn't go for the name. Said it would be interpreted as backbiting against Truman.

Jimmie thinks that Vaughan's influence is about the worst possible. At Potsdam, Byrnes said, Truman got very snappy with Stalin. During the first thirty minutes of his conference, long before Stalin had a chance to get recalcitrant and while he was in a very benign mood, Truman got up and made a speech as if he were lecturing a schoolroom. The substance of it was: "I expect this and this to be done and I don't expect to stay here all summer." Churchill looked shocked and later expressed his surprise to Byrnes. Driving away from the conference in an auto immediately afterward, however, Vaughan told Truman: "That's the way, chief. You certainly gave it to him. That was great. Give it to him some more." Truman beamed. He loved it.

At Washington, prior to the Potsdam conference, Molotov arrived to make a special call on Truman before going to the San Francisco United Nations conference, at which time, according to Byrnes, Truman gave Molotov the bawling out of his life. Chip Bohlen, who doesn't love the Russians, reported it later to Byrnes and said he was shocked. Stalin, because of Roosevelt's death, had sent Molotov to Washington at the last minute. He had previously not planned to send Molotov to the United States but wanted to pay this courtesy to Roosevelt's memory. Despite this, Truman acted as if he were bawling out a buck private. Byrnes said that he supposed the incident didn't change history since the Russians probably would have changed their course anyway, but nevertheless, it didn't help history.

I remember when I called on Truman once at the White House

how he also bawled me out as if I were a buck private. And on another occasion when I called on Truman, as a Senator, he proceeded to bawl me out because I had said something about the Canol pipeline in Canada. I had written extremely favorable stories about him and about his committee, but he remembered that one small item where I had given the Army's point of view. On another occasion, at a cocktail party, Truman came up to me and said, "It's all your fault." I didn't know what he was talking about and when I expressed some surprise he continued, "Yes, you were the first one to suggest that I should be Vice President. You got me into this."

Louis Johnson and Forrestal lunched with Truman today. I saw Louis afterward. He said he was as nervous as a schoolboy. He said that Truman had promised him Secretary of Defense. Forrestal doesn't want to get out until May 1 but Truman suggested April 1. Louis said that April 15 would be O.K. Louis still has his fingers crossed but the announcement is supposed to be made on Friday. Knowing the bad luck Louis has had in the past, I have my fingers double-crossed. Louis wanted to know if Bob Allen would take over his press relations. I told him Bob might if he were made Assistant Secretary of War.

March 2:   Flew to New York. Met Ben Sonnenberg* at the Stork Club. He says that John Cahill has already drafted Forrestal's letter of resignation. Forrestal's close friend Clendenin Ryan is out to try to block Johnson's confirmation. He told me that in November of '47, when France was tied up with the railroad strike, Forrestal asked him to raise money to break the strike. Ryan raised $25 million which was sent over to Paris in early December, after which the strikes halted. In February 1948 Forrestal again asked him to raise money to win the Italian elections. Ryan called a meeting of his friends and raised $70,-000 which was sent to Rome. Thirty thousand dollars of it was paid direct to De Gasperi. Afterward, Forrestal arranged for the donors to deduct this amount from their income tax, they having paid $5,000 apiece, but according to Ryan most of them refused to take the deduction and chalked it up as a service to their country.

Came back on the sleeper.

*A public-relations man and friend, Ben Sonnenberg had been responsible for getting Drew Pearson on the cover of *Time* magazine (the December 13, 1948 issue). He did it in part as a favor, in part to prove he—Sonnenberg—had the influence to pull it off.—ED.

March 3: Truman came through after all. He announced Johnson as Secretary of Defense.

March 4: Saw Louis Johnson. People change quickly. Before his appointment, he was all hot and bothered about appointing Bob Allen in charge of his press relations. Now he isn't. Looks like he is surrounding himself with various old cronies from the American Legion, plus some friends from big business. His hardest job is going to be to save himself from his friends. I must look up his connections, which I have a hazy recollection include not only Pan American Airways, but Victor Emanuel, the investment banker, financier Floyd Odlum, and all their farflung ramifications—and of course, General Aniline and Film.

March 7 [Palm Beach]: Joe and Marjorie Davies* entertained us at dinner. It was a big charity brawl at the Everglades Club with about 300 people present. Joe Kennedy donated $100,000 at an auction of an automobile, and then gave the automobile to the hospital—a Catholic one—for which the money is being raised. Mrs. Pillsbury, of Pillsbury flour, sat on my right. She spent part of the evening arguing that it is necessary for the Germans to rebuild the Ruhr, and for American steelmen to have cartels with Europeans.

March 10: Gave what I hope will be my last lecture in Palm Beach. This is the fourth at the same place. All of the great were there. Mr. Yarnall, of the crowd that runs Philadelphia, sat in the front row and snored. Charlie Munn, the New York stockbroker, was also present. I couldn't help but recall the time when Munn entertained General MacArthur after an Army-Navy football game when MacArthur was Chief of Staff. The highlight of the evening was a dozen George White Scandals beauties dressed in Army uniforms, and a dozen dressed in Navy uniforms, with MacArthur pivoting in the center. When MacArthur sued for $1,750,000,† I almost approached Charlie Munn for details on this party because there is a strict Army regulation against

*He was F.D.R.'s first Ambassador to the Soviet Union, she the heir to the Post-Toasties fortune.—ED.

†In 1934, General MacArthur, then Chief of Staff, sued Drew Pearson and Robert S. Allen on several charges of libel. MacArthur dropped the case when it appeared some even more damaging material about him would come out at the trial. —ED.

desecrating the uniform, and it so happened that these young ladies had certain vital portions of their uniforms cut away.

Left for Washington immediately after the lecture.

March 11: Arrived home. Cold. Went to dinner at the French Embassy in honor of Chief Justice Vinson. How I hate dinner parties where I have to meet people I have just criticized. Ike Eisenhower came up and twitted me about the piece I wrote on him Sunday in which I said that he wasn't needed in Washington. "You are so right. I wish I could convince Mr. Truman," he said. "There is nothing I would like to do better than to get away from here." Ike was very genial about it. During the conversation, General Gruenther came up and talked about the speech I had made before the Railway Progress Association in New York. "The last time he made a speech with me," said Eisenhower, "he nominated me for President. I don't want to be speaking with him again."

At dinner I sat beside Mrs. Royall, wife of the Secretary of the Army. A few seats away was Mrs. John Sullivan, wife of the Secretary of the Navy. I had just resigned the latter's husband and I have been resigning Secretary Royall for so long I can't remember. Johnny Sullivan was very cordial anyway. So was Mrs. Royall. It would be much easier to write about people if they weren't so nice. Mrs. Royall says I just don't understand Kenneth, and her dearest ambition is to get us better acquainted. After dinner she took me over to him and told him so. Kenneth was reasonably pleasant under the circumstances, but not pleased. Luvie played bridge with Eugene Meyer and won. Eisenhower, Vinson, and Gruenther played at another table—supposedly the best players in Washington.

March 13: The wire-tapping scandal in New York is getting hotter and hotter. I talked to Mayor O'Dwyer on the phone. It looks as if Clendenin Ryan was caught redhanded in a conspiracy to tap wires and may get five to ten years. The New York scandal has brought into the open what some agencies of the U.S. government have been doing for a long time, especially the Army and Navy. I hope that the New York airing will have a salutary effect on Washington. Incidentally, the New York police have seized one eavesdropping machine which doesn't even have to tap wires. You sit in an automobile 300 or so feet away from a window and pick up the conversation inside. In 1944, I wrote a story about Charles Wilson of General Electric, then vice chairman of the

War Production Board, and Donald Nelson, WPB Chairman, using a similar instrument to eavesdrop on Forrestal's home where a dinner was taking place; included were Bernie Baruch, General Somervell, Under Secretary of War Patterson, and Ferd Eberstadt; they were plotting to oust Nelson. Afterward, Nelson and Wilson took a transcript of the conversation down to Roosevelt, who had the record locked in his safe. Shortly thereafter Eberstadt was fired. When I wrote the story, however, Wilson screamed to high heaven, threatened suit; and somewhat against my better judgment, but because the proof was extremely difficult, I gave him a retraction. It caused cancellation of one important newspaper—the Rochester *Times Union.*

March 14: Breakfast in Philadelphia at 7:30 A.M. before the Russell Conwell Breakfast Club run by Reverend Dan Poling. Poling is not one of the Protestant leaders opposed to an Ambassador at the Vatican. He thinks the President should be allowed free rein in appointing an Ambassador there or anywhere else. But when he was one of many signatories to a statement pleading with the Spanish Francoites not to bomb open cities in Spain, he received a host of threatening letters and phone calls. Last year I asked Congressman Jack Kennedy to speak at Poling's dinner in commemoration of the Four Chaplains. Jack accepted and then he telephoned me at the last minute with considerable embarrassment stating that the Church had forbidden him to speak. He said he must follow the dictates of the Church. I am wondering if he also does in regard to legislation.

March 15: Income tax day. Harry Truman today lost the battle of the filibuster—in my opinion one of the most important battles in his political career and in the recent history of the country. It was handled with inexcusably poor strategy. Truman scolded Congressmen instead of soft-soaping them as did Roosevelt. He had no one on the hill offering jobs, warning, soft-soaping. Dave Noyes warned Truman not to go to Key West at this time. McGrath, a good-natured, very nice individual with his heart in the right place, has not been effectual. Scott Lucas has blown hot and cold. He never was much of a leader and has been a miserable failure now. If the situation had been handled more expeditiously, the administration could easily have won. Some of the more reasonable Senators—as Maybank of South Carolina, Sparkman and Hill of Alabama—on such things as the poll tax and anti-lynching, would have cooperated. They never will win the South over on the FEPC.

The tragedy is that a defeat for Truman is not merely a defeat for Truman. It is a defeat for all the liberals who elected him. The Republicans are in ecstasy. If the Truman debacle keeps up it will be many years before liberal leadership can come back in this country. Already the Republicans are counting the 1950 congressional election as won and they may not be too far off.

March 16: Received a tip that John Snyder was trying to persuade Truman to take drastic action to get me off the air. Apparently it was more true than I realized that he was encouraging the Coughlinites.

March 17: Had the unpleasant job of talking to Lamar Caudle about some alleged fixes on income taxes for North Carolinians. He is reported to have held up a case of a taxi company head in Charlotte, named Beaty, while Beaty gave him three Chevrolets. Also three other North Carolinians who hired Lamar's law firm there are reported to have had their income tax cases fixed.

I couldn't quite believe this of Lamar even before I went to see him, and was delighted when the story blew up. In the first place Beaty had no income tax case. In the second place, two of the North Carolinians whom his law partner is supposed to have saved already had been indicted. Apparently the police chief of Charlotte, named Littlejohn, has been gunning for Lamar for a long time and is spreading rumors. If I wrote on all the unchecked rumors that come into this office, I would be in hot water twenty-four hours a day. About 50 percent of them, however, do prove to be accurate.*

March 20: Ran a high temperature. Missed my first broadcast since I've been in the game. Bob Allen† took over.

---

*T. Lamar Caudle was a North Carolina lawyer Truman appointed Assistant Attorney General for the Tax Division, Department of Justice. He was later convicted of fixing another tax case. Drew Pearson always maintained he was innocent. President Kennedy later pardoned him at President Truman's request.—ED.

†Robert S. Allen, former co-author of the "Merry-Go-Round" and several books with Drew Pearson.—ED.

March 23:   Wrote Louis Johnson congratulating him on his new job and also warning him that as a friend I was going to watch him more closely than if he were not a friend, and call the shots accordingly. There have been a lot of rumors about Louis's high-handed lobbying for Pan American Airlines and other big corporations. I think they are largely exaggerated, and Louis tells me that he has broken entirely with Victor Emanuel, who is about the worst business influence I know in government.

There is no question Louis is making a very sincere effort to pick good men for National Defense. Jack Peurifoy, Assistant Secretary of State, has turned him down and so has Bob Hinckley, both of whom would have been excellent as either Assistant Secretary or Under Secretary.

March 24:   George Bowden dropped in. He reports that the mine holiday was actually inspired by the coal operators who met in Cincinnati about three weeks ago and decided that there would have to be a drop in the price of coal. However, they put the matter up to Lewis to save them. He called the mine holiday in order to prevent the price drop.

George has been tentatively approached by Louis Johnson to come into the national Defense Department, probably taking over Intelligence. He would be excellent.

The Internal Revenue Bureau, according to George, is shot through with politics. All the big tax dodgers are being protected while the little fellows are being punished. The new collector, Bolich, is a great pal of gangster Frankie Costello and has called off the dogs on the Costello investigation.

George thinks that Russia will make war this year.

March 28:   The Senate is beginning to receive mail from my broadcast on the Dutch East Indies and the United Nations. We began a personal lobbying drive on this issue which to me seems terribly important. The State Department started out with a very fine position before the United Nations against Dutch aggression. Since then, the Dutch have kicked the United Nations all over the map. They have flouted practically all United Nations requests and the State Department, after cutting off Marshall Plan aid to the Dutch East Indies, then pussyfooted on the major question of Marshall Plan aid to Holland itself.

This aid—approximately $400 million last year—was the exact amount which financed the Dutch Army in Indonesia. The $16 million cut off to Indonesia was merely peanuts. It's the $400 million to Holland that really counts. But so far the State Department has opposed the amendment introduced by Brewster of Maine which specifies that no Marshall Plan money can be sent to a country which is in violation of U.N. Security Council requirements or demands, [i.e.], is regarded as an aggressor. It is unfortunate that Brewster introduced this amendment because he is truly disliked on both sides of the aisle. However, most of the Republicans are going to vote for the amendment and, surprisingly, a large number of Democrats. I talked to Fulbright, Pepper, Sparkman, Kilgore, Hunt, Maybank, Lister Hill, Miller of Idaho, Young of North Dakota, and a few others. I think all will vote for the Brewster amendment.

Jack* talked to many others. Some of them, such as Ives of New York, were going to vote against Brewster largely because they don't like him, but changed their minds after getting an explanation of the background.

It seems to me that having kicked the United Nations around to a considerable extent and given the appearance of bypassing it with the North Atlantic Pact, it would have a most disastrous reaction in Europe if the Brewster amendment supporting the United Nations were defeated.

March 29: Believe we have lined up a majority of the Senate for the Brewster amendment. If the vote were held tonight, it would go through. I was a little afraid that Dr. Frank Graham, the new Senator from North Carolina, would feel his obligation to the State Department and officially side with them though in his heart I know how deeply he resents Dutch aggression. However, I talked to him today and he is not only standing 100 percent on his convictions but he is talking quietly among other Senators to give them the true background. It never was published but the Dutch finagled to get Graham out of Indonesia when he was representing the United States on the U.N. Commission. They found him too righteous in his wrath against imperialism.

*This is a reference to Jack Anderson. Anderson began as a leg man in 1947, later became a partner, and today carries on the column.—ED.

March 30:   Telephoned James Webb, Under Secretary of State, to warn him that he was going to be licked on the Brewster amendment and to urge the administration to save its face and accept the amendment. Jimmy had a lot of excuses, most of which didn't make too much sense. But he did somewhat surprise me by indicating that he personally had been working hard on the Dutch government and that Dean Acheson had been likewise. Obviously they have been putting tremendous heat on the Dutch in the last week or so. This may have been inspired by the fight over the Brewster amendment. At any rate, Acheson is meeting with the Dutch Minister of Foreign Affairs to demand that his government back down. Webb argued that the economic recovery of Europe had to be balanced against aggression in the Pacific. I argued that there was no use recovering Europe economically if you were going to destroy the peace machinery of the world. Telephoning Webb may have been a tactical error because he got busy during the day and the State Department has now worked out a compromise amendment to reply to the Brewster amendment. On the surface this substitute is fairly good. It emphatically supports the United Nations, in fact passes the question of European Recovery Program aid back to the Security Council and gives the Council considerable leeway in advising the United States regarding curtailment of aid to an aggressor nation. The amendment has one important defect in that members of the Security Council can always veto—and at present the French and the Belgians, worried about French Indochina and the Belgian Congo where they have been almost as bad as the Dutch, might well veto.

However, the amendment is excellent in that it supports the United Nations. It apparently will be passed overwhelmingly. Ernie Gross, Assistant Secretary of State, called me in the late evening to explain the amendment and to promise that Acheson would put all sorts of personal pressure on the Dutch Foreign Minister. He pointed out that the State Department people object to the Brewster amendment, also that the United States might well be placed in a position of vetoing sanctions against an aggressor nation if it automatically meant that ERP aid would be cut off to that nation. For instance, if Great Britain was found to be an aggressor, the State Department might consider aid to England more important than acting against an aggressor. It strikes me that this is a very theoretical argument, but I can see that it might happen. Anyway Senator Vandenberg will offer

Brewster a chance to introduce the State Department's new compromise amendment and if Brewster doesn't want to, Connally or Vandenberg will do so.

April 1: Forrestal seems to be off his bean. While Tom Clark was in Florida last week, Forrestal called him almost every day, worried about something, wouldn't say what. When Tom got back to Washington, Forrestal called him and said, "You've got your men over here. What are you trying to crucify me for?" Clark denied this. "Yes, they're investigating me," insisted Forrestal.

Clark did have a couple of men checking on the Arabian Oil Company but not on Forrestal. However, Forrestal, who was to retire as Secretary of Defense in about two days, insisted that he was being investigated.

Next day Jim called from his home and told Clark there were four men outside watching him. Clark tried to find out who they were, wanted to know if they were workmen. "They've tapped my wires; they've been all over the house," Forrestal claimed. "They're trying to get something on me." Clark offered to send some FBI men over immediately to see what was going on, but Forrestal was evasive. He said something to the effect that "Jo knows what's wrong." "Who's Jo?" asked Clark. "You know who Jo is," replied Forrestal. "She's my wife."

Forrestal finally said that Eberstadt was coming down from New York with a doctor. This fits in with a telephone call I got from Eberstadt early in the week. He made a special request that I lay off any criticism of Forrestal at this time. I didn't know exactly what it was all about, but promised to do so. After all, there's no use applying the whip to someone who is out of office.

Tom says that Forrestal has a peculiar way of calling up around six o'clock every evening and inviting him for dinner—"just as Mama has our own dinner cooking." Then Tom continued, "Jim doesn't seem to realize that when your wife starts cooking dinner, she doesn't like to stop in the middle of it."

Anyway, Forrestal called Clark again on Tuesday, March 29, one day after he was out of office, at twelve o'clock and invited him for lunch. Clark had already invited the New York Congressmen to lunch with him and asked Forrestal to join them. He declined. Then at 1:30, right in the middle of Clark's lunch, Forrestal called back, but when

he phoned Clark was at the lunch—he should have known anyway—
and Forrestal didn't press the call. Later that afternoon Tom called
back to find Forrestal had left for Hobe Sound.

Truman is going to make Forrestal a dollar-a-year man, give him
a Navy plane, and send him on a cruise around the world for a vacation.

I talked to Tom about making Ickes chairman of the National
Security Resources Board instead of Mon Wallgren. It would be a
ten-strike for Truman, not only with liberals of the country but almost
everyone else. Tom liked the idea and suggested I talk to Howard
McGrath [Democratic National Committee Chairman].

April 2:   The Attorney General of California [Fred N. Howser], who
is suing me for $300,000, now wants to duck out on having his deposi-
tion taken. We have to argue the deposition in court on Monday.*

April 4:   George Arnold† telephoned from Los Angeles while I was
in court and just before we were about to argue Howser's motion.
George says that Jim Mulloy is afraid to give a deposition in California
because he will be arrested by Howser as a bookmaker immediately
afterward. We are arranging to take his deposition in Washington—
at considerably more expense. I hope, however, he turns up.

Lunched with Ickes. Talked about flowers and trees. Not many
who have heard about the crusty curmudgeon would realize that he
would much rather be out in a garden than cussing people. Ickes
attempted to syndicate his column on a weekly rather than a tri-weekly
basis, but his efforts fizzled. He has seven papers who are willing to take
the column out of a previous list of fifty. His gross income would be
only $156 a week, out of which he would have to pay overhead. Ickes
has aged noticeably in the last few months. I think that the failure of

*Fred Napoleon Howser, elected in 1946, was repeatedly accused of shielding or
sharing in gambling operations. His $300,000 suit arose from Drew's charge, based on
information from James T. Mulloy (a gambler), that Howser had taken underworld
contributions for his campaign.—ED.

†George Arnold, married to Drew's daughter Ellen (and himself the son of New
Dealer Thurman Arnold), was representing him in the case along with William Rogers
(later, to be Attorney General under Eisenhower, and later still, Secretary of State for
Nixon).—ED.

his column has accelerated this. Last week the boys in New York offered me $750,000 a year to broadcast six days a week, which I turned down. In a few years I will probably be scraping around for nickels like Ickes.

Ickes told me what I had never known before—that he was responsible for appointing Bernard Baruch as rubber czar. He regrets it now in a way and considers Baruch one of the biggest phonies in the country.

Nobody feels very sorry for Forrestal. He never was true to any friend. The man who put him in the Roosevelt entourage was Brain Truster Tom Corcoran, who got him a job first as White House Secretary, later as Under Secretary of the Navy. But when Forrestal became Secretary of the Navy, Ickes approached him about making Tom Corcoran Assistant Secretary. Forrestal's reply was that Roosevelt would not like it. Subsequently Ickes asked Roosevelt if he would have any objection and Roosevelt, after thinking it over for about half a minute, said that he had none. "Do you mind if I tell Forrestal that you approve?" Ickes asked. "By all means," replied Roosevelt. Ickes saw Forrestal at the next meeting of the Petroleum Board, took him aside and told him that FDR had approved Tom Corcoran's appointment. Forrestal's jaw dropped. He mumbled something about having made a commitment to Struve Hensel. Shortly thereafter Hensel was appointed. The interesting thing to me—and I remarked on it to Ickes—is that Tom Corcoran was still lobbying up until the very end for the retention of Forrestal as Secretary of Defense.

Attended the signing of the North Atlantic Pact. Simple and reasonably impressive. The speeches generally were uninspiring. The Norwegian Foreign Minister made the best. He talked frankly about the hesitation his country faced regarding such a pact and how they had finally decided to sign. Luxembourg and Iceland were also forthright and inspiring. Ernie Bevin, the British Foreign Secretary, was disappointing. The Dutch Foreign Minister got a reasonably good hand, despite his country's aggression.

Worst boner of the ceremony was the State Department's failure to invite the Senate. They were really burned up. Meanwhile Truman's secretariat, looking third-rate even at their best, trooped in and occupied front-row seats. How much smarter if these seats had been given to Senators!

Harry himself came on the stage almost three minutes before the networks were ready for him to begin his speech. He grinned and shook hands with the Foreign Ministers and at any moment I expected him to come to the edge of the stage and clasp his hands above his head like a boxer in the ring. I listened to Truman for a brief interval. He was even less inspiring than the others and I walked out. The band, incidentally, played "It Ain't Necessarily So."

Called on Count Sforza at the Italian Embassy. Remarking on the North Atlantic Pact ceremony, Sforza said, "Why is it that diplomats think they have to yawn through life?" The Russians, he predicted, would not make war. They don't dare at this time.

April 5:   Governor Gruening of Alaska and Constantine Brown came to dinner. The rumor is that Eisenhower has cancer. Gruening claims that Ike is the best bridge player in the country, but Connie thinks that Al Gruenther tops him. The defense of Alaska is only 8,000 men whereas the Red Army's strength on the rim of Siberia is 250,000, plus 1,100 planes. What the Russians have inside Siberia is not known. However, Eskimo intelligence is reasonably good, from Kamchatka and all along the Bering Sea. The Eskimos come and go without passports and are very loyal to the United States. Gruening thinks Alaska may be the next Pearl Harbor.

April 6:   Forrestal spent three days at Hobe Sound, then flew back to Washington where he was clapped into the Bethesda Naval Hospital. The report is he tried to commit suicide.

There is a Marine guard on Forrestal's door at the Hospital, apparently to prevent another suicide attempt.

April 8:   An iron curtain of silence has been rung down about Forrestal's insanity.

April 9:   It now develops that Forrestal tried to commit suicide three times. He took a large dose of Veronal and had his stomach pumped out. He then tried to hang himself, then tried to slash his wrists. It was at this point that they flew him back to the Naval Hospital at Bethesda. Bob Lovett said he never spent such a terrible three days in his life. Forrestal was staying at Averell Harriman's house. Eberstadt flew two specialists down from New York and finally they gave him injections which put him to sleep for seventy-two hours.

The climax came on the night of April 1 when a fire siren blew and Forrestal jumped up, thinking it was a sign of Russian attack. The fire siren blew a second time and Forrestal rushed out of his house in his pajamas screaming. They had a hard time catching him and getting him back to bed.

For the last few weeks Forrestal has been calling up Truman almost every day, sometimes several times a day, asking him to decide the most trivial matters. Kate Foley, his secretary, has covered up for him on all sorts of things. Louis Johnson has also protected him. It has been known by his intimates that he was out of his mind for some weeks and perhaps unbalanced for six months. It got so bad toward the end that the date of Forrestal's resignation was advanced from March 31 to March 28. He had previously insisted on resigning June 1, but Truman pushed it up to April 1.

April 10:   ABC objected strenuously to the Forrestal broadcast. Forrestal's attorneys, knowing that I was working on the story, had their men in New York trying to crack down on the network. They partly succeeded. Bill Neel of ABC had orders to sit in the control room and cut me off the air if I mentioned the word insanity. I ad-libbed in part— called it temporary insanity and got by.

Significantly, the network also objected to any reference to the idea that Forrestal might have been out of his head while in public office, and that Truman knew about this. To me this was the most important part of the news. When a man is insane while in high public office, it affects millions. When a private citizen becomes insane it affects only a handful.

When Elliott Roosevelt's wife cut her wrists, newspapers front-paged it as attempted suicide. When James Roosevelt's wife took an overdose of sleeping pills, the newspapers did likewise. Both are private citizens and have no effect upon anybody's life beyond their immediate families. But Forrestal's decisions affected two million men in the armed services, billions of dollars, and the future of the entire country.

April 11:   Lunched with Jim Bruce. He is not going back to Argentina as Ambassador but probably to London. However, his brother Dave has been promised the Ambassadorship to Paris so it may be embarrassing for Truman to have two brothers on each side of the English Channel.

Bruce has known Forrestal a long time, had dinner with him last

February when he was feeling very sorry for himself because he guessed wrong on the election. "If I had made some speeches in New York State, I might have swung the election for Truman," Forrestal said. After the election, Forrestal went to see Louis Johnson and tried to get Louie to transfer $2,000 given by a friend of Forrestal's, though actually by Forrestal, back to Forrestal's name. Before the election, Forrestal did not want his contribution identified with Truman, but after November he did. Louie told him it was impossible.

"The admirals are against me," Forrestal also moaned. "They used to be for me, but now they're against me." Forrestal was feeling so sorry for himself that he was obviously in no state of mind to make decisions.

Bruce, who used to know the Dillon, Read firm well, says that Clarence Dillon and Forrestal never got along too well together. But Dillon had an ambition to have a man in the White House. Therefore, Tommy Corcoran was inveigled to get Forrestal appointed as Roosevelt's administrative assistant in 1938. To counterbalance the appointment of a Wall Street banker in the White House, Dan Tobin of the Teamsters Union was also made a White House assistant. Shortly thereafter, after breaking the ice of public opinion, Forrestal was quietly shifted to the Navy as Under Secretary. This was the build-up for Governor of New York and later the Presidency. Forrestal began warming up to Boss Flynn and to Paul Fitzpatrick, who succeeded Ed Flynn as chairman of the New York State Democratic Committee. Forrestal figured he could fix things up with the Cardinal [Spellman], despite the fact that he had not been a working Catholic and had been married to a divorced Protestant. However, trouble came when Roosevelt died. Forrestal figured there was no chance for him since Truman would run again and he began cozying up to the Republicans. I remember even during the war how I drove Senator Brewster of Maine down to the Navy one day for a talk with Forrestal. When he came out, Brewster said the chief thing Forrestal was interested in was who the Republican candidate might be, and whom he, Forrestal, should back.

Bruce tells an interesting story of how Stanton Griffis became Ambassador to Poland—despite the fact that Griffis once referred to Hitler as one of the greatest men in the world. Paul Shields, Forrestal's man in New York, was lunching with Paul Fitzpatrick, who complained that the Democratic party was broke. "You've got some good assets if you use them—Ambassadorships," advised Shields. "You can get $100,000 for London alone." Later Shields asked Griffis how much he would pay to be Ambassador to London. "Two hundred thousand dollars," replied Griffis. "O.K., you can have it for $100,000," replied Shields. But Truman didn't give.

Meanwhile Griffis wanted to be on the Cornell Board of Trustees and promised Governor Dewey $50,000 for the appointment. Dewey came through, but Griffis didn't, which has made Dewey sore as blazes and determined to block Griffis's confirmation to any important post. Finally, they gave Griffis Poland, which pleased him not at all, and he never did come through with a contribution to the party.

April 12: Went to Hyde Park to lay a wreath from the *Merci* Train on FDR's grave. A lot of the old Cabinet came back—Morgenthau, Miss Perkins, Bob Patterson, and Henry Wallace for the first time since FDR's death. Morgenthau placed one wreath on the grave and I the other. Fala, however, was the chief center of attraction. Mrs. Roosevelt was asked by the photographer to lead him up to the grave and Fala, not knowing very much what it was all about and being close to ten years old—the equivalent of eighty—wasn't too interested.

Mrs. Roosevelt took me over to the Roosevelt library after the ceremony to show me the aquamarine, given her by President Vargas of Brazil, which I had written about. I had pointed out that the people of Brazil would be hurt if Mrs. Roosevelt carried out her idea of selling it. Her point was that the stone was given to her, not to her husband; therefore she had a right to sell it, which is true. Mrs. Roosevelt has now informed me with mixed sadness and amusement that the aquamarine had now been given to the government and could not therefore be sending Brazilian students to school in the United States as she had planned.

Henry Wallace drove me to the station. We ignored politics and talked about inbreeding among chickens and pigs. Contrary to most experts, he believes that inbreeding among animals is not harmful. I told him this relieved me of a lot of worry about Stettinius* who was inbreeded with his daughter and his granddaughter.

April 13: Letters criticizing my Forrestal broadcast have been heavy. When anyone has a cabal of newspapermen around him that he has nurtured for years, it is amazing what a public opinion front he can

---

*A prize Hampshire boar hog, which was named after the former Secretary of State. The pig pen at the farm was known as the State Department.—ED.

build up. Forrestal had a committee composed of Lyle Wilson of United Press, Frank Kent, Arthur Krock of *The New York Times*, Marquis Childs, and the Alsop brothers, and Tris Coffin. And he consulted with them more than he consulted with his admirals. When Forrestal first went off his nut, Childs telephoned some of my friends and frantically pleaded, "Don't tell Drew." Apparently he doesn't realize that he has an obligation to the public.

April 14:   Louis Johnson says that the first time he realized Forrestal was mad was in February after Truman first asked Johnson to become Secretary of Defense. He conferred with Forrestal in the Goldfish Room and noticed that his eyes bulged and he betrayed some of the symptoms which Johnson had noticed in his own daughter Lillian, an incurable mental case. From that point on, Forrestal worked with Johnson almost every day. Sometimes Forrestal was clear and sharp, then his mind would wander. He gave the impression of taking dope. He had a direct telephone in his office to the Alsop brothers and in the middle of conversations would pick up the phone, call the Alsops and tell them what was going on. Sometimes he even told them things that had never happened.

At the moment Forrestal is being kept on dope and will have to take a long psychiatric treatment course after he comes out of it. Forrestal has obsessions about the Russians and the Jews and on the airplane trip from Hobe Sound to Washington he demanded that before the plane landed, the airport be cleared of all Air Force men and Jews.

April 15:   Tom Clark claims that he is really going after Frankie Costello. The people who seem to be holding things up are over in Internal Revenue. It is significant that Bolich, the new Assistant Commissioner, was given an ornate party by Costello when he first took office in charge of the intelligence unit in New York.*

April 17:   I got the impression that the American Broadcasting Company has given orders to protect Truman. For two weeks anything I mention even remotely critical of Truman is cross-examined from every angle. Tonight I had to leave out an item about the makers of White

*Daniel A. Bolich was later convicted of tax fraud.—ED.

House chinaware in Abingdon, Virginia, who protested against making china that might be used at profane Presidential dinner parties. The item appeared in the front pages of *The Washington Post* but unfortunately the network objected.

Dave Noyes came to dinner. We had a long talk afterward. He has had several sessions with the President and says that he is more worried than ever before. As he described it, Truman's brain has locked. "Sometimes the beating a man takes during a campaign affects him after election," is Noyes's explanation. "The four days FDR spent campaigning in the rain in 1944 contributed to his death in 1945.And the hundred days of punishment Truman took during the campaign are showing their effect today."

Dave says that Truman just has no conception of what's going on or any idea of how to put his program across. It looks as if the Russians are going to ease up on the international front, which will bring a severe economic turn on the domestic front and Dave thinks Mr. Truman hasn't the vaguest conception of how to cope with the latter.

April 18:   Took Mulloy's deposition in the Howser case. He substantiated under oath his previous allegation that he gave $1,200 in bills to Howser during the 1946 campaign.

Talked to Senator Flanders of Vermont about his idea of dropping leaflets behind the Iron Curtain. We both agreed this might not be the right thing, but that some start had to be made in cracking the Iron Curtain.

April 19:   Jim Lee [of Lee Hats] came down from Danbury for lunch. He wants me to go off the air in May instead of July. I told him I would not make any concession which might appear to be a victory for the Catholic Church.

Have had various calls from Wheeling, West Virginia, that Bill Lias, the gambler, was going to get out of his indictment. Went to see Caudle at the Justice Department. Something phony is taking place though I am quite sure it is not in Washington. Indictments against Lias are being dropped because an Internal Revenue agent was in the grand jury room when Lias's bookkeeper was testifying. However, Caudle today sent two assistants to Wheeling to bolster up the case and reindict Lias.

April 22:   Talked to Stuart Symington. He looks like a phony. He talks like a phony. But I still am convinced he isn't a phony.

May 1 [Atlanta]:   Had the same room at the Atlanta Biltmore that I had three years ago during the Klan broadcast. However, the atmosphere was considerably different. No conspiracy of silence. In advance of the Klan broadcast, the radio station pulled out all facilities and we had to fly an engineer in from Chicago, an announcer from Jacksonville, and equipment from Washington. The Georgia Power and Light Company, the Georgia Trust Company, and Alanta businessmen throughout the city brought pressure on the radio station to cancel all advertising if I were allowed to broadcast. Ellis Arnall, then governor, said he had never had so much pressure brought on him in his life. This time everybody was most hospitable. Caught a train to Washington immediately after the broadcast.*

May 2:   Lunched with Ickes. His first *New Republic* article came out today and he is feeling a little better. The administration, which sought him out and urged him to make speeches during the campaign, hasn't asked him to make one speech at the Jackson Day dinners. Truman has barely given him a scant thanks for his help.

Louis Johnson, on the contrary, has been smart enough to invite him to lunch a couple of times. Ickes gave Louis some pretty stiff advice about Curtis Calder. Louis claims that Truman wants Calder appointed [Secretary of the Army], but I have reason to believe that Louis is the guilty party. In the first place, Calder is a friend of Louis's intimate pal, Floyd Odlum, and in the second place, Calder contributed $3,000 on November 22, when Louis was scraping the barrel to make up the Democratic deficit.

May 3:   Received word from Detroit that the new U.S. Attorney Edward Kane made the amazing statement to the press that "there was absolutely no evidence that Father Coughlin was mixed up in the Gariepy tax case." This is exactly contrary to the long file in the Department of Justice, which states that Gariepy's attorney pleaded

---

*On July 21, 1946, Drew Pearson broadcast from the steps of the state Capitol in Atlanta despite a death threat from the Ku Klux Klan. In the broadcast, he charged that Talmadge, the Governor-elect, planned to appoint a Klan official to his cabinet. —ED.

that $68,000 had been received [by] Gariepy [from] Father Coughlin for payment of damages for the alienation of Mrs. Gariepy's affections. The record even shows how Gariepy came home one day to find Coughlin leaving the house, Mrs. Gariepy in a negligee, and the bed mussed up. The record also shows how Gariepy shadowed his wife and found her car parked outside the Coughlin rectory for long periods. The money was paid by Coughlin, according to Gariepy's attorney, the first payment of $50,000 in bills in a paper bag; the rest in installments of about $8,000 a year. Since the hospital at Royal Oak loses money and since Gariepy was not a wealthy man, it would have been difficult for him to have made this money in medical practice.

May 4: Showed Lamar Caudle the statement by U.S. Attorney Kane in Detroit. He was amazed and in favor of making Kane retract. Later he talked to other Justice Department officials who were afraid Kane wouldn't retract. They were of the opinion that the Church had carefully arranged for Kane's statement. They also disclosed that Treasury agents, in working with the Detroit district attorney's office, found that the latter was hell-bent on saving Coughlin. The attorney who handled the case, Joe Murphy, is a staunch Catholic, while Kane, the new U.S. attorney, is likewise. As a matter of fact, Gariepy's case was stymied in the district attorney's office in Detroit from October 15 to January 30, when I blasted it. Even after that it took a phone call from Washington to get the case before a grand jury.

Despite all this, Justice says it is afraid to reprimand Kane. The alternative is for the Justice Department to make a statement itself.

May 5: Called on Barkley. Suggested to him as diplomatically as possible that his son-in-law Max Truitt was getting him into trouble as the paid lobbyist for Franco of Spain, Trujillo of the Dominican Republic, and also representing a powerful Argentine shipping company—the three chief dictators remaining in the world. Barkley got a little miffed, at first at me, then possibly a little bit at his son-in-law. He said he could not control his son-in-law and that his son-in-law could not control his vote—even if he had one. When Max left the Reconstruction Finance Corporation, Barkley said he advised him to go back to St. Louis to practice law, but Max chose to ignore his advice. "And perhaps," said the Vice President, "Max was right, because he is now making a pile of money.

"After all," said Barkley, "he has to make a living for his family."

I suggested that he could forgo a few dollars and cents for the protection of his father-in-law, but Barkley replied that Max had lobbied vigorously for Tidelands Oil while he, Barkley, in the last Congress, had battled against Tidelands Oil.

May 6:   Saw Tom Clark, who says that Senator Virgil Chapman of Kentucky came in to see him about Prichard and the stuffed ballot boxes in Kentucky. He warned the Senator that anything that was said about the case would have to be used but Chapman, who was unshaven and half-drunk, proceeded to talk anyway. He said that Prichard had signed the ballots with his left hand, while the other partner, Funk, had signed with his right hand. Chapman urged that no harm had been done and the case be dropped. However, Tom says he got pressure from a lot of other people, chiefly Cassius Clay, formerly with the RFC, and ex-Senator Cooper of Kentucky, that the case be prosecuted. Since he was accused of not prosecuting regarding the Kansas City frauds, he decided to prosecute in Kentucky. The evidence against Prichard is flimsy and probably won't stand up in the final trial.*

I showed Tom the Kane statement in Detroit. He was noncommittal.

May 8:   Went to dinner with the Vournases and Peggy Palmer.† Peggy had been to the President's birthday party the night before. Sam Rayburn slept during the latter part of the party and groused audibly at the end—which was 2 A.M. "Why doesn't the son of a bitch go home at a reasonable time instead of keeping us all up early," said Sam referring to his so-called friend in the White House.

---

*Edward F. Prichard, Jr., a young lawyer with a promising political career who had been Justice Frankfurter's law clerk, had apparently stuffed the ballot box on a bet. Despite the intercession of many prominent people, Prichard was convicted. The Kansas City frauds concerned allegations of irregularities in a 1946 Congressional primary in which a Truman-backed Democrat defeated an anti-administration incumbent; a Justice Department investigation collapsed when the suspect ballots were stolen —ED.

†Both the Vournases and Peggy Palmer were close personal friends. A Washington lawyer, George Vournas was active in Greek organizations (he had immigrated from Greece) and in the Democratic Party. Peggy Palmer was the widow of A. Mitchell Palmer, Woodrow Wilson's Attorney General.—ED.

May 9:   More mail coming in re Coughlin. The National Catholic [Welfare Conference] News Service has sent out a story to all Catholic papers.

Jim Lee has been down from New York again wanting to cancel the contract. This time he didn't admit the Coughlin issue is in the background but he did inadvertently let drop the fact that McGuire of the Manufacturers Trust is the man demanding cancellation. Lee Hats owes banks a million dollars payable June 20, and McGuire is the man who heard the priest denounce me in Brooklyn last February and who demanded cancellation of the contract next day.

May 10:   Haven't been able to get the Justice Department to do anything about the Coughlin statement in Detroit. Caudle is in Florida fishing and the boys don't want to act without him. I finally got Caudle on the telephone in Raleigh, North Carolina, where he was grounded late tonight. I have written out a statement to be issued over his name setting out the true facts regarding Coughlin, which Turner Smith is going to put up to him.

May 11:   Talked to Caudle on the telephone and he is reluctant to issue the Coughlin statement under his own name. He wants to run for the Senate against Clyde Hoey next year and figures the Catholics would sabotage him.

May 12:   Caudle got back and is 100 percent for issuing some kind of a statement, preferably one by the Justice Department. However, his advisers want the statement to come from Kane in Detroit, who after all made the initial false statement. We finally drafted one and it was arranged that Kane would be given orders over the telephone, but now Peyton Ford, Number Two man in the Justice Department, has put in his oar. He is highly dubious, if not cool.

Everyone in the Justice Department admits that the Church maneuvered adroitly to get Kane to make the statement and they don't want to buck the Church. They also admit that in their opinion Coughlin did pay the money to Gariepy; even Jim McInerney, a staunch Catholic who is in the tax division, is convinced of this. But nobody wants to even slightly antagonize the Church.

May 13: Interior Secretary Krug hasn't been around Washington more than on Cabinet days for weeks. He spends a good part of his time in the New York apartment of a man named Marks, head of Publicker Liquor Company and now under indictment in connection with German properties. Truman is partially wise to Krug and has sent word to Under Secretary of the Interior Oscar Chapman that he would like to get rid of him if he could find the right out. Meanwhile, Krug, apparently seeing the handwriting on the wall, talked to Bernard Baruch April 19. Bernie urged him to try for Averell Harriman's job with the ECA in Europe.*

I am to get some Senate pressure on the White House regarding Krug.

Wrote a brass ring tribute to [Secretary of Agriculture] Charlie Brannan today. As a result members of the Cabinet today were eying him with suspicion as a possible "Pearson leak." The anti-Pearson Cabinet members now have spotted Oscar Chapman, Brannan, Tom Clark, and Louis Johnson as the Pearson members.

After a long series of huddles with the Justice Department, Peyton Ford finally agreed to a weasel-worded statement by the district attorney in Detroit whereby he will disavow part of his earlier statement that Father Coughlin was not connected with the Gariepy income case. It has been so watered down by Ford that I doubt very much whether any Detroit newspaper will publish it.

May 14: Went to the Women's [National] Press Club dinner. Truman sat beside Mrs. Roosevelt and cooed incessantly in her ear. He looked as if he loved all the Roosevelts, though it is becoming increasingly apparent that the exact opposite is the case. His friends say that nothing irritates him more than the mention of the name Roosevelt. I could hardly believe it at first, but the Democratic National Committee, which represents Mr. Truman, has sent an official endorsement of the Tammany opposition of F.D.R., Jr., in the New York congressional race. In the old days, Roosevelt always supported Fiorello La Guardia, though a Republican, in his fights against Tammany. Roosevelt never ducked. In the present, F.D.R., Jr., race, Truman at least could have avoided taking a stand, but he didn't. He came out against a Roosevelt.

*Harriman was at this time U.S. Representative to the Economic Cooperation Administration and held the rank of Ambassador.—ED.

During the dinner, Truman delivered the awards on behalf of the newspaper gals, one of them to Mrs. Roosevelt, and afterward he made a little speech pointing out that he was the first to discover Mrs. Roosevelt's diplomatic ability and appointed her to the U.N. I could not help remembering what Jimmie Byrnes told me—namely, that in 1945, when Truman appointed Mrs. Roosevelt, he particularly mentioned to Byrnes that this appointment would insure Roosevelt support for him when it come to his renomination in 1948.

Handing out the awards to the ladies of the year, Truman was at his best. He was homey, full of smiles, immaculately dressed in a white dinner jacket. He loved to do his job and did it well. If Mr. Truman had just been able to go through life in the position of a glorified hander-out-of-awards, instead of directing intricate affairs of the greatest nation in the world, we would all have been a lot better off.

May 15: Put in a hard plug for F.D.R., Jr., on the air. Compared his battle to his father's battle against Tammany three decades ago. Also compared Truman's flying out to the Pendergast funeral with his failure to place a wreath on the Roosevelt tomb.

May 16: As I suspected, the Detroit newspapers could find nothing newsworthy in the milk-and-water statement of the district attorney in Detroit re Coughlin.

Spoke on the radio in New York for F.D.R., Jr.

Van Heusen shirts made an offer for the radio program.

May 18: Truman is fit to be tied over F.D.R., Jr.'s victory. He took part of his ire out on me. At a White House staff conference, he unleashed another string of expletives, only this time he didn't use initials. "That blankety-blank Pearson," he said, "swung 10,000 votes for young Roosevelt."

Later in the day, Dave Niles came up to see Frankie to tell him that Truman was actually in his corner, but couldn't say so publicly because he had to go along with the "organization." Niles, who stayed on in the White House with Truman after F.D.R. died, extended Frankie an invitation to join up with the Democratic party in Washington and said Truman would be 100 percent behind him. Naturally. Truman has no other alternative.

May 22:   Jim Forrestal died at 2 A.M., by jumping out of the Naval Hospital window. He had the cord of his bathrobe tied around his neck. Beside his bed was a translation of Sophocle's "Chorus from Ajax" which included this line: "When Reason's day / Sets rayless—joyless —quenched in cold decay, / Better to die, and sleep / The never-waking sleep, than linger on, / And dare to live, when the soul's life is gone."

I think that Forrestal really died because he had no spiritual reserves. He had spent all his life thinking only about himself, trying to fulfill his great ambition to be President of the United States. When that ambition became out of his reach, he had nothing to fall back on. He had no church; he had deserted it. He had no wife. They had both deserted each other. She was in Paris at the time of his death—though it was well-known that he had been seriously ill for weeks. But most important of all, he had no spiritual resources.

I have seen Alben Barkley weather a great disappointment. He wanted to be Vice President in 1944, which everyone knew would have made him President. But Barkley fell back on his own wealth of spiritual resources and is a great man today. I have also seen Arthur Vandenberg of Michigan led up to the Presidential mountain twice. He suffered great disappointments, but he has been quite content to do a less sensational job, though in many respects an equally important one. He has grown with the years and with his disappointments, and without him in the Senate today American foreign policy would not be on anywhere near such an even keel.

But James Forrestal's passion was public approval. It was his lifeblood. He craved it almost as a dope addict craves morphine. Toward the end he would break down and cry pitifully, like a child, when criticized too much. He had worked hard—too much in fact—for his country. He was loyal and patriotic. Few men were more devoted to their country, but he seriously hurt the country that he loved by taking his own life. All his policies now are under closer suspicion than before. Interior Secretary Richard Ballinger, when he was forced out of Taft's Cabinet under great criticism, did not break under the strain. Apparently he had inner resources to fall back on. Since then, history has vindicated Ballinger. History can never vindicate Forrestal because he will not be alive to defend himself, and many of the policies he put across with such haste and with what now appears to be an unbalanced mental attitude, will probably be revised.

There have been other cabinet members who retired under great stigma—Interior Secretary Albert Fall of Teapot Dome fame; Denby, Harding's Secretary of the Navy, and Harry Daugherty, his Attorney General. Fall was an old rascal who had no conscience, and who was so calloused that nothing could hurt his soul. He died on his ranch after serving a term in jail. Denby was more sensitive, but in private life weathered the storm. The calluses on Daugherty's character helped him through the crisis and he died at an old age forgotten.

Forrestal not only had no spiritual resources, but also he had no calluses. He was unique in this respect. He was acutely sensitive. He had traveled not on the hard political path of the politician, but on the protected, cloistered avenue of the Wall Street bankers. All his life he had been surrounded by public relations men. He did not know what the lash of criticism meant. He did not understand the give-and-take of the political arena. Even in the executive branch of the government, he surrounded himself with public relations men, invited newsmen to dinner, lunch, and breakfast, made a fetish of courting their favor. History unfortunately will decree that Forrestal's great reputation was synthetic. It was built on the most unstable foundation of all—the handouts of paid press agents.

If Forrestal had been true to his friends, if he had made one sacrifice for a friend, if he had even gone to bat for Tom Corcoran who put him in the White House, if he had spent more time with his wife instead of courting his mistress, he would not have been so alone this morning when he went to the diet pantry of the Naval Hospital and jumped to his death.

May 23:   Pegler has published a column virtually accusing me of murdering Forrestal. Telegrams and telephone calls have been coming in singing the same song.

May 24:   Pegler has another column blaming me regarding Forrestal. His theme is that I kicked a man when he was down. Of course, Pegler makes no mention of the manner in which he persecuted Harry Hopkins when Hopkins was undergoing operation after operation. Nor is there any word about the way Pegler has dug up the dead body of Franklin Roosevelt week in and week out ever since F.D.R. died.

The Navy has been waging a very skillful undercover campaign to play up Forrestal as a martyr and a hero. Part of the campaign is aimed against Louis Johnson, whom the Navy hates with a bitter, undying hatred which borders close to mutiny. Part of it, I think, is also aimed against me. I now learn that Steve Early, new Under Secretary of National Defense, is the man whom the Navy used to glorify Forrestal. Louis Johnson was lunching with Joe Davies on Sunday when arrangements for the funeral, publicity campaign, etc., were being made. Steve called him away from the lunch time after time to report on the most minute matters such as whether or not he, Johnson, was to meet Mrs. Forrestal when her plane arrived. It was obvious that the Navy was coaching Steve from the sidelines. Steve, supposedly the smartest publicity man in the country, didn't realize that he was being used by the Navy against his boss. Of course, Steve has always been partial to the Navy. I remember him many years ago when he first came to Washington, when he covered the Navy for the Associated Press. He took himself almost as seriously then as he does now.

Late this afternoon I clapped a libel suit of $250,000 on Pegler.

May 25: Spent the day at Dover, Delaware, with Abe Spanel of International Latex, trying to decide whether or not I should go on the air for him. I like everything about him except the prospect of advertising baby pants and women's girdles. I asked Abe if the commercials would read pantie-girdles, and he said that they would. He promised, however, that they would not use such commercials as: "Don't hold a leaking baby on your lap."

May 26: The furor over Forrestal is continuing. *The Washington Post* is being bombarded with letters, some of which threaten to cancel subscriptions unless the column is canceled by June 15. It looks like an organized campaign.

I suppose the secret of mesmerism is to repeat a thing often enough and the victim will believe it. People are repeating the charge that I killed Forrestal to the extent that I am almost beginning to lie awake nights wondering whether I did. Certainly a lot of people have convinced themselves that it is true.

The truth is that my exposé of Senator Bankhead's speculation on the cotton market probably did kill him. The Alabama Democrat had a stroke a few days thereafter and died. I was always afraid I might be accused of his death, and in his case I undoubtedly would have been guilty. I have also been wondering why people did not accuse me of being responsible for Parnell Thomas's illness after the stories on his salary kickbacks.

But in the case of Forrestal my record is fairly clear. There was not very much I wrote about him of a personal nature. And if he had not been subject to my criticism of his policies, he probably would not have become a member of the Cabinet. I had forgotten it, but as early as 1929 when it was worth your life to write about the big bankers, I wrote an article for *The Nation* putting the finger on Dillon, Read, for loaning the money to Bolivia which started the Chaco War. I remember that Dillon, Read forced a semiretraction from *The Nation* at the time on the threat of a libel suit. My real gripe with Forrestal and what most people have lost sight of: that the same man who sanctioned loans for war purposes in Bolivia and particularly in Germany, was in control of the military establishment of the United States, and followed a policy in Germany almost identical with that which his banking firm followed from 1923 to 1930.

May 27:   Truman told Admiral Souers at a staff conference: "That son-of-a-bitch Pearson got the best of me on the SOB thing, but I'm going to get the best of him on the Forrestal suicide. I'm going to rub it in until the public never forgets." Following this conversation, at which General Vaughan was present, Vaughan got in touch with General Bolling, head of G-2, and called Hanson Baldwin of *The New York Times* in New York to play up Pearson as responsible for Forrestal's death. How many other calls Vaughan made I don't know, but the results of the campaign are obvious in Washington.

May 28:   *Editor & Publisher* carries a lead story on the Forrestal suicide with slanted news references to Winchell and Pearson being responsible.

May 29:   The Navy has sworn to get Louis Johnson. It is seething with rage over the way they have become the third-rate arm of the service. Under F.D.R., the Navy ruled the roost. There was nothing they couldn't get. The admirals never hesitated to go over the head of the Secretary of the Navy to F.D.R. direct. Now Truman, a former artillery captain, is not only partial to the Army, but his bosom friend, General Vaughan, is constantly at his side, while he has appointed as Secretary of Defense an Army colonel who leans toward the Air Force. So the

Navy is pulling every conceivable wire to smear Johnson. In addition, Forrestal's old friend, the investment banker Ferdinand Eberstadt, and the Wall Street gang are out to get Johnson. On top of this, the little group of newspapermen who were Forrestal's brain trust have also started a campaign to smear Johnson.

At first President Truman loved it—because it was reported that Louis was running for President. That was why Johnson came out at Clarksburg last night and announced that he had no political ambitions; that after his job was over, he was coming back home to West Virginia. Truman, finally seeing that the more they smeared Johnson the more they indirectly smeared him, called in Sam Rayburn and Senator Scott Lucas, demanding that they call off the investigation of the B-36, a plane Johnson is alleged to have favored because he was director and attorney for Consolidated Vultee, which manufactures the B-36. Lucas told Truman he could control some committees, but he couldn't control Appropriations, on which McKellar and Pat McCarran vote like Republicans.

May 30:   Telephones are being tapped again. After Forrestal left office, taps were pretty generally removed, but I got word yesterday that taps are on again.

June 3:   Spoke at luncheon [of the National Conference of Christians and Jews] at the Waldorf. When I first sat down at the speakers' table and looked out at the audience, I decided against going into the Forrestal matter. I decided to stick to mother, home, and heaven stuff. However, at the last minute I changed my mind. I went into a description of some of the problems of newspapermen in deciding what news should be printed and what should not, giving as an illustration the case of Congressman John Kee of West Virginia who is a dope fiend, and, without mentioning his name, told why I hadn't published this story —namely, because he is not in a position to make important decisions affecting the nation and, second, because he is over seventy and about to retire from public life. I then told of the decision I faced and other newspapermen faced regarding Forrestal, gave the reasons why Forrestal's decisions affected almost every person in the United States, told how some of the decisions in regard to Palestine, unification, etc., had been reversed, and pointed out that when a man in his position became temporarily insane, it was news to which the American public was entitled. And if I had to write the news again, despite the storm of criticism, I would still write it. I could not tell exactly how the speech went across, but at least, to put it mildly, they were interested.

Flew back to Washington. The Lee Hat people are still determined to take me off the air as of June 13, while International Latex is raising various objections to the terms of the new contract. Arrived at the farm for the tail end of Tyler's annual party. Spent most of the evening trying to write my Alumni Day speech for tomorrow.

June 4:   Arrived in Swarthmore shortly before lunch. It was my thirtieth reunion. Did reasonably well in remembering names of classmates I had not seen for years. I wonder if I looked as much older as they do. The Alumni Exercises were held in the outdoor auditorium which father had conceived about thirty-five years before, but which has now been dressed up with terraced seats thanks to the generosity of Tom McCabe and his Scott Tissue Paper Fortune. I rehashed the events of the first war and the class that graduated then. I did not remind anyone that I delivered the valedictorian address that year. But I did quote from some of it and recalled how miserably the world had fallen down on the pledges we took in 1919. It was much too serious a talk and probably I should not have made it.

Got home in time to write part of the broadcast and to spend most of the evening putting in long-distance telephone calls to prospective horse bidders. Joe Lebowitz has contributed an Arabian stallion which I wish I had never heard about.* It has to be auctioned off on the air tomorrow. And I am afraid the bidders will be scanty. I have been trying to get Rita Hayworth and Aly Khan in Paris to put in a bid, but they are unreachable.

June 5:   The Arabian stallion was auctioned off to Mrs. Louis Marx of Scarsdale. We had far more bids than I ever anticipated and the program was exciting, at least for me, though I hear from more intellectual listeners that it was a flop.

June 6:   Abe Spanel and the Weintraub cohorts descended on me unexpectedly to try to persuade me to advertise ladies girdles and babies pants. In many respects there is no one I would rather work for and

---

*A Chicago gambler, Joe Lebowitz specialized in covering the bets of bookies who needed to lay off heavy bets from their own clients. He also raised Arabian horses, and the horse in question was contributed to help one of Drew Pearson's charities.—Ed.

with than Abe Spanel. We think alike on almost everything. He has now conceived the very important idea that it is up to American businessmen to employ college and high school graduates. Otherwise we will have repetition of the disillusionment that occurred in the early 1930s and which produced the Alger Hisses and Whittaker Chamberses. Our radio negotiations, however, ended in a stalemate.

June 7:   After my speech in New York last Friday, I now learn that the head of the Adam Hat Company approached the Weintraubs with a view to sponsoring me.

June 8:   The Lees are getting nasty. They served me with an ultimatum that I was to get off the air June 12, though I have a two-year contract yet to run. They want me to cancel with no compensation. I have previously told them that I would cancel as soon as I got another sponsor, but now they want me to get off, sponsor or no.

June 11:   Flew to New Orleans, met by Mayor deLesseps Morrison's committee and was given a lunch by them at Antoine's.
     It has been just ten years since I wrote the series on the Huey Long gang which sent Governor Leche and about five others to jail.
     At Baton Rouge, I stayed with Governor Earl Long despite the fact that I had been a vitriolic critic of his brother toward the end, and had exposed the big contributions which put Earl Long in the governor's mansion. Both he and Mrs. Long are homey, delightful people. She has no children, considers Earl something of a son. He was much more at home on his farm than in the governor's mansion, and doesn't hesitate to say so. He is now raising goats plus some hogs, which he says are about as wild as the goats. Earl has incurred the enmity of the oil companies by socking them with a heavy tax, but on the whole has the people of the state with him and seems to be doing a good job.

June 12 [Baton Rouge]:   My broadcast was from the Louisiana *Merci* Car, which Fred Dent, chairman of the State Capital Memorial Commission, has enshrined on the grounds of the old state capitol. This was supposed to be my last broadcast. And it still may be. Faced with a quandary over a closing line: "Listen to Drew Pearson next week, etc." we simply ran the program a little long and filled in with the Marseillaise.
     After the broadcast I had to listen to Leander Perez, head of the

Tideland Oil lobby, about whom I have written in the past—and not too favorably. He is the man who contrived to take Truman's name off the ballot in Alabama and at first in Louisiana.

It was interesting to check on what became of the old Huey Long gang. Dick Leche was on his farm raising flowers and charges seventy-five cents to visitors to look through his gardens. George Carpenter, who served a jail sentence as a result of my accusations, is now the foremost builder in Baton Rouge. Seymour Weiss, once Democratic national committeeman, served a sentence for income tax evasion and is back running the Roosevelt Hotel, being a very good citizen.

Dr. James Monroe ("Jinglemoney") Smith, who got thirty years for embezzlement when president of Louisiana State University, finally was paroled and served as welfare officer at one of the state prisons. He did a good job there, but died a few weeks ago. Abe Shushan, who built the New Orleans airport, is back in the textile business; one other old man whose name I have forgotten committed suicide. With the possible exception of the latter, all have staged creditable comebacks.

June 13:   Edward T. Kane, U.S. district attorney in Detroit, finally rectified his previous statement that Father Coughlin was not involved in the Gariepy income tax case. Kane was a little evasive, but admitted to the press that Coughlin's name had figured in the investigation. It took three weeks to wring this statement out of him. During the three weeks, he was summoned to Washington once and got five telephone calls from the Justice Department reminding him that he had to come across with a rectifying statement. Finally this morning the Justice Department told him if he did not make the statement himself, they would make it for him.

June 14:   I telephoned Frank Hall of the National Catholic Welfare Conference News Service, asking whether he was going to carry the Kane statement. He told me in effect to go to hell.

Adam Hats signed up as a sponsor. I will miss Abe Spanel, but I still think I am better off advertising men's hats and shirts rather than ladies' pantie-girdles.

Pegler has been hounding the Lees with questions implying that the contract was canceled over the Forrestal suicide.

June 16:   The town is in a tizzy over rumors that J. Edgar Hoover has turned in his resignation.

June 17: At Cabinet this morning, Oscar Chapman and Charlie Brannan congratulated Truman on his statement to the press earlier in the week criticizing witch-hunting and inferentially casting aspersions on J. Edgar Hoover. This teed Truman off to quite a tirade on Hoover, to the effect that he was overrated and should not be collecting gossip about innocent people. He was particularly sore because Dave Niles had been mentioned in an FBI report in connection with a youthful love affair which had absolutely nothing to do with subversion. "Being a victim of Cupid," said Truman, "is not being a victim of Moscow propaganda."

Tom Clark confirmed the fact that Hoover had not offered to resign and, in fact, was far from it.

The Lees finally closed their cancellation contract with me, paying me $30,000 as a termination fee as of 1951. I predict that by that time they will not be in business.*

June 20: We received notice that Howser was taking a deposition from James T. Mulloy, our witness in Fresno. This sounds bad. Mulloy drew some [bank] drafts on me without permission and I declined to honor them. I suspect there might be repercussions.

June 21: The FBI is raising hell over the column for release tomorrow. As usual they got wind of it in advance. *The Post* is going to cut out all critical references to Lou Nichols [assistant director of the FBI]. They don't believe that it was Lou Nichols who spilled the Elizabeth Bentley story to Senator Homer Ferguson last year. However, this was the fact. At that time everyone thought Dewey was going to win. Ferguson was to be his Attorney General and Hoover's boss. The FBI at that time had no idea, first, that I would spill the story on Senator Ferguson's cowardly retreat from Senator Thomas of Oklahoma, or, second, that Truman would be reelected.† The Hiss trial in New York, the trial of Communist leaders, and any number of other repercussions

---

*Drew Pearson's involvement with Lee Hats made them the most widely worn men's hats in America, but his prediction of a business failure by 1951 was wrong. Lee Hats did disappear later—but so have most hats for men.—ED.

†Drew Pearson had disclosed that a scheduled grain-market investigation had been called off by Senator Ferguson after the Michigan Republican had been threatened by Senator Elmer Thomas with disclosure of his own business dealings.—ED.

all stem from the fact that Lou Nichols took the Elizabeth Bentley file up to Ferguson. While he did not leave the file with Ferguson, he prepared a brief digest from which Ferguson could ask questions.* George Boos got so sore that he walked out of the office and stayed out all during the Bentley hearings.

June 22: George Arnold has gotten in touch with Mulloy in Fresno and finds that Mulloy has gone over to Howser. We don't know why.

June 24: George went to Fresno and finally got the truth out of Mulloy. He says he was approached by the Howser crowd, who in the end offered him $18,000 plus a trip to Canada if he would retract all that he had testified to in his deposition for me. Ex-Congressman Bud Gearhart and [Walter] Lentz, who acted for Howser in dealing with Mulloy, told him that the Justice Department would never extradite him from Canada to face a perjury charge because Truman hated me.

June 25: George has persuaded Mulloy to stand with us. Mulloy is weak but I am convinced honest at heart. George stood in the lobby of the Fresno Hotel and watched the Fresno DA, who works for Howser, hand Mulloy some money.

June 27: Flew to New York and had dinner with my new sponsor, Elias Lustig, of Adam Hats. His first question was: "Well, are we going to have a welfare state?" We got along famously in regard to business matters. I discovered that Lustig had been one of the benefactors of the Bonus Army in 1932. We agreed that we had similar ideas regarding the danger of native fascist leaders.

Just learned that Harry Cooper, former Secret Service man, had committed suicide in Baltimore, leaving a note which indirectly blamed me.

*Elizabeth Bentley, who appeared before Ferguson's Senate Investigations Subcommittee in July 1948, testified to much of what she had told the FBI in 1945: that she had served five years as a courier of a Soviet spy ring in which thirty government employees were members.—Ed.

It was Cooper who broke up the American Joy Club in Kunming which was run by Mme. Chiang Kai-shek, supposedly for the entertainment of American troops but actually for her own personal profit. Cooper, who was provost marshal for General Joe Stilwell, once told me how Stilwell was worried over leaks regarding troop movements and ordered the Joy House closed. Following which Stilwell went south to the battlefront. Immediately thereafter he received instructions from General Chiang Kai-shek to report to Chungking. Stilwell wired back that he was busy at the front and a war was going on. The General replied, reminding him that Stilwell was the Chief of Staff. So Stilwell flew to Chungking, and he was confronted not by the General but by Mme. Chiang with Chennault. She chided him for closing the Joy House. "After all, this was established for the hospitality and amusement of American boys who are doing so much for us," she said. "But we have traced important war secrets to the girls in this house," argued Stilwell. However, Mme. Chiang was adamant. She insisted that the house be reopened and it was. Later Stilwell caught three Chinese girls and convicted them of espionage regarding troop movement information. However, they were the daughters of important Chinese politicians and, although given death sentences, Stilwell found out that subsequently three Chinese peasant girls were beheaded in their place.

Cooper also told me that Chennault had received about $250,000 from the Chinese during the war, which he kept in a strongbox in either New Orleans or Mobile. I cross-checked this story with the Treasury Department and found it to be true. The matter came up during the war when Treasury Secretary Henry Morgenthau wanted to collect income taxes from Chennault but was advised first that Chennault had made his money outside the United States so it was nontaxable; and, second, that the matter should not be raised because of bad morale reaction.

June 28:   Truman is still irked at J. Edgar Hoover. One reason is that the FBI file contained a report that Charlie Ross, going down the bay on a Norfolk boat, had chased a couple of gals around the deck.

June 29:   Practically all the Catholic papers have refused to retract the Coughlin story even despite the statement of District Attorney Kane in Detroit.

Saw Louis Johnson for the first time in his office since he became

Secretary of Defense. Louis has changed a lot since the days when he was begging for support to get this appointment. He spent most of his time arguing over whether or not he had declined to see me previously; also telling me that Curtis Calder of Electric Bond & Share was not his choice for Secretary of Army, but rather Truman's. "I have to play ball," explained Louie. "I have to take the rap for the chief."

I planted with Louie the fact that it was Secretary of Interior Krug who leaked the facts to Bernie Baruch about Truman's failure on the National Securities Resources Board. Louie was quite pleased with the information, said he would get it to the President right away. "There is no one the President hates more than Baruch," said Louie, and I was tempted to add, "Yes, the saying around the White House is the only man Truman hates more than Pearson is Baruch."

Interesting fact about the Krug-Baruch leak was that it came from a telephone operator in the Interior Department who listened to Krug telling Baruch about the National Securities Resources Board's failure.* It always pays to have the telephone operators on your side and in the Interior Department they don't like Cap Krug. I hope this will do a job for Oscar.

July 1:   I saw Sumner Welles for the first time since last summer. He has lost thirty-five pounds and aged ten years in ten months. At long last he is going abroad, on the old SS *De Grasse*. Ever since the war, Sumner has wanted to travel but Mathilde said no. Inevitably a man always pays when he marries a rich wife and Sumner, although he has had great advantages, has paid in the end rather heavily.

Dave Karr was in Steve Early's office when Louis Johnson rushed in to report on the Cabinet meeting. "Drew's name came up at the Cabinet," Louie reported. "The President wanted to know if I had mentioned Drew in my press release denying his story on the Joint Chiefs of Staff." (Louie was referring to a story in which I quoted the Joint Chiefs of Staff as being opposed to arming Europe under the North Atlantic pact.) "I replied that the State Department issued the release," continued Louie. "Ask Dean. Dean said to the President, 'No, we didn't mention Drew's name.' " Louie further reported that the

*On June 28, 1949, Baruch charged that the Truman administration had been negligent in failing to adopt a National Securities Board plan for war mobilization. —ED.

President seemed pleased. In that case I can't understand why he asked specifically whether my name was mentioned.

Steve Early, believe it or not, proceeded to give Louie a bawling out. Here's the gist of what he said: "Louie, you've got to quit lying. You lied to Drew about Curtis Calder (Dave had just reported our conversation of two days before). You said Calder was a White House choice and he wasn't. You can't lie and get away with it. And you lied to Drew about forty-eight air group.* You said it was fifty-four. You can't lie to your friends." "Well, I estimate that the forty-eight might be figured as fifty-four according to how you count the planes," replied Louie. "You know it can't be figured that way," shot back Steve. "You know it perfectly well, and you've got to quit lying. You can't lie to any newspaperman and particularly you can't lie to Drew who's been helping you."

July 5:   Cut ten acres of hay. This may have been a mistake, both from the point of view of sunburn and the Lees. While away from the telephone, the Lees jumped the gun with an announcement that they were now taking on a "noncontroversial" radio program. They had agreed in writing that there would be no announcement except by mutual agreement.

July 6:   Lunched with Bob Kerr of Oklahoma. He is a real diplomat. He remarked when we met: "You've lost weight. I told my wife," he continued, "that I'd reduce any way she wanted except through two things—diet and exercise." We then proceeded to eat a nonreducing lunch. The Senator was worried because I had reported that he was pushing the new bill removing the gas companies from regulation by the Federal Power Commission. His main argument is that natural gas is used chiefly by industry, not consumers, and that other commodities used in industry—coal, steel, labor—are not regulated. Therefore, it is unfair to penalize the producer of natural gas whose expenses are heavy anyway. I told Bob, "O.K., but why penalize a public servant, Leland Olds (who is now up for confirmation), merely because he had been against the natural gas companies and the Senator?"†

---

*Reference to the Presidential budget message of January 1949, which set financing for forty-eight Air Force combat groups.—Ed.

†A member of the FPC, Olds was up before the Senate for confirmation of his renomination to a third five-year term. A Senate committee rejected the renomination on October 5, 1949.—Ed.

July 8: Saw Tom Clark. J. Edgar Hoover wrote him a stinging letter accusing me of killing part of the FBI-Lou Nichols column in two papers, but lacking the courage to do it in the others. Of course, it was the editors who killed the story—not me. Tom thinks that Ward Canaday's appointment should be killed as Chairman of the Munitions Board. I asked him why Truman should appoint a man whose company [Willys-Overland Motors] was up for fraud before the Justice Department, who had boosted automobile manufacture prior to Pearl Harbor at a time when the New Deal economist Leon Henderson was urging that the auto companies be patriotic and curtail, and who was one of the big backers of Empire Ordnance, one of the worst scandals of our days. Tom has no answer.

Lunched with Ansel Luxford of the World Bank. He is pleased that McCloy is going to Germany. Eugene Black of the Chase Bank, now head of the World Bank, is improving. Trouble was that McCloy didn't belong to the Wall Street club so he always tried to be clubbier than the club members. He kowtowed to them. But Black does belong and now he wants to show that he is a good government man and not part of the Wall Street club.

July 9: *Time* magazine got wind of the story on Father Coughlin being responsible for cancellation of my radio contract. At first I weaseled. I can now understand how easy it is for a government official to lie to a newspaperman. The newspaperman usually doesn't know the facts, has to depend upon the honesty of the official he is trying to talk to. That is what I did with *Time*. Later I got conscience-stricken and called Oulahan of *Time* in and told him the truth.

Had lunch with Sam Pryor of Pan American Airways, who is trying to tempt me to take a South American trip—which I am not going to do.

Harold Talbott, who raised much of the money for Dewey, stopped by at the table to complain that Hugh Scott, the GOP chairman, wasn't able to raise a cent. Scott, he said, has got to go.

July 10: Some of the GOP boys held a secret meeting in Pittsburgh last night and in order to carry out Talbott's admonition, it looks as if Scott is on the skids. This means the Stassen-Taft crowd are determined Dewey will never have another smell at the nomination. I also suspect that Governor Duff of Pennsylvania and Harold Stassen, president of the University of Pennsylvania, made a deal. They are already laying their plans to get their own man in as GOP chairman.

July 12:   George Killion, the Democratic fund-raiser from California who is just back from the Orient, came to dinner, together with Jim McHugh, who for seven years was personal aide to Generalissimo Chiang Kai-shek. I knew he was not enthusiastic about the General, but I had no idea how bitter he was. Jim lunched, dined, and sometimes breakfasted with the Chiang family for years and says they were anti-American in the extreme. They not only hated the United States but joked about the way they were using American aid.

Killion reports that MacArthur got himself into an inextricably bad spot making himself higher than the Emperor. He now has to take all the blame for all that goes wrong in Japan.

The American military, once popular in Japan, is now hated. If MacArthur had trained a constabulary of Japanese, he could withdraw American troops into a few barracks in the background and let the Japanese do the policing. As it is, the American Army is entwined with the economics and politics of the country. In one hotel alone there are three different currencies—one for American military personnel, one for American businessmen, one for Japanese. You cannot unload a ship without permission of the military. You can't get a hotel room without permission of the military. There is nothing in fact that you can do without an American military O.K. Obviously the Japanese resent this.

July 13:   State Department has received a report from a special inspector they sent to Hungary on the Mindszenty case and on Selden Chapin, the Ambassador who was kicked out by the Russians. The report shows that Chapin was smuggling anti-Soviet agents out of Hungary in the trunk compartment of the Embassy's car. Chapin was working hand-in-glove with the clergy, including Mindszenty, in espionage matters and it looks as if the Soviet trial was probably not too far off base. Cardinal Mindszenty himself was not implicated as much as the clergy under him, though obviously he knew what was going on. The Russians apparently were quite right in demanding Chapin's recall. We would have done the same thing had we caught Russian diplomats up to the same tricks. Inspector also reported that Chapin ran such an inefficient Embassy that it would be difficult to appoint him to any other position except for the fact that such a furor was raised over his recall. In other words, the Russians did Chapin a favor.

July 14: Truman is making a speech on the importance of spending, and the Republicans are opposed. His idea is that spending will head off depression. It's the same old Roosevelt–Herbert Hoover fight all over again. When Roosevelt was running for President in 1932, he claimed Hoover was spending too much money. When he got into office, Roosevelt made Hoover look like a piker when it came to spending. I predict that if the Republicans come into office in the relatively near future they will outspend Truman.

July 17: My last broadcast for Lee Hats. Ohio's Senator Taft will take over the next broadcast.

I learned today in the course of probing General Vaughan and his lobbying links that he was behind the Tanforan race-track scandal. I now realize why I had such a hard time moving federal officials regarding Tanforan. More than two years ago I talked to the U.S. district attorney in San Francisco, and the federal housing authorities in California, all of whom were anxious to prosecute the race track for violating housing orders. The race-track people had used scarce building materials to which veterans were entitled, to repair their stables. And a federal judge finally held them in contempt of court. But although I can usually get action in Washington, this time I couldn't. Both the Justice Department and the Housing Expediter refused to budge. In the end the federal judge in California, together with U.S. Attorney Hennessy, proceeded with the case and sent several of the Tanforan officials to jail, though not until after I had worried them incessantly. Only today I learned the real reason. Harry Vaughan, the White House coordinator for veterans' activities and supposedly the protector of veterans, was working against the veterans at Tanforan.

July 18: More about Tanforan. The Senate Expenditures Committee has bumped into the fact that James V. Hunt, the five-percenter, first talked to Housing Expediter Creedon about Tanforan, but apparently didn't do a good enough job. Following this, Vaughan himself intervened with the Housing Expediter, who sent a memo to the Justice Department advising Justice that the criminal case against the Tanforan boys in San Francisco could be dropped. John Maragon apparently got a $5,000 fee out of the deal. In back of the whole thing was Bill Helis, who had bought the race track in about 1946 from Joe Reinfeld, one of the biggest bootleggers ever to operate off Jersey during prohibition days. Now I understand why Bill Helis contributed $3,000 to the J. Edgar Hoover Foundation.*

Frank Murphy died. I will miss him. The last time I talked to Frank was on the long-distance telephone. I said that Cardinal Mooney was now in Coughlin's corner after not speaking to him for six years and that the Church was determined to get me off the air. I asked Frank if he could help, but he said that the Church was almost as down on him as it was on me, because of his vote on the Supreme Court regarding Catholic education and the public schools. Frank and I have gone through some hectic days together. I remember when he was running for Governor of Michigan and I was speaking before the Michigan Educational Association all over the state, and put in a plug for him each time. I don't think it did any good but he never forgot it.

The only time I ever got sore at Frank was when I asked him how he felt about Franco in 1939. He was then Attorney General. He replied that he was opposed to him. Later, when I quoted this in the column, Frank issued a denial, which was smeared all over the Brooklyn *Tablet* and other Catholic papers. Frank later apologized to me and said he was under pressure.

I remember sitting in Harry Hopkins's bedroom one morning about 10:00 A.M. when Liz Whitney phoned to say: "Harry, I bet you don't know where I am. I'm in Frank Murphy's apartment. I spent the night with him. I was out with Frank until three A.M., and he couldn't get rid of me so he brought me home here. He still can't get rid of me." "Well, there's no place where you could be safer," said Harry, which was largely true. Frank loved the women, but according to Evie Robert, he died a male virgin, and Evie should know.

*John Maragon rose from Senate shoe-shine boy to Presidential envoy to Greece —a post he held only briefly after his five-percenter activities were exposed by Drew Pearson. The five-percenters—those who got a kickback on government contracts they helped obtain—were a part of one of the major scandals of the Truman administration. Aside from his race track operations, Bill Helis was a New Orleans oil man. The J. Edgar Hoover Foundation was one of Drew Pearson's charitable involvements.—ED.

Frank got mixed up with Mrs. Whitney in Warrenton last winter when Liz went on the warpath, got out a revolver and began shooting. One guest was shot in the fanny, others dropped out the window, and I don't know what became of Frank. Anyway the police hushed the whole thing up because Frank was involved.

July 20:   Jim Carter, the U.S. Attorney in Los Angeles, finally cracked down on the Howser crowd. They arrested Howser's DA in Fresno this morning. An hour or two later they arrested Walter Lentz, who used to be Howser's right-hand man and head of his secret service. They held Lentz on the charge of bribing a witness—namely, Mulloy.

July 21:   [Police Commissioner] Harry Toy called up from Detroit to say that Cardinal Mooney had employed William Gallagher to protect Coughlin in the Gariepy income tax case when it is tried. Gallagher is the man whom ex-Attorney General Eugene Black recommended I retain to sue the Detroit *Times*. Now I understand why Gallagher was not even polite in saying no. Toy also reports that a local Detroit football star, now an attorney, has been retained to sue me on behalf of Coughlin and Mrs. Gariepy—a Church deal.

Lunched with Ellis Arnall. He says no one can beat Senator George if he wants to run. Arnall would like to run later. He is only forty-one.

[*The entries from July 27 through September 20, 1949, as well as entries for September 29, September 30, and October 1, are transcribed from longhand notes, which were evidently intended as a basis for dictating full entries at a later time.*]

July 27:   Mrs. R. answers Spelly—"God is the judge as to whether I am an unfit mother."*

July 30:   Warned Spellman might ban column for all Catholics. R.S.A. [probably Robert S. Allen] asked quote from O'Mahoney, etc. None would criticize Spellman publicly.

---

*On July 23, Cardinal Spellman had called Mrs. Roosevelt's opposition to public aid for parochial schools "unworthy of an American mother." Mrs. Roosevelt replied in a letter made public July 27.—Ed.

August 1:   Lunched with Guy Gabrielson.

August 2:   Guy Gabrielson elected [Republican National Chairman, replacing Hugh Scott].

August 7:   McCarthy & Sparkman good job.*

August 8:   Costello reports from Detroit that Catholic fascism on upsurge due to Mooney's absence.

Hearings started on Vaughan. Tanforan. It was three years ago that I started crusading on Tanforan. Had no idea then Vaughan was behind it. Recall wall of silence and resistance I met in Washington. It was just five months ago that Truman unloosed SOB blast at me because I protested his [Vaughan's] receiving a medal from a dictator. Now I wonder who's the SOB?

Only history can tell how our lives influenced by the buffoon in W-H [White House]. Potsdam—Truman's lecture of Stalin.

Men who see any President every day have greater influence than Cabinet members.

Things to bring out on Vaughan & Maragon. Fired from Bituminous Coal. Fired by B & O—squeeze on hotels. Liquor deals—Vaughan—Kronheim. Fight in Nats' locker room. Fired from Greece—Grady. Killion wouldn't let him around Dem. Committee.

Yet he [was] taken to Potsdam.

August 11:   Finally left for California. Dinner with Geo. Bowden. Vaughan was to be governor of Guam after his Guatemalan vacation —Guam to be transferred from Navy to Interior. Then all hell broke loose in Senate.

August 12:   All day on Super-Chief—through New Mexico, Kansas, and Arizona. How many times I have traveled this route—as a boy to Kansas, as a news syndicate salesman, on my honeymoon, and the last time with the *Merci* Train. There was one other memorable time when I went to California to board [Herbert] Hoover's battleship for South

---

*This is apparently the first reference in the diaries to Senator Joseph R. McCarthy and it most probably referred to the Wisconsin Republican's participation in the five-percenter investigation.—ED.

America as the representative of *La Nación*. And at the last minute Hoover wouldn't let me go. I went out on a launch in San Pedro Bay to the gangplank of the ship, but that was as far as I got.

However, the story I cabled BA of the refusal to admit the correspondent of *La Nación* made such headlines that Hoover invited a special *Nación* correspondent to board the ship at Santiago. Everything went wrong on that trip—in fact during most of his four years in the White House. Sometimes I think I got him off to a bad start.

My friend Gen. Vaughan is still in the headlines. This time the perfume co. which hired Maragon sent a deep freeze to Vaughan, Mrs. Truman, & Vinson.*

Pegler sounded off again. One whole column. Beginning to think I'm important.

August 13:   Arrived LA. My grandson is as redheaded as ever—and divine!

August 15:   Saw Jim Carter; swell guy; will make A-1 judge. Told Mayor Fletcher Bowron his friends who helped elect him were on spot as result of police scandals. He agreed; promised to clean up.

Discovered that Howser's finagling with J. Mulloy was much deeper than I realized. He phoned his political stooge, Franklin, in Fresno, who contacted chief of police & asked to have cop with impeccable reputation pick up Mulloy, who [was] making book at ____ Hotel. Then phoned two judges to keep Mulloy in jail until after deposition. Also arranged that Demos was to call Mulloy out just before deposition & tell him: "We have recordings of your conversations." This would put Mulloy in position of perjuring himself one way or other.

August 16:   Saw Gen. Worton, a sincere, military-minded ex-marine who, as emergency Chief of Police, is trying to clean up the Police Department, but finds he can't fire anyone. Under civil service any cop goes before a committee of other cops. Previous chief slept every afternoon. Didn't know what going on. Sunset Strip is under county, not city. Can thumb nose at city police. Each sheriff is a king in his own county. State has only highway patrol. I told Worton as diplomati-

*A reference to the celebrated freezers sent by the Albert Verley Company of Chicago in 1945, in return for favors rendered its representative, John Maragon.—ED.

cally as possible that he could have beaten the papers to the punch by making public the Cohen recordings. Now he is fighting rearguard action. George went further & told the chief that newsmen wouldn't cooperate because they regarded him as a boy scout. This broke up the meeting.

Lunched with Gov. Warren. We discussed his political future. He admits he's lost ground with Republicans. But his program is the same as he announced it. Only trouble is that Republicans expected him to talk liberal & then act conservative. He hasn't. Warren says Howser is planning to run Goody Knight, now Lt. Gov., against him & he'll have lots of money. "There is nothing to be ashamed of in being defeated for political office," he said, "but I'm not sure yet that I want to go through another four years of the grind of political office." Already seen eight years as Governor.

August 19:   Phoned R.S.A. [Robert S. Allen] re Pegler. He doesn't want to help. Lunched with Manchester Boddy of the Los Angeles *Daily News*. Gen. Wm. A. Worton, Dick Dickson, & Sammy Hahn. Sam has a NC law client, Blumenthal, who's in income tax trouble & wants to plead guilty. Justice told Sam they didn't want to compromise case for fear of me. Sam is getting Mon Wallgren a $100,000 job with Douglas Aircraft.

August 20 [New Mexico]:   They stopped Super-Chief at Lamy to let us out at Santa Fe. I am going to stop off a day at the Clarks' ranch.

August 22:   Many years ago, before Luvie & I were married, we drove up a dusty trail toward a mt. range and lunched on the banks of the Rio Grande River. Today we drove in the same direction, passed the same river and the tearoom now closed, to the place where man may be plotting his own downfall. Or, he may be making war so terrible that it will never come again. The dusty trail we followed has been replaced by a three-lane highway now and the beautiful mesa above the Rio Grande has been transformed almost overnight to a thriving, teeming city.

Los Alamos, once the most secret city in the world, is divided into three parts. The outer rim is accessible through a gate to anyone with a pass, which can be obtained on a few minutes' notice. Inside this is the "tech area" to which a pass takes three months FBI clearance. And inside that is the super-super secret area. We visited only the outer rim.

Los Alamos (The Willows) is the research center for all atomic weapons. Oak Ridge & Hanford are production projects. Los Alamos is also the center for health projects & the Navy men who went onto Bikini too quick were here with hands swollen the size of catchers' gloves.

The Zia Corp. (McKee) illustrates the difference between government & private efficiency. They maintain all autos, buildings, roads, garbage, electricity, water for a fixed fee of $12,000+ a month, which is 1.47 percent of total cost. Once they mowed & watered every lawn —labor cost $1.20 an hour. Now every tenant takes care of his own lawn or if he doesn't, gets a bill from Zia.

Unique experiment in complete government control. No taxes. Nothing to tax. Government owns everything—even the theaters, the stores, radio station, newspaper office, & barber shop. However, it leases out to concessionaires.

Three reasons why government saves money by letting Zia Corporation run Los Alamos: 1. Government workers get twenty-six days leave + 15 days sick leave; 2. government doesn't pay on time so doesn't get discounts for cash; 3. AEC can't clear workers on time. [Illegible] law *all* AEC workers must be cleared by FBI. You can't tell carpenter or truck driver "I'll hire you in sixty days." He'll be off at some other job. So Zia hires 'em in outer city, then, after clearance, moves 'em into "tech area."

At lunch, two scientists discussed why scientists didn't like to work for government. Its a curse, a throttling, a stagnation. [Illegible] of Calif. is in charge of all research. The government leases this job direct to the University, which hires & fires. Capt C. L. Tyler in command of AEC is retired naval officer, not too brassy, interested in democratic government. Folks complained they had no power to run Los Alamos, but on June 10 they became a county, will elect officials in Nov. 1950. Youngsters first anxious to run town now cooling. Realize its a lot of work. Older folks are taking over.

Los Alamos is still a closed city. There are certain advantages to no peddlers, no thieves. No worry about crime. Leave doors open all summer. Oak Ridge became open city & in two weeks many wanted it to be a closed city again. Thronged with tourists & salesmen.

Los Alamos has reactivated sleepy Santa Fe. Girls who got $10 a week now get $35 taking care of LA dormitories. Mexicans who got

$15 now get $50. New wage is $1.20 for unskilled labor. You can't get labor any more in Santa Fe.

September 2 [Washington]:   Testified before the Senate Expenditure Committee re Vaughan & the Burton jury bribery case. Told how I had sat in Jim McGranery's office when Vaughan called to ask his support for the Burton jury-bribers.*

The committee couldn't make up its mind until the last minute whether to call me or not. The Republicans wanted me called, the Democratic chairman, Clyde Hoey, didn't. Funny that I should have gone to North Carolina during Hoey's first political race and helped him be elected Governor.

September 4:   Back on the air again. Had a hard time deciding whether to use an item on Nina Lunn, the granddaughter of Senator White of Maine, who was caught holding a bath towel round herself and the otherwise nude Argentine Ambassador in the apartment of George Abell. Her husband, Nat Luttrell, who owns Woodward & Lothrop, had hired Joe Shineman, a police lieutenant, to shadow the lady & he made the mistake of breaking into the apartment while dressed in uniform—something they do in Russia, Spain, & Argentina. So the Ambassador protested to the State Department & got the divorce proceedings sealed.

Later, Foreign Minister Bramuglia kidded the Ambassador so vigorously that the Ambassador challenged him to a duel.

After more debate, we used the story with emphasis on the dueling and the police-state methods.

September 5:   Labor Day. Spent it not at the farm where I should, but at the Retail Clothiers Association of the Carolinas. Many nice people & more would have been nicer if they hadn't been drunk. However, had a good swim and met a fine editor, J. A. Rogers of the Florence *News.*

---

*William T. Burton, a wealthy New Orleans oil man, had been tried twice in 1946 on income tax fraud charges and had twice wound up with a hung jury. Subsequently, he was indicted and convicted of jury bribing. At the time of the telephone call, McGranery was Assistant to the Attorney General.—ED.

In Washington they have no conception of the extent to which the South hates the Truman Democratic party. Also they have been sold on the idea that the Truman program is entirely a socialistic one & that all their taxes are squandered.

If you told them that far more Northern taxes were poured back into the South they wouldn't believe it. A preacher who grandstanded before the drunken convention talked of the high taxes Mississippi paid to Washington. He forgot the money Washington poured into Mississippi in the form of war plants, air bases, & in cotton subsidies.

In Washington last week, Ansel Luxford of the International Bank talked of Britain as being America's No. 2 Depressed Area—the No. 1 Depressed Area being the South. This is true, but the truth is fighting words in Dixie.

September 6: Jim McGranery has denied my testimony that Vaughan tried to influence the Burton case.

It's funny how low people behave re the truth under varying circumstances.

In the summer of 1946 when the Burton case was before the Justice Department, McGranery was sore at both Truman & Tom Clark for not making him a circuit court judge. But this week, with Justice Rutledge dying, Jim wants to be appointed to the Supreme Court. In fact, Jim came down to the White House just after Frank Murphy died and before Tom Clark was appointed to his vacancy.

September 7: Dined with Peggy Palmer and George Gillis, an American Express official just back from Greece, who says that no American who works in Greece wants to go back. He signed for a year but has left after ten months.

Peggy got started on Joe Guffey. The day Mitchell Palmer died, he told her: "I probably haven't long to live now. And if I had my life to do over again there is one thing I wish I hadn't done—saved Joe Guffey."

He told how he and Dave Reed had intervened when Guffey embezzled a lot of money; how Reed had gone to the Mellons in Pittsburgh & raised the money to make up the deficit.

Later of course, Joe ran against Reed & defeated him for the Senate.

I have always wondered why Guffey, who was under either indictment or default on his income taxes for about thirty years, always threw Democratic support to the Mellon [Republican] machine in Pittsburgh. That's how they controlled the city.

I have also wondered why Guffey, who didn't practice much of what he preached, always voted consistently and religiously for the New Deal. Finally I have wondered why Joe was able to build an expensive new house when he came to Washington, despite the fact that he couldn't pay his income tax. Of course the truth is that Roosevelt was elected, and kept his congressional support in line, through the help of some of the shadiest figures in the country. The support of Jimmy Hines, who later went to jail, could not have been examined too closely. But perhaps, like a modern-day Robin Hood, his help from the feudal barons of the big city machines was justified by his program.

Senator McCarthy called me in today to say that more about the Costello-Helis-Vaughan connection was developing—another illustration of underworld support for the New and Fair Deal.

September 11: Justice Rutledge died last night—a great loss to the country and especially to the cause of liberalism. I remember when he came to see the Friendship Train film, *Thanks America*, with Frank Murphy. The two were almost inseparable—if that could be said of any of Frank's male friends.

Hugo Black & Bill Douglas are going to be mighty lonesome on the Court, but I have a hunch Tom Clark is going to be a lot more liberal than both expect.

September 12: Lunched with Bill Boyle—new chairman of Democratic National Committee. He talks liberal & so far acts liberal. Maybe he will really prove to be a liberal. He claims Truman and I are too much alike to get along. Don't know whether this is a compliment or not—but he meant it that way.

Saw Howard McGrath, the new Attorney General, to tell him about the J. Edgar Hoover Foundation. His outer office looks a lot different from Tom's—full of old-line politicians. To appoint a chairman of the Democratic National Committee as Attorney General a man must have a will of iron or else merely become a political tool.

Bill Boyle confessed that Truman was sore at Sam Jackson in Indiana because Sam didn't mention Truman's name when campaigning for Governor in 1944. Alex Campbell, he says, will get the nomination [for Senator].*

September 14:   An ex-Communist named Rushmore† testified before the Senate Judiciary Committee that Dave Karr, "Drew Pearson's legman," was a Communist & had worked for the *Daily Worker*. Rushmore said he had seen Dave's card.

I issued a denial. Of course, Dave, like a lot of other youngsters, might have had Communist leanings or even been a party member. But if I am any judge of human nature, he was cured of this long ago. And even if he was, a lot of us would be out of luck if all the sins of our youth were held against us.

Louise Steinman came in to get some advice about publishing Frank Murphy's letters to his mother and his memoirs. She said Frank couldn't do a lot of things he used to do—during his last year.

Very few people knew that Frank was ten years older than he claimed to be—which made him sixty-nine. A Michigan professor wrote me this once & Frank more or less admitted it when I asked him.

At the Rutledge funeral, Hugo Black looked old and worn. Even Bob Jackson looked tired. Few people realize how much of a grind the Supreme Court is. Hugo told George Murphy that he would retire in a year or two. He seemed to miss Frank pretty badly. George Murphy wanted to be Ambassador to Hungary.

September 19:   Lunched with Ickes. It always makes me sad to lunch with Ickes. Here is a world champion, now seventy-five years old, who doesn't realize he's out of the ring. He is still beating his breast, still ready to take on all comers & is going up to New York to campaign for Gov. Lehman. He'll do a good job at that. But otherwise he doesn't realize—except in a vague sort of way—that the world doesn't listen to him much any more.

Or perhaps he does realize it & just has too much pride & courage to admit it. I am rather inclined to think the latter is the case.

*Alexander Campbell did get nominated by the Indiana Democratic Party to run for the Senate in 1950. He lost.—Ed.

†A former *Daily Worker* reporter, Howard Rushmore recanted his Communist affiliations. For a time, he worked on the Hearst-owned New York *Journal-American;* later, he joined Senator McCarthy's staff.—Ed.

When I see him I think: "There someday will be me."

But in contrast to some others, Ickes is a fountain of youth & enthusiasm. Sumner Welles is in terrible shape—his wife dead, his big toes gone, some of his fingers off. He has no interest in life, won't see his friends, can't sleep at night. I'm afraid he wants to die.

I have been sitting with Ernest Cuneo tonight trying to figure out how we can arouse Sumner's flagging interest in life.

I think I shall ask Eugene Meyer [*Washington Post* publisher] to make him foreign affairs adviser of the *Post.*

September 20: The income tax inspector went into my 1948 tax return & threw out $150 for a dinner for the Chief Justice as if they think the Chief Justice can be corrupted by a dinner or anything else!

I had rumors that the White House was waiting to pounce on my 1948 return & sure enough they examined it shortly after it was filed. The tip came from Admiral Souers of the National Security Council, who said that Truman had ordered my tax returns gone into twice this year—as far back as 1935.

September 23: Mr. Truman announced today that Russia had set off its first atomic explosion. Public reaction was varied. One Republican remarked: "Pretty soon he'll be announcing that the Chinese discovered gunpowder." It reminds me of the dull, dead days of the early '30s when almost anyone could see that a dictator was building up in Europe who would eventually cause war. Those were the days when the people were much more interested in the stock market and the nationwide wave of kidnappings than they were in storm clouds abroad. Today the Brooklyn Dodgers are one-half a game behind St. Louis in the National League and the Yanks and the Boston Red Sox are neck and neck. And the American public is basically probably more interested in this race than in the race of atomic energy.

Some Truman critics are saying that he held the announcement in order to get more appropriations out of Congress, but as far as I can see this was not the case. Although the Russian explosion occurred in mid-August, scientists had not completed their findings until just a few days ago.

September 24: Talked to Howard McGrath yesterday about judges. I talked to him about Dave Bazelon who wants to be a U.S. Court of Appeals judge here in the District but who bet on the wrong horse in

Illinois, figuring Truman would lose. He gave $200 to Senator Curly Brooks, the spokesman of the *Chicago Tribune.* McGrath amazed me by pooh-poohing this. He said he often contributed to his opponent in political campaigns just to help him get started.*

Lentz and Franklin, the two Howser stooges in Fresno who tried to bribe Mulloy, were indicted yesterday on the charge of tampering with a federal witness. George Arnold called me up from California to say that Howser had risen up in all his wrath and accused me of appointing Jim Carter, the district attorney, to a federal judgeship, in return for his indictment of Howser's pals.

I told George to issue a counterstatement thanking Howser for the compliment but reminding him that anyone who is called an SOB by President Truman does not appoint judges in the Truman administration.

September 25:   It now develops that Britain did not want Truman to make his announcement on atomic energy at all. Roger Makins of the British Foreign Office, an old friend of Dean Acheson's, flew up from Washington to New York, tried to persuade him to dissuade Truman. I talked to Charles Campbell, the British press relations officer, but as usual the British lied.

Followed up a mysterious tip from a man who wanted to see me about Senator Thomas of Oklahoma and his commodity speculation. The informant refused to give his name, refused to come and see me, and refused to even give his address over the telephone. Finally he mailed me his address, 1701 V Street, S.E., and asked me to see him Sunday evening. Thinking it over and knowing some of the threats made by the boys around Thomas, I began to wonder whether this could be an ambush. Fred† was even more concerned and wanted to trail me in his car. He decided that the dangerous moment in any ambush was when you parked your car. In the end and after about an hour of searching all over Anacóstia, we located 1701 V Street, S.E., Apartment 1, where a very nice and inoffensive clerk in the Civil Service Commission turned out to be the informant. Mr. Yearwood had sat on the grand jury which indicted Ralph Moore, Thomas's speculating pal, together with Bob Harriss, Father Coughlin's friend,

*President Truman nominated Bazelon to the U.S. Court of Appeals on October 15, 1949.—ED.

†Fred Blumenthal, a leg man during this period.—ED.

Tom Linder, the Agricultural Commissioner of Georgia, and James MacDonald, the Agricultural Commissioner of Texas. He told me that Senator Thomas had also appeared before the grand jury in defense of himself and his friends, but that the more he talked, the more he incriminated himself. The grand jury wanted to indict Thomas, but the government protected him. Yearwood told how the FBI had dug out the accounts from Harriss & Vose showing that Senator Thomas's trading account was carried out not by name but by number, together with the other accounts on the part of Tom Linder, Ralph Moore, etc. The grand jury received conclusive evidence showing how prices went up just after certain investments were made by Thomas and his pals —investments which could only come from inside knowledge. One man from the Department of Agriculture testified before the grand jury that he was not employed by the government. Later it developed that he was, but the Justice Department has not yet brought a perjury case against him. He was one of those who tipped off the Thomas gang.

It was also developed before the grand jury that Bob Harriss had given a DeSoto to Tom Linder because of his statements calculated to influence the cotton market. Yearwood thinks also that another DeSoto was given to MacDonald but isn't quite sure. To climax it all the Justice Department has now dropped two indictments against the four members of the Thomas gang.

It looks like, Yearwood said, Irving Kaufman, in charge of the case, did a mediocre job, and the real work was done by Dodd, his assistant.* Irving Kaufman is now slated to become a federal judge.

September 26:   Mr. Kenneth Giddens, who runs the CBS radio station in Mobile, came in to tell me about one Joseph Mitchell of Mobile and his partner, Sam Ripps, who had made a large fortune selling jewelry to the Army PX's but who failed to file a proper income tax. He said that they had ducked out of criminal prosecution by contributing $70,000 to Joe Blythe of the Democratic National Committee.

It seems to me that there has been more and more of this type of thing going on in the Truman administration. People in the rest of the country are beginning to say: "If the big boys in Washington get theirs, I'll get mine." They take Harry Vaughan as a symbol of graft and figure that if it exists in high places, they can get away with it in

---

*Ironically, this appears to be a reference to Thomas Dodd of Connecticut; from 1938 to 1954, Dodd served as a Special Assistant in the Department of Justice.—ED.

little places. I doubt whether there is as much graft as the public sometimes believes, but unquestionably there is far more today than ever before. I have always maintained that the federal government was relatively honest. I am sure that the Hoover, Coolidge, and Roosevelt administrations were. With all their faults, the Republicans did not raid the Treasury as far as I can see. But today all sorts of people are getting away with shortcuts.

I went down to see Turner Smith in the Justice Department to talk to him about the Mobile case. At first he said that no case was on file, and I am certain he was telling the truth. Then he said it might have been an old case so he looked in his back file and found that, sure enough, it was there.

It had been closed out in June 1949, which meant that it was sent back to the Treasury Department as a nonprosecutable case. Turner, who is one of the most conscientious public servants I know, read me part of the record, which showed that a conference had taken place in Birmingham, Alabama, between the U.S. district attorney and John Mitchell of his office, together with some others, in which they decided that the evidence was not sufficient. The books of the Gulfport company had been destroyed and thus the government was not able to prove the amount of revenue obtained. Turner said that Lamar had been worried about this case because [Joseph] Mitchell had tried to hire his ex-law partner in Charlotte, N.C., and for that reason Lamar had leaned over backward to make sure their decision not to prosecute was correct.

While I am convinced that the boys in this part of the Justice Department are completely on the level, I still suspect that there was some kind of a fix higher up from some place along the line in this case.*

September 29: Took Bill Roberts† up to see Senator Matthew Neely of West Virginia, the new chairman of the Senate District of Columbia

---

*Despite transmission of the Ripps-Mitchell case from the Bureau of Internal Revenue to the Justice Department for prosecution, no action took place for two years. Ultimately, through the persistence of a Justice Department attorney, John H. Mitchell (not to be confused with the defendant, Joseph Mitchell), Ripps and Mitchell were convicted and sent to prison.—ED.

†Roberts, a Washington attorney with liberal leanings, occasionally represented Drew Pearson and was also a source of information and news leaks.—ED.

Committee—a thankless job if there ever was one. Matt Neely is a peculiar guy, but in a way he represents the type of public servant who has thrived under the Democrats and who on the whole has done a pretty good job.

Back in West Virginia, Matt gets his support from the gambling underworld. Bill Lias, recently up for income tax evasion, has consistently contributed to Neely's campaign, and Neely went to bat hard for him when he was in trouble. But in Washington, Neely has had a consistently pro-public voting record, and furthermore has fought hard for the public interest. In a way he is like Harry Truman, who came to the Senate with the support of the corrupt Pendergast machine, again supported by gamblers, but again Harry went down the line in the Senate, and since, for the little guy.

It seems as if I have known Neely almost since 1922 when he first entered the Senate. He is now older than God, certainly at least seventy-five, but he looks to be sixty.

Bill Roberts gave him a pretty good picture of the way the District of Columbia is run by the big utilities. Bill was appointed people's counsel by F.D.R. and probably knows the situation better than anyone else. In brief, it boils down to the fact that while Harry Truman blasts the utilities of the rest of the nation, the utilities run the capital of the United States right under his nose.

The Board of Trade, which is run in part by the *Washington Star*, teams up with the Capital Transit Company, the Potomac Electric, the Washington Gas & Light Company, all three up until recently controlled by Stone & Webster and North American. Flanagan, head of the Public Service Commission and supposed to protect the public, formerly worked for the utilities and sees eye to eye with them on everything. The head of the D.C. Commissioners, John Russell Young, was a correspondent for the *Star* for twenty years.

Neely promised to blow open the situation but it is going to be a complicated job.

Ford gave his workers $100 pension at the age of sixty-five last night. The Newmyers, with whom I dined, were in on the negotiations. One week ago (Friday) they were almost agreed when UAW President Reuther said: "I've got to threaten you with a strike. This can't appear to come too easy."

So he broke off & bargained for another six days. The terms, however, remained the same.

If Reuther had secured the contract too easily his value to the union would have been lessened. He could afford bad relations between labor & management, but to lessen his own value to the union he could not afford.

September 30: Stu Symington is blazing mad at the Navy, compares 'em to the Jap military fascists who overthrew civilian rule before Pearl Harbor. Glenn Martin, who couldn't get Air Force contracts, even had the Burns Detective Agency checking on Stu.

Air Force strategy has been shifted suddenly. All bases in Caribbean being closed and planes then taken away from Panama to concentrate in Alaska, Canada, & Greenland—all as a result of Russian A-bomb.

Alaska—fifty-eight miles from Siberia—is woefully unprepared. The radar screen is inadequate to detect Russian planes & Congress appropriated no additional money for radar screen.

Russians could knock out Seattle Boeing plant—Consolidated Vultee, both on West Coast & sole makers of B-36. Thats why Stu's insisted that Boeing move to Wichita, Kansas, despite terrific pressure from Seattle business interests.

Stu thinks Russians will attack once they know they are stronger than we. They will stage another Pearl Harbor.

Stu kept coming back to the question of naval insubordination. In Japan they assassinated. Here they just try character assassination.*

The Chief Justice [Fred Vinson] and I have been trying to get Peggy Palmer a job in the State Department. He called this A.M. to say that Under Secretary of State Jimmy Webb had called him to say they had found a place—where she will work with women's clubs. Webb said it would help if House Speaker Sam Rayburn called about it. Fred was obviously a little quizzical about this. Apparently Webb didn't think the influence of the Chief Justice was enough. But, anyway, Sam called.

*In August 1949 an anonymous document submitted to the House Armed Services Committee had charged Secretary of Defense Johnson and Secretary of the Air Force Symington with irregularities in awarding B-36 contracts. The document was later revealed to have originated with an assistant to the Under Secretary of the Navy, who in turn admitted that he had consulted with Glenn L. Martin, Consolidated Vultee's competitor for the B-36 contract.—ED.

October 1:   Ray Wakefield of the FCC committed suicide yesterday. This time the rantings that attended Forrestal's death are absent. But Wakefield was a far better public servant.

Harry Costello got a phone call from Detroit saying that the Catholic leaders there had decided to promote the Gariepy libel suit against me after all. Mrs. Gariepy has finally been induced to bring suit even though some of the Catholic laymen have warned that a lot of her past is bound to come out. Meanwhile Harry reports that the record in Mrs. Gariepy's divorce suit has been lifted from the court files.

October 3:   Senator Hoey has called off the investigation of General Vaughan and Maragon—as I expected.

George Arnold called me from Los Angeles to say that he had moved in federal court to postpone Mulloy's deposition. The judge granted the motion without even listening to his argument; told him to "Sit down young man, and don't argue when the court is with you." In preparing his motion, George got affidavits from the district attorney in Fresno and one other city official stating under oath that Howser had approached them last May asking them to get Mulloy drunk in order to give the police an excuse to arrest and jail him for the purpose of getting him to change his testimony.

The significant thing to me is that the FBI must have had exactly this same information at the time Howser was up for possible indictment. Nevertheless the Justice Department sidestepped indicting Howser.

Had quite a talk with Ray McKeough, now a Maritime commissioner, who came up through the ranks of the Kelly-Nash political machine in Chicago. McKeough told how Mayor Ed Kelly of Chicago came to see the then Assistant Secretary of War Louis Johnson in 1940 to get his support on a Chicago waterways problem. Louis appeared distracted, didn't pay much attention, finally remarked: "How about some votes from the Chicago delegation for me?" This was just prior to the Democratic convention in Chicago which renominated Roosevelt and at which Louis aspired to be the Vice-Presidential candidate. Kelly is a thick-skinned politician, but he came out of the conference remarking to McKeough: "That guy is not for me." Louis got no votes from Illinois.

October 4:   Lunched with Dr. Townsend, of the old-age pension movement. He didn't mention the scathing editorials his papers used to write against me, nor did I mention some of the things my column used to carry about him. He is eighty-three years old and doesn't look it, eats like a sparrow, says the secret of living a long time is being thin. He also says he expects to live to be over a hundred.*

October 11: Went to see Bernie Baruch. He is lonesome. I arrived at 10:30, stayed for lunch, and didn't leave until after two. I think he feels rather deeply the Truman boycott. He said it didn't worry him, but he kept coming back to it from time to time.

Bernie says that one trouble with this world is that nobody has time to think. He told how, when they were discussing the Marshall Plan at Blair House [the temporary White House] in its very early stages, Bob Lovett, then Under Secretary of State, estimated it would cost $27 billion. Baruch wanted to know where he got that figure. Lovett fumbled in his papers, said he didn't know, finally cabled Paris, and later came back with the figure $17 billion. He had been in just too big a rush to get things straight. Later during the conference, Forrestal took out his watch and said he had to go. Lovett then said he was busy and left. Finally all departed except Baruch and General Marshall. Baruch turned to Marshall and said: "That's the trouble, General, none of us have any time to think. We don't plan things ahead."

Baruch's point is—and I think he is right—that nobody planned the Marshall Plan carefully. They didn't require Europe to form a United States of Europe. And so after all the money is spent, Europe will still be just as badly off as it ever was.

Bernie is worried about the lack of civilian defense in case of an atomic bomb raid on this country. He says about fifty laws have been drawn up ready to be passed to prepare for this, but nothing has happened.

Bernie told me in some detail about his personal relationship with Truman, how he suggested to Truman that he call a special session of Congress in the summer of 1948 after the Philadelphia [Democratic nominating] convention. He also told how he had picked up the telephone and called Harry Byrd to call off the Southern Senators in their opposition to Tom Clark's confirmation to the Supreme Court.

*Townsend came close: He died in 1960 at the age of ninety-three.—ED.

Later, I sat at dinner beside Howard McGrath and mentioned my visit with Bernie. McGrath seemed to think that things could and should be patched up between Truman and Baruch. And I gather that he will undertake to do so. From a human relationship point of view, I think probably Truman is right. Baruch's advice is 100 percent on the reactionary side.

McGrath has been worried over the fact that the newspapers won't publish the government's side of the case regarding antitrust suits, the row with the American Medical Association, etc.* I suggested that he hold press conferences, reminded him that the press conference had practically become nonexistent in the Truman administration. But I also reminded him that the only way to handle the newspapers was to be tough. They would never be on his side anyway, so he might just as well tangle with them via the antitrust laws. I mentioned cases which his antitrust division is working on against the Omaha *World-Herald*, the Rochester papers, the Kansas City *Star,* which incidentally he didn't know about. McGrath was a bit shocked. "Don't you suppose they'll learn a lesson from the Lorain, Ohio, case?" he said.† "Newspapers never learn," I told him.

October 12 [New York]:   Went to the U.N. General Assembly. The Polish delegate was answering Ben Cohen's charges regarding lack of freedom in Bulgaria. His answer was merely a recital of Ku Klux Klan incidents in the South coupled with a few incidents in the North. Read consecutively, it was a shocking record. Americans have no idea how this record sounds to Europeans. Of course, neither the Polish delegate nor the Moscow radio let it be known that the incidents in this country are small compared with its normal everyday life.

October 13 [New York]:   Morris Ernst came to dinner. We spent most of the evening talking about Frankie Costello, whom Morris has represented in one or two cases, notably when Costello was paying $1,000 a month protection money to the New York police to keep from being arrested every night, with $400 a month to Dewey's state police.

*McGrath's Justice Department was investigating local medical societies for possible antitrust violations.—ED.

†The government had charged the Lorain *Journal* with monopolistic practices. —ED.

Morris wrote to Police Commissioner Valentine, told him that his client was ready to answer any and all charges and would be available for cross-examination at any time; and that if any charges were to be brought they should be brought instead of harassing him with arrests. Valentine immediately stopped the shakedown racket.

Morris says there are some human sides to Costello. Among them is the fact that his psychologist urged him to go out and do something for other people. Following this advice he threw a big party in the Copacabana, which he owns, for the Salvation Army, and immediately got a rash of unfavorable publicity.

I told the story of how Jack Regan in Chicago had given me the inside story of the gambling racket and a few weeks after I had turned this over to Tom Clark, Regan was shot when his car stopped at a red light in Chicago. Regan wasn't killed—though badly wounded. However, the syndicate got to him in the hospital, bribing either a nurse or doctor, and he was found dead with a tube of mercury in his intestines. Morris says that Costello undoubtedly elected Fiorello La Guardia and also elected O'Dwyer. Yet both mayors castigated Costello unceasingly. What the payoff was nobody seems to know.

October 14: Dined with Sumner Welles. Had forgotten the fact that it was his birthday. Sumner looks better, but is still a long way from being his old self. When he was talking on Latin American affairs, he made good sense, in fact better sense than I have heard since the old days when he was steering those affairs.

Of course, it is useless to cry over spilt milk, but I still cannot help but think that if Sumner had remained on in the State Department in 1943 the peace of the world would not be so garbled. Sumner has plenty of faults and is a difficult man at times to get along with, but he has a perspective far beyond anyone else I have known in the State Department.

He recalled how when the U.N. was first being discussed and before it was actually announced to the world, [representatives of] South American countries were called into Blair House, lined up like schoolchildren, and given a lecture by Pasvolsky, Cordell Hull's White Russian adviser. They were merely told what was to be done, not consulted. Naturally their backs were up against the U.N. from the start.

Then when Secretary of State George Marshall went to the

Bogotá conference, he went out of the way to tell Latin Americans that they would not be included in the Marshall Plan—despite pledges given to these same nations shortly after Pearl Harbor that they would be included in all reconstruction plans after the war.

F.D.R., according to Sumner, had definite and concrete plans for the future of Germany. He planned a United States of Europe in which the individual German states would participate as separate entities, not as one country. F.D.R. had literally grown up in Germany, Sumner reminded me, and knew the German people intimately. His idea was to restore the principalities of Bavaria, Saxony, and Westphalia into the old German Federation.

Sumner pointed to one difference between Truman and F.D.R. which I expect few people realize—namely, the fact that Truman has never read a history book in his life. You can't mold history, according to Sumner, unless you know history.

We talked at length about Wendell Willkie and F.D.R. I told Sumner about my conversation with Willkie and the plan in the summer of '44 to have Willkie nominated as Vice President on the Roosevelt ticket. Willkie, according to Sumner, was the one candidate Roosevelt had run against whom he really liked.

We sat and talked in the same room where in 1932 we put together the first draft of the Roosevelt foreign affairs platform, later adopted in Chicago. It was verbose and lengthy, but when F.D.R. got through with it, he had kept in the essential portions but cut it down to readable size.

October 15:   Steve Early telephoned David Karr in New York wanting some help regarding the battle of the admirals. D.K. suggested they release the Bikini report but, believe it or not, Steve said that the admirals had it and wouldn't give it to them.*

October 20:   Went down to see Louis Johnson. Stuart Symington was in his office when I walked in, both looking quite pleased at the way the B-36 hearings were turning out and both ribbing me for my panning of their air junketing. I thought Stuart was a lousy witness before

---

*Drew Pearson had charged the Navy with suppressing information concerning the heavy destruction of target warships in the atomic-bomb tests at Bikini atoll in 1946.—Ed.

the committee. Johnson is going to testify tomorrow and it looks as if his statement will be pretty good. He says categorically that Denfeld will be kicked out and replaced by Forrest Sherman. Bradford won't be changed immediately. They don't want to make a martyr of him. Louis says that aside from these Navy diehards, most of the Navy is working in a full spirit of cooperation every day in the Pentagon Building.

I have suspected that the congressional hearings on Louis were not entirely unpleasant to Harry Truman, who doesn't like to have anyone nudge him for the political limelight—and Louis is definitely a Presidential possibility for 1952. However, as far as I can see, the President has given Louis complete support and is sore as hell at the admirals.

October 21: Walter Winchell, who got kicked all over the lot by the admirals during the war, has been called to Washington to their rescue. I gather that he is going to attack Omar Bradley [Chairman of the Joint Chiefs of Staff] and come out for Captain Crommelin.*

One of the most shocking stories of the Army-Navy row is the way the Navy has used Congressman Dewey Short of Missouri. For some reason or other, newspapermen do not seem to think that a Congressman getting drunk in public is worthy of news comment. I disagree. Dewey was the man who almost publicly, at least in the presence of a thousand dinner guests, shouted foul language at the Chief Justice of the United States when Vinson was trying to speak at Frank Boykin's dinner last summer. Chief of Police Barrett, in one of the few moments when I agreed with him, and himself slightly tight, started to beat up the Congressman from Missouri and had to be held off by one of his own cops. Whenever I criticize Dewey, he always reminds me that he was an old friend of my father's.

October 27: Showed the report of the Krug lawsuit to Bill Boyle. He hit the ceiling. Said if anything was written about it now, Truman would never fire Krug. Everything is all set, he said, for Krug's exit within seven or eight days. I won't write the story but I still have my fingers crossed.

Saw Louis Johnson just an hour before Truman was scheduled to

*In September, Captain George G. Crommelin, a veteran naval flier, had charged that Army and Air Force senior officers were trying to destroy the naval air arm.—ED.

announce Denfeld's exit as Chief of Naval Operations. Louis was purring. I suggested that in view of the Navy's continued bitter counteroffensive via Congress, he ought to indulge in a counteroffensive of his own and dig up the Senate committee's investigation of Arabian Oil. In my opinion, there was just as much crookedness in that deal as in Benny Meyers's airplane procurement, except that it reaches higher up. I don't think they'll ever prosecute.

Father Sheehy finally came out in the open yesterday as one of the top Navy lobbyists. He couldn't stand it any longer. When Secretary of the Navy Matthews, a Catholic, fired Denfeld, the good monsignor let out a blast against the Catholic layman whom he had helped appoint; said that Truman had appointed Matthews merely to win Catholic votes. If Father Sheehy spent as much time with his students at Catholic University as he does with the admirals, their scholastic record would surpass Harvard's.

October 28:   David Karr has a baby named for me. This now makes four youngsters—one nephew, one grandson, one Japanese-American, one Jewish—who have to bear up under the name of Drew.

Secretary Matthews telephoned me at Louis Johnson's suggestion to say that Father Sheehy had written him a hot letter back in May resigning as a Reserve Naval Chaplain because the Navy had not appointed Admiral Cassidy, his friend, to be Chief of Naval Operations.

October 31:   Jim Welsh, whom I helped about twenty years ago, when his daughter was kidnapped in Venezuela, came in to see me. He had been visiting with Gerald L. K. Smith, whom he knew during the Huey Long days. Huey put up with Smith for a while, then found he was too emotional, even for Huey's brand of politics. Welsh reports that Smith says: "Drew Pearson is the best —— —— friend I have. He's going to be a gold mine."

Apparently Dyke Cullum, Marty Heflin, and various friends of Senator Thomas of Oklahoma, together with Judge Armstrong, are putting up the money for Smith's literature attacking me. General Vaughan and Maragon are putting up the information. Colonel Mara of Vaughan's office has suddenly got chummy with John* and went out

*Probably a reference to John Donovan who, at the time, was working full time in Drew Pearson's office as his attorney.—Ed.

of his way to tell him over the weekend that Vaughan's office had nothing to do with the information contained in the Gerald L. K. Smith smear sheet. Obviously most of it, however, could have come from no other source.

November 2: Senator Claude Pepper telephoned from Orlando, Florida, to ask for help in his forthcoming primary. The big boys who have always opposed Claude have gotten smart this year. They are going to run George Smathers, liberal ex-GI Congressman. Claude says they have promised a campaign kitty of $200,000. I noticed that Smathers's votes in the last session already had begun to taper off to the conservative side and this probably is the reason. I didn't remind Claude of a speech he made after Forrestal's death inferentially blaming me. On the whole he has been a good Senator.*

Saw Louis Johnson. His old cockiness is back again; also his tendency for not telling the truth. Louis gave me an ecstatic account of the White Sulphur Springs banquet for Prime Minister Nehru, attended by the leading economic royalists of the country. Even Colonel McCormick was invited, though he didn't come. His wife said he had to see *South Pacific* for the fourth time so she came to the dinner in his place. I wonder what Nehru thought of the assembled royalists, most of whom were dead opposed to the independence of India, and all of whom are the exact counterparts of Eastern Cables, the P & O Steamship Co., Dunlop Tires, and the other big British cartels that so vigorously fought Nehru (and Johnson) regarding the independence of India. F.D.R., of course, would have featured prominent educators and legislators and social workers among the guests at such a dinner. Louis, always a boy at heart, reported that Nehru had the time of his life. But George Cameron of the San Francisco *Chronicle*, who also attended the dinner, told me that Nehru looked dead tired and slept in the plane coming back to Washington.

November 4: Went up to New York to breakfast with Milton Diamond, head of the Poletti and Franklin Roosevelt, Jr., law firm. He is taking on the Pegler case for me. Diamond is a tough fighter, looks like a straight shooter and should be just the man to engineer this battle. "This is one," he said, "that you can't afford to lose."

---

*Smathers was elected and served in the Senate until he resigned in 1968. As predicted, he did become conservative.—ED.

Flew back to Washington with Joe Hynes, an ex-Navy officer, who defended the Japanese war criminals but finally resigned because he said the other American lawyers were doing such a left-handed job in their defense. He agrees with the book on Yamashita, now banned by MacArthur, that Yamashita never should have been hung. Frank Murphy and Rutledge also dissented.

November 8:   Lunched with E. A. Stephens ["Steve"], who is flying to Germany with John Donovan. We talked as usual about the cause of liberalism in the South, which in some respects is getting less hopeful. The New Orleans *Item*, run by Dave Stern, is putting up a gallant fight, but not making much progress.

Leander Perez, in Steve's opinion, is one of the most pernicious influences in the South. He cloaks the oil companies' fight under high-sounding phrases about states' rights. Once Steve called him on it, but Leander said, "You've got to talk that way to put this across." The Civil War, of course, was caused by the big slaveholders who originated states' rights to protect their property. Now the oil lobby is doing exactly the same thing to protect its property. Nevertheless, because of the bugaboo of segregation, some very fine people are falling for this line, including my old friend Jimmie Byrnes. I talked to him on the telephone the other day and he seems to be quite serious in his opposition to about everything Truman is working for. The funny part of it is that when Jimmie was in the Senate, he was the spearhead of the Roosevelt forces which put across exactly the same type of program.

The reason I called Jimmie was because the Senator Olin Johnston forces are putting out one of the cleverest propaganda schemes I have ever seen. They are saying Byrnes has been calling on Monsignor Fulton Sheen for readmittance to the Catholic Church. If this story gets around, it will mean that Jimmie not only loses all Protestant support [but] will not regain the Catholics who have been against him.*

November 11:   David Karr rode back from the airport with Louis— who is Louis Johnson's chauffeur. Louis told what a pleasure it is to work for the Johnsons after having worked for the Forrestals. Louis

*Byrnes, whose public career had included terms in the Senate and on the Supreme Court and who had served as Secretary of State, was at this juncture getting ready to run for Governor of South Carolina. In 1950 he was elected, succeeding Strom Thurmond.—ED.

described Forrestal as a wonderful man and said, "He would still be alive if it were not for that woman he was married to. He should be where she is today and she should be where he is.

"In the beginning I wondered why he worked so late every night in his office, but he had nothing to go home to. Sometimes he was afraid to go home because he couldn't bear to face another fight with her. They used to think those circles under his eyes were from work. They were from worrying about her. She could change her mind more times than any woman I ever read about. She was the most unpredictable woman I've ever seen. If it hadn't been for Miss Foley (Forrestal's private secretary) who was always smoothing things over, he would have killed himself a long time before."

November 21:   Bart Crum* is still worried about a story involving a man named Nathan Lichtblau who has been indicted a couple of times but who has been a big contributor to the Democratic party and raised a million bucks for Palestine. Lichtblau got a relative, David Lewis, appointed to a War Claims Board and has been pulling all sorts of wires to keep his background from being published. He even spread the fantastic idea that Dave [Karr] is in on some kind of a take.

Crum told me that the "take" story had got to the White House and that Truman had remarked: "I am probably the one guy who has called Pearson an SOB, but he isn't that kind of an SOB."

November 22:   There seems to be more and more finagling around Bill Boyle. I have been impressed with Boyle as a straight shooter and a liberal, but some of the men around him certainly are not. And perhaps he is fooling me the same way that Bob Hannegan must have. After all, no man can make a million and a half dollars as Hannegan did in a few short years without cutting corners.

Twice recently those closely connected with Bill Boyle have tried to shake down applicants for RFC loans. One case was a man named Snowden who was about to get an RFC loan when he got a phone call from a man named Young, telling him he would have to pay a commission on the loan. The loan had been virtually granted prior to the phone call. When Harley Hise, head of the RFC, heard about this he required

---

*A California lawyer and, for a short period, co-owner of the New York *Star*, Bartley Crum had represented members of the Hollywood Ten before the House Un-American Activities Committee in 1947.—ED.

Snowden to sign an affidavit that he had paid no commission to anyone. To Hise's credit it should be noted that the conversation went somewhat as follows: "We have asked you to fulfill seven conditions. I am now going to add an eighth. You must sign an affidavit that no commissions have been paid on this loan."

And when the Kaiser loan was about to come through, Henry Kaiser, the company chairman, got a similar call from a man named Merl Young, apparently the same man, also stating that a commission would be necessary. Edgar Kaiser, Henry's son and the company's president, had put through the loan practically without a lawyer and purely on its merits. No commission was paid and the loan went through anyway.

Merl Young is the guy whose wife is secretary to Truman and who, though he denies being related to Truman, looks so much like him that he would be taken for his son.

November 23:   Cap Krug, not yet retired as Secretary of Interior, is reported to be in a terrible condition. The $750,000 loan borrowed on his textile mill has given him a lot of trouble. He is drinking heavily and terribly depressed over leaving his Cabinet job. His wife was furious when my column came out regarding the real facts in his resignation. His wife was so sore that she bawled Cap out right in front of the Interior Department chauffeur. Cap didn't go to work that day at all.

Clint Anderson now tells the real story of why Krug passed out while about to broadcast in Phoenix, Arizona, in October, 1947. Clint says that he and Cap were sitting up late that night in Phoenix drinking. Clint is a pretty good drinker himself, but toward midnight he reminded Cap that he had work to do the next day and should turn in. However, Cap insisted on staying up and pouring them in. Next morning he was on hand for his broadcast and shaky. The platform around the microphone was strewn with flowers which gave a sickening sweet odor. When Cap stood up to speak, this aroma of the flowers hit him and he keeled over. The story went out to the newspapers that he had had a heart attack. Clint also attended a football game with Krug in New York one night when Cap got so tight he could hardly get out of his auto. He even bawled out his wife for leaving a shaker full of cocktails at home.

Went to Elsie Little's funeral. Brought back memories. I remember having dinner with Elsie in Quantico when Louis Little was commander of the Marine barracks there. I got a phone call from J. Edgar Hoover during the dinner in effect threatening to put me in jail unless we killed the story giving the real truth on Pearl Harbor. I told Edgar that he was nuts, that there was no law by which he could put me in jail, and that he was not the man to interpret the law. He admitted all this, said that Steve Early at the White House had called him up and asked him to throw the fear of God into me.

November 25:   Saw Oscar Chapman for the first time since he was appointed Secretary of the Interior. He reminded me of how he had been one of Judge Ben Lindsey's "juvenile delinquents," just as I had been. He had gone to Colorado because of TB, finally persuaded Lindsey to let him work for him, and finally ran Ed Costigan's campaign for the Senate.

I remember meeting Costigan in Denver in 1924 and having lunch with him and Ben Lindsey. They were both waging a campaign against the KKK at that time and Costigan was a relatively obscure labor lawyer. The Klan was then sweeping the Middle West, and even my grandmother in Osawatomie, Kansas, who was the most pacifist-minded person in the world, told me in all seriousness she had been asked to join the Klan's Ladies Auxiliary and wanted my advice as to whether she should. She said that most of the ladies were joining and it seemed like a very nice social organization.

Ben Lindsey, who was always fighting the big companies, the utilities, and the big lawyers, was in hot water at that time as usual, and it looked as if he might not be reelected. I wired *Collier's* Magazine from Denver suggesting a story on Lindsey and boys and was surprised when I got back an affirmative reply. By that time I had gone over to Kansas City, but went back to Denver and got the story from Lindsey. It was the first magazine piece I ever had published.

Oscar Chapman has come a long way since I first met him in 1933 at a party given by Dorothy Detzer. At that time my father was still Governor of the Virgin Islands, having been appointed by Herbert Hoover, although the Democratic diehards in the Senate led by Pat Harrison of Mississippi and Tydings of Maryland were trying desperately to get him out. Chapman was the first to come to father's rescue. Talking to him today about the things he was most proud of doing in the Interior Department, he claimed credit for putting across the Virgin Islands Company. I diplomatically reminded him that the Virgin Islands Company had been started by father in a Republican Administration though Oscar certainly deserves credit for helping to put the idea through.

November 28:   Parnell Thomas's trial started this morning. Looking at him in the courtroom, I couldn't help but feel sorry for him. I can't relish helping to send a man to jail. Nevertheless, when I figure all the times Thomas has sent other people to jail and all the instances when he has kept men away from combat duty in return for money in his own pocket, to say nothing of salary kickbacks, perhaps I shouldn't be too sorry.

Miss Campbell* has been nervous, but has borne up pretty well. I spent last evening coaching her on how to answer questions under cross-examination. What I am afraid of is that she will let slip the fact that she was jealous of Vera Halyburton.

November 30:   The Parnell Thomas trial ended abruptly. Thomas got cold feet and threw in the sponge. He changed his plea of not guilty to *nolo contendere*. The case against Miss Campbell was immediately dismissed. It was a little over a year ago I think that Thomas was calling me a liar.

December 1:   It now looks very much as if my old friend, Larry Duggan, had been a member of the Communist party. The indication slipped out in the trial of Alger Hiss yesterday. Some peculiar things that happened back in the days when Larry was in the State Department now become clearer. Also it now appears to be conclusively the fact that Larry was a suicide.

In New York yesterday a memo from Adolf Berle was put in the record naming Larry as a member of the Communist party. His name had been deleted from one copy of the memo, but by accident his name remained on another copy and before the judge could strike it

---

*Helen Campbell went to Drew Pearson with the kickback story apparently out of jealousy over Thomas's attentions to Vera Halyburton. One sidelight of this episode: After the trial, Miss Campbell found it impossible to get another job, evidently because of this breach of loyalty. Drew Pearson hired her and for many years her job was transcribing the diaries.—ED.

out it was seen by the newspapermen. The memo indicated that Berle, during the war when he was Assistant Secretary of State, was checking on Duggan, a result of the fact that Whittaker Chambers or someone had reported Duggan to be a member of the Communist party.

During the war I remember calling Larry on a Sunday to ask him a more or less routine question regarding Argentina. There was nothing confidential in the nature of the inquiry. Larry reported to me later that the next day the Secretary of State [Cordell Hull] had called him in and asked him if he had talked to me over the telephone. Larry made the mistake of not admitting the call. He told me that Hull was noncommittal, but seemed to know all about what he had said. I had always figured that Larry's usefulness in the State Department was impaired as a result. But probably also the way he was gradually eased out resulted from the suspicion that he was a member of the party. He was shunted over to UNRRA and later left the government altogether. I also figured that the wiretap which Hull had on our telephone conversation was on my phone, not Duggan's. But apparently it was the other way around.

I am certain that Larry Duggan in his later years in the State Department was far removed from the principles and teachings of the Communist party. He was a farsighted and idealistic public servant under whom our Good Neighbor policy reached a genuine peak of success. If he was a member of the Communist party, as now looks to be a fact, it was back in the days of the Hoover depression when young people were groping for something and when the breadlines were blocks long in most of our big cities.

December 5: Lunched with Clinton Anderson, who says that the story I wrote about the President being down on him has now come true. Clint confirmed the on-again, off-again tactics of Harry S. Truman. He said that long before he resigned as Secretary of Agriculture, his zest for working with H.S.T. was lessened by two incidents. One occurred after [Charles] Luckman became food conservator and when he (Clint) was interviewed by the United Press on the telephone, an interview which later came out as criticism of the Luckman program. Truman bawled the hell out of him. Later, Clint said: "Mr. President, if I show you a transcript of what I actually said, would you like to take back some of the things you said?" "I've nothing to take back," said Truman.

The second incident came during the plans to tighten or relax price controls. Averell Harriman had been handling these and Truman asked Anderson to help out. Anderson argued against rigid controls. Whereupon Truman snapped, "A Cabinet officer doesn't give orders, he obeys orders."

I told Clint that Truman was passing out the word that he had long considered Clint disloyal and that Clint got out of the Cabinet in May of 1948 because he figured Truman was going to lose. Clint's review of the circumstances leading to his exit sounded to me exactly the opposite. In the spring of 1947, Truman talked to him about becoming Democratic National Chairman. He was hell bent to get Hannegan out. Snyder, an enemy of Hannegan's, also wanted Anderson to take over. Finally Hannegan came to Clint and asked if it was true that Truman had approached him. He said that if Clint would wait, he and Ed Pauley would put him up as a candidate for Vice President. Hannegan said that Truman was determined to make Bill Douglas his Vice President and that he and Pauley wanted to block this at all costs.

Truman became so insistent about the Democratic chairmanship that Anderson finally told him that in fairness to his wife and family he should have a physical check by General Wallace Graham. "My wife spent a long time building me up from a TB case and it isn't fair to take on extra work if it's going to set me back again." Truman agreed, and Dr. Graham, after a painstaking examination, decreed that Clint could handle one job or the other but not both.

Later in July of 1947, Clint bought tickets to take his family to Hawaii. Arriving at San Francisco, he got an urgent phone call from Hannegan to come to Los Angeles to a party given by Ed Pauley. Clint went to Los Angeles on a special plane provided by Hannegan and Pauley. Sitting around Ed Pauley's swimming pool at Los Angeles, Pauley and Hannnegan immediately began talking about the chairmanship. They didn't want Clint to take it. Eventually it became clear that their opposition to him was because they believed an Irish Catholic must be chairman. They said that a Catholic was necessary in order to keep big city bosses, such as Ed Flynn and Ed Kelly, in line. Clint's reply was that he had already told Truman he didn't want the job and that he definitely could not be both national chairman and Secretary of Agriculture. By that time Truman and Hannegan were at logger-heads. Truman was saying that Hannegan had used him to build up a fortune.

After Anderson came back from Hawaii in the fall of 1947, he went to see Truman and told him there was talk of his running for Vice President. He advised the President that he could do one of three things—kill the idea abruptly, let it ride, or encourage it. Truman's reply was: "Because of the states you and I come from, it would be disastrous." Clint then ended all talk of the Vice Presidency—though, remembering that at the time it was in the air, I know darned well he hated to do so. Clint was talking to the President at about that time about resigning.

Later, in January of 1948, Senator Hatch announced plans to resign and pressure became strong from Democratic leaders in New Mexico for Clint to take his seat. Finally, while at the White House one day in January, Clint got a call from Biffle, at that time Executive Director of the Senate Democratic Policy Committee, asking him not to leave until he had talked to him. Clint went back into the President's office, told him that Biffle was calling, and added: "You know what he wants to talk to me about. Do you mind if I take the call right here so you can see what happens?" The President listened while Clint was urged by Biffle to run for Hatch's seat. He demanded that Clint come up for a joint conference with him and Barkley. "We are going to lose the Presidency," said Biffle, "but we can win the Senate." In brief, that was how Clint happened to leave the Cabinet.

Clint told in some detail how Truman was surrounded by a little coterie of cronies and how not even Cabinet members could break through. Vaughan, he said, hated him. At one time Clint and Krug were supposed to go with the President on a cruise to the Virgin Islands but Vaughan and his cronies stepped up the departure date, knowing that Anderson had to make a speech and would not be able to get away. Once, Truman had agreed to have a breakfast meeting with the Cabinet once a week, but when the cronies heard about it they induced Truman to cancel.

Clint said he had repeatedly urged Truman to take some of the Cabinet members with him on trips. He [Truman] pointed out that neither Forrestal nor Krug played poker, therefore he didn't want to take them on poker trips.

In November of 1948, just after the election, Clint was motoring with Truman down to the yacht when they stopped at the naval gun factory to look at something the Navy was fixing up for Truman's ship. While there, Clint said: "You know, Mr. President, I think if you had called in Drew Pearson before the elections and told him that even though you still resented what he had said about your wife,* you appreciated what he had written about your policies, I think he would have swung a whale of a lot of votes for you." Truman's reply was abrupt and to the point: "He's a blank in my books," he said, "and always will be." Clint argued a little further, which was foolish.

December 11:   After some misgivings and various huddles with Commander George Craig of the American Legion, I finally launched the drive for Christmas toys to the children of Europe.

December 12:   Headaches have just begun. CARE, which had previously agreed to handle distribution of the toys, sent a battery of five lawyers, warehouse experts, and others down to Washington to raise a lot of bugaboos they hadn't thought of before, including warehouse charges, packing, violation of postal rules in sending messages to European children in packages, etc. Spent most of the day trying to iron these things out between the CARE people and the Legion. The Legion executives have been remarkably understanding and cooperative.

December 13:   Our old friend Arthur Ringland, of the State Department, now rears his ugly head. He is the guy who did his best to stop the Friendship Train and darned near succeeded. It was Ringland who first devised the idea of distributing Friendship Train food 25 percent to the Catholics, 25 percent to the Jews, and 25 percent to the Protestants, with 25 percent to American Aid to France. I suspect it was also Ringland who caused us to hold up the airplanes taking the special

---

*In 1945, Drew Pearson commented in his column that the wife of the new Vice President had something to learn about being a hostess, pointing out that Mrs. Truman had become tired during the inaugural reception and had had to stop shaking hands, whereas Mrs. Roosevelt had lasted the whole day. Vice President Truman bristled at this story and said that in Missouri they had a four-letter word for columnists like Pearson. The relationship between the two men stayed cool for a long time.—ED.

editions of *Il Progresso* and *Look* to Europe at Christmastime, until the State Department could censor those editions.

I sometimes wonder how our foreign policy functions as well as it does in view of some of the red tape snarlers in it.

1950

January 13 [en route to California]: Joe Lebowitz met me in Chicago. The "syndicate" is putting the screws on him as a result of my campaign against Costello and the gambling network. They want him to get me to shut up.

January 15: Broadcast from Los Angeles on the hydrogen bomb, devoted all of the broadcast to this one subject. So far, few people in Washington and almost no one in the rest of the country seem to know that a hydrogen bomb is in the making.

January 16: Got up early. Took the plane to Fresno. Who should be at the airport taking the same plane but Howser's attorneys, Messrs. Bingham and Robb. One never knows when previous columns will come home to roost. In the early days of the New Deal, one of the lobbyists whom Bob Allen and I took over the hurdles was Bruce Kraemer, Democratic National Committeeman from Montana who virtually ran Homer Cummings's Justice Department for him when he was Attorney General. Bruce Kraemer's stepson now turns out to be Bingham, one of those who has egged Howser on to sue. In the *Nine Old Men,* we pointed to the fact that one Court of Appeals judge, Justice Robb, had been responsible for preventing the enactment of a Child Labor Act for a quarter of a century. His son is also now representing Howser.

    At Fresno I changed hotels. El Rancho was too far out of town and on the ground floor where I figured my briefcase would not be safe.

January 17:   Checked on the jury panel. There seem to be some fairly good people on it—but also some farmers who get their irrigation water from projects which Howser has championed. Took Mulloy to the movies last night to keep him sober. His is our weakest point in this case. He finally got on the stand today and the opposition really opened up on him. He has been intermittently inebriated in Fresno and the whole town knows it.

Attorneys for the defense put up a big hue and cry about this case being brought by Pearson, not by the U.S. government. And to some extent I suppose this is true. Certainly the government is rather weak-kneed about the whole business. I can understand when I see how some of these government attorneys and the FBI operate why the goverment lost so many cases.

January 18:   Flew from Fresno to San Francisco. The trial is not going well. I finally persuaded Phil Woodyatt to testify for the government. He had several talks with Robert Franklin, Howser's campaign manager, in which Franklin offered to become a government witness if he got a certain amount of immunity. Then at the last minute Howser apparently came through with a big offer to Franklin and Franklin decided to stand pat. He even told Woodyatt if he had to take a three-year rap at San Quentin his family would be taken care of. The FBI had interviewed Woodyatt but got nothing out of him.

January 19:   Had a long talk with George White, the chief of the Narcotics Bureau for the West Coast. He told me an amazing story of the arrest of an Armenian narcotics peddler named Davidian at Bakersfield who later turned out to be a relatively small cog in the narcotics ring and who offered to help get evidence on the rest of the ring, especially on Joe Sica, who is a Costello man and who has virtually taken Mickey Cohen's place as the Number One gangster of Southern California. However, the California Narcotics Authority, under the attorney general of the state—my friend Howser—refused to cooperate. They insisted on prosecuting Davidian immediately, before he had time to help the federal government catch the rest of the ring. White had arranged a setup with dictaphones and phonographs by which marked money would be passed in the sale of narcotics by Davidian to the others. But the Howser crowd demanded an immediate trial for Davidian and secured it. Finally, at the last minute, the federal government persuaded the judge to delay sentencing Davidian for ninety days and as a result indictments were finally brought against Joe Sica and fifteen other members of the dope ring. Every indication, however, points to the fact that Joe Sica is one of the big "bagmen" for Howser.

January 20:   Spent the morning with Warren Olney of the California Crime Commission going over the Howser evidence. He suggested several leads, one of them Harold Wyatt, a gambler who worked for the Chinese in San Mateo County and who, after paying about $30,000 in payoffs to the Howser crowd, got double-crossed. I searched for Wyatt on the telephone all over northern California and finally located him in a Chinese gambling den just outside San Francisco. He was not cooperative.

January 21:   After writing the broadcast George [Arnold] and I went out to see Mary. She is Ralph Allen's sister and we have been trying to persuade her to give us a deposition telling how Howser was a frequent visitor at the Allen home and how, after Ralph had been indicted, Howser sent deputy sheriffs in a car to take him to the race track under state protection whenever he wanted to go. Later, of course, Howser railroaded Ralph to San Quentin, from which the Crime Commission finally extricated him. Mary finally agreed to give us a deposition. Among other things, she told how, when the Guaranty Finance Company got into trouble, the boys called Howser and he rushed over to discuss the matter. Howser at that time was district attorney for Los Angeles County and was supposed to be the chief law-enforcement officer.

January 22:   Got a phone call from Vince Lamb, an underworld character who is out on parole, stating that Howser had us followed last night. He knew that we had stopped at the Lankersham Hotel, knew whom we had talked to, knew that we had then gone out to see Mary. Lamb had the details so accurately that he could not possibly have made up the story.

   Got a phone call from Tom Young in Marysville. He is the gambler mentioned in the Crime Commission's report who had a deal on with Howser's close friend Curly Robinson, who circulated branded punch boards in northern California with an agreement that Howser would knock off the joints carrying unbranded punch boards. Young flew to Los Angeles, where George and I met him at midnight in the Roosevelt Hotel Bar. He brought us a branded punch board and told the story in detail. Also showed us canceled checks and letters signed by Curly Robinson. The Howser crowd had gone through with their deal up to the point of knocking off the unbranded punch boards, but after that the sheriff in Marysville got suspicious and the deal was called off. Young made the mistake last week of getting tight in his own bar and pulled out a revolver along with a local cop and shot a glass mirror off his establishment. He is now in danger of having his liquor license taken away and is willing to help if we can get his liquor license continued. I sent him up to see Warren Olney in San Francisco.

January 23:   Olney says that Tom Young's testimony is just what he's been looking for, will fill in the missing link and enable him to bring some indictments in the alleged conspiracy to control the gambling rackets of northern California. So far the Crime Commission has done a lot of work, made a lot of noise, but brought not one single indictment.

Called on Gladys Told Root, a very successful criminal lawyer who is the attorney for Vince Lamb. She is something right out of Hollywood, dresses as if she were Theda Bara except that her bosoms are more decolleté than ever would be allowed on the screen. She is the attorney for an abortionist ring which I gather is about to be indicted. Mrs. Root says that Howser is more involved than we have any idea about and that her abortionist criminals could buy their way out of an indictment if they put up $20,000. She offered to have dictaphone records of bribed conversations and supply pictures of Howser in houses of prostitution. But she wanted plenty of dough for it and I haven't any extra dough to spare. She did not get down to brass tacks but I gather that she expected me to put up the $20,000 for her clients. She is also the attorney for a call-house madame in San Francisco who came down to see us in Los Angeles and who is willing to testify that Howser has been a frequent visitor at her house and that he recommended the abortionist who was responsible for the death of her sister. Of course, the difficulty is that these are underworld witnesses against the attorney general of the State, and I am not sure that a jury would believe them, though the more I study Howser the more I am convinced that the information is true. Howser's sister Hazel was arrested in Long Beach not long ago on a charge of prostitution. And it is significant that although the press smears some people, not a word of this was published in the Los Angeles papers.

January 24:   Got up at five this morning and caught a plane to Fresno where I spoke for the Kiwanis Club. I read them the list of property owned by their ex-chief of police Ray T. Wallace—total 1,740 acres which he acquired during a period when he was drawing $450 a month salary. I also read a list of thirty-two houses of prostitution in their fair city which had recently been closed. They told me afterward that some members held their breath for fear I would read off real estate property which they held, but all-in-all the crowd took my exposé good-naturedly.

Afterward I dropped in to pay my respects to Mr. Lockwood, the editor of the Fresno *Bee,* who went on at great length at what a job the *Bee* had done to expose the underworld in Fresno. He halfway apologized for carrying a front-page story which had the effect of throwing down my exposé of Police Chief Wallace and his property holdings. "Of course," said Mr. Lockwood, "we knew about this property of Wallace's for a long time." "Did you ever publish it?" I asked. "No," he replied. "We never published it. We were afraid of libel." I suppose I should have told him what I thought but I didn't. In brief, a local newspaper sits on a local scandal for years when all they had to do was walk across the courthouse square and examine the tax assessor's records on Wallace's property in a few spare moments, as I did in Fresno last week. But after someone else sticks his neck out on libel to expose the facts, the local paper proceeds to try to throw the story down. All of which in my opinion is one reason why so many newspapers are not particularly respected in their own communities.

Fresno's mayor, Gordon Dunn, when he got on the witness stand, welshed slightly about Franklin's calling him up and asking to have Mulloy arrested because Mulloy was my witness. Dunn said on the witness stand that Franklin wanted Mulloy arrested because he might be making book. Meanwhile the scandal which Franklin started when he proposed opening the city of Fresno to the gamblers has died down in the public mind, but is even hotter under the surface. The lady who runs the chinchilla farm south of Fresno came down from the mountains on snowshoes and gave her testimony to Jim Theusen, the county district attorney. She said that Franklin had told her specifically that he would have to take the gambling scheme up with the heads of the crime syndicate in Chicago. Although we have always suspected it, this is the first definite link between Chicago and the local Fresno group. She also said that Max Cadwallader had never returned her books. Cadwallader is a member of the Fresno City Council, a professor at Fresno College, and a highly respected member of the community. Nevertheless he was to be the accountant for the whole gambling racket deal.

January 25:   The trial at Fresno appears to be on the rocks. If Ernie Tolin [the U.S. attorney] wasn't so sincere a person, I would believe the reports circulating in the Los Angeles underworld that the government was throwing the case.

January 26:   We finally took Howser's deposition. He looks somewhat like a race-track tout and judging from his testimony he spends most of his time at the races. He admitted knowing a good many gamblers and underworld figures, including Bugsie Siegel, though he minimized his acquaintanceship by saying that he had merely met them at the races. Reading over his testimony it would appear that that was where the attorney general of California spent most of his time. Significantly, Howser denied knowing Ralph Allen. Naturally he knew all about Allen because he had had him nearly beaten to death in Long Beach two weeks before, and had detectives following him at the Lankersham Hotel only two nights ago. However, he stuck to his story and flatly denied that he had ever been at Allen's house and known his sister Mary or any other member of the family except his brother Don, who is on the Los Angeles City Council.

Incidentally after the thugs failed to kill Ralph in Long Beach, Don Allen, his brother, proposed to Ralph's sister that they certify him for insanity. The steps taken by the Howser gang to put Ralph out of the way are almost too fantastic to believe.

Also when we reported that two detectives were following Ralph the other night, Ernie Tolin called the FBI and asked them to intervene since Ralph has been a witness before the federal grand jury. The FBI, however, refused. Their excuse was that Ralph was a witness in an income tax case and that was Treasury business. Like the CIO and the AFL, the FBI has its jurisdictional disputes.

Woodyatt's testimony finally was admitted in Fresno and was the most sensational part of the entire trial.

Pat Field has been urging me to talk to a lawyer named Avery Blount from Arkansas, who he says can get me some income tax records on the Long Beach racketeers. I finally talked to Blount and this evening drove to Long Beach to see a tax accountant named A. L. Burt. Burt turned out to be intoxicated, but I had quite a talk with him and his two assistants at about 10 P.M., having left Henry Kaiser, Jr., in the middle of a dinner to make the trip. The trip was futile as far as Burt was concerned. He was almost too intoxicated to talk. However, I made some headway with his two assistants and believe we may have struck something important.

Burt is the tax adviser for Curly Robinson, Pat and Joe Irvine, and possibly for Bones Remmer, all close pals of Howser. He admitted to me verbally that their income tax returns showed payoffs to Howser, though he refused to give me the amounts.

January 27: Lunched with Harry Warner. He is drearier than ever. I can understand now why the movies are so lifeless. His chief theme during the lunch was how terrible labor is, how this country was founded by men who knew how to work. I gather from Harry that the movies continue to be scared of their own shadow.

Lentz and Franklin were acquitted in Fresno as I was sure they would be. Tolin scarcely argued in rebuttal. Maybe now he will be confirmed by the Senate. The poor guy was betwixt and between with Sheridan Downey, his chief Senate supporter; the California Senator didn't want Howser to be convicted.

Goodykoontz, head of the Internal Revenue Intelligence unit, tells a story (via the Crime Commission) of Bill Benelli, the former chairman of the Los Angeles Board of Equalization, who was called in to explain an item of $60,000 on his income tax which he listed as miscellaneous revenue. Goodykoontz asked what that was for. Benelli replied, "You know the penalty for revealing this information?" "Yes," said Goodykoontz. "All right then," said Benelli, "It was for bribes."

January 28: Mary came through with her deposition. She told of seeing Howser many times. Perhaps even more important, she brought along a neighbor who testified that two deputy sheriffs had called at her house asking for Ralph Allen's home. They were in uniform, she said, and she remembered them vividly and even saw them later drive away with Ralph in their car. This was one of the occasions when

Howser sent deputy sheriffs to take Ralph to the races when he was under indictment.

March 6 [Washington]:   Lunched with Ickes. Next week is his seventy-sixth birthday. He was feeling blue—chiefly because he thinks Oscar Chapman is going back on him. Oscar, he says, has failed to move on appointing fresh personnel and has simply marked time. Ickes also says Oscar doesn't consult him.

March 12:   Beamed my entire broadcast to the Russian people. It was sent over World Wide Broadcasting Foundation, but afterward the Voice of America called and asked permission to rebroadcast it. They beamed it not only to Russia but to every European country plus Latin America and the Far East.

March 14:   Lunched with Oscar Chapman. Ickes had told me that Oscar was cooling off on him, but Oscar says he has lunched with Ikes religiously once a week. The only trouble is that it knocks about three hours out of his day. He says he is trying to get the Justice Department to reverse its ruling that Ickes doesn't like on tidelands oil, and make the Mineral Leasing Act applicable to the submerged oil lands along the coast.*

Ickes has forgotten, however, Oscar says, that not only did Cap Krug's solution rule that the Mineral Leasing Act is not applicable, but that Ickes himself when Secretary of the Interior had indicated this act was not applicable. I am to talk to Philip Perlman, Solicitor of the Justice Department, to see if it won't reverse previous Justice rulings.

Ickes is also peeved that Oscar hasn't appointed a new Under Secretary of Interior. Oscar has been trying to persuade Jim Rowe to take the job but Jim is now making money at law for the first time and doesn't want to leave. In addition, Truman isn't very anxious to have him, because he has been tied up with Tom Corcoran's law firm.

We talked about our old friend, Bob Hannegan, whom I always regarded as a healthy influence in the administration and a fighter for the underdog. Of late, I have come to have increasing misgivings about

---

*The question was whether the Mineral Leasing Act, under which the federal government granted oil leases on the public domain, would apply to tidelands oil. Interior ruled it would not, which left leasing arrangements to the states.—Eᴅ.

Hannegan's honesty, since he left an estate of a million and a half dollars following his death. Oscar had concrete evidence that Hannegan had been counted in by Ed Pauley on a couple of oil wells and that Hannegan was representing Northwest Airlines and TWA when he was chairman of the Democratic National Committee. Later he became Postmaster General, where he had to rule on airmail contracts. Admiral Vardaman, now with the Federal Reserve Board, is authority for the statement that Hannegan once came to him when Vardaman was naval attaché to Truman and suggested that Vardaman could represent an outside interest for a fee of $30,000 without violating any ethics.

The other day, after the Cabinet meeting, Truman was remarking to Charlie Brannan and a couple of others about a story I had written when Brannan volunteered: "I inherited Pearson from my predecessor. He's no particular friend of mine." The statement by Brannan was gratis and not particularly necessary. Afterward as they walked out of the White House, Oscar chided Brannan and Brannan replied: "You know how the President hates Drew." "Yes," said Oscar, "but in January 1946 there wasn't any man in the United States Truman hated more than Harold Ickes, but a time came when he called Ickes into the White House and asked him to do some favors for him." Oscar managed to put across the appointment of Governor Knous of Colorado as judge, despite Brannan's opposition and despite Truman's reluctance, in order to get John Carroll the senatorial nomination. Knous has not been particularly strong for Truman. It becomes more and more evident that judges these days are appointed not for their ability but because a Senator or certain interests want a friend on the bench; or because Truman wants to reward party loyalty.

March 16: I invited a group of Senators to dinner to discuss the question of penetrating the Iron Curtain. Among them were Brien McMahon [Connecticut], Tobey of New Hampshire, Ives of New York, Sparkman of Alabama; also several others, including New York lawyer Morris Ernst, Montana Congressman Mike Mansfield, Ed Stanley, formerly of OWI [Office of War Information]. Morris told about his experience with the Vogeler trial.* Although he never got to Buda-

---

*Robert A. Vogeler was arrested by the Hungarians in November, 1949, on espionage charges.—ED.

pest, he had some reasonably accurate information about the third degree through which they put Vogeler and the head of the Jewish Joint Distribution Committee, of whom I had heard the week before in Atlanta. Morris believes that the squeeze is on to run every American out from behind the Iron Curtain, and to take over satellite countries with Russian dictators.

His story made a profound impression particularly on Tobey, who deplored the political business on Capitol Hill. He said that every day Republican Senators gathered to ask "How's Joe doing?" meaning their colleague Senator McCarthy from Wisconsin. They all agree that Joe wasn't doing well, but that he was kicking up a political rumpus and urged him to keep on talking. Taft was the leader in urging Joe to continue. Tobey told how he had gone to the White House weeks ago for a talk with President Truman and was convinced of Truman's sincerity for peace, but he felt that in view of partisan bitterness in the Senate there was little the Republicans would cooperate on at the present.

Ed Stanley told in graphic detail of the many methods used during the war to get information into the enemy countries. He pointed out that families who have made a living smuggling goods across the border for generations are still in operation; that we haven't anywhere near exhausted our means of penetrating the Iron Curtain. Brien McMahon told me that he and Senator Douglas were planning to invite Scott Lucas and other Democratic leaders to a dinner to discuss this same problem of penetrating the Iron Curtain. I urged that Truman be approached by some intimate friends, possibly Chief Justice Vinson with a view to getting one or two real Republicans in the administration. Morris Ernst suggested that a Republican be made Coordinator of Government Agencies to wedge the Iron Curtain itself. Tobey suggested Charlie Taft, brother of Bob and a very good man.

We arrived at no particular conclusion except that Tobey emphasized the fact that the purpose of the meeting must not be allowed to taper off.

March 17: Lunched with Tom Clark at his apartment. It was the first time that I had had a visit with him since he went on the Supreme Court. He has Charles Evans Hughes's law books and seems to be getting a kick out of being a justice. He's just as delightful, placid, and slow-talking as ever. Tom always gives the impression of having a slow mentality but in the end he nearly always comes through. I spent most of the time talking to him about the Russian picture and the need of a real bipartisan approach. With Vandenberg ill, the bipartisan policy has gone to hell in a hack, and Truman has got to act fast if he is going to save anything from it. I also emphasized some of the points Ed Stanley made about getting through the Iron Curtain. Finally, I urged that Fred Vinson go to Truman and put all this before him.

The point that Tom liked best was my suggestion that Truman go to Europe himself on a whistle-stop campaign. I pointed out that Truman was at his best when he was out among the people, talking to them direct, and that Europe was not unlike the United States. If he went to Rotterdam, Amsterdam, Brussels, and not merely Paris, but the middle-size towns of Europe, as we did on the Friendship Train, he would not only become the great hero, but he would convince Europe that we are serious about peace. I pointed out that this is a war of propaganda as much as anything, and that although we want peace, people's minds in Europe have become confused. Such a whistle-stop offensive, I urged, would put Russia on the defensive, and carry the cold war right to her own doorstep. I suggested Truman should not call for merely a diplomatic meeting; he should call for a raising up of the Iron Curtain. This kind of campaign would really drive the Politburo nuts. Tom seemed to like the idea. He went to see Vinson that afternoon. Among other things, I had suggested—rather lamely, I admit—that Truman invite Stassen, Dewey, Governor Warren, and Taft to a conference in order to unify the country. This idea, however, didn't register. Even while I was expressing it, I realized that Truman would never rise to this occasion. Tom did agree, however, that some leading Republicans could be brought in and he liked the idea of Charlie Taft.

Learned that the man feeding Senator McCarthy is General Carter Clark, the colonel who fed the Republicans all the dirt on F.D.R. in regard to Pearl Harbor and who gave Dewey the information in 1944 that we were breaking the Japanese code.

March 18:   Vinson flew to Key West today. Carter Clark paid me a surprise visit in the country. There was no way he could have known I knew he was leaking to McCarthy except by tapping my telephone wire. Clark didn't mention McCarthy, and I didn't give him an opening. Ostensibly he dropped out to see about the purchase of a farm in Maryland.

March 19:   Spent most of last evening and part of the day trying to track down the McCarthy leak in the President's Loyalty Review Board. I have reason to believe it is a man named Thomas W. Beale. Interestingly enough, when Jack Anderson called Seth Richardson, Richardson denied that any such man was on the staff. And when I called the executive secretary of the board, he also dodged. But finally when I demanded a list of the entire staff he came across with it and, sure enough, the name was on the list. I finally got Beale on the telephone, but he denied knowing McCarthy. I still think he is the leak, but for safety's sake, I left his name out of the broadcast.

I got an immediate critical reaction to my editorial on McCarthy. At first, I did not think this represented the real sentiment of the country, and I still don't. Nevertheless, the Marine Corps veterans have now awarded McCarthy the gold medal of the year, and it looks as if he has ignited a potent though irresponsible segment of our public opinion. In other words, Senator Taft is right. As long as Joe keeps talking, the longer he can confuse 'em.

March 20:   Last night I left Carter Clark's name out of the broadcast but said that McCarthy's leak was a general in the Pentagon Building. This morning, shortly before an intelligence staff meeting in the Pentagon Building, several of the generals compared notes and had no trouble deciding who the leak was. They reported afterward that General Clark, who usually arrives at staff meetings bustling with an exaggerated idea of his own importance, this time slipped in quietly and took a seat in the rear. After the meeting was over, he reminded one of the senior officers that a mission had been planned to Japan and he thought he might very well go on that mission.

It was over two months ago that I told Louis Johnson about Carter Clark, but Louis as usual has done nothing. Could it be that Louis is delighted at McCarthy's excoriation of Acheson? I also warned Bill Boyle two months ago about Clark. Boyle I know has tried to do something, but apparently he had been unsuccessful. I have warned him again today.

Talked with Howard McGrath. McGrath strikes me as one of the most honest and straightforward men in government, but with a background steeped in the political routine. As a boy, he was brought up in the school which believes that the party boss has the last say. For instance, I talked to him today about Bob Wallace, the attorney for

Magnolia Oil in Oklahoma City whom Senator Kerr has nominated for the federal court. Wallace is sixty-five years old, has worked for the oil companies for twenty-five years, and will soon draw a pension from them for life. In other words, on the federal bench he will be drawing a salary from Uncle Sam and the oil companies. McGrath seemed a little surprised at this and said that this should not be. But he also said that when Bob Kerr and Governor Roy Turner proposed anyone as a judge, he, McGrath, had no alternative but to send the name on to the White House—which he has done in the case of Wallace. I reminded him that Roosevelt had looked around for good men to elevate to the federal bench and that after Mr. Truman leaves office, it is the federal judges who will carry on his philosophy. McGrath agreed but gave no indication that Wallace's appointment might be blocked.

March 21: Sentiment for McCarthy seems to be building. People forget that none of the people he has named so far are actually in the State Department. They tell me with all earnestness: "Don't you want to get the Communists out of the State Department?" Senator Taft amazed me by admitting publicly what I said about him—namely, that he was egging McCarthy on. I never thought he would admit it.

March 22: Lunched with Secretary General Trygve Lie, a very engaging personality who admitted quite frankly that the United Nations was in danger of slipping into a moribund, intimidated agency like the League of Nations. He is going to put the heat on other countries to try to get China seated on the Security Council and thus get over the present stalemate. Significant of the American attitude toward the U.N. now is the fact that at the dinner given for Trygve Lie last night at which he delivered a speech, Vice President Barkley expressed some embarrassment privately at being present when Trygve Lie delivered his espousal of the U.N.

March 23: The Frelinghuysens came to dinner. His father was Senator from New Jersey during the Harding administration, and a man who entertained heartily and frequently on his yacht. Yet young Harry is so disgusted with the Republicans he is on the verge of becoming a Democrat.

He says that McCarthy has paralyzed almost all the thinking in the State Department, also made it impossible to hire good men. They don't want to undergo the danger of a McCarthy attack. Harry is in charge of the Korean desk, paid $4,000 a year, and as he himself expresses it: "I could plunge the United States into war over night. And the State Department can't afford to pay me more than $4,000." The tragedy is that Harry is not exaggerating.

March 24: Tom Young of Marysville, California, who flew down to see me in Los Angeles, finally came through in the punch board investigation in Sonoma County. Young even named Howser as getting a $50,000 payoff.

Saw Gordon Gray, retiring Secretary of the Army, about Carter Clark. He didn't believe at first that Clark could be feeding McCarthy. Later I learned that he had called in some of his generals and asked them about Clark. He said he had heard various rumors, but when he tracked them down they "all came from Drew Pearson." The generals confirmed what I had said. Furthermore when they sent for Clark, they found him at the office of Senator Styles Bridges of New Hampshire.

March 25: McCarthy has now said that he would stake his whole case against the State Department on one man, whose name he has not yet divulged but who happens to be Owen Lattimore.

March 26: I finally decided to mention Lattimore's name on the air. No other newspaper had done so due to the fear of libel. I am now being called unethical by other members of the press. Actually the AP sent out an FYI message to clients that they had Lattimore's name but were worried about libel. When I take the risk of libel, however, I am unethical.

March 27: Dropped in to see Fred Vinson. He is a great human being but much as I love him, I can't see how he would make a good president. I fear, however, that he is Truman's candidate for 1952. Vinson exudes sweetness and light and is a square-shooting loyal friend, but I don't think he sees the big problems on the world's horizon today.

April 1: Congress has been debating the Kerr natural gas bill now for weeks. Yet scarcely a line has appeared in the local newspapers. I can't help but think that in the old days, when George Norris, Bob La Follette and even my old friends Henrik Shipstead and Gerald Nye—

who turned out to be such isolationists—were in Congress, the country would have had such fireworks that it would have been headline news everywhere.

Instead, I have been about the only newspaperman who has played up the story in Washington.

Yesterday Sam Rayburn finally pushed the bill through the House by the margin of two votes. In the first vote roll call he was behind six votes, whereupon Charlie Halleck induced four members to switch. It was the most brazen piece of wire-pulling seen on the floor of the House in years. It is now up to Truman to approve or veto.*

April 5:   It looks as if the military are getting a case of spring jitters again. Of course, in view of Pearl Harbor, the Fuchs case, and Russian development of the A-bomb, I don't blame them. Six Russian submarines have been discovered off the West Coast. Many more Russian subs have been seen off the Aleutians. Meanwhile, local draft board chairmen have been ordered to prepare for reactivation of their boards. A good many reserve officers also have received notices to stand by.

I haven't been able to find anything new in the European picture to warrant this except the previous concentration of Russian troops on the Yugoslavian-Hungarian border. And I don't believe the U.S. will really intervene in that far-distant area even though, in long terms, such intervention would be justified and probably wise.

April 6:   The Air Force has decided to pull all its bases out of the Aleutian Islands. It will even withdraw from the northwest part of Alaska in case of war. In brief, enemy troops will be permitted to occupy that part of Alaska closest to the Bering Sea. This is secret strategy which the Air Force at first denied but which I confirmed from other sources.

We have been shipping a lot of Air Force troops from Montgomery, Alabama, to Seattle. Looks as if Southern air bases would be largely closed up.

April 10:   Spoke for the United Jewish Appeal at Newark, New Jersey. They raised $550,000, an increase over last year. The biggest contributor was the brother of Joe Reinfeld, an ex-bootlegger whom I have been

*He vetoed it.—ED.

giving unshirted hell in connection with the Tanforan racetrack, income tax evasion, and other shenanigans. The Reinfeld family put up $110,000. In fact, they first contributed $100,000 and then raised it to $110,000 after my speech.

Later, I met Joe's brother and felt a little mean about going after him. However, when a man like Joe makes a fortune by flouting the law, I suppose I should not be too charitable.

April 11:   Heard the music for Leon's* musical show, which is based on Washington and features a newspaperman who makes predictions. The title is *The End of the War—Tra La.* The music sounds surprisingly good but the plot certainly makes a monkey out of me.

The Cuneos staged a very nice cocktail party. It is getting tough to stand through a three-hour cocktail party drinking no more than ice water and tomato juice.

Cuneo thinks that I am nuts to go after McCarthy, claims the tide is in the opposite direction and that the entire country is determined to clean out the Communists. I agree except I think that the Communists have been pretty well cleared out. Now it has got to a point where anyone who was sympathetic to Russia during the war is in danger of being called a Communist.

The Russians have shot down an American plane near Latvia. Maybe this was what the Defense Department was so jittery about last week.

April 12:   Lunched with Bart Crum and a member of his law office, together with Jack Wheeler, my Bell Syndicate boss. He read me a letter from the editor of the Troy, New York, *Record,* calling me a pinko and a radical because I told the story of who was behind McCarthy—namely the Chiang Kai-shek paid lobby and an assorted conglomoration of Coughlinites. I lean over backward to exonerate the Catholic Church, but I regret to say that Georgetown University, which is one of the outstanding universities operated by the Church, has been backing McCarthy with poorly concealed enthusiasm. Monsignor Walsh and my old friend Maurice Sheehy have been giving him all sorts of support.

*Leon Pearson, Drew Pearson's younger brother, for many years an NBC newsman.—ED.

Later in the day I visited with Maggie Swope and Aunt Lelia's family, where I was surprised to find almost everyone for McCarthy. Apparently he has renewed public faith by calling Louis Budenz as a witness.

April 13:   Talked to J. Edgar Hoover about the McCarthy charges. He says that Budenz will testify that members of the Communist party told him that they had used Lattimore. Hoover doesn't think Lattimore was a member of the party but that he was easily used and is a poor security risk. If Budenz springs this out on the witness stand, it will make McCarthy a hero. Furthermore it will swing public opinion just enough to mean the defeat of some very good Senators in November. And it will also mean a Republican Congress.

Yet with Truman's future for the next two years at stake and even more important with one of the most vital battles for public sanity an issue, there is no leadership, no cohesion, no initiative being taken by the White House. In fact, I think Mr. Truman is blissfully ignorant of what is going on.

I got hold of Abe Fortas and Morris Ernst to suggest that they get hold of some witnesses to refute Budenz. No one in the administration seems to have any desire or ability to act. What I know has happened is that McCarthy was promised an affidavit by Budenz stating that Lattimore was a member of the Communist party. However, the affidavit was not forthcoming or it never existed. So now the heat is on Budenz from Georgetown University via Fordham to produce enough to save McCarthy's neck. And although Budenz never gave the FBI anything about Lattimore in the past, he is now slated to produce just enough to muddy the water and fool the public.

April 14:   I saw Admiral Souers and Jack Peurifoy with the idea of having seven FBI men who testified at the Communist trial in New York go on the stand to refute Budenz after his testimony next week. They could testify that they were planted inside the Communist party to see what was going on and that they never knew Lattimore either as a top Communist spy or in any other capacity. I finally got hold of Howard McGrath to give him this idea but I doubt whether it will get anywhere with any of them.

Steve Early is terribly upset about the plane shot down over the Baltic. He believes it was a deliberate test of American public opinion;

that the Russians are planning to invade Yugoslavia in May, and that they want to see whether the shooting of the plane would show the American people to be in a belligerent mood.

Former Texas Congressman Maury Maverick has just had a typical Maverickesque interview with Dean Acheson. It went something like this: "I am not going to be polite. My time is short and I don't have time to be polite. I'm tired of hearing about you and Harvard and Yale and that you're witty. I've never heard you say anything funny yet. But one Jerome Frank says you are O.K. and this man Pearson seems to like you, so you must be O.K."

At this point Dean laughed a little sheepishly and said he couldn't help it if he had gone to Harvard and Yale.

"If Harold Ickes got caught in a whorehouse at three A.M. killing a woman," Maury continued, "a lot of people would go to bail him out. But not you, you've got no friends."

Dean protested at this point that he had done the best he could. "No, you haven't," Maury replied. "You've done nowhere near the best you could. You've got nobody up on the Hill to make speeches for you. You've done nothing to win friends. You are a lawyer. You are one of these big-shot defense lawyers and I am a poorly paid offense lawyer. But you know what it is to take pressure in court. Now, however, you are under pressure from 100 million people. The pressure on you is 1,000 times more intense than when you are in court. You are doing the most important thing in the world, and for the sake of the rest of us, you have to succeed. You are our foreign policy. So you've got to try a lot harder than if you were in court. And you've got to get over the idea that you are doing your best—because you ain't."

I still don't know exactly what was in Maury's mind and though what he said was so true, I doubt if it made much impression on Dean. He is too harassed, too tired and too numb. Nevertheless, it is so true that he has few friends and has lost public opinion.

Franklin D. Roosevelt was a past master of public opinion, knew that his only hold on Congress was to be stronger with the country than they were. Once Congress knew that they were stronger than he, they were ready to turn on him like a pack of wolves on a lame steer.

Neither Harry Truman nor Dean realizes that. That is why Congress has turned on them now. That's also why McCarthy's fight is more important than almost any other battle in half a decade.

April 15:   Tom Corcoran and Ickes came to lunch. Tom reminisced on F.D.R.'s relations with the Church. Told how Roosevelt had bet all his cards on Cardinal Mundelein, a great human being; then when he died, Spellman, a hard-boiled politician, stepped in. Tom also says that the fight over parochial schools is unnecessary because the Church can't possibly continue them. According to Tom, Mundelein used to say in a few years we'll be coming to them (the municipalities) and asking them how much they'll give us for our buildings. It is almost impossible, according to Tom, to get a sufficient supply of nuns as teachers; and parochial schools are built on a system of no salaries to teachers.

I remember during the height of the Spanish crisis talking to Tom about the embargo on arms to Spain. His reply was, "Talk to the Cardinal," meaning Mundelein. In more ways than one, he fixed F.D.R.'s foreign policy.

April 16:   The real story of the U.S. plane shot down over the Baltic is gradually unfolding. None of it has been in the papers yet. The Russians have been holding war maneuvers in the Baltic. This is their special testing ground for rockets. The American plane was not only loaded with secret electronics equipment and radar but the Navy made the mistake of putting the names of the crew and their ratings on a bulletin board in advance. Civilians had access to this bulletin and, the Russian spy system being what it is, Moscow undoubtedly knew the plane was taking off with electronics experts aboard. The plane's mission was to watch Russian rockets—getting a screening of their flight. This can be done much better from the air than on land. The American plane also had orders that in case of attack, it was to crash and destroy the instruments. This obviously was done.

Undoubtedly the Russians announced their note of protest because they knew the United States would be embarrassed in disclosing the real nature of the plane's mission. The plane had orders not to go near the coastline so it is almost certain that it was not overlapping territory as claimed by the Russians.

April 18:   Lunched with the American Legion. If you had told me a year ago I would be palsy-walsy with the Legion, I wouldn't have believed it.

April 19:   Flew to Detroit in Henry Ford's private plane. Lunched with him and his vice presidents, looked over the Ford plant, and talked to Henry about our proposed juvenile delinquency school. I couldn't help remembering the last time I was in Dearborn. It was the summer of 1924 and I was just out of teaching a course at Columbia and determined to make a name for myself in the journalistic world. I went to Detroit to try to interview old Henry Ford, then reputedly one of the interview-shy figures in the U.S.A. For one week I marked time in Detroit, pounded the pavements, went to the movies, and took the slowpoke electric line out to Dearborn every day to sit with a row of inventors, job seekers, and others craving an audience with the powers that be. Finally after half a week I managed to see Ford for a few scanty minutes. He said that the thing that he was interested in most was the diversion of big industrial plants; getting workers out in the country where they could farm in their off-hours. He suggested that I go to see his village factories on the River Rouge, then come back and talk to him. I did so. The village factories were spic and span, beautifully located, and the kind of places where I would like to work myself. After inspecting them, I went back to see Ford and in another scanty few minutes he told me that he considered that this type of factory was to be the industry of the future. The big city, he said, was doomed.

I went back to New York and wrote an interview which hit the front pages all over the country. I still remember the lead. It was : "The big city is doomed." When I saw Ford's grandson, I told him about that interview. We both laughed at the fact that the city of Detroit, which his grandfather thought was too big, is now almost twice its size in 1924.

I told young Henry about going to India later and writing a story about Gandhi, who also believed in the diversification of industry and who urged that every Indian peasant have a handloom to weave his own cloth during the off-farm season. When I put together Henry Ford's ideas and Gandhi's ideas in an article for *Asia* magazine, the editor asked me to interview Ford a third time and get his ideas on Gandhi and then interview Gandhi to get his ideas on Ford. I saw Ford and although I went on to India I never did see Gandhi. He was in the middle of a fast and my wife couldn't wait. She was pregnant.

At lunch with the Ford executives I was cross-examined by Graeme Howard, former vice president of General Motors in charge of their European sales. Probably no one at the luncheon table except he and I knew that he had been castigated by me some years before for organizing Franco's military transport during the Spanish Civil War. The vice presidents bombarded me with questions, most of them intelligent. We had a very good time—in fact, a much better time than twenty-six years ago when I, a very scared young newspaperman, lunched with the famous Ford reactionaries, Bennett, Sorenson, and Knutson. The first two were fired by young Henry. Knutson I got to know and like as chairman of the War Production Board.

All of the Ford executives were a little jubilant over McCarthy.

April 20: Lunched with Ed Barrett, the new Assistant Secretary of State in charge of propaganda. He tells me that at long last the State Department is coming around to my idea of balloons over Russia. He even proposes beer bottles containing messages which could be washed ashore along the Baltic. (What a job for Blatz Beer, one of the big contributors to the Democratic National Committee.)

I suggested to Barrett that the best man to answer McCarthy was George Marshall, that he was revered and respected by everyone. I bore down on him the fact that the State Department was losing the McCarthy battle and I think they are beginning to realize that they will have to act and act fast. Barrett rushed off after lunch to act on the Marshall idea—before he took a plane for a weekend in New York.

Budenz testified. It was worse than I expected. He accused Lattimore of being part of a Soviet spy ring. I am certain that Budenz was under terrific pressure from certain influences in the Catholic Church, and I am also reasonably certain that he perjured himself.*

April 21: McCarthy got a big ovation from the American Society of Newspaper Editors. Talking to them the next day, it was interesting to see that the western editors were against McCarthy and the eastern editors for him.

Assistant Attorney General Joe Keenan came to see me after the McCarthy speech very much worried. He said that by accident he had been with McCarthy and some of his friends after he had spoken to the editors, that McCarthy was drinking heavily, and that a plan had

---

*Budenz was, at this time, a columnist for the National Catholic Welfare Conference News Service. Between 1940–45, he had been Managing Editor of the *Daily Worker.*—ED.

been discussed to either bump me off or cause a little permanent mutilation. McCarthy pointed out to his friends that he would be a hero with many Senators if he could pull my teeth, break my insteps permanently, or break fifteen ribs. I don't know where he got the figure fifteen. Joe was so worried he wanted to talk to J. Edgar Hoover. He said that McCarthy was something of a madman and boasted after speaking to the editors that he had not seen the text of his speech until he opened it up on the rostrum.

April 23:   Winchell, believe it or not, carried a plug for McCarthy. He also used a long spiel eulogizing the editors and their fearlessness. Walter really must think he's slipping. I will probably lose some newspapers and get some people mad, but I wound up the radio program tonight with a comparison between Salem witch-burning and McCarthyism.

April 24:   Dean Acheson's speech before the editors has now been published in full and is fairly good but much too late. It had more vehemence than facts. The State Department is suffering from the same fault which bogs down the entire Truman administration—lack of organization and brainwork. In the old days of Huey Long, a battery of Senators—Hugo Black of Alabama, Shay Minton of Indiana (both now on the Supreme Court), Joe Guffey of Pennsylvania, Homer Bone and Lou Schwellenback of Washington—laid for Huey and pounced on him every time he got up to speak. I have tried to tell some of the administration people that that is the only way to handle McCarthy. Dean should not have to spend his time defending himself. He should have others do this so that he can concentrate on foreign policy, which today is the most important problem facing the nation.

I dined with a group of churchmen and others interested in helping the administration work out a bipartisan foreign policy. Father John Cronin of the National Catholic Welfare Conference seemed quite liberal. He is the man who stated that there were no Communists in the State Department. He confessed that he hadn't meant to make this statement publicly and was a little embarrassed by the wide circulation now given it. Also present were Frederick Reissig of the Federation of Churches, Raymond Wilson of the American Friends, Colonel Don Zimmerman, chairman of the Joint Advanced Study Committee of the Joint Chiefs of Staff, and Dr. Stuart Rice of the Budget Bureau. Zimmerman incidentally told how the Joint Chiefs of Staff had instructed him to chart the course of war fifty years in advance at which time the men might be fighting planet to planet or even taking refuge on the moon.

April 27: I prepared a list of questions to be asked by Senator Hunt of Wyoming of Frankie Costello. Hunt, however, showed them to Senator McFarland of Arizona, chairman of the committee, who said no. Apparently Costello was not to be embarrassed. All of which bears out my suspicion that this hasty Interstate Commerce Committee investigation of racing wires is chiefly a pretext to head off the Kefauver crime probe, which would really get to the bottom of things.

Wrote a full column on Claude Pepper and Congressman Smathers, which is raising hell in Florida. Simultaneously John Perry, who has staked everything on defeating Pepper, arrived as my house guest.*

April 28: A good many of the Florida newspapers refused to publish the Pepper-Smathers column. Every paper in the state except four is for Smathers. The Orlando paper not only refused to publish the column but refused to take it as a paid ad. This is the same publisher whom Pepper helped to get a radio license.

I had a big cocktail party for the Perrys attended by Senator Taft and various Republicans. I told Taft that my wife caused me a lot of trouble whenever his name was mentioned in the column. In fact, she even tried to exercise the one thing I will not permit from anyone—censorship.

May 2: Last Saturday Ed Morgan, counsel for the Tydings committee,† called to say that I could predict Senator McCarthy was going to be given the one-two punch. Morgan wouldn't elucidate further, but I am now beginning to find out what he meant. Peurifoy says that the administration has finally awakened to the damage McCarthy has done and they are going to try some of the tactics I have been urging. Senators Kilgore and Neeley of West Virginia will show the McCarthy lie, for which he will be cited for official censure. General Marshall,

---

*Perry owned many papers in Florida and was one of Drew Pearson's favorite publishers despite some differences in philosophy.—Ed.

†The Tydings committee—a subcommittee of the Senate Foreign Relations Committee—was investigating McCarthy's charges of Communist infiltration of the State Department.—Ed.

Cordell Hull, and James Byrnes have already issued a blast against him. However, thanks to the delay, it's going to take a lot more than it would have taken originally to put McCarthy in his place.

John Maragon was given eight months to two years for perjury.

May 3:   Claude Pepper was defeated. In fact, he was swamped. The Smathers victory was overwhelming. This means that we will probably have a Republican Congress in November. Much more important and serious, it means that Senators like Frank Graham of North Carolina, one of the finest in Congress, will have to fight for their lives. It will also mean that Senator Lucas and Frank Myers will be defeated in Illinois and Pennsylvania. What the administration hasn't realized is that McCarthy's charges really cut deep. Smathers made the most of them.

He printed a booklet throwing up every conceivable move Pepper had ever made which could be linked even remotely with Russia, and circulated it all over the state. It even contained references to Dave Karr as a card-carrying Communist and said that Karr and I were responsible for Pepper's short-lived Presidential fling at Philadelphia in 1948.

Truman, as usual, didn't realize the issues that were at stake in Florida, and failed to give Pepper the slightest nod even while he was in Key West. Bill Boyle, who knew what was at stake, sent $25,000 secretly to Pepper, but this was just a drop in the bucket compared with the Republican money Smathers had to spend. Smathers used some of the foulest tactics in recent political history and I, for one, do not propose to let the public forget about them.

Truman's stock has dropped so low that even in Alabama the more enlightened Democrats, loyal to him, barely won their race to control the Democratic State Committee.

May 4:   Truman says that the Pepper defeat had no significance. He doesn't know what's hit him.

May 11:   Constantine Brown* has been telling me that I am all wrong about McCarthy. We had lunch today and I tried to convince him that

---

*Co-author with Drew Pearson of *The American Diplomatic Game* (published in 1935), Brown had his own column for many years. The two men fell out over McCarthy as Brown grew increasingly conservative.—ED.

he was wrong. I don't believe I succeeded. However, the more I talked, the more I convinced myself that I was right. I recalled the events that he and I had written about in the *American Diplomatic Game*—the attempt by Henry L. Stimson to mobilize the world's peace machinery against Japan when the war lords first invaded Manchuria in 1931; Franklin Roosevelt's attempt to invoke the world's peace machinery against Japan in 1936 when Admiral Leahy urged a naval blockade in the Pacific; Stimson's attempt in 1930 to sign a merely consultative pact at the London Naval Conference. All of these moves to head off war were stymied because of a confused public, because of lack of confidence in our leaders, because the American people were not sufficiently educated on the basic issues and dangers. Today the thing that McCarthy has accomplished best is to confuse the public and destroy confidence in leadership.

Today if Acheson proposed that we take drastic steps to head off a war with Russia he could get nowhere; the people would not follow him, would not believe in him. The seeds of war never sprout suddenly. They are planted, cultivated, nurtured, and grow over a long period of time. It's in the fairly early stages that you prevent war. And today the United States must be in a position to move and move rapidly to prevent war at the first signs, wherever they may break out.

If I directed the machinations of Moscow, I can think of nothing more helpful than to have the American public confused at this vital time.

May 12: Talked with Howard McGrath. He does not want the real story of the Amerasia case* published because it would reflect on the FBI, which illegally entered Larsen's apartment. The Fourth Amendment is not suspended during wartime, contrary to some people's impression, and the FBI apparently forgot there was such a thing as the U.S. Constitution.

*In June of 1945, John Stewart Service, a State Department Foreign Officer, and five others were arrested and charged with the theft of confidential documents from the Departments of State, War, and the Navy as well as from the Office of Strategic Services. *Amerasia*, a magazine edited by Philip Jacob Jaffe, allegedly reproduced some of these documents, which were found when the FBI raided the *Amerasia* offices. Service was never indicted although Senator McCarthy later used his arrest as part of his evidence of Communist infiltration of the State Department.—ED.

Senator Chavez of New Mexico has delivered an extremely courageous speech for a Catholic, attacking Budenz and calling him a liar. It will be interesting to see what the reaction is in Catholic circles. The *Washington Star*, incidentally, published an editorial which for that conservative paper is almost revolutionary, warning that alleged ex-Communists may still be Communists after all.

May 13:   Attended the Gridiron Club dinner. As I was walking in to the dinner, who should come up behind me but Senator McCarthy with his hand outstretched and a smile on his face. He said: "Someday I'm going to break your leg, Drew, but for the time being I just wanted to say hello."

I am more and more convinced that there is a screw loose somewhere.

May 18:   Peggy Palmer had a dinner last night for the Vice President. However, the President also turned up, together with about fifty others, and during the course of the dinner Mr. Truman rose and said this is the first time in history that the "President of the United States" (he always likes to use the entire phrase "of the United States") and the Vice President of the United States, the Chief Justice, and the Speaker of the House of Representatives, have all been together under the same roof.

It was quite an evening and you could not help but remark on the difference between Democrats and Republicans. I suppose it's the difference between the rebel yell and the austerity of Northerners.

Anyway, even the few staunch Republicans who were present seemed to like Harry, and Mr. Norton, who was Peggy's best man at her wedding, got up to say that as Bob Taft's old roommate in Ohio, he wanted to pay his respects to the President. And the way he said it, you could see that though he would die before he ever voted anything but the Republican ticket, he could not help but like Harry.

There were a lot of speeches touched off when the Chief Justice described himself as the second substitute, and then hurriedly corrected himself as the "third substitute" (I suppose he meant by that that Sam Rayburn is now in line to succeed after Barkley) and proposed a toast to the President. The first substitute, Barkley, then gave a brief speech and though I hope it was just my imagination, Barkley seemed a little old and tired. It was about the first time that his speech wasn't all it usually is.

Sam, who was reasonably sober, kidded Peggy and Perle [Mesta] about the competition over him and said he also hoped that the photographers would be present to take a picture of all three together. Sam incidentally was only invited at the last minute by Peggy at the insistence of Mrs. Truman. Sam, whom I have ridden pretty hard over the Kerr bill, was quite friendly but complained that Bob Allen had been mean to him.

After it was all over, the President played the piano; not being a musician, I couldn't judge his talents, but the way he played was certainly appealing. He looked a little bit like a small boy who had been studying hard and has to watch every key on the board. Afterward, Clark Clifford told me that he had been practicing and had developed one or two new tunes. In fact, the President remarked that one of the tunes he had learned from Margaret and in the middle of one—I think it was Mozart—he stopped and said: "That's as far as I can get."

I debated whether I should go up and shake hands with the President but finally didn't.

May 22:   Went to Harrisburg to lunch with Governor Duff, who has achieved the biggest primary victory in the history of Pennsylvania. The last time I called on a Governor of Pennsylvania was in 1932 when Gifford Pinchot was in the Executive Mansion. Bob Allen and I dined with him and Mrs. Pinchot. Those were the dark days of the depression when Roosevelt had just been elected, but had not as yet taken office.

Unless I am very fooled, Duff has been just as liberal a Governor as Pinchot, possibly more so. He has accomplished what Pinchot and all of his fine ideals never could get accomplished: the redemption of the Schuylkill River; has built more bridges and improved more schools than any other recent Governor. The only trouble is that he is sixty-eight years old, an age which probably precludes him as a Presidential candidate. We talked for two hours. He is the most refreshing practical Republican I have met in a long time.

[*The entries for July 17 through 27 are transcribed from longhand notes.*]

July 17: Jim McHugh at dinner, a former aide to Chiang Kai-shek, thinks our greatest mistake was when General Marshall didn't come out openly against Chiang. Chiang and his wife had gotten a build-up with the American people—glamour, American background—it was unpopular to criticize them. Marshall should have told the truth instead of saying "a curse on both your houses." Then we could have started winning over Communists.

Our chief policy was one of drift. We did nothing.

MacArthur has moved so slowly on Korea it may be disastrous. Today Tito bid for peace with Moscow. MacArthur doesn't seem to realize time is working against us. He has four divisions and has kept three in Japan. He held back two-thirds of the air force. His tactics are similar to those of people who proposed to defend California after Pearl Harbor.

No air strips near Sasebo. No nets for strips in South Korea. No LSTs. General Stratemeyer is stuffed shirt. Did poor job in China-Burma Theater. He waited, as he waited at Clark Field. Takes nap in P.M. Orders not to wake him.

Maybe we should get out of Orient altogether: This is a deficit area and Russia might get indigestion trying to swallow them. We certainly can't keep on feeding Japan forever. She has to trade with China.

July 26: Saw Senator Hunt re probe of police wire-tapping Senator Brewster. He thinks crime committee should do it. Lunched with Robinson, chief investigator for crime committee.* They all shy away from probing California. Senator Brien McMahon of Connecticut makes more sense than any of them. He will have Scott Lucas take up wire-tapping probe at Democratic policy meeting tomorrow. Brien is worried. He wants to make speech for disarmament, but fears he will be pilloried before election. Thinks he can urge total mobilization at same time. We mobilize to hilt and at same time offer to disarm—in fact we consider it an act of war if another nation refuses to disarm and refuses normal intercourse of peoples.

I think Brien has a great idea. Wish there were more like him in the Senate.

Jim McInerny has discovered that McCarthy forged an FBI re-

---

*The Senate Special Committee to Investigate Organized Crime in Interstate Commerce, chaired by Senator Estes Kefauver of Tennessee.—ED.

port on Mr. X—the State Department official whom he branded as a
Communist yesterday. The date of the report is July 1948. But in the
body of the report is a reference to a report made in September 1948.

Also one paragraph is completely inserted in McCarthy's alleged
FBI report. In other words, McCarthy is not only a perjurer but a
forger.

The Justice Department phoned me today that the Attorney
General had a report I had been beaten up. So far—untrue.

The Russians are calling in all their diplomats as of August 31.
Also all their gold. It begins to look as if they really meant business.

Meanwhile MacArthur, believe it or not, continues optimistic
about Korea.

July 27:   Mike Monroney finally defeated Senator Elmer Thomas in
Oklahoma. This culminates a four-year campaign beginning May 1946
to expose Thomas for his dishonest speculating. Significantly, the administration people in Oklahoma supported Thomas—farm agents,
internal revenue people, postmasters. If you've been a Senator twenty-
four years you can build up a powerful machine.

Bernie Baruch testified before Congress yesterday urging controls
on everything. He is so right. Truman, however, remains timid. Our
greatest danger is a weak dictatorship. Truman will never withstand the
military the way Roosevelt did. He hasn't strong men around him and
won't have. If we had strong leaders, I am sure the Russians would
never risk a war.

September 12:   Louis Johnson was fired today. Knowing Louie, it
must have been the worst blow of his career. But also knowing Louie,
I know he will blame others. Yet actually it was entirely his own fault.
It is true that Truman had to have a scapegoat for the Korean War,
but you can't make as many enemies as Johnson has made inside the
services, inside the Congress, and the country generally without automatically nominating yourself as the scapegoat.

I was pretty sure that Johnson was on the way out ever since the
Chief Justice came to dinner last month and asked me confidentially
whether Johnson was knifing Acheson. I confess that I was delighted
to tell him that he was. And I held back no details. The Chief Justice
was also interested in what the public reaction was to both Acheson
and Johnson—in effect, whether both should go. I stood up for Acheson. I gathered that both Truman and Vinson were strong for Acheson;

in fact, the Chief Justice went into some detail regarding Acheson's ability.

Vinson mentioned the difficulty of finding a successor for Johnson and wanted to know who I thought could do the job well. I called him back two or three days later to suggest Jack McCloy, a Republican, who knows the Pentagon better than almost anyone. Apparently the suggestion didn't click, for General Marshall was nominated today. Marshall has the reputation of being a civilian-minded general, but I have my fingers crossed. He has a great knack of putting on an intelligent press conference, and I think in his heart has become reasonably civilian-minded.

But I will never forget how, shortly after Pearl Harbor, two of his generals, who could not very well have acted without his O.K., called NBC officials to Washington and demanded that both Winchell and I be put off the air when the first opportunity arose. NBC acted within two weeks to remove Winchell, merely because he had inserted two words without prior approval in writing.

I have always wondered also just how J. Edgar Hoover found out about the meeting of the two generals with NBC. He called me on the telephone and read to me the brief transcript of what happened at the meeting.

Paradoxically, the FBI telephoned last night to say that they were being forced to investigate me in connection with the alleged leak of atomic secrets to Fred Blumenthal while I was away. Fred wrote a story about the trigger mechanism which sets off the atom bomb—a story which probably is no longer much of a secret but which never should have been written purely from a public reaction point of view. The FBI was loath to investigate, but the Atomic Energy Commission says they have to find out where the leak came from.

September 22:   Truman vetoed the anti-Communist bill. The House passed it over his veto, scarcely reading his veto message. Some members wanted to vote even before the message was read, and, of course, no reading by the clerk ever does justice to a Presidential message.

September 23:   A handful of Senators filibustered all night to support Truman in his veto against the anti-Communist bill.* My old friend

---

*Despite these efforts, the veto was overridden, and the Internal Security Act of 1950 became history.—ED.

Senator Langer of North Dakota collapsed on the floor at five A.M. after speaking most of the night. Senator Lehman of New York will probably be defeated as a result of his battle to uphold the veto. Though he has consistently fought for minorities, especially the Negro, the American Labor Party has put up a leading Negro from Harlem as a candidate against him, and it will probably swing enough votes to count him out.

I was rather young when the last tide of anti-Communism swept the country in 1920. But A. Mitchell Palmer, who delivered the baccalaureate address when I was graduated from Swarthmore, was then Attorney General and was charged with leading the wave of hysteria. Of course, you can't particularly blame him in view of the fact that his home was bombed. However, there is a significant difference between the 1920 wave and the current one. In 1920 the administration in Washington rode with the wave—in fact almost led it. Today the administration has bucked the wave. Tom Clark consistently refused to be stampeded, and so has Howard McGrath. I am frequently amazed also at the courage and basic convictions of Harry Truman himself, in the crucial issues where the interests of a great number of people are at stake. Truman is right almost 99 percent of the time. If his appointments and his execution were as good, he would be a truly great President. But unfortunately some of his flubs, such as the statement about the Marines, seriously impair his effectiveness.

September 25: Just before my broadcast yesterday, Tris Coffin [a staffman] called the White House and suggested to Charlie Murphy that the President listen. I devoted part of the broadcast to upholding him on his veto message. Today Tris got a call from Charlie Murphy saying that they were in "ecstasies" at the White House over the broadcast and wanted a copy in order to cheer up some of the downhearted. I doubt the ecstasy business—certainly it couldn't have applied to General Vaughan.

Senator McMahon delivered quite a long speech in the closing hours of Congress against the Hearst press and asked for an investigation of the draft records of three of the Hearst boys. It is one of the most carefully prepared and devastating diatribes against a newspaperman in a long time. But hardly a word got into the newspapers. *The New York Times* and the *Herald Tribune* didn't touch it. The AP waited five hours before carrying the story.

Simultaneously Senator William Jenner of Indiana let loose about ten minutes of invective against me. Every press association carried the story, and I have had repercussions all the way from Florida to Texas. Reason: I control no newspapers; I am not a member of the AP Board of Directors; I buy no press services.

I don't mind being attacked by Jenner. In fact, it's an honor. But when the newspapers show such discrimination in favor of a powerful newspaper chain, how is the American public ever going to know the truth? The last time Hearst got any really unfavorable publicity was when he carried a series calling Senators Borah of Idaho, George Norris of Nebraska, and a couple of others Communists and accused them of plotting in Mexico.

Had Hearst picked on some inconspicuous Senators, he might have got off, but Borah was too powerful and Hearst was hauled before the Senate Foreign Relations Committee. I well remember what a pathetic spectacle he was. He mumbled, stammered, and had absolutely no alibi for the tissue of lies he had published. Incidentally, Ernest Gruening, who was called a Communist in this series, made himself independently wealthy for life by suing and collecting from every Hearst paper.

Since then, nobody important has tangled with Hearst or the Scripps-Howard chain. The nearest to it was when Franklin Roosevelt started to investigate Roy Howard's income tax. And when Bob Allen wrote a story, not in the column but in the *Nation*, about Roy's tax deductions regarding his yacht, the column was promptly canceled in all Scripps-Howard papers. Roy even refused to let us mention Pan American Airways in a critical manner because he had had a free ride on Pan Am to Australia.

Someday I'm going to try to do a job on the "Lords of the Press" —but I'll have to wait until I am just ready to retire from the newspaper business.

October 31 [California]:   I received word that two mysterious callers were checking up on me. One report was that they came from the attorney general's office in California. Another was that they came from two banks in Rockville [Maryland].

Today, part of the mystery appears to be solved. Arnold Gary, the dairyman, told me that Charlie Lowery had permitted a dictaphone to be put in his house and recordings were made of Ralph's [Ralph Allen] conversations. This was done through two investigators from Rockville, apparently retained by Bingham and Robb. Gary said that he had been trying to figure out whether he should tell me about this and finally decided to do so. He learned about it through Leon Lowery. The reason two investigators came to see Leon was that when Charlie moved out of the house, he apparently left some of the recordings behind. This is another version of the story that investigators were trying to check on my telephone conversations, as well as Ralph's.*

November 1:   Ralph gave his deposition today. It was an incredible story but he seemed so familiar with every detail that to me it was convincing—especially when Warren Olney says that every detail of it they have checked has stood up. However, Ralph gave away the names of so many prospective witnesses that we will be spending most of our time now interviewing witnesses and taking depositions.

During the middle of his testimony word came that two assassins had attempted to break into Blair House, where the President is living temporarily. I had to continue with the deposition, but afterward learned that two Puerto Rican nationalists, obviously linked with the Communists, had staged a desperate and obviously impossible attempt to break into the President's residence. Had they been shrewder, and waited until he crossed between Blair House and the Executive Offices, they might have killed him.

Personally I have always felt that the President took far too many chances. When he walks along F Street or up Connecticut Avenue, he has a Secret Service man with him, and a couple in front and behind him, but they would be very little protection in case an assassin was willing to risk his life. The other day also the President was walking through Brooklyn early in the morning, when it would have been easy for someone inside a house to have operated a machine gun. However, the President says, "When my number is up, it will be called." And perhaps this is not a bad philosophy to have.

November 2:   Last night, William Power Maloney came to see me. The last time we crossed each other's paths indirectly was at three o'clock in the morning in the Washington Hotel when Jack Anderson and an investigator for the Pepper wire-tapping committee routed him

---

*Ralph Allen, a key witness in the Howser case, had been moved for safety to the Pearson farm in Maryland. Charles Lowery, one of the farmworkers, quit at this time; Leon, who also helped on the farm, was his brother.—ED.

out of Henry Grunewald's apartment. Bill gave me an interesting idea about Lt. Gov. Joe Hanley of New York. He said that Hanley was more and more fed up with Dewey, more and more convinced that Dewey would let him down and therefore was ready to spill the whole story about the payoff. He also gave me some interesting new details on the manner in which Dewey tried to recover the Hanley letter to Congressman Kingsland Macy, after he first learned of its existence. Today the Maloney story is borne out by the fact that Hanley was taken by car from Albany to Hudson City Hospital, where he is confined with a state trooper guarding his door. Significantly, Albany is a Democratic city whereas Hudson is a Republican stronghold. Dewey can get his way in Hudson, but not in Albany.

I immediately put in some phone calls—one to John Bennett, another to Duncan Just, and another to Raymond Richmond, all good friends of Hanley, to see whether we could talk to him. Just was ready to drive up to Hanley's with me, but first talked to Hanley's daughter, Mrs. Josephine Wilcox, who flatly refused to let anyone see her father. Finally I got Mrs. Wilcox on the telephone myself and suggested to her that if Dewey lost, her father would be out of luck, and that if Dewey won, he wasn't going to carry out his promise of appointing Hanley to the Thruway Commission because that automatically would confirm the Hanley letter. Instead I suggested that her father might publish his memoirs and fill some speaking engagements for a lot more than Dewey would ever pay him through political patronage. However, I got nowhere. All the reports are that Hanley is a beaten and discouraged old man, probably doesn't care much whether he lives or not. Meanwhile, reports from Upper New York State indicate that Dewey is going to run with a lower vote than ever before in history. Even his old friend publisher Frank Gannett has come out against him.

Incidentally, I think Gannett has become definitely gaga. His wife and his chief editor, Paul Miller, in effect kidnapped and took him up in the country away from the telephone to try to keep him from coming out against Dewey. However, he got loose and made the anti-Dewey statement just the same.

November 3: Dined with Sumner Welles. After dinner, he reminisced at great length and, for the first time, went into some detail about his emotions when Roosevelt fired him. Unlike most people who came to the parting of the ways with Roosevelt, Sumner has never been bitter. And this time he pointed out how wise Roosevelt was to get rid of him when he had become a political liability. He even compared his position with that of Dean Acheson, who, politically, without any doubt has become a liability to Truman. Sumner pointed out that Roosevelt was playing for higher stakes than friendship—namely the peace of the world, and that Cordell Hull was essential to the ratification of a peace treaty. As I look back on it we have gone so much further than the limited U.N. setup put across at San Francisco, it seems incredible that the Senate would not have ratified almost any peace treaty. However, at that particular time—1943—probably Roosevelt was right. For at that time unquestionably the Senate lagged far behind the people in thinking about peace.

Sumner had just had a visit that morning with Anthony Eden, now Deputy Leader of the Opposition, who told of his visit to Moscow and a conference with Stalin in 1942. During that conference, Stalin had remarked to Eden: "Hitler is a genius but he doesn't know when to stop. "Does anyone know when to stop?" asked Eden. "I do," was Stalin's reply. Eden asked him when, to which Stalin replied, "I'll stop when we recover our prewar boundaries and before the army runs away with things."

Eden and Sumner have both clung to the opinion that Stalin had been stampeded by Red Army leaders and that they were responsible for Russia's avariciousness since the war. They also believe that Stalin, in his dotage, did not actually know what was happening in the rest of the world. Sumner believes that the British Conservatives will come back into power fairly soon. Eden is completely confident.

Sumner also reminisced about Churchill, whom he described as one of the few men who could literally float in brandy and yet keep his head. When Sumner was in London last summer, he had lunch with Churchill, who received him at about twelve o'clock with glasses of port at his side. He consumed most of the port before lunch. During the lunch, Churchill consumed a bottle of champagne. After lunch he takes a nap from two until four and explains that he cannot sleep unless he puts on his pajamas. From about five until dinner time, he reads. Then after dinner he works until 4 A.M.

This is what killed the British Cabinet according to Eden. They had to be on call at all hours of the night up until 4 A.M., and then had to get up and go to work at 9 A.M., whereas Churchill did not get up until noon.

Sumner said the only time he had ever seen Churchill drunk was on the battleship in the North Atlantic when he and Roosevelt were drawing up the North Atlantic pact. At dinner one night, Churchill had had too much to drink and Franklin Roosevelt, Jr., finally led him to the nearest men's room, which happened to be Harry Hopkins's bathroom. Harry had become ill early in the evening and had gone to bed. Churchill, however, was so potted that he missed the bathroom and proceeded to use Harry's bedpost instead. Harry was most irritated, but was so sick he could not get up. Judging from my own conversations with him, it did not dilute his undying love for Churchill.

November 5:   I finally got my election predictions off my chest. When Election Day rolls around and I have to predict yes or no on various types of races, I sometimes wish that I was not such an exponent on making democracy live. From the point of view of having to predict, it would be much better if we didn't have elections.

I finally stuck my neck out by predicting that Dewey would lose in New York, though almost everybody else feels he will win. However, I figure there will be a strong silent vote against him. And in California I stuck my neck out for Congresswoman Helen Gahagan Douglas for the Senate though everyone else says she will lose. However, reaction in her favor has been growing. The only trouble is that people sometimes change their minds at the last minute and the reverses we have suffered in North Korea as a result of Chinese intervention may change the picture overnight.*

At any rate I can be fairly certain of predicting that if I am too wrong and if the Republicans score large gains, a lot of Republican newspapers will proceed to cancel the column.

December 19:   McCarthy issued another blast on the Senate floor today and again vigorously called upon the public to boycott Adam hats. Most of his tirade was devoted to David Karr. Dave called just before the tirade to tell me that he had a firm offer from the Dumont network, but I suppose it will be pulled out from under us when they read the papers tomorrow.

---

*Dewey won with 53.1 percent of the vote. (In the New York race for the Senate, Lehman won by 300,000 votes.) Richard M. Nixon, with 59.2 percent of the vote, swamped Douglas.—ED.

December 28:   Lunched with Joe Davies. He reminisced on his early days with Truman and whether we could have kept Russia in the peace orbit if Truman had not antagonized Stalin and Litvinov.

Joe said that immediately following Roosevelt's death. Forrestal and Admiral Leahy began pulling Truman into the anti-Russian camp. I had always suspected it though never knew it categorically. Joe and Harry Hopkins urged that the sole hope for peace was to have some understanding with Russia. Forrestal and Leahy on the other hand, backed by Harriman, urged that this was impossible and that our best policy was one of the straight-arm diplomacy and preparedness. Truman continued to be torn between the two camps until the Potsdam conference. Here he did pretty well and on the whole got along with Stalin. It looked like there was a new lease on American-Soviet friendship. Stalin, for one thing, promised the use of the Red Army against Japan even before Truman told him about the atomic bomb.

Of course, this may have been purely a surface gesture of help, since the Soviet spy ring in Canada was trying to get the secret of the atomic bomb during 1943 and 1944. But even at Potsdam Truman was torn between the Forrestal-Leahy anti-Russian group and, on the other hand, the friends-with-Russia group. Henry L. Stimson was one of those who used his influence in favor of friendship with Russia. But Churchill was vehemently on the other side. He had already begun his campaign for reelection and the keynote of his campaign strategy was to appeal to right-wing labor by attacking Communism in the left-wing. Joe felt that if Churchill had not had to run at that particular time it would have helped allied relations with Russia materially.

I don't know whether Joe is naive about all this or not. At the time I heartily agreed with him that our sole hope of peace was to get along with Russia, and I still think this is right. However, I also fear that it is almost impossible to get along with a police state, no matter in what country it operates.

I am almost convinced that if Joe's views were to be published now, Joe McCarthy and the pack of jackals who follow him would hoot Joe out of the country.

1951

February 26: Dan [Dan Moore, Luvie's brother], Luvie, and I left Istanbul on British-European Airways and landed in Athens two hours later. This is a trip that used to take about two days by steamer when I was last in these parts.*

In Athens, Ambassador John Peurifoy met us at the airport to get all the latest gossip about McCarthy. We also had time for a brief automobile trip through the city. Athens hasn't changed much in the 2,000 years-plus since the Acropolis was built, nor in the thirty years since I was there. The hotels look about the same. The King's palace still has its royal guard with skirts to the knees standing in front, and the only difference I understand that has taken place in the city is that the shepherds no longer cut off the water supply up in the hills so that you are not left standing in the shower bath covered with lather, waiting for the water to come on again.

In general, however, Greece looks up-and-coming. I was particularly impressed with the fact that we were able to leave our baggage at the airport for an hour. It would have been impossible to go away and leave our baggage in the old days even when it was checked, unless each piece was carefully locked. We left that afternoon for Salonika by plane—a Greek plane which on the whole was just as efficient as the British, probably more so. Greece now has airlines joining Athens with almost every part of the country. It once took me two days to go by

*In 1919, after graduating from Swarthmore College, Drew Pearson traveled to Turkey, Greece, and Serbia (now Yugoslavia), where he worked with the American Friends Service Committee rebuilding war-ravaged villages. He returned to the United States in 1921.—ED.

boat from Athens to Salonika and a day and a half by train. The trip by air took one hour and ten minutes.

Salonika hasn't changed too much in thirty years. In fact, thirty years is relatively little in the life of Salonika. Even the gate erected by Alexander the Great is still standing. I missed, however, the miles and miles of British, French, and American dumps left by the Allied Armies when I was there in 1919. It was my job to [pick] through these dumps, which were strewn with locomotives, locomotive tracks, piles of dynamite, corregated-iron roofing, kegs of nails, gasoline tanks, beaten-up trucks, good trucks, more and more trucks, all stretched out for ten miles along the bay—the leftovers of a great invasion army which had pushed up against the Germans and the Austrians in the late summer of 1918.

I suppose that I was one of the most expert pilferers of the Allied dumps, for I managed to persuade the British to give me two threshing machines, twenty tractors, and about two freight-car loads of iron roofing, together with the nails and a lot of other odds and ends to build houses in Serbia. At that time I used to live at the Russian hospital, then run by the remains of the czar's army, where I fell in love with a Russian nurse. I used to take her down to the open-air nightclub along the Aegean when I spent much more money than I could afford and listened to her tell me about the gallantry of Italian officers. At that time Salonika was still occupied by the French, the Italians, and British. On the night of February 26, however, Luvie and I enjoyed the luxury of a bath and hot running water, the last we would see for some time.

February 27: The Embassy had arranged for us to tour through southern Serbia with George Trett of the American Food Mission in one of its jeeps. We had dinner with him that night at the Hotel Macedonia, a dinner which cost about $20 for a bowl of soup and some indiscriminate meat and cabbage for the four of us. I have never seen prices so high anywhere.

February 28: We finally got started, with a trailer hitched onto the jeep to carry our baggage. George Trett was introduced to me by Dick Allen of the Food Mission as being an expert in the Serbian language, but after a couple of conversations with traffic cops in Skoplje trying to find our way out of town, I discovered that George was not much of an expert. It was left to me to be the interpreter for the party.

Finally we found the road up toward the Kachanik mountain pass toward Mitrovitzea and the Albanian border—the area which once was headquarters for the American Friends Service Committee for two years. In the old days, it would have been impossible for us to go by road but now the road is reasonably passable. Furthermore all the railroad bridges were intact, and although there were the remains of two or three locomotives still in the river and a lot of freight cars burnt out by bombing along the tracks, I could not tell whether these were the remains of World War I or World War II. Some of them looked like the same war wrecks I had seen thirty years before. The trip up the railroad to Mitrovitzea took only two hours. In the old days it used to take me pretty much of a day by train and I remember one New Year's Day spending more than a day sitting on the wrong side of the river waiting for a railroad bridge to be rebuilt.

Thanks to our late start we did not hit the base of the Albanian Alps until about three in the afternoon. This should have been the most interesting part of the trip. Here Yugoslavia is actually populated by Albanians—Albanians who came in under the Turks around 1350 and were given to the Yugoslavs by Woodrow Wilson's "self-determination of peoples" idea.

At Prizerend we stopped to let Luvie look at the Albanian market. She was scared almost to death. The Albanians apparently considered her mink coat and cellophane "Rain-dears" as unique as a woman from Mars, and they thronged around her as if she was a museum piece. Instead of our watching the market, they watched her. Prizerend is a city of narrow cobblestone streets, beautiful old Turkish buildings set on a hill, and if we had not been in a hurry we would have had a wonderful time looking it over. However, we were trying to reach Pec by dark, and the road along the base of the Albanian mountains was through restricted territory, forbidden to anyone without a pass. We had no pass and time after time were stopped by Yugoslav soldiers. However, we found that the word "Amerikanski" worked magic and we never had any real trouble getting through.

The monastery of Dêcani, which we could not see in the dark, is now pretty much a military fortress. We were stopped in front of the monastery and as usual asked for our passes. Dêcani is where we once had an orphanage and where the Serbs in their tragic retreat in 1915 stopped before they started up on the mountains and across to the Adriatic. Approximately one-third of the Serbian nation in the course of this retreat was lost.

In 1921 Andy Simpson and I covered the route of the retreat on horseback. It was then March and the snow was so deep that in places it was up to our horses' bellies.

March 1:   Pec was a little disappointing. Of course, I expected to see the old Turkish-type hotels, clustered around the marketplace, instead of which Pec now has one five-story hotel called the Hotel Stalingrad. It is run by the government under the Communist system and there are no bellboys or porters. You carry your own baggage. The rooms, of course, are without heat, the beds are passable, though not exactly up to Waldorf standards. The old gypsy orchestras are gone from the *kafanas,* but the food, though scarce, was reasonably good. Most of the time we stopped out on the road to cook Army rations on little stoves.

Parts of Pec have also been built up to an amazing extent. There are even two trains a day entering and leaving the town.

I went over to the Presinik's office to find a rather tough-looking Montenegrin, obviously a Communist appointee, now running the town. I explained that I had lived there many years before and wanted to see some of my old friends, especially Nejib Beg. The new mayor remembered Nejib, said he was about eighty years old and sick, and gave me one of his stenographers to take me to Nejib Beg's house. However, we went to his son's house by mistake. His son was a teacher and by the time we finally tracked him down at the school, which by the way was very good-looking and rather modern, the time was getting late. Furthermore, he said that his father was ill and not able to see many people.

I then hired a *fiacre* and started on a tour of Pec. We went to the old hospital which is now taken over by refugees with cattle on the ground floor, and then to our old house which was the most beautiful Turkish house in town. It had burned down. The garden was still beautiful and the little streams of water which served for both irrigation and washing were still running through the garden. My old office which was above the garage was still intact and so was the old kitchen. I also passed by our old warehouse where we once ladled out wheat and corn to our Montenegrin settlers. It is now a shop which sells wolf and fox skins; but by accident in front of it I met a graduate of Roberts College who offered to take me to Nejib Beg's home. It was just around the corner. In fact, believe it or not, he was occupying the house which we once ran as a guesthouse and where I had spent a good many weeks myself. It is a house with many vivid recollections, chiefly recollections of taking a kerosene lamp at bedtime and going around the walls smoking bed bugs into the flame. We always put each leg of our cots on four sardine-cans full of kerosene, but even that did not keep the bugs away as they dropped down from the ceiling. Nejib Beg, whom I met in his garden, looked reasonably well. At first he did not recognize me, and who could blame him after thirty years? However, when I reminded him about the hospital and the fact that I had served on the Citizens' Committee for the hospital, his memory came back and he insisted on calling me "Doctor."

I was interested to note that although Nejib Beg had two wives in the days when I knew him—one a Mohammedan and one a Christian, he being a politician who had to get both Montenegrin and Albanian votes—only one wife was still alive, the Montenegrin. I reminded Nejib Beg that the last time I had seen him was at a farewell dinner in my honor just before I left Pec, where I made one of two public speeches in Serbian. It was true that I read the speech and probably read it very badly. The next day I left for Rome and the United States. And the next day also Nejib Beg was shot. He was then a candidate for reelection. Fortunately he was not seriously wounded. In fact, I think he has been shot twice during his stormy career as mayor of Pec. Today the Communists do not permit elections so there is no problem along that line.

I was interested in the fact that many of the Mohammedan women in Pec still wore veils although they did not clutch them around their faces with the same frenzied modesty as in the old days.

We were able to get some gasoline from the Yugoslav government and proceeded out on the road to Mitrovitzea. The road is just about the same as far as the bumps go. In fact, I think it is a little bumpier than before, perhaps due to the fact that the military do not keep it up as well since the railroad was built. But the houses along the road almost remind one of a surburban area in the United States, at least compared to the old days. I had no trouble recognizing the first village which we built—Viti Moritza. The houses were in excellent shape, and although new houses have been built around the village and in the village most of them have thatched roofs and few of them are as good as those we put up. I stopped and talked to some of the Montenegrin women living in the houses and asked them who had built them. Without any hesitation they replied: "The Amerikanskis." I have forgotten whether we put floors in these houses or not, but if we didn't most of the houses now have floors. After I had identified myself one old woman came around to complain that her house needed some repairs. She seemed to think that we would stop to fix it up for her.

Djurakwatze, the second village we built, is now a thriving metropolis. The government has built a magnificent school and city hall, and the population of the town has about doubled. I would never have recognized it. The old Albanian headquarters is still intact and looks just about the same. I could not help but remember how I had once given my brother the honor and almost impossible task of driving a cow and calf eighteen kilometers from Djurakwatze to Pec. He was on horseback, but even so, it was an exhausting all-day job and if I had known as much about cows as I do now, I wouldn't have given the job to my worst enemy.

We drove on past the windswept hills over the once-extremely muddy roads. The roads are still extremely muddy but nowhere near what they used to be. I remember one steep hill where a three-ton truck loaded with nails, dynamite and black powder got stuck for three days. It just happened that this truck also contained nine million dinars which the Serbian government had asked us to take across to Pec to pay its officials. The gendarme guarding the box of dinars sat there in the rain for three days and fortunately did not toss any of his cigarettes on the black powder. I never knew exactly why.

We stopped in Kurshumlje for dinner. It was then nearly 9 P.M. Many a time I have ridden by horse between Kurshumlje and Nis and it always took two days, but on this night we drove by jeep to Nis in about three hours, getting to Nis and the main line of the railroad at 1 A.M.

By that time it was about as cold as I have ever known it in Serbia and we had to wait until three-thirty before our train came in. This was Luvie's first taste of a railroad station. The floor was packed with humanity. It was difficult to walk without stepping on someone. There were no benches in the Serbian railroad station, only a stone floor where you could sit or lie. You could go into the restaurant, but it was equally crowded. So we stood or sat on our suitcases until the train arrived. We had purchased first-class tickets (all berths in the Wag-en-Laye being taken), but the stationmaster explained that all seats were taken in first-class, so we rode second-class and were lucky enough to get a compartment to ourselves. It was bitter cold, and Dan and I spent the night putting on more socks and more shirts until we were wearing a layer of about three socks and three shirts each. Fortunately Luvie had her mink coat.

Next morning we noticed that there was insect powder in the corners of the upholstery and a little later it was easy to discover why. We were covered with bites!

March 2: Belgrade has changed considerably. It is no longer the old, overgrown Turkish village it used to be. Furthermore the people look more sophisticated and far less interesting. Gypsy orchestras no longer play in the restaurants. I suppose they all belong to the union now and the restaurants can't afford orchestras.

I talked to the former Ambassador to Washington, Sava Kosanovitch. He thinks that Tito is not going to be able to see me. At the closing of the Schupstina session yesterday, Tito left for military maneuvers. Kosanovitch says that he really wanted to see me, and George Allen, our Ambassador, says the same. I wonder whether Tito and those around him may not recall my prediction of some years ago that he would be assassinated.

March 3: I have been so busy working up a broadcast that I haven't seen much of the city. We dined at the Embassy and met the British Ambassador, who was most charming, and the French Ambassador, who was stationed in Washington with de Gaulle's Free French at the time the State Department was snubbing him.

My broadcast at midnight over the Yugoslav government radio station was quite an ordeal. After fifteen minutes of trying to get New York on the radio telephone, but failing, I went on the air anyway and had the feeling that I was talking to 5,000 miles of trans-Atlantic vacuum. In addition, I figured that some of the things I was saying would not be particularly pleasing to the Yugoslavs and I could not help but wonder whether I would be cut off.

It was the first broadcast the Yugoslavs have given to an outsider in a good many years, and when I finished my manuscript was covered with perspiration that had dropped off my face. However, New York came through immediately and reported that they had recorded every word.

After the broadcast we had a drink in the former residence of the Foreign Minister. It was quite a palace, beautifully furnished with choice portraits but significantly had been expropriated by the government and turned over to the Belgrade Press Club. Of course, the United States frowns upon expropriation by the Communists but I can't help remembering thirty years ago when I wanted a horse, I went to the *natchonlik* and he expropriated it. He not only commandeered a horse from a wealthy peasant, but he expropriated bridle, saddle, and sometimes he expropriated a bed for me to sleep on at night. At first, I did not realize that this was the way my horses were being secured. When I discovered what was happening, I bought an old German cavalry nag that went at a terrific pace all day, but wore itself out after a week's travel so that it never was good for much again. And I traded it off to Major Hardwicke, the head of the British Serbian Relief Fund. It was the only time I ever got the better of the British.

March 4:   Left for Trieste on the Simplon Express. Before doing so we had lunch with Ambassador Kosanovitch who is now a member of the Cabinet. Significantly he is one of only two Cabinet members who are non-Communists. After dinner, he brought in Save Voukasavelatz, who had been Minister of Agrarian Reform in the days when we worked in Pec. Voukasavelatz was the second man I met in all Yugoslavia who remembered me. He and I had taken some rather hectic trips together over the Metohjia Okrug, and there was good reason why we should not forget them. I recall that on five different occasions he proposed that I and other members of our mission receive decorations from the Yugoslav government. We politely declined. Undoubtedly it is a sign of old age and ego, but since that time I have accepted decorations from France, Italy, Denmark, and Chile; but in those days I did not think foreign decorations should be accepted by one engaged in reconstruction work. Perhaps also I was a little soured by the fact that almost every American who came to the Balkans spent part of his time euchreing for decorations.

I remember being in the office of Colonel Edwin Erskine Hume, then head of the American Red Cross for Yugoslavia, when he received a telegram from Colonel Andrews, head of the Red Cross in Rumania, which read: "I am sending you one carload of sugar as per your request. How about that order of St. Savaa?" Colonel Hume had about as many decorations as General MacArthur.

I always remember the decoration given to Mrs. Leavitt in Turkey, the Order of Chastity, third class. At any rate Voukasavelatz and

I had a most pleasant visit. He is now over seventy years old and a professor at the University of Belgrade.

March 5: Arrived in Venice after a reasonable comfortable train trip. We took the midnight sleeper to Rome.

March 6: Italy after the Balkans is like arriving in modern civilization. We stayed at the Hotel Excelsior, from which I directed the Italian Friendship Train three years ago. Italy has changed almost beyond belief. Of course, Rome itself was not hit by war, but all of Italy outside of Rome is rebuilt, rejuvenated, and there is a fresh energy and confidence in the Italian people. In fact, they are so confident that they are now a little cocky. The most optimistic development, however, is that the Communists are really on the retreat.

March 10: Arrived in Frankfurt last night. I now understand why the American Army and other American personnel like to live in Germany. A reasonable number of servants are furnished by the German government free as part of the occupation costs, while additional servants can be hired for almost nothing.

Dined with Jack McCloy at his hunting lodge just outside Frankfurt. Mrs. McCloy, whose father was born in Germany, has been criticized by Americans for her friendship with Germans, particularly her sympathy for some of the Nazi war prisoners recently given a stay of execution.

McCloy in my opinion is doing a good job as U.S. High Commissioner. It is probably the toughest job in Europe. He is damned by the pro-Germans, and damned by the anti-Germans, and damned by the Germans themselves. However, he has managed to set up a government in Bonn which is operating reasonably well and which has a chance of avoiding the tragic pitfalls of the German Republic after World War I.

March 12: Finally arrived in Berlin after a trip about as bad as anything in Yugoslavia. I had lunch with Mike Fodor, whom I had met in Vienna in 1923 when he was with the *Manchester Guardian*. I reminded Mike of how we had sat in a restaurant in Vienna and listened to a twenty-piece orchestra play "Yes, we have no bananas." Mike is now the editor of the American government paper in Berlin, and, I found, had more contacts with the political underground then anyone else. He put me in touch later in the day with a refugee from the Ukraine, who was formerly head of the Ukraine underground. He reported that resistance against the Russians had practically ceased in the Ukraine. There were too many people killed. It was no longer possible to flee from the Ukraine across the Polish and Czech borders. The opposition continues, but it is silent, and not by force of arms.

Berlin is the most vigorous city I have been in on this entire trip. There is a sort of feeling here among both Germans and Americans that is hard to describe, a vibrant quality. People here live within the shadow of the Russians. They know that they could be wiped out almost overnight. Yet there is no fear, no pessimism; there is more cooperation with the United States and gratitude for the help of the United States than in any other country with the possible exception of Turkey.

I dined with Mayor Reuter at the home of the American Military Commander, General Matthewson. At the dinner was a German senator and a German publisher. The senator had spent twelve years in the United States in exile during the Hitler regime; Mayor Reuter himself had been to the United States many times, chiefly during his exile. Talking to these Germans, you get the feeling that they are really fighting for the preservation of democracy. I don't know whether these are typical of the other members of the Bonn government, though Jack McCloy says they are.

I was not particularly impressed by the attitude of the Germans in the south though I did not meet any members of the government there. But I was impressed by the people of Berlin.

March 14:   Flew from Frankfurt to Paris last night on Air France. It was freezing cold and we were delayed by sixty-mile winds. As a result we landed at Orly Airport instead of Le Bourget. I had no idea anyone would meet me, but when I stepped off the plane, there was Luvie, together with the entire committee of the French *Merci* Train— Messrs. Cast, Picard, Artiguenave, et al. They were just the same as ever, except that they had learned two or three words of English. They have outlined a schedule which is not going to give me much time for newspaper work. It began with a luncheon today at the restaurant "Chez Cou-Cou," consisting of fifteen courses, all of them delicious.

Picard says that French public opinion is in a bad state. It is not particularly friendly to the United States. And he believes that if Russia should invade, most of France would go under to Russia in a couple of weeks. After talks with various Americans and other Frenchmen, I felt that the picture is not quite as pessimistic as this. The Communists are somewhat on the downgrade, with de Gaulle coming up. However, de Gaulle is vigorously anti-American.

March 15:   The mayor of the Department of the Seine had a little reception at the City Hall today and presented me with a medal, after which we had lunch at the railroad's Chemin de Fer Club—another long ceremony accompanied by some rather touching speeches.

I cannot help but think that despite the criticism of the United States, the French are quite vigorously in our corner. Certainly of all the countries I have visited, the French remember the Friendship Train and the other things that we have done perhaps more vividly than anyone. Of course, it is asking a lot for people to remember the Friendship Train three years after it happened, but the French certainly did. I am still convinced that periodic gestures of this kind create more good will than we generally realize.

The big question in western Europe today is the Shumann Plan. It is being initialed this weekend. I recall visiting Le Creusot in 1923 and interviewing Charles Schneider, then head of the Schneider Steel Works, in regard to French and German steel cooperation. He was a hard man to interview because he was so colorless, and I confess that I had to drag ideas out of him and embroider on them afterward. But I got him to go on record for cooperation. In a way he couldn't help it because one of his biggest plants operated in Skoda, Czechoslovakia, now taken over by the Russians. However, the interesting thing is that both the French steel magnates and the Germans are now bucking the Shumann Plan. For the most part they managed to get through the war without having their factories bombed, and now they figure that they can make deals between themselves as they have for years without government interference. Incidentally one of the amazing things about Frankfurt is that of all the vast destruction in that city, much of it unrepaired, the I.G. Farben buildings remain in their pristine purity. Even the fountain with its surrounding willow trees was unscathed by the bombs we poured on the city. You can't tell me this is just luck!

The most interesting thing about the debate over the Shumann plan is the opposition of the British, undoubtedly due to the fact that the British always hate to see the continental countries getting along together. Even under the Labour Government the British still believe in the balance of power. They do not seem to realize that a United Europe makes a peaceful Europe. All they can see is that a united Europe means less opportunity for British trade.

I had an interesting talk with General Eisenhower. He looks older. However, he has not lost his energy and his contagious charm. With one exception, whenever I have talked with Eisenhower, he has exuded something similar to what Franklin Roosevelt had—an ability to make people like him and the ability to inspire confidence.

However, I think that Eisenhower really has more of it than Roosevelt. Roosevelt used to tell stories. Eisenhower talks about ideals and aims. I had a hard time seeing Eisenhower. General [Buck] Lanham informed Luvie before I arrived that I could not see him at all. However, I more or less told Lanham where to get off and in a few minutes got a call that he, Lanham, had managed to squeeze in a minute to see Eisenhower personally and that Ike had said: "Why, of course I want to see Drew." I suppose this was an act.

At any rate, although I tried to leave a couple of times, Eisenhower insisted on talking. And he talked like a man who is really wrapped up in what he's trying to do. I remember talking to him once when he was Chief of Staff and when I thought he wanted to run for President. At that time he was expounding on the importance of free speech. I wasn't quite sure at the time whether he was doing this for my benefit or not. But the longer I know him the more sincere I think he really is.

March 16:   Arrived in London by air. We are staying with Jean Beliard.

When you have lived in London twenty-four hours you sometimes wonder how the British can put up with their own country. Their homes are unheated, the water is cold, the food is still rationed, and their allotment of meat is only eightpence a week, about one pound of hamburger steak. However, the British are amazingly cheerful, and you have to admire their courage. They are really about the only country in Europe which has tightened its belt and is living on its budget. The others are all living on Uncle Sam. Of course, the British got a huge subsidy from Uncle Sam too, but you have to consider the fact that they have lost India, lost some of their other colonies, and their resources are running very thin indeed. What we in the United States don't remember is that every time we ship a ton of steel abroad or every time a battleship is sunk in the middle of the Atlantic, or every time we fire an artillery shell, we are using up the Mesabi range in Minnesota just as the British have used up all their iron; and their coal is down so deep the cost of mining is such they can't compete easily with other countries. Someday we will be in the same position. Few people realize what tremendous resources we have or how extravagant or profligate we are with them.

March 20:   We suddenly got tired of Europe last night and asked Pan American to take us home a day early. Since the planes were practically empty, they obliged. Left London at 7 P.M. and arrived in New York at 6 A.M. I remember the first flight we took to London required three days.

The customs inspector informed me that New York wasn't much interested in Europe any more. It was all Frankie Costello.

March 26:   Ben Sonnenberg telephoned from New York. He had flown up from Key West to have lunch with A. Lyons, president of the Philip Morris Company and of Bond Street tobacco. Bond Street had been about to close with ABC for my sponsorship when suddenly the deal went up in smoke.

Ben said that he spent two hours with Lyons and virtually got down on his knees begging Lyons to go through with the deal without success. The last-minute reason for the blowup was that a Philip Morris executive named Foley, who is a high member of the Catholic Church, vigorously objected. Lyons, who is Jewish, told Ben that while I might bring in a few more customers for Bond Street, I would probably alienate an equal number of Catholics. I suspect that some of the McCarthy forces and the Church went to bat at the last minute— possibly as a result of a tap on my telephone.

March 28:   John Maragon came to see me regarding income tax violations by Bennett, the perfume manufacturer. In the course of the conversation, he said that it had been Bill Helis, during a dinner at the Carlton Hotel in honor of General Vaughan, who had demanded of Vaughan that George Vournas not be permitted to go to Greece. Maragon said that he saw the G-2 record on Vournas and that it stated that Vournas had been flown back from Egypt to face court-martial as a Communist and that I had used my influence to prevent his being court-martialed. None of which, of course, is true. The G-2 file also stated that I had tried to get George a commission in Naval Intelligence—equally untrue.

Bill Helis, according to Maragon, raised about $6,000 to $7,000 dollars for Truman's Kansas City campaign against Congressman Roger Slaughter; but contributed more heavily in 1948 when Louis Johnson became Democratic treasurer. Helis contributed about $10,-000 to help pay Truman's expenses on the western trip and later contributed $17,500 to the National Broadcasting Company to pay for a broadcast by Mrs. Roosevelt from Paris. This money, which does not appear on the campaign contribution list, was probably partly raised through the Greek War Relief Committee, with probably some given by Costello.

Congressman Paul Shafer of Michigan now turns out to be the legislative spokesman of Milton Kronheim, the liquor dealer. He has introduced various bills for Kronheim, who in turn has contributed heavily to Shafer's campaign and keeps him well-supplied with liquor. After Shafer made a statement in 1948 critical of General Vaughan, Kronheim telephoned Shafer from the office of Tim McInerny and told Shafer to pipe down. I remember that Jack Anderson went to see Shafer at about this time and found him unusually uncommunicative.

April 16:   It looks as if Harry Truman is going to have to fight his battle almost alone. None of the military men on whom he has leaned so heavily in the past appears ready to face MacArthur.* I talked to several Trumanites, but they don't seem to realize that once public opinion builds up too strong, it's difficult to stop it.

April 17:   Spoke in Cincinnati for the United Jewish Appeal. Lunched with Lloyd Taft, son of the Senator—a very swell youngster and a lot more sensible than his old man. The Cincinnati papers give nothing on the other side of the MacArthur dispute. Yesterday, Senator Millikin of Colorado told the press, following a meeting of the

*On April 11, 1951, President Truman relieved General of the Army MacArthur of command of the armed forces in Korea and recalled him to the United States. —Ed.

Senate Republican Policy Committee, that the Republicans have decided not to endorse MacArthur's visit officially. Obviously they were afraid of the reaction. Yet not a word of this appeared in the Cincinnati papers.

April 18:   MacArthur arrived in San Francisco last night. The town went wild.

April 19:   Washington also went wild. The most ironic spectacle was a group of brass hats, Marshall, Bradley, et al.—who had recommended MacArthur's dismissal—at the airport at one o'clock in the morning jostling each other in an effort to shake hands first. When did a man who was fired ever receive an ovation like this? Of course, MacArthur's greatest asset is Harry Truman. If Truman had played his cards a little more carefully, if he had fired MacArthur last December during the tragic Korean defeat, or if he had brought him home first for a moderate welcome and fired him afterward, the Democratic party and all the fundamentals Truman really stands for would not be placed in such jeopardy.

April 20:   Debated the American Society of Newspaper Editors on the value of columnists. I had expected a lot of heckling, but got by relatively unscathed—perhaps because I took it easy and jazzed it. I defended Westbrook Pegler and kidded myself. The editors were not swayed in MacArthur's favor. I think that fundamentally this was because they recognized the real issues—namely, military dictatorship vs. civilian government. Also, some of them were not happy over the way MacArthur kept them waiting three hours yesterday while he took a nap. Apparently the old boy is not as agile as his dyed hair indicates.

Arthur Vandenberg died last night—simultaneous with the arrival of General MacArthur in Washington.

Vandenberg, if he had arrived from a peace conference—of which he attended several—never would have received the ovation that was given MacArthur today and which did not pause even in the Senate, where Vandenberg was loved and revered.

Yet in my opinion, Vandenberg's contribution to world peace was far, far greater than anything the glittering general has given the world. The trouble is that we get too close to our political heroes. They are called names, criticized in cartoons, and though they suffer pain and agony as Vandenberg did, the public seldom knows it until too late. They cannot be surrounded by drawn bayonets; they do not have troops to maul photographers when they get too close and might expose aging features. They are not surrounded by the folderol of the military.

That of course is the fundamental danger of Europe, and although it has not been much of a danger in the United States, it may be so now.

I recall vividly two conversations with Vandenberg: one was when he returned from Detroit in the spring of '48, and I told him half-jokingly that some of his friends in Michigan had quoted him as saying that he would not run for President because if he did "Drew Pearson would bring out the facts regarding the 'Senator from Mitzi-Sims.' " I told Vandenberg: "Senator, I would not write that story, though if I did it would elect you President."

Vandenberg laughed. "I don't regret any of the indiscretions of my youth," he said. I really think that it was his affair with Mitzi Sims, glamorous Danish wife of a Canadian attaché, that helped to prevent his getting the Presidency—though another affair with a Mrs. Patterson, beautiful British widow in Washington, also contributed. The *Chicago Tribune* crowd claimed that the British had planted these two women on Vandenberg in order to make him pro-British and cure him of isolation. Knowing Mitzi Sims, I don't think so. The Patterson woman affair might have been deliberate.

There were other conversations with Vandenberg; during the battle of the Marshall Plan, he complained that a group of Republican cutthroats were running him ragged. Jenner of Indiana, Kem of Missouri, Bricker of Ohio, he said, were the leaders, and they carried along such nitwits as Ecton of Montana, Watkins of Utah, and others who were natural isolationists and easily swayed by rabid leadership. Vandenberg looked sick and old then, and this was in 1948. Today, following his death, it develops that he was incurably ill during all this period.

My last talk with Vandenberg was last December, after MacArthur's disastrous defeat in North Korea and when the Republican wolfpacks were straining at the leash to kick overboard all vestiges of unity. I had tried, through a friend at the White House, to get Truman to invite Senator Taft in for a personal conference. Taft was eager to be invited. He had even canceled a trip to Yale University when word was sent to him by Tris [Coffin] that he might be invited.

Then Truman got stubborn, or perhaps it was somebody close to

Truman. I will never know. At any rate, Taft was not invited and did not get to the White House until he was included with a group of other Senators a week later. By that time he was fit to be tied and in no mood for reconciliation. Meanwhile, however, I telephoned Vandenberg in Grand Rapids and asked him what he thought could be done to bring the two parties closer together. Originally I wanted to quote him on such a policy, but after talking to him for two minutes, I realized this was out of the question. Vandenberg seemed older and tireder than ever. He had almost given up any thought of bipartisan foreign policy. My suggestion of more and franker conferences between the White House and Republican leaders, he threw out as difficult.

"The boys have gotten the bit in their teeth and are running with it," he said. "I doubt anything the White House could do would whip them back into line. God knows I had a hard enough time when I was there."

April 21: The clay feet of the military are getting colder and colder. General Bradley at Chapel Hill, North Carolina, last night blurted out the statement that the decision to fire MacArthur was a political one and he refused to comment on MacArthur's statement before Congress on Thursday, that the Joint Chiefs of Staff had agreed with him regarding the bombing of China.

The White House tried to rally a little support from the brass in the Pentagon last night, but the military boys were siding with their fellow military men from Tokyo.

Clayton Fritchey spent most of the day at the White House trying to work up a statement. Finally he got out a very lame excuse for one.

April 23: Went to the Associated Press lunch in New York. I stayed on the twelfth floor of the Waldorf, with MacArthur on the thirty-seventh floor. It was interesting to note that the U.S. Army is supplying military police to guard certain entrances to the Waldorf, and of course, the taxpayers are paying for the special Army plane with which MacArthur tours the country. The people of New York are still talking about the great hero.

April 24: John [Donovan] telephoned this morning that the McCarthy crowd was elated over a new development and were going to spring something soon. They called him to say that [Edward Bennett] Williams, the attorney for [Norman] Littell, McCarthy, and Donald Surine [a McCarthy aide] would give him a good job if he cooperated.*

This afternoon McCarthy sounded off with another speech on the Senate floor claiming that the Justice Department had now finished its investigation and had a complete espionage case against me. He also pontificated that I had received State Department documents from the State Department via Dave Karr, whom he described as a top member of the Communist party. McCarthy also claimed that the column today, which dealt with developments in the atomic bomb field, paraphrased a secret report and was a violation of security.

Of course, the paradoxical fact is that a newspaperman can be stopped from writing almost anything of inside news variety if a Senator wants to hammer on the Senate floor every week. Today's column on atomic energy had been read over the telephone to the Atomic Energy Commission, whose chief comment was that most of it had been published in one form or another before. I suspect that McCarthy's diatribe was calculated to coincide with the beginning of my new sponsored program. I had a drink yesterday with the new sponsor, Harry Hoyt of Carter's, who seems to be a tough little guy and capable of standing the brickbats. I hope so because he will get plenty of them.

May 16:   Bill Boyle called to say that Frieda is ducking. She isn't going to vote at all on WBAL. Yet she wants to be a federal judge, where she will have to make decisions at the rate of twenty or so a day.†

May 18:   Talked to Clayton Fritchey, who has jumped from the Cleveland *Press* to the New Orleans *Item* to the Chief Press Relations Officer at the Defense Department. It's the first time the Defense Department has ever had a really good man. I pointed out the miserable way in which the administration has been handling its public

---

*Donovan was Drew Pearson's lawyer for all libel cases. During his lifetime, Drew Pearson lost only one libel suit—the Littell case. He never appealed the Littell decision because tax attorney Randolph Paul convinced him it would be cheaper to pay the $50,000, but he always regretted breaking his record.—Ed.

†Frieda Hennock was an FCC commissioner at a time Drew Pearson joined several others in a suit opposing renewal of WBAL's license. The suit was brought on the grounds that WBAL was not being operated in the public interest. The Drew Pearson group—the Public Service Radio Corporation of Maryland—lost this landmark case by a 4–3 vote.—Ed.

relations in the MacArthur controversy and I suggested that Senator Fulbright of Arkansas should ask certain pointed questions of General Bradley on Monday as to whether the Joint Chiefs of Staff had warned MacArthur of his failure to have battle liaison between General Almond of the 10th Corps and General Walker of the 8th Army; whether this warning had not been made twice; what MacArthur's replies were; and whether the Joint Chiefs had not ordered MacArthur to withdraw the 10th Corps from its exposed position; also the role which the Navy had played in extricating the 10th Corps.

Clayton wanted me to plant the questions with Fulbright but I said that since he was paid officially by the U.S. government, he should do it himself. However, if he finally decided not to do so, I told him that I would be glad to help.

May 20:   Winchell let loose one of the worst diatribes at the State Department and the Truman administration I have ever heard. He concluded by reminding the public that with Maragon going to jail, the Democratic National convention might well be held in Alcatraz. I have talked to Cuneo several times about the way Winchell hopped on the MacArthur and McCarthy bandwagon. Cuneo is frank to say that it's because: "we are not consulted." In other words, Roosevelt used to get Winchell down and hold his hand once a month so that Walter became his great companion. Now Cuneo can't get near the White House or in to see the Secretary of State. I think the real reason for Winchell's ire goes deeper, and back to the fact that Truman once called him a "kike." Also Walter sees which way the wind is blowing and wants to get on the bandwagon.

May 21:   Had lunch with Tom Finletter, who, since he became Secretary for Air, has been tight-lipped. Today, however, he let his hair down a little and admitted things were going to the dogs politically. He put up a great defense of Truman, however, pointing out that in the big and courageous policies such as civil rights, housing, the Marshall Plan, and the North Atlantic Pact, Truman had more courage than Roosevelt. I had to agree that he was right.

Tom asked how they could improve their public relations. I suggested a couple of things: one, a public relations task force such as operated under Roosevelt, and second, a few adroit policy statements by people who had a few vestiges of prestige still intact.

For instance, I suggested that one reason why MacArthur had

made such a hit with the American public was that he had emphasized that he was saving the "blood of American boys." This struck home with every mother, wife, and in fact the whole public. On the other hand, the facts were that MacArthur had wasted American blood most of his career, not only in Korea.

I urged that the Joint Chiefs of Staff, when they testify, should show up MacArthur's glaring errors and his well-known "extravagance with his men." For instance, General Eichelberger, who commanded the 8th Army during World War II, could testify to MacArthur's shameful laxness on New Guinea and his refusal to visit the front at Buna even once. Eichelberger has hinted at this in his book and was quite bitter in his personal conversations to me. He even told how, in Japan, MacArthur expected to be drafted by the Republicans in the 1948 election and told Eichelberger to stand by to take over Japan.

I also urged Finletter to have Bradley tell the real truth about the ghastly errors in North Korea and the failure to corrolate the Walker-Almond commands. Tom made some interesting observations about the Truman administration's failure to rely on civilians. He had great praise for Bradley and the Joint Chiefs of Staff, but pointed out that Louis Johnson had taken unfair advantage of them by sending them up to Capitol Hill to testify regarding appropriations, when it was not their job to be put on the spot in this way. Obviously they wanted more appropriations, yet they had to go up to tell Congress they did not need any more. Having played up the military end of the Defense Department, Tom pointed out, the fate of the Truman administration was now in the hands of the military. Upon their testimony, the President had to rely to extricate himself from the MacArthur mess. Tom recalled how Winston Churchill had refused to permit any general to testify before the House of Commons, and that this was the tradition of all British politics and parties.

May 23:   General Bradley has been testifying for two days, and no word has come out as yet regarding MacArthur's errors in North Korea. This morning I phoned Senator Fulbright and asked him if he had received some questions from Clayton Fritchey. He had not. I then gave Fulbright the questions. He wanted more dates and I phoned Fritchey with a request that he phone Fulbright direct. He promised to do so. I don't know whether he did or not. But later in the day,

Fulbright did ask the questions I suggested that did draw out from Bradley for the first time in the entire MacArthur debate the fact that the Joint Chiefs of Staff had warned MacArthur against splitting his command.

Sometimes I think that this administration is so dumb it is not worth saving. The tragic thing is that the Republicans at the moment are worse. And if the things Truman stands for fall, the whole liberal era in this country collapses. I sometimes wonder why I should be trying to help out a Defense Department and a White House which three times has demanded of the Attorney General that I be prosecuted for publishing one of MacArthur's intelligence reports which showed up MacArthur in his true light even as early as last December.

In talking to Finletter on Monday, I reminded him that I had come to see him as early as last October, warning him that either MacArthur had to be fired or Acheson, or Truman would go down the drain, and suggesting to him that some of MacArthur's reports be leaked to the press. I told Tom at that time that if he did not want to get them out through me they should put them out through some other newspaperman in order to show the public what was really happening. I got no cooperation from Tom, but when I did manage to get hold of a couple of MacArthur's reports the result was a demand from Senator McCarthy that I be prosecuted and, believe it or not, a follow-up by the Defense Department supporting McCarthy.

May 25: General Collins finally blurted out the truth about MacArthur's military mistakes. He even told how MacArthur had ignored a JCS order to use only South Korean troops around the Yalu River. I don't know whether this was the result of prompting from Finletter or whether Collins still is loyal to his old friend Eisenhower. I did not think Collins had sufficient courage. He has gone to Tokyo for conferences with MacArthur more than any other member of the JCS and it was reported that MacArthur had twisted him around his finger. MacArthur always called him "Joe" while Collins called MacArthur "General," though Collins, of course, was his superior.

I gave a luncheon talk at the Radio Executives Club in New York and took as my subject a defense of the State Department's basic diplomacy. I compared Acheson with Hull and pointed out that Acheson was a boy who worked in a cloistered room and couldn't get out in front of the klieg lights. His policies will probably be recognized by historians as among the greatest of this century, but he can't perform before television as MacArthur or Cordell Hull.

Perhaps our Secretaries of State have got to be more actors than statesmen in the future. Meanwhile the Republican din for Acheson's removal has been reinforced by many Democrats. Down in Texas, Tom Connally, who has defended Acheson and supported his policies, is probably going to be defeated just for this reason.*

May 28: I saw Dean Acheson at the Norwegian Embassy. He looked his usual smiling self. The barrage of criticism doesn't seem to affect him, at least outwardly.

May 29: Senator Capehart demanded that the Banking and Currency Committee meet early today in order to take up the question of "Drew Pearson." It turned out that they got involved with this question all morning—while price controls, affecting millions of housewives, waited.

Capehart demanded that I be subpoenaed before the committee, put under oath, and asked from whom I got the suppressed B&O report and copies of committee minutes.† He figured I would not reveal my source and then could be cited for contempt. Blair Moody of Michigan argued against it. He said, "Pearson will just refuse to give his source and then where do you go from there?" Senator Benton remarked: "It will just give Pearson a million dollars' worth of publicity. He'd love it." (My friend.) Senator Bricker, strangely, argued to the same general effect. He pointed out that there was a law in Ohio whereby a newspaperman did not have to disclose his source and that it would be foolish to call me before the committee. Capehart, I understand, got terribly miffed. He also demanded a vote of confidence in him, which the committee brushed aside. Senator Douglas of Illinois said that he had not read the report and on the face of it it looked as if Capehart had suppressed something because the minutes stated that he, Capehart, demanded that the report be put under lock and key.

---

*For whatever reason, Senator Connally retired at the end of the term.—ED.

†In 1947, Senator Tobey, Chairman of the Banking and Currency Committee, convened a subcommittee to investigate an RFC loan to the B&O Railroad. The loan amounted to $800,000,000, the largest ever made by the RFC to that point and the investigation was concerned with the possibility of criminal fraud. The Tobey report had, however, been withheld for four years.—ED.

Afterward Capehart called a press conference, having mimeographed and passed out in advance the copies of my column, plus the Senate committee hearings of July 1947, at which time he, as acting chairman, had suppressed the B&O report. I went to the press conference, which was affable, perhaps too affable. Capehart called me "our friend," and I kidded him along about scooping me by getting a copy of my column one day in advance.

Capehart is such a nice fellow when you talk to him that I always hate to be in disagreement. I always remember how at Elkhart, Indiana, he took the trouble to come to the *Merci* Train reception and made a nice speech from the flatcar, paying tribute to me. But when I look at his voting record, there isn't any way to get around the fact that Capehart has almost never voted with the general public. His big campaign contributors perhaps tell the reason why.

May 30: Abbott Washburn of the Committee for Free Europe came down from New York. They plan to release balloons to Europe this summer with a big battery of the top brass doing the releasing— MacArthur at Independence Hall; Clay from New York; Eisenhower from Paris; also Eddie Rickenbacker from West Germany to Czechoslovakia. It looks as if I have been left out in the cold.

June 1: Senator Maybank finally made public the B&O RFC report. *The New York Times* played it up with headlines bearing out everything I had said.

June 2: The Italian Embassy finally presented me with the Star of Solidarity medal which Count Sforza had given me in Rome in December 1947. That occasion was the coldest luncheon I have ever attended. [Prime Minister] De Gasperi sat with his overcoat on and so did most of the others. Italy had no coal and the luncheon was held in an ancient palace that had not been heated since the Roman Empire. Today, in contrast, the Italian Embassy in Washington was sweltering. I was glad that the Embassy presented Dave Karr with his medal, which also had been technically awarded him in Rome four years ago. At that time, however, Italy had no metal.

The Ambassador could have ducked the ceremony with both of us, but he did not. He gave a very fine talk about the importance of building friendship.

June 8: The FBI has started another investigation. An agent named Frank Dunne got hold of my friend* and quizzed him at length about a Russian, allegedly brought over here by Joe Davies, who was supposed to have been a friend of mine; also a newspaperman named Barger. The agent was particularly interested in whether Leon [Pearson] had known these men and who Leon's contacts were in the State Department. I don't remember either man. It was six years ago that Leon covered the State Department and it would seem that they are going an awfully long way back to discover my leaks.

June 10: Leon says he never knew a newspaperman named Barger, nor a Russian that Joe Davies brought over to this country.

June 12: Went to New York for the Kate Smith TV show. Lunched with Henry Morgenthau. He seems strangely removed from things today. He was once the hub of some of the most active and effective work in Washington—tried to cut off war supplies to Japan long before Pearl Harbor, tried to freeze funds to Perón in Argentina, tried and succeeded in arming the French and British long before we got into war, and did his best to put the finger on Hitler in Germany. Now he says he is content to raise apples.

I talked to Henry about the China lobby and the way in which the Soong-Kung dynasty had hidden its money in the United States. He says that one Chinese bond issue for five hundred million dollars was subscribed by about 75 percent and that H. H. Kung and T. V. Soong, former head of the Bank of China, had subscribed the balance at twenty-five cents on the dollar. The loan was payable in the United States within a few years so that in this way they were able to collect dollars in New York.

Already the apologists for the Chiang Kai-shek crowd—David Lawrence, Scripps-Howard, et al., are trying to get a propaganda fire against any probe of the China lobby.

June 13: Tipped off Lock Currie that the McCarran committee† was about to brand him as one of the top Russian informants in the Roosevelt administration. Lock was administrative assistant to Roosevelt, now is adviser to the Colombian government. He looked as if the

*There is no clue who "my friend" refers to.—ED.

†The Judiciary Committee, chaired by the Senator from Nevada.—ED.

ground had fallen out from under him. His contract with the Colombian government is up for renewal and if charges like this are made, obviously he is finished.

Lock is a meek and mild little man who I think would have been the last to have played ball with Russia. Of course, during the war a lot of people were hastening the shipment of supplies to Russia and it should be very easy to pillory someone for that activity now.

June 14:   My friend has had another visit from the FBI agent, Dunne. He is still harping on Leon's activities ten years ago. He also made the remark to my friend: "What is it that Pearson has on J. Edgar Hoover?" I have had a suspicion for some time that there wasn't too much loyalty inside the FBI.

This is the second or third time the FBI has been prying into me this year. Two or three months ago they had one of their top agents, Maurice Taylor, and a lesser agent, Charles Lyons, interview about thirty witnesses. Taylor is the man who cracked the Hyattsville bank robbery and is now assigned to one of the minor cases. He tried to find out the names of my servants, whether I had a night watchman, when I went away to the farm, whether the house was unguarded during trips to the farm, where I kept my files, what my files were like, to say nothing of whom I talked to.

He even asked questions as to how I felt toward the FBI and whether I was a real friend of Hoover's. He even went so far as to help a former employee of mine get inside a federal agency if this man would talk to him about me.

This is the kind of Gestapo tactic which they had in Germany and Russia. But the FBI has built itself up—partly with my help—to an impregnable position where it can do no wrong. Apparently, civil liberties and the sanctity of a man's home or office now mean nothing.

June 15:   Lou Nichols, Hoover's assistant, asked me to come down to see him. Half apologetically he said that he supposed I knew the FBI had been investigating me and he wanted to know the circumstances. He said that he was afraid that I had been getting sore at Hoover and he wanted me to know that it wasn't Hoover's fault. The first investigation, he said, was asked for by Jim McInerny of the Criminal Division, and Hoover turned it down. Then came a request from Peyton Ford which Hoover also turned down; following which came a letter from

Secretary Marshall demanding an investigation. This checked with what McGrath had already told me several weeks ago.

Nichols surprised me, however, by saying that there had been a total of five investigations. The first was over the December 30 column, giving the real strength of the Chinese Army as outlined in MacArthur's intelligence report; the second was the column of December 31 giving some information regarding the State Department. Lou said it might amuse me to know that the State Department, upon being queried, went to my defense. They replied that the information I had published was similar to some material already published in European newspapers. The next column was that of January 30 giving a confidential Chinese estimate of American strength, and, following this, a broadcast from Munich, March 11, in which I said Stuart Symington, then Chairman of the National Security Resources Board, proposed a complete withdrawal from Korea. The final investigation is over a column of April 30 that General Matt Ridgway's promotion to be a full general was overruled by MacArthur.

An interesting thing to me is that most of these columns were written in defense of the administration during a time when it was engaged in probably the worst political death struggle of its years in office.

June 16: A State Department official just returned from Cairo telephoned the office today saying that he had some information regarding the two missing British diplomats.* Miss Schimmel told him that Mr. Blumenthal would be glad to see him in a couple of hours. About an hour later, the diplomat called back to say that he had some further notes that he had forgotten to give Mr. Blumenthal.

Funny part of it was that Fred Blumenthal had not yet been to see him. Jack [Anderson] and Fred immediately went to see the diplomat, who said that twenty minutes after his first phone call a man had appeared introducing himself as Mr. Blumenthal and proceeded to take notes but seemed a little nervous and wasn't a convincing substitute for the real Fred Blumenthal.

Obviously the FBI had tapped my phone and decided to send an agent around to the diplomat immediately to get concrete evidence of a government leak to me. No evidence secured by tapping a telephone

---

*Guy Burgess and Donald Maclean, officials of the Foreign Office who defected to the Soviet Union in May of 1951.—Ed.

is admissible in court so the agent rushed around to see my diplomatic source to get the goods on him direct.

June 17:   Judge Goldsborough died last night. His passing brought back memories of the hectic Tydings campaign and the circumstances under which Goldsborough was appointed. The first time I talked to him was in the early spring of 1938. Goldsborough was then in Congress from Maryland's Eastern Shore and considered a potential political factor. He was cagey about helping Roosevelt against Tydings and wanted to know what would happen to him if Tydings was not defeated.* I suggested that Goldsborough might be interested in a judgeship. He replied "Are you in a position to make me a judge?" I replied that I wasn't, but that I thought I could get a definite commitment; after checking with Harry Hopkins I later informed Goldsborough that the White House would go through with the judicial appointment. Actually Goldsborough did not do very much to help the Maryland campaign. He was so afraid of being seen at the headquarters that he used to meet the campaign manager in the back row of a movie theater in Baltimore.

However, he did come across with the invitation to Roosevelt to speak at Denton, Maryland, Goldsborough's home town, on Labor Day. Politically this was a mistake and the mistake was made by F.D.R. himself, due to his love for the water. He conceived the idea of spending the Labor Day weekend on his yacht, cruising around the Chesapeake and driving up through the Eastern Shore on Monday, Labor Day. We had originally arranged with Mayor Howard Jackson of Baltimore for Roosevelt to speak at Baltimore, a big industrial-labor city, on Labor Day. But when F.D.R. made the other proposal, we did not argue. In the first place I was in no position to argue; secondly I discovered that Harry Hopkins almost never argued with the President. And third I realize how difficult it is to argue with any President.

So F.D.R. made the trip through rural Maryland on Labor Day and most of the newspapers hooted and howled over the fact that he was visiting a rural community where no organized labor lived.

I was called upon in advance of the trip to write the speech to

---

*For years, Drew Pearson had held a grudge against Tydings because of the Senator's opposition to Paul Pearson, Drew's father, as Governor of the Virgin Islands. In 1938, Tydings was on F.D.R.'s "purge" list, and Drew's grudge had led him to campaign actively for Tydings's opponent in this Senate race.—ED.

be delivered at Denton. I spent several nights at it and finally rushed a rather badly botched job over to the White House. It was pretty well rewritten and deserved to be. Only about two lines of mine were used.

Anyway after the Tydings campaign was over and the Senator was reelected, Goldsborough raised the ante and wanted to be made not a district judge, but a Court of Appeals judge. The President stuck to his bargain and Goldsborough was appointed to the district court.

Most of the lawyers did not like him but he had courage and by and large, his decisions are probably more memorable than any other district judge in the last decade—namely, his historic fine of John L. Lewis for violating a court injunction and the death-sentence awarded Collazo, the attempted presidential assassin.

Though Goldsborough and I remained close friends, he called the shots as he saw them as far as I was concerned. In a libel suit brought against me by the secretary of Congressman Thorkelson of Montana, Goldsborough threw the case out of court without even listening to my attorney. On the other hand in the WBAL case, he sided with the Hearst papers against the FCC, thus tying up our litigation for months.

I have scarcely mentioned Senator McCarthy since my return from Europe but tonight I gave him the business. I compared his war record to General Marshall's, against whom McCarthy launched a 60,000 word blast on the Senate floor this week.

June 18: Telephoned several Senators including Lehman, Brien McMahon, and Clinton Anderson of New Mexico suggesting that they follow up McCarthy's blast against Marshall by asking the Republican party whether they concurred. I urged that this was the time to put Taft right on the spot and make him come out one way or the other for or against McCarthy.

June 19: Brien McMahon reports that the Democrats have decided not to press the Republicans on the Marshall issue. Brien says that they are hoping the Republicans will nominate Taft, in which case they can defeat him. Therefore they are planning to pull their punches on embarrassing Taft re McCarthy, etc. It looks like the Democrats never learn. They pulled their punches on MacArthur for months until Truman finally fired him at the most inopportune time of all. And they are going to do the same thing on Taft. What the Democrats don't realize is that the public has a very short memory. They will not remember that Taft is a great pal of McCarthy's unless it is punched home now and repeated frequently.

June 26:   Flew to Lenox, Massachusetts, to confer with C. D. Jackson and the Commiteee for Free Europe. It's apparently definite that we will release balloons at the rate of about 2,000 a day to Poland beginning the latter part of August. The State Department hasn't given its o.k. yet on Czechoslovakia.

July 1:   Walter Winchell took an indirect poke at me tonight for comparing Senator McCarthy's war record with that of General Marshall.

July 2:   Released some balloons from Franklin Field containing a Russian translation of the Declaration of Independence. It was supposed to be a symbol of what might be done if the balloons were released from Europe.

July 3:   Senator Millard Tydings of Maryland asked me to drop in to see him. A few years ago I wouldn't have considered this even remotely possible. He wants to circulate some literature in Wisconsin against McCarthy.

Either I have become mellower as the years go by or else Millard has. His ideas on life generally, as he talked today, made pretty good sense.

The St. Thomas [Virgin Islands] Municipal Council has just voted to name the new housing project the "Paul M. Pearson Gardens" in honor of Father. I suppose that most men who accomplish real things get recognition only after they are dead. Today the Virgin Islands is thriving thanks to the tourist trade which Father started and his many other projects to get what Herbert Hoover once called an "effective port island" back on its feet. The greatest thing he did, however, was to wipe out the color bar and to work toward the appointment of a Negro as Governor. I remember also when Tydings crucified him and forced his ouster, how he campaigned for slum clearance and housing projects—some of them in states where federal housing projects were forbidden by law. Now, of course, a bill has been passed by Congress appropriating money for them.

I have wondered whether Tydings realizes the injustice he was guilty of and that he sacrificed a great man and a great enterprise because a Missouri politician wanted to become judge in the Virgin Islands.

July 4: Paul Gore-Booth of the British Embassy came out to the farm and helped me spray trees. He says that his government still hasn't heard from the two missing British diplomats. One of them, Burgess, was personal chauffeur for Anthony Eden when Eden was here last spring, and also was a friend of Sumner Welles.

July 5: Bob Allen and I went to Baltimore for what we thought might be the last meeting of the Public Service Radio Corporation of Maryland. After a fight, however, the directors have authorized the filing of a petition for rehearing. I don't think anything will come of it and in a way perhaps the battle is not worth continuing. However, the basic issue to me is about the most important in the country when it comes to freedom of speech. If the Federal Communications Commission is to require radio stations to put across any kind of decent program, they have to exert their right, given by law, to transfer a wave length. If a wave length becomes owned by the user merely by his right of erecting a transmitter and furnishing a studio, then the air waves belong not to the people but to people with money enough to exploit them. It's like ruling that the channel of the Hudson River in New York belongs to anyone who stakes out a certain slice of waterway. The man who threw the case against us was Senator Kerr of Oklahoma, who got FCC Commissioner Walker to switch his vote. Walker had voted for us but after Bob and I opposed Kerr on the Natural Gas bill, Walker suddenly reversed himself.

July 6: Lou Nichols of the FBI informs me that I am no longer under investigation. He says that questions were asked about Leon's friends because they are trying to track down a Russian agent in this country who knew Leon. However, Leon is in no way involved.

Lou says they got out of the last investigation of me by asking the National Security Council whether they would be willing to declassify the Symington report recommending that we pull out of Korea altogether. The FBI pointed out that unless the report could be declassified to use in a trial, there was no use continuing with the investigation.

The Security Council refused to declassify the report so the investigation was dropped.

The Un-American Activities Committee has just made public some secret testimony by a woman undercover agent who belonged to the Communist party and who listed Andy Older as a member of the party. I hear that Senator McCarthy is going to make a speech again blasting me.

Of course, it is always difficult when you have to explain things, but the fact was that I fired Older when I learned that he was a member of the Communist party. I confess that at the time I felt I was a little unfair because I was convinced that Andy was trying to force himself from his Communist surroundings. He joined when he was a youngster just out of college. In view of what has happened since, however, I am certainly glad that I did fire him.

Of course, Andy is dead now and it isn't going to be too happy for his children to read about their father having been a Communist. And the public generally will not know the truth, which is that once a man joins the Communist party it's hard for him to get away from it. Comrades threaten to expose him if he leaves. Andy did not tell me that in so many words, but that was pretty much what happened to him.

July 8: I had more trouble with ABC today over my broadcast than at any time in about eight years. They almost cut me off the air because of an item which read: "Attention Walter Winchell—Before you defend the war record of Senator McCarthy against General Marshall's, please investigate why Red-Card Joe resigned from the Marines at the very heart of the war." ABC's Velotta demanded that I cut out any references to Winchell whatsoever. He confessed that Winchell had been raising hell with him and that his life would be miserable if the item went on as written. I finally had to compromise by omitting Winchell's name and merely referring to a certain commentator to be heard "later this evening." When I went on the air, however, I did not know whether even this would get by or whether I would be cut off when I came to this particular item. However, I wasn't.

Winchell flatly refused last winter to go on a TV program at 9 P.M. with me following him at 9:15 or 9:30. He has forced the network to rule that no commentator will follow him before about eleven P.M. Sunday night.

October 10:   Last Friday, Clayton Fritchey suggested the Czechs were looking for an opening to release AP correspondent Bill Oatis, and that if I approached the Czech Ambassador a way might be found whereby an open letter written by me to the Czech government could outline the principle involving freedom of the press, and perhaps give them an opening for Oatis's release.

Accordingly I asked for an appointment with the Czech Ambassador and saw him today. It took three days incidentally to get the appointment, which is longer than it takes to get one with a cabinet officer.

The Ambassador is a pleasant, not too prepossessive person, whose English is fairly good but who was assisted by a younger man who has been in this country longer and who from the conversation is a bit more hardboiled than the Ambassador. If Communist practice was followed in this case, it was the younger man who was the chief Communist representative in the Embassy.

I explained to the Ambassador that in my opinion, without going into the merits of the case, the imprisonment of Oatis had worsened relations between the Czech and American people. I explained that sometimes when relations between two countries were deadlocked, private individuals could serve as a sort of fulcrum or crowbar to get them undeadlocked, and I explained the idea of an open letter which might serve as a wedge for the release of Oatis.

The Ambassador listened carefully and then asked some rather pertinent questions. One was whether I did not believe that relations had become so deadlocked that even with Oatis released, the State Department could not change its trade policy toward Czechoslovakia. He pointed out that many people in the United States now felt that "the Reds are on the run and we should continue to keep them on the run." The Ambassador's assistant emphasized this in pointing out that newspaper influence would continue pressure on the State Department even if Oatis were released. I told him that I could not answer the question except to say that I was certain pressure would not be relaxed as long as Oatis remained in jail.

I pointed out that the State Department was to some extent a prisoner or a creature of public opinion and it could not change its policies until public opinion changed. I also mentioned the fact that no one in the State Department knew that I was coming and that this was entirely a private matter.

Finally the Ambassador said that he would think over my suggestion and let me know in a few days. He said that he agreed that the deadlock was such that not much could be done by governments. He pointed out that Czechoslovakia could not bow to economic pressure from the State Department.

I pointed out in passing that the United States had made the most important overture possible toward economic cooperation by extending Marshall Plan aid to Czechoslovakia. The Communist assistant immediately said that there was an answer to that—namely: "Strings attached to dollars."

As the younger assistant showed me downstairs he asked if I had read John Fenimore Cooper. I told him that I had read James Fenimore Cooper, and he said there was a quote in there from the French that "I have always remembered—'We use spies but we despise them.' Today," he said, "apparently spies are not despised."

I still don't know what he meant by that remark. Possibly it was meant as a crack at me as a spy for the American government. Or again he may have been referring to our balloon messages into Czechoslovakia. Probably he meant that Oatis is considered a spy by the Czechs, yet since I intervened for him, spies are no longer despised. Anyway I chose to ignore the remark in favor of a large black cat which was sitting in the middle of the hall of the Embassy and which I addressed as *matchka*. The assistant corrected me. He said the proper name was *kotchka* in Czech. The word *matchka* for cat is Serbian.

October 26: Went to see the Yugloslav Ambassador and suggested that now was the time to release Archbishop Stepinac, thereby improving Catholic public opinion in the United States toward Yugoslavia. I suggested that I write Tito a letter, that Tito write back, then immediately release the Archbishop.

The Ambassador's reaction was immediate. I suggested that he query Belgrade and let me know. He suggested that I go ahead and write the letter.

October 29: The Yugoslav Ambassador called to ask whether I had written the letter to Tito. They wanted to see a draft of it immediately. I had not written it and told them I would get it around tomorrow.

October 30: The Yugoslav Ambassador liked the letter, made a couple of changes, and cabled it to Belgrade immediately. I was surprised that they acted so promptly. Dr. Bruner [counselor of the Yugoslav

Embassy] even came by the house at 6 P.M., though I had only given him the letter at 4 P.M. I still don't think the letter is what it should be.

November 11:   The Yugoslav Embassy telephoned and asked me to come by immediately; they apologized for the fact that it was a holiday. Tito's letter to me regarding Stepinac had arrived. It was dated November 9. The letter was not what it should have been as far as appeasing Catholic public opinion was concerned. It took a lot of digs at the Vatican, and I tried to persuade Dr. Bruner to eliminate them. I suggested that I rewrite the letter and see him later.

November 13:   I read Tito's letter to Paul French, head of CARE. Paul thought it would arouse the Catholics and not do much good.

November 16:   Dr. Bruner called, wanting to know what I had done about the Tito letter. I promised to see him next week, after my return from Boston.

November 19:   I had breakfast with the mayor of Boston and an assortment of citizens representing the Crusade for Freedom. The last time I was in Boston I was given a luncheon by Mayor Curley shortly after his release from jail. Curley started to run for reelection this fall but pulled out. Apparently the people of Boston, who carried him on their shoulders after he got out of jail, are finally wise to him.

I called on Harold Wheeler, editor of the Boston *Traveller.* He apologized for not being at the breakfast, said a crisis had come up but did not say what. But later I found it was the resignation of John Crider as editor of the *Traveller's* sister paper, the *Herald,* because the *Herald* refused to publish Crider's critical review of Senator Taft's book. Bob Choate, publisher of both papers and representative of the First National Bank of Boston, which owns them, refused to let the editor publish even a mild critique of Taft's book. I remember Bob when he was a young newspaperman in Washington, a most charming and an apparently innocuous person. Apparently age and the banking surroundings do things to a man. Bob was one of the great pals of Dean Acheson in the early days. Now his papers are severe critics of Dean's.

November 26: Saw Dr. Bruner. Belgrade has been getting impatient regarding the release of Tito's letter to me and the release of Archbishop Stepinac. I had cooled off a bit on the idea after Tito put so much propaganda into his letter. However, we fixed up a proposed elimination of a couple of paragraphs which Bruner cabled to Belgrade.

November 27: Ed Prichard came for dinner. He says that the Chief Justice [Fred Vinson] would have definitely liked to run for President if he had been able to step into the State Department about nine months before the nomination—in other words, last fall. Now he doesn't feel he should go into the State Department. It would be too obviously a makeshift springboard for the Presidency.

Something apparently happened at Key West to curtail Vinson's visit with the President. He had expected to stay several days but got back Sunday. He is coming to dinner tomorrow and perhaps we can find out.

Lamar Caudle was raked over the coals by the House income tax investigating committee regarding his fishing trips by airplane to Florida. I recall that I was invited on one of these. In fact, Lamar made a great issue out of it. Sometimes I think I'm lucky to be in the position of having to write one column a day, including Sunday, Christmas, and the Fourth of July.

The Yugoslavs telephoned to say that Tito had planned to release the correspondence in Belgrade almost immediately. Accordingly I sent out to all newspapers subscribing to the column copies of my letter and Tito's letter on a "hold for release" basis.

November 28: Tito published his letter in the newspaper *Borba* in Belgrade. Brief stories were carried by the AP and UP. The Philadelphia *Bulletin* and *New York Post* are playing up the news and for the most part it looked as if I would be scooped on my own story. The Embassy telephoned later, indignant because part of Tito's letter to me had been left out by some papers.

The Chief Justice came for dinner. He went home early, saying he had to work the next day. I still can't tell whether he wants to run for President or not. But I am beginning to think that his original enthusiasm—if any—has diminished considerably in view of the tax scandals and the probability that Eisenhower will run on the Republican ticket.

Clayton Fritchey also was at dinner. This was the first day of the truce in Korea and Clayton seems to be fairly optimistic.

I can't help but think, however, that the Commies have outsmarted us again. They are not going to yield to any lasting peace in Korea and it is going to be impossible to get the American public and the American Army, to say nothing of our U.N. allies, to get back any enthusiasm for war if it has to be resumed.

The greatest tragedy in Korea is that we fumbled the ball—the first real test of the United Nations and an international police force. Perhaps we should not have made Korea a test case. But once we did so, we should have achieved a quick, decisive victory. I suppose it will take a long time for history to fix the blame. But I, for one, am convinced that the blame rests largely on the shoulders of the man whose army in Japan was not prepared, and who either should not have told Washington he was prepared or else should have warned Truman that he couldn't win in Korea.

At the time of Truman's decision, I remember Constantine Brown writing me a letter quoting MacArthur as having told the White House: "I guarantee success whether Russia comes in or not." Mr. Brown, of course, is by no means infallible. But at that time his close friend, General_____,* was in charge of decoding all messages in G-2. Furthermore, the message sounds like MacArthur. I cannot conceive that Truman would ever have taken the decision without an O.K. from MacArthur even though MacArthur in his Senate testimony claimed the contrary.

November 29:   Wally Jordan, my alleged radio agent, telephoned to say that ABC would not renew my contract for another year. They will renew for another six weeks beyond February 18—this six weeks being the remainder of a thirteen-week period which Carter's wants to contract for.

Meanwhile, the Ted Bates Agency phoned that Carter's had decided against television at this time. I am a little suspicious as to whether the decision was taken because of unfavorable Catholic reaction to the Stepinac release. Probably not, because Mr. Hoyt seems to

*The General was not identified.—ED.

be quite enthusiastic. However, I am more and more convinced that anyone who gets caught between the Communists and the Catholics gets killed. Unfortunately a large part of the American people, especially the liberals, are now in that position.

December 1: Archbishop Keogh of Baltimore has issued a statement protesting the release of Stepinac. He virtually admitted that they wanted Stepinac kept in jail as a martyr.

December 3: Monsignor McCarthy telephoned me this morning, with a polite though rather forceful reference to Archbishop Keogh's statement. I told the monsignor that I had referred to it on the radio last night, which set him back a little. He then admitted that he had not heard me. He remonstrated that Tito was propagandizing against the Church and the Church was "in chains in Yugoslavia."

I told him that I had been to Yugoslavia fairly recently and that I was convinced that there was complete freedom of worship. I also quoted the representative of the Catholics, a Yugoslav lawyer sent by CARE on the recommendation of the National Catholic Welfare Conference, who reported that food was distributed impartially to priests and nuns as well as to other churches.

McCarthy apparently did not know that this representative of the Church had been sent to Yugoslavia. Nevertheless he continued to protest.

I recall that in Los Angeles two years ago it was Monsignor McCarthy who wrote a violent attack on me in the Catholic newspaper *The Tide* at the time I reported that Father Coughlin was involved in the Gariepy income tax case.

December 5: Tito was as good as his word and released Archbishop Stepinac today. He is being sent to his old home in Croatia. A press dispatch from the Vatican indicates that reaction there is favorable— quite different from the reaction of the hierarchy in the USA.

A Vatican spokesman said that Stepinac would not be satisfied until he was restored as Archbishop but it was interesting that the Vatican put this squarely on Stepinac's shoulders and, as for the Pope, indicated that the release was a step in the right direction.

December 6:   Arrived in Detroit for the deposition in the Coughlin-Gariepy case. We tried to take the testimony of the tax accountant of Dr. Gariepy, but it was obvious he was in league with Mrs. Gariepy's attorney. He refused to answer all questions and we had to go to court to compel answers. Significantly, however, Dr. Gariepy's lawyer, ex-Judge Gillespie, who is a staunch Catholic, said that he had gone down to see Dr. Gariepy in jail and received permission from him to testify. He did so at length and told of Coughlin's alleged payments to Gariepy. I remember that Dr. Gariepy's brother Louis was a surgeon, and is up for a $400,000 tax fraud. It may not be significant but the case sat in Washington for two years. It is now gathering dust in the office of the U.S. attorney in Detroit. Meanwhile, the statute of limitations has run on the best year of the tax fraud.

It will be interesting to see whether they let the statute run on the balance of the case, which will expire about March 15, 1952.

December 7:   We appealed before Judge Frank Picard, who, after a lot of palaver and an hour's hearing, finally ruled in our favor that the tax consultant, Whitfield, would have to answer our questions.

Afterward I went in to see Judge Picard, and he recalled what I had forgotten but pretended to remember—that he had met me in Saginaw, Michigan, with Frank Murphy when Frank was running for reelection as Governor. The judge told how he had sat on the original Gariepy case, and said it was a tough one to handle.

"Here am I a Catholic, the U.S. attorney was a Catholic, the assistant U.S. attorney was a Catholic, the attorney for Dr. Gariepy was the brother of the Bishop, and the defendant was a Catholic," the judge said. "However, I was convinced that Dr. Gariepy was using Father Coughlin as an excuse."

Henry Ford came to the Adcraft Dinner where he spoke and introduced me. Before dinner I had a drink with him and Malcolm Bingay of the *Free Press*. They were panning Caudle—and Bingay was reprimanding me for defending Caudle.

Apparently Caudle's name is mud throughout the entire U.S.A.

December 9:   Dined with Sumner Welles, met his bride-to-be. They are getting married January 8 and going to South America. He is still drinking too much, and confided to me that he had never spent such a lonesome period as that since Mathilde died.

December 13: I now begin to understand why George Bowden was so solicitous about Henry ["the Dutchman"] Grunewald.* Several times before he died, George asked me to ease up on Grunewald, even told me how Grunewald had been offered $250,000 by high Republicans to "get me," but he had turned it down.

It now looks as if the secret of George's interest was Grunewald's close affiliation with Charles Oliphant, then the Chief Counsel of IRS. Apparently Grunewald could get anything he wanted out of Oliphant —and of course, George, as a tax attorney, had to find out the score inside Internal Revenue.

John Service was fired by the State Department today after six years of loyalty reviews. The man who fired him was Hiram Bingham of Connecticut, one of the few Senators in recent years who has been publicly reprimanded by all the members of the Senate for using influence in a Senate committee. He permitted manufacturers association lobbyists to sit in on committee sessions when the tariff was being written. The only time I remember meeting Service was at a party where he gave me some rather startling information about Pat Hurley having a Cadillac car shipped over the Hump by airplane during the height of the war when the Chinese were desperately hard up for supplies. Service was probably indiscreet when it came to talking to newspapermen, but I doubt whether there was any real reason to doubt his loyalty.

December 24: Erna Grunewald, daughter of the Dutchman, came around to the house immediately after the broadcast. With her was her brother-in-law, Hartzell, in a most belligerent mood, who said he had just been fired by the Justice Department as a result of my broadcast stating Grunewald had been living at his house while the Justice Department was trying to locate him.

They seemed to blame me for the congressional inquiry of their father; said if it hadn't been for me it never would have been started.

*Grunewald, described by *Time* magazine as "an influence peddler," was ultimately indicted on thirty counts involving his refusals to answer questions put to him by House investigators probing tax scandals in the Truman Administration. During the course of these hearings, Owen Brewster testified he had used Grunewald as an intermediary to contribute $5,000 each to the Senate primary campaigns of Richard Nixon and Milton Young. Grunewald's troubles did not end here, as the diary entries in 1954 and 1958 show.—ED.

Miss Grunewald, I gather, is the divorced wife of John Sorrenti, though we did not mention him. I sometimes wish that the people I have to criticize did not have children.

Ted Acheson, brother of Dean, also phoned after the broadcast. Dean has been trying to keep Ted out of trouble for a long time but not too successfully. He has been working to get the release of the steel mill which the Czechs ordered in the United States some time ago, but which has been held up. I remember the days when Ted and I used to ride at Dean's farm. Personally I would have preferred not to use this on the broadcast.

December 25:   George, Ellen, and Little Drew arrived last night and we hung up our stockings.

Luvie says that we are getting fewer presents this year, and it's all my fault. My campaign against Christmas presents to win government favor has been too successful.

1952

❯❯❯·❯❯❯·❯❯❯·❯❯❯   ·   ❮❮❮·❮❮❮·❮❮❮·❮❮❮

January 1: Maury Maverick joined the Arnold-Pearson families in seeing the New Year in. In the afternoon we had a neighbors' party at the farm. Luvie is still worried for fear I will start a mink farm. I maintain that with mink coats in the news in Washington, minks are what we need instead of cows.

January 2: Lunched with Clayton Fritchey. Clayton has written a memo for the white House on the importance of a United States of Europe. He has timed it to coincide with Churchill's arrival.

Harold Ickes is still in the hospital and not doing too well. His wife told me after I saw him that one doctor said he could not pull through. He is almost seventy-eight. The tragedy of Ickes is that he is now so bitter. I think it's because having been an active man all his life, he is now on the sidelines. And knowing very little about other parts of the government today he takes his venom out on the only department he knows well—the Interior Department.

January 3: Brien McMahon has sent a memo to Truman on the importance of the United States of Europe and emphasizing this to Churchill. I put Brien in touch with Fritchey and they are exchanging memos. I doubt, however, whether Truman will be able to move his aged visitor. Churchill is now about the same age as Ickes and, although in better health, is in no position to take new and daring steps. Everything he is proposing seems to revert to the past.

The more I see of old men in important places, the more accurate I think was the general thesis of Franklin Roosevelt's Supreme Court bill barring oldsters on the bench. If General MacArthur had been forced to retire at sixty-four, it would have saved the world a lot of grief. And while George Marshall did reasonably well as Secretary of Defense and Secretary of State after the age of sixty-four, younger men have done far better since they succeeded him. Likewise Jimmie Byrnes at seventy is no man to be Governor of South Carolina. He is bitter and living in the past.

January 4: Lunched with Oscar Chapman. Ickes has been writing him letters apparently to build up a record putting him on the spot. I urged Oscar to ignore them as much as possible. There's no use getting into a fight with an old man who hasn't much longer to live.

At the Cabinet this morning Truman went out of his way to allay the resignation fears of Howard McGrath. He referred to the reports he had seen in the newspapers that McGrath was going to be fired and said he wanted them to know that none of his Cabinet was going to be fired. Previously Truman has been quite cold to McGrath, especially when he refused to deny press reports that McGrath would get the ax.

In the interim overnight, however, Archbishop O'Hara of Philadelphia made strong representations to the White House. I also understand that Cardinal Spellman got word to the White House—through what channel I don't know since he is in Korea. However, I understand that the President's Appointments Secretary, Matt Connelly, did part of the funneling. Anyway, the effect on Truman was almost instantaneous.

Marcus Cohn and Leonard Marks* informed me that word has been dropped all over the radio industry that Paramount is being influenced by FCC Commissioner Bob Jones and that is why my ABC contract is not renewed. ABC executive Bob Hinckley had told me earlier that Jones was holding up the ABC-Paramount amalgamation because of me, with the inference that if I were dropped, FCC approval would go through. Jones was formerly represented by Hogan and Hartson, the law firm which now represents Paramount.

January 5: Mike DiSalle called Thursday night re McGrath's exit.He said that he would give up running for Governor of Ohio if he could get the Attorney Generalship, and indicated the White House was

---

*The law firm of Cohn and Marks specialized in practice before the FCC. They represented Drew Pearson at times and both men were personal friends.—ED.

seriously considering him. I called him back this morning to tell him what had happened at the Cabinet meeting. He was a little discouraged but seemed to think that McGrath would still leave.

Later in the day Oscar [Chapman] had lunch with McGrath and apparently McGrath figures that his tenure is extremely dubious even though the hierarchy has gone to bat for him. McGrath is organizing a fight to stay on—one move being the crime cleanup campaign, which he should have started two years ago. He is ordering crime juries all over the country to investigate rackets, the Mafia, etc. The tragedy is that this comes two years after Senator Kefauver of Tennessee introduced his crime resolution and two years after I began my series of stories on income tax frauds, the Mafia, and various other forms of corruption.

I talked to McGrath repeatedly two years ago regarding Costello and a lot of other problems that were stymied in his department, but got nowhere. McGrath is one of those sweet and likable characters whom you hate to tangle with, but he will not move.

January 6: Cabot Lodge finally staged the long-awaited nod from Eisenhower today announcing that Ike's name would be entered in the New Hampshire primary. He still hasn't the official word from Ike, however, and explained that this could not come under Army regulations until the General had taken off the uniform.

January 7: Frank McKinney [Democratic National Committee Chairman] came to dinner. I seated him beside Senator Kefauver but they didn't strike up any bosom companionship. Nothing uncordial, but just no great warmth.

Senator McMahon of Connecticut was also there. He and Kefauver apparently are not going to get along as far as the Presidency is concerned either.

After dinner, FCC Chairman Wayne Coy got to talking about the Commission, and I asked him about Bob Jones's alleged threats to hold up the ABC-Paramount merger unless I was taken off the air. With amazing frankness, Wayne confirmed the whole thing, said there was no question that Jones was doing his best to block the merger and had made no secret about his demands that I be taken off the air. Senator Moody, who was present, immediately suggested that he make a speech. I told him I thought that would rock the boat too much at that time.

January 8:   Had lunch in New York with Chris Witting, head of Dumont. He is interested in a TV program, and apparently would pretty much take up my contract from ABC.

Discussed with Mel Evans of Doubleday the idea of doing a book on Washington and corruption. I would sure like to do it but I don't see where I could get the time.

New York is agog over the *New York Post* exposé of Winchell. Cuneo is particularly agog. Reporters have been lurking downstairs in his apartment trying to get a shot of him.

January 9:   Kintner [ABC president] telephoned from New York, very much disturbed over my inquiries to Eddie Weisl, attorney for Paramount, regarding the Bob Jones threat. Kintner insisted that failure to renew my contract would have no relation to the Jones threat. Also that Paramount did not even know about my contractual situation. The more I think of it, however, the more it appears more than coincidental that ABC refused to renew even last November when Carter's had made them a definite TV offer.

January 13:   I ducked the Cardinal Spellman issue again. Meanwhile Bob Allen has published in the *New York Post* the fact that Spellman intervened to save McGrath's hide. It is all over town. But I suppose that when my future is so tenuous with ABC I had better not risk the wrath of the Church—even though I have been putting on a battle on the Cardinal Mindszenty issue and helped get Archbishop Stepinac out of jail.

January 14:   Kefauver asked for advice on what he should say to Truman tomorrow. Jack and I advised him to go in very humbly and remind the President that he had supported all of his platform even on the tough civil rights' issue, and then to ask the President's advice on what he should do about running.*

Tydings has an amazing letter which a young Army lieutenant wrote to Senator Bill Benton of Connecticut telling how McCarthy performed an act of sodomy on him after picking him up in the

---

*Senator Estes Kefauver of Tennessee wanted to run for President, but Truman did not withdraw until after the New Hampshire primary, which Kefauver won. This breach of protocol cost Kefauver Truman's friendship and thus the nomination.—Ed.

Wardman Park bar. The letter was sent to Benton about January 1, but two weeks have gone by and apparently nothing has been done. Tydings and I, knowing how McCarthy operates when he knows a witness is against him, thought we had better interview the lieutenant immediately. So Tydings got Benton on the phone in New York. Benton was evasive and appears to have done little. Therefore, Tydings thought I should arrange for Jack to go to New York.

However, when I called Benton as a precautionary measure, he told me that the White House had stepped in and that the lieutenant was being handled by the FBI. I am a little skeptical as to how the FBI interviews certain witnesses, especially with James McInerny, head of the Justice Department Criminal Division, playing cozy with McCarthy for the last two years.

January 15: Ruth Hagy of the Philadelphia *Bulletin* dropped in to tell me of an amazing interview she had with Eisenhower. A mutual friend had arranged the appointment. She spent three hours with the General, said she found him surrounded by top brass so he did not know what was going on in the world, lonely, worried about the future, and somewhat frustrated. He told her he wished that Paul Hoffman, the ex-Administrator of ECA, would run. He was skeptical about Cabot Lodge, not at all confident about the people who are guiding his political destiny in Washington such as Senator Duff of Pennsylvania, and troubled by his amazing ignorance of things political.

Ruth is an engaging talker and I can understand how the General would spend three hours with her. Apparently he kept Field Marshal Montgomery forty-five minutes outside, and then brought Montgomery in to talk to him with Mrs. Hagy present.

She feels—and I think she is probably right—that the Eisenhower campaign is bogged down, that the Eisenhower leaders here have concentrated on getting Eisenhower to run rather than concentrating on local leaders who can corral delegates, and that if things continue as they are, Taft will win. She feels Lodge ought to be kicked out and a tough political operator put in. Young & Rubicam had been given the public relations job for Eisenhower and from my knowledge of advertising agencies, they are likely to be political bumblers. In New York, a group of Eisenhower enthusiasts are holding a meeting at Madison Square Garden from 11 P.M. to 1 A.M. at a time when it would be extremely difficult to fill the arena.

And if it is only half filled, it will be a terrible black eye to Ike.

The difficulty is—what can be done by a lot of well-meaning, enthusiastic supporters, with no mastermind at the top. It looks to me as if this is a campaign that Eisenhower will have to win purely on his own—perhaps by coming back here for a couple of really statesmanlike speeches. In these he should emphasize the lack of moral leadership in the U.S.A., the fact that the Soviets could ask for nothing more effective than our present despondency and disintegration; the fact that our youth today is blasé, discouraged, and lacks any real vision for the future. It will take a real leader to weld this world together. Taft can't do it—but I think Eisenhower can.

Aside from this one ability to pump in new blood, I would prefer Kefauver to Eisenhower. Kefauver has the know-how and the idealism, but I am afraid the Republicans would immediately begin to tear him to pieces. What this country needs most of all right now is unity.

Kefauver said after he saw the President that he followed our advice. He reported that Truman was extremely friendly, rather fatherly, and said that the Democratic party needed new blood. Kefauver told him that he planned to run.

January 16: Ambassador [Chester] Bowles is back from India to try to get one billion dollars from Congress for Indian relief. He is having a tough time. I saw him at a cocktail party given by Bill Benton. Benton told me that McGrath and the President both were working on the matter of the young lieutenant involved with McCarthy. This is the third report on McCarthy's homosexual activity and the most definite of all. Others were circumstantial and not conclusive.

Bumped into Clayton Fritchey, who said the President had ordered an investigation of my story on the White House conference for the Joint Chiefs of Staff. This was the column that General Bradley himself read over and O.K.'d after suggesting a couple of changes.*

The President went into quite a tantrum saying "I'm going to have this man jailed for treason." He then ordered an all-out FBI probe, which resulted in interviewing about thirty witnesses. Two FBI agents spent more than an hour with Clayton. Apparently he had rather an

*In this column, Drew Pearson reported extensively on this Presidential conference, and stated that "the chief theme of the meeting was that a cease-fire agreement [on Korea] may be close at hand [probably] within the next 20 days."—Ed.

amusing time with them. After he had let drop a few facts about the story, they asked him, "How did you happen to know this?" "Oh, I was at Pearson's house for dinner," Clayton replied. "Oh, you were?" said the FBI men in amazement, thinking they had really run across a clue. "Yes," Clayton continued. "Pearson had just received a call from General Bradley's office and I looked over the story with him. I suggested a few changes in it but General Bradley did not even go as far as I did." "How's that?" asked the FBI, getting more incredulous. "Yes, General Bradley read the story over too."

This seemed to amaze the FBI and they wanted more details. So Clayton told them how I had sent the story down to General Bradley, how he had read it over and O.K.'d it with certain slight modifications. The FBI dropped the remark that I had killed the story. Apparently they gathered this from the fact that *The Washington Post* did not use it and they did not bother to look at the other columns published throughout the country. "By the way," said Clayton, "did you know that Pearson did not have a scoop on this? His old partner, Bob Allen, beat him to the punch by about two days." This sent the FBI agents off more puzzled than ever.

January 18: Skipped the Churchill lunch to lunch with Bob Hinckley of ABC. Signing my contract seemed more important. Bob professed not to know much about it but predicted it would be signed. He confirmed to the hilt that Commissioner Jones had threatened to hold up the ABC-Paramount merger unless "that SOB Pearson was taken off the air." Hinckley said, however, that ABC was not going to give in and would ride the storm out.

January 19: Drove out to Ickes' home. They took him back from the hospital yesterday chiefly as a move to cheer him up. He is not much better. I wired Henry Wallace, who telephoned him just as I arrived. He gave the old man a great lift. I also called Kefauver, who phoned and asked Ickes for advice on his campaign. This made him feel that he still had some usefulness left in life.

January 20: Lamar Caudle and his wife came for supper. He is so grateful for the few kind words I said about him, it's pathetic. I still can't make up my mind if Lamar was one of the dumbest public officials in office, but I am inclined to think so rather than that he was dishonest. He told me incidentally that in the Shoe Styles case in St. Louis that I had written about, when he got a call from the White House, he went ahead and prosecuted. I reminded him of the recommendation for prosecution he had made against Emmitt Warring, the gambler, but he doesn't seem to be astute enough to defend himself even when the facts are 100 percent on his side.

January 21: Just learned that two FBI agents called in Harry Costello and quizzed him about me. They reminded him he was an "American first" and "an ex-Pearson employee second." They told him they were working on a tie-up between Pearson and the Commies and asked him specifically about the leak of one of MacArthur's cables to the Pentagon a year ago January. They said they had had information leading them to believe the leak came from a Commie. Harry put up quite a gallant defense, pointing out that he was a Catholic and an American and that in his opinion I was one of the greatest Americans he had ever known. The interview lasted three hours and was accompanied by frequent FBI references to a huge file on the desk presumably on me. Harry said at the end of the interview that the agents admitted he was their last hope and that the past year they had met a brick wall in their research for the source. The FBI contacted Costello through Jim McInerny, who instructed them to see him. There have been more and more indications of late that McInerny was playing cozy with McCarthy.

I heard from Benton and Tydings that the FBI's interview with the young lieutenant in New York flopped. He denied writing the letter, claimed it was planted by another homo who was jealous.

Gael Sullivan called me from Los Angeles to talk over the idea of being campaign manager for Kefauver. He claimed he could not be released by the Theatre Owners. I called George Skouras immediately who said they would give Gael a leave of absence. However, I am still not sure whether Kefauver really wants him and whether he is exactly the right man.

January 22 Went to Reidsville, North Carolina. Had a most delightful time visiting with people though there were very few I actually remembered. It's hard to realize that it's been thirty-eight years since I was in Reidsville. I compared notes with P. W. Glidewell, the man who defended me there, and we believe the year of the famous bath was 1915, which would have made me sixteen years old. Anyway the visit in Reidsville made me realize how old I am getting and how much has happened since those carefree days when nobody worried much about anything. Later, I sneaked off to go down to the railroad yards to try to find the old spigot where Dean Widener and I took the memorable sponge bath. I remembered a lot of places in the railroad yards but I couldn't find the spigot. Perhaps the old building was gone.*

January 23: Wyn Nathanson of the Watch Institute came down from New York for lunch. He seems to think that there's a chance of Benrus Watches as a sponsor.

January 24: Henry Morgenthau came down for the Bob Patterson funeral and we lunched. I had wired Morgenthau asking him to call Ickes and cheer him up but he hasn't done so. In fact, I now find that he probably will not do so. I had not realized that the old feud between Ickes and Morgenthau was so intense.

Morgenthau told me that at no time had Roosevelt ever asked him to fix a tax case. Doubtless true. But Roosevelt was too smart to ask Henry to do anything like that. He knew Henry's straightlaced conscience too well. Roosevelt used to go over Morgenthau's head to the boys in Internal Revenue.

Morgenthau also told me that he had not wanted to appoint Hannegan as Collector of Internal Revenue in St. Louis. Therefore, he made a very careful check of Hannegan's past operations, going back for years. He said that Hannegan came up with an absolutely clean record. Furthermore, all of his record as collector in St. Louis was clean. When it came time to appoint a Commissioner of Internal Revenue, Hannegan's office had the best record on collections. Morgenthau said he did not know whether anything had happened to Hannegan later, but his own experience indicated that he was honest.

*This incident came up again and again throughout Drew's life. After working all night taking down the Chautauqua tent he helped his father operate, Drew had decided he needed a bath. A horsewatering trough in the rail yard was convenient, but, as dawn broke, an overzealous policeman arrested Drew for indecent exposure. The Judge ruled for Drew, but in later years a succession of enemies raised the incident in an effort to prove him of poor moral character.—ED.

January 25:   Brien McMahon has suddenly pulled out of the Illinois primary against Kefauver. It was Scott Lucas and the President who put him in; but Senator Douglas got hold of Jake Arvey while in Washington yesterday and persuaded Arvey to be neutral. Without the support of Arvey's Democratic machine in Cook County, naturally McMahon did not have a chance. In the end, Truman telephoned him, advising him to withdraw, which he has just done.

January 26:   An investigator from the Marine Corps has interviewed Henshaw [a former part-time Pearson staffer] about leaking to me regarding McCarthy. The investigator says that the information I gave on McCarthy's war record at the time I compared it with General Marshall's could only have come from McCarthy's confidential file inside the Marine Corps.

   The interesting thing is that my defense of General Marshall occurred nine months ago and today the administration is suddenly lumping all these leaks together in an attempt to pin something on me —I don't know what. Yet I don't recall anyone else going to bat for General Marshall against McCarthy as I did.

   Went to see Ickes. Jane told me before I went that he had been talking about having nothing to live for and no more battles to fight. He did not talk quite this way to me but I could see that the old man was pretty well gone. However, he still talked about the importance of the preelection battle and the forces that were lining up which could pull the country to pieces. This, he said, would be his last fight.

   I tried to encourage him about the importance of getting into the fight and the forces of liberalism which could be rallied by few other people than him. I am not sure that I stirred much of a spark. I had the feeling when I left that this was Ickes' last fight in more ways than one, and that I might not see him again.

January 27:   At the session of the House Judiciary Committee last week, New York Congressman Manny Celler, who previously talked about investigating the Justice Department took exactly the opposite track. So to a lesser extent did Frank [Francis] Walter of Pennsylvania. Of course, Celler is extremely vulnerable. His law firm has been representing the A & P grocery firm at a time when he was supposed to be investigating monopoly. And at a time when the Justice Department had moved against the A & P for monopoly. He has also dropped

Pan American Airways when his financial
nerous—I suspect with Manny's law firm,
isiness.

Tom Clark told me about Walter; how he
e government while a member of Congress,
tentiary offense. A clever Attorney General
hatever he wanted from them.

ner given by Paul Porter. For some strange
e Justice [William O.] Douglas. I don't know
effect a reconciliation following my broadcast
orce, but at any rate it was a little awkward,

ice talk with Oscar [Chapman]. He is going to
call Ickes.

an Embassy to a reception there, and much to
myself going through a receiving line, consisting
, whom I criticized the night before on the radio;
ham, about whom I had just written a column for
day; and my old pal, General Harry Vaughan—
all of them just having been decorated by the Cuban government.

January 30: Kefauver and a political leader named Robert Blaikie
from New York came in for lunch. Blaikie emphasized to Kefauver that
he could not carry delegates in New York City unless he took a firm
stand for civil rights, which, of course, would alienate him with the
South.

The thing that impresses me most about Kefauver is that he is
fighting a completely one-man battle. He even carried home a bunch
of correspondence that he was trying to answer late in the evening and
which he should have had somebody helping answer for him. He has
no campaign manager, no one out rounding up delegates, merely a
group of very fine people who spend all their time talking to him.
Furthermore, the impression has gotten out that he is being run by the
New Dealers—namely, Leon Henderson, Wendell Berge, Powell
Davis, and David Cohn, all wonderful people but the political tides of
today are running in the opposite direction.

We finally got Estes back at about 6 P.M. and talked to him about
getting someone good to go out and tour the country very quietly

shaking hands with potential delegates. He indicated to me privately that he was skeptical about Gael Sullivan because of Gael's Hannegan connections. So I suggested Silliman Evans, publisher of the *Nashville Tennessean*. We finally got Silliman to drop down to the hotel room and he agreed to start out for California next week. The only trouble is that Silliman has not been on the wagon for a long time and needs to take the pledge.

On the face of it, I don't see how Kefauver can win the nomination unless he gets an organization or unless the organized support behind Adlai Stevenson is weak indeed. The most interesting factor, which incidentally I told Estes, was that [California Attorney General] Pat Brown, when he was here last week, told me he did not want to become a favorite son in California if he had to run against Kefauver. Kefauver, he said, was too strong.

January 31:   Lunched with Joe Davies. The rumor is that he and Marjorie, after all their honeymooning and after her three previous divorces, are now on the edge. She is in Florida and Joe is about to leave for India. Obviously he has been quite ill.

We talked about the thing that interests him most and which has stymied peace more than any other factor in the world—the break between Russia and the United States. I gather he has written voluminous notes on this, but we both agreed that this would be a bad time to publish them.

Joe had read some of the columns I wrote during Churchill's visit, in which I blamed him for disrupting peace. Joe remarked that I was completely accurate. He then went on to tell me about his own experiences, some of which I had not known about.

Joe said that in October of 1944 Roosevelt had refused to make a deal with Churchill for spheres of influence in the postwar era. Victory by that time was obviously just around the corner so Churchill and Eden flew to Moscow where they worked out a deal with Stalin for separate spheres of influence in Southeast Europe, the British taking over Greece and the Mediterranean coast of Yugoslavia; Stalin taking over Bulgaria, Rumania, and the rest of Yugoslavia. Joe was not clear as to where Hungary and Austria were to fit into the picture. Shortly thereafter, Joe said, the twenty-nine German divisions fighting in Yugoslavia had offered to surrender. The surrender offer was made through Mikhailovich and was relayed to Allied Headquarters in

Caserta, where General Sir Harold Alexander stymied it. Alexander wanted the British Army to fight up through the Italian peninsula and get into Austria ahead of the Russians, therefore, the last thing he wanted was the surrender of twenty-nine German divisions in Yugoslavia. Later Mikhailovich was captured by the Tito forces and flown to Moscow, where he told the Kremlin about the surrender offer. After that, the Russians were so sore and so savage that at times it was nip and tuck whether the Allies would break up. Stalin began a series of brutal notes to Roosevelt which ended only a few days before his death. Finally Roosevelt wrote a letter to Stalin shortly before he died in his own handwriting, which Joe thought put the situation back on a fairly even keel. Joe is optimistic that if Roosevelt had lived, it could have continued on an even keel and the postwar peace of the world might have been saved. The fighting in Yugoslavia against the twenty-nine divisions which did not surrender cost the Russians 200,000 men and delayed the final VE day by three or four months.

Much later, in fact immediately after VE day, Davies was spending the weekend at Chequers, where he found Churchill so bitter in his denunciation of Stalin that Davies reproved him. Churchill admitted that he was partly motivated by the need to win the British election and that the only way to do it was to denounce Russia. Ironically that tactic failed. Churchill was overwhelmingly defeated even while he was meeting with Stalin at Potsdam. Later, just before Churchill's Fulton, Missouri, [Iron Curtain] speech, Joe said he was having Truman out to his Russian chateau (where we lunched today) for a game of poker. He said that he took Truman aside and warned him that Churchill might be using Truman's presence on the platform in Fulton to put across proposals which were directly contrary to American policy.

"I told him," said Joe, "that Churchill has only one ambition— to preserve the British Empire and to drive a wedge between the United States and Russia."

I don't believe that Joe will live to see the day when historians will tell us who was right, and, judging by current bitterness, I doubt if I will either.

Truman called McCarthy a pathological name-caller who doesn't need facts to make charges. I remember when McCarthy made his first speech attacking me. Harry Vaughan rushed a copy in to the President and I'm told remarked: "I hope they both kill each other off."

February 1:   ABC offers me a contract at four-fifths of what I am getting now, subject to cancellation at thirty-days' notice.

February 2:   Dined with Oscar Chapman. *Fortune* magazine has just published an issue on Washington in which a critical chapter is devoted to Oscar; among other things, it quotes Forrestal as saying he would not attend Cabinet meetings with Chapman partly for fear of leaks to me. The irony is that Forrestal's diary said this of Ickes, not Chapman. I suspect that since *Fortune* gets a great deal of its advertising from the power companies and since Oscar had actually secured more public power appropriations than Ickes, the article was inspired.

February 3:   Ickes died ten minutes after my broadcast. The Chief Justice came for dinner. Like most people in Washington, he had rowed with Ickes—in his case, over the price of oil. Ickes wanted it increased during the war and Vinson, who was then Economic Stabilizer, wanted it held down. It was funny how Ickes went to bat for his friends, in this case the oil companies. Most of the time his friends were little people, but when his friends happened to be important people, he went to bat just as vigorously for them too. The Chief Justice, however, made no recriminations, he was always a staunch booster of Harold's. Mrs. Vinson came to dinner for the first time in about two years; she looked extremely well, though she has been quite ill. She explained that she was late because she had been baking bread and was waiting for it to rise for the third time. She also told the story of how she tried to prevent Fred from becoming Chief Justice. She heard of the appointment over the radio after Fred had told her the President had casually talked to him about it, but that he, Fred, was not interested.

She drove home to give Fred hell. He acted like a boy who had been caught stealing cookies. "I was just getting ready to settle down on one of these nice farms that you folks have," said Roberta, "with Fred in private law practice. Now you have the farms and I do my own cooking in an apartment."

February 4:   Harry Vaughan spoke at the Blue Lodge in Anacostia last night, where he said his first trouble in Washington came when he stopped Pearson's stooge, George Vournas, a Communist, from going to Europe. He said the Greek Archbishop had come to him and complained about Vournas; as soon as he crossed wires with Pearson, his troubles began.

February 5: Lunched privately with Frank Waldrop, publisher of the Washington *Times-Herald*. Joe Borkin* brought us together. It has been about ten years since I have talked to Frank; in fact, just about the time of Pearl Harbor. Frank was cordial and so was I. In a way it was rather interesting to talk about old times and rehash some of the incidents in the life of my late ex-mother-in-law. One thing he told me that I had not known before was how Burt Wheeler had tried to horn in on the will contest. Burt had represented the *Times-Herald* in some matters before Cissy died, but Cissy got sore at him because he went off to Europe, leaving a libel suit in the hands of Ed Wheeler. So she fired Burt. After she died, Wheeler called up to say that "the other side" was talking to him and insinuated that he should be brought into the case. The other side, of course, was me. I had one talk with him, I think on the suggestion of Walter Trohan, chiefly for the purpose of getting information. Nothing important resulted.

February 6: Henry Wallace came down for Ickes' funeral and we had lunch. Henry Morgenthau was supposed to come, but wired at the last minute that he was ill. Dave says his new wife is getting him down.

Wallace opened up at lunch in a very frank way about the third-party movement. He realizes now how the Communists used him.

His secretary at that time, obviously a member of the Communist party, listened in on conversations, screened visitors, and planted other visitors on Wallace. For instance, when Wallace was considering whether to start a third party, his secretary brought in various labor leaders, probably all Commies, but scattered among different unions, who gave the impression that the entire labor movement wanted Wallace to launch the movement. Wallace indicated that Louis Bean was the worst deceiver of all.

Wallace referred to this incident as the worst mistake of his life. Wallace said he wished Morgenthau had been there because he wanted to ask him one question: "whether he thought Harry White, his late Assistant Secretary of the Treasury, was a Communist." The question

*Joseph Borkin—a former Department of Justice official and close personal friend.—Ed.

went unanswered, however, Morgenthau not being there. However, Morgenthau asked me that question about a year ago and I replied that I thought White was.

Wallace is trying to develop a new type of chicken which will lay more eggs and yet have enough weight to be a broiler. The chickens that lay the most eggs, he says, are thin and die after they have produced for a certain period.

President Truman attended the Ickes funeral. He sat almost alone on the front pew with old Joe Short beside him. Two rows back sat the mainstays of the old Roosevelt Cabinet, together with many of his own —Francis Biddle, the Chief Justice, Dean Acheson, Justices Jackson and Douglas, Henry Wallace, Oscar Chapman, etc. I could not help but think how much stronger the Roosevelt Cabinet was than Truman's, and how, almost as he sat alone in the church, Truman operates alone as a President. Roosevelt had strong men around him to take the share of the criticism and the heat. Truman takes it all on his own shoulders.

It seemed hard to realize that I had first known Ickes twenty years ago when he fought the battle of the Virgin Islands to defend Father.* The Southern Democrats are still gunning for the best policies Truman stands for.

February 7:   Lunched with Oscar. He pointed out the injustice of the *Fortune* piece, particularly in regard to his lack of courage. He recalled how he had battled the Senate Rules Committee on public power and on the Southwest power project for eight hours and refused to yield to them. He recalled how he had put across [racially] mixed use of swimming pools in the District of Columbia and not run away from the fight as had Krug. By so doing so, he aroused every Southern Congressman and jeopardized his appropriations. He also recalled how he had secured 163 million dollars' worth of appropriations for public power last year —three times as much as Ickes' highest appropriation.

He said: "I can't operate like Ickes. I can't get out and call names and make speeches. Furthermore, Mr. Truman wouldn't like it I did." We both talked over the idea that perhaps Mr. Truman, strange as it

---

*Paul Pearson was the first civilian Governor of the Virgin Islands and was appointed by Hoover. Southern Democrats objected to his liberalism, especially on racial matters.—Ed.

may seem, prefers to have the abuse or criticism heaped upon his shoulders rather than on those of his Cabinet.

Oscar said Truman had reversed him only twice, once in regard to the Anaconda-Harvey Alliance deal where Charlie Wilson had told the President that Tom Corcoran represented the Independent Oil Companies. Truman hates Tom so much that he issued the contract to Anaconda while Oscar was in the Far West. Later Oscar explained to him that he personally had asked Corcoran to bring the independents in in order to create more competition. Truman was sorry, but felt it was too late. The second point where Oscar lost out was in regard to Tidelands Oil and his plan to deal with them under the Surplus Property Act. He had sufficient legal ground to justify this though McGrath opposed. However, Truman argued that to apply the Surplus Property Act while Congress was adjourned would make it look as though the administration was circumventing Congress. Oscar argued that the Tidelands Oil bill had been kicked around in Congress for years and he had to get action out of Congress soon or get completely snarled up. However, Truman overruled him.

Oscar is trying to get Helen Gahagan Douglas appointed Assistant Secretary of the Interior. Truman is a little skeptical, said, "We may be taking on too many fights at this time. Let me think about it."

Harry Hoyt of Carter's Products called out of the clear blue to offer me a year's contract.

February 11 [Utah]:   Dined with Governor Bracken Lee of Utah, who is about as reactionary as any Republican I have ever met. We kept the dinner on an even and pleasant keel however.

My old friend Reuben Clark, one of the highest moguls of the Mormon church and a reactionary of the worst sort, has finally been demoted by the new President of the church, David O. McKay. It has brought rejoicing among the many people of Utah. McKay is a former schoolteacher and fairly liberal. It is interesting that the Mormon church which once had parochial schools has given them up. The church has returned all the schools to the state of Utah.

February 12:   Drove to Ogden [Utah]. Lunched with Governor Pitman, who drove in from Nevada. He gave me a long story of the despotism of Senator McCarran. It was so shocking that it was hard to believe—more like a story happening in Russia. McCarran has even refused to let some of Pitman's old friends get jobs. Companies that wanted to hire them were afraid of having their taxes investigated too thoroughly by Internal Revenue.

Afterward I spoke at Weaver College. During the question period, I was asked about Senator Watkins and replied that he was of no consequence in Washington. Later Senator Watkins's son was introduced to me. He did not appear to be pleased.

February 13 [California]: Spoke in Long Beach. Had a friendly session with Larry Collins, publisher of the Long Beach *Independent* who is thoroughly disapproving of everything I have written on Tidelands Oil but nevertheless has been a good sport about publishing it. Tidelands Oil is a real battle cry in this part of the world. The city of Long Beach virtually escapes taxation as a result of the wells which stud its harbor.

February 14: Spoke at Chico, a little town which in the old Ellison White Chautauqua days was considered one of the most conservative on the circuit. It is an area of huge rice and wheat ranches interspersed with fruit farms, where most of the people have voted Republican ever since the gold rush days. I had a wonderful audience at Chico, however, and perhaps gave my best lecture of the trip.

February 15: Flew to San Francisco, where Thurman Arnold had arranged a luncheon with Henry Kaiser, Paul Smith, Judge William Denman and Judge Homer Bone of the Ninth Circuit U.S. Court of Appeals, and various others.

February 18: My last day in Los Angeles. Lunched with Jack Leighter, Jim Geller, and Maxwell Shane. Shane is trying to sell a movie on Washington corruption featuring some of my stuff, but every studio so far has turned it down. They are scared to death of offending Washington. Darryl Zanuck has some income tax troubles and I guess some of the others do too. If they only knew how in-wrong Washington is with the rest of the country.

Bob Smith had a big dinner for me featuring the Mayor; Charles Skouras, the head of the Hilton hotels; Terrell Drinkwater, head of Western Airlines; and about twenty others. It was one of those occasions where it's almost impossible to say the right thing. I took the plane to Texas around midnight.

February 19 [Texas]: Visited the Wagoner ranch just outside of Vernon—570,000 acres studded with oil wells. It's easy to understand why Texas is one of the most reactionary states in the union. It lives on vast cattle and cotton plantations plus oil. The 27 1/2 percent oil depletion allowance could not be knocked out of the tax bill without Texas definitely revolting.

I wonder how carefully tax returns of these big cattle men are scrutinized. The new Commissioner of Internal Revenue, John Dunlap, is from Dallas.

Kintner called from New York with a proposal by Carter Products for a year's contract on the radio plus a year on television, though with cancellation clauses at the end of every thirteen-week period on TV. I accepted.

February 20: It is spring in Beaumont. Azaleas bloom in the suburbs, and the trees are greening. All through Texas, where sentiment for Eisenhower is overwhelming, Ike is just as popular as Truman is unpopular.

February 21 [Washington]: Louise Steinman came in before dinner. She wants me to fly to Paris to talk to Eisenhower and get him either to come back and campaign early or persuade him to call for Senator Duff. Apparently her boss Duff hasn't the temerity to arrange an appointment with Eisenhower himself. He says that Dewey and General Lucius Clay have spiked his guns, have told Eisenhower that Duff is a bungler and that Ike should not see him.

Net result of all this is that the Eisenhower crowd are at sixes and sevens, and the Eisenhower boom is being deflated fast. I have long wondered how Cabot Lodge got into the picture as Ike's campaign manager, but the story is now unfolding. General Lucius Clay, it appears, is the Number One political adviser to Ike. I can't think of a worse person. He antagonized labor to such an extent that Truman had to ease him out of Washington. He thinks in strictly military terms. There is nothing liberal about him. Yet Clay sold Ike on bringing Dewey into his campaign and also Cabot Lodge. The latter two are not so bad except that they are not trusted by Republican leaders.

Meanwhile, Ike has indicated to ex-Senator John Cooper of Kentucky that he was not coming back to campaign. Meanwhile also Averell Harriman has been in Paris trying to dissuade Ike from running.

And the more strength Eisenhower loses, the cockier Truman gets about running. He is now about persuaded that he can defeat Taft.

I returned from Texas this morning to a front-page story by Phil Graham of the *Washington Post* that Vinson definitely would not accept the nomination even if drafted. Luvie reports that the Chief Justice had passed up several bridge games because he had to be at the White House almost every night this week. Later I found he has been busy trying to tell the President that he should not run. The palace guard had about persuaded him that he should run, but Vinson has argued that Truman's place in history is already complete on the bigger issues and he would only hurt himself and the country if he ran again.

The palace guard is so vindictive against Kefauver that when Governor Adlai Stevenson made a brief compliment or reference to Kefauver, they rushed the statement in to Truman to feel him out. Stevenson had betrayed him. One of the things apparently that is inducing the President to reconsider his previous decision not to run is jealousy of Kefauver.

John Bennett stayed for dinner. He thinks Ike is afraid to come back for two reasons: one, he doesn't want to face the Kay Summersby* charges, and two, he doesn't want to face MacArthur's blasts. John thinks that Mrs. Eisenhower never knew the truth about Summersby—namely, that Ike wanted a divorce. MacArthur has been saying: "That boy will back out in the final showdown." And now some of the Republican leaders think MacArthur may be right.

[*The entries from March 19 through March 26 are transcribed from longhand notes.*]

March 19:   Taft boom seems to be collapsing.

March 22:   Ellis Arnall's changed tune re steel. The pay boost was too high. Murray's got old and crabby. Wilson hates labor.

March 23:   Truman disavowed McKinney [?] on Korea & 3d term because of Lovett and Acheson. Lovett & Dulles bolting—see handwriting on wall.†

---

*A WAC officer on Eisenhower's staff during World War II.—ED.

†A New York banker and partner in the firm of Brown Brothers Harriman, Robert H. Lovett had served in several capacities in the Roosevelt and Truman administrations. In 1951, he became Secretary of Defense, a position he held until the end of

March 24: TV luncheon with Ted Bates ad crowd. 5 year—no raises, they cancel. Swope getting old. Dave Scoll: H. H. Kung was behind N. Morris.

March 25: Publishers afraid of McCarthy book. American Legion boycott of anything liberal. Doubleday—Schuster said no.

March 26: Blank wall in Gariepy case. Tom is Catholic—everyone afraid of boycott. Dinner with Vinson. Thinks Barkley will run and win.

March 29: Dined with former Governor Jack Dempsey [New Mexico] and his wife. After dinner we turned on Truman's Jackson-Jefferson Day speech. Having been on a sleeper for two nights I sat back and dozed intermittently. (Luvie would say I would have dozed whether I had been on a sleeper or not.)

Suddenly the room was electrified and even I woke up. Truman announced that he would not run again.

March 30: Washington is agog. Democratic candidates are everywhere. I had to throw out a good part of my broadcast to concentrate on political news. Fortunately I had predicted on June 17 [1951] that Truman would not run and played the record of the broadcast back on the air. After the broadcast I met Senator Anderson of New Mexico at dinner, one of the Trumanites who had consistently and vigorously predicted that the President would run. Late this afternoon the White House announced that there would be important announcement at 5:30 P.M. Then some of the boys at the White House realized I would get a scoop at 6 P.M. so the announcement was delayed until 6:20— five minutes after I got off the air. However, I had a suspicion that the announcement was to be over Charles E. Wilson's resignation as Defense Mobilizer and managed to get a line into the broadcast at the last minute.

---

the Truman Administration. John Foster Dulles had served in the Truman Administration with the rank of Ambassador in the Japanese peace treaty negotiations (1950–51), but it is more likely that the reference is to Allen W. Dulles, Deputy Director of the CIA from 1951–53, and Director from 1953–61.—ED.

March 31:   Ellis Arnall apparently was the man who forced Wilson's resignation. He blocked giving the steel companies an increase in price to compensate for increased wages. I talked to Ellis briefly today. He said he had told Truman in their joint session with Wilson: "I've been trying to protect the little people, Mr. President, as you wanted me to do, and I don't think I'm wrong. This increase in the price of steel is not going to do it."*

Dined with the Israeli Ambassador in honor of Lord Samuel, first British High Commissioner to Palestine. He is eighty-one years old. Talked at dinner to Byrode, in charge of Germany for the State Department. He is generally enthusiastic about the United Europe. Thinks that miracles are being accomplished, and that Germany will serve in a joint army with France. He is chiefly worried today about the French. They are getting jittery about coming into the deal. Charles Brannan, who was at the dinner and who has been having a lot of headaches over surplus grain that has disappeared from government warehouses, seemed delighted at the recent plethora of political news. "If anyone wanted to commit murder," he said, "this is the time to do it. It would hardly get on the front pages."

Clinton Anderson has been trying to get the Vice President to enter the [primary] race in California against Kefauver. He wants to corral the Truman delegates and switch them over to Barkley. Senator Clements [of Kentucky] said he had talked to Truman, who had no objection to Barkley's entering the race, but that he should clear the matter of the California delegates with Frank McKinney. When Clements called McKinney, he said he was trying to clear the delegates for Senator Kerr. McKinney finally urged that neither Kerr nor Barkley file.

He said it would be a bigger blow to Kefauver to have him win in California by default. Clements offered to go to California to put Barkley in the race. However, Anderson said he did not want to have the old man break his heart on an uphill game and asked my opinion on the political atmosphere in California. I told him that I thought Barkley would lose. However, just to make sure, I called up Paul Smith

---

*On April 8, in the midst of the Korean War and in the face of a steelworkers strike, a pay hike authorized by the Wage Stabilization Board, and a demand by industry that the increase be passed on to the consumer or there would be no increase, Truman seized the steel mills. The action was reversed by the Supreme Court two months later.—Ed.

of the *Chronicle* and Bob Smith of the Los Angeles *News*. Both seemed to agree with my opinion.

However, I learned that Pat Brown, who says I elected him Attorney General, is now going to file as a favorite son.

April 1: Oscar called to say that his plans for an Easter memorial for Harold Ickes were falling flat. Marian Anderson, who had been refused an appearance in Constitution Hall in '39 and then invited by Ickes to sing on Easter Sunday at the Lincoln Memorial, refused to sing at the Lincoln Memorial again in honor of the old man, now that he is dead.

She is going to sing on Ed Sullivan's program instead. Oscar called up Henry Ford, who sponsors the Ed Sullivan program, but he washed his hands of the whole business. I called Sol Hurok, Miss Anderson's agent, but he was equally uncooperative. It seems that she wants the $2,000 bucks she gets from Ed Sullivan and isn't much interested in Ickes, now that he is gone.

April 2: Newbold Morris came for a dinner with Clinton Anderson, Harry McDonald, Schenley head Lewis Rosenstiel, and some other people. Morris was expecting word any minute that he would be fired from his job as Special Assistant to the Attorney General and finally went back to his hotel to await the word. He said that McGrath had blown up after Morris and his counsel, Sam Becker, had lunched with McGrath, and Becker had told him: "Mr. Morris wants to get through as soon as possible and he thought we better finish the Justice Department first, so on Monday I am going to bring a squad of lawyers in and we are going to start going through the records. We want a list of your phone calls and your diary."

Next day Morris was given orders that no more positions were to be filled, and when he tried to protest this order, McGrath wouldn't see him. This was the beginning of the end. Clinton Anderson suggested that McGrath was trying to cover up, probably the income he received from the gun factory that he operated with a big politician in Indiana.

April 3: Morris was fired by McGrath at noon today. At four P.M., Truman fired McGrath. I think that Truman did not know McGrath had fired Morris. However, Oscar told me that at the dinner given for

Queen Juliana last night, McGrath was talking like a wild man. He and the President also had a row at the airport while waiting for the Queen.

Jim McGranery has been appointed the new Attorney General. It will be interesting to see how good he is. Under Biddle, he was excellent, but always with a weather-eye out on the White House. And I remember when I testified how Harry Vaughan had intervened at the Justice Department to save Joe Cawthorn from jail and that McGrath had taken a stand against Vaughan, McGranery in New York immediately issued a statement denying what I said. In other words, McGranery had his eye on the White House even then, for the future—I think a circuit court judgeship. He never dreamed that he was going to become Attorney General.

April 13:   Gave my first radio broadcast on Winchell's nine P.M. spot. Caught the train afterward for New York en route to Paris. I hope April 13 is lucky.

April 14:   This time took TWA to Paris. Plane was late as usual though held up by fog. It seems like a long time since I last crossed the Atlantic by ship. It was in 1937 on the *De Grasse* when Luvie and I came back with Tyler from the famous Isle of Sark. Since then, I have crossed the Atlantic four times, round trip, always by air and always with other members of the family.

April 15:   Arrived in Paris about six hours late. [General] Buck Lanham's car met me at the airport and drove me out to SHAPE for lunch. Flying the Atlantic, I tried to figure out the best way I could persuade Eisenhower to stand still for a newsreel shot of me and him, plus a TV interview. I figured some good questions and even wrote down his prospective answers. However, I might as well have saved my time. At lunch, Lanham made it clear that there were to be no statements, no interview, no pictures, etc. I did not press the point.

Lanham is one of the few good things to come out of the proposed station [WBAL] in Baltimore. I met him when we were trying to figure out radio educational programs. He was then in charge of Information and Education in the Army, and I have always thought he was one of the most refreshing brass hats in the Army. He confessed to a lot of trouble with Ike's press relations and privately wrung his hands over what was going to happen to Ike when he got back to the U.S.A. So far, he has made no plans for a press secretary, a political secretary, or anything else. He plans to hold no press conferences until after the conventions, and so far has held no real press conferences in Paris. When Ike made his report on his first year in NATO, he refused to make a separate TV and radio record so that the radio broadcast was full of "uhmmms" and "ahhss"—the result of Ike's improvisation. And he refused to read a written text for the TV cameras because he has to wear specs. So all in all, his report on NATO, cracked up to be a reverberating public relations success, was a bust.

Buck has twenty-eight years in the Army with two years to go before he retires; otherwise I think he would like to handle Ike's press relations after the campaign starts.

I had a long talk with Eisenhower after lunch. He had seen Walter Lippmann in the morning, and, according to Buck, spent forty-five minutes talking to Lippmann pretty much in the way F.D.R. used to monopolize conversations with visitors. In many respects Eisenhower reminds me of F.D.R.—the same contagious charm, the same ability to talk, and the same tendency toward pleasant-sounding generalities.

Whenever I talked to Roosevelt I felt sort of lifted up during the conversation, but when I left I always wondered what it was that he had said that was of any importance. The talk with Eisenhower this time was a little bit more specific; or perhaps it was because my ego was flattered by the fact that I did part of the talking. Anyway Eisenhower seemed tremendously interested in what I told him about Taft's efforts in the South to steal delegates. Apparently Senator Lodge had not reported to him in detail on this. He was also mildly interested in the China lobby, though he did not react one way or another when I urged that he take two counterattacks which would be just as effective as Patton's tank runs around the German army. These I suggested were an investigation of delegate-buying in the South, which I had already discussed with Senators Monroney and Hennings, Democrats, and Lodge and Duff, Republicans. The other counterattack was to investigate the China lobby, which I pointed out was overripe and an exposé of the bribery and graft would cut the ground out from under his critics who claimed he knew nothing about any part of the world except Europe. This teed Ike off on a discourse in which he said: "People forget the world is round. They forget that what affects us in Asia, affects us in Europe, and vice versa." Indirectly alluding to the French problem in Indochina, he emphasized that his problems of arming western Europe were naturally affected by what happened in Asia.

In trying to gauge which is most important, Europe or Asia, he said: "I think we can reduce it to very simple terms—the areas where there is the greatest intelligence, the greatest skills, the greatest production, the greatest amounts of iron and steel. And it has been my feeling that Europe fits these details. If an enemy wants to go to the superhuman task of conquering Asia as a back door to Europe, well, that's something we have to reckon with. But I personally don't think we can send American troops into Asia to stop it."

I asked Eisenhower quite bluntly what he was going to do about his press relations when he came back. I also reminded him that Taft had primed some of the press to be ready. Ike laughed at this. "I don't think any man can talk glibly about every problem in the world," he said. "But he can get experts to come in, study the situation, and say this is what the score is. From this he can make up his final judgment. I don't believe the American people want me to talk glibly on every subject. It wouldn't be true to form, because they know that I don't know. I have been over here concentrating on a job and obviously can't be an expert on every problem."

I made an indirect reference to the fact that I thought Ike would have been better running as a Democrat. I led into this accidentally by mentioning the fact that he was going to be up against some powerful isolationist opponents in the Senate if elected. He interrupted, however, and the subject never did get back on the track of his isolationist opponents.

"It seemed to me," he said, "that if I ran as a Democrat, I would be obligated to a great many party leaders. And also it seemed to me that what Washington needs more than anything else is a good cleaning out, at least for four years."

Thinking back on it later, it seemed to me that this "four year" statement was rather significant on Ike's part and meant he would not run for a second term.

He went on to say: "I hate bureaucrats. I saw enough of them when I was in the Pentagon—people striving, concentrating on building up bigger bureaus and more power for themselves. It seems to me the administration is bogged down with bureaucrats."

I got a chance to say: "It seems to me that the administration is bogged down for lack of idealism. Mr. Truman's policies on the whole are good, but he hasn't been able to sell his ideals to the country and to the world. People have to have more than just a dollars-and-cents livelihood. They need to be lifted up and led."

Eisenhower jumped up at this, pulled a coin from his pocket and handed it to me. It had a cross on one side with the word "freedom," and the word "God" on the other. "You are so right," he said. "That coin represents my religion. Somebody gave it to me out in Kansas some years ago."

He then gave in a very few words one of the most convincing and sincere lectures on the futility of war that I have ever heard. He didn't use the exact words "I hate war," but the way he said it carried all of that meaning and was even more convincing. He told how once you finished a war, you just had to begin over again to build up the nation you had destroyed, how wars led to more wars, and so on.

I told him that I thought he should say some of these things during his farewell visits to the different NATO countries. However, I don't believe I pushed my point hard enough. I figured that I had already emphasized this at some length in my earlier letter which Lanham said made a great impression.

Afterward Lanham expressed the opinion that Ike didn't want to talk too much on these NATO farewell visits because he would be accused of playing politics in his European job; and on the whole, I am convinced Lanham had the situation sized up correctly.

Eisenhower also talked at some length about the problem of North Africa. "I wish there was something you could do to awaken the American public regarding the Muhammadan World," he said. "There's a great stretch of country running from Gibraltar to the Philippines where their hatred of us is measured by our aid to Israel. We cannot dump this problem on the laps of the British and we cannot dump it into the hands of the French. It's our problem as well as theirs and we have to help work out the solution. We have to win them over as our friends. The Arabs tell me: 'Isn't our oil just as important to you as Israel? Israel doesn't want to become part of NATO for fear of endangering the relatives of Jews behind the Iron Curtain, so why should we reverse our stand of neutrality, in regard to your defense pact?' "

Ike talked at some length on this. I could not help thinking that he was right, but I also could not help thinking that he would really blow the lid off politically if he said these things publicly in the United States.

I started to tell him that Truman's chief campaign funds had been raised by the Jews in '48, and that when the President had absolutely no money to pay radio for time at the start of the campaign, the Jewish contributors had moved in with help. However, I thought better of it and changed the subject.

The thing that Ike seemed to be most interested in during the course of our hour-and-five minutes' conversation was the manner in which Louisiana and South Carolina Taft delegates had stolen his delegates and also my story of how Johnson had offered me $10,000 if I would make a favorable reference in the column to Dr. H. H. Kung.* I haven't told this to many people, but I did tell it to Eisenhower as an illustration of how the China lobby works. He asked some rather naive questions about Congressman Judd of Minnesota, a conservative Republican who would head the Foreign Affairs Committee if his party gained control of Congress, and he wanted to know whether the China lobby wasn't really motivated by the sincere belief on many people's part that we should save China. I told him that on the contrary, more money had been spent on the bribes on behalf of the China lobby than any other major matter in Washington.

Dined with Leon in a hole-in-the-wall restaurant where he took me to dinner in 1946.† He is pessimistic over the chances of the Germans and French getting together.

April 16:   Lunched with Dave Schoenbrun of CBS. He says that the French are hanging back regarding the unified army with Germany but believes that by the time the pact is up for ratification in the fall, they may approve. He claims that Dean Acheson pushed the French too hard at the Waldorf-Astoria meeting in New York in the fall of 1950, when he demanded that Germany be given the right to rearm.

Acheson was under terrific fire from the Senate isolationists and the Senate economizers who wanted to shift the military burden and saw what they thought was an untapped reservoir of German manpower going to waste.

McCarran and McCarthy were among the leaders; also Taft and most of the Republican extremists. With things not going well in Korea and Acheson under heavy political fire, both on the McCarthy-Communist issue and otherwise, he put the heat on the French. While Schoenbrun is in a better position to judge than I regarding the French,

---

*Brother-in-law of Chiang Kai-shek and former Minister of Finance (1933–44), a U.S. resident since 1948.—ED.

†Leon Pearson was then with NBC in Paris.—ED.

there is no question but that the McCarthy-McCarran clique did the United States a great disservice in playing up the demand that Germany should rearm.

When I was in Germany last winter and summer I noted that the Germans had two dangerous reactions—one, they were getting cockier and, two, they were getting less willing to extend military cooperation. The more the Germans feel they are essential, the more impossible they are to deal with.

Dined with Jean Beliard and the Lanhams. Beliard, who is an integral member of the NATO staff, is quite pessimistic. The French are in the same never-never land that they were in in 1939, Beliard contends. In 1939 the French expected the Czechs to fight against Hitler. Today they expect others to fight—but not themselves.

Beliard agreed that Acheson had jumped the gun on western Europe at the Waldorf conference in 1950, demanding that Germany rearm. This pressure, he said, was what put Germany in such a good bargaining position that it may be the undoing of European unity.

April 17:   Also visited with Anna Marie Max's brother, who publishes the magazine *Réalités*. He seems more optimistic about French public opinion than the others, says the French Assembly always lags behind the public just as Congress lags behind the American people.

April 18:   Lunched with Ambassador Hervé Alphand, the French representative on the NATO Council. He seems optimistic about German-French *rapprochement*. However, most diplomats are. Dave Schoenbrun, who was with us, makes the point that General Bradley pushed the French too hard at the Lisbon NATO conference. He told the French: "We've got to show Congress that France is doing her share. France is the hub of the entire North Atlantic Pact. She must be a show window for European defense." As a result, French rearmament was increased; but not French taxes, and of course, that meant more inflation. Most newspapermen are peeved at Ike's press relations. They like him personally, but he has held no public press conferences. It seems reasonably obvious to me that Ike is going to have a difficult time when he gets back with his press relations unless he has such a predominant number of powerful publishers on his side that they forgive him his transgressions just as they forgave Hoover's and Coolidge's.

April 19:   Few people realize how the American election is holding up everything in Europe. The Europeans figure that the proposed unified army cannot be voted on until after November because they want to see what we will do. If Taft is elected, the European army, they figure, will be out the window. The other thing that could spoil unity is peace in Indochina. If the Russians were smart, they would bring about a real truce in that area, permitting the French to bring their army home, whereupon France would say: "We can defend ourselves without Germany's help. To hell with the Boche."

Recorded my broadcast and decided to fly back home a day early. I don't like the idea of spending Sunday away from home.

April 20:   Flying a few hours out of Gander the pilot told me that he had picked up a radio message that convicts rioting at New Jersey state prison at Rahway had asked for me to mediate their dispute. Arrived in New York at 10 A.M., and got a phone call from Jack Anderson in Washington urging me to go to Rahway. Somewhat against my better judgment, I put my bags in a taxi and drove an hour and a half to the prison. One wing of it was draped with bedsheets featuring messages from the prisoners to the public. The New Jersey state police let me go up to the front entrance but that was as far as I got. The guard grudgingly took a message to the warden, William Lagay, but forced me to wait outside. I have been in a lot of jails, but never one as ominous-looking as this one. The best was probably at the federal penitentiary at Lewisburg, Pennsylvania, which is sometimes called a country club. The worst, next to this, was at Atlanta, Georgia, where the scum of the city is locked up every Saturday night. I also visited San Quentin in tracking down Howser witnesses and also Folsom penitentiary near Sacramento. Both are clean and hospitable compared with Rahway.

Perhaps I should add a note for posterity that my visits to the above jails were in line of duty, not compulsory. The only time I have been forcibly detained was in a Soviet prison in Havarsk, Siberia, for a brief interval; and part of a night in the 13th precinct in Washington, D.C., for failing to post $15 collateral for speeding. Actually I had the $15 in my pocket, but did not want to say so. However, after lying on an iron cot for a few hours listening to other prisoners yell and groan, I finally relented and paid the $15.

Anyway, after waiting an hour or so with no word from Mr. Lagay, I gave up, drove back to La Guardia and caught a plane to Washington.

April 22:   Perry Patterson, attorney for Colonel McCormick, got in touch with Bill Roberts yesterday and hinted at a settlement of the McCarthy suit. He begged that McCormick be let off the hook from answering questions. Bill was adamant and refused. It appears that the *Tribune* crowd is sore at McCarthy.*

April 23:   Went to New York to work out my first television program, which begins in about ten days. I have a premonition TV is going to be worse than war.

April 24:   Holmes Baldridge, the Assistant Attorney General in charge of Justice's Civil Division, made an atrociously bad argument for the government in the seizure of the steel mills. In Europe, Truman's taking over the steel industry had an extremely favorable reaction. It cut the ground out from under the Communists. Even the more conservative English and French seemed to think it was a good move, but back in the United States, I have heard nothing good about it.

The worst tragedy happening in the world today is that the United States is so engrossed in an election, corruption, and a bitter internal feud over Harry Truman that we have almost completely forgotten the rest of the world. There is almost no interest in what has happened in Europe, today, and the peace of the world for decades to come hangs in the balance. If the French and Germans can really unite in one army, wearing one uniform, then I think the most important milestone for peace in a century will have been laid. But the American people don't realize it and don't particularly seem to care.

April 25:   Lunched with Joe Davies and Marjorie. As usual, the conversation got around to the question of whether we could have had

*In 1951, Drew Pearson sued Senator McCarthy and eight other named defendants, charging the Senator with assault (the notorious Sulgrave Club incident) and alleging the Washington Times-Herald Publishing Company, Fulton Lewis, Jr., and Westbrook Pegler, among others, had conspired to libel him and deprive him of his livelihood. After Senator McCarthy was censured, Drew Pearson felt he had been vindicated and he dropped the suit.—Ed.

cooperation with Russia, if it had not been for Churchill. Joe reviewed the chapter of the war with which I was only vaguely familiar: how Molotov, then still Minister of Foreign Affairs, had come to the United States in June of 1942 and secured Roosevelt's pledge for a second front across the English channel. This, of course, was worked out and Eisenhower had been sent to England to prepare for it. General Marshall, Joe said, was strong for opening this front within the next six months. I recall talking to Marshall during 1942, though I think it was earlier in the year, about a second front and he seemed rather discouraged about its prospects at that time.

At any rate Joe said that Churchill had come to Washington with Sir Alan Brooke, then chief of staff, to oppose the second front. They laid down an ultimatum that if it was opened, it would have to be with 80 percent American troops. British troops would not be available. It was Harry Hopkins, according to Joe, who tipped the balance in favor of Churchill and against the second front. Harry was always susceptible to Churchill. I remember rather vividly how Harry always fell for those with wealth and charm. I remember also how Harry told me and a group of newspapermen in the winter of 1942 how he had gone to England to help bolster Churchill's slim and restless majority in the House of Commons. At any rate, Marshall was badly disappointed. Finally we compromised on the North African front, which was a long, slow way to Berlin. Joe thinks that if we had carried out the pledge to Molotov, made in June of 1942, the present picture with Russia would have been entirely different.

April 27:   I predicted that Judge Pine would overrule the government on the right to raise wages in the steel industry, but uphold the government on the right to seize.

April 28:   Called on Dean Acheson to give him some ideas on the propaganda battle in Europe. I suggested two things: that Eisenhower make a few remarks during his farewell tour emphasizing the importance of peace and the fact that a United Europe army is the first step toward unity and peace. I suggested to Dean that inasmuch as the United States for twenty years had argued that the way to peace was through disarmament, the people of Europe could not reverse themselves so quickly and believe that the way to peace was through rearmament. They must have it explained to them that when nations can work together through a unified army, it's the first step toward European unity. Second, I suggested that next October, when the unified army pact comes up for ratification, Truman go to Europe and make a few speeches about peace. By that time, Truman would be out of politics and a disinterested world figure who should have great appeal on the Continent. I had tried the idea out on several Frenchmen and they'd liked it. Dean seemed interested in both ideas though I couldn't tell whether he was just being polite. It was the first time I have talked to him to any extent in almost fifteen years. He was pleasant, though slightly cool.

I got so interested in talking to him about Europe that I completely forgot one of the main ideas I had wanted to talk to him about —namely, the China lobby. Bill Roberts has turned up some secret instructions from the Chinese to their military attachés ordering them to spy on almost every phase of American activity, including the atomic bomb.

April 29:   Judge Pine reversed the government completely on the steel strike, but Judge Morris handed down a more important decision as far as I was concerned. He threw the Gariepy case out of court. This is the case which really lost me my contract with Lee Hats.

Lunched with Oscar Chapman in Ickes' old [Interior Department] dining room. I told him this was the first time I had ever lunched there without a big Manhattan cocktail. He told me he once received a case of Virgin Islands rum and that Ickes had euchred it away from him.

Went to the Guggenheims' dance. Was very embarrassed to find that I was dancing with the wife of the dean of the diplomatic corps a good part of the evening without knowing who she was. However, she was a good dancer.

July 1:   Senator Kefauver came for breakfast. I told him that I thought his most difficult hurdle in getting the nomination was Truman. Truman couldn't get the nomination for himself, but he could block anyone else. I suggested that he deliver a couple of speeches praising Truman, and he said he was giving one at Richmond that night. Oscar Chapman had told me previously that Senator Ed Johnson of Colorado seemed to be warming up to the idea of Kefauver for President, provided Kefauver would take Ed for Vice President. I passed this on to

Estes but told him I thought it would be a mistake to take Johnson. Estes asked that I write a couple of speeches for him—one on foreign affairs, one on the general subject of Eisenhower.

July 2: Clayton Fritchey got Kefauver's speech at Richmond put on Truman's desk.

July 3: Wrote the first foreign affairs speech, which Estes used at Topeka.

July 4: Left for the Republican convention at Chicago.

July 5: The convention is going to be hard to cover. First, it is spread all over town; second, this is the first time television has really played a part. I have to handle TV every night as well as write a column, which isn't going to be easy.

Eisenhower has a real issue on the question of Southern delegates, and he's using it. Hitherto he had no issue with Taft which appealed to Republicans. His issues with Taft were of much greater appeal to Democrats. But the issue of whether votes have been stolen in the South smacks of the corruption issue against Truman and is very effective. The swing to Ike has already started.

July 6: In my regular television program tonight I virtually predicted Eisenhower, though with reservations. I also went out on a limb and predicted Kefauver for the Democrats.

July 7: This convention has more and more resemblance to that of 1912 when Teddy Roosevelt was euchred out of the Southern delegate picture by the Taft machine. Only in those days, the *Chicago Tribune,* then young and virulent, was on Teddy Roosevelt's side and one of the delegates at the convention was none other than Bertie McCormick, then vigorously for Roosevelt, but now beating the tom-toms for the son of the man who opposed him in 1912. John Perry, who is staying with the Colonel at his summer place, says that McCormick is in his dotage.

General MacArthur, who had a great opportunity to stampede the convention with a key speech tonight, was a flop. Even the conservative AP admitted that MacArthur had even lost the chance to be Vice President.

July 8:   Staged "Pearson's Parade," my first TV show covering the convention. It was a dubious success. My only consolation is that when it comes to flops, the reverberations from MacArthur's speech last night make him a worse flop.

Taft's force appears to be crumbling. Senator Knowland of California has received an offer from Taft which really takes him up on the mountaintop. Taft proposed that Knowland switch California's seventy-six votes to Taft on the first ballot. If Taft failed to get the nomination on the first ballot, he, in turn, would switch all his delegates to Knowland.

July 9:   Had a visit with Governor Warren. Knowland resisted Taft's offer. However, I detected—more from Knowland's tone of voice than what he actually said—that he was peeved with Senator Nixon. Rumors are already cropping up that Nixon will be the Vice Presidential candidate with Eisenhower.

Warren told me that he was standing pat, was making no deals, and would support neither Eisenhower nor Taft.

I couldn't help feeling sorry for him. Three times Warren has come to the Republican convention as a possible candidate and three times it has passed him by. He knew, as I knew, that it was going to pass him by this time. In fact, he said so.

"I haven't the money and I can't go out and make the deals necessary to raise the money to stage a real campaign," he told me. "You have to hock your soul in order to do it."

Early this morning I had published a story that the Republican who would be surest of winning against the Democrats was Warren. However, the Chicago *Herald-American* did not publish it, as it has also failed to publish anything else I have written on the convention. Warren told me that he had hunted all over town to find a copy of the column after his office in Sacramento had told him about it, and only found it in *The Washington Post.* The papers in Chicago were publishing exactly what they wanted published according to the candidate they wanted nominated. The *Tribune* published nothing favorable about Eisenhower, the Chicago *Daily News* nothing favorable about Taft; while the *Herald-American* is 1,000 percent for MacArthur.

July 10:   Tom Dewey is really running things at Chicago. His old campaign manager, Herbert Brownell, sits constantly with Eisenhower.

Ike seems bewildered by it all, constantly asks: "What do we do next, Herb?" Dewey had the slickest machine I have ever seen function at Philadelphia in 1948, and he has just about as efficient a machine here.

July 11:   Eisenhower was finally nominated on the first ballot when Stassen switched his votes after the first ballot was taken.

I couldn't help remembering Stassen's talk with Eisenhower in Paris at which time he planned to go into a lot of political strategy, but Ike carefully invited a bunch of other people to dinner so that Stassen couldn't say a word about politics. If Eisenhower had spent a little more time on politics and domestic problems, he might be better prepared today. As it is, it's now clearly apparent that he's a political babe-in-the-woods.

July 13:   On television tonight I called attention to Eisenhower's statement in Chicago that the French were 50 percent atheist and that their moral fiber had deteriorated. In contrast, I showed the film of the French farmer, Marcel Hertault, who had given 100 acres of his land to Eisenhower for his headquarters. I had taken the film when I was in Paris in April.

July 14:   Had a birthday party for Bob Allen. Some of the old New Dealers were present, including the Randolph Pauls, Thurman Arnolds, Oscar Chapmans. No one present thought Eisenhower would be any kind of a President.

July 15:   Lunched with Joe Borkin. He proposes that I go into partnership with Frank Waldrop in producing television programs on film, giving the inside lowdown on Washington. I told him that I did not see how I could go into a partnership with Waldrop. His argument was that I need some kind of political counterbalance to my liberalism in order to keep on the air. Otherwise, he argued, the reactionaries would raise so much hell with the FCC that I would lose out. I told him that I thought I could overcome that obstacle.

July 16:   Was awakened at one o'clock this morning by the AP which had a story from Huntington, West Virginia, that my television program was being kicked off station WSAZ because I had criticized Eisenhower's religion. The interesting thing is that the Huntington

Advertiser has a complete news monopoly on not only two newspapers but the chief radio station and the only television station in West Virginia. Young Rogers, son-in-law of the owner, had the gall to state that they would not permit my views to reach the people of West Virginia during the election, but I might be taken back after November.

Clayton Fritchey says that Truman will not do a thing for Kefauver, but probably will not oppose him.

Talked to Senator Moody about the new Republican National Committee Chairman, Arthur Summerfield, who was embroiled in various campaign contribution frauds in Michigan. It seems to me that the Republicans have left themselves wide open by appointing Summerfield, but I don't see any Democrats on the horizon who have the sense to go into it.

July 17:   Lunched with Oscar. He promised to try to talk to Truman about Kefauver. However, the President has gone out to Walter Reed Hospital to nurse a strange virus infection and will not even see his alternate delegate from Missouri, who wants to know how he is to vote in Chicago.

The Chief Justice came for dinner. I drove him home and talked to him at great length about Truman's attitude toward Kefauver. Vinson made it fairly clear that Truman would never support him. I urged that the man who could best win for the Democrats was Kefauver, who had a tremendous personal following and whose name was a household word throughout the nation.

"But how," asked Vinson, "can you expect the President to support the man who humiliated him in the New Hampshire primary?"

Vinson kept coming back to the idea that Barkley was the man. I couldn't believe this, though the Chief Justice was rather persistent, throwing out hints that Barkley was the man Truman really wanted.

July 18:   Oscar has not been able to see the President. I suspect that the President's illness is a political one.

July 19:   Lunched with Estes and Nancy [Mrs. Kefauver]. Reported that Oscar was trying to warm up Truman, but that it was apparent from my talk with Vinson that Truman leaned toward Barkley. The White House expects Kefauver to lose strength after the first ballot.

Nancy remarked: "It seems strange that after all the work you put in on a nomination, everything can be decided in just a few days. We tramped through the snows of New Hampshire, we stumped almost every town in Florida, we toured all over California, and almost every other state, and now, in a just a few days, all that work will either pay off or be washed away." It was obvious she felt very deeply.

July 20:   Went all-out on the telecast regarding the Kefauver foes in Chicago. Frankie Costello, Artie Elrod, the other hoodlums and their friends who are pulling the wires to block Kefauver.

Stevenson made another statement tonight urging the Illinois delegates not to put up his name. His statements have a ring of sincerity, but a powerful organization is working for him just the same.

July 21:   Stevenson opened the convention, made an excellent speech. Jake Arvey had stacked the galleries and they staged a real demonstration. Driving home afterward, Arvey asked Stevenson: "What do you mean, there's no draft?" referring of course to the demonstration. "Yes," said Stevenson, "I guess I'm hooked."

That evening Stevenson came down to the convention floor to take his seat as an Illinois delegate and heard that ex-Senator Francis Myers of Pennsylvania was working for his nomination. He demanded that Myers quit. About 10 P.M. I bumped into Senator Hennings of Missouri who told me the Vice President was preparing a statement, presumably withdrawing as a candiate. I went on the air almost immediately and scored a pretty good scoop for ABC.

July 22:   Put Joe Clark, the new mayor of Philadelphia, on television as a guest. He told in somewhat guarded language how Francis Myers and Mayor David Lawrence of Pittsburgh were pressuring Pennsylvania delegates not to vote for Kefauver. Privately he elaborated on the manner in which the old bosses do not want a new control of the party. They saw what had happened in Pennsylvania during the write-in vote, also what happened in New Hampshire. Yet a change in party leaders is the only hope for the Democrats. I arranged with Western Union to collect telegrams from all over the country in a "People's Poll." This has shown a tremendous sentiment for Kefauver—about 73 percent.

July 23:   The Chicago newspapers are blitzing for Stevenson. Also the radio commentators. CBS is all out for him. So is ABC's Martin

Agronsky and some of the others. The effect on the delegates is important. However, even the *Herald-American* poll shows that Kefauver is
running 2 to 1 as the most popular candidate in the state of Illinois.

Sam Rayburn, the permanent chairman, is using the same tactics
on the convention that he uses in the House, but not getting away with
it. Public reaction is very sour. The political bosses don't seem to realize
that everything they do and say is recorded before the eyes of millions
of people. This is democracy in the rough and the most important
experience in democracy the American people have had perhaps since
the early days of the nation.

The Democratic battle over the Southern delegates is somewhat
similar to the Republican battle, but in this case the party bosses have
reversed the field and are doing their best to seat the reactionary
Southerners in an effort to keep the party together. This may drive the
Harriman-Kefauver forces into a combination. They are working closer
and closer.

Harriman still seems to think that he has a chance for the Presidency. I have talked to Jim Rowe and some of his other henchmen and
they can't budge him. If he said the word, most of his delegates would
go over to Kefauver, but he won't say it. Stevenson is the man who put
Harriman into the race on the promise that he, Stevenson, would not
run, but Harriman remains loyal to him just the same.

July 24:   All last night the convention battled over seating the Southern delegates.

Previously it had been agreed that they were to be seated if they
took a loyalty oath to support the delegate who was nominated. But
when Senator Byrd of Virginia and Governor Byrnes of South Carolina
threatened to bolt, Blair Moody, Franklin D. Roosevelt, Jr., went along
with McKinney and Arvey in a reversal. They proposed seating the
Southern delegates even without a loyalty oath. Kefauver and Harriman
opposed, but were defeated.

Several times Kefauver forces tried to get Sam Rayburn to adjourn
the convention in order to reinforce their lines, but Sam was intent on
holding a first Presidential ballot that night. He was following exactly
the reverse tactics of Senator Sam Jackson of Indiana, chairman of the
'44 convention, when Henry Wallace wanted to go ahead with the
balloting. At that time the Truman forces, afraid they might be licked,
adjourned the convention through Jackson. This time, Rayburn, figuring he had Kefauver on the run, wanted to continue.

Finally, about 3 A.M., a fire on the floor of the convention, plus a warning from the fire marshal, ended things.

Afterward, the Kefauver and Harriman forces met from 4 to 6 A.M. to try to reach an agreement. They got nowhere. Harriman still thinks he can win.

July 25:   The first ballot showed Kefauver ahead. On the second ballot he picked up strength. Michigan and Minnesota switched to him. This was a real blow to Stevenson and the Truman forces.

It has become increasingly evident to me that Truman is bitterly resentful against Kefauver and that Oscar and Clayton Fritchey were either kidding me or else ignorant of the facts when they thought he was being warmed up. The Truman forces at Chicago are pulling every possible wire to defeat Estes; and having alternately backed Harriman and Barkley, are now determined to nominate Stevenson.

I talked to George Backer, ex-husband of Dottie Schiff, and one of the strong Harriman backers. He told me that Harriman would swing his votes to Stevenson on the third ballot, when it began at about 8 P.M. I went to the Stockyards Inn immediately and told Kefauver at 7:30 that the jig was up, unless he had some strong supporters in the Pennsylvania and Massachusetts delegations who could break down the pull of the party bosses he was lacking. Kefauver asked me what I thought about taking the Vice Presidency. He added that his supporters had urged him to do so but that he was not in favor of it. I told him this was a very difficult thing to advise anyone on, but that I would be inclined to take it. After all, the Vice President, I said, is the second most important job in the nation and could lead to many other things. He said he would talk it over with Nancy and decide. Of course, he never got a chance to decide.

Later that night, Truman, Rayburn, and Stevenson had a huddle in the little room just behind the rostrum, at which time Stevenson proposed Kefauver's name, but Rayburn and Truman were bitterly opposed.

If this campaign has done nothing else, it has healed a marital breach which a year or so ago I thought was fairly certain between the Kefauvers. Nancy has not only been one of Estes' biggest assets, and he not only has appreciated it, but the campaign has brought them together as never before.

Figuring that the convention was about over, I took a plane back to Washington. Sitting in the airport, I saw Kefauver battling his way on the convention floor to the rostrum, Senator Paul Douglas by his side.

July 25: Stevenson was nominated on the third ballot, early this morning, after Kefauver switched his support. Later I talked to Estes on the telephone and also talked to Bill Roberts who was one of his closest advisers at the Stockyards Inn.

Here is a pieced-together picture of what happened. When Kefauver heard that Harriman was going to support Stevenson, Paul Douglas and Rudy Halley, immediately afterward, urged him to go to the convention floor and throw in the sponge. Douglas, who had loyally supported Kefauver and thereby incurred the wrath of Jake Arvey and Stevenson, wanted Estes to turn his delegates over to Douglas, then let Douglas make a speech and turn them over to Stevenson.

Accordingly Kefauver went out on the convention floor and tried to get up to the rostrum and obtain recognition from Rayburn. However, Sam Rayburn refused. Sam of course, hates Kefauver. He had interrupted the course of the balloting on behalf of Virginia and South Carolina, but he refused to interrupt the balloting for Kefauver, despite the fact that Kefauver was ready to make a speech. His delegates stuck by him loyally until the end. Not one vote in California, Ohio, South Dakota, Tennessee, or elsewhere deserted him.

It is Bill Roberts's contention that if Kefauver had not gone out on the floor and thus discouraged other delegates, he could have increased his lead on the third ballot. Bill contends that he had delegates in Pennsylvania and Massachusetts ready to switch to Kefauver.

Roberts also contends that Phil Murray in Washington was ready to call up Jack Kroll and make him reverse his stand. Kroll, who was defeated by Kefauver as a delegate from Ohio, had instructed all CIO delegates to vote for Stevenson, and Murray was ready to countermand this.

I don't know whether Bill Roberts is right, but I do know that the Kefauver delegates were terribly loyal. George Arnold told me that there was not one move inside the California delegation to desert even after the third ballot and that they were stunned when Kefauver threw in the sponge. I also detected a tremendous popular disappointment over the Kefauver defeat. When I finished my last telecast in Chicago after a prediction that Stevenson would win, every electrician and member of the technical staff crowded around me to express their concern.

My daughter, who managed to wangle her way onto the convention floor every night to sit near her husband, talked more optimistically over the telephone from Chicago. She said that after hearing Stevenson's speech she felt that the convention had nominated a wonderful candidate.

This, incidentally, is the first time a political convention has been observed by three generations of Pearsons—my daughter and her husband, who was a delegate from California, together with my grandson, who was not too much impressed with this historical precedent.

October 21:   Spoke in St. Paul. This is about where I came in twenty years ago.

Last time I spoke in St. Paul was on March 3, 1933. The city was in the throes of a depression, the banks were closing. The Dillinger gang had made St. Paul one of the crime centers of the nation. After I spoke, I caught a train to Chicago and an airplane from there to Washington. There were no planes then running between St. Paul and Chicago and the plane I flew in out of Chicago was a decrepit Ford with a leaky gasoline tank. I had to call the pilot's attention to the fact that gasoline was streaming through a petcock before he turned it off. I got back to Washington just in time to see Roosevelt inaugurated.

I have the feeling that I will get back to Washington this time a little early and a little more efficiently, but for the election of another President—probably Eisenhower.

Sitting in the Minnesota Club waiting for the people for whom I was to speak, I noticed Frank B. Kellogg's picture. It reminded me of my experience with the man we called "Nervous Nellie" and who made such a miserable botch of relations with Mexico, Nicaragua, only to go on to fame and idealism as author of the pact to outlaw war.

I have often wondered whether Kellogg's trouble in Mexico wasn't really that of a gentleman who has since caused a great deal of trouble elsewhere—Arthur Bliss Lane. Kellogg, relatively green and a progressive Republican Senator from Minnesota, entrusted Mexican relations to a Wall Street Ambassador named Sheffield and a careerman named Lane. It was Lane who really drafted the now-famous notes "Putting Mexico on Trial Before the World," which soured our relations for the next decade. It was Lane also who toured Wisconsin a month or so ago whipping up sentiment in the Polish communities against the State Department and in favor of Joe McCarthy. He has become one of the most fascist-minded influences in the country. That night, speaking before a rather unfriendly and dyed-in-the-wool audience, I told them of my early experiences with Kellogg and his pact to outlaw war, trying to draw a comparison between Kellogg's successful efforts to get Democratic support for his treaty and the current Republican bitterness over foreign policy. I tried, rather unsuccessfully I think, to show that Eisenhower's current partisanship on foreign policy was a tragic mistake.

October 27:   McCarthy finally made his long-awaited speech tonight. His tactics were somewhat like those against me. He put out publicity teasers indicating what a terrific speech it would be so that his audience was probably terrific. However, the speech was a relative flop.

He didn't speak from the safety of the Senate floor as he did when he went after me. And he dwelt more on Stevenson's associates than he did on the Governor himself.

Jim Farley has declined to answer McCarthy. Stevenson had asked him to as a personal favor, but Jim welshed.

October 28:   The State Department is finally making public the Nixon correspondence to the American Ambassador in Havana, asking for intervention on behalf of Dana Smith,* his "bagman" who dropped $4,200 playing *chockalato* at the Club Sans Souci and then stopped payment on his check. If this had been anyone close to the administration, the AP and UP would have bombarded the State Department with queries immediately after my broadcast Sunday. In contrast, the State Department got one query only, from the Sacramento *Bee.* However, they are going to publish the correspondence anyway. And apparently there are some Republican spies in the State Department

---

*Dana Smith was a Pasadena lawyer and leader of the Southern California Citizens for Eisenhower and Nixon. Questioned about large campaign contributions to Richard Nixon ($18,235 over a two-year period), Smith explained that the money—donated by seventy-six wealthy Southern Californians—had been part of a "supplementary expenditure" purse that had ceased to exist when Senator Nixon received the nomination for Vice President. Disbursement of the committee's monies had been in the hands of the committee headed by Smith. The special fund led directly to Nixon's famous Checkers speech.—ED.

since the Dana Smith letter has been filched from their files. They had to send to Havana to get the original.

More cancellations of the column. The most I have had in any other election has been one or two, but this time we already have a dozen. In addition, papers all over the country are leaving the column out, and I have twenty or so angry letters threatening cancellation.

Sumner Welles and his wife came to dinner. They have sold their house at Oxon Hill, which makes me feel a little old because I remember going down there before the foundation was laid, when Sumner was chopping trees. That was about twenty-five years ago, in which time Sumner built one of the most palatial mansions in Maryland, entertained for Presidents and potentates, dominated the State Department, also was fired, and is now almost a forgotten man. He said that it gave him a strange and unhappy feeling to come to Washington on the train and realize for the first time that he had no place to call home.

Of course, he isn't too badly off because he still has a house in Palm Beach, another in Bar Harbor, and his new wife has quite an estate in New Jersey. The other day I had lunch in his wife's old home on Massachusetts Avenue, now the Cosmos Club. The upper part of the house hasn't been changed too much. It features ornate decorations of the Gay Nineties. The last time I was there at a big dance, Douglas MacArthur was still Chief of Staff and Pat Hurley had just retired as Secretary of War. I remember it so vividly because Hurley accosted me in one of the most disagreeable scenes I have had in a semipublic place —and since then, I have had many. It was shortly after I had been fired by the *Baltimore Sun,* largely thanks to him. His language was unprintable and finally I suggested that he retire to the basement where I could properly answer. He turned on his heel and left.

Stevenson spoke from Madison Square Garden. We watched him on television. He was in top form with a tremendous crowd.

October 29:   Stevenson headquarters have debated backward and forward how they should answer McCarthy. They finally decided that Adlai will not do so. A lot of his stuff is easy to answer because it was so packed with misquotes and lies. For instance, he named a Negro Communist named Cummings as the first Attorney General under Roosevelt, referring I suppose to Homer Cummings.

Lawrence Westbrook telephoned me from Texas, where he is helping Sam Rayburn, to tell me about a conspiracy which began about

two years ago by H. L. Hunt, the big oil man, and a publicity firm called
Watson Associates, to put Nixon into the Vice Presidency. He claims
an untold amount of oil money has been behind Nixon for some time,
and that all this was put over on Eisenhower without his knowing it.

Later, some calls to Texas indicated the story is probably true, but
I am wondering whether Westbrook called me to see if I was wise to
a story which the New York *Herald Tribune* had just broken to the
effect that he was to receive a 5 percent commission on a $9 million
tungsten deal with a Portuguese firm. The Democratic Committee, for
which Westbrook now works, promptly fired him. Reading the facts
carefully, it looks to me as if Lawrence had been made the goat,
inasmuch as he virtually completed the deal before he joined the
National Committee. However, for political reasons, I don't think the
committee had any other choice.

November 1: Joe Borkin claims the undecided vote will go for Stevenson. Gallup refuses to make any prediction. His latest poll shows
Stevenson and Eisenhower running about even.

November 2: I finally predicted an Eisenhower victory. I base this on
two factors: first, my own observation is that the undecided vote is not
going to go for the Democrats, the way it formerly did.

Second, cowardice.

I figure that if I am wrong on Eisenhower, I can still live with my
Stevenson friends. But if I am wrong on Stevenson, I can never live
with my Eisenhower friends.

Nixon is demanding a lot of retractions. In a speech at Long Beach
this week, he threatened jail to critics of himself and Eisenhower. A
gang of roughnecks in his entourage beat up several people in his
crowds carrying anti-Nixon signs.

November 3: I was just able to get through the telecast last night
before coming down with a high fever. I guess it's the election.

November 4: Still have a fever; unable to go to New York and report
the election returns. Watched them on TV, however. Winchell was
jubilant. At midnight he predicted Eisenhower—a fairly safe prediction because it was obvious even at eight o'clock that Eisenhower was
going to win. Winchell even conceded on behalf of Stevenson.

November 5:   It's pretty much of a landslide for Eisenhower. However, there are several very important state victories for the Democrats: Montana, where Mike Mansfield won out for Senator; Washington, where Scoop Jackson defeated Senator Cain; and Massachusetts, where Jack Kennedy defeated Cabot Lodge. I don't know whether this latter is a plus or minus. Lodge was a good Senator. Kennedy probably will revert to the thinking of his old man.

Tom Mechling lost in Nevada by a very narrow margin, due to the boneheadedness of the ILGWU's Dave Dubinsky. He had sent some money out to Mechling and made the mistake of sending the record to the clerk of the House of Representatives at an early date. He could have held it back perfectly legally until after Election Day. In Nevada, they connect Dubinsky with Communism, though his union has been one of the foremost battlers against Communism.

At 8 P.M., when Eisenhower went on television last night, he was tight. It was a little obvious from watching him, but the newspapermen say he was really something of a potted palm.

November 6:   Art Hachten, formerly of International News Service, now with Senator Brewster, came up to the press gallery to tell the superintendent that about fifty mush-mouths and socialists who had been writing anti-Republican news would be cleaned out of the gallery.

November 7:   Harry Hoyt called up from New York. Wants me to go on television again December 24 on Dumont, but with a 50 percent cut in salary. I think it may be a smart move for me to go to Korea briefly, just before Eisenhower gets there.

November 9:   My last telecast.

November 11:   The head of my news syndicate called from New York to urge that I not go to Korea. He thinks I should stay and write the news from Washington. I argued that it was necessary to give a change of pace to the column to keep recalcitrant papers in line. The Kansas City *Star*, one of the oldest papers, has just canceled, also a monopoly paper. It will be interesting to see just how soon the Justice Department drops the present grand jury investigation of the *Star*'s monopoly tactics.

Dinner with Kay Halle and the David K. E. Bruces. I remember twenty-five years ago when Bruce was courting Ailsa Mellon. He had just been admitted to the Foreign Service and she was the most eligible debutante in town, daughter of the Secretary of the Treasury and good-looking in addition. Now Bruce is Under Secretary of State and married to his former secretary, who is a lot more beautiful than Ailsa, and more charming—in fact, the most beautiful woman I have seen in a long time.

Bruce thinks that if the U.N. sends a commission into North Africa to study the French-Arab question, France will bolt the U.N. Likewise, the Union of South Africa would bolt if the U.N. studied the race question there.

November 12:   The hearing on McCarthy seems to be all set except that the chairman is missing. He went out to Lincoln, Nebraska, on Monday but hasn't been heard of since.* Senator Carl Hayden has come back from Arizona ready to bolster the committee and seems determined to go through with it. At lunch Bill Fulbright said that he would pep up both Hennings and, if possible, Hendrickson.

I talked to Senator Ives, who later talked to Hendrickson, pointing out that the best thing that could happen to Eisenhower is for McCarthy to be blocked from the Senate. It would take a recalcitrant Senator out of his hair, a man who would never support him, and it would permit Governor Kohler of Wisconsin to appoint a new man who would.

Also talked to General Ted Clark, formerly on Eisenhower's staff, who promised to get hold of some New Jersey Republicans to put more backbone into Hendrickson. Clark has just come back from the Far East. He says Eisenhower will equip and activate ten regimental combat teams from Formosa for use in Korea; also will use Navicerts to blockade the Chinese coast. I asked him if this did not involve considerable risk. He said that there was no risk greater than that of prolonging the Korean War.

Performed the unforgivable sin of forgetting my wife's sixteenth wedding anniversary.

---

*Senator Thomas Carey Hennings, Jr. [D-Mo.], chairman of the Senate Elections Committee, had frequent bouts with the bottle. Sober, he was tremendously effective. He made a strenuous effort to block the seating of Senator Joe McCarthy.—ED.

November 13:   Senator Benton telephoned from New York to say that Tom Hennings had been located at the Plaza Hotel, Room 1627, where he has been locked up, dead drunk, since Monday. He was seen at Joe Madden's nightclub, guzzling martinis. This is the first time I have known Tom to get off the wagon since he was in the House of Representatives, though I had suspected that he has sometimes fallen by the wayside. I had the unpleasant task of calling Elizabeth [Hennings].

She had telephoned Lincoln, Nebraska, and talked to Jim Lawrence of the Missouri Valley Commission. Jim was embarrassed as the dickens because apparently Tom never came to Nebraska at all.

I offered to go up to New York to bring Tom back but Elizabeth called later in the day to say that he had come back under his own steam, apparently sober. She has put him to bed and it will take him a couple of days to get back to normal. She is not sure whether he is going to be able to preside at the McCarthy hearing Monday or not. Joe Madden, whom I reached on the telephone later, swears that he had never given Tom a drink.

Lunched with Johnny Hays, who was on Ike's staff for three years. He says that if you don't oppose Ike on anything you can get along fine by just saying: "Let's not do it that way now; let's do it that way a year later."

Dined with the Tom Finletters and met at least one general and his wife, the Nate Twinings of the Air Force, who were for Stevenson. The Egyptian and Austrian Ambassadors had the probably interesting experience of listening to all the Americans present bemoan the election and predict what was going to happen.

None of the predictions were very rosy.

The military men present say that Ike's chief trouble is that he hates to read or study anything.

November 16:   Gordon Dean announced the explosion of the hydrogen bomb at five-thirty today just before I went on the air. Public reaction is blasé, rather numb.

Two years ago when I first revealed that the United States was considering a hydrogen bomb, there was a terrific furor. Papers were full of the news. I bumped into the story in a peculiar manner. I was calling on Louis Johnson, then Secretary of Defense, and was shown into an outer waiting room when Dean Acheson walked out.

He and Louis were at loggerheads on most things, especially Formosa, and I asked Louis afterward whether they had had another wrangle over arming China's troops on Formosa. He said no, they were talking about the hydrogen bomb. This was the first intimation that the question of building an H-bomb was even under discussion.

November 18:   Ellis Arnall, calling on Truman today, was shown a series of books Truman had prepared for Eisenhower. "I wish that someone had prepared some of these things for me when I took over," Truman said. He told Ellis that he was going to do his best to cooperate with Eisenhower in every possible way for the smooth transfer of government, and he really seems to mean it. Though he was sore as blazes at Ike during the campaign, his temper has cooled and he is terribly anxious to have this transition period run smoothly.

He showed Ellis various charts giving information on defense production and with a touch of pride he said: "We haven't done as badly as our critics say we have."

Basically Truman, with all his faults, has a great feeling that this country must come ahead of personalities. If he had showed this more frequently during his seven years in office, there wouldn't be such bitter resentment against him today.

Eisenhower arrives for his conference at the White House today and it will be interesting to see what happens.

November 20:   Eisenhower appointed John Foster Dulles Secretary of State; Charles E. Wilson, Secretary of Defense; and Governor McKay of Oregon, Secretary of the Interior—all of them a surprise to me. He told me in Paris last spring that he had been talking to Dulles about foreign affairs and seemed to set great store by his advice. However, I figured that Dulles, who is a didactic, somewhat domineering person, would rub Ike the wrong way. Apparently, however, Eisenhower is going to appoint executives and let them run their own show pretty much as he did with his field commanders during the war.

Bernard Baruch had recommended Charles E. Wilson of General Electric for Defense, but Eisenhower appointed the General Motors Wilson instead—a better man. Wilson will be good in directing production but whether he can curb the turbulent military chiefs is something else again. He is going to have a terrific battle on his hands from the Navy and the Air Force almost immediately over atomic-powered aircraft carriers.

November 21:   Gael Sullivan says that when he, Gael, became Assistant Postmaster General and Bob Hannegan first took him over to the White House to introduce him, Truman said: "There are just two things I want you to do. Never talk to Drew Pearson and stay away from Tom Corcoran."

Eisenhower is continuing the same big business trend for his Cabinet, with George Humphrey for Secretary of the Treasury and Herb Brownell as Attorney General. Stassen, who I thought would get Labor, has been made Mutual Security Administrator. I remember in Munich a little over a year ago Stassen was trying to see Eisenhower but missed connections. Humphrey is head of one of the biggest holding corporations in the U.S.A. He is certain to want to reduce taxes in the higher brackets.

November 22:   Senator Wayne Morse of Oregon came for breakfast in the country. He was critical of Governor McKay's appointment as Secretary of Interior; says he is a small-town garage-owner who wired Morse asking that if he couldn't vote for Tideland's Oil to at least not vote at all. Morse wired back that he was not elected by the people of Oregon to run out on voting. Morse says he will make a pretense of opposing McKay's confirmation though in the end he will vote for it.

Morse thinks he is licked for reelection in 1956.* The Republicans are ganging up on him as never before. He also thinks the Democrats will see this as an opportunity to elect their own man. However, he says he isn't going to pull his punches. I suggested that he might at least give the new Cabinet members an opportunity to show their lack of worth before criticizing them and that his immediate criticism might turn public opinion sour on him. However, he argued that you might as well call a spade a spade.

The new black Angus bull we got is played out. Nineteen cows were too much for him. He had to be locked up.

---

*Morse had been a Republican until 1952, when he became an independent; by the time his election rolled around in 1956, he was a fully converted Democrat.—Ed.

Luvie and I dined with Hugo Black alone. He is fearful that the new administration will bring on fascism and war. He sees increasing encroachments on freedom of the press. Hugo is still somewhat bitter, though in a way philosophical, about the terrible treatment the press gave him at the time he was revealed as a former member of the KKK. There were threats on his life and the Justice Department offered to send a guard. They hounded him all through Europe. Sulzberger of *The New York Times,* according to Hugo, said he was going to drive him off the Supreme Court, while Roy Howard made similar threats. However, Hugo says that the press has got to be protected just the same. Newspapers don't realize that when a man is prevented from talking on a street corner that curtailment of free speech also may become a curtailment of the press.

He told of a minority opinion he had written permitting a man to use a loudspeaker which disturbed the neighborhood. The majority of the Court felt that the city had a right to curtail the loudspeaker but Hugo felt that this might be a small beginning of erosion on civil liberties.

November 23:   Dined with George Baker. He is resigning from the State Department, feels John Dulles is a tragedy. George knows some of Dulles's children, points out that the driving ambition of their father to become Secretary of State has alienated all of them. Avery became a priest, at which time the family gave him up as dead. The daughter married a truck driver, seldom sees her father, while John, Jr., has gone to Mexico to be as far away as possible.

I have not seen Allen Dulles, though he lives across the street from me, for about twenty years. But today, just before the broadcast he hailed me from across the street. I don't know why he did. I was in a hurry to get to the radio station and didn't get much chance to talk with him. But coincidentally, I had just got out the file on his brother, preparatory to writing a critical series on him.

November 25:   Senator Humphrey of Minnesota came for lunch with Ilya Lopert, the movie producer. Lopert, just back from Paris, says that everyone over there is laughing at us for barring Charlie Chaplin. They think we have gone nuts. He also has held up showing *High Noon,* not so much because the American Legion has protested, but because its producer is also working on *The Caine Mutiny* and too much publicity from the Legion would probably sour the Navy from helping out on the *Caine Mutiny.*

Meanwhile, Senator Nixon is going to campaign for removing all federal art from post office buildings if it was painted by anyone remotely connected with the many so-called front organizations of the 1930s.*

Humphrey says that the Republicans are planning to run Congressman Judd against him and that the blackout on the press in Minnesota is working toward that end.

November 26:   Clayton Fritchey said he just discovered at the White House that Attorney General McGrath had him tailed last year and warned Truman not to hire him because he was a friend of mine. Truman hired him anyway.

Drove to Swarthmore with Hugo Black for Thanksgiving. Luvie was already in New York. I tried to persuade Hugo to go by train, but he insisted that he liked to drive. We had a good time except that he drove so slowly. Finally I got the wheel and I think he didn't have a good time because I drove so fast. Anyway we got there in time for a pleasant evening with his daughter and my family.

November 28:   Wayne Morse telephoned to say that he was going to announce that he would vote with the Republicans chiefly because he believes Eisenhower should have full responsibility and that a divided control of Congress would given him an excuse to duck that responsibility.

November 29:   Eisenhower left for Korea last night. The security was so tight that not even the Pentagon was sure he was going. No written indications passed between New York and the Pentagon regarding the time of departure or anything else. Eisenhower's headquarters kept on announcing the important appointees just as if Eisenhower were still in New York. The press was informed that he watched the Army-Navy game on television, and a list of appointments for Monday was issued.

---

*Despite Nixon, the works stand today in many older federal buildings, monuments to WPA's efforts to help depression-starved artists.—Ed.

November 30: In order to keep up the myth of Ike's presence, Eisenhower headquarters announced the appointment of Winthrop Aldrich as Ambassador to Great Britain and Nelson Rockefeller as head of a committee to study the executive branch of the government.

The FBI called the Washington police to say that somebody in California was threatening my life, and so a detective went to the broadcasting station with me. I think it was nothing.

ABC balked at letting me mention Eisenhower's heart condition on the air. Of course, it should have been mentioned before he was elected. I hinted at it as best I could, but tempers run so high that people won't believe you even if you do try to report a candidate's health. One heart specialist said that Eisenhower could not possibly live out his four years. He had to have a scooter carry him between golf holes at Denver because of the altitude, though he got along better at Augusta, which is almost at sea level.

December 1: Talked to Tom Hennings about the foolishness of emphasizing at a recent press conference that he was at Lincoln, Nebraska, when actually he was at the Hotel Plaza in New York. I reminded Tom that the McCarthy boys were watching him and that he ought to be careful about his whereabouts and about stating he was one place when he actually was in another. Tom unfortunately lied. He said he was in New York on a law case and that his office and wife knew where he was. I couldn't very well tell him that I had been talking to his wife and that she had called Lincoln, Nebraska, and had a very embarrassing experience with Jim Lawrence about the fact that Tom was not there.

Tom insists that he is going to push the McCarthy case to a finish; explains that the failure to call witnesses is not going to prejudice the final report inasmuch as the report will consist largely of documents and that every document introduced will be accompanied by a sworn oath by the investigator who obtained it.

He stalled on doing anything about Nixon. Meanwhile, however, Senator Fulbright has given both to Hennings and to Senator Hayden a copy of the Union Oil Company letter to Frank Wolckman* of Sun

---

*In the diary entry for December 7, the name appears as "Wolkmann." Neither spelling appears in *Poor's Register of Directors,* but there is a listing for a Franklyn Waltman of the Sun Oil Company in the 1959 edition.—ED.

Oil stating that Union had paid Nixon $52,000 in 1950. This was the first year he became Senator.

December 3:   Taft let loose the first inevitable break with Eisenhower. He blasted the new Secretary of Labor, Martin Durkin. Durkin was appointed at the last minute because Ike suddenly found he had failed to appoint either a Catholic or a Jew to his Cabinet.

December 4:   John Bennett, here for dinner, told about his talk with Eisenhower last Christmas when I sent Bennett to Paris with the Eisenhower Christmas cards. What Ike was chiefly concerned about was the General Patton letters and the fear that Mrs. Patton would release them. These are the letters in which Patton tells of Eisenhower's affair with Kay Summersby and his desire for a divorce. Eisenhower wanted to know what the effect on the public would be if Mrs. Patton did release them and seemed chiefly worried because apparently Mamie didn't know he even contemplated a divorce.

December 5:   Eisenhower announced from Korea that there was no panacea for peace—exactly what Stevenson had repeatedly said all during the campaign.

Mike DiSalle has come back to help out on price control. He tells me that Tighe Woods did not resign as he indicated to the press but was peremptorily fired by Truman because of a personal entanglement.

I remember when I was in Rome about this time in 1947, getting a trans-Atlantic telephone call because Truman was firing Jim Landis from the chairmanship of the Civil Aeronautics Board. The real reason was pressure by Pan American Airways, whom Jim had opposed; but knowing Truman's ideas on morality, they used the weapon with Truman that Landis had been living with another woman for years. He had, but he also married her.

December 7:   John Moore, of the Senate Rules Committee, went up to Philadelphia to interview Frank Wolkmann [sic] of Sun Oil regarding the Nixon letter. They kissed it off as a phony and Moore seemed to be satisfied.

December 11:   Truman held a press conference in which he blasted MacArthur for his statement that MacArthur had a solution to the

Korean War, but had never been consulted. One of Truman's secretaries with whom I dined later in the day, said that the press conference had been very carefully staged with cameramen and newsreels admitted. Truman handled the first part of the press conference very well. He told how he had flown three-fourths of the way across the Pacific to get MacArthur's advice on the Korean War, how MacArthur had told him the war would be over before Christmas, how he had relied on MacArthur's advice, and how that advice led to one of the most tragic military catastrophes in American history.

But after the cross-questions which followed, someone asked Truman whether he also considered Eisenhower's trip to Korea "demagoguery," the same word he had applied to MacArthur. Truman replied "yes." As a result, the press has been bellowing all day that the President called Eisenhower a demagogue. Actually, he didn't. It was a question he never should have answered—just like the question as to whether he considered the Alger Hiss case a red herring, which again were words put into Truman's mouth.

December 12:   Talked to [Secretary of the Senate] Leslie Biffle about the Nixon letter, the one from Union Oil in California to Sun Oil in Philadelphia, stating that the former gave Nixon $52,000 in 1950. Biffle promised to talk to Senator Hayden about the letter and get it investigated. I left a carbon copy with Biffle. I told Biffle that Moore had made a very sketchy investigation in Philadelphia, and it looked as if the matter would be dropped.

December 14:   Eisenhower returned home. He's been resting on the cruiser *Helena* and was in Hawaii. He has held no press conferences, announced no press conferences regarding Korea. Yet there's been no squawk from any publisher or newspaper editor. If Truman had remained this silent it would have been headlined.

December 19:   Tom Hennings has been away all week. The Senate Elections Committee is nearing a showdown on the McCarthy report. In fact, it's completed, but Tom has not been around and queries by Senator Hayden get only evasive replies that Tom is in the Middle West working on the Missouri River Commission.

December 20:   The [Senate] Elections Committee held a final meeting to put together the McCarthy report. But Tom did not show.

Senator Hendrickson of New Jersey came down for the meeting, but nothing was accomplished. Another meeting will be held Monday.

December 22:   Again Hennings, the Chairman of the Elections Committee, did not show. I called Elizabeth and found that he finally straggled in at 1 A.M. She had not heard from him for more than a week. He usually telephones her when he is late, but this time she heard nothing. He is pretty well under the weather and the doctor said he couldn't possibly get to the Senate until Wednesday. Elizabeth said with a little luck she might be able to get him back to his office by Tuesday though she warned that he would be very irritable.

My family arrived from Los Angeles. Bad weather. The plane was about three hours late. George and Ellen slept most of the way and apparently Drew and Georgie had the run of the plane with the passengers taking care of them.

December 23:   Tom has not sobered up yet. Hayden had postponed any meeting until next Monday, December 28. They lost one whole valuable week in getting the McCarthy report out to the public.

December 26:   I called Elizabeth. Tom is still not sober. He has been sleeping all day and getting up in the evening to drink again. Since Elizabeth keeps nothing in the house he walks out and gets it someplace, returning early in the morning.

I finally went up to his home about 5:30 when Elizabeth said he would be getting up and sat downstairs until he came down. He was apparently sober but shaky. I told him that I had been through a lot of things with him and hoped to go through a lot more, but he had simply got to cut out drinking. I told him that it was all over the capital and so far the press had protected him but they wouldn't do it much longer.

He took it extremely well, thanked me and seemed quite grateful. Then I suggested that we go out to dinner and to a movie. I was a little afraid that he might stray back that evening and that if we could get him through one evening, he would be O.K. He agreed.

So Elizabeth, Tom, and I went out to dinner at Fan and Bill's. Tom was in pretty good shape, had a good meal, after which he said he was tired and thought that he would rather rest than go to the movies. So Elizabeth took him home.

December 28: Tom was in good shape for the Senate meeting, but Hendrickson didn't show. However, Hayden and Hennings decided to send the financial report up to him and get his approval by telephone. He had already seen most of the report the week before, and Hayden had taken the bull by the horns and ordered the Government Printing Office to get it into type.

I talked to Biffle about organizing a drive to prevent McCarthy from taking his seat. He agreed to work on it. Then I also called Bill Evjue of *The Capital Times* in Madison [Wisconsin] and asked him to organize petitions and perhaps a delegation to come to Washington.

December 30: The messenger carrying the report did not get to Hendrickson last night as expected. Hendrickson's executive assistant did not take it to him direct but went to New York instead. He gave no explanation why but it looks as if it was delaying tactics.* Meanwhile, Hennings got hold of Hendrickson and sent the report to him direct by his own messenger. However, it did not get there until the middle of the afternoon. Meanwhile, I talked to Senator Ives, who called Hendrickson and asked him to get busy on the report. Hendrickson said it had not arrived but Ives quoted me as saying it had been sent to him. Nothing is likely to make Hendrickson sorer than to know I am in on this.

December 31: Went to New York for the telecast. Meanwhile, Hendrickson did not give his O.K. Most of the day Jenner, Welker, and Dirksen phoned him and finally McCarthy flew up to see him in New Jersey. Meanwhile, also, Hayden and Hennings held a five-hour conversation with him trying to work out detailed changes in the report.

Hendrickson interrupted the conversation every so often to talk to other people—probably McCarthy or various Republicans. Anyway the report was not signed. And tomorrow is New Year's Day, when the Government Printing Office will not be open.

---

*Time was critically short to get a committee vote before the new Senate convened in January under Republican control.—ED.

1953

–»» · ««–

_____

January 1: Hendrickson let drop the remark early in the week that the report would not be published until Friday [January 2]. His tactics now also become obvious. If the report is not published until Friday, only twelve hours will be left for the Senate to consider it and for public opinion to get steamed up.

Finally he came to Washington at noon today. Hennings met him about one o'clock and, putting his arm around him, said: "Bob, let's go over and get something to eat. This is a holiday."

Tom then poured six martinis into him before lunch. How Tom was able to do this without getting plastered himself is a miracle. I think Tom must have stuck to Coca-Colas, which he always does at my house anyway. However, Tom remained sober, and Hendrickson, virtually pie-eyed, finally signed the report.

Tom and Hayden had detected indications over the telephone the day before that Hendrickson had been drinking heavily, so they decided to apply McCarthy's tactics themselves.

However, Hendrickson managed to extract one promise—namely, that the report would not be released until 4 P.M. Friday. This prevented the Democratic caucus from considering it on Friday morning. It also prevented the press from having a look at the report before the Senate meets Saturday noon.

January 2: Jack Anderson and I talked with about half the Democratic Senators and three or four Republicans about stopping McCarthy. The Democratic caucus met at 10 A.M. and we posted Anderson of New Mexico, Kilgore of West Virginia, Green of Rhode Island, together with Hunt of Wyoming, Kefauver, Douglas of Illinois, Murray of Montana, and Fulbright to raise the question

245

It was raised with a fairly favorable reaction.

Just before the caucus, Hennings told me that he and Hayden were bound not to discuss the report until 4 P.M. I asked Tom, however, if he wouldn't agree at the caucus to say that the report was coming out at 4 P.M. and that another caucus should be called afterward. Fulbright proposed such a resolution—namely, to call a second caucus, whereupon Hayden came over and asked him to withdraw it. He said it would embarrass him with Hendrickson if it became known that a second caucus was called. Therefore, it was left to the discretion of Lyndon Johnson to call a caucus.

I talked to Lyndon late in the afternoon. It was obvious that he was going to call no caucus. He had just been made Democratic floor leader by Southern reactionaries and he felt supremely in the saddle. Jack talked to Senator Richard Russell of Georgia who said that he would vote against McCarthy taking his seat, but he would not ask Lyndon to call a caucus.

I remember the days when Lyndon used to call me from Texas saying he had a tight primary fight and asking me to make this or that prediction regarding him.

January 3:   Russell, Johnson, and Hennings remained in Biffle's office until midnight last night figuring out various strategies but most of the time was taken up with plans to kill the filibuster. I talked to Tom just before breakfast and they have no intention of calling a second caucus.

Fulbright said he was so upset over the runout powder that he couldn't sleep. However, last night I remained on the telephone until about midnight and talked among other people to Don Dawson, who had President Truman call Hayden at 8 A.M.

I supplied him with quite a little ammunition regarding the vote setup, including the fact that three Republicans, Potter of Michigan, Payne of Maine, and Purtell of Connecticut, would not be able to vote, due to the fact that their names came after McCarthy's. This, together with three or four [anti-McCarthy] Republicans, such as Morse, Mrs. Smith, and Ives, I argued, would tip the balance against McCarthy.

However, Truman was not able to sway Hayden. He remained adamant. He argued that McCarthy would be seated and this would be publicized as a terrific victory for him. He said that Taft was cracking the whip to get McCarthy seated and there wasn't a chance of winning any Republican votes. Hayden was certainly right on the latter point. Earlier, Young of North Dakota had promised to stay away when the vote came up, but this morning he said he would have to renege. I talked to Langer, who also said that he would have to vote with the rest to seat McCarthy. However, Tobey told me that he would certainly vote not to seat McCarthy except without prejudice to remove him by majority vote later if the question came up. Tobey was as good as his word in that he talked to Mrs. Smith and also called Hayden. However, Hayden discouraged him.

In the end, nothing happened. Chavez of New Mexico and Langer were seated only without prejudice to removal by majority vote later. But McCarthy took his seat completely unchallenged. There was not one objection. The press rose in the gallery and looked forward expectantly, but not one Senator had the courage to raise his voice.

Jack [Anderson] urged Kefauver to make a request that the Senate seat McCarthy in the same category as Chavez and Langer on the ground that the report was 400 pages long and impossible to study. But Kefauver said he had enough trouble getting reelected in Tennessee without having McCarthy campaign against him. Matt Neeley, whom Jack also approached, said that his office would be right across from McCarthy's, and he just felt that it would be unpleasant to tangle with him.

Duff, with whom I talked, weaseled; Maybank also weaseled; Ed Johnson of Colorado, Ellender of Louisiana, and Magnuson of Washington would have voted but they lacked the courage to do the challenging.

McCarthy put out a blatant statement that the Democrats did not dare unseat him. If what they said was true, then I did not deserve to sit in the Senate, McCarthy told the press. But even this did not faze the Democrats. It was the most cowardly exhibition I have seen in Washington since I came here twenty-seven years ago.

January 9: Went to see Senator Tobey, who has been trying to block the ABC merger with Paramount. I saw him on Monday [January 5], when he promised to let the FCC know that he was reversing himself and was not opposed to the merger. I argued to Tobey that whether you like combines or not, this looks like one which is essential to compete with RCA and NBC's combine, and the vast resources of CBS. Without some kind of financial support, ABC will go to the wall, which is exactly what Tobey's friend David Sarnoff of RCA wants.

In talking to Tobey today, however, I made no headway. He has sent a telegram to the Justice Department demanding an investigation and in an embarrassed sort of way made it clear that his previous promise to me was out. The reason, I finally discovered, was his old friend Montana's former Senator Burt Wheeler. Wheeler represents Zenith radios, which doesn't want the merger. I also hear that Wheeler's law firm has hired Tobey's son.

January 12: Gardner Jackson, now with the CIO, lunched with me. Gardner is worried over the religious issue inside the CIO. The Catholics are making a tremendous play, he claims, to take over the union, and there was much bitterness against Walter Reuther, a Lutheran, when he became president. A priest spoke at Phil Murray's death and talked about the "agnostics" who opposed Murray inside the CIO.

January 13: Went to see Senator Russell to suggest that he look into the background of Harold Talbott, the new Secretary for Air. I showed him copies of the Charles Evans Hughes probe on Talbott at the end of the first war. He seemed interested.

Lunched with Jack Kennedy, the new Senator from Massachusetts. He has the makings of a first-class Senator or a first-class fascist —probably depending on whether the right kind of people take the trouble to surround him. His brother is now counsel for McCarthy's committee and he himself has been appointed on McCarthy's committee, though Jack claims against his wishes. There was a time when I didn't quite understand why F.D.R. broke with Joe Kennedy. But the more I see of Jack, the more I can understand it.

January 15: The editor of the Grand Island, Nebraska, paper, threatened to cancel the column because I told about the Republican liquor club opposite the capitol. It will be amazing if the public knows one-tenth of the news going on in Washington with 80 percent of the newspapers anxious to hush up any Republican scandals.

Dr. Bruner of the Yugoslav Embassy came to see me about the Vatican. He reported the amazing fact that the seven Catholic bishops who came to see Tito not only asked for the interview but waited until relations were broken with the Vatican before so doing. The Vatican opposed any settlement between the Church and the government.

I suppose there will be hell to pay if I write this.

January 16:   Lunched with Oscar. The new Secretary of the Interior is moving in so we lunched at the old dining room on the fifth floor where Ickes and I have lunched hundreds of times. I felt a little sentimental about it.

Oscar let his hair down about a lot of things: how McGranery is miffed over his stand on the oil companies in the Near East, how the Cabinet is conspiring to keep Truman from getting lonesome on the afternoon of January 20. (They are beginning lunch at 2 P.M. and plan to keep him pretty well oiled until his train leaves at 6:30.) And how he persuaded Truman to switch Tidelands Oil over to Naval Reserve. I asked Oscar about the report that Continental Oil had promised him a retainer and that was his reason for opposing the Justice Department on its prosecution of oil companies in the Near East. Oscar denied this. He then told me of the tremendous pressure the oil companies had put on him regarding Tidelands Oil; one company offered him a $100,000 retainer.

I think I can honestly say that Oscar is one Cabinet member who will go out of office untainted and untouched. I don't mean by that that he is the only one, but his record of liberalism has stood out consistently and valiantly through the twenty years. I helped a little bit in working out Oscar's arrangement with Marcus Cohn and Leonard Marks. He will be their senior partner. He turned down several offers from more affluent firms.

January 29:   A "Miss Brown" phoned me. Obviously not her real name. She said that a tall man who had worked for Senator Thomas of Oklahoma and whose name began with a "C" had been using Room 840 of the Washington Hotel with a girl from the Hibbs Building to do some investigating for McCarthy.

I couldn't quite make out whether Miss Brown was Mrs. Cullum or not. She said that previously Cullum had learned about the source of some of my information through a member of my staff, and had found out that a member of his family (his wife) was talking to me.

Miss Brown said they went into the room about noon, and were typing up some material for McCarthy regarding election probes. I couldn't make out whether this was supposed to be a sex case. Miss Brown said they had been chased out of the Willard, where they once had a room, said they were going after former DNC chairman Bill Boyle and some others around Truman. Most interesting information was that Cullum had been seen at the Shoreham with Li Kung, who was working with him on buying soybeans. Kung, she said, also visits McCarthy. The Chinese have enough money in their bank in New York to corner the soybean market but they were afraid I might find out about it. This fits into the fact that McCarthy was buying soybeans and that the Chinese Nationalists did just about corner the market before Korea.

Clem Norton of Boston called me last night to say that McCarthy hung out in what is called the Bird Circuit around the Grand Central Terminal in New York. The Bird Circuit refers to the Blue Parrot and Golden Pheasant, two shady bars used by homos.

Clem said he was sitting in the Carroll Arms Hotel at 10 A.M. yesterday when a man rushed in, sat down at a little table, and the bartender scarcely looked up, and without a word from the visitor poured a double Scotch and soda. The man was our friend McCarthy.

February 4: Lunched with Harry Hoyt and his advertising vice president. They are definitely canceling the television program, also want me to take a 50 percent cut in radio.

February 5: Left for Berlin on the Belgian airline—Sabena—with some misgivings. Luvie, as I left, was running a temperature of 103.

February 6: Arrived in Berlin relatively on time. Mark Sullivan's son-in-law had met me at the Brussels Airport for a short visit. Ambassador Myron Cowen did not meet me. The last time I talked to him was by transatlantic telephone regarding the $12,000 payment he made to Congressman Keogh of Brooklyn in regard to a liquor license which had been denied by the Alcohol Tax Unit.

In Berlin, Leo Cherne and I stayed at the Hotel Kempinski, rather a gaudy place, newly built with the help of Marshall Plan money. Hitherto, I always stayed at one of the American Army hotels in Berlin. They are much cheaper, but I think it is time we got back to living on the German economy. Cherne is newly elected president of the International Rescue Committee.

February 8: Lunched with Mayor Reuter. He is by all odds the most militant and effective anti-Communist in this part of the world. He was a little worried, as was the State Department, that Eisenhower's message to Congress proposing the end of secret agreements would land Berlin in the soup. He recalled that Eisenhower had made a secret agreement with the Russians himself—in London, prior to the Normandy landing—that Berlin would be under a four-power control. That was the reason Berlin is now surrounded, an oasis of democracy with the Red Army round about.

February 9:   Flew to Paris by Air France, always a precarious journey in their rather dilapidated planes.

February 10:   Had a fine talk with General Ridgway. He strikes me as a more practical and down-to-earth person than Eisenhower. He doesn't have the same charm and gift of gab, but he is a military man who I felt had a strong understanding of civilian problems. He told me that he is completely hedged in, however, by civilian politicians on NATO, particularly the British. Originally, they had estimated that infrastructure—namely, air bases, telegraph lines, roads, and buildings —would cost £400 million. The military men whittled this [by] £176 million, whereupon the civilian chiefs arbitrarily cut it by £83 million more. When Ridgway made a speech at a NATO meeting recently regarding the foolhardiness of this cut, he was not permitted to give his speech out to the press.

Also I had a visit with General Gruenther. He is getting along fine with Ridgway, despite the fact that he wanted Ridgway's job. Gruenther strikes me as a man deeply devoted to the United European Army. It was significant that both he and Ridgway talked about the difficulties of building a military establishment when they had no civilian unity on which to base it.

They both wanted more friendship on the part of the people of France and Germany and urged me to try to help out on it. They pointed out that as military men they could not meddle in civilian matters. When I talked to Eisenhower about this a year ago, he did have the power but refused to exercise it. Since then, Ridgway's power has been drastically curtailed.

Lunched with Pierre de Luce of the Foreign Office, who was extremely frank in telling me that the United European Army Pact would never be ratified. His argument, obviously sincere, sounds very much like the argument of the isolationists who defeated Wilson's League of Nations. However, I am quite sure that a great many Frenchmen feel that same way. Apparently Bidault, Minister of Foreign Affairs, is one of them. De Luce said that Bidault had not been at all frank with Dulles in describing the French attitude toward the European Army pact.

Flew back to Washington.

February 23: Tom O'Conor, former editor of the Scranton *Times*, now with the government, has been talking to a Secret Service man who is concerned about the way things are going at the White House. There has been more wire-tapping ordered than ever before. The Secret Service, hitherto not in the wire-tapping business except on counterfeiting cases, placed a tap in the office of Senator Wayne Morse. It has been picking up everything he says.

Two perverts have been fired from the White House. The chief telephone operator, Miss Hachmeister, has been fired, though she only had a short time to go before getting retirement. Reason was that she lived near Mamie at the Wardman Park Hotel during the war, and Mamie used to confide her troubles about Ike's girl friend.

February 24: I went up to Wayne Morse's office, told him about the microphone. We made a superficial search, couldn't find anything. However, these new microphones are not much bigger than a half dollar and don't have to have any wires attached. The Secret Service man said that the plant had been arranged in Morse's furniture when he sent it out to be upholstered.

February 25: The Kefauvers and the Tobeys came to dinner. Tobey brought his third wife. At the age of seventy-two, he is more dynamic, and more liberal, and more human than almost anyone else in the Senate.

Eisenhower tore the White House apart over the column this morning. It was the column quoting from his notes at his first press conference. If Ike only knew where that story came from, he would lose more sleep over it.

February 26: Talked to Harry Truman for the first time since the fall of 1945. I had heard that Senator McCarthy was investigating him, so put in a call to Independence to get Truman's reaction.

The call came through without any delay and before I could say "This is Drew Pearson," Mr. Truman said: "Hello, Drew."

I told him that a lot of people missed him in Washington, and he replied that he hoped that they did. He said he would hate to feel that "nobody missed me back there." I added that more were going to miss him as time went on.

Then I told him that McCarthy was investigating a report that he had taken about $10,000 worth of steel filing cabinets when he left the White House.

"That," replied Truman, "is a damned lie. It's a lie out of whole cloth. I bought those filing cabinets and have the receipts to prove it. The only thing I have are some old wooden boxes about to fall to pieces which General Services lent me for my papers until I could get them sorted out and put away in my new building."

I then told Mr. Truman that McCarthy was also investigating an allegation that the Army had moved two carloads of the President's personal effects out of the White House. To this Truman replied: "Every President is moved out of the White House at the expense of the government. It was done for Mr. Hoover. It was done for Roosevelt, and it was done for me. McCarthy had better get his facts straight if he's going to tangle with me or he'll get his ass in a sling."

I then told Mr. Truman a little bit about McCarthy's terrorizing the State Department and how Assistant Secretary McCardle had called Eisenhower's Press Secretary, Jim Hagerty, to plead for the President's support to back up the State Department and get McCarthy called off. But, I added, Eisenhower ducked at his press conference yesterday.

"I saw that," Truman replied. "What Eisenhower doesn't seem to realize is that when a man doesn't back his subordinates, the whole morale of government is shot to pieces. Don't quote me on that part, however. You can quote me about the stuff involving McCarthy."

We had some further pleasant, inconsequential words, and I expressed the hope that he might be coming back here sometime soon and that ended the conversation.

The last time I talked to Mr. Truman, I had taken a petition of about 30,000 names of GI's in the Philippines who wanted to get out of the Army, and, with this under my arm, I had attended a White House conference.

Charlie Ross made me deposit the petitions in another office because of the rule that no petitions can be given the President at a press conference, and afterward I stayed for a second to tell the President about the petitions. Whereupon the President proceeded to bawl me out almost before I could open my mouth.

"You are upsetting my foreign policy," he stormed. "You are demanding that GI's be released from the Army. It's weakening our armed services and upsetting what I'm trying to do."

He went on at some length in a high, nervous, and semicontrolled voice. He did not, however, use any cuss words as was later reported in *Newsweek*, nor did he pull out the drawer of his desk and threaten me with a pearl-handled revolver as later was told by Arthur Krock.

Leonard Lyons, who dined at the White House the last night the President was there, said he would try to get Truman to write me a letter taking back the SOB business.

I told Leonard that I hope that the President will not write such a letter, at least at this time. It would only make matters more difficult with my Republican papers.

Carter's notified me that the radio program is canceled. This makes both radio and TV canceled.*

March 4:   Stalin died last night. I junked our TV program and concentrated on the aftermath of Stalin's death. The State Department seems to think there's a chance of a row between Stalin's successors, also that there may be a lot of unrest, even revolt in the satellite states and some parts of the Soviet Union.

March 5:   The FBI came to see me regarding Chip Bohlen. He's up for appointment as Ambassador to Russia. I was amazed when they asked me whether he was a homo and then quoted me as having once said he was. I disabused them as far as any statements by me were concerned, and told them further that I had never had the slightest suspicion or thought along this line. Actually I have known Bohlen only slightly, he having highhatted me every time I have asked for an appointment in recent years.

I told the FBI how young Walter Chrysler, who lived next to me, had been eased out of the Navy on some kind of a rumor that he was

---

*This was the end of network broadcasting, although he continued on the air by establishing his own syndicate of stations, which used taped radio programs and filmed TV shows—ED.

a homo, though I always suspected it was a false charge based upon the suspicion that he had been leaking news to me. He was married to an ex-Follies girl, one of the most beautiful I have seen.

March 6:   Malenkov has been appointed as Stalin's successor, as I predicted and as was generally expected. However, the administration has been caught with no program. This is a day which the Russian advisers have looked forward to for years. Kennan and Bohlen have been talking about the day when Stalin would die, but the boys in the State Department and around the White House have no strategy. This could be a moment when it would be possible to pry open the door for peace, even win away some segments of the Soviet Union, but as far as I know or can see, there are no concrete plans.

Lunched with Oscar Chapman. The FBI has been to see him regarding Cap Krug. They are looking into the $700,000 loan Krug received under the peculiar circumstances that he did not have to pay it back. Also his many women, his trips to New York at government expense, and a reported fee which he is supposed to have taken from Ed Pauley. I doubt that Krug would have taken money; however, he has never quite explained how he got an interest in the Los Angeles Rams. The FBI is going into this also, and doesn't believe his alibi that the stock was purchased for him on a long-term deal by some friends in Louisville.

March 8:   Isaac Don Levine and his wife came for dinner. He had been meeting all afternoon with C. D. Jackson, Abbot Washburn, and a man named Comstock on the next move to make regarding Russia. They were floundering all over the place, have no idea what they should do. Levine advised not to be too hasty in sending an Ambassador but to let the Russians send someone over here. That, he believes, would give us the chance to look at their people better and not make us so eager for a truce. He feels that the same old truce terms will be trotted out in Korea and that they will lead nowhere.

According to Don, when Bedell Smith was Director of the CIA, he got sore when his men paid $100,000 to the Polish underground. His men were naive and got sucked in. The men to whom they paid the money in large rolls of bills were actually Communist counterintelligence agents and the Warsaw radio had a great time razzing us.

ABC refused to let me say much about my exit from the air.

Velotta was on the job in New York and raised Cain about my proposed statement. I finally yielded.

March 9:   Chris Witting of Dumont called to say that the sponsorship deal with Dunhill Cigarettes collapsed. The advertising agency was all for it and it seemed on the verge of going through, but after several meetings, the Dunhill boys finally replied "too controversial." This is the same crowd which almost signed me up for Bond Street Tobacco two years ago, but at the last minute one of their directors, a high Catholic layman, raised Cain and the deal was off.

Called on Brownell, the new Attorney General, and asked him about his moving of his personal effects from the Lee House to the Justice Department in a government truck. He admitted it, claimed it was ordered without his knowledge, and, it being Washington's birthday, he couldn't get another truck. He said he had paid the government back for the truck, driver's time, etc. I suspect that he arranged this alibi after he had received some queries, but I did not argue the point.

I asked him what he was going to do about appointing a chief of the antitrust division. He admitted that this was a tough one. I pointed out that the entire nation would be watching him and that he had some highly sensitive cases such as that against Ike's friend, Roy Roberts, of the Kansas City *Star;* that against the investment bankers, which involved some of Ike's best friends; and that against Dupont and General Motors, which involved members of the Cabinet. He admitted that these were ticklish matters.

Called on the new Secretary of Interior, Douglas McKay, a nice guy but a political phony if I ever knew one. He has no conception whatsoever about the basic fundamentals of protecting the public and would give away the entire national domain if he thought he could get away with it. He employs the tactic of talking fast and lengthily, a strategy frequently used by smart politicians who want to avoid embarrassing questions.

March 12:   Called on Dean Francis Sayre at the National Cathedral —a quite young but quite wise and sympathetic gentleman who looks like his grandfather, Woodrow Wilson. I suggested that the idea of a committee of prominent clergy and others who might promote the idea of friendship with the people of Russia, might be worth consideration. He was a little timid about the idea, partly, I suspect, because he took quite a beating after his criticism of McCarthy. He said the mail had been terrific and although it was 3 to 2 for him, nevertheless he received some highly caustic, critical letters. I suggested in turn the idea of prayer for the Russian people. Later that day, I called on Bishop G. Bromley Oxnam of the Methodist Church, an equally sympathetic and delightful man. It made me realize that specializing on politicans in Washington really causes the neglect of some wonderful people.

Bishop Oxnam was also timid about the idea of friendship to the Russian people. He pointed out that he had once appeared on the same platform in New York at a meeting of the Friends of Soviet Russia, and while he was there in company with Ambassador Joe Davies and other distinguished gentlemen, the McCarthyites have tried to smear him ever since. However, he had already talked to Dean Sayre about the idea of prayer and they are planning to do something.

March 13: A British plane was shot down today between Hamburg and Berlin. I waited all day today to hear from Weinrott regarding the possibility of going on Mutual. I had talked both to Harry Hoyt and to him about this and there was a meeting scheduled for today. However, no reply. My suspicions increase that one of my troubles is not only ABC but the Ted Bates Agency, which was so rabidly pro-Eisenhower during the campaign. Harry Trenner talked to Kintner today about a sponsor, but met a blank wall of resistance. Kintner wasn't open to any sort of proposals whatsoever. Meanwhile, some people I never suspected have contacted ABC, including Senator Ed Johnson of Colorado, of whom I have sometimes been critical. Also I understand that Senator Taft exploded against ABC. Alf Landon has sent them a very strong letter. There seems to be no doubt that the fix went in at the time the Paramount merger was approved.

March 14: Eric Johnston [head of the Motion Picture Association] told me of his talk with Len Goldenson, chief mogul in Paramount. Goldenson was polite but emphatic that I was not going to be on the air, said they had already sold the time. Actually they merely transferred Monday Morning Headlines from 6:15 to 6. They did it in an awful hurry, however, in order to claim that the time was sold.

March 15: ABC had an engineer in New York standing by ready to cut me off if I stepped out of bounds tonight. They also had Velotta prepare a statement in reply to my generalized statement on the concentration of channels of expression in the hands of four networks. I had to surrender forty seconds of time to let them give it. Joe Davies, whom I talked to about General Foods, hasn't even bothered to call back.

March 26:   Saw Warren Olney [Chief of the Criminal Division of the Justice Department] regarding the prosecution of Congressman Bramblett of California.* I told him of the rumors going around town: one of them being that Nixon had stepped in to stop the prosecution of Bramblett; another being that a feud was on between the Warren forces and Nixon forces in California regarding Bramblett.

The four Justice officials whom Olney kicked out over the Bramblett issue have been spreading rumors either directly or indirectly.

Olney finally broke down and told me the whole story off the record—namely, that the file on Bramblett had been placed on his desk in a routine manner. He glanced at it rapidly and noticed that four lawyers had recommended against prosecution. It was a rather thin file, Olney said, and he put it aside to take a look at it the next day. When he went through it, there was definite evidence warranting prosecution. In order that he should make no mistake, he gave it to another man to study independently.

Other parts of the file which were missing began to turn up, including a flat and categoric recommendation by Attorney General McGranery to prosecute. This was made on January 14, six days before McGranery left office. It was accompanied by a six-point outline of the points of the issue on which prosecution was to be based. The instructions were clear and clean-cut that these were to be presented to a grand jury.

Also in the files there turned up a memo from a Washington attorney, purporting to be a friend of Olney's, and interceding for Bramblett. Olney said he hit the roof. Obviously, if the file had stood, it meant a clear-cut indictment of his integrity, since he would have been reversing a Democratic Attorney General, presumably at the behest of a personal friend who represented Bramblett.

Olney said he couldn't figure whether this was a plan by someone in the Department to embarrass him or not. At any rate, he said he

---

*Ernest Bramblett was in fact indicted a few months later on charges of perjury in the matter of staff salary kickbacks that had been made to him in 1950 and 1951. —Ed.

could not work with men who were either slipshod or whom he could not trust, so he told the four who had recommended against prosecution that he would accept their resignations. He said he hated to do this because he had come to Washington expecting to use the men already on the job.

I told Olney in advance that I had already written a story about the matter, although I didn't tell him I had it in my pocket. He assured me that no one at the top is going to stop prosecution.

March 27:   Called on Senator Taft. It was the first time I had with him for a personal talk in about two years, during which time I had been pretty tough on him. However, he was extremely cordial. I asked him about McCarthy, told him that one reason many people liked the idea of a Republican administration was so we could get away from the constant harassment of government departments. He replied to the general effect that investigation of government departments was pretty much standard procedure; that he agreed with McCarthy on the Voice of America. He felt it should have been cleaned out or abolished long ago. Regarding Bohlen, he said that he thought McCarthy was wrong and while he wasn't too enthusiastic over Bohlen, he never thought it was wise to buck the President on every issue that came along. He said he reserved the right to differ with the President, but he wasn't going to do it on the ambassadorship to Russia.

I asked him about a story that he had remarked in a conference with Eisenhower that "we didn't need any more generals." This was in reference to the proposed appointment of General Van Fleet to replace General Hershey. Taft laughed and said the story was essentially true, but that Van Fleet was to be Veterans Administrator, not replacing Hershey. He said the story wouldn't have been embarrassing if Eisenhower had laughed, but that nobody in the conference smiled except him. The interesting thing is that Congressman Joe Martin, whom Tom McNamara had queried about the same story, carefully quoted Eisenhower as laughing and agreeing with Taft. Martin also denied the fact that he had reproved Eisenhower for not letting him know about the job appointments in his district. Taft, however, confirmed the latter, and I am sure that Taft was telling the truth.

Regarding patronage, Taft added that appointments were a little slow, but he said you have to realize that the ten men who came down here were very good men but they knew nothing about government, so naturally they were slow in making appointments. It's somewhat like the Churchill administration. When they took over, there were only two men who knew anything about government—Churchill and his Foreign Secretary, Anthony Eden. At first, the Churchill government was not popular and Labour would probably have been voted back in office. But now they have developed some new men, and I am informed that if elections were held today, the Conservatives would be elected. On the way out I noticed a statue of Taft's father and was tempted to tell him that my father had given Taft his first job after he left the White House. He paid him $4,000 a week lecturing on the Chautauquas. I did tell him, however, that my father-in-law [Dan Tyler Moore] had been Teddy Roosevelt's military aide when his father was Secretary of War, and that Colonel Moore was down on the Secretary of War for the same old reason—namely, cutting the budget. I didn't tell him that Colonel Moore was so vigorous in his denunciation that Teddy Roosevelt used to say: "Hide the carving knife; don't let Dan get it. Taft is coming for dinner."

March 30:   Ed Hart called David Lilienthal from my office to ask him to talk to David Sarnoff, for whom he now works, to persuade Sarnoff to permit me to broadcast over NBC. Lilienthal politely but quickly said no. I recall that one of the fiercest denunciations of me on the Senate floor was by Senator McKellar of Tennessee, after I had defended Lilienthal and exposed some of McKellar's charges against him. McKellar filled approximately three pages of the *Congressional Record* with his diatribe.

April 2:   Have been working on ways to line up a transcribed radio broadcast, replacing the network. It's been only four days since the last broadcast and since we started the idea and so far 140 stations have signed up.

April 3:   Flew to Detroit with Dave Beck [of the Teamsters]. Some years ago, John Boettiger in Seattle told me that Dave Beck was the most statesmanlike labor leader on the West Coast, despite his reputation for high-handedness. I talked to Beck most of the way to Detroit and found him all that Boettiger said he was.* He is placing certain

*The assessment of Beck as a statesman may have been colored by his need for

material before the Justice Department pertaining to a racket by his own local leaders in Oakland. In fact, I had placed it before the Justice Department some years ago without action. Now he thinks with the change in administration it may be acted upon. He was vigorously critical of Joe Ryan of the Longshoremen and other labor leaders who let the rackets get mixed up with their unions. He says the reason for dope peddling and pimping by taxi drivers in New York and Washington is the fact they are underpaid and unorganized and can't make a living otherwise.

On the West Coast, where all cab drivers are tightly organized, wages are high and drivers are the highest type in the country. His union, I was surprised to learn, is now the biggest in the United States with 1,200,000.

At Detroit we discussed with Roy Fruehauf the idea of a television program sponsored three ways, by the Teamsters Union, the truck manufacturers, and the Trucking Association. I told them that I was a little skeptical of the idea. After watching a portrayal of the trucking side of the picture presented by Leslie Allman I had to admit that they have an awfully good case. Beck and Fruehauf say they want to go ahead. It's now up to the Trucking Association.

April 5:   Spent my first Sunday without a broadcast in a good many years.

April 6:   Mrs. John Cowles telephoned the office last weekend while I was away and dictated a statement to Bill Neel critical of her sister-in-law, Fleur Cowles, whom Eisenhower has appointed Ambassador to Queen Elizabeth's coronation. It was obvious from Mrs. John's language that she doesn't think much of Fleur and frankly I can't blame her. I telephoned her back in Minneapolis to make sure she wanted to stand by her statement and sent it out in the column today.

There were immediate repercussions from John Wheeler [president of Bell Syndicate] in New York, who urged that the story not run. He argued that it would get me in wrong with publishers. I told him that when publishers are appointed to ambassadorial posts or other high offices, they become just as subject to fair comment as anyone else.

---

help in fighting a news blackout. Beck eventually landed in prison, convicted of embezzling union funds.—ED.

Kraus came down from New York to discuss the Pegler case with Roberts and me. We decided to try to take Pegler's deposition in all four cases, then probably drop the New York case and push the Washington and Detroit actions.

April 7 & April 8:   Russ Wiggins of the *Post* telephoned at a rather early hour for him to say that he was worried about the Cowles column and thought it should be killed. He argued that Mrs. [John] Cowles was menopausal, and the story would hurt me with publishers. I told him that when I had talked to her she seemed to be a perfectly calm and balanced lady, and that on three separate occasions she had indicated her desire to have the story published.

I had hardly hung up when John Wheeler was at me again from New York regarding the story. Wheeler had received a telegram from Mike Cowles threatening a libel suit and demanding that all subscribing newspapers receive a copy of his telegram. I told Wheeler to send the telegram to all papers together with a statement detailing that Mrs. John Cowles's statements had been read back to her for correction, and reminding editors also of the long-established British ban on divorced persons at Court. Later in the evening came a call from Phil Graham of the *Post.*

Meanwhile I had talked to Senator Humphrey of Minnesota, who said that all his relations with Mrs. John Cowles have indicated that she was not suffering from menopause—in fact, she had been to India and written a very fine series of articles from there. Phil Graham let the cat out of the bag as to why Russ Wiggins had called me earlier —namely, Mike Cowles had been on his neck.

Phil came forward with the same old excuse of the menopause, wept copiously though with some dignity over the telephone about taking advantage of a poor lady who was not in her right mind. I pointed out that Mike Cowles had put me in a position, with his telegram threatening libel, where I could not possibly kill the story.

Phil agreed, but added he was going to urge Mike to take the softer approach. Phil called back during the evening but I was at a dinner and did not reach him until next morning, by which time Mike Cowles had been trying to get me, to say nothing of his emissary Mr. Karr.

I was in the middle of a deposition in the Littell case, plus various legal conferences between depositions. I got the advice of Cuneo, who did not want to kill the story, and Luvie, who also thought it should run, plus my office staff, who also exhibited no great tenderness for the former Fannie Feinberg. In the end, however, I finally followed the old dictum that where publishers are concerned you should bow three times from the waist and apologize for anything ever written about them. I finally took Cowles's telephone call.

He was so apologetic that I felt sorry for him. I dictated a telegram which he sent me withdrawing his libel threat, and in turn I sent a telegram to all newspapers embodying the text of his wire, together with a statement from me that inasmuch as delicate family programs were involved, the story should be killed. I am still a little provoked at myself for yielding, chiefly because of the fact that publishers seem to think that they are beyond the pale of fair comment.

The [Cowles] Des Moines *Register* not only killed my column during much of the campaign because I tried to tell the truth about Nixon but they demurred at printing a paid ad which reprinted one of the columns on the Ford Motor Company which they had killed. In addition, *Look* magazine, headed by Mike Cowles, carried a libelous reference to me in a grossly unfair story defending Nixon.

I mentioned this over the telephone to Mike, incidentally, and he apologized for it, said he agreed it had been unfair and uncalled for. I did not mention the fact that his dearly beloved wife, the Ambassador to the Coronation, had remarked to Oswaldo Aranha in New York last December that, "While the Cowles papers believe in freedom of the press, they could not possibly print my column."

Of course, when Dolly Gann and Alice Longworth tangled over who should sit where at dinner, it became the biggest story of the Hoover administration, and the many scoops I published regarding it helped to launch my budding journalistic career. I expect we will have to save this one for the book.*

Release Thursday, April 9, 1953: *Sister-in Law of Fleur Cowles frowns on her Appointment as Coronation Ambassadress*
Mrs. John Cowles, wife of the publisher of the Minneapolis *Star and Tribune,* has asked me to make clear that she is not to be confused with her sister-in-law, Fleur Cowles, wife of the publisher of the Des Moines *Register-Tribune* and of *Look* magazine, who is

*Since he wanted it saved for the book, here it is.—ED.

to be one of Eisenhower's Ambassadors at Queen Elizabeth's coronation.

Furthermore, Mrs. John Cowles states that she does not approve of sending a divorced woman as an Ambassadress on this important occasion.

Mrs. John Cowles, whose husband was recently appointed by Eisenhower as an adviser on the National Security Council, is a lady of charm and dignity, married thirty years to one man, who feels that the customs of the British Court regarding divorced women should be observed by the United States in the appointment of Ambassadors. The Queen of England, she points out, did not attend the wedding of Foreign Minister Anthony Eden—though a very old friend—because he had been divorced.

"The John Cowles family," Mrs. Cowles points out, "was in no way responsible for the enormous bad taste of sending a divorced woman and third wife—all of them living—to the coronation."

Mrs. Cowles said that the first she knew of her sister-in-law's appointment was when Jim Milloy, Washington vice president for *Look* magazine, sent her husband a clipping from the Washington *Daily News* which read: "Wife of another magazine publisher, Fleur Cowles, will be content if she's named to represent President Eisenhower at Queen Elizabeth's coronation."

This referred to the fact that Clare Boothe Luce, the wife of the publisher of *Life, Time,* and *Fortune,* was made Ambassadress to Rome. Mrs. Fleur Cowles' husband, Gardner (Mike) Cowles, is publisher of *Look* magazine.

Attached to the clipping was a scribbled notation from *Look*'s James Milloy indicating that he was the man who arranged the Fleur Cowles appointment. The notation read: "John: when Mike was here Jan. 20 he asked me to do this. It's all set. Jim."

Mrs. John Cowles made it clear she did not think much of this haphazard method of making ambassadorial appointments based upon whether her sister-in-law would "be content."

"As a member of the Cowles family for thirty years," she said, "I wish to be completely dissociated from the bad manners of those who made and confirmed the appointment, and from the bad taste of the woman designated, who is going where she is not truly wanted.

"And as a grandmother and the wife of one man for thirty years, I am sorry that out of all the millions of American women who represent the highest standards of American family life, someone better qualified could not have been selected as our representative at the coronation of a queen who stands for all that is fine in the family life of England."

Note—Both Cowles brothers threw the powerful support of their publications to Eisenhower during the campaign and there was speculation that Eisenhower might appoint John Cowles as Secretary of the Treasury. His father was appointed a member of the RFC by Herbert Hoover. The family is related to the Thomas Lamonts of the J. P. Morgan banking firm.

From the Bell Syndicate, Inc., Note to Washington Merry-Go-Round editors:

Mr. Gardner Cowles has sent the Bell Syndicate the following telegram regarding the column of April 9 which in fairness both to him and to Merry-Go-Round subscribers I am relaying to you:

I am reliably informed Bell Syndicate has distributed a Drew Pearson column for release Thursday which contains clearly libelous material relating to me and my wife. This is to inform you and I request you to so advise each of your clients receiving the Pearson column that we regard reference to us as libelous and expect to take action against any paper publishing this inaccurate and libelous material.

Gardner Cowles, President
Des Moines *Register-Tribune*

After due consideration the Bell Syndicate and I do not feel justified in withdrawing any part of the April 9 column for the following reasons:

1. The references to Ambassadress and Mr. Cowles are not libelous. They were carefully checked with attorneys. The quotation from Mrs. John Cowles was volunteered by her, and was read back to her over the telephone for correction. The corrections she made were carefully embodied in her statement. Mrs. John Cowles also sent a photostat copy of a clipping bearing the handwritten notation of James Milloy, vice president of *Look* magazine, regarding the Fleur Cowles appointment. Following receipt of this, one day later, Mrs. Cowles was queried by me personally in Minneapolis to make sure she wanted to stand by her original statement.

2. The appointment of Mrs. Fleur Cowles has become an international incident. It may not have been publicized in the United States, possibly in deference to the feelings of a fellow member of the newspaper fraternity, but it has aroused plenty of comment in England. It should be remembered that the Duchess of Windsor,

despite the passage of years, is not yet received at the British Court, and that no divorced person is received within the Royal Enclosure at Ascot. Various divorced Americans have been tentatively considered for appointment as Ambassador to England but always turned down because of this old British tradition. This is the first time in history, as far as the State Department can recall, that the tradition has been broken.

3. There is no disposition on my part or on the part of the Bell Syndicate to single out a newspaperman for comment. However, when he or his wife is appointed to high public office, the manner in which he or she secures the appointment and the reverberations it causes, whether national or international, must be the subject of journalistic reporting. Mrs. Oveta Culp Hobby, now entering the Cabinet [as Secretary of HEW], cannot be immune from journalistic scrutiny either because of her sex or because she is the wife of a newspaper publisher, any more than could Secretary of Labor Frances Perkins, nor Mrs. Fleur Cowles.

4. I have defended all libel suits in the past and am prepared to defend this one, should it develop.

Drew Pearson

April 9: *The New York Times* featured a story this morning to the effect that the Eisenhower administration would accept a new boundary in Korea at the narrow waist and would also relegate Chiang Kai-shek to the background. The White House immediately denied the story, despite the fact that it had come from John Foster Dulles himself.

Eugene Meyer and the Chief Justice came to dinner. They both thought I was right in killing the Cowles story. I reminded Eugene that when he had tangled with Cissie Patterson through no fault of his, and when Jesse Jones had knocked his glasses off at a dinner, the press had carried the story widely. Despite this, he seemed to think that his fellow publisher, Mr. Cowles, should be protected.

I reminded Eugene that last fall he had told me that what we needed in the White House was a man who at 4 A.M. on June 5 could decide that an Allied Army would make a Normandy landing.

"Are you satisfied?" I asked. "With the prompt decisions made by the new President?"

Eugene, of course, will never admit when he's wrong.

"I sometimes think from reading your column," he said, "that you don't understand he is the new President."

April 20:   Went to New York at the request of the Dumont network to talk to a sponsor. Dumont had called twice last week to say the sponsor was ready to start as soon as I was, and urged me to clear the decks for action as soon as possible.

In New York the Dumont people introduced me to a gentleman named Green with two advertising associates who put out what they call a motor additive. At first, I thought I was going to be sponsored by a battery additive which I have been writing about critically in connection with the firing of Dr. Astin as Director of the Bureau of Standards. I was ready to say "no" in a polite way but found I did not have to. Mr. Green politely explained that they decided Senator McCarthy was more than they can take and that if they sponsor me, McCarthy was sure to attack them.

Green pointed out—and I agreed with him—that McCarthy might demand a federal trade investigation of their product, which might seriously handicap if not terminate their entire business.

April 22:   The Littell libel suit was postponed until tomorrow, giving us one more day of preparation. We have been working night and day, perhaps harder than for any other case, though in my opinion this should be one of the easiest. Graham Morison has had the jitters, however, and wanted to settle. I finally tracked down the fact that Littell was confined to a sanitarium in Seattle in 1940 and that he had a nervous breakdown while in Harvard in 1924. However, Morison refuses to use this.

April 23:   The Littell case is postponed until next Monday. We now hear that Ambassador Winiewicz will retire from the Polish Embassy and seek asylum in the United States. This means he will probably testify for Littell, which may be quite damaging.

April 27:   Started the Littell trial. Unfortunately I had a lecture engagement at the University of Florida, Gainesville. This is the first time I have ever been absent during any part of a libel suit, and I am superstitious.

April 28:   The trial judge in the Littell case—ex-Congressman McLaughlin—doesn't look too promising. I had dinner with him one evening when Secretary of Navy Matthews took us down the river on his yacht. He seemed like a nice and friendly person, but the people who surrounded Matthews were always professional Catholics, and I am suspicious that [Edward Bennett] Williams, Littell's attorney, who teaches law at Georgetown University, may have a sort of access to McLaughlin.

May 7: The Littell trial has dragged out interminably. McLaughlin has let all sorts of evidence get before the jury and Graham Morison has dragged out the cross-examination of Littell interminably—beyond all reason.

The jury is bored. McLaughlin upheld Judge Schweinhaut's ruling that what I said about Littell in the Dutch case was libelous per se. From this, the right of comment in the District of Columbia will be seriously abridged from now on.

McLaughlin turned around and made an amazing ruling that what I said about Littell in the Polish case did not imply that he was a pro-Communist. I would have disagreed with McLaughlin on this because the inference was reasonably clear that Littell was working hand over foot for the Polish Communists. I think that McLaughlin is confused in his own thinking and leaning over backward to be fair with both sides.

May 8: Went to the first White House Correspondent's dinner in a good many years. Eisenhower made a speech about one-minute long. In contrast to those which Truman and Roosevelt made, it was a flop. Truman was probably at his best in these informal speeches, while Roosevelt was always good. Eisenhower seemed bored and anxious to get away.

May 9: Lamar Caudle came to lunch yesterday. He told me that when he first became Chief of the Criminal Division of the Justice Department, he heard of a file on Alger Hiss. It was the most secret file in the Department. It was called the "Gregory" file rather than the Hiss file.

At first Tom Clark did not want Lamar to have it. He had to ask for it several times and had to tell Tom that as Chief of the Criminal Division, he had to know what was in all the criminal files.

Finally he got it. It was about one foot thick and he did not have time to read it all before he was transferred to the Tax Division. However, it showed that Chambers had pressured Hiss to obtain the State Department's secrets by threatening to expose him.

Lamar said he also looked at the Dexter White file. It showed that White had planted Silvermaster in the Treasury as a Soviet spy and also planted Frank Coe in the Treasury. Elizabeth Bentley was in cahoots with them all, at that time being in love with a Russian courier.

Lamar said he called Tom Clark's attention to the White file after the FBI had told him about it. Tom at that particular time was at Johns Hopkins getting a physical checkup, and since White was about to be confirmed to the International Monetary Fund, Lamar called Fred Vinson, then Secretary of the Treasury, urging that confirmation be stopped. But he had already been confirmed.

A few weeks later, Lamar said, he saw the picture of Vinson and White taken together at a Monetary Conference at White Sulphur Springs. Later, J. Edgar Hoover had telephoned Jimmie Byrnes that White's confirmation was pending in the Senate. (Byrnes had phoned Matt Connelly who in turn called Senator Lister Hill, but White's confirmation had already gone through.)

May 10: Few people realize how little time Eisenhower spends at work. He golfs at least three days a week and is spending a three-day weekend in Phillipsburg, New Jersey, and gets away for an equally long period during most weekends. The newspapermen protect him. I think it boils down to the fact that Ike is really not at all well, also probably rather lazy. I understand he has colitic poisoning, as well as high blood pressure.

May 11: Churchill spoke in the House of Commons today urging a Big Three conference with Malenkov. This is likely to widen the chasm with Eisenhower, certainly with the United States. Dulles seems to have little idea of what it's all about, and Eisenhower, though he undoubtedly has an idea, does little about it.

It seems to me that we are drifting in the same direction we did from 1930 to 1941—toward more dissension with our friends, toward more encouragement of the dictator nations. It is getting more and more difficult to get American people to understand foreign policy. They are more concerned with baseball and television, and more and more calloused to what's going on in the rest of the world. There was a time when Forrestal or the White House could whip up patriotism by citing Russia's armed power. But now the public is blasé. Meanwhile, there is more isolation, more religious dissension, and less money for schools.

May 12:   Williams called in as his final witness a notary public who swore that she had taken an affidavit signed by John M. Henshaw on March 10 (I think this was the date), 1951. We were able successfully to object to use of the affidavit; however, I had a chance to read it. It stated that the Littell case was prepared entirely after the story was written, that we had rigged an alibi with Alex Campbell, that Joe Borkin had placed a predated letter in the files of the Justice Department complaining about Littell's activities re the Dutch; that the tip about Littell had been planted by Randolph Feltus on Blumenthal and that Henshaw sat in on the staff meeting in which these things were discussed. The date of the affidavit was March 1951, shortly after Henshaw left my employ. I had kept him on the payroll considerably against my better judgment for some time but gave him notice on January 1, 1951, that with the loss of the Adam Hat sponsorship he would have to get another job. He actually left the payroll on March 1, and obviously went immediately to either McCarthy or Littell— probably both.

Yet at the same time he was asking me to get a job for him at the Office of Price Stabilization, which I did. When he was about to be fired by OPS, I intervened for him and after he was fired by OPS, I found further work for him. In the winter of 1952, when I was in the Virgin Islands, I remember the frantic telephone calls I got that Henshaw was up before the Loyalty Board. Later, when I came back, I signed an affidavit attesting to his loyalty. And I still have his unpaid note for $700 plus a lot of other loans I have made him. It all reminds me of Alben Barkley's story on "What have you done for me lately?"

May 13:   Last day of the Littell trial. Graham did a pretty good job of summing up to the jury, though Williams did a better job. We did not use the Francis Biddle letter telling how Littell jeopardized the secret of the atomic bomb at Camp Washington. We also failed to introduce the record of Littell's many rows and his two nervous breakdowns. All of these in my opinion were grave mistakes. I think that Graham refused to use the nervous breakdown because he himself once had one.

May 14:   Jury is still out.

May 15:   The jury awarded $50,000 to Littell in the Dutch case, plus one dollar punitive damages. In the Polish case, the jury was hung. One man, Frank Thomas, stuck to the bitter end. He was the disabled war veteran. He told me afterward that the other jurors had unmercifully pummeled him verbally and it was only because of this that he finally yielded in the Dutch case.

I confess that when I first took a look at the jury, composed of rather complacent, self-righteous, middle-class people, I had grave misgivings about the outcome of this suit. In addition, I have never worked with a lawyer who was more stubborn about the way of trying the case. And today, I learned for the first time that Graham had never before tried a libel suit.

May 23: Breakfast with Dave Beck. Talked to him about the AF of L buying a national newspaper—particularly the Los Angeles *News*, which I feel is going bankrupt. He reacted favorably. He said that Chandler newspapers had pilloried him for weeks when he was organizing the milk drivers in Los Angeles.

May 26: Finally had lunch with the AF of L regarding the newspaper idea. It was promising but inconclusive. Scott Milne of the Electrical Workers was most enthusiastic. Morris Novak, representing Dave Dubinsky, who incidentally now has $160,000,000 in his treasury, was also enthusiastic. Bob Allen was the only other newspaperman there. He favors buying the San Francisco *News*. Consensus was that the livest wires in the Federation—among them Beck, McGowan of the Boilermakers, George Harrison of the Railway Executives, Petrillo of the Musicians, and Dubinsky—should confer further and meanwhile we should keep our eyes open for good newspaper bargains.

Later I talked to George Harrison, who liked the idea in a general sort of way, but was worried about a boycott of advertisers in case a paper were known to be labor-owned. He said that AF of L members had been talking about sponsoring me on the radio, instead of buying a newspaper.

June 15: The Chief Justice was supposed to come to dinner. He called at 7:15 to say he couldn't get there. Usually he arrives five minutes ahead of time. He finally arrived after dinner in time to play bridge and remarked he had had a hell of a day. One guest was indiscreet enough to ask whether the delay was over the Keating Committee's demand that Tom Clark testify, to which Fred replied, "Further than that deponent sayeth not."* I gathered that the real reason for the delay was the Rosenberg case. The court had just ruled five-four against any further stay of execution.

June 16:   Bill Douglas took the unusual step of granting the Rosenbergs' stay of execution despite the ruling of the court the day before. I presume this was what Vinson was kept late at the Court arguing about last night. Probably he and Douglas had quite a set-to.

June 17:   Douglas reaffirmed his stay with an opinion which I, as a noted lawyer, couldn't help feeling to be right. He ruled that the atomic energy act of 1946 superseded the espionage act of 1917, and that the Rosenbergs should have been tried under the latter. This does not provide for the death penalty unless so recommended by a jury.

June 18:   The Supreme Court met and overruled Bill Douglas. Only Hugo Black stood with him.

I think the real thing in Vinson's mind was, first, that the majority will of the court had been challenged by Douglas; second, that the prolonged discussion of the Rosenberg case had caused devastating reverberations around the world. Even the Vatican radio had asked for a sympathetic hearing, while two cardinals in France had sent messages on their behalf. The issue was taken up by all sorts of people not even remotely Communist, though the Communists unquestionably teed off the whole business. I could not help but think that guilty as the Rosenbergs unquestionably are, it might have been wiser to give them life imprisonment.

June 19:   The Rosenbergs were executed.

June 20:   The riots in East Berlin are continuing. To me they are far more important than anything happening in Korea.

June 22:   The lawyers called up to say that I had to raise $50,000 by 4 P.M. to satisfy Littell. Judge McLaughlin has ruled out our motion for a new trial. Later, Littell's counsel gave us until the end of the week.

---

*Congressman Kenneth Keating of New York was Chairman of the Subcommittee of the House Judiciary Committee investigating the Department of Justice.—Ed.

June 24:   Had an interesting visit with Harry Truman—the first since
he bawled me out in the White House for handing him a petition from
30,000 GI's who wanted to come home.

Harry was looking extremely well and was most cordial. Neither
one of us mentioned the unpleasantness of the past. When I remarked
on his health, he said: "Well, I got that seven-ton weight off my head.
People don't realize the responsibility of the Presidency. That's why I
have every sympathy with my successor, especially at this time when
the problems have so increased."

He had turned a bedroom in the Mayflower into a little office,
which we entered. He remarked: "I wouldn't invite you in here, but
I've turned this darned air-cooling off. They make me sick." I told him
I had the same trouble at home.

I said: "I don't suppose you know it, Mr. President, but I sent a
suggestion to you by Dean Acheson about a year ago, and told him not
to tell you that it came from me—namely, that you should go abroad
to try to build up our sagging prestige."

"Yes, I know about that," he replied. "Dean talked to me and he
told me that the suggestion came from you. I could not get away at
the time."

I told him that I thought now might be an even more appropriate
time, that inasmuch as our prestige had skidded terribly in the last few
months, it would be a wonderful thing if he could go to the Vosges
Mountains where he had once fought. "If you drive your own car and
just mingle with folks the way you did across the continent, it would
make a terrific impression. You would just be your good-natured self
and would win a lot of friends for us. It would first of all remind our
friends of our contribution in two wars, and, second, you would have
a chance to give some interviews here and there in which you could
drop a few words that would help the whole picture."

"I sure would like to do it," he said. "I remember all those roads
in France. I rode over them on horseback and I think that I could
remember them even now. But I don't know that it's a good idea. I
thought when I got out of office I could go back to being a private
citizen. But this trip has proved it's difficult. Maybe when I can get rid
of this glamour, I can go. But if I went now, the President of France
would feel he would have to entertain me, reciprocate for his visit over
here. So would Churchill. Even the Queen would probably feel she had
to entertain me. And I would end up making a lot of speeches in which
I would say nothing important—just platitudes. I wouldn't be able to

travel on my own. Some day I want to go to Greece and Turkey. I would like to spend a couple of months in Italy. And I want to visit the Arab countries and Israel. But I want to go when I can really be a private citizen. I would like to see if those old women that we knew in France are still there. I suppose they are all dead now, but when we were in the Vosges Mountains, there was no one there except little kids and old ladies. They took awfully good care of us, sewed our clothes, made us feel at home, and when we left, they ran alongside the road with us weeping. But I suppose they are all dead, though I would like to see them."

I remarked that our prestige wasn't likely to improve much so this trip would be worthwhile then too. He said that he was distressed at the drift of the world. I told him about having been to the State Department that morning where Jimmie Riddleberger had told me of his efforts to get the White House to make some statements encouraging the East Germans. All sorts of plans were ready in the State Department to demand elections and exert leadership before the Russians set their house in order. But Riddleberger had not been able to get to first base. All he got was a blank wall. I told Truman that he did not know whether it was Dulles's or Eisenhower's fault.

"Dulles's trip to Europe was the most distressing thing that's happened to our foreign relations," Truman said.

I also told him about ex-Premier Mikolaiczyk, who dined with me on Saturday. "I know him well. He's a wonderful man," Truman said. "He might have been killed over there if it hadn't been for Stanton Griffis."

I went on to say that Mikolaiczyk, Osusky, and other refugees felt that if the world drifted much longer, Russia would be able to drive a wedge between France and Germany and that war would be inevitable. I told him that's why I thought he should go to Europe soon.

"Well, I might be persuaded," he said. "In strictest confidence," he added, "if this administration gave me the cooperation I gave [President] Hoover, it might be different, but they are watching everything I do." He appeared to be in the middle of telling me something extremely interesting when Mrs. Truman walked in. This ended the interview. He had a dinner engagement and I left.

July 3:   Finished taking Pegler's deposition today. His counsel objected repeatedly and cleverly to a lot of pertinent questions. Despite this, we struck a gold mine of information. Pegler got his original stuff against me from John Maragon and Harry Vaughan, and later from McCarthy.

After the deposition was over, Pegler and his troop of lawyers went to the Statler for lunch. Later in the afternoon, Arthur Watts, a waiter at the Statler, called me up to say that they were conspiring as to how they could get hold of John Henshaw. "If we could just find Henshaw, we can break the s.o.b.," quoth Mr. Dempsey.

July 5 [Philadelphia]: Broadcast from Independence Hall. Vice President Nixon was there the day before. Had a nice talk with my sponsor who tells me that the Philadelphia *Bulletin* refused to take an ad regarding my program because I am on a competing station.

July 16: Flew up to Topridge, Joe Davies' camp in the Adirondacks. It's the most fabulous camp I've ever seen. An escalator carries you from the boat landing up to the camp. There are small cabins for guests and different members of the family, plus a huge lodge filled with everything from stuffed foxes and bears to an Eskimo kayak. The room was so crowded that Fred Vinson looked around and said: "I could get interested in some of the things in this room if there weren't so many of them. That boat, for instance, hanging from the ceiling," he said pointing to the kayak, "must have quite a history. But there's just too darned much here to inquire about."

On the other side of the camp are two small lakes; behind the camp is a virtual village given over to about twenty servants. They have their own movies, recreation area, even their own private bathing beach and boats. I imagine there are about four servants for every guest.

Joe insists that his guests dress for dinner though the Chief Justice rebels mildly though politely, and twice has broken the rule. I don't think Joe likes it much—but then, Joe has quite an array of maroon and purple dinner jackets.

July 17–18: I am the only non-bridge player here. Everyone else plays bridge from 2:30 P.M. until midnight. This is rather nice for me because I have had a chance to read, do whatever I please. Yesterday we went on a camping-boating trip at one end of St. Regis Lake. The lake is studded with summer camps, most of them occupied only thirty days of the year. Mrs. Ogden Reid has one near us, and the Ed Foleys, who are now at camp with us, used to operate one nearby.

Joe asked me to look over his memoirs. And we talked about his days during and immediately after the war. He's still of the opinion that the forceful reactionary ideas of Churchill spoiled the peace.

At Potsdam he watched the argument between Churchill and Stalin. They were two great masters of direct diplomacy. Churchill was oratorical, swayed his listeners. Stalin was direct and forceful. After a series of questions asked of him, Stalin, without any beating about the bush, replied: "You have asked me thus and thus. My answer is thus and thus." Then he sat down. Churchill, according to Joe, was working for the preservation of the British Empire, the long-cherished route through the Balkans, the Near East to India. Stalin was out to capture the same route. At one time, Stalin told how the United States had failed to deliver supplies, how Russia was fighting without weapons. Truman then made an eloquent speech telling of the seventy-five American ships lost out of one hundred en route to Murmansk, and the heroism of the American crews. It was such a touching story and so dramatically illustrated the point that though the United States might not have delivered the supplies, she tried; even Stalin seemed moved.

Prior to Potsdam, Joe said that Stalin had been so sore at Churchill for failure to start the second front and for nondelivery of supplies that he actually refused to see Churchill. Churchill had proposed coming to Moscow for a conference, but Stalin balked. Finally Joe said he smoothed things out and Stalin agreed to let the British Prime Minister come to Moscow.

July 20:   Not much bridge this evening.

Fred Vinson gave his view at some length regarding China. He showed little understanding of the problem, said General Marshall had been a miserable failure as Ambassador. Joe and I argued that the failure had taken place three years before at the Cairo Conference, when Churchill had refused any kind of compromise regarding the restoration of Hong Kong to China and had refused to operate any kind of belligerent action up the Burma Road. Fred understood little of the necessity of keeping Russia in the war though Joe argued that if Russia had backed out of the war at any time prior to the fall of 1944, we would have been defeated.

Fred told of a Cabinet meeting in 1945 when Secretary of War Henry L. Stimson had argued in favor of giving Russia the secret of the atom bomb. The Secretary of Commerce, Henry Wallace, Jimmie

Byrnes, and the Secretary of Labor, Mrs. Perkins, supported him. Vinson and Forrestal led the opposition with Tom Clark backing them up. Ickes was not present and Abe Fortas, who substituted for him, said nothing. Stimson claimed that Russia would get the atom bomb anyway (how right he turned out to be), and argued that the United States might as well get their good will by offering the A-bomb secret to Russia now. The entire world would applaud and we might be able to break down a certain amount of Russian suspicion, he claimed. In the end, Truman ruled otherwise. He further said that thirty minutes after the Cabinet meeting broke up Leo Crowley leaked the story to Arthur Krock.

July 21:   Mrs. Vinson almost never goes out with Fred, partly I think because she's just as bored with bridge as I am.

Fred said that the only time he was ever defeated in a political race was in 1928 when he ran for Congress from Kentucky but campaigned for Al Smith. The anti-Catholic feeling, he said, was beyond current understanding though he felt it was being revived somewhat by the issue of McCarthyism.

I asked the Chief who he thought had done the best job of controlling prices—Chester Bowles, Leon Henderson, or Prentiss Brown. He answered that beyond all doubt Leon Henderson had. Henderson, he added, may have rubbed people the wrong way but he ended up with prices a little bit lower than they were when the war started.

July 23:   Flew home with Fred Vinson, Julio Heurtematte, and Linwood Harrel. The Chief Justice didn't seem to worry about his safety in the air though he did ask some questions in advance about the weather.

At La Guardia our 7:30 connection from Boston to Washington was late, and by accident I got word of this fact and secured reservations for our party on the 7:55 plane. But American Airlines refused to transfer the baggage from one plane to another and so the Chief Justice carried his own heavy suitcases out to the plane, as did the rest of us. That plane trip was one of the most rugged I have ever been through. We hit a storm over Baltimore. There were eighty-two passengers in the plane, and we remained circling between Baltimore and Washington for an hour during a tropical thunderstorm which almost shook the passengers out of their seat belts. As far as I know, no one aboard the plane, except a couple of us, knew that the Chief Justice was aboard. He said nothing, made no complaints about the lack of ventilation, though the plane was steaming inside and everyone else was complaining.

July 25:   Tom Clark came for dinner in the country with his daughter, Mimi. He swam in the pool for the first time since around 1945 when the famous picture was taken of Thurman Arnold floating on his back with the cigar in his mouth and Tom Clark lighting the cigar. That picture, which was supposed to have been private, has been circulated in more embarrassing publications than almost any picture I know of. Tom recalled it with considerable amusement.

October 16:   Flew to Springfield, Missouri, where I spoke before the Southwest Missouri Teachers' Association. A terrific crowd. I gave McCarthy what-for. On the whole, they seemed to like it. In the evening I spoke before the Community Chest drive. The editor of the local paper told me afterward how he had tried to cancel the column but got too many protests.

October 18:   I got home about 10 P.M. to find that Ernie Cuneo had been calling about a broadcast by his client, Walter Winchell, who indicated that I was going to be indicted by the Justice Department. Ernie was more upset than my wife. Her bridge guests told her she apparently wanted me indicted.

October 19:   Five cancellations on the column. I don't know whether it's the Littell suit or criticism of Eisenhower, or the difficulty of getting inside news.

October 21:   Lunched in New York with the Matty Fox outfit [Motion Pictures for TeleVision]. They apparently mean business about a TV film show. Talked with Bob Wagner, candidate for mayor. He looks very much like his father and I hope he will be as good.

We talked about Kefauver's making a statement supporting Wagner. Later that evening I talked to Kefauver about this and after considerable hesitation, he decided that he had better not come out against Halley, his former Crime Committee counsel. He felt it would have a bad reaction in Tennessee, though personally he is for Wagner, not Halley.

Talked to Dolly Schiff, publisher of the *Post*, about buying the Los Angeles *News*. She was frigid. She now has a new husband—her fourth.

David Karr says the cancellations are because the column is slipping. No news and poorly written.

October 23: Jack Anderson called late in the evening to say that one of his high friends in the Pentagon reported I was to be indicted next week. Later in the evening he got the same report from a girl reporter working for the Niagara Falls paper. The reports were that the indictment was to be rushed in order to influence the election in California.*

Cuneo is full of grandiose statements about the way to beat an indictment before it takes place, not afterward. He wants to come down to be defense counsel.

October 24: Decided to write a letter to editors using the column, plus sponsors and radio stations, telling them to get prepared for possible Justice Department action. I drafted such a letter and the staff prepared to send it, but at the last minute John Wheeler and Cuneo dissuaded me. Perhaps they are right. I am beginning to think this is partly a war of nerves. The rumors, of course, have been spreading ever since Winchell's broadcast. However, I am inclined to think that except for a few weak papers and sponsors, I could weather the storm, and I would like to have a showdown on this question of suppression of an individual newspaperman for publishing allegedly restricted information. I looked up the columns McCarthy has been yelling about and which have to do with MacArthur's poor intelligence during the Korean retreat in 1950; also the column on Tank Turrets which came from Don Murray, Jack Small's assistant in the Munitions Board. Frankly, I don't think that a jury would ever take action on these.

Bob Smith called from Los Angeles. He has been getting the runaround from Ray Lehaney, Dave Beck's representative there. Beck seems to be very much interested in buying the *News*, but Lehaney won't even talk to Smith. I finally put Smith in touch with

*Drew's son-in-law, George Arnold, was running for Congress in a special election.—ED.

Dave Charnay, who is representing the Teamsters and is in Beverly Hills.

October 25: Bob Smith called to say Sheldon Sackett of the Coos Bay, Oregon, *Times*, had made him a definite offer and deposited a check for $25,000. Simultaneously Joe Keenan [of the AFL] called to say that Beck had offered to put up $250,000 in cash and asked the other unions to come in with him so that it would not be exclusively a Teamsters' project. Keenan was delighted and said that AFL President George Meany was 100 percent for the program. Keenan is trying to get other unions to go along.

Last night, Jiggs Donohue finally got hold of Bill Rogers in the Justice Department. Bill said that no action regarding me was pending that he knew of.

October 26: Jiggs saw the Acting Chief of the Criminal Division, who says that no action is pending. Meanwhile, Marquis Childs called up to say that he understood definite action would be instituted this week, possibly before he could get a column published. The funny part about the Justice Department is that two good friends of mine are in key positions—Warren Olney as Chief of the Criminal Division and Bill Rogers as Deputy to the Attorney General.

October 27: Supposed to get the new TV programs and scripts ready but way behind.

Dropped in to see Chief Justice Earl Warren. He was reading some law books when I entered, says he spends all his time studying law, is a little lonesome with his family away. We had a pleasant talk in which he diagnosed the situation in California and advised that George would be better off without Kefauver or other outsiders helping. Warren said that when Alben Barkley came in to help Jimmie Roosevelt run against him, he made capital out of it. He described the two candidates running against George—Lipscomb and Collier—as "One can't talk; and the other ought not to talk."

Warren brought up the question of Joey Fay, the convicted labor leader who has become so controversial in New York City and for whom Warren supposedly intervened to get a parole.

The Chief Justice said he frankly couldn't remember whether he had done anything for Fay but didn't think he had. I told him that I recalled an incident where I had asked him to give a pardon to one Ralph Allen and that he had declined; and inasmuch as this was a case in California, I couldn't conceive of his going outside of his own jurisdiction to intervene in an outside case. Warren said he sometimes sent letters on to other people with a covering letter saying that "such and such person had sent the enclosed letter" and that he may have done this in the case of Fay.

Sumner Welles came for dinner; seems to be in pretty good health. We didn't have a chance to talk very much.

October 28: I advised George against having Kefauver and Wayne Morse come out to California. He was lukewarm about the idea but those around him are pushing it. They seem to think he needs more support. Talked to both Morse and Kefauver, who said they would do whatever George finally decided.

Julius Klein, representing Schenley's, has been pressuring Collier, the other Republican running against Lipscomb, to withdraw from the race. Artie Samish, the big liquor lobbyist, is apparently in the picture, also Senator Dirksen of Illinois and Postmaster General Summerfield. All are trying to get Collier out of the race so the Republicans can concentrate on Lipscomb. Lipscomb has voted right down the line for Samish's liquor and racing bills in the State Legislature. He also has one of the gals who was Howser's right-hand money raiser working for him.

October 30: Marquis Childs published a column today stating that the Justice Department was planning to bring action against me regarding the argument among the Joint Chiefs of Staff re a bigger air force. The line in the column which got the Pentagon in a hubbub was a statement that General Twining added a line to the JCS minutes reserving the right to work for a 137-wing Air Force. Obviously no military secret was involved since this demand by Twining has been well publicized. But what irked Defense Secretary Wilson was the fact that few people knew this line had been added to the minutes. He called in Air Force Chief of Staff Twining, also Air Secretary Talbott, and various others to ask if they had been talking to me.

November 1: The Nelson Rockefellers came for dinner. He had just spoken at Yakima, Washington, and is worried over sentiment toward Republicans in the West. He remarked on how hard it was to take over a new administration. The problems of personnel and policy, he said, were terrific, as contrasted to the days when one Democratic administration succeeded another. I told him, incidentally, what he had not known—that Alexander Hamilton founded the Public Health Service, now charged by the Republicans as being the right arm of socialism.

November 5:   Flew to Los Angeles.

November 6:   Spoke at the University of California at Los Angeles last night and flew to Tucson immediately thereafter. Arrived in Tucson at 2:20 A.M. Just before leaving Los Angeles, I heard that Herb Brownell, speaking in Chicago, had told how Harry White had been kept on the payroll and, as he claimed, promoted to the International Monetary Fund after Truman knew he was a Russian spy.

Spoke three times at Tucson. And each time, they asked about the Harry Dexter White matter. I told them in some detail about my experience with him and how I had warned Vinson about him. To the best of my recollection, this was about July of 1945, though it may have been September. I recall that I went in to Vinson, then Secretary of the Treasury, and told him that I happened to know some of the people working with him fairly well. I mentioned Luxford as very efficient; I mentioned Joe DuBois as a man who I thought had no Red affiliations, but was a man who would disagree with Vinson and argue vigorously for his position though always do it to his face. I mentioned Harry White as one whom I was suspicious of, as being either very pro-Russian or else linked with a Russian club. I told Vinson I couldn't be sure, but that he ought to be watched. I don't believe I told Vinson, but one reason why I was suspicious of Harry White was not only his reported activity with the Russians at the San Francisco conference but because he had come to see me late one night while I was having a dinner party to argue about a story I had written critical of the Russians. He called in advance, and although I explained I had guests, he said he wanted to see me anyway and arrived around 10:30. He told me he thought the story I had written about the Russians was very unfair and that we had to get long with them somehow or other. I agreed with him that the peace of the world depended on our cooperation, but that when the Russians deserved criticism, they could not be spared from getting it.

Later I remember sitting with Mrs. Vinson at the "Make Democracy Live" dinner which I gave to award prizes in a contest. I told her about the Harry White matter and by that time I had learned that Jimmie Byrnes had called the President on the day White was confirmed and that the White House, in turn, had called Leslie Biffle to stop his confirmation—too late. I told this to Mrs. Vinson in a semijocular manner as one of the few things Fred had been not quite on the alert about. But I remember vividly that she did not take it as a joke.

Tucson is sometimes called Peglertown. However, I had a nice time there. Governor Pyle, the Republican who I predicted would not win, sat on the platform at one meeting. I can understand why his radio station boycotts my program.

November 7: Flew back to Los Angeles. The White story is raging. Lipscomb, George's chief opponent, has made a statement praising Brownell and castigating Truman. The statement had the effect of putting Lipscomb squarely on the Brownell elephant.

November 8: Spending most of my time baby-sitting. George appeared on three television programs today and did pretty well. He faced some tough questions on the Taft-Hartley Act and the loyalty oath, but did not hedge on either. I felt he could have protected himself better on the loyalty oath by saying that he stood for Governor Warren's modified loyalty oath rather than the new "McCarthy" oath. His answers, though honest, left him wide open to all the fascist critics who are going to be more vociferous in view of the Harry White exposé.

November 9: George didn't jump in to put the bee on Brownell for raising a Red herring on the eve of the California election. All the Democrats, however, say that George will win and this includes some of the Republicans. I have been a little afraid that they were too overconfident.

November 10: Lunched with David Noyes and Joe DiSilva. Noyes talked to Truman about becoming publisher of the Los Angeles *News*, but Truman is too busy with his memoirs. Ray LaHaney, the man who painted up the boxcar with Teamsters' insignia for the Friendship Train, but put not an ounce of food inside of it, has been giving Bob Smith the runaround. Dave Beck has put up $250,000 as a down payment on the *News* but they seem to be getting nowhere. DiSilva tells me that LaHaney is negotiating a new health contract for the Teamsters in which he has asked for a $90,000 cash rakeoff for himself.

George has a pretty good organization—the best this district has seen in years. Ellen is worried sick for fear there won't be enough poll watchers. They need 215. Lipscomb could count George out. Late in the afternoon one of George's headquarters gave me a list of thirty people to call to see if they had voted. They were all regular Democrats. I was able to get 90 percent of them and practically every one of them had voted. I suspected, however, that a good many had voted against George, though they did not say so. If the Democrats are deserting, he will not do so well. At 7:30 we went to his first headquarters. The returns are coming in somewhat against him.

I went back to baby-sitting. Drew had a fever of 101. I couldn't bear to tell him that his daddy is losing. He has looked forward so much to going to Washington. During the campaign, he told George he wished he wasn't running for Congress, that he never stayed home to play with him any more. But he was consoled with the story that he would come to Washington to see me and visit on the farm.

Sam Yorty drove me to the airport. He wants to run for the Senate. What punishment!

November 11:   Flew back to Washington. Armistice Day. The city is anything but peaceful. In fact, it is wild over White and severely split. Truman has been subpoenaed by Velde, Chairman of the House Un-American Activities Committee, who was probably drunk when he did so. Byrnes has piped up against Truman, reviving the old and bitter controversy. It now develops that the Harry White exposé by Brownell was part of a Republican smear campaign which was pretty well planned and timed to break just before the California election. The Republican National Committee was alerted in advance. It was J. Edgar who sold part of the idea to Brownell, just as he took Tom Clark to the mountain and told him he could become Vice President. However, Eisenhower yesterday backtracked on part of it. He underwent about the toughest barrage of newspaper questions a recent President has ever experienced during which he said that Truman should not have been subpoenaed and he did not consider Truman to have been disloyal.

I learned that the man at the Justice Department considering my indictment is Cecil Heflin, a member of the Criminal Division. The

FBI has been coking him up, though I understand he is against prosecution. The returns against George were 43,000 to 34,000, which on the surface is not good, but when you consider that no other Democrat has won more than 9,000 votes in the last ten years, it isn't bad. I'm afraid I was a jinx. I had a hunch I should not go to California.

November 13:   Went to New York for conference on new TV film.

Ed Prichard phoned from Kentucky to say that it was Fred Vinson who really kept White in the Treasury, not Truman. Vinson was convinced that the accused should have a chance to face his accuser and J. Edgar Hoover refused to divulge the name of the informant against White.

Uncovered important story showing that Eisenhower knew White despite his press conference statement to the contrary and that they lunched together at Ike's headquarters in New York in 1944. After I had sent this out in the column, the *New York Post* dug up the same story and I had to kill mine. Dictated new lead under difficult circumstances from La Guardia airport.

November 18:   Hoover turned on Truman and testified that he had vigorously recommended that White be taken out of government. He was against leaving White on the International Monetary Fund, he said, because he was then under international jurisdiction. This, of course, is not true. It was a simple matter to tap White's wires in the District of Columbia every minute of every day, and this was done. The FBI even knew when he came to my house uninvited.

Hoover has been waiting a long time for this moment. He hated Truman and almost everyone around him. He used to say that he considered Frankfurter the most dangerous man in the United States. The Democrats are sore. Representative John McCormack of Massachusetts recalls how in 1933 when F.D.R. was about to fire Hoover because of his alleged membership in the Ku Klux Klan, McCormack and Congressman Oliver went to the White House twice to urge that Hoover be kept on.

I recall how Attorney General Homer Cummings invited Bob Allen and me to dinner in 1933 or 1934 and told us he believed the best cure for kidnapping was to build up the FBI, not only in actual strength but in the strength of public opinion behind it. If the underworld came to believe the FBI was invincible, Cummings argued, there would be less kidnapping. To that end, he asked our advice about the appointment of a top-notch public relations man and those of us present, including Cummings, all agreed on Henry Suydam. Henry was appointed and did a terrific job. He really went to town with Hollywood, the radio industry, and everyone else to make the FBI invincible. A couple of years later, an amendment appeared in the Justice Department appropriations bill specifying that no money from it could be expended for the salary of an assistant to the Attorney General who did not have a law degree. It was aimed, of course, at Henry—a newspaperman. It was Hoover who got this amendment inserted in the bill. After the head start Henry gave Hoover, he had no trouble with his public relations.

November 19: On Monday, Dave Beck, Joe Keenan, and I dined with Charnay; Beck promised to put up a million dollars if necessary to buy the Los Angeles *News* if George Meany would bring in other AF of L leaders and get them to underwrite a note for approximately ten to twenty thousand per union. Keenan agreed to see Meany immediately.

Both Beck and LaHaney, who was also at the dinner, agreed to remain in Washington during the week to try to perfect the deal. It is now Thursday, however, and Keenan has not yet talked to Meany. He flew to Duluth, and I have been pestering him on the long-distance telephone, but so far no results.

November 21: Drums of fascism are beating louder. Brownell has the bit in his teeth and intends to dig up a lot of alleged spies both dead and living. Though he struck at Truman, he actually hit Morgenthau. All of the so-called spy ring worked under Morgenthau and most of them are Jews.

November 22: Went to Philadelphia to speak before a large Jewish gathering. A few days before, Velde's Un-American Activities Committee was in Philadelphia, where it called twenty-two teachers. All of them were charged with Communism and all of them invoked the Fifth Amendment. All turned out to be Jews. There's no question that anti-Semitism, though hitherto latent, is on the rampage again. After my talk, a young Jew asked me to step aside and asked me in dead seriousness whether it would do any good to bump off McCarthy. I discouraged him.

November 23:   Dined at Charnay's with Alben Barkley and Joe Keenan. Keenan completely missed the boat on George Meany. We have
lost a week's time during which Beck is now on the West Coast and
the *News* has lost another $20,000. It is losing at the rate of $20,000
a week and Smith has wired me that he has to have a definite date of
a conference or else fold.

November 24:   LaHaney, Charnay, Keenan, and I finally sat down
with Meany. He is definitely interested in buying the *News*. "Labor has
got to get hold of a paper sooner or later, and we might just as well start
in Los Angeles." He said he would see Smith the next day, Friday, or
at anytime thereafter. LaHaney gave Meany rather low figures regarding the *News's* indebtedness. I suggested that the debt was considerably larger, though I did not know how much. LaHaney seemed to be
stalling off a meeting, but finally it was agreed that he would call Smith.
This was done, and a meeting is set for Monday, November 30.

November 25:   McCarthy spoke last night blasting Truman and also
taking some pretty vigorous digs at the Eisenhower administration.
This may be the break in the McCarthy battle we have been looking
for. It's barely possible that Ike will now get off his fat fanny and realize
that the chips are down, that he can't temporize with a would-be
dictator.

November 27:   I telephoned Henry Kaiser in Oakland to try to inter-
est him in a television series. He was about as helpful as a large pillow.
I should have known better than to call him. I remember when he
wanted a blast furnace from the government in Cleveland that Tom
Clark was about to give to Republic Steel, I managed to swing it to
Kaiser on the ground that the government should help small business.
Then Kaiser turned around and sold it right back to big business—
namely, Republic Steel.

Lunched with Ray Morison and Charlie Murphy. They called me
some days ago for advice on answering McCarthy's broadcast. It seems
funny to have the Trumanites asking me for advice. I previously told
them the best man to answer McCarthy would be General George
Marshall. However, Marshall has now left for Sweden to get his Nobel
Peace Prize and on his departure paid tribute not to Truman, who put
him in the Cabinet, but to Senator Vandenberg. Second, I suggested
Dean Acheson or Alben Barkley. Dean we ruled out because he has

been too badly spattered, but Murphy thought that Barkley was just the man.

I suggested a broadcast by Barkley reviewing the history of another famous general who became President of another country—Germany —and who shrank from tangling with a bumptious politician, product of a Munich beer hall, who served as Chancellor of Germany under Hindenberg. Murphy was enthusiastic, said he would put the idea up to Truman and Barkley.

November 28: I now learn that the plane which crashed at Fort Bragg during the paratroop maneuvers was manufactured by Kaiser, not Fairchild. Last Sunday I chided Secretary of Defense Wilson for accepting entertainment from Fairchild when he was switching airplane orders from Kaiser to Fairchild. If I now go on the air and correct this, it would look to Henry Kaiser as if I were retaliating for his aloofness in buying my television film. I ought to stay away from selling.

November 30: Bob Smith arrived from Los Angeles. Saw him at lunch and dinner. In between he saw Meany.

I was not present, but Charnay, who was present, told me that Smith made a very bad impression. In the first place, the *News*'s indebtedness is fantastic. They owe $279,000 to the government on back taxes, to say nothing of $150,000 in current bills, $29,000 to the Guild and $375,000 to the Jefferson Life Insurance Company, plus some others which I can't remember. However, Smith wanted $750,- 000 for the property, which means that labor would have to put up an additional $750,000 to cover back debts. Yet Smith talked as if he weren't particularly anxious to sell.

Before he went to see Meany, Smith borrowed $5,000 from me to pay his own taxes, and he has just shelled out another $21,000 to keep the paper alive for a week.

After dinner Charnay and I called up Keenan, arranged to meet him early in the morning, to see if he couldn't put through the sale.

December 1: Met with Keenan at the Old State Department building at 8:45. It was arranged that we would talk to Smith and get him to be more realistic. Simultaneously, Keenan would try to arrange an appointment for Meany later in the afternoon. Spent all morning with Smith. He was not too reasonable. We finally agreed on $425,000 for the paper; $350,000 down with $125,000 in notes over five years. He held out for a million dollars on top of this to be paid only if the paper made that much profit during the next ten years.

December 18:   Went to the Yugoslav Embassy for dinner. Under Secretary of State Bedell Smith was there. He asked me to write something favorable about the Foreign Service. He said that McCarthy's attacks on the Foreign Service had undermined morale to a lamentable extent.

December 20:   There's more bickering among the public today than ever before; the same kind of drift toward intolerance as occurred before Pearl Harbor. The country needs a leader now as never before, yet Ike is not leading.

December 21:   Talked to Senator Kefauver about Lyndon Johnson, and the way he is failing to lead the Democrats. I urged Estes to issue some pungent press releases about conditions generally during the Christmas holidays when newspapermen will be hard up for news and will give him a real play.

December 23:   Clinton McKinnon has finally bought the Los Angeles *News*.

December 26:   Got up about 5:00 A.M. and caught the train to Detroit to work on the Gariepy case. It being Saturday, not many people were around. Lemaux has gone back on his affidavit given to Fred Blumenthal, that Mrs. Gariepy was a frequenter of a house of ill fame where she spent various nights with Schmidt, a circulation man for the Detroit *Times*. Lemaux refused to see me or talk to anyone. He tried to touch me for $1,000 after he gave the affidavit and apparently is sore because I refused to come across. Dr. Steinberg, who practices in Royal Oak and who previously was aloof, this time, however, was willing to talk. He says that it was common knowledge in Royal Oak among the police that Coughlin has had various girl friends and in recent months has driven downtown frequently with a blonde.

December 27:   Drove to Lucas, Ohio, to visit Louis Bromfield on his famous farm about which he has written two books. Rather a dull day. The farm was interesting but not much different from ours. In fact, his cows, cattle barn, etc., are nowhere near up to ours. He has the advantage of being on some very fine glacial fill, giving him a rich soil about 100 feet deep. If we had this in Maryland, we could farm with equal profit.

Met a theatrical agent named Loesser, who was at dinner at Bromfield's, and who was the agent for Mistinguette, whom I first saw dance in Paris when I went through with Felicia in 1925. Now over eighty years old, she came to the United States last year, and was a failure. After all, not even French women can remain attractive to the age of eighty. When I evidenced some sympathy for Mistinguette, Loesser said she was worth about $10 million. He also added that Maurice Chevalier, for whom he is likewise agent, is worth about $12 million. Chevalier is slightly out of his mind, and is now banned from getting a visa to visit the U.S.A. Winchell takes credit for banning him. What actually caused the trouble between Winchell and Chevalier, and perhaps the visa refusal also, was that some years ago Chevalier was wearing a rather natty, embroidered shirt which Walter admired. Chevalier remarked: "I'll send you some," which he promptly did. However, when the shirts arrived, Winchell had to pay duty on them, which made him so sore that he immediately wrote a column cussing Chevalier out as a skinflint and he has been panning Chevalier ever since. Thus run the motifs of our great opinion-makers.

December 28: Officiated at the opening of the Capital Bank, a small but modern bank which sponsors me on the radio. It's run by a very nice Jew who was born in Hungary and speaks with a very broken accent. I am constantly amazed at the manner in which immigrants can come to this country and roll up terrific fortunes in a few years. This man has not let wealth go to his head and sometimes I wish there were more people like him in the country. Boarded the plane for Kansas City to have my first TV interview with Harry Truman.

December 29: Called Truman's office and got word from his secretary to come up to see him immediately. He has rather a pleasant office in the Federal Reserve Bank Building. Shelves around his office are filled with new books, most of them history books. He had a pile of Christmas correspondence on his desk and he is meticulous in answering mail. We talked for a long time, probably forty-five minutes, prior to the interview.

December 30: Several radio stations have canceled at the end of the year. Wheeler is also worried over the number of newspaper cancellations. Lyndon Johnson, who says that I was responsible for electing him to the Senate, went to great pains to telephone Texas publishers who are friendly to him, asking if they canceled. Several of them did.

Broadcasting magazine carried an item early this week stating that the FBI for years has been trying to get something on Pearson and now they think they have got it. As a result, the Don Lee Network on the West Coast has written a Seattle advertising agency a letter stating that they would not carry the program.

1954

January 1: Spent New Year's Day on the farm. In the evening the Eugene Meyers and the Tom Hennings came for dinner. We razzed Agnes Meyer rather vigorously about Eisenhower. She didn't take it too well. She claims Ike is going to stiffen his backbone on McCarthy and take a fine new liberal policy. I asked her how she knew, and she said she had been to the White House. Presumably Ike gave her the usual brand of soft soap.

January 22: Left for Toronto by all-night train to interview Igor Gouzenko, the Soviet defector. We had been promised that at long last he would consent to a TV interview wearing a mask. So far, he has never had his picture taken, masked or unmasked.

January 23: I had taken the question of interviewing Gouzenko up with the Canadian Ambassador before leaving Washington. He was quite encouraging and said his government would impose no objections. Meanwhile, Matty Fox flew his attorney, Basel Esterich, up to Toronto, and he made the arrangements with Mr. Gouzenko. We purposely went to Toronto early so that there would be no slipups. However, the slipups began to occur all too rapidly. In the first place, the missionary work I did with the Canadian Embassy backfired against me. A member of the Secret Police called on Igor telling him that if he did appear before a TV camera, his Royal Canadian Mounted Police bodyguard would be withdrawn. Naturally, this caused the little man considerable concern. And he remained elusive all morning.

Finally we were given an address in suburban Toronto and told to be there at three o'clock. We arrived, were greeted cordially by the hostess, who did not know anything more about the business than we did, and fifteen minutes later Gouzenko himself arrived. He speaks English quite well, is still young and has a wife with all the vivaciousness of a Russian and some of the beauty of an American. She travels with him wherever he goes. We talked together for approximately two and a half hours. It was rather wearing, but I wanted to cover the whole ground of the interview carefully, especially since MP-TV [Motion Pictures for TeleVision] wants me to make the equivalent of three interviews. I did my best to persuade him to go ahead with the filming that night while it was fresh in our minds, but while I argued myself blue in the face, and Basel did the same thing, we failed. It was then I came to understand that the young man who had the courage to ransack the code room of the Soviet Embassy in Ottawa was a man who had very definite opinions on almost everything and a stubborn determination to carry them out.

However, we finally agreed to meet at a small house outside of Toronto at 7 A.M. Sunday.

January 24:   Promptly at 6:55 I turned up at the appointed address; with me were a motion picture cameraman, two sound men, Charles Curran, the producer, and Basel Esterich. We drove in two cars, and inasmuch as we had a lot of camera equipment, the taxi drivers were a little suspicious and possibly suspected a bank robbery. The people at the house were not up when we arrived, but the housewife, pattering around in her bedroom slippers and kimono, was kind enough to produce toast and coffee. Little did we know that we were to wait exactly eight hours before His Nibs was to arrive.

During that eight hours, we were unable to telephone him because his telephone number is one of the most carefully guarded secrets in Canada. However, we were able to call his agent, who did his best to produce the elusive Mr. Gouzenko. I suppose that if it hadn't been for my training in the Balkans, I would have gotten disgusted and left long before 3 P.M. But having had to wait a week or so for Slav officials, an eight-hour wait for a Slav in Canada probably did not affect me as much as it did the others. Anyway he finally turned up. Reason for the delay was his worry over the threat from the Royal Canadian Mounted Police that his bodyguard and secretary would be removed. Well, we went through with the interview. Had a hard time with his English and I'm not sure many Americans will understand what he was saying, but for the first time in history Gouzenko was put on film for TV and the movies.

February 1:   Flew to Mexico City to see former Ambassador Bill O'Dwyer. Interviewed him for TV. The interview was not too good but his conversation with me was extremely candid. There is no question that he is still the most popular American in Mexico City and although he is bitter at some things, he doesn't act at all like an exile. His bitterest feeling is toward Sloan Simpson. Apparently during her latter months in Mexico City, she was careless of her reputation, which was confirmed not merely by Bill, but by various others. Mexican society ostracized her and Bill finally moved to a hotel. He now says it was the greatest mistake he ever made. In a subsequent conversation, however, he begged me not to say anything critical of her, so I suspect he still has a sneaking affection for her. While I was in his office, furthermore, a priest telephoned to talk to him about the annulment. I gather Bill does not want an annulment.

February 2:   While in Mexico City I got Jimmie Roosevelt on the telephone and arranged for a TV interview. Persuaded American Airlines to hold a plane in Dallas for a connection and managed to get to Los Angeles by 7:00 A.M.

Interviewed Jimmie Roosevelt in Ellen's garden. Drew, Ellen, and George helped with the production. The only difficulty was the birds. They kept up a constant chatter so that you could hear them over Jimmie's voice. Jimmie was rather frank with me in private conversations. I don't think he told me the whole story. When I asked him why he had written the famed letter mentioning twelve women, he said that he had come back from the Pacific in February of 1945 and was told by his father's massage man that F.D.R. had very little time to live and that any shock would mean the end.

"At about this time," Jimmie said, "Romelle tried to force a showdown and was going to divorce me." To prevent the divorce, he signed the letter. In piecemeal form, other scraps of information came out which, put together, give a more comprehensive story. Jimmie said that Romelle took her religion most seriously and was a great believer in confession. Apparently, she got advice from a priest to get a list of names from Jimmie and then both a priest and a lawyer drafted the famous letter which Jimmie finally signed. The names of the twelve women were not given by him at one time, but were picked up over a period of months by Romelle. Of course, there must be an awful lot of truth behind the letter even though Jimmie had nothing to do with some of the women.

I remember Harry Hopkins used to tell me "The Roosevelt boys are all bed-hoppers. But you can't blame them because every girl wants to get into bed with them."

Jimmie told me that not all the Romelle story had come out, and that she had some other things on him. His father had a coonskin coat of the old college type which he remade into a coat for Romelle. However, Romelle didn't like it. It was too heavy, and she wanted to sell it. So Jimmie said he bought it himself from Romelle and gave it to a girl in Cleveland. This, I gather, happened fairly recently. Jimmie said that they had a detective shadowing him and the girl in Cleveland, who was acting as a sort of business adviser, and in that capacity they spent several evenings together. Jimmie said it was quite platonic but he did not quite explain how the coat happened to come into platonic friendship.

February 3:   Flew to New York on the new fast plane from Los Angeles which is not supposed to stop in Chicago. However, we stopped. This makes the third successive all-night sleep in an airplane. However, I managed to finish the TV filming the next day, though the two columns I had to write are not much to read.

February 6:   Used the Jimmie Roosevelt interview ahead of the second Gouzenko film. I got a deluge of critical reaction, mostly from women. They thought I was too kind to Jimmie.

February 10:   Talked to Warren Olney regarding the indictment that McCarthy is trying to have the Justice Department bring against me. He says that it came to his attention some time ago and he thought it was cockeyed.

February 14:   I have been in correspondence with Jack Peurifoy, now Ambassador to Guatemala, and have been talking to the State Department about what could be done to stop Communism. It seemed to me that the United Fruit refusal to surrender land is part of the trouble. As a result, about a quarter of a million acres have been seized by force.

In Swarthmore, I talked to a couple of Quaker leaders about the idea of establishing a summer camp in Guatemala with perhaps the sending of a thousand young Americans, 4-H Club members, people of all religious groups, to work with Guatemala and show them that we are real human beings, and not all executives of United Fruit Company.

When I talked to the State Department, they were at first highly skeptical. Their reaction was about the same as their original attitude toward the Friendship Train. Jack Peurifoy also did not seem to have much imagination. His idea is to slap a coffee embargo on Guatemala to make them yell "Uncle." In this case, however, Russia has already agreed to buy all of Guatemala's coffee crop; and the effect of a boycott would just about ruin us in the rest of Latin America. In Swarthmore, I found a couple of leading Friends interested, but rather inclined to think of the project on the basis of a dozen or so people, which, of course, would not make much of a dent, at least in one summer.

I suspect, what with a TV program and everything else I am trying to do, I shall not get too far in Guatemala. However, a project like this is something which really needs to be done and which would have a terrific impact throughout all of Central America.

February 15: Talked to Jack McCloy, now board chairman at the Chase Bank. He is always eloquent but not usually impassioned. This time he was passionate on the question of McCarthy. He told me in some detail how he had been at Dartmouth when Eisenhower made his book-burning speech and how Eisenhower had heard McCloy tell about the libraries McCloy and Lucius Clay had set up in Germany— libraries which included criticism of American officials. It was because Germans could go in and read criticism of McCloy and Acheson and Truman that they knew they were getting a cross-section of American books. And it was for this reason that they jammed our libraries, McCloy told Eisenhower, and left the Russian libraries empty. It was McCloy's eloquent description of the American libraries, which were then being attacked because of McCarthy, that led Ike to make his book-burning speech. "McCarthy talks about twenty years of treason," McCloy told me. "I was part of that administration and I served with Republicans and Democrats, men like Henry Stimson, Bob Patterson, Bob Lovett. I had been a Republican all my life and my father was a Republican and I'm not a traitor. We managed to win a war. We won a war that extended all over the world and touched every shore and after the war we managed to keep the economy of the world prosperous. That was a great achievement and I'm proud of it. And it was not accomplished by traitors."

I asked McCloy if he would appear on my television program, but he declined.

Went to New York last night in time to have dinner with Rita Hayworth and her new husband. Went to a little French restaurant where the food was passable and at least we were not recognized. I confess that despite some experience at being able to hold my liquor, I had a hard time keeping up with Rita and husband. They seem to have the idea that the world is "agin 'em" and it's everybody's fault except theirs. Or should I say perhaps that this is primarily the point of view of Dick Haymes. How long Rita can stay with him is in my opinion a matter of some doubt. My prediction would be approximately one year. I was not successful in persuading them to go on my television program, and I am not sure that I would want both of them together, with Mr. Haymes doing all the talking as he more or less suggested.

I shot Bob Young, formerly of the Chesapeake & Ohio, for TV. He is now frantically trying to take over the New York Central. He is a dynamic and contagious little man, though just how he happens to be such a power in the financial world I don't quite understand.

February 17:   The Joe Caseys came for dinner. Joe has just been indicted on the sale of surplus tankers.

He says that at the time Pat Flanagan's company in Baltimore was indicted Brownell had been his personal attorney and had recommended in favor of the transfer of the tankers. The legal question at issue is whether an American citizen can transfer tankers he purchases from the United States government to foreigners. Brownell apparently O.K.'d such a transfer. Lionel Perkins, according to Casey, organized the Landmore Corp., named for Landover School and Swarthmore College, which his boys attended, to buy tankers for both institutions and transfer them to foreign nationals. But the bank didn't accept it (thank God for Swarthmore). As a matter of fact, I heard about the deal some years ago and telephoned John Nason, then president, to warn him against it. I suspect my phone call may have had some effect. Casey says that Onassis the Greek bought up various T-2 tankers which had been anchored in the Hudson and James rivers, where nobody wanted them. He also has been indicted and he also retained Brownell as his legal adviser. He paid Brownell $10,000 personally.

February 18:   Clayton Fritchey said that when he was about to be appointed to the White House staff Truman received a warning from Howard McGrath that he was a friend of mine. So Truman asked him about it.

"Yes, that's true, Mr. President. I am a friend of Drew Pearson's. But you wouldn't want me to give up my friends. After all, you have some friends that I don't approve of and I trust you."

Harry slapped him on the back and hired him.

February 22:   Made some frantic efforts to get a TV guest. It being Washington's birthday, almost everybody important was out of town.

February 24:   [Secretary of the Army] Bob Stephens, after taking a heroic stand against McCarthy in regard to McCarthy's bulldozing of General Zwicker at Camp Kilmer,* was called up before the Republican members of McCarthy's committee, and he was brain-washed and persuaded to agree to a statement which pretty much backtracked on his previous brave pronunciamiento. Among other things, he agreed that Army officers would be produced before the McCarthy committee and would answer questions, whereas previously he had threatened to defy McCarthy. Stephens, who was at our house just last week, is an honest, sincere person whose motives and reactions are 100 percent right, but whose brain is a little slow on the uptake. Obviously when Messrs. Dirksen, Mundt, Potter, and McCarthy were finished with giving him the works, he didn't really know what he had agreed to. Stephens's son is married to Louis Bromfield's daughter, and the family spent a very pleasant evening with us.

*On February 18, 1954, Brigadier General Ralph W. Zwicker, Commandant at Camp Kilmer, appeared before a closed session of McCarthy's Permanent Subcommittee on Investigations, where he was questioned about the promotion and honorable discharge of Major Irving Peress, whom McCarthy accused of being a Communist. Zwicker refused to reveal the names of the officers involved in the promotion and discharge and Stephens, upholding Zwicker, had then directed him not to appear again before the committee. The Senator's abuse of Zwicker was a major factor leading to the subsequent Army-McCarthy hearings.—ED.

February 25: Dinner at the Portuguese Embassy. Bill Fulbright was there—the only Senator who has had the courage to vote against McCarthy's appropriation. He attended a Foreign Relations Committee meeting this morning at which Dulles reported on his Berlin trip. Bill said that Knowland of California heckled Dulles to such an extent that tears came to Dulles's eyes and that he almost wept. "It seems to me," Dulles said, "that you gentlemen are not actually interested in the foreign relations of your country."

February 26: Flew to Miami.

February 27: Interviewed Bill O'Dwyer a second time in Florida. The Mexico City film didn't come out right due to the fact that Mexico's electricity is on fifty cycles whereas our film is on sixty. So Bill met me in Miami where we did the picture over again. Bill is terribly anxious to have Senator Kefauver make a statement exonerating him. I have talked to Kefauver about it and think he will do it, though I am not quite sure.

Flew to Havana later in the day, where we got quite a reception from a battery of Cuban officials plus the local TV station, plus the Embassy. Luvie and I have not been in Havana for years and we decided to go out for dinner on the town. However, we started at the Hotel Nacional, which is in a ritzy area far from the real people of Havana, and we didn't see very much. Besides we were both tired.

February 28: Lunched at the American Embassy. I was a little embarrassed by the fact that when Arthur Gardner was appointed Ambassador I wrote a not-too-kindly story saying that Susie Gardner would wear the pants at the Embassy. However, they went out of their way to be nice and I suppose that all in all Arthur should be grateful; because about three weeks ago he called me from Havana to say that he understood I was writing a story about him and the manner in which he had allegedly insulted the daughter of a former president of Cuba. I had heard the story but hadn't paid too much attention to it and Arthur swore over the telephone by all that was holy that the story was untrue. Later I was interested to see that John O'Donnell published it plus another story, both highly uncomplimentary.

What happened was that Arthur was lunching with various Cuban leaders when he said that "all Cuban presidents were crooks." One lady immediately pricked up her ears and raised her voice. "I am the daughter of a president of Cuba and a granddaughter of a president of Cuba," she said, "and I'll have you know that Cuban presidents are not crooks." It was the daughter of Mariano Gómez. Even the American Embassy admitted to me that the story was true, and naturally it has had all Havana laughing. Probably Arthur was more correct than not.

March 1: Interviewed Fulgencio Batista. He is an extraordinarily gracious person, not at all the military tyrant he is depicted. The interview began about 5 P.M. in his office and lasted until about seven. He was extremely patient. Furthermore, he had rehearsed his lines, which were written out in English in large type on cardboard held behind my shoulder, with the result that he spoke as if he were almost a past master at English.

Lunched with the staff of *El Mundo* earlier in the day and talked to various newsmen. I gather that Batista has the following of business and the conservative elements, but probably not the majority of the Cuban people. Actually he has put across rather liberal policies and although he is reputed to have lived pretty well off the country there is no question but he has given Cuba a far more honest administration than his immediate predecessor, President Prio. I couldn't help but think during the interview that the last time I had been in Cuba President Machado was still in power, probably the worst tyrant Cuba has ever seen. The first time I was in Cuba, along with Calvin Coolidge and Charles Evans Hughes and Frank B. Kellogg (though they probably didn't know I was there), Machado had arrested about 10,000 people, put them in jail for fear of riots during the Coolidge welcome.

I was surprised at the manner in which Cubans apparently of all walks of life go out of their way to be nice to Americans. Batista made it quite evident that his policy, first, last, and always, is to cooperate with the U.S.A.

March 2: During my interview with Batista last night, we got word that five members of Congress had been shot by Puerto Rican assassins from the gallery of the House of Representatives. I immediately tried to get Governor Muñoz-Marín on the telephone in Puerto Rico with the idea of going to San Juan for an interview with him immediately. However, it was impossible to get through by phone so we went to Miami last night where Luvie took a plane on to Washington and I, plus the camera crew, stayed all night in a hotel near the airport, scheduled to leave for San Juan at 8:25 A.M. As luck would have it and thanks to being an early riser, I got up about 6:30 to call San Juan, where I got Muñoz-Marín's secretary. The Governor had flown to Washington. So we finally were able to recheck our 600 pounds of baggage to Washington, arriving shortly after lunch. Had dinner with the Governor this evening at Abe Fortas's home just around the corner. Two bodyguards were with him, plus a couple of others outside.

March 5:   Jack Kraus, my attorney in the Pegler case, committed suicide. I can't understand why. He had just written me a note setting a date for the Pegler trial, but two days later he jumped off the Washington Bridge. A difficult man to know, I had come to like him.

March 27 [Los Angeles]:   My grandsons Georgie and Drew were at the airport with George [Arnold] to meet me. Ellen is expecting the baby in late May. We went to the zoo, also rode the ponies and on a miniature train, which seems to be the rage for youngsters in California. Drew ate too much popcorn and candy and got sick. The last time I was in Los Angeles he also got sick, so I have a black mark against me.

March 30 [Washington]:   Interviewed for TV Anna Lee Moss, the Pentagon colored lady who McCarthy claimed was a Communist. She has been reinstated by the Army and exonerated by the Senate Democrats. McCarthy's attack on this lady, I think, has boomeranged, and hurt him worse than almost anything else of late.

April 5:   Talked to Bob Allen about the idea of coming back as a copartner in the column. He was receptive.

April 6:   McCarthy answered Ed Murrow. In my opinion, he did a savage and effective job. He did not actually answer Murrow, but used the usual McCarthy diversionary tactics, talked about the growth of Russia. This is what the rest of us have been talking about for years, but which McCarthy actually has been voting against—the Marshall Plan, the Voice of America, etc. I couldn't help but remember how Ed Murrow vetoed my going on CBS after McCarthy's first attack on me in December 1950.

April 7:   Lunched with Joe Volpe, one-time counsel for the Atomic Energy Commission. He told me that Lilienthal had been sore over a story I wrote several years ago telling of the differences between him and Admiral Strauss over the hydrogen bomb. I had been trying to get Lilienthal on the telephone to ask him to be a TV guest, but he will not even take the phone call.

For two Sundays I have passed up an item about Dr. Oppenheimer being under investigation for security. Volpe confirmed that Oppenheimer is under investigation. I have not used the item chiefly because I did not want to play into McCarthy's hands.

April 8:   Dulles has gone abroad to try to whip the British and French into line regarding Indochina. He is not succeeding. However, the National Security Council definitely voted to send American troops into Indochina if the French pull out.

April 11:   There is no question but what the administration is trying to whip up more and more public sentiment for Indochina. The Pentagon is definitely considering the use of small atomic bombs in that area.

April 13:   The Oppenheimer story broke. Tremendous spread in the New York newspapers. His counsel, Lloyd Garrison, gave out the full text of the AEC charges against him and Oppenheimer's reply. [AEC Chairman] Strauss and the Eisenhower people are certainly getting petty. I can conceive of no move more calculated to bolster McCarthy and to encourage witch-hunting than this throwback to the prewar years and this attempt to search under the bed of Oppenheimer's past to see whom he was talking to or meeting with in 1939 or 1940. Naturally I am a little sorry that I failed to use the Oppenheimer story when I had it two weeks ago.

April 15:   The investigation of Oppenheimer looks more and more as if it was a case of Strauss revenge. Strauss is a smooth article, but vindictive. More scientists are withdrawing from government work, and it looks as if even Strauss is worried over the hornet's nest he has stirred up. Lloyd Garrison is down from New York to represent Oppenheimer at the hearing, and his wife insisted on coming along to keep an eye on him.

April 16:   Nixon addressed the editors. He spoke off-the-record for an hour, and Bob McKinney of the *New Mexican,* who dislikes him, was impressed. There is no question but Nixon is the man the Democrats are going to have to figure in the Presidential election in 1956. Eisenhower, if he had had any thought of running, would have been around to speak himself before the editors. Instead he was in Augusta despite the Indochina crisis.

Nixon laid it on the line cold to the editors that we would go into Indochina with ground troops if the French pull out. Eisenhower made a belated statement today that American troops would stay in France as long as there is danger to France. This is the kind of statement he should have made two years ago when he was at NATO or immediately after he became President. In that case he might have gotten a European Army long ago. Instead, Dulles went to France last February and proceeded to beat them over the head with the threat that we would withdraw European aid. Nothing could have backfired worse.

April 19:   Have been trying to locate Oppenheimer to persuade him to go on TV. No luck. His friends act as if he were the Virgin Mary.

April 20:   The French are almost certain to lose Dien Bien Phu. It will take a miracle to get any kind of agreement at Geneva, and John Foster Dulles is not a miracle worker.

April 21:   *Variety* has given me one of the three annual TV awards of the year. This is the best boost I could have and means, I presume, that MP-TV will sign up for another year. They seem to be even more delighted than I am.

April 22:   Went to see George Hayes, Negro attorney for Mrs. Anna Lee Moss; he also has represented Paul Robeson. I had a tip that Robeson was going to renounce Communism in a public statement, and I offered to put him on my television program. Hayes hadn't heard from Robeson for some time, but said he hoped it was true. Not long ago, he told me, Robeson had addressed a meeting in Washington; Walter White of the NAACP had refused to attend because he had heard that Robeson was to be present. In talking to Hayes, I realized how many Negroes probably have joined left-wing fronts at one time or another. Ralph Bunche is now under the same kind of security check being given to Oppenheimer. And Secretary General Dag Hammar-skjold is so sore over it he has promoted Bunche to be Under Secretary just to spite the State Department. The promotion obviously puts the State Department in a terrific spot because if his security clearance doesn't go through, the entire world will tag the United States as anti-Negro.

Later I called Robeson myself. Trying to be as polite as possible, without using the word Communism, I told him I understood he was thinking of renouncing some of his past political ideas and said that, if so, I would like to invite him to appear on TV. The brush-off I got was about as curt as anything I've got from anyone in thirty-five years of journalism.

"I don't know what you're talking about, Pearson," said Mr. Robeson. It was obvious that he was not renouncing Communism.

Went to a dinner in honor of Joe and Marjorie Davies arranged by all the people who have been entertained by them at Camp Top-ridge. General Heslep gave a toast to both, and Joe was tragically pathetic in responding. It was obvious to almost everyone there, and there were about 300, that Marjorie would like nothing better than to see him on his way. This is her fourth husband and gossip is she has already picked out the fifth. There was a day when I didn't feel at all sorry for Joe, he having left a very nice wife for one of the most glamorous heiresses in the U.S.A. But now, at the age of seventy-five and his health failing rapidly, Joe looks on his last legs and my sympathies are with him.

It was a trip to Europe on the same boat together that brought about the romance. At any rate, Marjorie has stuck with Joe longer than her niece Barbara Hutton has stuck with anyone.

April 23:   Bart Crum came to see me about noon. While here he got a phone call from New York that Rita Hayworth's two daughters were being taken over by the Westchester court on a charge of neglect and cruelty. Rita and her new husband, Dick Haymes, are due to arrive tonight for dinner. Bart left immediately for New York with instructions to break the news to them when they arrived and to get in touch with him. Luvie and I waited dinner until about 8 P.M., then gave up the idea of entertaining the Haymeses. However, I sat up until about midnight without putting my pajamas on. However, no Haymeses!

April 24:   Had arranged a stag dinner in honor of Carmine DiSapio, new head of Tammany. He has the reputation of being the cleanest-cut executive of that motheaten and sometimes graft-ridden organization in three decades. Ten or twelve others were invited, including Senators Lehman, Langer, and Earle Clements of Kentucky. Langer looked like a ghost. I can't help but think that he hasn't got too long to live. Lehman, now over seventy, looks as young as ever. Yet he served as Governor of New York more terms than any man in history. Once one of the wealthiest men in New York, he hasn't lost his liberalism or his perspective. I wish there were more like him. I believe he is only the fifth Jew to serve as a U.S. Senator, one of the first having been in the early days of the Republic.

Dinner was scheduled for eight o'clock. I had completely given up Rita and Dick when they telephoned at seven-fifty. I had specifically asked that they telephone from Virginia to give us a couple of hours' notice. But they just don't operate that way. So during the course of the party they walked in—Dick with a three-days' growth of beard on his face, Rita looking lovely, as usual. How she can continue in love with a beachcomber like Haymes is beyond my understanding. During their entire visit they were interested in very little except themselves. They wouldn't come to dinner that night. They wouldn't come to lunch the next day. They had their meals in their rooms and when Margaret went up to help make them comfortable with some of their baggage, Haymes jumped up as if Margaret were an eager-beaver autograph seeker.

They didn't take the trouble to call the children until the next day. They didn't hop on an airplane to get up to see the children. And they didn't bother to take their leisurely drive to New York until twenty-four hours after they arrived here. All they did was sleep and eat and moan about being persecuted. Their dog, Brutus, is much better behaved. Dick has the idea that Harry Cohn of Columbia Pictures is trying to break up their marriage and I suspect that this is probably correct. They want Rita to come back to Hollywood, which is, of course, not a proper motive for breaking up anyone's marriage. But I suspect if they let Rita alone, she would break up the marriage herself, and would have done so long before this. I suspect that persecution has driven them together.

While part of the persecution is probably true, a good part of their troubles stems from their own boneheadedness and selfishness. In a mistaken moment I tried to give them a friendly talk about getting along with the press. I suggested, for instance, that it would be a simple matter to talk to the newsmen who had been calling all day and tell them that they had done what any ordinary parents would do, picked the best governess possible and left the children with her, this governess having known the children for many nonths. But they kept wailing that the newspapers doublecrossed them, were unfair to them, etc. Of course, when you get the press sore, they can be very unfair and that is exactly what's happened in this case. Rita owes most of her success to favorable press notices, but her new husband is a long way from realizing that. Last time Rita was here, I was in Hollywood, and Luvie entertained her at the farm. This time she kept an engagement in New Jersey with Marian Frelinghuysen, and I entertained Rita, dog, and husband, at the house. After Rita left the last time, Nellie, who used to be Luvie's Scotch nanny, remarked: "Luvie, why do you put up with that trash?" This time Melvin was asked by Margaret whether he was going to stay to see Rita, and he remarked: "I'd rather see Mrs. Lost World across the street." (Referring to a spinster lady who looks as if she lost out on the world.)

April 25: Last night at dinner, the chief topic of conversation was the McCarthy hearings. Democratic Senators present thought that Symington, Jackson, and McClellan had played it smart by not intervening and letting this be a row between Republicans and the Army and among Republicans in the Senate. I am not sure that they are right. The country got the impression that Democrats were afraid to tackle McCarthy. Furthermore, if McCarthy does win this row, the chance of a Democratic election in November will get slimmer and slimmer.

Everyone has agreed, however, that Ray Jenkins, a Tennessee lawyer picked by the Republicans as special counsel, is up to his eyebrows in sympathy for McCarthy.

April 27: When I watch the McCarthy hearings on television, I get so sore that I can hardly think straight. Luvie gets so upset she can't sleep afterwards. However, looking at it from a cold-blooded point of view, I think that McCarthy is losing friends as the result of these hearings. People have begun to realize how slick he can be and how ruthless. Gradually it is dawning on people that he is employing exactly the same type of delaying tactics that the Communists always employ at the United Nations. The hearings are dragging on interminably.

April 29:   While the country is absorbed with McCarthy, Dulles is letting the peace of the world go down the drain at Geneva. He committed a terrible error telling American newsmen the day before the conference opened that the United States was not going to use troops or intervene in any manner, shape, or form in Indochina. Next day *The New York Times* and other papers all carried a flat story attributed to no one, but obviously a very important person, stating that the United States would not intervene.

I did not know at the time the source of the story, but I have since learned that it was Dulles. Result of Dulles's press conference was that Molotov, the Soviet Minister of Foreign Affairs, went into reverse. He called the Red delegates together and told them to hold out for unconditional surrender rather than appeasement. Prior to Dulles's statement it looked as if Moscow was ready to appease.

The whole thing reminds me of the London conference of 1930 when Stimson was at odds with Herbert Hoover. Stimson wanted to sign a consultative pact agreeing to consult with our European friends in case of war. But Hoover vetoed it. He was under pressure from the isolationist wing of the Republican party. In Dulles's case, he wants to go much further than Eisenhower, Knowland, and the Republican isolationists will permit. The National Security Council had decided that the United States would intervene in Indochina but having made that decision they then found that neither the Congress nor the American people nor our allies were prepared for such a step without some educational buildup.

That, of course, was why Dulles pulled the rug out from under himself at Geneva. The amazing thing of it was that he called a press conference. He kept his cards close to his chest without telling anyone that Eisenhower had reversed him.

April 30:   Flew to Detroit to work on the Gariepy case. Spent most of the day interviewing members of the Royal Oak police, some of them being most sympathetic and cooperative.

The dislike of Coughlin in Royal Oak is kept very much beneath the surface but it is strong. Everyone I talked to figured that Coughlin had an affair with Mrs. Gariepy and also with various other women. He is the most powerful man in the community and was considered the most unscrupulous.

May 1:   Flew home. Arrived at 4 A.M. Republican leaders are pulling wires to stop the McCarthy hearings. Eisenhower is so furious over the investigation that when questioned at his press conference Wednesday he walked out, with visible signs of emotion. For Eisenhower, the hearings are not only a disruption of the Republican party but a terrible reflection on the Army. They show there was pull and special privilege which, of course, a lot of people have known, but which has never been brought out with such official force and emphasis. They also show that the Secretary of the Army was a weakling. All in all, the organization to which Eisenhower devoted forty years of his life comes off badly— though McCarthy comes off a little worse. Ike is so sore that he will probably fire Stephens shortly after this hearing cools off. He has made no move, however, to do a thing about McCarthy.

May 2:   Joel Fisher has the best description of Eisenhower. "Ike said before the election that he wanted to be like the President of France and just go around pinning medals on people and kissing babies. That's exactly what he's doing today, with Dulles running foreign affairs and running them into the ground, and McCarthy tearing the country asunder. Kay Halle says she talked to a White House photographer who took a picture of Dulles when he came in to see Eisenhower before leaving on a recent trip. Ike posed for the photographs, shook hands with Dulles, and was his usual pleasant self. Then he said: "Now, just where are you going, Foster?"

May 3:   Lunched with Jiggs Donohue. Decided not to take Father Coughlin's deposition. From all I picked up in Royal Oak, Coughlin was probably guilty of having an affair with Mrs. Gariepy, but Jiggs figures there's no use stirring up the charge, and I believe he's right.

May 5:   Lunched with Paul Richman, Joel Fisher, and a young man who is raising money for Mrs. Roosevelt's "Fact" organization which is trying to rebut "Facts Forum" and the Texas millionaires. The latter now have four different radio and TV programs which they give free to various networks as a "public service" and inasmuch as Mutual and ABC are running on a very tight budget or else in the red, these free package deals are very attractive. On the other side, there's almost no one to present the liberal point of view, and Mrs. Roosevelt's organization is supposed to be the answer. So far, it's pretty ineffective.

May 7:   Dien Bien Phu has fallen. Actually it was not an important fort, but has been played up to such an extent that it is the worst psychological defeat in the Free World that the Eisenhower administration has taken for some time. It puts Eisenhower more on the spot than ever, and he simply hates being on the spot.

The National Security Council has now changed its tune. In February they came to the hard and fast conclusion that Indochina was essential to the free world and that the rest of Asia would go Communist if it fell. Now the NSC has officially come to exactly the opposite point of view.

May 10:   Jane Ickes came for breakfast to go over the next installment of Harold's diary. I have the feeling that they are cheapening the old man by retaining a lot of gossip that he noted in his diary. (Even as I am.) The first years were terrific, but when he retired from the Cabinet, he had nothing to do but brood and gossip and this comes out rather vividly. I told Jane that I thought she should use the pruning shears rather drastically in the later volumes.

May 11:   Lunched with an East German who was here as a guest of the State Department. He emphasized the importance of keeping up our contacts behind the Iron Curtain and encouraging people there. I reviewed with my luncheon guest the efforts we had made to get balloons into Czechoslovakia—rather successfully; and also the promise Eisenhower and Dulles had made during the election campaign to stir up the Free World. Promises unfortunately which haven't been fulfilled. I couldn't help thinking, however, that perhaps the best strategy in regard to Indochina right now would be to concentrate on causing trouble for Moscow right in its own front yard—namely, Czechoslovakia, Poland, Hungary, all the countries far more important than Indochina.

May 12:   Eisenhower and Knowland both made appeals to the Democrats to come back to a bipartisan foreign policy. They say the Democrats aren't traitors after all.

Got a squawk from WTOP regarding the cigaret–lung cancer interview with Dr. Ochsner. They said they had too many cigaret companies buying time on their station. Dumont in New York would not carry the cigaret–lung cancer program at all.

I'm beginning to think that the debate over Indochina between ourselves and the British and the French is like the debate on March 7, 1936, when Hitler invaded the Ruhr. The French and British debated all day and did nothing. If they had done something, they would have found, as was discovered after V-E Day, that Hitler's troops had a double set of orders, one to advance, the other to retreat in case of opposition. The Indochina problem is more complicated. But the Air Force would like to use the atom bomb in Indochina on the grounds that Communist opposition would immediately fold up. The State Department and British say no on the argument that the vast populations of Asia would be inundated. I think the State Department is right, but likewise I think the war would be over if the atom bomb was used. I can sympathize with Eisenhower in being faced with this decision. If I had to make it, I think I would vote with the State Department.

May 13: The Scripps-Howard newspapers are featuring editorials: "Get Going Ike." They demand he show some leadership regarding the McCarthy hearings and really run the country. It reminds me of the editorials published in the late summer of '52, during the Presidential campaign, entitled: "Ike's running like a dry creek." It was this editorial as much as anything which got Eisenhower to blast the Democrats, especially on Korea, and really caused him terrific headaches as of now regarding the bipartisan foreign policy. Yet he would have won anyway. The White House still worries about these Republican editorials and it will be interesting to see what effect this one has.

As of last weekend, however, Eisenhower was still trying to appease McCarthy. I now learn that he took Secretary of the Army Stephens for a drive in Virginia with Nixon, and they both poured it on Stephens to agree to terminate the hearings. Stephens is showing more backbone than I ever thought he had. He refused.

May 14: Dined last night at the Argentine Embassy. It made me think of the time I had picketed the Embassy when Harry Vaughan was given a medal by Perón. It was that picketing that caused Harry Truman to call me an s.o.b. which, as far as my relations with Republican newspapers were concerned, was the best thing that could have happened to me. I have always felt a little foolish, however, about that incident. I don't think I should have gotten myself into it.

Senator Dirksen is still trying to appease McCarthy and call off the hearings. McCarthy has been a very silent spectator all week. Instead of interrupting constantly, he has said almost nothing, while the Army counsel has been on the stand. I think this is because he got a very sour reaction from the public for constantly heckling Stephens. Dirksen mentioned almost plaintively my column of yesterday in which I said that he was trying to call off the hearings. I couldn't help but remember with a twinge of remorse when I had once imposed on Dirksen to spend a day in the Charles Town, West Virginia, court-house, testifying to my good character and the fact that I was no Communist. This was the libel suit against Funkhouser, who had called me a Communist. However, I once went all the way to Pekin, Illinois, to speak for Dirksen, so I guess it's even. And I shouldn't feel too badly about criticizing him.

May 16:   I've been reading Claude Bowers's book on Spain. It's a revealing document, especially in light of the current campaign to make anyone who sympathized with Loyalist Spain a Communist.

Oppenheimer is now on trial because he helped to raise money for Loyalist Spain. Jack McCloy has been pilloried by Pegler—as I have —because McCloy advocated commissions for Americans who fought in the Spanish Civil War. I wrote columns along this line and in fact conferred with McCloy on the subject. In contrast, Bowers tells in great detail the story of the strong Republican forces in Spain at that time and the pressures against them by both the Monarchists and the Communists. Bowers, who was our Ambassador during the Civil War, reveals something that I should have known but didn't, and which explains much of the propaganda and bitterness in this country. The Spanish Republican government had voted to bar teaching by Catholic priests. In other words, parochial schools were abolished. This made the clergy see red, and in retrospect I can now understand the violence of the Catholics in this country toward the Republic. It also explains the determination of the Catholic group to get a substantial loan for Franco in these later years to insure his economic and political position. In a way, it also explains the bitterness of Father Walsh and some of the Georgetown Jesuits against Dean Acheson. For it was Acheson who stood steadfast against any aid to Spain, as did Truman. Of course, there were other factors coupled with it, such as the fact that Dean refused to take the graduates of the Georgetown Foreign Service School in large numbers and reached out into other universities and other walks of life for his embryo diplomats.

But someday the entire story of the McCarthy attacks on the State Department and the part Father Walsh had in inspiring them will be told in relation to the Spanish Civil War, and the present propaganda to make anyone connected with the Loyalist side of that war a Communist.

May 17:   My third grandson, Joseph Patterson Arnold, born today. The Supreme Court also ruled today against school segregation. Governor Talmadge of Georgia is raving. Jimmie Byrnes of South Carolina is strangely silent. He had done a lot of talking in the past but now, being a former Supreme Court Justice, I presume is loath to buck the Supreme Court.

Filmed a TV program on Indochina. Men in public life should learn to be a lot more careful about what they say in these days of television. I showed Nixon making a speech in which he promised there would be no new "small wars," and pledged that we would depend upon massive retaliation. Then I quoted him a month later telling the newspaper editors that we are going to send troops to Indochina for a "small war." When Dulles's speeches have been put end to end, they will face worse contradictions than Truman's. I sometimes wonder whether anyone bothers to collate Dulles's or Nixon's speeches.

May 19:   Bill Benton came to see me. Is bubbling over the excitement of the drubbing given to McCarthy. This looks like the first real stumbling block for the man from Wisconsin. Dozens of people at dinner parties used to look at me coolly, but now come up and congratulate me. Most of them are Republicans.

Bill, who is making money hand over fist, has chartered a swank yacht to cruise through the Mediterranean. He is a mass of social and economic contradictions. He talks about the great job the liberals are doing and when in the Senate voted amazingly liberal, and simultaneously he tells how he's fired six girls who used to turn the records for Muzak, and now hires one girl who does it all.

Ex-Senator McFarland asked me to drop in to see him. He is planning to run for Governor of Arizona, but complained about the radio and news blackout. Eugene Pulliam tosses my column out of the Phoenix papers whenever it suits his convenience, which is frequently. Governor Pyle, the Republican, received a Ford convertible from a dealer in Flagstaff in payment for his help on Tidelands Oil. But nobody will print the story.

May 28: Senators Duff, Lodge of Massachussets, Smith of New Jersey, and Paul Hoffman, Board Chairman of Studebaker-Packard, are very cool on Ike. They feel he gets his policies completely from General Lucius Clay. At a White House breakfast of Republican leaders recently, one Senator, identified as Griswold,* was reported to have told Ike, "We promised to lead the nation and are not leading. Unless we show some leadership, we are finished."

Joe Davies says that Churchill is so sore over the rebuff Eisenhower gave him at Bermuda that he wept for days and would have nothing to do with Eisenhower. This was one reason why he has been so cool regarding our overtures on Indochina. Dulles made the tragic mistake of exhibiting his own weakness to the Russians by going to London on a mission that he should have known was futile before we went—namely that Churchill would not do business with us.

The irony is that Churchill, who is now flirting with the Russians, once was responsible for alienating the Russians. Today he says that Molotov is one of the great statesmen of Europe. He has sent emissaries to talk over trade with Russia and was delighted to have labor groups visit Red China.

Last December Joe was at a dinner where he sat at the head of the table next to Eisenhower. Eisenhower asked how he was doing and then asked how he thought things were going with his administration. Joe replied, "They're cutting your guts out. You should have taken my advice and gone with us. These people don't think the way you do, don't act the way you do, and they're undercutting you every minute."

Eisenhower said, "Come have lunch with me soon. Let's talk about it." But Joe never got the invitation.

I recall that in the summer of '48 I went to see Joe shortly before the Democratic Convention and urged him to help get Eisenhower to run on the Democratic ticket. Joe said that he would. But today, apparently forgetting this conversation, he told me that he was the one who urged Ike not to run as a Democrat in '48, but to wait till '52. "Then you will be a shoo-in. If you run now you have two strikes against you. The wife of MacArthur's aide is out to get you, and this other woman is writing a book. The Baptists, Methodists, Congregationalists, will all be against you. Wait until the book blows over."

*Possibly Dwight P. Griswold, Republican Senator from Nebraska, who had died six weeks earlier.—Ed.

June 1:   Sailed down the river on the Sequoia as the guests of Assistant Secretary Fred Seaton and his wife. The last time we were on the Sequoia was with Francis Matthews, Secretary of the Navy under Truman. The Republicans, however, shop the Sequoia around so that any member of the Cabinet can borrow it, which seems to be a better idea. Matthews used it practically every night for himself.

On the cruise were Len Hall, chairman of the Republican National Committee, who turned out to be quite a songbird and a very enjoyable gentleman. Also Mrs. Catherine Howard, Republican National committeewoman from Massachusetts, now with Civil Defense. General and Mrs. Davidson (she is Al Gruenther's sister) were there and various others, some of them not in government. I was the only newspaperman present and was not sure whether this was an olive branch or not. I am inclined to doubt it though God knows the Eisenhower administration in the face of the McCarthy attacks needs to toss out a few olive branches. Mrs. Howard traveled on the Eisenhower train with Seaton and they told some interesting reminiscenses, among others how Ike had been given an elk's head at one western town and she had put it in Bobby Cutler's bed, very carefully tucking the sheets around the elk's ears so he peered out in the most affectionate though somewhat startled manner. Then they all listened to see what Cutler, the Boston banker did when he went to bed. Unfortunately, like most Boston bankers, he was too restrained.

June 2:   Senator Symington of Missouri, whom I panned for being a molly coddler at the McCarthy hearings, is really doing a job; he has turned out to be the best cross-examiner of all.

Dined at the Greek Embassy. Mrs. Myron Cowen, whose husband I was critical of when he was U.S. Ambassador to Belgium, was most gracious and went out of her way to praise my stuff on McCarthy. It made me feel like a heel.

The Minister of Luxemburg wants me to buy a cottage at Seal Harbor, Maine. I did not tell him how broke I was.

June 3:   Clayton Fritchey came to lunch to discuss ideas for interviewing Adlai Stevenson on Saturday. He said that Adlai was doing a lot of thinking about the encroachment on the Executive branch by the Congress and the need for protecting the President's powers. For years it was just the other way around.

Dined at the Brazilian Embassy. Seldom have I sat down at the same table with more people whom I have panned, beginning with Senator Dirksen, whom I panned in the broadcast recorded no later than this afternoon though he won't hear it until Saturday. Also Capehart of Indiana and Frear of Delaware, whom I once referred to as "pay-toilet" Frear. The only familiar friendly faces besides our host and hostess were the Ambassador of Italy and Madame Tarchiani. She still talks about the Friendship Train, which of course always makes me feel at home.

However, I had quite a talk with Dirksen. He has the happy faculty—though sometimes it isn't too happy from his point of view —of being all things to all men. If he hadn't switched sides so many times, I would respect him more. However, I can never dislike him. He is one of the most gracious people I know and if he only had more backbone he would be a terrific Senator.

I also had quite a talk with Capehart after dinner. The last time I saw him was in his office where he had called a press conference to bawl the hell out of me regarding the B & O Railroad scandal, which I had accused him of suppressing. He told me how he had put the public housing bill through the Senate, and I must say he did an extremely efficient job. It even turned out better than I thought it would.

June 4:   Took the midnight train to New York. Lunched with Carter's Harry Hoyt. He had his attorney, Hanaway, present, who is still fighting the Federal Trade Commission on the right to use "liver" in regard to Carter's Little Liver Pills. The question of Oppenheimer arose.

Oppenheimer was OK.'d for loyalty yesterday but denied security clearance. Hanaway and Harry Hoyt immediately jumped on him.

Then the question turned to McCarthy and Hanaway praised him as a great American. I threw in my two cents' worth rather vigorously, and Harry agreed with me. As I look back on it, it's a wonder I stayed on the air for Carter Products as long as I did, though I am sure that if matters were left to Harry Hoyt alone I would probably still be operating for him.

Dined with the Karrs. General Hugh Casey and his wife were present, and as the evening progressed, each took me aside individually to tell me what an s.o.b. I was for having written about their daughter's marriage in Germany and the fact that they were sending some packages to her by air. For the life of me, I can't recall the incident. It made me realize, however, how many people's toes I've stepped on and how many enemies I've made over the years.

June 5:   Interviewed Adlai Stevenson for TV. He received an honorary degree at Columbia University at noon and left me in his suite at the Savoy Plaza until about three o'clock. I must say that Adlai is just as attractive to meet personally as he is cracked up to be. I had not talked to him as far as I can recall since he testified against me in the libel suit brought by Monroe Kaplan. Actually, Adlai wasn't exactly a hostile witness though he did deny some of the things I had written in the column. However, the effect on the jury was pretty well removed when I jumped up when he left the witness stand and shook hands with him. He was caught in a place where he had to be equally cordial. I didn't remind him of this today, though, nor did I remind him of the letter I had written him in 1948 urging that he let his friends build him up for President. This was the first TV interview he has given aside from a Lincoln Day appearance with Ed Murrow and I think he was a little sorry he had consented. During the warmup, he remarked that Dave Karr's yellow-and-red necktie looked like the "Spanish Armada," told him not to bring his grandfather into the picture as a buildup because he wasn't born when his grandfather was Vice President. And when the producer asked him to keep his head in the same place because "your head is on the wall," referring to his shadow, Adlai replied: "I've been wondering all day where my head was."

He was amazingly spontaneous during the interview and when he had recounted some of the Republicans who served under Roosevelt, including Jack McCloy, Henry L. Stimson, I remarked: "Were these some of the traitors that we hear have been operating for the last twenty years?" To which he replied: "Yes, and Eisenhower was one of them too."

Privately he told me that he was very much puzzled as to how we could get back on a bipartisan foreign policy—first because the Attorney General had insisted on calling the Democrats traitors no less than a couple of days ago; second, because it was only human nature for the opposition political party to pick the policies that are not going well and disapprove them. "Our policy in China during the war," he pointed out, "was not a success, so the Republicans have seized on that as a

campaign issue." Privately he made some remarks about Dulles that
were not too favorable, and I was tempted to draw him out on this on
the air, but didn't. It is a fairly easy thing to take the ball away from
the average person on interviews, but not Adlai. He was pretty much
master of the situation.

June 6:   Roy Howard came out editorially today, in effect, for a preventative war. On June 17, the Joint Chiefs of Staff meet at Quantico
with various military leaders, more and more of whom are talking about
a preventative war.

Ansel Luxford, who used to be in the Treasury under Morgenthau,
has suggested to me today that I stage a television program with a
so-called Fifth Amendment Communist and he believes he could get
some important person, such as Fred Coe or Harry Glasser, both
formerly in the Treasury, to answer questions on TV which they would
not answer before a congressional committee. He points out that the
public doesn't understand why people plead the Fifth Amendment.
First, because once they answer one question they then have to answer
every question; second, the expense of a trial if they make some small
error. They have all noticed how Lattimore tried to answer questions
but was caught on some irrelevant questions where his memory was
bad, and thus indicted for perjury. Luxford suggested that if I were able
to arrange with a prominent lawyer to handle their case if they were
subsequently prosecuted, he might persuade them to appear on television.

June 7:   Heard over the radio this morning that Maury Maverick was
dead. I don't know when I have been more saddened. It was only two
months ago that I had dinner with him in San Antonio, together with
about fifty of his friends and liberal leaders at which they organized the
Society for the Perpetuation of Drew Pearson.

Maury did not say so but I gathered that he was having a hard
time with his law practice and I know that his son was having a very
tough time as a member of the legislature. The legislators are paid ten
dollars a day when they meet and it's impossible to live on that in
Texas, as a result of which most of them are subsidized directly or
indirectly by oil, gas, and cattle lobbies. Maury, Jr., was trying to decide
whether he should run again, especially in the face of the fact that the
Texas Manufacturer's Association was planning to drop $20,000 into
his district to defeat him.

Maury, Sr., told me that at long last a little ray of light was beginning to creep above the political horizon in Texas and that people spoke to him once again as he walked down the street. Now he is dead. I shall miss his provocative letters and his goading telephone calls encouraging me to stay in and fight.

June 9: Senator Hunt of Wyoming has announced that he will not run again. He gave as his excuse his health. Unfortunately I am afraid that the morals charge against his son and the experience Hunt suffered was the main factor. Welker of Idaho and Bridges of New Hampshire attempted to blackmail him out of running in one of the most scandalous pressures ever exerted on any Senator. I remember meeting Hunt on the Friendship Train riding through Wyoming. He began as a dentist, made a good Governor of Wyoming, and an excellent Senator. He was reasonably sure of reelection and the fact that he has dropped out of the race has made it harder for the Democrats to control the Senate.

June 10: Went to the British Embassy garden party. They were lucky it didn't rain. I remember Lady Makins when she was Alice Davis, and one of the most beautiful debutantes in town. She is still beautiful. Met Art Sylvester of the Newark *News* at the Garden Party, and talked to him about admitting a Negro to the Press Club. The Negro is Lewis Lautier. Art will go for it, but thinks that I shouldn't sponsor Lautier since I am one of the more controversial members. However, Art is on the board of governors, is confident that the application will go through.

Dined with Kay Halle, and General and Mrs. Twining were there. He agrees with General Ridgway that it would be foolhardy to go into Indochina. He was discreet in what he said but I gather that he chafes a bit at Eisenhower's mercurial tendencies. He told the story of how he had once gone in to see Truman on a very delicate and important bombing problem in Korea. General Vandenberg was away and Twining, as second in command, had to take the matter up direct with the Commander in Chief. He said he was scared to death when he went in to see Truman and carried a map showing what the Air Force planned to do. Before he had quite finished, Truman said: "Fine. That's an excellent idea. Why didn't we think of it before? Go ahead." Twining didn't say so, but I gathered he can't get the same decisions out of Eisenhower.

General Ridgway called in a group of newspapermen last Saturday night and told them that if the Army was forced to intervene in Indochina, he would feel called upon to resign.

June 13 [Amherst, Massachusetts]:   Luvie stayed awake most of the night worried over the idea that Tyler was either married or getting married. Despite my assurances, she wouldn't think otherwise until I had a talk with Tyler.

At the graduation, Tyler was the first to receive a degree, thanks to the accident of the alphabet. He was not the first in his class scholastically though this last year he has done far better than I expected. Had a hard time realizing that the youngster who was born in the depression days of 1932 was now graduating, and I couldn't help but wonder, as I watched the long line of 230 graduates file by, what the future held in store for them—the jungles of Indochina, atomic war, or what?

June 14:   The Republicans are determined to end the McCarthy hearings and they have the votes to do it. They are riding roughshod over the Democrats. Apparently Eisenhower is also 100 percent behind them.

June 15:   Got a telephone tip last night that one of McCarthy's typists, Madeline Grotnes, is ready to tell the truth about the memos which McCarthy's secretary claims were typed during the height of the Army controversy. Actually Madeline is the girl who typed them and is willing to tell the truth.

I took this information to Stuart Symington at breakfast and to my amazement he refused to touch it, argued that the Republicans would refuse to call any more witnesses and that McCarthy would only accuse him of smearing. He also refused to ask Cohn whether he had ever attended meetings of the Lawyers Guild, which is reported to be a fact, or any other controversial question.* Stuart didn't explain why

*The National Lawyers Guild, a favorite McCarthy target, was a radical counterorganization to the American Bar Association. Because of its members' active involvement in liberal and leftist causes, it was accused of being a Communist front. Presumably, "Cohn" is Roy Cohn, the McCarthy Committee counsel.—ED.

but he made it obvious that he just wasn't going to tackle McCarthy any more. Later I learned that he had received a bushel basket full of telegrams berating him for going after McCarthy on his finances.

Senator Jackson also is going to take the rest of the hearing lying down. Last week Cohn threatened to "get Jackson" and it was learned that Cohn had prepared a file on Jackson's alleged left-wing connections. However, Jackson, though urged to answer Cohn and urged to put Cohn on the witness stand, so far has refused to do so. He hasn't even forced a showdown on the file Cohn has brazenly displayed on the Senate committee table.

Interviewed Senator Margaret Chase Smith of Maine regarding her primary race with a McCarthyite. She is a lot more liberal privately than she is publicly.

Churchill has agreed to come to Washington to see Eisenhower. I understand that Eisenhower will fix the date only when he knows the McCarthy hearings are going to end.

My old friend Jack Peurifoy has made three attempts at revolution in Guatemala and it looks as if the last one might be successful. He persuaded six generals to call on President Arbenz and threaten him with revolution unless he gets out.

June 19: Senator Hunt of Wyoming committed suicide early this morning. I am not sure whether it had to do with the threat Senator McCarthy made yesterday that he was going to investigate a Democratic Senator who had fixed a case, or whether it was Hunt's concern over his son's homosexual troubles. About two weeks ago Hunt went out to the Naval Hospital and afterward announced that he was retiring from the Senate because of health. Actually Dr. Calvert says there's nothing wrong with his health. Personally I think he just didn't want to face the innuendo and rumors regarding his boy during the election campaign. Also he had been bludgeoned by Senator Welker of Idaho to get out of the race. I was on the verge of writing a story about this last December, but got a call from Tracy McCraken of the Wyoming newspapers, who pleaded with me not to. Hunt also told Jack Anderson at the time that if the story was written, his wife would die. He said she had suffered agonies and had eaten nothing for a week during the boy's trial.

June 20:   Debated Congressman Clarence Brown of Ohio and Congressman John McCormack of Massachusetts over NBC on the obligations of the press. Opinions differed as to whether I got the worst of it. I was on the receiving end and had to admit that 80 percent of the press is Republican and that much of it is biased. I didn't get a chance to mention it, but General Motors has just withdrawn $250,000 worth of advertising from the *Wall Street Journal* because the *Journal* dared to print the advance models of the new GM cars. Certainly this indicates that big business is determined to control the press.

June 21:   Talked to the Chief Justice about making an address on the Fourth of July reminding the nation about our basic freedoms. He said that he had been invited to speak at Gettysburg on July 4 at the centennial of Pickett's charge, but declined because he was not qualified. "I'm going to have to pass on a lot of questions dealing with our basic freedoms," he said, "and McCarthy might say I'm prejudiced if I take a strong stand today. Furthermore, I'm not sure that I'm qualified to talk on these things. I'm doing an awful lot of reading and it's something I want to approach very carefully." Warren said that he was speaking before the American Bar Association in the late summer and the John Marshall centennial in the fall, and that he might take the opportunity to speak on the subject at either one. Talked with Senator Ed Johnson of Colorado about the FCC and about Commissioner John Doerfer. I didn't need to talk to him. He launched forth in a tirade against the Eisenhower administration as the most graft-ridden in history. He said the Harding administration had turned out to be a piker in contrast. He pointed out that commission after commission is bent on robbing the public, that the quasi-judicial process has disappeared, and that all you had to do was to know Presidential Assistant Sherman Adams to get TV licenses, oil pipelines, and increased utility rates. Ed, who is the ranking Democrat on the Senate Commerce Committee, is considered quite a conservative, and I was surprised at his outburst. He said that he had voted against Doerfer and would demand a hearing regarding Ted Lamb. I suggested to Ed that John Carroll, now running for the Senate in Colorado is an old enemy of Doerfer, and he should make up. They have been political enemies since Carroll ran against Johnson in the primaries. Johnson smiled and said he thought that could be arranged. I called John afterward in Denver and suggested he might make some overtures to Ed and I believe they are going to get together.

Cuneo called from New York to say that he had received a stiff telegram from Senators Welker and Bridges demanding a retraction on a special column I distributed yesterday telling how the two Senators had pressured Senator Hunt to withdraw from the Wyoming race or his son would be prosecuted. Both Cuneo and John Wheeler* wanted to kill the column. I finally persuaded them to stand pat though I had a whale of a time trying to do so.

June 22: Cuneo came down from New York especially to see me re the Welker-Bridges column. He still wants to send out some kind of an apology. I hear that Welker and Bridges are busy lining up Inspector Blick, the vice-squad chief who was told by Bridges and Welker to resign unless he prosecuted.

Talked to Senator Duff of Pennsylvania about the Flanders resolution censuring McCarthy. He squirmed all over the lot and talked big, but made no commitments. His alibi was that the Senate rules should be changed to prevent such behavior as McCarthy's. He didn't seem to realize that no matter what the rules, McCarthy would violate them.

Talked to Warren Olney about the Madeline Grotnes matter. He promised to investigate, though I have my fingers crossed. He says that newspapers are most unfair to the Republicans, especially my column.

June 23: Ted Lamb testified before the Senate Committee regarding the manner in which his TV licenses had been threatened because he had contributed heavily to the Democratic party. Commissioner Doerfer immediately denied all this, and I gather scored heavily with the Senators. Howard McGrath, Lamb's counsel, has been sitting on his big fat fanny, doing nothing in the same brilliant way he performed as Attorney General. Senators don't vote until they are educated. They are too busy. And McGrath has done no educating.

July 2: Two Internal Revenue men came to see me to discuss the Patullo-Modes case. They wanted to know, first, the date of a broadcast in which I had mentioned the Patullo-Modes case. Made a thorough search and could find nothing either in the column or on the radio. They also said they had checked on Edward Martin, who was involved

---

*At this time, Ernest Cuneo was a part owner of the Bell Syndicate, which distributed the column; John Wheeler was president. Later, Bell was purchased by Drew Pearson and two partners.—ED.

in the Chinese aviation gasoline deal, which in turn involved Senator Bridges. They indicated that they were looking into Bridges also, but I couldn't draw them out. I gave them information regarding the money Bridges had received from Phillips Petroleum when he voted against the Kerr natural gas bill. They took the information but were noncommittal. I had the feeling that the agents down the line would like to do a real job on Bridges but those up above didn't.

July 6: Subpoenaed to testify before a federal grand jury regarding Grunewald and the Patullo-Modes case. I told them that I couldn't find copies of anything I had ever written or said on the radio about it.

July 20: A filibuster finally started against Dixon-Yates, the steam power contract given to private interests in competitition with TVA. I have spent the last two days talking to various Senators, including Lister Hill of Alabama, Magnuson of Washington, and Wayne Morse, urging them to filibuster. I didn't have to urge Wayne. He was all for it. The others didn't take much urging either.

July 21: Tried to get Joe Dodge, former Budget Director, on the telephone to check on a story that he employed a public utilities man for three months to work out the Dixon-Yates deal, after which this man went to work for Dixon-Yates. Traced Dodge to San Francisco, where he finally answered the phone—but hung up on me.

Went to Mike Monroney's for dinner. It was Peggy Palmer's birthday. Sam Rayburn was quite expansive. He thinks the Flanders resolution against McCarthy will fail. I suspect that Sam reflects Lyndon Johnson's views. Monroney didn't get to his own dinner party until 10 P.M. because the Senate was still filibustering.

July 22: Lamar Caudle let drop something that I always suspected but never could prove. He says that Joe Blythe, former treasurer of the Democratic National Committee, received $60,000 from Ripps and Mitchell of Mobile, the two income tax violators I finally tracked down some years ago. I had heard that they gave Blythe $25,000, and at the time of the story, which was 1950, I asked Lamar about this. He said he didn't know anything about it. However, he did get to work and did prosecute and convict Ripps and Mitchell. But today he told me that Congressman Boykin of Alabama, who was a good friend of Lamar's, had told Harry Truman: "Lamar knows about that $60,000 that was given to you in Mobile." "I didn't keep it," Truman replied, according to Boykin. "But Lamar knows about it," Boykin says he told Truman. "So you had better not fire him."

Lamar says that Truman passed the money on to Joe Blythe and it was found in his strongbox on his death. He did not give it to the Democratic National Committee but kept it.

Grunewald* was indicted today. One of the counts against him was that on which I testified—regarding the Patullo-Modes case. Grunewald had told a congressional committee that he had heard nothing about the Patullo-Modes case until "Druly Drew" told about it on the radio.

I went to the airport to see George and Georgie [George Arnold and his second son, George, Jr.] off. Georgie looked very wistful under his big cowboy hat. He wasn't much interested in me but was in his elder brother. "Come, Gu, come," he said, holding out his hand to Drew.

July 25:   The filibuster against Dixon-Yates is broadening out to one against the entire atomic energy bill to permit private industry to develop atomic power. But the filibuster began to cave in last night. Lyndon Johnson cracked it.

Governor Shivers has been forced into a runoff in Texas. This is quite a defeat for Eisenhower. Yarborough, the candidate against Shivers, had almost no money and not much of an organization.

Lunched at Colonel Grady Gore's. His son-in-law, Gordon Dean, had a big blowout—ostensibly for Ben Sonnenberg—but actually it seemed to feature Atomic Energy Commissioners, and Senators and Congressmen who are members of the Joint Atomic Energy Committee. Gordon Dean is now working for Lehman Brothers, and even before he left the chairmanship of the Atomic Energy Commission he had come out for releasing atomic power to private industry. He is now back in Washington lobbying. I suspect that he was responsible for

---

*Grunewald was indicted on several counts of perjury, including earlier testimony in which he had lied about his tax-fixing activities during the Truman Administration; in particular, he had lied when he had said he never discussed tax matters with Daniel Bolich, the Assistant Commissioner of IRS who was himself indicted and convicted of tax fraud.—Ed.

helping to get Senator Gore of Tennessee and Lyndon Johnson to break the filibuster last night.

Drove Luvie and Drew to the beach. Later went to the Abe Fortases. Stuart Symington and his wife were there for dinner. Stuart talked about ducking out on the Flanders resolution against McCarthy. I was interested in the fact that his wife, who I have always thought was pretty much to the right of center, chided him. "You can never do that," she said. "You have taken a stand against McCarthy and you can't possibly duck a vote on him." Stuart, however, is hoping they will postpone any vote on the Flanders resolution.

July 28: Abe Fortas called to say that Senator McClellan of Arkansas was running out on the McCarthy-Flanders debate. McClellan was renominated in Arkansas only because he had taken a firm stand against McCarthy during the Army-McCarthy hearings; now he is not going to come back to Washington to vote on the Flanders resolution but will stay in Arkansas. I should have realized that neither a leopard nor a Senator ever changes his spots. McClellan was a conservative phony from the first day he entered the Senate and will always be one.

I called Senator Flanders to tip him off about McClellan. He said he was not too surprised. Also talked to Senator Fulbright. He said that he had had a hard time getting Flanders and McClellan together in the first place. They finally met about 10 P.M. in McClellan's hotel to work out the alleged agreement on McCarthy. But apparently it was a rather one-sided agreement, and the publicized promise by McClellan that he would vote against McCarthy was rather reluctant.

Senator Gore called me a liar on the Senate floor today. He didn't like what I said about his having caved in on the Dixon-Yates filibuster.

July 30: Went up to the Senate for the beginning of the Flanders debate. Haven't been up there for over a year. The anti-McCarthy Senators were trying to hold it up until McClellan got back from Arkansas. I think they will succeed.

July 31: Visited the Phil Grahams at their place in Virginia. Phil doesn't think much of Kefauver. He tells how he and Wiggins finally persuaded Kefauver to introduce a crime probe and that after Kefauver's book came out he didn't give the *Post* credit—only Phil Graham —which Phil was not interested in.

The McCarthy debate was held and is continuing.

August 3:   The Senate finally compromised on McCarthy. They will hold a special session of the Senate to take up the censure resolution and nothing else.

August 5:   The Senate finally appointed a committee to investigate McCarthy. Ed Johnson of Colorado, who is a member, said privately, "I will have to vote against McCarthy." The committee is rather nondescript and includes no one who has ever expressed his views on McCarthy publicly before.*

August 6:   Senator Kefauver won by a tremendous majority in Tennessee. The three columns I wrote at the very end regarding his opponent, Pat Sutton, seem to have helped. Pat Sutton was a young man who came to see me at the end of the war in a naval uniform to tell me what an s.o.b. General MacArthur was. Among other things, he told how he, Sutton, and others had swum ashore at Leyte as frogmen, and after they had captured the beachhead and the fighting had gone further inland, he, together with the other frogmen, were asleep on the beach when they were awakened, given rifles and told to pose as if they were shooting at the enemy. It was all staged because General MacArthur was wading ashore to the tune of the newsreels. He didn't like the way the cameras had filmed his so-called "I have conquered" bit of acting, and insisted that the newsreels do it over seven times—according to Sutton.

Later, when MacArthur was fired by Truman and Truman needed a little support, I asked Sutton to give a speech on the House floor regarding the incident. At first he said he would, but he never did.

August 9:   The Austin *Statesman* didn't publish my story on Governor Shiver's wife and mother-in-law getting illegal printing contracts from the State of Texas. Neither did many other Texas papers. The so-called freedom of the press—yet the story was quite completely documented from official records. Reminds me how in 1952 no Texas

---

*The Committee was carefully picked by Earle Clements of Kentucky, the Democratic whip of the Senate, so that no member of the committee could be accused of prejudice. The strategy worked, but McCarthy felt Clements had been so fair he even tried to help reelect him. "I'll speak for you or against you," said McCarthy. "Whichever you feel will do the most good." Clements refused the help and lost his 1956 reelection bid, but for other reasons.—ED.

papers would publish my story that Governor Shivers had received $425,000 on a quickie land deal, even though a sworn deposition on this was in the files of the Hidalgo County courthouse.

Lyndon Johnson came to Wayne Morse for help on the Atomic Energy Bill. This is almost revolutionary. Lyndon had refused to give Wayne his old committee appointments, and Wayne had taken some pretty stiff gibes at him during speeches in Texas. Perhaps Lyndon now sees the writing on the wall. The strong anti-Shivers liberal movement is developing inside the Democratic party in Texas.

August 25:   I wrote Harry Truman some time ago, in fact before he was taken ill in June, suggesting that now is the time for him to go to Europe if our hoped-for unity of Europe was going to be salvaged. I received a letter from him today—the same day the French vetoed the European Army plan. In the two months that have passed since I wrote the letter, European unity has been going downhill fast.

August 28:   Governor Shivers finally won the runoff. It is reported that he spent over a million dollars.

August 31:   Drew was in the office. He knows that he is going to go home soon. Miss Spendlove asked him if he didn't want to go back to see his baby brother. "No," he replied, "I have seen him." I lost my toenail, thanks to an accident, and told Drew I thought I would put it under my pillow to see if the good fairy brought me something—following his practice with a pulled tooth. He advised, "That's a good idea, but you better tell Luvie so she'll make sure you get the money."

September 3:   Wayne Morse came to dinner. Luvie has finally come around to liking Wayne. Mrs. Morse, like most wives, thinks Wayne's election chances are slim. Personally, I predict he will be reelected easily. In my opinion, he has done the most outstanding job of any Senator this year.

September 4:   It now seems definite that secret indictments have been brought against ex-Secretary of the Treasury Snyder, California Congressmen Chet Holifield and Cecil King, and former Assistant Secretary of the Treasury Ed Foley; also Tom Lynch, former counsel of the Treasury. This puts me in an incongruous position. I was Snyder's most bitter critic while he was in office and also went after Cecil King hammer and tongs. However, I can't help but feel that the secret indictments are brought only for political purposes and are being purposely sprung during the election campaign. It's a typical Brownell trick. And I am more or less put in the position of defending the people I once criticized—with the exception of Holifield. He has been a fine Congressman. And I can't understand how he could have been in the Long Beach case, though I am sure Cecil King is in up to his eyebrows.

September 7: Erna Grunewald came to see me. She had come to see me two or three years before quite unexpectedly with her brother-in-law to raise Cain about what I was writing about her father. The meeting at that time was not pleasant. I heard the other day that her brother-in-law had died of cancer, and she told me this morning that she wanted to apologize for intruding on me a couple of years ago and now wanted to consult me about her father. He has been under indictment on six counts for perjury, served a brief time in jail for violating the judge's instructions, and went off the deep end with a gal in the Wardman Park Hotel and in Jersey City where the gas stove was found turned on. I told a Revenue agent when he called on me the other day that I was beginning to feel sorry for Grunewald, and when I listened to his daughter's story I felt more so. At any rate, she asked me to cooperate with her father in writing a book, and when I said I was interested, she kissed me.

September 8: Grunewald and his daughter came for lunch. The story he outlines is not as good as his daughter indicated. He doesn't want to tell the real story about either Bridges or Brewster or even implicate Joe Shimon, the police lieutenant who tapped Howard Hughes's wires for Pan American Airways. However, he says that he once gave $5,000 in cash to Dewey and a similar amount to Brownell. He says that Bill Rogers got his job with the Brewster committee through him and then proceeded to make love to his daughter. This explains why when I asked Rogers to testify before the Pepper committee on the Grunewald–Brewster–Pan American wire-tapping case he declined. Bill had volunteered that Grunewald helped him find an apartment when he first came to Washington and that he had been introduced to Grunewald by Brewster, but didn't tell me about boarding out for a time with Grunewald, etc. Grunewald says that I did write about the Patulla-Modes case, and that was the first he had heard about it. He says he has the clipping. I told him I had searched my files but couldn't find anything, and had so testified before the grand jury, which is now one of the perjury counts against him.

Grunewald claims that they are out to prosecute him before the elections. I asked him if he would go to New York and testify before Arnold Bauman's* grand jury regarding Bridges, but he declined. I told him that Bauman was really out to get the higher-ups, not the little fellows, and that if he testified before Bauman it would help to delay his prosecution here. But even so, he seemed adamant about protecting Bridges.

As he left, two squad cars followed him down the street. The Internal Revenue agents waved at me as if they realized following him was quite a joke. There are three squad cars around his house most of the time, and many of the Russian diplomats living next door are scared to death and run into the house from the garden whenever they see Grunewald with his squad-car entourage coming home.

Spoke at the Silver Spring Board of Trade. I am not sure I am going to relish the job of being a local publisher. It will mean a lot of handshaking, speaking engagements, and local headaches. However, the Silver Spring *Shopper* is making some money and the Maryland *News* is about breaking even. I will probably need something for my old age.

September 16: The Republican National Committee leaked the story of my tax litigation before the U.S. tax court. They called up the *Chicago Tribune* first to tip them off to the story, then the press associations.

Dulles is flying to Germany, ignoring France. I don't think this kind of pressure tactics is going to work. Dulles is flying thither and yon, more scatterbrained than ever.

September 17: Televised Henry Grunewald. He was very frank in answering questions, almost too frank for his own good.

*Bauman was Chief of the Criminal Division of the U.S. Attorney's Office for the Southern District of New York.—ED.

October 6:   Grunewald came in for a session. He says that Senator Brewster went to see Brownell to ask, "Why are you going after Henry? After all, he gave you a lot of campaign money." To which Brownell asked, "What's he trying to do, blackmail me?"

My television interview with Grunewald told how he had given $10,000 to Brownell in cash for Dewey and also how he had gotten Bill Rogers his job with the Senate Investigating Committee when Brewster was chairman.

Bill Rogers called Luvie while I was out of town. First time he has called since he assumed public office—in contrast to the difficulty I have had in getting him on the phone. He was all peaches and cream. Said he wanted to talk to me and give me the full story about Grunewald. I recall that when a Senate subcommittee, headed by Senator Pepper of Florida, was investigating Grunewald, I tried to persuade Rogers to testify before it regarding the fact that Brewster had introduced him, Rogers, to Grunewald. Rogers ran away from the idea awfully fast, but I was never suspicious of it until recently when Grunewald was giving me the whole story of his intimate relations with Rogers at that time.

October 7:   The Atomic Energy Commission is determined to ram through the Dixon-Yates contract. Talked to Senator Langer about this. He is going to do his best to stop it. Sidney Davis, an old friend of mine, is his committee counsel. At the same time, Eisenhower and Nixon are meeting in Denver to see how they can win the November election yet simultaneously flout Congress.

The interesting thing to me is, why the urgency? Why the determination to push the Dixon-Yates contract through? Is it Eisenhower's friendship with Bobby Jones? Is it Admiral Strauss's connection with Kuhn Loeb? Is it Congressman Cole's connection with Corning Glass and General Electric? I don't know. But I do know that all this hurts Cooper in Kentucky and Cordon in Oregon and helps Democratic candidates all over the USA. And it's policies that count in the long run in an election—not speeches.

While Nixon and Eisenhower were talking in Denver, Assistant Secretary of the Interior Orme Lewis has another oil giveaway on his desk—to permit oil drilling in game refuges for the first time in history.

October 19:   Brooke Lee came to see me. He looks years older. He says he is being indicted for income tax evasion. I didn't tell him that I had heard it previously. Perhaps I should have told him a long time ago. The Republican administration has reopened his case—against a Democrat—and closed the case against Funkhouser—a big Republican in West Virginia—although the Funkhouser case is one of the most flagrant in history.

October 21:   The Gariepy trial finally got started. Judge Jennings Bailey, eighty-six years old, is the judge. He was appointed by Woodrow Wilson, according to court gossip, by error. Wilson wanted to appoint a judge from Tennessee and sent the commission to the court where it was wanted by the clerk of the court—namely Bailey. When the commission got back to Washington, Bailey's name was picked up by Wilson, and he was appointed instead of the judge. However, he is considered one of the best judges on the bench.

This case has now gone up to the Supreme Court, has lost me a sponsor, has required innumerable trips to Detroit, plus various depositions; and I still don't know where we are. I have talked to various people in Royal Oak, including the police force, but still don't know whether Mrs. Gariepy was intimate with Father Coughlin or not. Lots of people in Royal Oak suspect it.

October 22:   Nixon is pouring on the smears. He has resurrected the old Reds-in-government technique which he himself used to get elected to the House over Jerry Voorhis, and which he also used unfairly against Helen Gahagan Douglas. He has also persuaded Eisenhower to get into the fight. There is more money being poured into this campaign than any midterm election that I have ever seen.

October 25:   Another day in court. I sometimes wonder how many days of my life I have spent in court. More cases have been named for me in the District of Columbia court than anyone else so far. I may have pioneered some new libel law, but I would just as soon forgo this distinction.

Two Negro ladies arrived from Detroit as witnesses. We only have one Negro on the jury. The clerk of the court apparently has worked out a new system for picking jury panels by which Negroes are partly eliminated. Whenever we have a jury with a large quota of Negroes I have no great worry about the outcome. I was called as a surprise witness by the other side. I had no chance to explain that I had to reimburse the American Broadcasting Company if the verdict goes against me.

October 27:   Eight Republican Senators have gone into Oregon to try to rescue Guy Cordon in his Senate race. Wayne Morse says privately the tide is going against Neuberger. The Republicans have too much money, and the Democrats began their campaign too soon.

George Pennington, Democratic State Chairman in Pennsylvania, called regarding Norman Rothman, owner of the Sans Souci gambling casino in Havana, who got chummy with Governor Fine of Pennsylvania. It recalled my report of two years ago that Nixon got mixed up with the same gamblers. Nixon emphatically denied this, but Rothman in talking to the District Attorney of Mifflin County, Major Horace Culbertson, stated quite categorically that Nixon was in Havana and was gambling. Rothman further stated that I had come down to Havana to talk to him about the matter and that he had lied to me. Of course, he was referring to the fact that Harry Costello did check on the case for me. It's amazing how people have forgotten Nixon's background, particularly the $18,000 private expense fund. It illustrates what television and a favorable press can do. People have evidently forgotten that Nixon pulled the most colossal boner of the past year when he stated that the United States would send troops to Indochina.

October 29:   We went to the jury. Eisenhower went to the people. He went by special plane to four different cities to try to turn the tide.

John Carroll called me from Denver. His race for the Senate doesn't look too good. He didn't exactly tell me this, but I could read it between the lines.

Tony Akers, candidate for Congress in New York City, also called, together with various others. They don't realize that my radio program is already transcribed and that there is nothing I can do at the last minute to help them.

George is trying to raise $1,000 to let all the congressional candidates from southern California go on television to answer Nixon, who has called them pro-Communist. They want to go on television with their families to show what kind of Communists they are. I got another $700 out of the Democratic Committee.

October 30:   The jury was still out this morning. At twelve noon the judge called them back and finally dismissed them, although only after Mrs. Gariepy's attorney put up a powerful argument that they be continued. Personally I was glad to see them go. Of course, it may mean another trial, but you never can tell what a jury is going to do. After they were dismissed, I called one of the jurors who told me the vote had been eleven to one in my favor. A lady in the front row, named Cecilia Lambert, held out. The jury thought it might be able to budge her if they sat longer. Paradoxically, she was a secretary in Internal Revenue, and this libel suit had considerable to do with my efforts to help collect income taxes.

Went to see Riley Campbell about Brooke Lee's tax case. He says that there is nothing in the works about Brooke and that he would know about it if there were.

Many years ago I recommended Riley to Henry Morgenthau for promotion—as a result of which he was transferred from Chicago to Washington. I have never gone to see him since. I talked to him, however, this time about the fact that his old friend and mine, George Bowden, had received $10,000 from Grunewald on behalf of the S and G Syndicate in Miami. George is now dead; and I had heard that Internal Revenue agents were going through his papers regarding the $10,000. Campbell didn't seem to think it was important. He pointed out that George had represented the S and G Syndicate as its attorney and that this was a matter of public record and there was nothing wrong with receiving $10,000. Campbell thinks the Grunewald case is one of the worst instances of tax bribery and influence in recent years. He is certain that it went to higher-ups.

1955

[*The entries from January 1 through January 25 are transcribed from longhand notes.*]

January 1:   Ellen called at 7 A.M.: Tyler and Bess have eloped.

January 25:   I can see why people become anti-Semites. Sat beside [illegible] of Chicago Monarch foods. Brought in his yacht, his collection of Peruvian ceramics which he bought himself (didn't collect it), his thirteen and a half acres of food processing plants in Chicago where he sells everything made in canned goods. Remember five years ago when I was kicked off the air by McCarthy how I called him in Chicago, tried to get him as sponsor. He was afraid. Still afraid. Didn't talk to him but I can see it in his eyes, in his manner.

March 1:   Senator Benton dropped in. A former Senate investigator, Harvey Fosner, came to see him together with Grace Johnson, who has long worked for the Senate Rules Committee. They said that Tom Hennings had held out some of the most damning reports against McCarthy, not because of Senator Hendrickson as alleged, but because Tom was scared of McCarthy. (The old liquor trouble.)

Grace said that the damning documents were now locked up in Senator Hayden's safe. They had reports that McCarthy was going to steal them; as a result she had slept in Hayden's office for four nights watching them.

Paul Cotter, who got excoriated by McCarthy for putting a mail cover on him, is now out of a job. Hennings actually ordered the mail cover to see where McCarthy's funds were coming from and where they were going to. But when McCarthy raised hell, Tom let Cotter take the rap.

Benton is going up to see Senator Hayden to see if he can't pry loose the documents and get Hayden to finish the job on McCarthy which was left suspended by Tom Hennings.

I went to see Stanley Barnes, Assistant Attorney General in charge of antitrust. He was cagey but pleasant; maintains that Brownell backs him in going after big business. He said that Brownell knew that hell would break loose regarding the Pan American Airways suit. But Brownell brought it anyway. Brownell sometimes kids Barnes, but Barnes says that both Eisenhower and Brownell definitely want to enforce the law.

I told Barnes how Thurman Arnold had tried to bring suit against Pan American Airways but was told by Bob Jackson that if he went ahead and pushed the suit he might as well quit. I also told Barnes how RCA had a complete in with the Truman administration and how Harry Truman had once held up Clement Attlee, then Prime Minister of England, while he finished lunch with David Sarnoff, head of RCA, in order to consolidate Margaret in her NBC job.

March 2: Senator Benton called from New York. He said that Hayden had been cagey and uncooperative except in one thing; namely, he wanted Benton's support for his own reelection in Arizona. New people are moving into Arizona, Hayden claimed, who don't know him.

Benton wanted a resolution introduced asking the Justice Department to take action regarding the unpublished documents and McCarthy's income taxes. He also suggested an investigation by Kilgore's subcommittee, which is supposed to scrutinize the Justice Department.

But Hayden balked. He said that if someone would get Sherman Adams to ask the Justice Department to take action it might do some good. But it would do no good to pass a resolution which would be ignored by Ike.

I am supposed to contact Nelson Rockefeller to see if he will talk to Adams. Don't think he will.

Three young fellows from Crusade for Freedom came to lunch with me. The balloon drive has really expanded and they have now dropped a total of one hundred million pieces of literature. They have permanent barracks in a field where we used to launch balloons, and they are expanding operations to Hungary and to some extent Poland. Polish Catholics, however, oppose. They claim that it stirs up the people unnecessarily and prematurely. One Swedish businessman back from Prague reported that he found leaflets under his pillow in his hotel room.

March 3: Went to see Sam Rayburn. Expected to be there fifteen minutes but stayed an hour. Sam told how he had gone to see Eisenhower with ten Democrats and ten Republicans and found himself in the room alone with Eisenhower.

"I told him what I told Harry Truman when he first became President," said Sam. "Truman was in my office and had just started to take a drink when he got word to come to the White House immediately. He knew and I knew, though we didn't say so—Roosevelt had died. Later I went to see Truman and told him: 'Now you ain't gonna be Harry to me any more. You are Mr. President. But as an old friend who has known you a long time I'm gonna give you some advice. You ain't as big a man as some people think you are.'

"To this Truman replied: 'I sure ain't.'

"When I told this to Eisenhower he leaned back and roared.

"Then I told Truman he was going to have two great problems. One with the people around him who find themselves in a high position close to the President for the first time in their lives. They will be afraid to let anyone else get near you, and they will be afraid of superior minds. They won't want to argue with people. They will surround you and, if you are not awfully careful, make you their prisoner.

"The second thing you have got to worry about is the big-business sycophant. Now the fellow from Missouri who is a friend of yours will come to town and will find himself with an hour on his hands and will call up and ask for an appointment; he'll find you booked weeks in advance and will take the Baltimore and Ohio back to St. Louis. He won't hang around.

"But the big-business boys will wait for you. They will make it their job to wait. They will be like the king who waited in the street to see the Pope and couldn't piss until he saw him. They will hang around Washington until they finally see you, and if you are not careful you are gonna get too much advice from them. And their advice isn't gonna be like the fellow's from Missouri.

"Well, I told this to Truman and I told it to Eisenhower," Rayburn concluded. "Truman made some mistakes along this line, but Eisenhower didn't even understand what I was talking about.

"Sid Richardson called me up the other day from Texas," Sam

continued. "Sid is a Democrat though he voted for Eisenhower, and I asked him, 'What does Eisenhower mean by saying I am irresponsible? When I put through the Reciprocal Trade Treaty on that motion to recommit I was a statesman. When I push the twenty-dollar tax reduction to give the little fellow a break I am irresponsible.'

" 'The trouble with Eisenhower is,' said Sid, 'that he probably didn't even know you put the Reciprocal Trade Treaty through. He doesn't know what's happening. He never reads the papers.' "

Sam was pretty sore about Eisenhower's blasting him over the tax bill. He said that he was planning to tack all sorts of amendments on future tax bills that the administration sends up to him. "We're going to knock out that dividend provision which gives the Treasury about three hundred sixty million dollars," he said. "We're also going to knock out that phony business that permits corporations to deduct funds that they set aside for the future.

"Congressman Zelenko of New York came in to see me the other day. He's a conscientious Congressman and a very smart fellow and called this to my attention. We're going to knock that out as soon as we can."

I asked him why Senator George of Georgia wasn't with him. "George doesn't follow a consistent course," Sam replied. "He is a fine man and I have admired him for years, but he just isn't consistent. Last year he wanted to pass an eight-hundred-dollar personal exemption provision which would have cost the Treasury four billion six hundred million dollars. Now he balks at my provision which would cost only about three to four hundred million dollars."

I told Sam that some Senators were irked at him because he didn't consult them in advance. "I never had a chance to. We had a meeting on Saturday night and had to spring the proposal on Sunday. We didn't know Ike was going to send his tax bill up so fast."

Sam also talked at length about commissions.

"I was in on the borning of every one of these Commissions except the Interstate Commerce Commission. I wrote the law that passed the Federal Communications Commission and the Securities and Exchange Commission, and I was in Congress when we planned the Federal Trade Commission and the Federal Power Commission. And I wrote the law for the Civil Aeronautics Board.

"The people don't know that these commissions are an arm of

Congress. They do what we don't have time to do. Yet Eisenhower has taken over and even appoints his friends.

"This fellow Hoover helped him do it. This fellow Hoover is the worst curse that has come to government in years.

"You can take a bad law and make it work if you have good administrators. But if you have a good law and appoint bad administrators, you just about kill the law. That is what Eisenhower is doing today. They haven't changed one of these commissions by law. They haven't amended a thing but they have appointed the worst commissioners this country has seen.

"Take this man McConnaughey.* He wasn't even honest enough to admit he worked for telephone companies. His appointment is going to cost the taxpayers millions. Even if he does his best to be honest he can't be unprejudiced.

"Most businessmen bucked these commissions when we first established them, but afterwards they realized they were the best thing that could have happened. When we passed the Holding Corporation Act, John H. Carpenter, head of Texas Light and Power, stopped by my ranch and told me that he had been against the Holding Corporation Act but now he realized how good it was. He said that now he didn't have to pay several million dollars to Ebasco; could keep it right in Texas.

"And when we passed the SEC, Wall Street bucked; but Emil Schramm, who was head of the Stock Exchange, came to see me—sat where you're sitting now—and told me you can't run the Stock Exchange without the SEC.

"But Eisenhower is sabotaging these commissions. The trouble is he doesn't know any more about what's going on than Ulysses S. Grant. Grant was a fine man until he got to be President. When Lee surrendered he told Grant: 'My men are starving. They haven't had anything to eat but hog hominy.'

"So Grant gave an order: "Every man in my army with three rations is to give two of them to Lee's army.'

"But when Grant got into the White House they ruined him.

"Some of us tried to tell Ike he should run as a Democrat, in which case he would have had men around him to tell him how to run things. But the people around him now don't want him to know."

*George C. McConnaughey, chairman, FCC (1954–57).—Ed.

March 4: A ghost-writer for Admiral Zacharias named [Ladislas] Farago came to see me with Ed Hart. He has a copy of the famed Patton diary. He made the mistake of giving his copy to Bill Hearst prior to the Chicago convention, and Hearst published a small excerpt from it, whereupon Mrs. Patton raised Cain, and the diary was returned.

Patton was most critical of Eisenhower as a military leader and told how in January 1944, he (Patton) opposed "Overlord," the plan for the cross-Channel invasion. Eisenhower refused the Patton plan, and General Patton began writing the diary for history.

Among other things he pointed out where Ike would get bogged down with the British. It happened exactly that way.

Patton was sore at Kay Summersby. He went to see Eisenhower on one occasion at headquarters. Summersby was present. Ike remarked: "We have no secrets from Kay." Patton replied: "Well, I have secrets from her." She left. Patton tells how Ike wrote to General Marshall when Marshall complained of relations with Summersby. Ike explained that he was a young man, vigorous, etc. Marshall wrote back advising him to "take a cold bath and have a masseur."

Patton says he knew Ike was going to run for President even when he was in North Africa; said he could tell by the way he talked.

In Sicily, Patton was court-martialed, though it never leaked out, for the massacre of ninety German prisoners. He was exonerated. What happened was that he had given the American troops a tough dressing-down before going into battle, and while he did not say to take no prisoners, the handful of officers either interpreted his remarks to mean that or else trumped this up as an excuse. At any rate, they shot the Germans in the stockade, and Patton was court-martialed along with the others.

Most significant parts of the Patton diary pertain to the closing days of the war when he was racing across France and could have marched right through Germany. When Eisenhower cut off his gasoline, Patton raided British supplies but couldn't get enough to go much farther. He sat and watched the Germans consolidate their lines, knowing that if he had had the gasoline he could have marched right into Berlin. General Bradley confirms this though his book is not as forthright as Patton's diary.

Patton used to keep his diary on little slips of paper which he would stuff into his pockets. Later his stenographer transcribed them.

One slip of paper contained a note that he owed his Negro orderly $615.

Farago bought the diary from Patton's secretary in Paris. Mrs. Patton, now dead, was vigorously opposed to publication because it would embarrass Eisenhower, and she once bawled out Farago.

Sam Block has been telling me that the underworld is behind Florida financier Louis Wolfson's efforts to buy Montgomery Ward and that most of the money to buy Montgomery Ward proxies had come from Las Vegas or the Purple Gang in Detroit. Jim Hoffa, head of the Teamsters Union, is reported mixed up with the Purple Gang. He has bought two-million dollars' worth of Montgomery Ward stock.

Today Sam came by with a new theory on the Rubenstein murder. He had been buying up Montgomery Ward stock, and the underworld came to him through P. S. Stanley, a Polish refugee, to say they wanted his proxies. Rubenstein refused. He also threatened to tell the Justice Department in order to ingratiate himself with them and prevent his deportation. That was why he was murdered.

March 5:   Lee Brooke, who is in the oil business with Franklin Roosevelt in Jamaica, came to see me along with Mike O'Shea, formerly with MP-TV. Someone had given me quite a dossier on Brooke's record, which didn't look too good. I went over it with him at breakfast, and he seemed to have a pretty good explanation of the record, in addition to which he had just gotten a complete retraction from the Hearst newspapers who published part of his record. Brooke went on to tell me about Rubenstein, whom he knew well. He said that Rubenstein always wanted to be respectable, which was why he bought heavily in Boeing Aircraft. Walter Germann of Interhandel also bought heavily on Rubenstein's recommendation. Brooke thinks Rubenstein was killed accidentally by someone who tied him up while he ransacked his home looking for documents. Rubenstein was a great blackmailer and he probably had some papers somebody else wanted. Brooke went into great detail about the intricate deal between Blair Holding, Stanwell Oil, which Brooke owned, Rubenstein, Germann, and Joe Rosenbaum. It was the most complicated financial setup that I have ever listened to.

He said that Rubenstein had put a girl in Wolfson's office to spy on him and also placed a man in Wolfson's accounting office. The latter had formerly been with Maxwell Zabell, Rubenstein's own accounting firm.

Brooke thinks that if Fulbright would subpoena P. Stanley's trading account and bank records they would get to the bottom of the Rubenstein murder, instead of studying the stock market transactions. However the police are looking at the rogues' gallery.

[*The following letter was included among the diary papers.*]

August 15 [The Farm]:
Dear Georgie and Drew,

It rained and it rained. It poured and it poured. The rain came down in buckets and in soup tureens. It came down in barrels and in canteens. We never saw so much rain.

The river down below began growling and rushing. It said: "How am I going to carry all this rain away? Its too much to carry. They dont give me any rain for months, and I get small and puny, and now they give me a lot of rain and it gives me a stomach ache."

So old man river began growing and rushing. He rushed more and more and grew more and more. And Grandpa looked down and said to himself: "That river is going to come right over the canal. He may even come up to the house. He's going to put all of Georgie and Drew's little friends out of a home. The turtle and the chipmunk and the squirrel and the snake wont have anyplace to live. Even the bird wont have anything to eat."

So Pazzy said: "We'll have to do what old Noah did and build an ark."

Pazzy got busy with Harry Clipper to cut down some trees and build an ark, but what do you suppose those animals said? They said: "We dont like these wooden arks. That's old-fashioned. You've got a nice aluminum canoe and we want something made of aluminum. We want an aluminum ark."

So Pazzy looked around for an aluminum ark. He went to Henry Kaiser but Henry Kaiser said: "We havent got any aluminum to spare for such a thing as animals. We're selling our aluminum to the big boys. Phooey on you."

Then Pazzy went to Reynolds Metals. And Reynolds Metals said: "Why should we sell you aluminum for an ark, when we can sell to our old customers and be sure of a regular return? After all you can only build one ark, and we wont have a stable market. We've got to take care of our old customers first."

So Pazzy went to see the Aluminum Corporation of America, and they said: "We're very sorry but no aluminum for you. You're a new customer and we can't spare any aluminum. Its very precious."

So Pazzy said: "I'll have George Arnold investigate you. He's a good lawyer and a good investigator and he'll expose your refusal to take care of these little animals and the way you want to deal only with big people."

But the aluminum companies said: "We're not worried, because we have friends in Congress. Our friends wont let you investigate us."

So Pazzy went back to the animals and told them they couldn't have an aluminum ark. He also went to the zoo in Washington and told the lions and tigers and elephants that they had better pack up and start moving, because the Potomac River was going to come right up to their cages.

But what do you think they said? "We would rather stay right here with Dr. Mann. If we go with you we'll have to work, and if we stay here the taxpayers and Dr. Mann feed us. Thank you very much."

By this time it had stopped raining. So Pazzy went back to see the little animals at the farm and said: "I guess if you members of the modern generation have to have an aluminum ark we just won't have one after all. We'll just hope the river doesn't grow any more."

"That suits us," said the animals, "but when are Drew and Georgie coming home?"

And if you don't think that happened, you can ask the animals yourselves. Love,

[*The entries from September 24 through October 7 are transcribed from long-hand notes.*]

September 24: At Cuneo's having dinner when Dave Karr called that Ike had heart attack. My radio program out. Nothing I could do. Fortunately, [I did] a story last week that Hall [Leonard Hall, chairman of the Republican National Committee] should take out candidate insurance. Also, editorial on health.

September 26: Bart Crum lunch. Rita—Aly Khan. Winchell on TVA—what I did for Howard Hughes.

September 30: World Series with O'Dwyer. No ovation. You sit in left field. Sorrowful.

October 3: Dr. White said Ike had bad day. Fatigued. Funny how I'm praying that he get well. With all his mistakes and flubs. Future with Russians depends on him. Alternative—Nixon.

October 6: Bill Rogers—Wiggins argued Nixon never asked for ruling. He never called Brownell. Wiggins seemed swayed—left called down like schoolboy in front of teacher. Recall fact that he once represented me.*

November 18: I have just come back from the tip end of northern Greenland which isn't too far from the Pole. It was a great experience which I am glad I did once, but wouldn't particularly want to do again.

We went in a special Air Force plane placed at my disposal because I organized a group of about fifteen entertainers for the troops. The purpose was to entertain the troops and at the same time give me a chance to do a TV program and write something about the Air Force in the Far North.

Our first stop was Goose Bay, Labrador, which we reached at 8:30 P.M. Friday, having left New York at about 2 P.M. About 2,000 men were waiting for us in a big hangar and we finally put on a show at 10 P.M. They were standing and I don't know how they ever waited that long. However, they seemed to like the program, which consisted of some comedians, a dance team, Ella Logan, the singer, and seven fashion models. I introduced the group and felt rather extraneous and unimportant, because although it was my show, I actually played a very small part in the whole business.

Next A.M. we were supposed to leave at 9, but couldn't get all the women awake and aboard the plane until ten. It's a long flight to northern Greenland—more than seven hours. However, our plane was a sort of flying theater. Miss Logan and the orchestra entertained us most of the time, so much so that I couldn't get my usual sleep.

Thule Air Base in Greenland is really something of a modern

---

*The entry refers to the allegation that the Vice President had tried to have Attorney General Rogers (formerly a lawyer for Drew) declare that Nixon should perform as President during Eisenhower's illness. Russell Wiggins was editor of the *Washington Post.*—ED.

miracle. It's more than a base, it's a city, spread out on the ice where there never was a city before. In fact the nearest humans are about one hundred Eskimos 65 miles away. They are not permitted near the base because mumps, colds, or our ordinary diseases would kill them. They have built up no resistance to the diseases of civilization.

When you first get out of the plane, the cold is so sharp that you feel a little sick. Actually it wasn't too cold—only a little below zero. In Labrador it was about 28 above, and just like Washington. Inside the barracks however, it is hot, so hot that you suffer if you have long underwear on; so that you're too cold outside and too hot in.

I had to stand outside part of the time doing a TV show in a parka. I had to stand in the snow to make it realistic, otherwise no one would have believed I was in Greenland. When the temperature goes down to 30 below and there's a 40- or 50-mile wind, your skin freezes in thirty seconds. But we didn't have any weather like this.

On Saturday night the officers had a cocktail party and dinner for us, after which I went to bed, leaving the rest of the party to entertain our hosts. There are, by the way, 6,000 men at Thule and only three women nurses.

No sooner had I got back to my quarters than the phone rang and a Captain McPherson got on the phone.

"Why is it that you aren't here entertaining us," she wanted to know. "You left a lot of girls to entertain the officers. Why aren't you coming back here to entertain us women?"

I told her I'd had a long day and had to write a column. As a matter of fact I was way behind in preparing my TV scripts. But she kept arguing. I told her that she had 6,000 men in Thule, but it didn't do any good. I had to hang up. The cast told me in the morning that they had taken two or three more calls later.

I have told this to my wife in order to prove that I have not entirely lost my appeal.

However, I must say that the trip made me feel old. The commander at Thule was only thirty-six years old. The commander at Goose Bay wasn't much older. The girls in our party were about eighteen to twenty-five. And I will be fifty-eight in about two weeks. And when I got home at 4 A.M. Tuesday after spending all night on the plane and putting on one more show at Goose Bay I felt over sixty.

After all it's a young man's world and I think both I and Eisenhower should face it.

December 23:   Finally did some Christmas shopping. Interrupted it to lunch with Louis Johnson. He is raising money for Kefauver, but chiefly I think as a means of stopping both Harriman and Stevenson. He claims Stevenson can't win, and he hates Harriman because he thinks Harriman got Truman to fire him as Secretary of Defense. Maybe he did. I always thought it was Acheson, but Louis says he has now discovered that Averell was sore because he, Louis, wouldn't hide some foreign aid spending in his Defense appropriation. I doubt this motive, though Averell may well have been the man. He was also the man who urged Truman to fire Douglas MacArthur in that late midnight conference.

Louis says he's going to raise about $100,000 for Kefauver and hints that some of it was coming from Republicans. When I suggested that the way to win was to make sure Ike didn't run and to start Senate investigations to that end now, he shied away as if he wanted Ike to run rather than Averell or Adlai. Claimed twenty or thirty men could put up the money to nominate any one candidate. Said he was worried that Harriman might squeeze in in case of a deadlock between Adlai and Estes. Truman might maneuver him in.

Louis was really bitter against Harriman, kept coming back and back to the idea that he might squeeze in.

He said that Ike had had a previous heart attack about ten years ago. This was not when he went to Key West as chief of staff in the summer of 1949. Louis said this was because Ike had peeling of the stomach lining, which could have been serious. He, Louis, went to see him in Key West to clear the idea of canceling out the airplane carrier which Admiral Denfeld had concurred in but later said he hadn't. Ike concurred too, after Louis went to Key West to talk to him.

The interesting thing to me was the manner in which the civilian leaders of the Defense Department had already begun to kowtow to the military. Here was the Secretary of Defense going all the way to Key West to get the Chairman of the Joint Chiefs of Staff to O.K. the cutting out of a carrier from the budget.

Louis says that George E. Allen is now in wrong with the White House staff. They feel he is using Ike, won't let his flowers and messages get through to him. He finally got through himself for a game of bridge.

Louis was in a loquacious mood, but it's hard to believe everything he said—namely, that the Chase Bank has sent word it won't take Warren for President; that Bernard Shanley was fired because he put across the Dixon-Yates deal (he's a director of Public Service of New Jersey); that the *Chicago Tribune* has the goods on a pansy party given by Adlai in Paris. He says the *Tribune* offered him a chance to look at the evidence. (I do know that the ex-Mrs. Stevenson offered some of Adlai's letters to Kefauver through Bill Roberts.)

December 25: It was the first Christmas in years that Luvie and I have been alone. Tyler was in Kentucky with Bess. George and Ellen and the children were at home in Alexandria. We hung up no stockings but got up early and went to church. Then to see the children's tree. They were completely uncontrollable and like little savages tearing open any and all packages.

George and Ellen were one hour late for dinner. I learned later that they had had a big row and Ellen almost went back to New York. Dinner was a grim affair.

December 26: Ellen did go back to New York. She had been ready to stay all week. I drove her to the station. She has got so she doesn't seem to care much whether she stays married or not. I think George feels the same way. She would have stayed if he had given her a little encouragement, I think.

1956

–≫≫ · ≪≪–

[*The entries from February 7 through February 8 are transcribed from longhand notes. Bracketed question marks indicate difficulty in deciphering the name or word.*]

February 7: Went to dinner with Jim Barnes. When I went in I noticed Jim looked glum. But I didn't see anyone in the room I ought to duck. However, pretty soon in came Sam Rayburn. I had just written how Sam had pushed the gas bill through by subsidizing Congressmen, including George Miller of California, to the tune of $2,500, etc. Sam came up to me however and said: "George Miller's going to sue you but I'm trying to persuade him not to." He was, as usual, as comfortable as an old shoe. Later, we talked about Kefauver and Stevenson. He was still bitter against Estes, said the South would never take him, that he wouldn't even consider him for Vice President. He doesn't like Stevenson too much, thinks he'll probably wash out, and that HST isn't for him. In a deadlock, he'd go for Symington, never Kefauver.

After dinner, Millard Tydings told about campaign contributions in Maryland.

Last night, Senator Matt Neely phoned me to intimate that he's been offered $5,000 to change his vote on the gas bill. I picked him up at the Willard Hotel at eight-fifty this morning and drove him to the Capitol. He said Louis Johnson offered him $5,000 for the Mollohan [?] campaign for Congress if Matt would change his vote. Matt refused. Louis represents Col. Gas Co. [?]. He donated $1,000 in cash with no strings attached but wants a pledge on the gas bill before he puts up the $5,000. Matt thinks that Kilgore was wobbling on the gas bill and that Louis had approached him.

February 8:   Breakfast with Tom Hennings. He had a terrific brain-washing from Lyndon yesterday. Earle Clements sat in on it. And tried to pour on the oil. Bess isn't going to like some of the things I'm writing now. Albert Gore also sat in and is standing up to Lyndon in a surprising manner. At one time he said: "Let's go Tom. Case is due at our meeting and we'll be late." "Go ahead," said Lyndon. "I didn't invite you here."

After breakfast I called Jim Rowe to get some help from Senator Mansfield on the Rules Committee; also phoned Senator Green. He had been wobbly about any full probe of the gas lobby. Tom came to dinner and told me what happened at the Rules Committee. Jenner of Indiana and Curtis of Nebraska were there with resolutions, he suspected, to make him resign as a Senator who was running for reelection. So he beat them to it with a statement that he would get out before April 29. He also demanded a full probe of the gas lobby, which, however, he won't handle. He's convinced Gore will do a good job. The problem is to get a good man in Tom's place on the elections committee, and the only man available is Mansfield. Whether he will stand up against Lyndon is doubtful. I urged Tom to call Louis Johnson in executive session and ask him about the $5,000, and he said he would. He's going to sell Gore on this without mentioning my name. Francis Case [of South Dakota] has been behaving like a fool and a coward. He is supposed to be a dignified and independent Senator; yet he accepted George Brown's instruction not to appear before the Hennings committee.

February 10:   I went to Bucknell University to speak. Officially I went there at the urging of my niece Betty Anne. She did not know it but I went there to see a lady with whom I had once fallen desperately in love. I met her when I was sixteen on a Chautauqua tent crew at Annapolis, Maryland. She was a soprano with an Italian band. Pontrelli, I think, was the leader. It was in the days before radio, and before many records, and before bands toured the country. She was older— I suppose eight to ten years older. I saw her that summer; her mother and she were nice to me that winter when I was in Exeter—spent my Thanksgiving vacation with them in Boston. And two summers following we became quite in love. Then suddenly she drifted away. I was rather sore at the time—even bitter in a schoolboy sort of way. But I surmised or learned afterwards that she, wiser than I, took steps to get transferred. I saw her infrequently after that—and for twenty years not at all—until tonight. She is white-haired, plump, buoyant. She was not invited to the dinner in my honor, seemed surprised when I insisted she come. She did come. There were some awkward moments, when we didn't know what to talk about—when memory was dim and groping—when we both wanted to consider ourselves the youthful flirts we once were, necking in automobiles or behind the Chautauqua tent, or sitting in parks in the moonlight. No one at the long table or in the audience of a thousand had any inkling that the cold embers of a youthful romance were being stirred—by a potbellied, baldheaded old newspaperman and a white-haired singing teacher who once was the most beautiful woman I had ever seen. I can understand how F.D.R. went back to see Mrs. Rutherford.

We parted at 8:30 P.M., right after my talk, I to sit for thirty minutes with more professors, then catch a little sleep before taking the 4:04 A.M. sleeper to Washington.

February 11: Ellen was due back in Washington last night to see the children, but didn't come. All day she didn't come. I have not heard yet whether she has come or not.

Before leaving for Lewisburg yesterday I talked to George, hoping that this meeting might begin to effect a reconciliation. George seemed willing to try. I had heard from Dave Karr in New York that Ellen was also willing to try.

George told me that Congressman Wright Patman had asked Jimmie Roosevelt to drop George because the Republicans objected to George as a staff member and leak to me. They threatened to hold up Small Business appropriations. George refused and Jimmie, after some hesitation, backed him up. Ironically, it now develops that the Superior Oil $2,500 to "bribe" Senator Case came from Patman's brother, Elmer. This explains how Sam Rayburn got $2,500 to give Congressman Metler and how Patman offered Jimmie Roosevelt $10,000 to vote for the gas bill. It's a small world! Yet Patman has been a genuine champion of small business. Ironically, Superior Oil supplied a good hunk of money to defeat George for Congress.

February 17: Congressman Jimmie Roosevelt of California asked me to come see him. He said he was worried over an item carried in the newsletter that he had been offered $10,000 to change his vote on the gas bill. He wanted me to know that if he was asked about it, he would have to call me a liar. He couldn't afford to tangle with his chairman, Wright Patman, cousin of Elmer of Superior Oil. He also said the Speaker had run across the item in the newsletter, coupled with the item that Jimmie and Randolph Churchill had dined with me, and put two and two together. I told Jimmie I understood. It looks as if much chance for a real lobby investigation is fading.

Later in the day Senator Neely of West Virginia phoned me with a plea that I say nothing more about the $5,000 offered him by Louis Johnson. He said my brief mention of Louis's lobbying had already cost him more trouble than anything else, had also hurt his boy in West Virginia (I think he referred to Mollohan), and he had told me about Louis only to cheer me up and get me to know I was on the right track. He pled with me in such a way that I finally promised. He said the President's veto of the gas bill, which came today, was my victory, that everyone on the Hill was saying "Drew Pearson won his battle." I told him it wasn't a victory unless we could clean up the rottenness in Washington, and that I wanted to come and talk to him about it. However, he shied away.

Jimmie also talked about the flagging leadership in the House. Barden of North Carolina hasn't held one committee meeting (Education and Labor) since Congress convened. Sam Rayburn does nothing about it. The school bill is stymied in the Rules Committee and won't come out till near the end of the session. If it does, Sam knows it will cause a holocaust of a debate. There will be an open rule (open to amendments) and every one of 400-odd Congressmen will speak. It will keep Congress in session for weeks. So the school bill simply won't pass. Jimmie says the House is going ahead with housekeeping bills and appropriation bills—just the routine. But there is no program, no leadership, no inspiration. The only way to put across such leadership is to get a Democratic President who can break through the Southern barrier with the weapon of patronage.

[*The entries from April 16 through June 11 are transcribed from longhand notes.*]

April 16:   Jiggs Donohue phoned, wanted me to come see him. He was at the Kefauver headquarters. He said Lyndon Johnson's former aide has approached him about a deal: If I would quit criticizing Lyndon's tax deal for Brown and Root, etc., then Lyndon would throw his weight to Kefauver when the fighting got tough in the Democratic convention. With some reservations and considerable doubt I agreed. I warned Jiggs that Lyndon probably would walk out on the deal; also that I would continue to write about Lyndon on other matters if they arose. But inasmuch as I had about exhausted the Brown and Root tax case anyway, I figured I might do that much for Estes. This is the first time I've ever made a deal like this, and I feel a little unhappy about it. With the Presidency of the United States at stake, maybe it's justified, maybe not—I don't know.

April 17:   Estes lost badly in the New Jersey primary. It put a bad crimp in the bandwagon rush to Kefauver.

April 21:   Televised all A.M. Lunched at the [Walter] Ridders'. Senator Knowland was there and found myself at the same table with him and Helen Knowland, both swell people personally. Whenever I talk to her, I wonder why she wanted to take sleeping pills as she did in a suicide attempt two years ago. Yet it's probably tough living with the Senator—about as tough as living with a columnist. He thinks Kefauver will probably carry California—depending on whether he first carries Florida.

Went to the big Democratic dinner. Lots of Democrats were sore at me because of Wednesday's column in which I said the dinner was going to be a flop. It was Ernie Cuneo who wanted me to write the story and it was Ernie who more than anyone kept the dinner from being a flop. It was pretty dreary at that.

Afterward we went to a party given by Phil Stern, Research Director for the Democratic Party Headquarters. Harriman was there, looking quite young: invited me to come up to Albany again. I must say that when you get a bunch of Democrats together they have so much more on the ball than the Republicans that you wish for old times again.

Carmine DiSapio told me Estes made a mistake when he challenged the Meyner machine in New Jersey. He should have confined his campaign to southern farm areas where Meyner is weak.

April 23:   Flew to New York for Bell Syndicate cocktail party for publishers. Not too many showed. I had invited Ellen but didn't even hear from her. Luvie and I went to see Eddie Robinson in *Middle of the Night*. It's a big hit. We saw him later and remarked how the atmosphere had changed. It was only a few years ago that he was virtually blacklisted because he had befriended some liberal causes.

As we waited for Eddie outside his dressing room, who should walk down the stairs but June Walker! I didn't recognize her, but she did me. It was just a few short years ago that June was the toast of Broadway, and I almost married her. I remember it was when I took her driving in Washington with Ellen, aged about nine, and Sarah the poodle and Sarah wanted to sit in the front seat, that things began to cool. Thank God they did.

April 24:   Had a terrible siege over last Saturday's column on Dewey and Elliott Bell. Bell got hold of Wheeler and Phil Graham demanding a retraction and publication of a letter full of half-truths. When publishers get together, a plain newsman doesn't have a chance.

April 25:   *The Post* published the Bell letter after a long hassle and snafu, despite the fact I promised Bell a retraction.

Ike said at his press conference that Nixon hadn't come in to tell him how he'd "charted his own course"—a lot of hogwash—but it started speculation that Tricky Dick was going to be dumped. Simultaneously Murray Chotiner, the Nixon lawyer who's been writing to all my newspapers and radio stations, got involved in a Senate investigation. Thanks to his squawks against me, a lot of editors are now familiar with his background.

April 26:   Brownell has been down in Houston talking to Governor Shivers about being the VP with Ike. Brownell doesn't favor Nixon. This plus yesterday's press conference, plus the Chotiner probe caused Dick to barge into the White House today and tell Ike he's running. If he waited until after the Chotiner probe it might be too late.

April 28:   You get twenty minutes of spring in Washington. Yesterday you needed a topcoat. Today it was sweltering. We televised the farm—two shows. The children came out last night so Drew could have his picture taken riding the donkey. At the end of the day, I was exhausted, Luvie was irritated, the donkey was impossible. When I got home Ellen and George were waiting for me to tell me they were getting a divorce. Or rather George did the telling. I suppose it was inevitable, but I have prayed that it wouldn't happen. I have prayed for few things in my adult years, but I have for this—almost every night. I can see them making the same mistakes Ellen's mother and I made all over again. I can see Ellen becoming more and more like her mother.

April 29: Went to see Ellen and George. Georgie was playing across the street with his friend Stevie. Drew was down the street some place. Joe was upstairs in his room. George brought him down, and he sat solemnly in a chair or paddled around the dust of the porch while his mother and father and I discussed a divorce that was going to affect his life more than anything else in the world.

I had rehearsed some of the things I was going to say to them, but I couldn't get them out—at least not effectively. Ellen says she has someone she wants to marry, but I can tell she doesn't really mean it. George kept repeating that they had to get the divorce, and in a way I don't blame him.

Ellen admits that after Little Joe came, she just quit trying. They both quit trying about a year and a half ago.

June 4: Televised last two shows. They will probably be *the last.* Either I am not good enough or the political atmosphere is agin' me. In brief, TV for me has been a flop.

Took the train to Chicago. One of the few times I ever get to relax. I used to duck speaking engagements. Now I'm anxious to get them if they pay anything—to meet the payroll.

June 5: Visited with Jake Arvey. He's dead opposed to Harriman, seemed very strong for Symington, and thought Adlai had made a mistake by going into the primaries because he's been seen too much, like a TV star who's been on too often. He was very friendly to Kefauver, said that there was a chance of a Stevenson-Kefauver ticket. Reason Estes couldn't get together with Adlai for VP last September, Arvey said, was because Adlai wouldn't make an advance deal with anyone—"irregardless." However, he would have taken him in 1952.

June 6: Flew back to Washington at 2:50 A.M. Lunched with Tom Corcoran—an amazing man. He hasn't lost his vivaciousness despite the years. He's been masterminding Lyndon Johnson, but says he's actually for Stevenson. Stevenson swept to such a victory in California yesterday that I think he's as good as nominated.

June 7: Chris Witting says he sounded out utilities about me—if Westinghouse sponsored me for their appliances. The hostility he found was deep. He'd run a check on what I've said. (Waste of time.)

June 8: Eisenhower was taken sick last night. The White House announced acute indigestion, but then carted him off to Walter Reed, which is not what you do with acute indigestion. I had to rewrite a whole column on people-to-people friendship—or rather, junk it. I don't see how the Republicans can possibly run Ike now, though they may try to prop him up and make him last through the campaign.

The Greek Embassy awarded me the Gold Cross of the Order of Phoenix today at lunch. I remember the days when I was young and swore that I wouldn't accept decorations from foreign governments— it influences a newsman's judgment. I wonder whether my judgment has been warped. I've been writing some very critical things about France and Norway lately, despite decorations from both. I note that the Norwegian Ambassador doesn't like it much and has stopped inviting me to his social functions.

June 9: Ike was operated on at 3:00 A.M. for suspected malignant tumor. They didn't announce it as such; rather, as a partial obstruction of the small intestine. Took out ten inches of intestine. The medical bulletins sounded like campaign documents. Operation lasted two hours, so they must have been scraping for possible cancer. Took him six hours to come out of the ether. Yet ten hours later it was announced he would run again.

Ellen came from New York for a conference with George and the attorney. It looks as if everything is washed up.

June 11: George Vournas is back from Greece. About one-quarter of Greece is left-wing or near-Communist; another one-quarter is reactionary. There is no real middle class. So unpopular in Crete that American fleet advised not to land there. We've left everything to the generals. All the emphasis is on the military. Greek security has a file on everyone, even vegetable peddlers.

July 18: Bill Roberts called this morning and asked me to set up a telephone call to Governor Stevenson at one-thirty.

Estes has been going through some difficult moments. Some of his advisers want him to stay until the end; some are worried about his campaign deficit. He also faces the fact that Jiggs has already been talking to DiSapio and worked out a tentative plan for Harriman to take Estes for Vice President with Jiggs as National Committee Chairman.

At 2 A.M. Estes decided that the unity of the party was more important than anything else, and authorized me to call Stevenson.

I called him, and at first had to deal in some double-talk because I was speaking from a phone booth in the Cosmos Club with other people using the adjacent booth.

I proposed that he meet with Kefauver tomorrow in Washington, and indicated in quite clear language what the result would be.

He began to alibi about having a full schedule. I told him to come early and have the meeting before the rest of his schedule took place. Stevenson suggested that he and Estes meet in Colorado, where they are both supposed to be at the end of this week. I told him that would be out of the question; first, because Estes was under pressure from others (I did not tell him about the Harriman proposals); and, second, because the psychological moment for the announcement was tomorrow night, at the Senator George dinner.

Stevenson then countered that he thought it was a mistake for him and Estes to sit down together; that it would be better for third parties to make arrangements between them so he could honestly tell the press that he'd had no meetings with Kefauver, made no commitments and no deal. He kept harping on this at some length.

I told him that the essential thing was not a deal but that two men sit down together and work for the unity of the Democratic party. I pointed out that Estes was somewhat like him—namely, shy and reticent in talking privately—and that it was important for them both to know each other. I told him there should be no deals.

Stevenson then said he thought any announcement at the George dinner might "be unfair to Averell. We don't want to take the spotlight away from Senator George. This is in his honor."

I pointed out that this would be in tribute to Senator George; that he would be in the position of inspiring unity; that Kefauver would say that in the tradition which Senator George had followed to keep the Democratic Party together, he . . . etc.

"Of course," I added, "George doesn't deserve it. And Estes will not say anything about F.D.R. and the purge in Georgia."

Stevenson laughed at this and said he was thinking of making a statement in his speech referring to the 1938 purge and the fact that George was the only man who survived the purge and had Roosevelt say he regretted it. He asked me what I thought of it, and I said I thought it would be fine.

At the end of our conversation I couldn't help thinking that Stevenson's friends are right that he's a very difficult guy to pin down and has trouble making up his mind on anything.

He said he would look at his schedule; I said I would talk to Estes about the third-person business and we would get in touch with each other later in the afternoon.

I did not call Stevenson, but if this particular opportunity goes by, Estes is going to be in the convention for keeps. He'll probably lose his shirt, but he'll go down fighting. And it will mean a long-drawn-out, deadlocked convention.

July 30:   I had dinner with Joe De Silva, head of the Los Angeles Retail Clerks' Union, and his attorney, Sol Lipman. Joe was here to attend the Kefauver confidential meeting of advisers on whether he should throw in the sponge. Joe reported that at the morning session everyone present was in favor of Estes caving in now. Joe made a speech in which he was the lone dissenter. He repeated the speech to me somewhat like this:

"Suppose I am the candidate. Let's see what we have got to lose. First, the organization of the convention is against me. Leonard Rensch may be way off in a corner behind a pole.

"Second, the page boys will be against my delegates. You know how it was at Chicago last time when those Arvey boys told you where to go and when to go.

"Third, Sam Rayburn will be against me. I will have no chance to be recognized.

"Fourth, Lyndon Johnson will be working backstage against me while Rayburn works against me on stage.

"Fifth, the Harriman boom has slowed down. It is dead; it is a bust. But if I throw in the sponge now, where am I. I am licked not only now but forever. I have got to run true to my past and go down fighting."

De Silva said that the Kefauver leaders were afraid they would lose seventy delgates on the second ballot. Jiggs Donohue and Howard

McGrath were the chief advocates of withdrawal. If so, Jiggs might become national chairman or might work out a deal whereby he would become national chairman and build for Kefauver in 1960.

Three plans were discussed at the meeting:

1. To throw in the sponge now and hope for a groundswell for Kefauver for Vice President.

2. Have Kefauver and Harriman sign a declaration of plans on civil rights. It was argued that this would put Stevenson's delegates on the spot, especially the Negroes who have lined up with Stevenson despite his moderate pro-South stand.

3. Fight it out to the very end and go down fighting with no compromise.

"Let's call a spade a spade," De Silva argued, "and let the Negro people face the civil rights issue. They don't want civil rights. Therefore, Harriman and Kefauver had better come out with a strong civil rights program and put the Negroes on the spot."

Strangely, Kefauver was not present during any of this meeting. Jiggs had told me that Kefauver would listen to the advice of his friends and then issue a statement at the end of the day announcing in favor of Stevenson. But with Kefauver not present and not listening to the advice of his friends, obviously something has gone wrong. I know that Estes is under great pressure from both sides. Bill Roberts was one of the few who supported De Silva and urged that he stay in the race. The more I think about it, the more I am convinced that he will have to stick it out or face political suicide.

Lipman says that Jim Hoffa of Detroit is going to replace Dave Beck at the next Teamsters' convention. Hoffa confided that he had paid $20,000 to get George Connolly, the Teamsters' leader in Minnesota, out of a conviction in connection with a bombing in St. Paul or Minneapolis.

By strange coincidence, I was talking to Governor Freeman of Minnesota on the telephone this morning about the fact that Stassen was working with the Teamsters in Minnesota to nominate a Vice President on the Republican ticket. Governor Freeman told me that he had been trying to prosecute Connolly for two bombings and had secured a conviction in Hennepin County, but that Connolly had been acquitted in Ramsey County where a Stassen-appointed judge, Robert V. Rensch, had refused to let the case go to a jury.

July 31:   Kefauver called me. He was afraid my phone was tapped and I went up to see him. I knew what he wanted to talk about, of course.

He asked me whether he should withdraw from the race. It was fairly obvious that his mind was made up, and that he was leaning toward a withdrawal.

Before I went to see him, I talked to both Joe De Silva and Bill Roberts, who didn't want him to withdraw; and to Jiggs Donohue who did. I leaned toward the De Silva-Roberts view, but the more I talked to Estes the more I thought he would be better off if he got out of the race. So my advice wasn't very firm. I told him I thought that if he made a withdrawal speech at an occasion like the Senator George Dinner or before some other big Democratic meeting it would be better than a mere press conference.

I also told him that I thought it was the hardest decision in the world to make and whatever he did his friends would be with him.

At four o'clock that afternoon he called a press conference and issued a withdrawal statement. It went over very well; much better than I had anticipated. Newspapermen were friendly and didn't heckle him. The radio broadcasts were all favorable.

Late that night Luvie and I telephoned. Estes was still at his office and feeling better. We certainly felt sorry for him. But I think he has enhanced his prestige, and certainly his political bargaining power.

August 23:   I wrote the story of Eisenhower's nomination three days before he was nominated and left San Francisco for Washington. Nothing could have stopped his nomination. Even if he had died en route to San Francisco, Len Hall would have stuffed him and run him anyway.

Some editors aren't going to relish my leaving the U.S.A. during an election campaign, but I have a hunch bigger news is brewing in the Near East.

August 24:   En route. Worked until 2 A.M. to finish last installment of "Confessions of an S.O.B." for the *Saturday Evening Post.* Dictated one column on the plane en route to New York. Finally left on Israel Airlines at noon.

Stopped in London for two hours and was interviewed for TV at the London airport, which made me a little ashamed. I have flown over England during my last three trips to Europe and never stopped. We're getting so we take England for granted—which is a bad thing to do with an old friend. The chief thing they want to know over here is who will win in November. They hope Eisenhower will not.

August 25:   It's rugged traveling on the plane toward the end of thirty-three hours. Crowded and hot. Far different from the first trip I ever took to Europe. It was in the same month—August—but in 1919, nine months after the end of World War I. It took us nineteen days on a slow Italian boat, the *Sofia,* to get to Greece. Leisurely, lovely stopovers at Gibraltar and Malta. Now we touch down two hours at London, an hour at Paris, don't even bother to stop at Rome.

We flew over Rome. It was beautiful even from the air—the Colosseum, the avenues radiating into plazas. Rome never changes. It hasn't changed in ten years. It hasn't changed since I first trudged through it with a knapsack on my back as a young goggle-eyed relief worker from the Balkans visiting the wonders of Ancient Rome. That was before Mussolini. Many political changes since then, but I could see from the air that despite wars, despite revolutions, despite cabinet upheavals, Rome was still Rome. In two minutes we had passed on, and in two more hours we were in Athens. Beautiful Grecian night. It reminded me of the nights I spent in Greece as a young relief worker thirty-seven years ago, looking out at the moon over the Aegean, madly in love with a Russian nurse in the hospital in Salonika. Salonika was still crowded with French and British troops, remnants of the Balkan push which ended the war. Today, Athens is crowded with American personnel, part of the Truman doctrine to keep out Communism.

August 26:   Got to Tel Aviv at 3:30 A.M. Sunday. Some Israeli officials had stayed up to meet us. They wore neither coats nor neckties. A little dog was also up to meet us. Luvie seemed more interested in him than in the Israeli dignitaries.

We drove to the hotel in the suburbs, a drive beneath cool, shaded trees, almost like a suburb on the Main Line of Philadelphia, except that it's tropical. No barbed wire, no sentries, no troops, none of the impression you get from reading American newspapers. Our hotel is modern and beautiful. We went to sleep with the gently rolling Mediterranean just below our balcony. If this is like the rest of Israel, this trip will be more vacation than work.

The work began, however, Sunday afternoon: After a few hours of sleep, we went out to Tel Hashomer Hospital for the first in a series of filmed interviews I am doing for Baruch Diener, head of ORB films. The hospital reminded me somewhat of the one I used to operate in south Serbia—a series of informal, rambling barracks, only with excellent modern equipment.

August 30: Drove to Beersheeba for the first night to get an early start for the Dead Sea. Beersheeba is a town of camels and donkeys, trucks and modern cars, squat shops and modern Israeli skyscrapers. From it rises a hostel for youth built by an American benefactor—modern, white, clean. We stayed there. It was hot. I pulled my bedding out on the balcony. It was cooler, but an Arab singing in a nightclub kept me awake most of the night. His plaintive wail floated over the still night air—with the help of a loudspeaker—as if he were fighting all the Arab wars against the Jews. Finally at four-thirty they called me; we bolted some sandwiches and left for the Dead Sea. It was beautiful driving through the desert in the morning twilight. The tents of the Bedouins and their goat herds looked like dim, black shadows against the sands. Coming back, those same sands were hot and cruel in the noonday sun.

The Dead Sea is a long lifeless body of gray water surrounded by almost molten salt and sand. It is so hot you can't walk in your bare feet. When I went in swimming I had to run. The water is so buoyant that I read *Newsweek* with two hands, my feet on the surface, and my hat on top of my head. We shot some scenes of me reading the Bible on the shore of the Sea.

I can understand how, and perhaps why, the Lord destroyed Sodom and Gomorrah. It is so hot here that sin probably bred easily. And the asphalt around the lake could well catch on fire if lightning hit in the right place. Rising above the lake is the pillar of salt that is supposed to be Lot's wife, and underneath it is the cave where Lot's two daughters got the old man tipsy. It all looks as if parts of the Old Testament had been written to fit the scenery.

Across from the Dead Sea is Arab territory. It is too bad that all this area is not under one country. Harry Truman once told me of his plan to run a canal from the Mediterranean to the Dead Sea to generate electricity by the 1286 foot drop. But it probably couldn't be done with the Dead Sea in the hands of two unfriendly countries.

Driving down to Beersheeba we passed near the Gaza Strip where

Egyptian and Jewish troops face each other. It seemed peaceful. Next day we learned that thirteen Egyptians had been killed in night skirmishes.

August 31:   Parts of this country are so narrow the Arabs can fire across it. The Tel Aviv airport is two and one half miles from the Jordan border.

Abdullah, King of Jordan, who was assassinated, was strong for Israel-Jordan friendship. Golda Meir, now Foreign Minister, went to see him toward the end of the war disguised as a Muslim woman. The Minister of Defense also had profitable talk with him.

Arab-Jewish bitterness is a problem for all of us, not just for Jews. The more bitterness there is here, the more Russia can take over the vital Mediterranean.

The Truman policy re Greece and Turkey was aimed at stopping Russia in the Mediterranean. (Row with Roosevelt over calling me chronic liar was over the Mediterranean. The Russians wanted to send diplomatic representative here.) Truman policy worked. Russia was stopped in regard to one great waterway—the Bosporus—but slipped down a little further south, bypassed the Bosporus and is reaping success at Suez. Under Nasser, Africa and Asia may become consolidated. Then it won't matter much what happens in Turkey and Greece. They die on the vine.

September 1:   Up at six-thirty and off to northern Galilee; it's rough, rocky country, though the most intensively cultivated in Israel—olive trees, terraced fields, tobacco grown among rocks where we wouldn't even tether a goat.

Interviewed Dr. G. Mer, director of health, on malaria, flies, and insect control. He was supposed to go back to work in Jerusalem today and would agree to stay over and be interviewed only if he received a letter from the Prime Minister that he could be late returning to work. We got him the letter.

In the late afternoon I interviewed a housewife, a businessman, and a public accountant as to what Israel needs most. All had come here from Germany just as Hitler got into power. The housewife answered: "Young people to develop the country"; the businessman, "Peace"; the accountant, "Arms to ensure peace."

Luvie is bored and wants to go home.

September 4: Up at five-thirty to go to Jordan canal. This is where the Syrians have threatened war if Israel completed the canal to tap the Jordan for irrigation. It's also a hot, rocky desert where David defeated his son Absalom and where Absalom, trying to escape, was caught by his hair in a tree and killed by one of David's generals. There are no trees here now, but there are the rocks behind which Jacob's daughter tried to find Joseph on that night before his envious brothers sold him into slavery in Egypt. In fact, rocks, rocks everywhere, with the hot sun pouring down on their unprotected surface.

Interviewed Paul Doran, the irrigation engineer in charge. It's an ambitious project, to carry water the entire length of Israel right down to the Negev desert. Work on the canal in the disputed area has stopped in deference to the U.N. But the rest of the canal is going ahead. Two Syrians eyed us suspiciously from the hilltop across the Jordan while we worked. Two jeeploads of Israeli troops protected us, but didn't seem much worried.

September 8: Drove to Nazareth. Attended Greek Catholic church services of Archbishop George Hakim, a very astute man, who doesn't like the Jews. He told me he was an Egyptian, travels back and forth to Amman, Syria, Egypt. This is amazing. No other resident of Israel could do this, and it indicates considerable tolerance on the part of the Jews that they let him. I buttered him up a bit; I also suggested, and this was not exactly buttering, that he could play a real part in bringing peace between the Arabs and Jews. He says there must be some territorial concessions to the Arabs just as well as financial payments to the refugees. He says Israel is ready to make the latter, though not if they are to remain enemies. The payments must be made as part of a general peace.

Nazareth, where Christ lived, is now completely Arab, though about one-third of it is Christian Arab. I recorded a telecast in the old synagogue where Christ taught as a youth.

Drove to Jerusalem, arriving at 10 P.M., a long day.

September 10: Couldn't sleep. We have a lovely balcony in the King David Hotel looking out over the palm trees and the cypress trees and the city of Jerusalem spread out below. The city seems very peaceful tonight. The stars seem brighter than I have ever seen them, and I can understand how bright they must have been on that night in Bethlehem 1956 years ago. Somehow they seem brighter and closer and more personal in this setting. But across the way, only a few hundred feet away in the old city, machine guns look down upon the new, making it anything but a city of peace.

This is the most fascinating of all Israeli cities—the blending of the old with the new, the presence of danger, make it so. Yesterday I interviewed Rev. William Hull, a Protestant missionary who expressed a view I had not heard before but which may be true—that this Arab threat has been a blessing to Israel, that the Jews never could have buried their differences and got along together without this threat. He also told how the Arab people, as differentiated from their leaders, want peace, how they gathered at the post office (the only place permissible in 1948) to whisper to each other while writing letters: "Are you all right?" The Arab leaders have found the Israeli issue an excellent political issue to keep their people whipped up over.

1957

March 21: Miss Canty* told me that there was someone on the telephone who said he was Joe McCarthy and that she thought he was telling the truth. I picked up the telephone and it was Joe. It was the first time we had spoken to each other in exactly seven years—since our melee in the cloakroom of the Sulgrave Club. The following conversation took place: "Drew, are you sitting down?" "Yes," I replied. "Well, I wanted to make sure you weren't standing up or you'd faint. I just wanted to tell you that I'm putting your column today in the *Congressional Record*. As you know, I don't always agree with what you say but this column I know tells the truth. So I'm putting it in the *Record* and I just thought I'd better warn you in advance so you wouldn't faint when you saw it." We exchanged a few pleasantries and I thanked him. That was the end of the conversation.

The column pertained to the double-cross given to Israel at the United Nations by John Foster Dulles.

March 27: I went down to the Pentagon today for the first press conference I have attended in the entire Eisenhower administration. I shouldn't admit this but press conferences don't really give out much news that I can't get by reading the ticker tape. However, I wanted to beard Charlie Wilson in his own den. I went early—too early—and had to sit for thirty minutes in a front row. But I wanted to be in the front row. The TV cameras were all set up and finally Charlie bounced in. He handled his press conference very well. I was surprised at his knowledge of the intricate operations of the Pentagon. I had typed out

*Marian Canty was Drew Pearson's personal secretary for many years.—Ed.

375

some good stiff quotes from the Nickerson memorandum showing how Wilson apparently favored General Motors in the missile race. I fired the questions, which he handled amazingly well. After it was all over I couldn't help but feel that Charlie had done pretty well by himself and was a decent human being. We shook hands and said hello.

One question during the press conference asked by the other newsmen pertained to the secret report on Pan American Airways which I had tried to get several years before under Louis Johnson. It tells how Pan American rooked the American people for about $100,-000,000 in building bases in Latin America during the war. They bribed Latin American officials right and left, which is one reason the report isn't being made public. Wilson, in reply to the queries, said he would take it under advisement. I popped up with the question: "Did you know that one of your predecessors as Secretary of Defense who suppressed that report later became counsel for Pan American Airways?" Wilson grinned and said something to the effect that that was a double-barreled question.

Wrote a nice column about Charlie Wilson. He wrote me a letter expressing his thanks, which sort of floored me. I guess he was floored by the nice column. I suppose it will be difficult for me to criticize Charlie in the future. But he won't be around long anyway. Mrs. Wilson has told him he has to leave. Charlie and I have the same masseuse. She tells me what a nice man he is and I tell her not to tell him that she operates on me, too. When he comes home in the evening he has a highball but Mrs. Wilson says, "Now, Charlie," and he puts his glass down. Mrs. Wilson apparently wears the pants in the family. She has been unhappy in Washington. In Detroit she was the whole cheese in the macaroni. Every automobile mogul in the city kowtowed and bowed before her, but here she is just the wife of another Cabinet officer where Cabinet officers and ex-Cabinet officers are a dime a dozen. She wants to go back to Detroit.

April 16 [Los Angeles]:   Spoke at the Los Angeles State College. Had a really live-wire audience with plenty of good questions afterward. They don't like Ike out here. Howard Hughes offered to drive me to Fresno for my next talk.

April 17:   It ended up with Hughes supplying a private plane to take me to Fresno. I wonder what will happen the next time something comes along critical of Trans-World Airlines. Will I write it or won't I?

April 19: Back in Washington. We went to Bill Douglas's for cocktails. The Chief Justice, Earl Warren, was there and I got a little fresh with Senator Symington. Kidded him in front of the Chief Justice about voting for Justice Whittaker's confirmation, which I told Stuart he should not have done because he wasn't going to be any good as a justice. I am pretty sure that Whittaker will line up against both Warren and Douglas in the future.

Went to Philadelphia to speak at a Jewish Passover service. I had not realized before how beautiful these services can be. They commemorate the exit of the Jews out of Egypt.

April 21: Spent Easter in Swarthmore. It was beautiful. I walked through the Crum Woods where our family used to picnic when I was a boy. It has hardly changed a bit. There are a few more paths and since I'm a little bigger than I was at the age of ten, I can navigate the steeper ones along the hillsides a little better.

April 26: Lunched with Edward Bennett Williams—the only lawyer who ever was able to win a libel suit against me. Asked him about the fact that the indictment of Jimmie Hoffa shows that Cheasty,* the McClellan Committee plant to entrap Hoffa, had called Williams's office in advance of his arrest, which would have indicated that Williams might have been in on the conspiracy.

He explained that Bobby Kennedy had asked Eddy Cheyfitz, the former public relations director of the Teamsters, to arrange for a dinner with Hoffa, which had taken place on February 14. Hoffa came to town, stopped at Williams's office in advance of the dinner, received the telephone call, then had dinner with Kennedy and Cheyfitz that same night at Cheyfitz's home.

*John C. Cheasty played a key role in the arrest of Teamster Vice President Jimmie Hoffa. An agent of the Secret Service and the IRS, Cheasty had been hired by the Senate Select Committee on Labor and Management Practices—the McClellan Committee. His testimony that Hoffa had hired him in an effort to get data from the Committee's files led to Hoffa's arrest on bribery charges.—ED.

Kennedy did not tell Hoffa that night that he had set a trap for him. Williams remarked that the ethics of decency should have required that Kennedy at least stay away from the dinner.

When Hoffa was arrested, the press had been tipped off by Mrs. Kennedy, on behalf of her husband, to be present at midnight at the District Attorney's office. About fifty of them were there. The New York *Herald Tribune* had received a special tip that Hoffa was to be arrested.

At the appearance before the commissioner, the District Attorney asked for a two weeks' continuance. This was at 2 A.M. Williams said, "O.K., provided my client has a right to a hearing." The District Attorney remarked that he considered this an insult. "That," said Williams, "is exactly why I insist upon a hearing."

In the end, a two weeks' continuance was given. But at 2 P.M. the next day Hoffa was brought before a grand jury and indicted— without the hearing. Williams has appealed on the ground that this was illegal.

Williams thinks that the FBI is tapping wires wholesale. He points out that the Judy Coplon case was never brought to trial on the appeal because two FBI agents perjured themselves by swearing that Judy's wires had not been tapped. When Judge Albert Reeves of Kansas City requested the record and took a look at it, he saw the wire-tap records. No Attorney General has since brought the case to trial.

April 29:   Flew to New London to do a TV show on a submarine. I was supposed to stay on the submarine all night. But I found out that I was going to occupy a tiny bunk and that all crew were going ashore to stay with their families. I figured it wasn't really worth my while being cramped all night just for the sake of saying I had been on a submarine for the night. We dove, traveled submerged, and went through all the other maneuvers. So I went back to the Mohican Hotel and got a room.

April 30:   Lunched with the top brass at the Groton Submarine Base. I never was surrounded by so many captains before. They are a little skeptical about me and not quite sure whether I will do a good job for them with this TV show. The crew of the submarine is terrific and I must say that they have real esprit de corps. Flew back to Washington late in the afternoon.

May 1:   Senator McCarthy has been drinking heavily His wife tried to use the knee injury to alibi his current trip to the Bethesda Naval Hospital. The doctor, however, refused to accept the alibi. Joe is in an oxygen tent and has delirium tremens.

Still unable to locate Tom [Hennings]. Tried three New York hotels where he usually goes when he is drunk.

May 2:   I was in New York when Bill Neel called to say McCarthy had died. Bill was able to catch my radio tape in time to eliminate my references to McCarthy's illness. I had reported that he had the DT's, which, of course, was correct but I would have caught hell had it been broadcast. I wrote a column that night in the hotel in New York on McCarthy. In some respects I am sorry to see him go. He caused this nation all sorts of pain and setbacks in the field of foreign affairs. But toward the end I couldn't help but feel sorry for him. He was a very lonesome guy. All the glamour that once surrounded him was gone. The newspaper men who had once hounded him wouldn't pay any attention to him any more. He used to carry press releases through the Capitol and try to hand them to newsmen. They were polite. They accepted the press releases but that was all.

May 5:   Spoke in Cleveland. Bill Friedman, my radio sponsor in Cleveland, says they get quite a few protests from McCarthyites. He called up Nat Howard of the Cleveland *News* to ask what he should do with them. "Throw them away," said Nat.

May 6:   I went to see Nat Howard. He hasn't been publishing much of the column. Nat told me how the publishers had tried to cancel the column last fall after the boo-boo on Eisenhower's health published out of Minneapolis and St. Paul.* He refused. He warned me, however, that he sometimes had a rough time with his publishers.

---

*During the 1956 campaign, Drew Pearson had written that Eisenhower called off two days of campaigning due to illness. His Press Secretary, Jim Hagerty, issued a denial saying the President wasn't ill but had gotten a "piece of confetti in his eye." —ED.

Flew to Kansas City, where I had a pleasant though unprofitable visit with young Joe Pulitzer of the St. Louis *Post-Dispatch*, who hardly publishes the column at all. I urged him to let us cancel so I could place the column with the St. Louis *Globe-Democrat*, but he refused. I also talked to him about Tom Hennings to see what we could do to get Tom back on the right track. I felt foolish in the end doing this because Pulitzer didn't register. He is very nice but rather ineffectual.

May 7:   I called Harry Truman's office for an appointment. I was surprised when he got on the telephone himself to say he was a little busy but would be delighted to see me at eleven o'clock. His office is on the eleventh floor of the Federal Reserve Building. His name is not listed on the directory downstairs but everyone in the building seems to know who he is.

I reminded him that when I had seen him last, in February 1956, he had predicted there would be war over Suez, and I asked him how he had known this.

"I remember," he said, interrupting me, "and the whole thing could have been avoided. We surrendered in Korea and we kowtowed at Geneva. All of our trouble has come from those surrenders.

"I proposed at the Potsdam Conference that all important waterways be internationalized, Suez, the Dardanelles, Gibraltar, the Black Sea straits. I offered to internationalize the Panama Canal. Those waterways have got to be internationalized to keep peace in the world. We should have done it before Nasser seized Suez."

"What happened to the proposal at Potsdam?" I asked.

"The British were lukewarm. Stalin said he couldn't do anything about the Dardanelles until the Montreux (Truman hesitated on the pronunciation and asked me how it was pronounced) Convention expired. He wanted to control the Dardanelles himself and take it away from Turkey.

"Stalin always wanted a base in the Mediterranean. Now Russia has got one, in Albania. I'll bet Stalin is standing up in his grave laughing. The Sixth Fleet was off up here where the boys could have a good time" (Truman pointed to the Adriatic), "not down here where they should have been" (he pointed to Suez) "when trouble broke the other day."

When I pressed him for an answer as to how he knew war would break out, he said, "Those Russian arms in Egypt."

"How would you stop them?" I asked. "They are still coming in now."

"No, they are not coming to Egypt any more. They are going to Syria," he corrected me. "We have enough ships in the Mediterranean," he said, "to throw a blockade against any vessel bringing in Russian arms."

I didn't have a chance to ask him if this wouldn't mean war. He jumped on to other subjects.

"I am just back from stirring up the animals in Washington," he said. "Somebody has to do it. You have been doing it. I have been following you. I've got you right on my desk." (He picked up *Personal from Pearson.*)*

I told him that the stuff I wrote in *The Washington Post* was better. He said that he had seen that too.

"Did any Cabinet officer ever buck you or Roosevelt on the budget?" I asked.

"Not on the budget," Truman replied, "but Morgenthau came in to see me and said he wanted to go to Potsdam. I told him the place of the Secretary of the Treasury is in Washington. 'In that case,' he said, 'I will have to resign.' 'All right,' I said, 'you can write it out now.' Morgenthau turned white.

"Then there was Ickes. He was a great old boy. I liked him. He opposed me on Ed Pauley for Secretary of the Navy. But I had a special reason for appointing Pauley to that job. I figured he was tough enough to keep the admirals in check. Pauley went over to Russia and did a terrific job on reparations. He was the only one tough enough to do it. But I couldn't make Ickes understand that. And after he opposed Pauley's appointment, he came to me and said he wanted to resign in six weeks. 'You have resigned already,' I told him.

"Later he came to see me, I think in 1950, and said, 'I have got to get into this campaign. They are taking the country away from us. I want to make some speeches.' "

I asked Truman if he had ever had any word from Eisenhower about going abroad.

"No. You know what happened last winter. They called me up and said, 'We will pay your expenses to Greece and Turkey, and the Greek and Turkish governments will take care of you after that.' I told

---

Personal from Pearson was the Drew Pearson newsletter.—ED.

them, 'I don't need your goddamn expense money. You can jump in the lake.' "

I have never talked to Truman that he didn't lapse into Missouri mule-driver language. It is obvious that he hates Eisenhower with an undying hatred. At one point he said, "Ike likes the royal folderol and the shits. I like the people. The trouble with him is what Admiral Leahy used to say about him." Truman then assumed a deep, bass voice, imitating Leahy: " 'That guy's got no guts.' "

I told Truman that General Omar Bradley had said the same thing about him. "When some of us made the mistake of talking about Eisenhower for 1948." I said, "Bradley sent that message regarding Eisenhower."

"I didn't really want the nomination in '48," Truman interrupted, "but somebody had to take it as I wasn't going to be pushed around."

I told Truman the reason no Southern Governors turned up at the Democratic meeting in Washington was because Lyndon Johnson had discouraged them. But I couldn't get a rise out of him.

"Well, it won't hurt us to fight among ourselves, just so long as nobody is underhanded. The Democrats are like the Irish—if they are not fighting the enemy they fight among themselves. We used to have factional fights in Kansas City. It did us good to have those fights out of our systems. We had a big fight once over a new highway, and an old fellow in Independence said, 'The more cats fight, the more cats there are.' "

I told Truman that since I had seen him last, I had gone to Israel.

"What do you think is the way to bring peace to that country?" I asked.

"Just what I told you before," Truman said. "That's where history began, American history, not the history of this part of the world." (And he pointed on the globe to Russia.) "Most of our wars began down here or in the Balkans. That's what Hitler was after—oil, and a route through Suez. But we are not going to have peace until we readjust things. Two hundred families own most of the arable land in Iran. I had a survey made when I was in the White House and it showed that the only way we can have peace is to settle all these problems—from the Adriatic to Morocco—together. We have got to give the people here a chance to live and to eat. There's no reason why they can't get along together. I told that to Ibn Saud when I saw him.

" 'You're all cousins,' I said, 'you ought to get along with the Jews even if they do call you bastards. You can call them that too.' "

"What did Ibn Saud say?" I asked.

"He laughed and laughed and laughed. 'We don't deny that Abraham's wife drove us into the desert,' he said."

I asked Truman how Eisenhower could be so vindictive toward him.

"I am glad he is," he replied. "If he wasn't I couldn't throw rocks at him. Somebody has to fight. You've been pouring it on. That's why I talk to you. You're doing such a good job of pouring it on 'em. Somebody has to fight for the country and this guy just won't fight."

As I left, Truman said in a voice which indicated he really meant it, "I would appreciate it if you would come out here on July 6th when we dedicate my library. I am going to turn twenty-one million dollars' worth of historical documents and keepsakes over to the government."

"I hear a strike is delaying construction of the library," I said.

"We will dedicate it anyway. I won't interfere with their strike but we are going to dedicate on July 6th, and I would appreciate it very much if you would come out."

The next day was Truman's birthday but I forgot to mention it to him. He looked no older than when he was in the White House, though I confess that I didn't see him much in the White House during his later years—we were not exactly on speaking terms.

May 8: Flew to New York for a big luncheon with Hadassah where they awarded me some kind of plaque. They are a little too professional. They also talked so long that I missed my plane back to Washington. In the morning in New York I had a session with Ted Ashley regarding future television prospects. He was a little bit bored, has no formula.

Went to the Marjorie Post square dance which probably was foolish but Luvie wanted to go. I couldn't sleep on the plane flying from Kansas City to New York, and this makes about twenty-two hours in a row out of a bed. However, I had an interesting talk with Senator Fulbright. Bill sees a steady drift toward war similar to that prior to World War II. He sees the same blasé isolation developing in the American people. He has reversed himself from two years ago when he championed Lyndon and is now sore as hell at him. We speculated as to why Lyndon had made a deal to confirm Scotty McLeod, the State Department's Joe McCarthy, but we couldn't find the answer. It was not natural gas because the Republicans will vote for the natural gas bill anyway. Bill Fulbright is unquestionably one of the most intellec-

tual and intelligent members of the Senate. But sometimes I think he
doesn't fight with both fists.

May 9:   Al Friendly and Phil Graham killed the Smathers item in the
Column. Phil once went to the University of Florida with Smathers.
I have received about a hundred letters raising Cain with me about the
Joe McCarthy column. Only a few are favorable. Hinson Stiles, editor
of the *Mirror*, phoned to say that they had never received so many
protests. He asked me to write something to take the heat off.

[The entry for May 18 is transcribed from longhand notes.]

May 18:   Went to Guggenheims' for dinner. Sat beside Mrs. George
Dixon, which I figured might be painful because I had written some
scathing things about her father and brother spending taxpayers'
money abroad and was just getting ready to write some more. It's going
to be difficult to write it in the future. She told me how she had
influenced her father to come out against Franco and how she'd influenced her husband to be against McCarthy. George lost a couple of
papers over McCarthy, and Bill Hearst, she said, didn't like his stuff.
She surprised me by saying the country would be better off under Nixon
than Ike. "People do change," she said. "And I really think Nixon has
changed." She said she had heard him speak before a Toledano group
of extreme reactionaries, yet he kept a liberal line. This is the second
time I've heard this from people who have deep convictions—the other
from Bill Fulbright at the square dance last week. Maybe I shouldn't
go out to dinner.
     Jack [Anderson] yesterday reported that Nixon paid $25,000 cash
for his new house and got a $50,000 loan from Riggs at 4 1/2 percent,
on which he pays $300 a month. I had to pay 6 percent the other day
and am paying $500 a month on the $40,000 I borrowed from Riggs.
Nixon still hasn't sold his first house, so where did he get the $25,000
cash?

May 28:   Elizabeth Hennings came to see me very much upset. Tom
has not been home since their dinner party May 11. That night he went
to the Naval Hospital, but has now disappeared. He called his Senate
office yesterday and when they asked where he was, he said, "At the
top of the Washington Monument."
     The Navy doctors said he didn't need a gallstone operation, which

seemed to disappoint him. They pronounced him in good shape. I suggested that we get three other Senators who are good friends of his to call on him when he gets sober and warn him that his usefulness in the Senate will be about over unless he stays on the wagon. Elizabeth says she is not going to give him a divorce.

Hank Greenspun* talked to me about Hoffa of the Teamsters. He wants me to ease up; said that Hoffa was a good man, and had been entrapped. I pointed out that I had given Hoffa a chance to reply to everything I had written before I had written it, but that the facts as given to me by his lawyers just did not jibe with the true facts. Greenspun has been talking to the head of the Teamsters in St. Louis, a man named Gibbons who he thinks will be new head of the Teamsters. Hank met Hoffa when he flew to Israel last fall, and was impressed with him. I agreed with Hank that Hoffa probably couldn't get a fair trial in Washington, but I did not agree that he was the knight in shining armor some of his friends seemed to think. In fact, I am convinced he is just about as crooked as Beck.

Congressmen Bolling, of Kansas City; John Dingell, of Detroit; and Judge Saund, of the Imperial Valley, came for dinner, together with Joe De Silva and others. Wayne Morse was kept in the Senate having a battle with Homer Capehart, of Indiana. Wayne called me earlier in the evening to say that he considered Capehart "a tub of rancid ignorance." I did not realize he intended to use this phrase on the Senate floor, but later he did. He and Hubert Humphrey did not get to the dinner.

Dingell, who succeeds a good congressional father, has turned out to be a brilliant Congressman. He had the courage to tangle with the FCC over the *Boston Herald Traveler* monopoly and I note that not one newspaper picked up the story. He has also been trying to expose Kuykendall, the Federal Power chairman. I suggested first that the Congressmen demand that Senator Magnuson hold hearings on Kuykendall. This seemed to startle them. They indicated that a Congressman doesn't demand of a Senator. However, they haven't even suggested. I then said that they ought to impeach Kuykendall, which the House has the power to do, but this seemed to horrify them. Bolling and Dingell are among the most courageous young Congressmen, yet I have the feeling that the hand of the oldsters and the reactionaries

*Publisher of the Las Vegas, Nevada, *Sun.*—ED.

is so strong over the House that even the courageous are afraid to move. They won't start anything unless they are sure it will succeed, and they don't realize that you can't get newspaper headlines unless you do something drastic.

June 4:   Betty Beale of the *Washington Star* called up to write a story about the Hennings divorce and the divorce by Senator Russell Long of Louisiana.

I talked to Paul Douglas and to Wayne Morse about a "visitation" on Tom. Paul was dubious, said he didn't know him well enough. Wayne was emphatically for it. It seems one trouble is that Tom doesn't know many other Senators.

Luvie and I stopped in to see the Mike Monroneys. Mike says he doesn't know Tom very well either, and doesn't know who does. Apparently, Tom has led quite an aloof life as far as his colleagues are concerned.

Senator Magnuson called me back and has now agreed to hold hearings on Kuykendall's confirmation to the Power Commission.

June 5:   I talked to Dingell of Michigan and Macdonald of Massachusetts about opposing Kuykendall's confirmation and testifying before Maggie's committee. They liked the idea. I also talked to Neuberger, who is going to appear as a witness against Kuykendall. The funny thing is that these Congressmen are afraid to urge a Senator to hold hearings unless a newspaperman intervenes first.

June 6:   Elizabeth Hennings came for lunch. She had taken Luvie's advice and saw her doctor for a tranquilizer pill.

Went to dinner at the Chad Calhouns'—a big jamboree they hold annually for all the friends of the Kaiser Company, the outfit that parlayed friendship with Roosevelt into a billion-dollar industrial empire. Though Kaiser climbed to fortune on the backs of Democrats, most of the people at the dinner were Republicans. I found myself sitting between Senator Norris Cotton of New Hampshire, who I have strongly suspected has been suspiciously close to the big utilities, and, on the other side, Mrs. McGregor, wife of the Congressman from Ohio. It just happened that the day before I had written a scathing piece attributing to Congressman McGregor the $2 billion increase in the cost of federal highways because the utility companies are going to be paid for moving their poles, water mains, conduits, etc. Through some whim of fate, I didn't actually send the story out. I didn't tell Mrs. McGregor I had written the story, and I suppose she will think I am much more than what Harry Truman said I was, when she reads the papers.

Senator Cotton, I found, had followed me at Exeter by about three years. He has done a pretty good job on some things at this session of Congress, but his voting record on the utilities is strangely contrary to the best interests of New Hampshire.

Neil Tolman, former assistant to Senator Bridges and the man who is paid by Phillips Petroleum an additional amount to siphon money off to the New Hampshire congressional delegation, was also at the dinner.

I have told the FBI and the Justice Department for some years how they could pin down the evidence on the bribery of two Senators by Phillips Petroleum, but the FBI doesn't want to tangle with Senators.

June 13: Reminisced with Phil Graham regarding war days—especially Wendell Willkie and his love affairs and his trip to China. Willkie's relations with Roosevelt were a lot different from Truman's relations with Eisenhower. Before Willkie went to China he had been at the White House, at which time someone suggested that F.D.R. write a personal letter to Stalin for Willkie. Roosevelt retired to his desk, wrote a letter in longhand in about thirty minutes and brought it back. Willkie's aides kidded him that he'd lose it. However, he didn't. In Moscow, Willkie asked for an interview with Stalin but nothing happened. He and his party waited and waited and waited. Finally, Willkie, who was furious, got ready to leave. That last night an English voice came on the phone stating that Stalin wanted to see Willkie. At the last minute somebody remembered Roosevelt's letter and they tried to find it but couldn't. A car picked Willkie up at about 2 A.M. to drive to the Kremlin. He always remembered his staff and took them to see Stalin too—namely Joe Barnes of the New York *Herald Tribune*, author of Willkie's book, and Mike Cowles of the Des Moines *Register*. They returned from the Kremlin at about 5 A.M. and began looking for the Roosevelt letter. They looked and looked. Finally, in a pile of old clothes they found it all crumpled up. The letter was never delivered.

In China, Willkie spent some time at Chiang Kai-shek's headquarters in Chungking. He came back to Mike and Joe Barnes from an audience with Madame Chiang telling them that there was never anything like this before. It was the only time he said he had ever been in love. He said he was going to take Mme. Chiang back to the United States. At one time the Generalissimo came through their quarters with about sixty secret police looking for Willkie. The staff was alarmed but nothing happened.

On the day they were to leave, they stopped to say good-bye to Mme. Chiang. Willkie went in. The door closed; they waited. They waited one hour and twenty minutes. She accompanied the party down to the plane and as he was about to get on the plane, she jumped into his arms. Willkie picked her up and gave her a terrific soul kiss. No wonder at one time the Generalissimo was looking for Willkie.

[The entry for June 15 is transcribed from longhand notes.]

June 15:   Dinner in honor of Ambassador Robert Hill, just appointed to Mexico. I once knew him when he was assistant to Senator Tobey, but have scarcely seen him since. He's done a good job for Dulles on the Hill under considerable handicaps. He said that Dulles didn't need to crack down on Lyndon Johnson's plan for penetrating the Iron Curtain. He had a phone call from Lyndon, fuming. "What does he think he is? Does he want his foreign aid bill passed?" Later, Dulles had a forty-minute session with Johnson to smooth him down.

When Fulbright made a remark to Dulles backing an immediate Eisenhower Doctrine in the Near East, Hill tried to get Dulles to write him a note. He didn't. Fulbright suggested that what Dulles and Ike wanted was a quick resolution from the Senate saying it was the general sense of the Senate that it supported Ike. Dulles, however, demanded a stronger resolution, though it took months to get it.

Hill thinks there never has been so much bitterness on both sides as today. I suggested things were just as bitter in Truman's day, but he pointed out that Republicans were now bitter at Democrats for opposing them.

Bill Douglas, who listened to my broadcast, expressed interest in disarmament talks. Mercedes made an interesting remark to me: that if she got sold on the Arabian slave market, she could write her memoirs for enough money to retire. (She's going through Iran and Arabia.) I told her the country couldn't afford to have Bill retire. She said it was a tough battle. "But you're winning," I said. "You don't win when you only have four votes." I suggested that some of the new justices were doing all right—meaning Brennan. She said: "You mean Whittaker." We were interrupted at that point.

She is taking a 1956 Chevy from Karachi to Istanbul; says the chief danger is breaking the springs. She's taking along a repair manual. One interpreter for each country. No guard or weapons.

June 18:   Senator Wayne Morse telephoned. Paul Douglas bawled him out in a secret caucus of leaders planning strategy for the Civil Rights bill. Here are two of the finest liberals in the Senate, now rowing with each other. I told Wayne to keep his shirt on. He wants me to write the story. Paul can be a bit vindictive at times and can lose his temper.

June 19:   I talked to Torbie Macdonald, the young Democrat from Massachusetts, also John Dingell of Detroit, and Vanik, the new Congressman from Cleveland. They are going to go to bat against Chairman Kuykendall when he comes up for confirmation. They have a chance to oppose him if they ask Senator Magnuson for the right to be heard when Kuykendall comes up for confirmation before the Senate Interstate Commerce Committee. Kuykendall has been accepting favors from the gas and oil people in Texas even though he's chairman of the Federal Power Commission, which is supposed to work for the public.

June 20:   I called Magnuson and asked him to try to defeat Kuykendall. He says he will vote against him and will be delighted to have the young Congressman testify, but he doesn't think there's a chance to defeat him. Apparently, there's a deal on Hell's Canyon. The Southern Senators will vote for Hell's Canyon if Maggie gets Kuykendall confirmed. I think I gave Maggie enough of a pep talk to at least delay the Kuykendall confirmation for a while.

The young Russian Air Attaché who came to lunch, invited me to the Russian Embassy to see a movie. I went. On the way I bumped into the Military Attaché of Syria who knew me, but I didn't know him. He made some remarks about my reports on Israel. In the Russian Embassy I found myself surrounded by military and air attachés. I didn't know there were so many in Washington and I could not recognize a single soul. Finally I sidled up to a Canadian Attaché who seemed friendly. His wife was just as much at a loss as I was. There were two or three Americans there. I had a vodka but wished I hadn't. It was far more potent than American vodka and nearly blew my top off. We went in to watch a movie which was of the Red army and air force on May Day. Quite a terrific picture. Afterward I sneaked out early. I felt anything but at ease in the Russian Embassy surrounded by military and air attachés.

June 27: The young Congressmen are really putting up a battle against Kuykendall. We won't defeat him but at least he'll be careful in the future. There will be quite a few votes against him in the Senate. We may even reach the June 30 deadline, when Kuykendall will have to leave office because he isn't confirmed.*

August 28: Arrived in Athens at 8:30 P.M. I feel as if I were reliving part of my life, except that, in 1919, the seas were rough, most of the passengers were seasick. The war was just over. I had been waiting to try to go abroad on a relief mission and when somebody suggested that I go to Serbia I had to look it up in the encyclopedia to find out the difference between Serbia and Siberia. This time Luvie and I came by TWA plane.

August 29: We left by Greek military plane to Corfu to visit King Paul and Queen Frederika. The bucket seats on the DC–3 were uncomfortable; the plane was frigid. No heat. Corfu, however, was lovely.

As a result of sightseeing, we were late for our audience, which is not the thing to do. The Queen greeted me with, "Mr. Pearson, you are an old friend." I couldn't help wondering whether she remembered me or whether she had been briefed. If she remembered me, it was probably in connection with my comment that she at first had refused to take the train to Washington from New York in 1953 when she learned that Eisenhower was not going to meet her. This is a mark of respect he reserves only for Arabian royalty.

After being received by their Majesties we adjourned to the other room for cocktails. I found myself talking to the Queen. "It's very good of you," I said, "to take time out from your holiday to see us."

*Kuykendall, who had been renominated to the FPC on May 1, was confirmed by the Senate on August 15 by a vote of 50–25.—ED.

"We are not especially on a holiday," she replied, "and we are so delighted to see you. We remember how wonderful you were to us during our visit to America."

Phil Clark of *Newsweek*, told her of going to her orphanage. The Queen obviously was pleased. "My daughter is working there," she said. "She has been there one year and will be there next year. I think it's the first time that a member of the royal family has trained in that way."

Talking about her trip to the United States, the Queen said: "I have never held a press conference in my life but your State Department said we had to have one; so every day we did. I must say that your newspaper people were extraordinarily nice to us. In fact, they couldn't have been nicer. Toward the end of the trip, in Los Angeles I wanted to do some shopping. I had heard so much about the stores of Los Angeles. But there were fifteen newspaper people waiting to go shopping with me. I asked the State Department to ask them to go away, but the State Department said, 'No, it wouldn't do any good.' So finally I told them, 'At home I can't go shopping. But here I have my only opportunity—provided you let me. If you follow me, however, I can't shop.' So they were very kind," concluded the Queen, "and left me alone."

I asked her what happened when she shopped in Athens. "It stops the traffic," she replied. "People are so friendly."

I had always heard that Queen Frederika was by far the most charming of the royal couple, also the most intelligent. In Washington, when I met them at the reception given by the Greek Embassy, I had no opportunity to judge, but talking to both of them, I concluded that the King is just about as charming as the Queen—which is a compliment to him. He has the ability to carry on small talk, which in itself is a gift, and make that small talk both charming and important. I asked him how many languages he spoke.

"Five," he replied, "Greek, German, French, English and Italian. I am not very good in Italian," he apologized. "When I go to see my sister in Florence they laugh at my Italian accent."

August 30: Luvie's cold was sufficiently better for her to attend the press conference with Archbishop Makarios. She said she had to be able to report to George Vournas. I did not get a good impression. His Beatitude is more a politician than a churchman, and I began to sympathize with the British for exiling him. From the American

Embassy I learn that the British are ready to give self-rule to Cyprus, also ready to discuss the whole matter. But Makarios won't consent to any conference unless he attends and dominates it. This is almost what he said in his press conference. He even indicated, in reply to a question from me, that he was opposed to American intervention to settle the problem.

Yet you can't tell this to a Greek. To them Makarios can do no wrong.

September 13 [Beirut, Lebanon]:   I left at seven-thirty in the morning to drive to the summer home of President Camille Chamoun. We passed many apple orchards, literally clinging to the hillside on stone-walled terraces. Lebanon is a great apple country and has lost its apple market in Egypt because of its friendship for the West. As a result the U.S. Sixth Fleet is buying its apples. Harry Byrd won't like that at all.

President Chamoun received me in his office looking out over the valley. He is rather a handsome figure who speaks excellent English and was quite frank in talking about all sorts of things. He did not think much of Arab unity, said that it was a long way off. Of course, Lebanon is half Christian and the President himself is a Christian, so that Lebanon can't be too happy about unity with the Arab world. He expressed the opinion that the refugee problem could be settled with Israel if Prime Minister Ben-Gurion would offer to take back the refugees, in which case he thought a hundred thousand might go back, but most of them would not stay. They would sell their land and then choose to live in an Arab country.

When I asked President Chamoun whether the United States could trust Nasser, he replied: "Not for twenty-four hours." The American Ambassador told me that he once expressed the opinion that the biggest mistake the United States made was not to have let the Israeli Army continue for another fifteen days [during the Suez War]. At the end of our talk, which was interesting but unquotable, the President asked me for my card. I was embarrassed by the fact that I never carry a card. Most people know the name. So, unembarrassed, he said, "Now would you tell me then your full name?" I told him. "What?" he replied, "You are the most dangerous newspaperman in America. I have been reading your memoirs in the *Saturday Evening Post*. The Ambassador," he said, "didn't tell me whom I was to meet —merely that I was to talk to a very important newspaperman."

The Ambassador later told me that this was not correct. At any rate, the President unbent a little more after that and we had a good time taking each other's picture with my new camera. He has exactly the same camera.

In the evening, an Arab newspaperman from *Le Soir* came to see me for an interview, bringing a photographer. I made a deal with the photographer to go to the Syrian border in the morning to take a picture of me in case I was turned down at the border. The photographer was afraid to ride with me in my car, but said he would take a taxi with some other people to the border in advance and wait for me. There seems to be quite a bit of fear of Syrian authorities in these parts.

September 14: I drove up to the Syrian border, arriving there about ten. At the Syrian border there were Iraqis, Jordanese, Syrians, people from Kuwait, and Saudis. Of course, there were also some Americans, some French, and some other Europeans. They were all clamoring to cross the border and I had to wait almost an hour in the security office to get cleared. The passport officer was harassed and anxious to finish his job, so perhaps that was why I got through. The Syrian Embassy in Washington and the Syrian consulate general in New York had both refused me a visa.

As I went into the passport security office my photographer was present and snapped my picture a couple of times. However, since I was not turned back at the border, the picture isn't worth much.

I went to the American Embassy, which arranged an interview with General Bizri, the military strong man and chief of staff of Syria. He was a thin-lipped, thin-mustached forty-three year old army officer who looked as hard-boiled as his reputation. He started out by asking me if I didn't want to take some notes. Usually, in an interview of this kind I don't take notes because it scares the interviewee. However, he spoke slowly and obviously for quotation.

The General professed to want American friendship. He repeated this several times. I left with rather a depressed feeling, however, that either he was hand-in-glove with Russia, or else he did not understand that when you accept arms and financial aid from Russia you are almost certain to become a satellite of Russia.

I had lunch at almost 4 P.M. with Bob Strong, the *chargé d'affaires* of the American Embassy, a very intelligent but rather pessimistic young man who doesn't think there's much to be done about Syria. By the end of the day I was inclined to agree with him.

In Washington I had heard that it was definitely true that some of the American officials with the Embassy had tried to overthrow the military regime in Syria by plotting with other army officers. General Bizri spoke about this at great length and said that the Syrians who conspired with the Americans would soon be up for trial. Naturally, I did not tell Bizri that I had heard his charges were true. But when I lunched at the Embassy I did try to find this out on a confidential basis. Strong protested that there is absolutely nothing to it. However, knowing how Central Intelligence operates, I am still skeptical.

September 15 [Amman, Jordan]:   I got a phone call from the American Embassy almost immediately after registering at my hotel that King Hussein would be able to see me in thirty minutes. I changed my shirt, hired a photographer, and drove up to the King's palace immediately. There I waited and waited and waited.

My photographer got terribly bored but in some respects the wait for me was interesting. All sorts of people were waiting to see the young King. They included members of the Muslim Brotherhood, who in the past have assassinated some Arab leaders and who are now on the outs with Nasser in Egypt; the Jordanian Ambassador to Iraq; the Turkish Ambassador to Jordan; the Chief of Staff; and two sheiks, one of them smartly dressed in brown robes with tan shoes and brown headdress, the other dressed in rather less impressive garb. He was a friend of the King's grandfather and had had some trouble entering the palace grounds, which are heavily guarded. He was sputtering as he came in and finally reached into his flowing robes and pulled out a wad of Jordanese pound notes. The Jordanian pound is worth $2.70 and I imagine he had about $5,000 worth of currency in his fist. He was protesting that the young guard who had held him up was of no importance, while apparently he, the sheik was. I asked him through an interpreter how many sheep he had and he replied: "Enough." Then, addressing the young assistant to the King who was my interpreter, he said, "When they cut your salary as a government worker, I shall be getting the same amount of money I always got. I don't have to depend on the government's salary."

In all, I waited four hours before I saw the King. However, it was worth it. The king himself was not too impressive. But for a twenty-three year-old, I must say he handled himself with great agility and common sense. It is not easy to be interviewed by a newspaperman from a foreign country in a different language. You are inclined to make mistakes. However, he made none. He said the right things and didn't go too far. I had heard that he was rather moderate toward Israel but he did not indicate it in his conversation with me. He insisted that Ben-Gurion was anxious to take the high land up to the mountain ranges of Lebanon in order to improve his defense position.

September 30: Flew to Boston. Governor [Foster] Furculo sent a car to meet me. I drove to his office in the ancient State House, which was crowded with people wanting to see the Governor. He gave me the impression of not being a very efficient executive. He was spending most of the morning with the Governor's Council, figuring out what to do about three Catholic boys who had been sentenced to death for murdering one Jew at a Jewish wedding. The Church wanted to get them commuted to life sentence and the Governor was for it. The Governor's Council is one of these antiquated institutions dating back to 1790. The Governor had me meet them, including Chris Herter, Jr., son of the present Under Secretary of State. He looks like his dad.

The Governor told me that the Kennedy family is running like mad to put Jack in the White House. He says that most of the enmity between the Italians and the Kennedys had died down and that one interesting benefit has been the fact that Joe Kennedy has been contributing heavily to all Italian charities.

At dinner I met Leon Kowal, former executive of the National Youth Administration and a great friend of Harry Hopkins and Aubrey Williams. He told me how he was managing the Kennedy campaign in 1952 when the issue of McCarthy came up. He had prepared a full-page ad to be signed by Governor Dever, Congressman John McCormack, and young Jack Kennedy. Dever was a little hesitant, but initialed the ad. John McCormack agreed without even seeing the ad, and Pat Jackson, speaking for Kennedy, said Kennedy would sign. However, about thirty minutes before the ad was to go to press, Jackson called up and said that Kennedy wanted to wait and study the ad carefully. Kowal replied "He can't, we go to press in twenty minutes. I want to come over and see Kennedy." "I don't think he will see you," replied Jackson. Kowal went anyway, demanded to see Kennedy; but Kennedy refused to see him despite the fact that he was one of Kennedy's campaign managers. That's the way Kennedy has ducked out on McCarthyism.

October 1:   Breakfasted in New York at the Harvard Club with the Lebanese Minister of Foreign Affairs, Charles Malik; a most enlightening but at the same time frightening interview. Here is the gist of it:

"We have three months to head off Russia in the Near East—after that we are gone. After Syria feels sure of Russia's support, both domestically and abroad, Syria will move. The Russian timetable working through Syria will be: to take Jordan in six months, Lebanon in nine months, Suadi Arabia in nine months.

"Saud will go down fighting. He will probably be assassinated. There was one attempt on his life about six months ago which almost succeeded and another about one month ago.

"Saud is greatly concerned. He fears Russia just as much as the United States. However, Saud seems to think he can switch the Syrians over to a Western policy and the State Department is inclined to give him a chance. In fact, they have no other alternative. His policy in Damascus is to see the old Syrian families and try to get them to defeat the young Syrian pro-Russian officers.

"Saud has a primitive mind but his motives are good. He is surrounded by Egyptian advisers but he's useful as an operator right now. Also, he is handicapped somewhat by his brother, Crown Prince Feisal, who is terribly jealous of the King and wants to take over. Feisal hates the United States, and the American Ambassador, George Wadsworth, had to work on him for some time to get him to come to the United States for American medical help. His hatred dates back to his visit here when Israeli boundaries were under discussion and two Zionist girls chased him at the Waldorf into his limousine. There he kindly rolled down the limousine window and they spat on him.

"In all his private talks, Saud has been intent on thwarting Syria. He is very worried.

"One month ago Turkey almost invaded Aleppo. It did not do so, partly because it feared Russia, partly because it had no pledge from the United States. Turkey was somewhat like the British on July 27, one day after Nasser seized the Suez Canal. They just weren't ready. The Turks are still talking almost every day with the United States and with Lebanon and with Israel about taking over Syria. The United States has refused to give any commitments. Syria says they have complete assurances of protection from Russia but some doubt this. It's a situation where nobody quite knows how far Russia will go.

"Turkey is determined to take over Syria once Syria starts moving on Jordan, but this may be too late. Syria is almost certain to become an integral part of the Soviet system. She can't help herself."

I caught a plane to Washington immediately after the Malik breakfast but was stacked in the air over Washington for over an hour. I was in a hurry because Eisenhower was meeting with the Southern Governors. I tried to see Governor [Luther] Hodges of North Carolina. The Governors were at the White House for about three hours, then conferring further by telephone with the White House. The whole meeting was a flop. My friend [Orval] Faubus of Arkansas played hard-to-get and crossed up the signals once again. Hodges left for North Carolina in disgust and Governor [Leroy] Collins flew back to Florida to try to keep his legislature in line. Eisenhower stood pat on keeping the troops in Little Rock. For once he was right.

Saw the Israeli Ambassador. He confirms all that Malik said. When Ambassador Eban came back from Israel, he went to see Dulles and told him it was no longer the Arabs versus Israel, but the United States versus Russia in the Near East. Russia has been establishing three bridgeheads—Yemen, Egypt, Syria—and is rapidly pushing forward. He told Dulles that Russia had made so much progress in a short time that NATO would be useless. There's no use in having a NATO army sitting in Europe when the oil to operate that army is cut off by Russia in the Near East. Dulles listened carefully and began to agree. But he had no solution. He merely agreed with Eban.

Eban said he had just come from the Turkish Ambassador who asked Eban if he had read my column. It stated that Turkey was terribly concerned and ready to move on Syria. Eban quoted this as not only accurate but that the Turkish Ambassador agreed. A Turk has been down at the State Department repeatedly. He gets a certain amount of support from Loy Henderson, whose fear of Russia outweighs his dislike of Israel. Turkey wants assurances that if it moves there will be no action by the United States similar to our action in Suez. Suez sticks in the minds of everyone. It stands out as the greatest mistake the Eisenhower Administration has made in the Near East. However, the Turk can get no assurance. The State Department simply says nothing. It hasn't pressured Turkey. It just will not give any assurance, and Turkey will not act until it gets assurances of NATO support.

The State Department, according to Eban, is terribly disappointed with Saud. They built him up and bet on him. He is now undercutting Dulles's policy with statements that there is nothing to fear from Syria. He is also undercutting Henderson's trip and our hasty dispatch of arms to Jordan. Eban thinks Saud's passion for air immunity is greater than his fear of Russia.

Eban remarked: "When the United States stopped Russia in Berlin, Russia moved to the Far East, where they were stopped in Korea. Belatedly, they were stopped in Indochina, but they have now moved to the Near East, where they have not been stopped. The chief thing the United States needs to do is get a firm policy in the Near East, draw the line. Say this is it. But you always act too late. You slapped Nasser on the nose with the Aswan Dam by withdrawing your offer and he, quite rightly, is still smarting."

Hoffa was elected president of the Teamsters today. All sorts of government agencies, including the Justice Department, threw roadblocks in his path to stop him. If the Republicans had not intervened in Michigan, particularly Postmaster General Summerfield in 1954 to stop the House probe of Hoffa, things might have been different today.

October 5:   Last night the Russians launched the first earth satellite, thereby beating us to the punch. In July 1955, when the Senate investigating committee started probing the conflict of interest of Harold Talbott, then Secretary of the Air Force, Hagerty plumped an announcement that we were working on an earth satellite in order to take the play away from the Senate Committee. But that seems about as far as we went. Since then the Navy and the Army have been in a hassle as to who should do the earth satellite; the Navy took the project away from the Army, and now we are behind Russia.

One good thing about this plus the World Series is that it's taken the spotlight away from Little Rock. Jack Anderson proposes that we start a friendship exchange of white students with Negro students in the South, namely some kind of plan whereby moderate white students in Southern schools would visit a Negro school for a day in order to see how things are going and express some friendship. I telephoned Jonathan Daniels in Raleigh for his reaction and he said that such an idea might lead to mob violence. I also talked to Philip Furnas at Guilford College, North Carolina. He was skeptical. Even though Guilford is a Quaker college, they have not integrated. The American Friends Service Committee has urged them to do so but the local North Carolinians say no.

October 19: Got home from Springfield, Missouri, last night where I talked to the Southwest Teachers of Missouri. A very live-wire group. They are for integration and against Governor Faubus. It makes you realize the strength of the backbone of the American people in the Middle West. I have on my desk a letter from Harry Truman. Considering the publicity he gave me over his former military aide, General Vaughan, it is a unique letter. Last August, Vaughan wrote me a letter squawking to high heaven over the column in which I said that Truman had opposed putting Secret Service and Central Intelligence under J. Edgar Hoover but that Vaughan had been working with J. Edgar Hoover and was more or less Hoover's man inside the White House. Vaughan sent Truman a carbon copy of this letter and Truman wrote me that every word in Vaughan's letter was true.

When I got back from the Near East I wrote Truman sending him a carbon copy of the column in question and suggesting that perhaps he had read it. Knowing that Truman dislikes Hoover and knowing how Hoover had castigated Truman in regard to the Harry Dexter White case, I figured that I had Truman in a box at long last regarding his old friend and my old *bête noir*, Harry Vaughan. However, Truman was equal to the occasion.

Here is what he wrote me: "General Vaughan has been very badly misrepresented in several quarters and undeservedly criticized, and I won't get personal in the matter, but eventually it will be discovered that in every instance he was working solely in the interests of his boss. Unfortunately, he is not a diplomat and does not understand columnists as I do."

A lot of people would wonder just when Harry began to understand columnists. Perhaps it dated from the time I began visiting him in Kansas City.

October 20: I went to the cocktail party given by the Advisory Committee of the Democratic party. Adlai Stevenson was there looking fat but quite genial. He addressed me as "How you doing, kid?" Nancy Kefauver looked wonderful. She spent a month in Scotland with seventeen relatives and one bathroom. "Under those conditions," said Nancy, "you have to get along with your relatives."

Averell Harriman thinks that the Little Rock situation is going to hurt the Democratic party with Negro voters in the North. He wants to coin a new word, "Faubus," synonymous for a lynching party. The

Democrats are really beginning to take heart. Sputnik has been a big boost. I haven't seen so much cheer among Democrats for a long time.

Had dinner with the Cuneos and the Jim Rowes. Ernest told a story that I have never written, though I have reminded him of it from time to time. He was bringing a pro-U.S. Italian agent up from Washington to New York during the war. Pullman space was scarce and a baggage car had been converted to a Pullman car by putting seats in it. A man who had never seen such a car began taking pictures of it and took pictures of Cuneo with the Sardinian agent. Ernest became suspicious. Later, the traveler put down a copy of *Time* magazine on his seat and a girl picked it up. Ernest immediately pounced upon this as evidence that he was transmitting a message to a fellow agent. Shortly thereafter, the traveler went into the men's room. Ernest followed him, called an MP, and told the MP, a lieutenant, to break down the door and get the secret agent out. Ernest flashed his OSS card to the lieutenant.

The lieutenant order his private to break down the door. "I can't," said the private.

"Then shoot through the door," Ernest ordered.

"Shoot through the door," the lieutenant ordered.

"I'd like to have that order in writing, sir," replied the private.

"Let me see your OSS credentials again," said the lieutenant to Ernest.

The private was the only smart man in the group.

By this time the train had passed Wilmington and Ernest called the conductor, ordering that the train be "arrested." There were 700 people on the train and the conductor demurred. However, Ernest insisted, flashed his OSS credentials, and finally when the train arrived in New York it was "arrested." Every person on the train was examined by the FBI, and the man who had taken the pictures was detained until about four or five in the morning. He gave as his reference a classmate of Ernest's at Columbia who vouched for him one hundred percent. He was released. He threatened to sue Ernest for false arrest and cited as his attorneys the Donovan law firm. General Donovan was head of the OSS and Ernest's superior.

As Ernest tells the story, he got to bed at about six-thirty and at about seven-fifteen the telephone rang and I was on the phone kidding him about arresting a whole train. It is true that I had all the details, but it is not true that I called him quite that early. What I didn't tell Ernest was that J. Edgar Hoover had tipped me off.

Elizabeth Rowe told how during the war, when Jim was in the Navy, she was having dinner with Speaker Sam Rayburn. He had a new piano given him by Gene Cox of Georgia (which may shed some light on why Sam went to bat for Gene with Attorney General Biddle to keep Gene from being indicted for taking money for lobbying with the FCC). Libby Rowe said she couldn't play the piano, but she told Sam she would dance and took off her shoes to dance.

"I'm going to get even with this fellow Lyndon Johnson," said Sam. "You call him up and tell him you are in grave danger and want some protection." So Libby called Lyndon.

"Jim told me to be sure to call you if I got in trouble," she told Lyndon. "I'm down here at the apartment of an old bald-headed man and he's got my shoes off and I don't know what he's going to get off next and I need help."

"Where are you," asked the excited Lyndon.

"I'm down here near Dupont Circle," she said. "But you'd better come in a hurry. I don't know what's going to happen. This old man is terrible."

Lyndon was very excited and promised to come immediately. By this time, however, Sam was on the line listening and chuckling, audibly. He couldn't resist the temptation of interrupting and telling Lyndon that he was the old man in question. Lyndon concluded that Elizabeth didn't need much help.

October 23: Bill Rogers today was made Attorney General. Brownell resigned. It's a small world. It was only a few years ago that Rogers was my attorney trying the Howser case. It was less time ago that Rogers called from some place in Montana to warn me that Nixon might retaliate if I was not kind to him. This was during the 1952 campaign.

October 25: Elizabeth Hennings came to luncheon. It looks like the end of a long and tragic chapter. She has locked Tom out of the house, changed the lock on the door, and plans to sue for legal separation.

The climax came after a hectic and unhappy trip to the Inter-Parliamentary Union in London. Tom was drunk most of the time. He went to Sir Roger Makins' luncheon out in the country and had to be literally carried out. Congressman Hale Boggs did his best to help Elizabeth.

The tragedy is that Tom is ending one of the most useful careers I have seen on the part of many in the Senate. The last time I talked to him he was smug about the whole matter and pointed out that he had been reelected [in 1956] by the biggest majority in Missouri history. I am tempted to write the story. It's the only thing that will make him begin to change.

Held a luncheon of civic leaders to get the Big Brothers fund drive started. I was a little embarrassed by not knowing a lot of people there, but they seemed quite enthusiastic and old hands at fund drives told me that we got off to a good start. They want me to invite Nixon to the big luncheon on November 19. I am not sure that I will do it.

October 27:   Flew to Minneapolis, arriving 2:30 A.M. Called on Governor Orville Freeman in St. Paul, a young dynamic liberal, governing a state largely dominated by U.S. Steel and the big iron and steel companies. We recalled that two years ago I had interviewed him and Orval Faubus of Arkansas, who at that time impressed both of us as being a decent, fair-minded gentleman on the race issue.

En route back to Minneapolis, I stopped at Station KSTP for a TV interview and there was tipped off by the station manager to a big story: Judge Clarence Magney, the retired judge who was called back from Europe to write an opinion regarding the ownership of minerals under lake beds, had sold some of his land to the Erie Mining Company. Back at my hotel I got on the long-distance telephone to the Recorder of Deeds, the Attorney General, Judge Magney, and the Director of Mines, who gave me the ownership of Erie Mining. The Attorney General, strangely enough, begged that I not write the story. Judge Magney refused to comment. I shall probably get into all sorts of trouble with my local newspapers if I write it. The Ridder papers in St. Paul and Duluth have played very cozy with iron and steel.

October 30:   Rushed back from Philadelphia last night to take a 9 A.M. plane to San Francisco; the Jewish National Fund are demanding that I get there early. I finally arrived at four-thirty, which pleased them highly. Then I had to wait around at cocktails and an early dinner. Finally, didn't speak until 9 P.M. I could have taken a later plane as originally scheduled. This is a deal whereby I give five speeches, practically for nothing, in return for the radio sponsorship of my program in Los Angeles.

Had a jam-packed audience in San Francisco—about a hundred standing.

October 31:   Up at 4 A.M., finished the column, caught a 6 A.M. plane to Los Angeles. Finished the broadcast and gave it by special leased telephone to Washington at 2 P.M.—another special extra cost as the result of rushing out here.

November 1:   California is seething over Goodie Knight's retreat. Knight wrote me that he would be unable to see me at Sacramento, which, on the surface, seems strange, because Goodie is a glutton for publicity. He's now hiding out in Phoenix, Arizona, evading everyone while reports circulate that he is to run for the Senate and bow out of his death battle with Knowland for Governor. When he was in Washington last June, he told me he would do just the opposite. "We are in there to the end," he said, "and we are going to win."

I dropped in to see Ed Murray, editor of the Los Angeles *Mirror-News*, whom I first knew in Rome when we organized the Friendship Train. Norman Chandler, owner of the paper, has just fired Virgil Pinkley, the liberal publisher, replacing him with his son. Everyone in Los Angeles is figuring the paper will go Republican. Murray confirmed this but said the column would be anchored from now on on the editorial page.

Bill Bassett, Nixon's old public relations man, came in for a chat. He remarked: "It's hell when you have a lot of news that you can't write." He was referring to the fact that Chandler had persuaded, or rather pressured, Goodie Knight to get out of the gubernatorial race. Goodie had appointed Mrs. Chandler, better known as Buffie, to be on the Board of Regents for the University of California, but this sop cut no ice. She turned against Goodie and for Knowland. The powers that be in southern California, and they are really powerful, particularly the publishers, have determined that there must be no split in the Republican Party, that Knowland must be Governor, but, above all, that nothing shall stand in the way of putting tricky Dick Nixon in the White House.

If I write all this, and it's unquestionably true, I'll be out of luck as far as the future publication of the column is concerned in southern California.

Went to the $100-a-plate dinner for Harry Truman. After Truman spoke, he went back to his seat at the head table, where he was congratulated by various people. Mrs. Truman, however, who was standing close by did not congratulate him. Finally, he stuck out his hand and shook her arm himself. You could see that while Harry was delighted with the praise of other people, the praise he wanted most was that of his wife.

November 2: I took the children out to Disneyland. They had a wonderful time. It was a little tiring for their grandfather, however, who hasn't had much sleep lately. I can't seem to sleep out here, partly because of the change of time, partly because I wake up in the night to cover Joe. He gets uncovered every hour or so.

Mr. and Mrs. Truman were also at Disneyland and we barged in on them while they were lunching in a semiprivate dining room. I told Mr. Truman that I wanted to initiate him into the Grandfathers' Club. Drew shook hands with both the ex-President and Mrs. Truman, but Joe was tongue-tied. Afterwards, Drew seemed to realize that he was in the presence of one of our two living ex-Presidents and wanted to know more about Mr. Truman. I didn't tell him about my past relationship.

I made one bad *faux pas* with Truman. I referred to his "granddaughter" forgetting that it's a grandson. He replied, "Well, I would just as soon have had a girl."

November 3: Went on television with Chet Holifield, the Congressman from southern California, who has just returned from Moscow. He was impressed by the fact that practically all the workers in Russian factories are women. They even do very hard labor. He attributes it to the loss of men during the war.

Russia put its second Sputnik into the air last night. This one contains a dog. Even the people in southern California are beginning to wake up to the fact that Russia is miles ahead of us in scientific development.

November 4: I drove to Oakland with Bill Birkett, who has done a terrific job of cleaning up the banking-treasury scandal in California. He told me that he had been with Goodie Knight when Charlie Blythe telephoned to say that no money would be coming in if Goodie ran for Governor. Blythe is the man whom Goodie mentioned to me in Washington last spring as certain to support him. He's head of the Blythe Investment Company and previously a strong backer. Goodie paced the floor of the executive mansion night after night in Birkett's presence, telling how the moneybags were pulling the rug out from under him and refusing to let him run for Governor.

Spoke in Oakland, and then caught a plane home. This has been a long and weary trip. I don't know when I've been so tired.

November 5: Arrived in Washington around noon. The Ridder papers in St. Paul, as I suspected, have been raising hell with me over publishing the story on Judge Magney. They claim I maligned a fine man. It seems to me that Judge Magney, if he had been that fine, would not have taken this case. The big publishers always object to having you clean up their front yards. It's true, whether it's St. Paul and the steel companies or Los Angeles and Nixon-Knight politics. Went to dinner for the St. Albans School. George Wharton Pepper, whose family founded the Wharton School in Philadelphia, where I once taught, was an honored guest. At the same hotel where we dined—the Statler— Governor Knight was bowing his knee and his head to those who refused to contribute to his campaign and withdrawing from the race. He needed about a million dollars. Goodie went to the White House this morning and formally withdrew from the race for Governor of California.

November 6: Pat Brown came for dinner. He is bubbling over with enthusiasm for his chances to become Governor. He didn't say so, but if he becomes Governor of California, he has a good chance to be President of the United States. He would be the first Catholic in American history. He still claims that I was responsible for electing him Attorney General of California. He is a wonderful guy personally, but I wish he had a little more backbone. Last week for the first time I met his wife, who is the lady who doesn't want him to step forward and run for anything. She is a beautiful, charming gal, but I can see that she doesn't like the limelight. Maybe, however, her timing has been best for Pat because he now may be in for really big things.

I talked to him about campaigning vigorously on the banking scandal which Bill Birkett unearthed. Pat was somewhat lukewarm. I think, however, that he will wage a good campaign.

November 7: Went to Marjorie Post's square dance. Stopped in the middle of dinner to listen to Eisenhower's speech. Found myself standing beside deputy Secretary of Defense Quarles and also beside Postmaster General Summerfield. Sherman Adams was near by, together with the Director of the Budget, Percival Brundage. I asked Summerfield afterward what he thought of the speech and he naturally said it was great. I told him I thought it was a little too defensive. This was an understatement of what I really thought. Compared with F.D.R.'s terrific speeches rousing the American people before Pearl Harbor, it stank.*

November 12: Our twenty-first wedding anniversary. Our cook, Margaret Brown, remarked: "I wouldn't stay married to one man for twenty-one years." Miss Canty remarked: "Mrs. Pearson, we think you are a really remarkable woman." I consider both of these highly uncomplimentary to me.

December 6: At eleven forty-five this morning the satellite Vanguard sputtered to a complete and tragic fiasco at Cape Canaveral, Florida. The shock that fell over the nation was appalling. The reaction abroad was terrific. The London *Daily Mail* carried the headline "Oh dear!" The Russians played it smart. They said absolutely nothing. All they did was to quote American press comment—which, of course, was bad enough. Had they exulted over the American failure, it would have served to bring the NATO allies together. Someone is running their strategy far more shrewdly than ever before. The suspicion is that it is Khrushchev himself.

Abe Saperstein has been balking about playing two civilian cities in Morocco and Libya with his Harlem Globetrotters. The U.S. Information Agency is enthusiastic over this as a means of putting the quietus on Little Rock, but Abe has refused to play without a $2,500 fee for each game. I finally got him on the telephone and he agreed to a compromise. We are to announce that he is getting his regular fee, and we will hand him a check. Later he will return the check to the government. I suppose I will end up giving him the check. I hope I get it back. He seems like an all-right guy, and this should be a very fruitful trip from the point of view of morale and good will.

The Air Force tells me, on the q.t., that they hope Lisa Faraday

*In this post-Sputnik speech, Eisenhower announced the appointment of Dr. James Killian as his science adviser and discussed a program for aiding science education and missile research, and for sharing the fruits of this with America's allies.—ED.

can be discreetly left at home. She is the Hungarian refugee who went with us to Greenland last year. Quite a talented actress. However, the Intelligence people say that during the war she acted as a Nazi agent, later became a double agent, and as the war ended went over to the side of the United States. I shall have to get out of bringing her somehow or other, I don't know how.

December 7: Went to the farm but the telephone rang most of the day and I had to bone up for the Mike Wallace program in the evening. The last time he interviewed me, he really put me over the hurdles. This time he was gentler. We went into the American scientific Pearl Harbor. He also put me over the hurdles, however, regarding the Truman-Roosevelt charges of liar and SOB. When he talked about Senator Jack Kennedy I blurted out the statement that Kennedy was the only man in history to win a Pulitzer prize for a book which was ghost-written for him. This seemed to cause a consternation and various fears that Kennedy might sue. He would be foolish if he did. However, I had to sign a statement before I went on the air that I would defend all lawsuits and hold the network blameless.

December 8: Lunched at Marjorie Post's. Ricardo Arias, ex-President of Panama, now the Ambassador, was there. He says that the fizzle of the American sputnik on Friday is going to lose Guatemala to the free world. It will go Communist. He says that the repercussions in Chile, Argentina, and Brazil will be serious. The Administration, according to Dickie, doesn't have any idea of how serious the American prestige and position is around the world.

December 9: ABC is in a dither over my statement that Jack Kennedy had a ghost-writer for his book. Their lawyers calling up all day. I identified the ghost-writer as Ted Sorensen, Kennedy's assistant.

Went to a cocktail party for Ed Dickinson of Averell Harriman's staff who is going to run for the Senate against Senator Ives in New York. Met Merriman Smith [White House UPI correspondent], who was tight. He complained vociferously that I had put him in the column twice. I was embarrassed by not recognizing Smith, but later came to my senses, and asked him how he liked the Mike Wallace program, in which I had praised Smith as a great newspaperman.

"For God's sake, don't mention me any more. Every time you do, you get me in Dutch," he said. "Sixteen minutes ago, Jim Hagerty accused me of leaking to you. If you are going to say anything, say something nasty but for God's sake keep me out of your goddamned column."

Smith has gone out on a limb that Eisenhower will go to Paris [for the NATO Conference]. Otherwise, he says, he will have to resign and admit that he is incompetent to carry on the duties of the President. And, says Smith, Ike doesn't want to resign.

George E. Allen, Ike's [bridge] partner, is also saying that Ike doesn't want to resign. If he does, he'll have to put up with Mamie twenty-four hours a day, which he has never done in his entire life before. Also he wouldn't have the advantage of an automobile, private airplane, and a private doctor. He could go to Walter Reed Hospital at times, but Dr. Snyder would not be around to nurse him. Most important, however, is that Ike resigned his permanent military commission and if he left the White House he would give up his pension and just revert to civilian status. In other words, he would have to be like Harry Truman and make a living. He would be off the public dole for the first time in his entire life.

Chet Bowles called me from Connecticut this morning. He says he is going to run for the Senate even if Bill Benton runs, though not if Dick Lee, mayor of New Haven, runs. Dick Lee would be unbeatable. Chet says that Adlai would still go to Paris if the Administration really asked him to go. They were so lukewarm about it, however, that Adlai got the impression that he wasn't wanted. Adlai says that Dulles is going to Europe with no program whatsoever, other than some technical arrangements for arms. Dulles already has the final announcement written for the end of the NATO meeting—he is so sure of what is going to happen.

December 13: Took off for North Africa. The entertainers from New York didn't get passports until today. I had to keep the passport office open until midnight. We finally left at twelve-thirty—an hour and a half late.

Arrived in Azores 3:30 P.M. A green, wet island, with almost no trees, 3,000 Air Force men and a little Portuguese village of 2,500. I was taken on a tour by an army engineer who knew very little about the base. Had I been the commander, I would have had someone on the job who knew his stuff. The commander is Brigadier-General Harold L. Smith. I have been wondering whether I ever wrote anything about him. He didn't come to meet us, or introduce the two shows.

Certain amount of friction between O'Shea, who organized New York entertainers, and the Harlem Globetrotters. The latter are 6-foot-3 Negroes, very quiet. After the shows we were given a dinner in a private room at the Officers' Club. I could see some of the Air Force wives look shocked when the Globetrotters walked through, but there have been no incidents. Lots of Portuguese in the audience, including the Governor. Everyone seemed to like the two shows—though the entertainment isn't as good as last year. We miss Ella Logan and Adolf Green.

The men seem happier here than in the Arctic. Not quite so isolated and wives can live with them.

December 16–17 [Tripoli]:   This is a primitive city on the edge of the Sahara. It's where the Marines landed in the war against the Barbary pirates, which is featured in the Marines' song "From the Halls of Montezuma to the Shores of Tripoli." What the Marines don't tell, however, is that a boatload came ashore loaded with explosives, and they exploded it by accident so many of the Marines were killed and the others taken prisoner.

The more I see of these new, independent, nationalist countries, the more I am convinced they can't possibly exist without some outside support and ought to be joined together into some alliance or federation. There should be a United States of Africa or of the Mediterranean. Otherwise, these little African nations will be sucked into the Russian orbit.

About 200 people govern Libya. They are friendly to the U.S.A. But 90 percent of the remaining 1,500,000 people are for Nasser and Russia. We're not reaching them.

The Catholic chaplain bawled me out for exhibiting girls in bathing suits. This is the first squawk we've had.

December 18:   We left at 10 A.M. for Nouasseur, Morocco, a big air base just outside Casablanca. It took us about five hours to fly about one-third the way across Africa. We couldn't go over Algeria because of the French, who force down foreign planes; so had to fly over the Mediterranean and Gibraltar. Nouasseur is a supply base for the Strate-

gic Air Command and impresses me as the most efficient base we have
visited so far. The base commander, Colonel Sam Smith, has thought
of every device under the sun to improve morale and better relations
between Morocco and America. He spent ten years as an Air Force
non-com and lives and breathes the Air Force.

We had heard of the fascination of Casablanca, its night life, its
intrigue, its espionage. We found it a sleepy, humdrum, though quite
modern city. After a long search for a nightclub, our chauffeur finally
located one restaurant that was open—an unexciting Spanish joint,
where we got a small steak.

December 19:   Wrote a column on Christmas in North Africa and
cabled it home. The Christmas spirit is really stirring. Lights and
decorations going up over barracks.

Drove to Casablanca to meet the USIS man, Arthur Bardos, and
prepare for basketball game. Five thousand people. The police couldn't
handle them. I carried in some folding chairs for the players, but the
minute I got them in, Moroccans grabbed them. I tried to argue, but
it was no use.

The Crown Prince was there incognito. After the game, he drove
away in his car, and really crushed some of the crowd. The consul
general and I were in part of the crowd and I have never been so pushed
by such a panic-stricken mob. Henry Ford, the consul general, who is
a little bald-headed man, grabbed my arm and said: "Let's get out of
here."

Dave Zinkoff, the Globetrotters' announcer, and I dined at the
consulate at about 9 P.M. Jim Henderson, the consul general from
Naples, was there en route to his port. These consuls lead rather a
humdrum, prosaic life, but they are the backbone of our diplomatic
service. Ford was very grateful for my bringing the Globetrotters. He
said it had helped American prestige and his work immeasurably.

December 20:   It's so cold here at night. Getting into cold sheets is
worse than being in the Arctic. There, the beds were warm. Here the
rooms are freezing. It's quite comfortable in the daytime. But once the
sun goes down the cold of the desert permeates everything. I got up
early to take a special plane to Rabat, the capital, for an audience with
the King. Before leaving, however, I went to the PX at eight-thirty, and
by special dispensation did my Christmas shopping.

I shall have a hard time writing about special VIP airplane junkets, in view of the special plane that took me to Rabat, then on to Sidi Slimane.

King Mohamed looked extremely well on his gold throne, sitting in a room of beautiful emerald tile. Afterward I met the Crown Prince. I asked him how he liked the basketball game, but didn't tell him he almost mashed me in the crowd.

Sidi Slimane is our most important bomber base in the world. I drove past a long row of sleek B-47's, capable of flying 600 miles an hour, and each one holding a hydrogen bomb, with more power than all the explosives fired in World War II put together; $75,000,000 worth of aircraft, crews ready, all set to fly four hours to Moscow.

This is our chief answer to the Russian IRBM and ICBM. It's an adequate answer for the moment, but won't be for long. I climbed up inside one of the B-47's and sat in the pilot's seat. He's strapped in, can't get down even to go to the bathroom, and must sit for eight to ten hours. These planes fly once in every sixteen days back to Shreveport, Louisiana. They make it in a day. However, one day strapped in that seat must be agony. Only a few feet from me was the H-bomb. I couldn't see it, but it was there.

We gave the whole basketball game and two theatrical performances, then flew back to Nouasseur to a cold bed. The performances were among the best we have given.

December 21: This is the shortest day of the year, but it seems like the longest. We have been flying all day across the Atlantic. One-hour stop at the Azores and now on to Bermuda—fifteen hours. We have now flown 10,000 miles in ten days.

December 22: Arrived last night in Bermuda and this morning it appears we have our first real snafu. I got a call from Zinkoff that the Globetrotters didn't want to play their game. Last night I had gone to the hospital with Miss Cedrone and some of the others with flu and sore throats, and while I was away, the Globetrotters were shown to a big open barrack with a dirty latrine. They didn't like it. Abe Saperstein came from the Castle Harbor Hotel where the rest of us were staying and ordered them to a Negro motel. There is segregation in Bermuda. He has gone fishing this morning and Zinkoff tells me that he left word that the Globetrotters were not to play a game. Major Weurth says the

Air Force goofed. With Clara Cedrone in the hospital with a 104 temperature, this left our theatrical cast badly limping, and I finally called off everything. To have gone on with the theatrical show and announced that the Globetrotters weren't playing would have made a bad impression.

Afterward I learned that the Globetrotters were not anywhere near as upset as Zinkoff reported. They told me they were quite willing to play. Saperstein also said that he had laid down no flat edict. By this time, however, it was too late. The time for holding the show was past. We relaxed in Bermuda and left for the U.S.A.

December 24:   Dined last night at the Belgian Embassy. Bob Silvercruys, the Ambassador, had just come back from the NATO conference. We listened to Eisenhower and Dulles report on it. I thought they were pretty bad. Ike talked for ten minutes only, and I learned afterward that his aides had refused to let him talk any longer because of the strain. Dulles talked for twenty minutes, but did a pretty bad job of interpreting what the conference was all about.

Silvercruys was discreet in his comment. From everything I can gather, however, NATO was a big bust. European nations are getting more and more fed up with us. The rumor at the State Department is that Dulles's health is so bad and he is so tired that he will have to get out.

December 25:   With the grandchildren in California and Bess and Tyler in Kentucky, things were quite quiet. The Thurman Arnolds and the Chip Robertses came for dinner. The conversation drifted around to Louise Cromwell MacArthur, now Heiberg. She is almost alone. Has gotten as broad as she is tall and is inebriated most of the time. When I first came to Washington, Louise was married to Lionel Atwill, the English actor. I met them at the Sumner Welleses'. She told me how MacArthur had gotten her to get her father, Edward T. Stotesbury, the J. P. Morgan partner, to go to Washington to see the Secretary of War, Mr. Weeks, to get MacArthur promoted from brigadier general to major general. Later, when MacArthur sued me for publishing this, Louise refused to stand by what she had said. After the suit was dropped, she apologized to me for it.

I learned a new phase of Louise's life today. During the war [World War I] she was living in Paris with General Pershing, and hoped to marry him. After the Armistice, she remarked to him that "this ends everything for me." She hinted that she would have to leave Pershing if there was no matrimony. He replied: "Marrying you would be like buying a book for someone else to read."

Pershing by that time was getting along in years and Louise was not only young but one of the most hot-blooded bitches around Washington or Paris. Later, when she married MacArthur, Pershing sent him the portrait which the Hungarian artist Laszlo had painted of Louise. With it was a card which read "With my compliments." Apparently, he was as fed up with her as MacArthur later became.

This country has a habit of making saint; out of its military heroes and protecting them with an immunity which is sometimes bad for them and bad for the country. If Eisenhower hadn't had this immunity while he was in France and England living with Kay Summersby, he would not be President today.

Pershing got his job solely because he was married to the daughter of Senator Francis E. Warren of Wyoming, the top Republican member of the Military Affairs Committee, and because Woodrow Wilson needed Warren's help in waging World War I. Because Pershing was the son-in-law of Senator Warren, he was picked to be commander of the American Expeditionary Force—though he was one of the most routine, humdrum generals in the U.S. Army.

Somewhat similarly, Eisenhower was picked to be Allied commander because of his ability to charm people. He was a good diplomat, not a good soldier. The decisions were made for both Pershing and Eisenhower back in Washington. They carried out orders.

Someday I'm going to have to write a book on the love lives of our heroes. Though it wasn't Anthony Eden's fault, his first wife spent a good part of World War II living in Paris with anyone who wanted her, particularly C. D. Jackson, now publisher of *Fortune* magazine.

December 26: Tyler and Bess came back from Kentucky. It begins to look more like Christmas. I still haven't been able to get Ellen or the children on the telephone. The telephone company is doing more business this year than ever.

1958

January 7: Talked to Doubleday Doran in New York about a proposed new book on our snafus on guided missiles. Doubleday Doran
used to be courageous, published the *Nine Old Men* and the *American
Diplomatic Game* when Harper got old-maidish regarding libel. But
this time Doubleday Doran raised the point that they had published
Eisenhower's book and that their president, Mr. Douglas Black, had
secured Eisenhower's appointment as president of Columbia. They
wanted to know whether the book would be critical of Ike. The answer
was affirmative.

January 8: Went to the Cooperative Forum to hear Dr. John Hagen,
Director of Project Vanguard. Slept through part of the discussion.
Suddenly sat bolt upright when I heard my name mentioned. He
complained, good-naturedly, that "even Drew Pearson had called the
Project Vanguard a failure." Dr. Hagen thought I and others should
have been more charitable, that the test at Cape Canaveral was only
one of many tests and therefore the Project was not a failure.

We went out for a drink with Dr. Hagen and Admiral Bennett,
Chief of the Naval Research Bureau. They were both extremely frank,
quite intelligent. I learned that the scientists had repeatedly urged the
propaganda value of the satellite on "the policy-makers," but were
rebuffed. The people at the top, apparently Eisenhower and Dulles, felt
there was no propaganda value in the satellite, no urgency. The project,
according to Dr. Hagen, was underbudgeted and quite leisurely. There
was no high priority.

The United States has listening devices so carefully geared and
placed that if Russia gets a satellite off the ground for any distance we

will know about it. Admiral Bennett disagreed with me that the White House had been responsible for the publicity given to the Vanguard launching. He said that Murray Snyder, Assistant Secretary of Defense, was under such pressure from the Moss committee to make everything public that he had publicized the advance launching. Admiral Bennett had made a statement in New York that this was not to be made public, and shortly thereafter was hauled over the coals for saying it.

January 9:   Doubleday Doran called from New York to say they would not accept the book. I suspected it. Simultaneously, Morris Ernst called to say that he had put the book before Harper and they turned it down, too. Morris says the publishers are getting like the big TV advertisers —too timid, no more crusading spirit. I called E. P. Dutton & Sons, who had been after me to write a book and they turned it down also, although on more legitimate grounds. They have a book of their own in the works. They came after me to see when I was going to write my memoirs, and I told them not for a long time. I should have told them, but wasn't quick enough on the trigger, that if they didn't have the courage to publish some other books, I would not give them my memoirs.

Eisenhower sent his message to Congress. I watched him on television. He looked well and did a good job. The message was reasonably good, though it certainly won't lead the nation forward in the missile-satellite race. I was interested in senatorial comment afterward. The three men who are obviously running for President—Lyndon Johnson, Jack Kennedy, and Estes Kefauver—all praised the message. The Senators who were not afraid to let the chips fall where they may, like Wayne Morse, Hubert Humphrey, Mike Monroney, told the truth. They called it a mediocre, warmed-over sermon delivered five years late.

January 10:   The President's brother-in-law, Colonel Gordon Moore, managed to get a juicy airline certificate for his friends, Trans Caribbean, of which he was once vice president. If Harry Vaughan had done anything like Colonel Moore, the Republican press would be raging.

Lunched with Cohn and Marks. Bob Allen is chewing nails over my lag in paying him. I just haven't got the money.*

---

*When Robert Allen went on active duty during World War II, Drew Pearson decided he liked doing the "Merry-Go-Round" by himself and bought his partner's

January 11: We are going ahead with the book even though we haven't got a publisher. Hope to do two chapters over the weekend.

January 12: Kay and Phil Graham came for dinner. Phil was more like his old relaxed, liberal self than ever before. We had a good talk. He is working to get Jack McCloy in Dulles's job and seems to think he has a fair chance of success. Lucius Clay and Milton Eisenhower, he says, are working on it. The other day, according to Phil, Ike remarked that he realized Dulles was a handicap and must go. This is directly contrary to my understanding, but it may be correct; I hope so.

"The trouble with this guy is that he has never had criticism," says Phil. "Now for the first time he is getting it and he is really worried." Omar Bradley agrees with this diagnosis, and looking back during the war years you can see that Ike certainly led a charmed life. Nobody ever said anything bad about him. Phil plays golf with Nixon occasionally, seems to think he is getting more human. We reminisced over the Supreme Court and how Stanley Reed, Bill Douglas, Hugo Black, and Felix Frankfurter were all appointed by Tom Corcoran. When Roosevelt balked at appointing Felix because he was too radical, Tom got George Gallup to do a poll of lawyers to show that Felix was acceptable. After that, Roosevelt broke down and appointed him. The irony is that today Felix won't speak to Tom or to me. I remember the day when Tom got Bob and me to write a column on Felix, praising him to the skies. We wrote not one but several columns. Yet Felix is the guy who tried to get me prosecuted for contempt of court.

Phil, who used to be the law clerk to Felix Frankfurter, told how, when the Court was deadlocked over appointing an administrator, the vote continued split four-to-four for some months. Tom had his own candidate for the job and was sore when Hugo, Felix, and Bill Douglas decided to vote for another man, Chandler. Tom got Felix and Bill Douglas whipped back into line, but not Hugo—he refused to change. Finally, Tom blurted out, "I put you on this Court." "Yes," said Hugo, "but I'm here now and I'm going to stay."

---

interest. When Drew Pearson's income declined, it became more difficult to make the payments, which had been stretched out for tax reasons.—Ed.

January 14:   Went up to see Senator Jack Kennedy. He called me last week. Talked to him for about an hour. He showed me his original notes and unquestionably he did conceive the idea of his book *Profiles in Courage*, the story of several courageous Senators and their battles against overwhelming odds. Sometimes I'm a sucker for a nice guy who presents an appealing story. I'm not sure whether this was the fact in my talk with Kennedy or not. He didn't ask me for a retraction, but I think I shall give him one.

He got a whale of a lot of help on his book. I'm still dubious as to whether he wrote too much of it in the final draft himself. He showed me the rough chapters—some of them worked out by Harvard professors. But he also showed enough knowledge of the book, had lived with the book, made the book so much a part of him, that basically it is his book. Furthermore, it is quite an inspiring book. I don't think it deserves a Pulitzer prize, but nevertheless it is good. I didn't bear down too hard on him in regard to the very liberal quotes he had taken without attribution or quotation marks from the Bumgarten book on Senator Edmund Ross of Kansas. He admitted that he had used this book and explained that there were practically no sources on Ross so he had to do so. "I don't claim this is original research," he said. "I never expected the book to sell and I was surprised that it did," he said.

He was quite frank in admitting that Harper had paid direct royalties totaling $6,000 to Ted Sorensen of his staff. "Ted did an awful lot of work," he said. He also paid $25,000 of his royalties to Harvard. *Life* magazine paid him $5,000 for one chapter which he didn't use and this he plowed into advertising which helped the book's sale. "I didn't want to plow in more advertising money," he said, "because it wouldn't have helped my income tax." He made a total of $50,000 in royalties, which is awfully good for a book.

We talked about the multitudinous other magazine articles he has written and he admitted that he got help on them. But he said, "When I have members of my staff working on these, I just consider it efficiency. I have to turn out as much as I can. There is no ghost-writer outside of my office; Ted Sorensen does a lot of work for me right here in the office. Most of the magazine articles are speeches that have been rewritten." I asked him about his article in *Foreign Affairs* on Algeria. He said it had come from a young Harvard professor, George Holman, who had been in North Africa and had worked up his original speech. Holman is coming back to work for him this winter.

We talked about some other things, including his father. He says he doesn't mind getting criticized because of his father, that he has to expect this. I couldn't help but think as I talked to him that he was very much like his father. His dad was a warm-hearted liberal Irishman who did a fine job in the early days of the Roosevelt administration, then went sour, got bogged down with too much money, and considered himself a law unto himself. Kennedy started as a fine Congressman and is still a good Senator. I told him as much. "I thought you were a wonderful Congressman when you first came here," I said, "but now that you are in the Senate it seems to me you're wobbling," was as near as I can remember. I didn't tell him that if he had stuck to his original courageous policies I would be 100 percent for him for President. Now Jack Kennedy's leaning more and more toward the pussyfooting of his old man, trying to please everyone, trying to vote liberal but yet be with the conservatives. Last week Senator Pat McNamara of Michigan, a fellow Catholic, made this amazing statement to me: "As between Kennedy and Nixon if they both were running for President, I would have a hard time making up my mind who to vote for." This is about the way I feel at the present time.

January 15:   Got word from New Mexico that Bob McKinney had dropped the column from the *New Mexican*. He had been bombarding me for years wanting me to write critical stories against Senator Chavez, also against Eisenhower. He wrote me a letter not long ago that the column rated highest—about 60 percent readership. He kicked out some features but kept the column. I looked through the file. It was full of letters from McKinney suggesting this or praising that. When he was Assistant Secretary of the Interior he used to drop by the house all the time—once lived here for a while. I called up Clint Anderson, who said that since McKinney was appointed by Eisenhower to the International Atomic Energy Commission in Vienna he had laid down a policy of no comment or criticism of the Eisenhower administration. Clint said that his editor, Joe Lawlor, had resigned. I called up Lawlor in Santa Fe. He confirmed all this and added that there was to be no criticism of the Republican Governor of New Mexico, or John Foster Dulles, or any domestic or international policy. McKinney laid down the rule when he left: "All I'm interested in is the monthly balance sheet."

January 16: I called Senator Chavez to see whether he was going to buck McKinney on confirmation. Chavez has been drunk most of the time; his son has been up to all sorts of lobbying operations, including taking fees on the side. McKinney was after him and I had reported some of these things, particularly the spending of about $50,000 in counterpart funds* by Chavez and son on a recent trip to Spain. Chavez, however, said he was not going to oppose McKinney. He didn't elucidate but some kind of deal has been made.

January 17: Senator Neely, of West Virginia, died. He was eighty-three years old, one of my best friends in the Senate, had been in Congress since 1913. He was one of the few you could always rely on. You never had to worry about where he stood.

Talked to Wayne Morse about opposing McKinney. He will make a speech against him. Also talked to Anderson again. Clint has changed his tune since two days ago. He now says he has to support McKinney and push him through in a hurry. I asked him to hold off for a couple of days but he declined. I asked him to wait until I could send a cable to McKinney in Vienna to get his point of view; again he declined. I sent the cable. I am also sure that Clint will run to Lyndon Johnson and urge speedy confirmation. Clint told me early in the week that it was Lyndon who had pushed McKinney's appointment. McKinney got to know Lyndon through George Brown of Brown & Root. He's the man Lyndon got out of income tax troubles for about $100,000 during the Roosevelt administration and is one of the chief lobbyists on the gas bill. McKinney is the nephew of Bob Young, president of the New York Central; also a director of the Rock Island Railroad and of International Telephone and Telegraph, of which George Brown is also a director. This a formidable lineup if you want to stop anyone from confirmation in the Senate.

January 21: I talked to Senator Pastore and Senator Gore, both members of the Atomic Energy Committee, which passed on McKinney. They said they had O.K.'d him because he was in Vienna and they didn't want to call him back, also because he had been on the panel before and they knew his views. Talking to Gore is like talking to a wet

*Nonconvertible local currency paid to the United States by foreign countries and spent locally by U.S. embassies—and sometimes by junketing congressmen.—ED.

rag. Pastore is a little more vigorous. Senator Neuberger of Oregon, an old and dear friend, also an ex-newspaper man, was a little disappointing. He said he would vote against McKinney if someone else got up and led the way. I pointed out that this is one of the few occasions when the Senate had an opportunity to speak out on monopoly of the press and the prostitution of the press; here was a publisher who had been for Truman when Truman appointed him to a job, and for Eisenhower when Eisenhower appointed him to a job.

January 22: Earle Clements came to dinner. I didn't talk about Lyndon Johnson or McKinney. We both agreed that if we were going to gamble on who would be the Democratic nominee, we would pick, as of today, Governor [Robert] Meyner of New Jersey. Unfortunately, the reason is that he's a pig in the poke. He hasn't made enemies, hasn't had to take a stand on controversial issues. It's a shame that a Senator who has to stand up and be counted makes so many enemies. He's a far better man usually than the Governor. We also agreed that Senator Clark of Pennsylvania might be the best President. And Clements surprised me by speaking very highly of Governor Williams of Michigan. He thinks Williams would be in a better position if he came to Washington as Senator and got himself a little national publicity.

January 23: Went to dinner at Kemper Simpson's. I have known Kemper since the Hoover administration, when he was working on the Tariff Commission. It seems like a long time. Senator Green, Democrat of Rhode Island, was there, aged ninety, and that made it seem longer. Theodore Francis Green is aging somewhat. His hearing is getting bad. But he took the streetcar to dinner and complained a bit that the motorman had not let him off at Third Street. We drove him home. The Senator still has a beautiful house overlooking the bay at Providence, built about 200 years ago. Every Christmas he opens the house up and has twenty-six of his relatives in for dinner, all named Green. In between times, he goes there occasionally but there is no one to cook for him and he cooks breakfast himself. He has a caretaker. He is worth several millions but seldom spends it on taxi fare. Senator Kennedy tells a story about him that when he got out of a taxi on a rare occasion en route to the Capitol he gave the taxi driver a nickel and said: "Be sure to vote for Eisenhower."

Jimmie Riddleberger, whom I have also known a long time, was there. He is newly appointed Ambassador to Greece. He has just spent four years as Ambassador to Yugoslavia, where he did a good job. Jimmie is not a prepossessing person but competent. He got his job because, during the closing weeks of the Truman administration, Dulles's sister came to him and said she had to get reappointed to the State Department under the Democrats. "If I'm appointed under the Democrats, my brother says he can keep me on. If I wait, then my brother says he can't appoint me because it would be nepotism." Jimmie appointed Miss Dulles and became Ambassador to Yugoslavia.

January 24:   McKinney was confirmed. There were only five Senators present. Wayne Morse telephoned Lyndon urging that the appointment be held up for a couple of days so he could be present. Wayne said he had to be on the West Coast. Lyndon refused. "There's only one man against McKinney—Drew Pearson," Lyndon stormed. I had talked to Hubert Humphrey, Pastore, Monroney, Chavez, McNamara of Michigan, Gore of Tennessee, and Neuberger, but not one would get up and talk about freedom of the press except Wayne Morse, who says he will do so early next week when he returns.

We have been trying to track down a story on Adam Clayton Powell, the Negro Congressman, and the fact that he withdrew several thousand dollars' worth of counterpart funds to keep a mistress in a villa along the Adriatic Coast. We find that about $5,000 worth of counterpart funds were withdrawn from the American Embassy in Rome by a member of the Labor Committee, of which Powell is ranking Democrat.

January 25:   Dave Karr phoned from New York to say that Bob Young, head of the New York Central Railroad, had shot himself in Palm Beach. It was only a couple of years ago that I interviewed Young on television during his fight to take over New York Central. He had promised great things, including an $8 dividend. Last month he had to skip dividends entirely. He has mortgaged his house in Newport, Rhode Island, and for six months has tried to sell his house in Palm Beach. No takers. Dave thinks there'll be a slump in the stock market Monday because Young's holding company has some heavy loans for Zeckendorf, the big real estate outfit which talks big but produces little. Bob McKinney, Young's nephew, had to take a revolver away from him a couple of times before.

January 27: Sat beside Mrs. Warren at the theater. She told me when the Chief Justice is working, he reads briefs in bed but like I do, he usually falls asleep. She says she turns out the light but he usually wakes up and goes back to reading.

She was interested in my report on Governor Goodwin Knight and felt very sorry for the way the reactionary Republicans had made him bow out of the Governor's race. I sometimes wonder how Eisenhower happened to appoint such a wonderful Chief Justice as Warren. Obviously, he didn't quite know what he was doing and probably Herb Brownell didn't either.

January 30: All week the Moulder committee has been stewing regarding the confidential memo I published last week showing corruption inside the Federal Communications Commission. Sam Rayburn, who wanted the investigation, has now got cold feet and Bill Kittrell called me in anguish last week to say, "Why do you sacrifice a thirty-year friendship with Sam Rayburn?" It isn't pleasant to sacrifice friendships, but somehow or other these scandals inside the FCC must be investigated. It now looks as if they will hold some whitewash hearings next week and merely go into such superficial matters as gifts received by the Commissioners. They will not look into the grants of TV licenses worth millions of dollars given to people like Senator Lyndon Johnson and the newspapers.

January 31: Talked to [Former FCC Commissioner] Frieda Hennock on the telephone. She, as usual, was almost hysterical. She has been called to testify Tuesday regarding the $200 color TV set which she paid for after she resigned from the FCC. Her skirts are clean and she should make a reasonably good witness on this one point. However, she has been yapping at me for a couple of years about the inequities and scandals of the TV industry. Now she tells me she will not testify on these points. I urged her to take the bull by the horns and give the committee the works, but she pulled a lot of yak about how she was a lawyer and she had to keep her reputation as a lawyer. She ought to go back to living with [ex-N.Y. State Supreme Court Justice] Ferd Pecora.

Trevor Gardner, the missile expert who resigned from the Eisenhower Administration in protest over our failures, came to lunch. He has a fascinating story. It should be a chapter in the book all by itself.

Went to the Czech Embassy for dinner. Bill Douglas was there together with Chalmers Roberts of *The Washington Post* and the Turkish Ambassador. This was rather surprising because the Turkish government has been at odds with Czechoslovakia over the importation of Czech arms into Syria. The Turkish Ambassador remarked to me on the side that he figured that Jordan would be the next country to fall under the axes in the Near East. He asked me what I thought of the Syrian-Egyptian partnership just announced this week. I told him that General Bizri had predicted it when I was there in September, but I hadn't really expected it would ever happen.

The Turk and I didn't get much chance to talk, however. I was seated next to a rather friendly and quite intelligent correspondent of *Rude Prova* which means "Red Truth" and it is the leading newspaper of Prague. He has been over much of the U.S.A., including the South, and it was interesting and significant that he had interviewed the Negro leader in Alabama, Rev. Martin Luther King. He feels that the Negro churches of the South have taken on a new moral crusade and now have become much more important than in the past because of the courageous stand they have taken for integration. He was quite impressed with King. He remarked that the South was like a young man with a wooden leg—full of vigor but handicapped by the color problem.

February 3: Arrived in Chicago last night. People out here think the race with Russia is over because we launched the Explorer. The *Chicago Tribune* is treating the investigation of the FCC as if Commissioner Doerfer is a hero. *The New York Times* and the Chicago *Sun-Times*, however, gave the story a pretty fair treatment. I understand that such valiant champions of a free press as Eric Sevareid and Ed Murrow are either ignoring the story or playing it as if Doerfer was a hero.

February 6: Televised in New York yesterday. Congressman Morgan Moulder of Missouri has bucked up and is doing a pretty tough job as chairman of the TV investigating committee. Jack tells me that our column on the way Congressman Oren Harris of Arkansas was sticking his nose in the picture did the trick. The committee almost fired Bernard Schwartz. The committee got him into a secret hearing and demanded that he be put under oath to answer questions regarding who leaked to *The New York Times*. He confessed that he had leaked and then he put each member of the committee under oath and demanded to know which one of them had leaked to Drew Pearson. He told Jack later that he had taken Jack's advice to go after the committee members belligerently.* Jack told him that when he had first come to Washington he had faced a Senate hearing on Bob Jones and his membership in the FCC after we had published reports that Jones was a member of the Black Legion in Ohio. I advised Jack to go in and testify and call a spade a spade. The average witness, Jack told Schwartz, is afraid of a senatorial or congressional committee. If you spit in their face they get afraid of you. That's what Schwartz did.

Sam Rayburn is trying to kill the investigation of the Federal Communications Commission because his nephew is involved. Yet it was Sam who started the investigation in the first place.

I was supposed to have lunch with Chairman Moulder today, but he postponed because his subcommittee is raising Cain with him. They want to hold the investigation of Commissioner Mack in secret. Mack has been caught with his fingers really in the cash register, as I tried to bring out two weeks ago. They will probably fire Mack and then try

*Congressman Moulder chaired the House Subcommittee on Legislative Oversight, which had undertaken the task of investigating the regulatory agencies. The parent group of the Moulder subcommittee—the House Committee on Interstate and Foreign Commerce—was chaired by Oren Harris. The rules Harris drew up for the subcommittee were odd in two ways: first, the power to subpoena and control over the $250,000 expense budget were to remain in the hands of Harris rather than Moulder; second, Harris and the ranking Republican on the parent committee could vote in the subcommittee whenever they wished, though neither formally were members. By the fall of 1957, Dr. Bernard Schwartz, who headed the subcommittee staff, was centering the probe on the FCC. Schwartz drew up a memo detailing charges about the acceptance of gifts, favoritism, and fraternizing with litigants on the part of FCC members. The memo was stamped secret, but it was leaked to Drew Pearson and *The Washington Post*. Questioned about the leak, Harris disclaimed all knowledge, saying the memo was Schwartz's and he, Harris, knew nothing about the charges. Schwartz was able to get a hearing on his charges and it was confirmed that FCC members had accepted color television sets from NBC/RCA; under oath, FCC chairman John Doerfer admitted to accepting $575 from the National Association of Radio and TV Broadcasters in 1954 after he and his wife had appeared at the group's convention in Spokane. In the face of these admissions, Harris agreed to call five of the seven commissioners. —Ed.

to discontinue the hearings. Mack is the Commissioner from Florida whom I criticized some years ago when he was first appointed, and the Miami *Herald* raised hell with me as a result.*

Frieda Hennock called to point out that the subcommittee was treading very gingerly regarding the most important thing of all, namely the manner in which the big networks dominate the TV industry and the FCC. This apparently is the last thing the Congressmen want to investigate.

The Vanguard failed again.

February 8:   Lunched with Congressman Moulder. A very nice but somewhat ineffectual gentleman with a fondness for involvements with everyone in his office. Last year I queried him as to why he had voted for the gas bill. He had a rather inane excuse. It's now reported, and I am sure true, that the payoff was that he would become chairman of an important committee. Sam has now given him his reward and wishes he hadn't. He's on the hottest spot of any Congressman in Washington. He told me about the closed door meeting where Schwartz had insisted that all the Congressmen be put under oath, and he in turn had cross-examined them as to who had leaked the secret memorandum to Drew Pearson. Wolverton of New Jersey, the ranking Republican on the Committee, was the first to take the oath. He administered it himself. "I swear to tell the truth and nothing but the truth," he said. They all swore that they had not leaked to Drew Pearson. However, Moss, of Sacramento, was absent and the next day he came in to explode: "I never heard of such outlandish and extraordinary procedure. Since I was not present and since some might get the impression I was absent by design, I want to make it clear under oath that I did not give the memo to Drew Pearson." Moss was sore, not at Schwartz but at the entire procedure.

Harris, Flynt of Georgia, and O'Hara of Minnesota went to Rayburn with Moulder afterward about firing Schwartz. Rayburn listened carefully, finally said, "It would not be wise at this time."

Schwartz had ended the earlier secret session by saying, "And I want you to know that I am not going to resign."

When the transcript of this testimony was delivered at the next

---

*Schwartz disclosed that Mack had received checks amounting to $2,650 from attorney Thurmond A. Whiteside, who represented the firm that was awarded a hotly contested Miami TV channel .—Ed.

closed committee hearing, it was stipulated on a piece of paper prepared by the stenographer that Moulder should sign a receipt stating
that this was classified material. He read the statement and then announced to the committee: "This is the most unusual procedure I have
ever seen. I want to know who has ordered this. Everyone knows this
material is not classified. It is taken in the public interest. If this
information is to be given to me under these circumstances I don't
want it. I shall refuse to take it." Harris then spoke up and said he
would take it and put it in the committee's safe. However, Schwartz
demanded a copy.

Moulder told me how he was district attorney in mid-Missouri in
1930 when the Union Electric Company started to build a dam across
the Osage River; he tried to stop it, got an injunction against it, but
failed. The Missouri Legislature was ridden with utility lobbyists and
Union Electric gave a party at the clubhouse to celebrate the construction of the dam. Moulder raided on the grounds that they were gambling. Lons, the Union Electric lobbyist, stormed, "I want you to know
that you'll be out of office in two weeks." Moulder wasn't out. He said
Union Electric had spent millions on the state legislature.

I reminded him that it was at about the same period that the
Roosevelt administration indicted high officials of North American, of
which John Foster Dulles was attorney, because of the expenditure of
$5,000,000 to influence the Missouri legislature. North American is the
holding company for Union Electric. I did not get a chance to go into
the details of how that criminal case was fixed when the *Chicago
Tribune* planted a woman on John Rogge and then had a camera in
the ceiling over the bed taking pictures of them. Rogge promptly
dropped the criminal prosectuion. This was probably one of the most
historic cases in the last fifty years. The case involved Jim Forrestal, as
well as John Foster Dulles. If it had ever gone to trial fully instead of
being stopped in the middle, Dulles would never be Secretary of State,
and Forrestal never would have been Secretary of Defense.

Moulder mentioned rather casually that Harris was trying to investigate Schwartz on the ground that Schwartz had spent some committee money illegally for moving his furniture and family down to Washington. Moulder said that there was nothing to the charge.

Later that evening, Jack Anderson told me that the committee
was meeting Monday to fire Schwartz on the ground that he had
fudged on his expense vouchers. Actually, Harris's plant inside the

committee—a man named Beasley—had prepared the vouchers. They were for four trips to New York when Schwartz was interviewing staff members. He lived at his apartment rather than at hotels, but charged up the equivalent of hotel bills because he had to continue renting his apartment a little longer. I got hold of Moulder and urged him to call off the Monday morning committee hearing until I could get some speeches made on the House and Senate floors supporting him and Schwartz. He agreed.

I called Jimmie Roosevelt and sold him on the idea of a series of one-minute speeches on the House floor Monday noon which would help stall for time on the vote on the Civil Rights Commission. The House Appropriations Committee had knocked out $750,000 to finance the Civil Rights Commission and the vote was coming up Monday, when big-city Congressmen from Negro areas would not be present. Jimmie agreed to make a speech and get some others to go along. This would give time for Moulder to get some public opinion behind him and Schwartz.

Schwartz, meanwhile, has leaked a copy of the secret transcript when he put the Congressmen under oath. It spoils a good scoop for us but it's probably in the public interest to have it out.

February 9:   Spent most of yesterday afternoon and evening at the farm on the telephone. This is no way to spend a weekend at the farm. Talked to Senators Kefauver, Sparkman, McNamara, and John Carroll of Colorado. They all agreed to give speeches Monday, supporting Schwartz and demanding a full investigation. They all suggested, however, that someone else kick off the speechmaking. Neuberger especially urged that if someone else would take the lead he and others would chime in. Kefauver is willing to do this but preferred to have someone like Paul Douglas or Fulbright lead off, since they originally investigated the mink coat and ham scandals under Truman.

On the House side, I talked to John McCormack, of Massachusetts, who liked the idea of the one-minute speeches. He said he would not be in the chair, that Rayburn would. I hope he doesn't leak our strategy to Rayburn. Also talked to Harry Sheppard of California, who was all for some hot speeches; also Jack Shelley of California, who suggested that there be a meeting in his office at 11 A.M. Monday to rally the forces. Others who are cooperating are Gene McCarthy of Minnesota; Mrs. Edith Green of Oregon; Frank Thompson of New Jersey; Stewart Udall of Arizona and Henry Reuss of Wisconsin. Gene

McCarthy promised to get a whole slew of his people there.

I still haven't been able to get Morse or anyone else to do the kickoff.

Spent most of the evening writing speeches for tomorrow. Schwartz came by with three speeches he had written at Jack's request. I'm afraid they won't do. You can't criticize your colleagues, either in the House or the Senate, and his speeches ignore this rule. Just as he arrived, Earle Clements came for dinner. Earle thinks that sentiment is building up behind Schwartz and Moulder and he suggested that if Moulder was any kind of chairman he could filibuster all Monday morning to prevent a vote throwing Schwartz out. With one favorable committee member to ask him questions, Moulder could drag out the hearings for hours until the Congress convened, at which time he could adjourn at twelve noon sharp. I called Moulder regarding this strategy and he reluctantly agreed. I also called John Moss and he agreed. He was not reluctant.

Stayed up until midnight writing speeches. Finally got Bill Welsh of the Democratic National Committee on the telephone and he agreed to get some of his staff to work early in the morning to dig out quotes by Republicans promising to rid the nation of corruption.

February 10: Got hold of Senator Talmadge of Georgia last night and asked him to talk to Flynt of Georgia to change his vote re Schwartz. Herman said that he didn't have much influence with Flynt because he had not been favorable to having Flynt run for Governor of Georgia. He said Flynt had mentioned to him the fact that he didn't like Schwartz. Herman said he would do his best, however.

Got hold of Morse at 7:30 A.M. He came in from New York at 1:20 this morning but called me early. He agreed to kick off the debate on the Senate floor. By getting two secretaries in at 7 A.M. I managed to have ready speeches for Kefauver, Morse, Sparkman, and McNamara. I also had a lot of material ready for the one-minute speeches in the House side which I sent up to Jack Shelley's office just before eleven o'clock. The quotes from Eisenhower which I got from the Democratic National Committee are priceless. Ike pounded the theme of ending corruption more than any other issue in '52. Had a last talk with Moulder, who promised to stand firm, but I was surprised to hear that he had agreed to a committee meeting at 2 P.M. as well as in the morning. He doesn't have to do this. Under House rules, a chairman can just refuse to meet while the House is in session. Moulder had been telling me over the weekend that if he was not present the had been telling me over the weekend that if he was not present the Committee would meet anyway without him. But they can't do it while the House is in session.

I took the speech up to Morse and he seemed to like it. We delivered a pretty hot speech to McNamara, enumerating all the gifts received by Eisenhower at Gettysburg from deep freezes to shrubbery for his farm. I don't know whether he'll go for it or not.

Went over to the House of Representatives for its opening. It was the first time I had been there in a year. Sam, however, stopped the one-minute speeches. I suspect that John McCormack leaked. Someone leaked at any rate and the speeches are off. In the Senate, however, Morse really went to town. Sparkman, McNamara, Carroll, Neuberger, and Clark also helped out. They asked some fine questions. Kefauver came in later and delivered quite a speech. Only one Republican was present, but the press got the story and did all right by it. The one Republican present was Javits of New York, a Jew. He did not lift his voice once in support of Schwartz, also a New Yorker, also a Republican, also a Jew.

Meanwhile, I learned that the vote in the Moulder subcommittee was 6 to 5 in favor of Schwartz. Wolverton switched to Schwartz's side and I think Flynt of Georgia did likewise.

In the afternoon, however, Schwartz got his righteous backbone up, insulted some of the members or at least so they said, and late in the day was fired. The trouble with Schwartz is his personality. Actually, he's a hero. If it hadn't been for his determination and courage, nothing would have come from this investigation at all. He has done the public a great service. And probably it's better that he should be fired. Some of the members, this afternoon, asked him if he would stay on and he replied that he would if he was given full authority and if Moulder was given the right to sign subpoenas. This was a reasonable request but the committee wouldn't go for it. I'm afraid that Schwartz was so rough with the committee members that the young Turks who had promised me to make speeches for him will back out. The House will not be in session again until Thursday anyway.

February 11:   Last night Schwartz learned that he was going to receive a subpoena to appear at a closed-door session today and bring all his documents. His wife called up to ask what he should do. Jack relayed the message to me and I advised that he should take his documents over

433

to the home of Senator Morse, the man who had made a speech demanding a full Senate investigation of what the House was failing to investigate. Jack tried to phone this advice back to Schwartz, who by that time was at his apartment. But the telephone was busy. By the time he finally got through, Mrs. Schwartz told him that her husband had left with the documents and with Clark Mollenhoff of the Des Moines *Register Tribune* to take the documents to Senator Williams of Delaware at the Mayflower Hotel. This was the last place where we wanted them to be. It means, first, that Williams, who is up for reelection and needs Republican money, will probably not cooperate in a full investigation. It also means that the documents will be in Mollenhoff's hands. He just barged into the story recently, and we have been nursing the story ever since last July. Jack finally got hold of Mrs. Schwartz and sent a message to her husband to get the documents away from Williams and over to Morse. Mrs. Schwartz must have remarkable control over her husband, because he picked up the documents, which were already in Williams's apartment at the Mayflower, and took them out. He brought them to my house. Jack Anderson met me here and Mollenhoff trailed along behind in order to try to salvage some of the documents for himself. I called Wayne Morse and he agreed to accept them. We got them up to his apartment around midnight and before Schwartz went back to his own apartment. He knew that a U.S. marshal was waiting for him outside to serve him with a subpoena. The marshal didn't get to him until after the documents were already in Morse's possession so he was not in contempt of Congress.

Around midnight I called up various people to get a lawyer for Schwartz. He wanted an ex-Senator or a man of Cabinet rank. I called Jim McGranery, the former Attorney General, but he declined; Graham Morison, the former Assistant Attorney General, but he was busy; Charlie Murphy, counsel to Truman, but he was ill; Jiggs Donohue, the former District Commissioner, but he was not in; Abe Fortas, the former Under Secretary of the Interior, but he was tied up. Schwartz didn't want ex-Congressman Joe Casey, who was playing bridge with Luvie unsuspecting of what was going on in the next room. I offered him George Arnold, my son-in-law, but he was skeptical. I also offered him my personal attorney, John Donovan. Next morning he said he would take Donovan, but John was busy so George Arnold went up to be with him in the closed-door session.

George told me afterward that they had a field day. They ran circles around the committee. George discovered that the subpoena for Schwartz to produce the documents was made out to the full committee and only the subcommittee was present. They were minus a quorum by about ten members so George refused to let his client answer any questions. It would have been a simple matter for the committee to have written a new subpoena and handed it to Schwartz while they were talking to him. They could have written it sitting at their desks. But they weren't smart enough to think of this. They did not know at this time that Schwartz had given the files to Morse. And he refused to answer questions as to where the files were. So they were very excited. They kept asking him over and over again whose property was this. They thought he had hidden the files in his apartment. Finally Harris said, "All right, Dr. Schwartz, I'm going to ask you to stand up and take the oath."

"No, Dr. Schwartz will not take the oath," replied Herbert Wachtell who was co-counsel with George.

Harris looked punctured. At one point Schwartz called the proceeding a kangaroo court. "That's enough, Dr. Schwartz, I'm not going to take any more from you."

The Congressmen acted as if they were really afraid of him. Finally, they requested Schwartz very humbly if he would go out at the noon hour and see if he could find any of the documents. He agreed to come back at three o'clock. Shortly after three, Bennett of Michigan, who by this time was getting smart, moved: "I move to recess and the committee immediately call for a special meeting at which time we will subpoena Dr. Schwartz." At this point, Schwartz agreed voluntarily to testify and told the committee that the documents were with Senator Morse. This took the wind out of their sails. They then asked: "Will you please ask Senator Morse to give us back our documents." Schwartz said he would. Shortly thereafter Schwartz was in the position of acting as unpaid counsel of the committee, not as a witness. They were asking his advice as to what they should do.

Earlier in the morning Mrs. Schwartz had brought some of the most important files to the House, including the canceled checks of money paid by Whiteside to Commissioner Mack. I called Senator Morse and she delivered them to his apartment.

I have read over part of the files. They substantiate all we said about Mack and then some. They also substantiate some things I have suspected about Governor Dewey. He has consistently and emphatically told me he never intervened in any matter in Washington. But there is ample evidence that he intervened in several airline cases up to the hilt.

Senators Kefauver and Carroll still believe that there should be a special investigation in the Senate. So does Morse. WTOP suddenly got hep to the censorship they pulled on my radio program Saturday night and sent for a copy of the original text. Morse's speech did it.

February 12: Wayne Morse telephoned. He has had the time of his life. I wrote a full column on his operations with Sam Rayburn and Congressman Harris in turning back the files. We didn't really mean to do it this way but coincidentally it has helped to dramatize and publicize this investigation, so it will be difficult now to stop. It's somewhat like the Whittaker Chambers pumpkin papers. Whenever you hide secret files some place, the public gets so aroused that the Congressmen have to investigate. Wayne says he will introduce a special resolution demanding an investigation by the Senate.

Dug up the correspondence I had with people in Miami when Commissioner Mack was appointed. The Florida newspapers gibed at me for describing Mack as too cozy with the utilities. I shot out a special column on Mack to try to beat Congressman Harris with his investigation tomorrow.

Lunched at the National Symphony Fund Raising Drive where I sat beside Mrs. Sherman Adams. I did not tell her that I had just seen two letters from her husband to Murray Chotiner in the secret files of Dr. Schwartz. We remained cordial but slightly aloof. On my right was Mrs. Burton, wife of the Supreme Court Justice I have panned from time to time for not doing any work on the Supreme Court. I suppose that I disappointed the ladies by talking not about the Congressional investigation, but about people-to-people friendship and music. I told them that I didn't know any more about music than the difference between a symphony and a philharmonic orchestra.

February 13: Schwartz was called upon to testify, this time in open session. Quite a contrast to the closed-door hearings the committee has held in the past where they said they wanted to invoke Rule 11 to protect Commissioner Mack. This time they received second-hand, hearsay evidence from Schwartz about Mack without Mack present to face his accuser. But they loved it just the same and even purred over the man that they had recently fired, Dr. Schwartz. Schwartz as a witness, not counsel, scored a smash hit comparable to the comeback of Maria Callas after her Roman fiasco. Schwartz was practically pelted with valentines from his former critics, who parted with him most reluctantly and let him go on the promise that he would give them an encore on Monday. They even overlooked the fact that he referred to members of Congress as "you people."

I wore my eyes out reading over the reports on Dewey and Eastern Airlines, only to find that the St. Louis *Post-Dispatch* plunked out a story on the same subject today. I had a column written and on the wire but had to hold it. I published the correspondence between Frank Stanton of CBS and former FCC chairman McConnaughey's son instead. This means I will never get a job with CBS in the future.

February 21: Interviewed Admiral Hyman Rickover at lunch. A cup of consommé, one hard-boiled egg, soda crackers, and an apple, plus a glass of milk. No wonder he keeps thin. He is gaunt, wiry, slightly stooped, crusty disposition. His left arm was tucked inside his shirt, apparently suffering from bursitis. During the interview he kept telling Jack and me that we were asking the wrong questions, told us how to conduct the interview. You could understand how other Admirals don't like him and why they nearly kicked him out of the Navy. When I asked him where he got the idea for the atomic submarine he replied, "The idea probably originated with Jules Verne." He put in quite a plug for the Navy idea that you had to have a lot of different kinds of ships, not just atomic submarines. I couldn't help but recall his telephone conversation with me when I asked to see him. He kept harping on the fact that you can't change the military mind and that if I wanted to change the military mind I was crazy. Rickover apparently has decided to get along with the military mind on superficial matters while he works on atomic matters. He says that it becomes increasingly difficult to put atomic engines in smaller ships. The bigger the ship, the easier it is but also the more expensive.

I learned from others there's a lot of opposition to his idea of an atomic airplane carrier—it will cost twice as much as a conventional carrier.

Went to the Polish Embassy for a concert given by Sidney Harth, the young Louisville violinist who went to Poland last fall and won high honors in a violinist competition. Jane Barkley, widow of the Veep, was there. As Harth played, a picture of Ignace Paderewski looked down over the piano. It was my father who brought Paderewski to the United States just as World War I was closing and just before Paderewski became the first Prime Minister of Poland. A lot has happened since then. Poland has shifted from a republic to a Communist police state but now seems on the way to getting back to a certain amount of freedom.

The Polish Embassy is quite attractive. I couldn't help but remember the days when the aristocracy were running Poland and when Jan Ciechanowski, the Minister, was making love to Alice Davis, wife of the Secretary of War in the Coolidge Cabinet. She wanted to go away and live with him but Ciechanowski was more interested in his Washington post. Her daughter, Alice, now Lady Makins, wife of the British Ambassador and a schoolmate of Luvie's, never did know what was going on.

February 22: Lunched with Oscar Chapman. Truman had quite a poker party last night given by Scott Lucas. Most of the Democratic bigwigs were there and although Harry vowed to take some money away from Clint Anderson, Bob Kerr, and Clark Clifford, they ended up by taking money from him. Harry will never learn.

Went to the big Truman dinner. Harry made a pretty good speech but Adlai, I'm informed, made a better one. I couldn't hear it because it was in the second banquet hall. I get the impression that Adlai may be willing to run again. The only trouble is that the Democratic stalwarts will never support him. Lyndon Johnson made the most boring speech of the evening.

February 23: I spoke in Indianapolis. The Indianapolis *Star*, published by Eugene Pulliam, one of the worst fascist publishers in the United States, continues to black out the column. So does Pulliam's Phoenix paper. Ike was in Phoenix today. Pulliam played golf with him.

The *Chicago Tribune* correspondent really got under Jim Hagerty's skin yesterday regarding Ike's 3,000-mile detour to Phoenix to take Mamie to the Elizabeth Arden reducing beauty ranch. Mrs. Ellis Slater of Seagrams Distillers and Mrs. Gordon Moore, whose husband is in the spotlight as an influence peddler, also took the 3,000-mile detour and a special White House limousine was driven all the way to Phoenix to meet the plane. Wonder what would have happened had H.S.T.

done this. I get the impression that Ike is getting sore at the press, which once treated him so royally, and is also figuring that he isn't going to have to worry about political life much longer.

February 24:   There were breadlines in Indianapolis at seven o'clock this morning as I drove to the airport. The depression is really hurting. The *Star* did not publish my column giving the wire recording of Commissioner Mack's confession to congressional investigators. It was a sensational column but nothing appeared in this part of Indiana. Pulliam has been trying to get a TV license for himself.

In the Pittsburgh airport I bumped into Pete Akers, executive editor of the Chicago *Sun-Times*. He thinks that Adlai would run at the drop of a hat if he was urged. Pete is editor of a paper started by Marshall Field to bring liberalism to the Middle West, but Marshall Field IV, its present publisher, insisted that the paper should support Eisenhower.

In Wheeling, West Virginia, and the Ohio towns on the other side of the Ohio River there is continuing evidence of depression. Some of the unemployed who came to see me at the Men's Shop, which sponsors the radio program, were quite depressing. One of them, a Negro coal miner out of work for some time, wanted to know when I thought the depression would end. When I told him July he remarked: "There's a lot of meals to be eaten between now and July." I spoke at the Board of Trade in Bellaire, Ohio. A very fine group of people. The Republican candidate for Congress insisted on heckling me. Wayne Hays, the Democratic Congressman, sat at the head table.

The Wheeling *News Register*, one of the Ogden newspapers, uses the column only intermittently. If I say too much about Eisenhower —it's omitted. The Ogden chain has a near monopoly on newspapers in West Virginia.

February 25:   Arrived back in Washington to find Truman's Secretary of Agriculture, Charlie Brannan, awaiting to have breakfast with me, together with Glen Archer and Paul Blanshard of the Committee for Separation of Church and State. The latter are trying to oppose the TV license given to Loyola University in New Orleans, on the ground that it is an organization controlled from Rome. The FCC law does not permit a license to be given to a foreign group and, previously, a license was denied a Mormon group because one of them lived in

Canada. Brannan, who had nothing to do with the others, gave me some interesting figures regarding the way Secretary of Agriculture Ezra Taft Benson has balled up the farm surpluses.

Went to the Truman lunch at the Statler. At a private cocktail party in advance, I found myself with Republican and Democratic leaders, including Lyndon Johnson. He shook hands cordially and we had quite a talk. He said that he agreed with the column this morning, adding that he didn't usually agree. He said it was correct that the Democrats were in part to blame for confirming people like Commissioner Mack. The trouble, he said, was that Senate committees bring in unanimous recommendations and it's difficult for the Senate leadership to go beyond their recommendations. Lyndon said that he and I have one thing in common "we both outmarried ourselves." He made quite a little argument that both he and I had the same things in common, but that he had one disadvantage in that he had to represent the oil and gas people. "You forgive Hubert Humphrey when he champions the dairy people in Minnesota," said Lyndon. "You forgive Tom Hennings his faults. You forgive Kefauver his problems. But you don't forgive me mine." I had to concede that Lyndon had a point there. I didn't tell him this, but I've got to have someone among the Democrats to criticize and he is, after all, the leader. I can't be criticizing Republicans all the time. Furthermore, when any politician gets in high position he has to be fair game.

February 26: The Harris committee* is really sailing into Commissioner Mack. Harris himself is asking some potent questions. No one has replaced Dr. Schwartz, but the committee is doing a pretty good job. Even John Bell Williams of Mississippi and John Bennett of Michigan are getting peppery. I think the column blast got under their skin.

February 27: Went to dinner at the F Street Club given by Senator Joe Clark of Pennsylvania. Had quite a talk with Hubert Humphrey. He's a wonderful guy if he would only settle down and stick to one or two issues instead of running off in all directions. I still think he would be the most effective campaigner the Democrats have for President,

---

*In mid-February, Moulder resigned as chairman in protest over Harris's actions in regard to Schwartz, in particular, his part in firing him.—ED.

but I'm afraid he hasn't any real chance. Over a month ago I wrote him that I wanted to talk to him and he still hasn't bothered to acknowledge the letter. A lot of Philadelphia Republicans were at the dinner, all enthusiastic over Joe Clark, but none of them running to vote Democratic in a national election.

I caught the 2:30 A.M. sleeper to New York.

February 28: Harry Cohn of Columbia Pictures died yesterday. I shall always remember him for having paid $750 for the title of "Washington Merry-Go-Round" in 1931 and made a million dollar movie out of it. He used to laugh when he saw me in later years. My share was $375. Latterly he has been chiefly famous around Broadway for paying $25,000 to the Negro nightclub singer Davis [Sammy Davis, Jr.] not to sleep with Kim Novak. Cohn claimed he discovered her first.

March 3: Lunched with Paresce of the Italian Embassy. He wants me to go to Italy before the Italian elections, feels that what I reported from Italy would be cabled from Washington and New York back to the Italian papers and would help in the final elections outcome. It looks like a close race. I told Paresce that I would try to go.

Commissioner Mack finally resigned from the FCC. The White House demanded it. Until the end, he seemed to figure that he could get away with continuing in office. It has now been almost two months since we first broke the story on Mack. The White House could have moved a long time ago. So could the FCC. The Congressmen who now give the appearance of being eager-beaver investigators did their best to hush up the investigation. It has been a long battle.

March 4: The Harris committee is now digging into Colonel Gordon Moore, the President's brother-in-law. They have found that he is linked up with a shipyard in the Dominican Republic. We reported Moore's operations in the Dominican Republic about two years ago, but he has led a charmed life. It's part of the fact that no newspaper either dares or wants to criticize Ike.

March 6: Vice President Nixon got back from Los Angeles where it's reported his arms were sore, slapping so many Negro, Mexican, and Japanese leaders on the back for the benefit of cameras. He attended the Ghana reception today where he was photographed with more African leaders.

The Soviet Ambassador spoke at the Press Club today, which is unprecedented. He has become the most effective glad-hander among the diplomats in Washington. Simultaneously, Secretary Dulles said no regarding a summit meeting under the current Russian terms.

March 7: Lunched with Max Friedman of the Manchester *Guardian* who is concerned over the bitterness in Canada against the United States. The movement in England against American missile bases is also strong. The American public has no realization of its intensity. A Parliament member who champions these bases is almost certain to be defeated.

Earle Clements called me up to suggest a story on Lyndon Johnson's skillful maneuvering to end the recession. He has put the heat on various committees to report out new highway bills, new public works bills, etc. Actually, Lyndon operates as if he were planning to be the next Democratic candidate and as if the different committee chairmen were his Cabinet. However, I wrote a story.

March 8: Ike is moving to catch up with Lyndon Johnson. He has come out with a recession program himself. The Claiborne Pells came for luncheon. He was in Russia last summer, says that he couldn't buy a meal for himself on the Russian trains. Everyone wanted to pay for his food because he was an American. When he arrived, instead of being hounded, nobody was there to meet him and they paid no attention to him, which was refreshing.

March 9: Planted azaleas. It began to snow while I was planting them. Finished the chapter on Eisenhower. It is a revealing document, but may go too far. It's amazing the public relations façade he has managed to build up.

Dined with Alfred Friendly [managing editor of *The Washington Post*] and his wife. We called the roll of potential Democratic candidates, found they all have flaws. However, we agreed that the Northern liberals will control the next convention if they want to exert the control. It will be the Governors, such as Soapy Williams, Averell Harriman, Pat Brown, who will control the delegations, not the Senators from Washington.

Senator Anderson of New Mexico called me last week regarding the insurance tax loophole bill which he says will give the insurance companies a $124,000,000 tax rebate. I wrote a story on it. What this administration and most of the Congress don't appreciate is that the tax loopholes are bigger and bigger for the higher brackets and the corporations, whereas the small taxpayer gets his taxes deducted from his salary. This is the situation which helped to encourage Communism in France and Italy.

March 10:   I talked to Earle Clements about lining up Lyndon Johnson to block the insurance tax giveaway. I gather that Johnson was lukewarm. He passed the buck back to the Senate Finance Committee. Talked to Anderson, Morse of Oregon, McNamara of Michigan, Javits of New York, and Humphrey of Minnesota to get them to block the tax giveaway. They promised to operate. It was interesting that Clint Anderson asked me to line up Morse to do some talking.

Dined with Sumner Welles. He was more intelligent than I've seen him in a long time. Completely sober, but looked like a ghost. He can't walk well without a cane. He agrees with John Foster Dulles that you can't meet with the Russians until you have some kind of agenda and some willingness to discuss disarmament.

March 12:   Took Perle Mesta to a Big Brothers luncheon at the Mayflower in honor of Professor Sheldon and Elder Glueck. They are a couple teaching at Harvard who have done some wonderful research on juvenile delinquency. A study of 500 cases showed that it's the family that makes the difference, not the surroundings. Children raised in slum conditions turned out to be fine children if the family was careful and adequate. Religion made no great difference they found but rather the family. Even television, etc., didn't count very much in their research. A family which took pains with its children and was not divorced worked wonders. There was almost no juvenile delinquency.

I was invited to go to Nixon's office for a presentation of an award to Dr. and Mrs. Glueck. I didn't go.

Emil Mazey, secretary of the United Auto Workers, is in the headlines as one of the witnesses before the Senate Rackets Committee. He was active in inspiring the Kohler strike. There's nothing showing that he was corrupt, and he has a fine record in that respect, but the interesting thing to me is that he was the guy who, when in the Philippines, inspired the 30,000 signatures which he sent me and which I later took to Harry Truman on that famous occasion when Truman bawled me out. I had no idea at the time that the signatures were coming from Mazey.

March 13: Went to dinner with Estes Kefauver at the Ansberrys'. Lyndon Johnson, instead of taking my suggestion on the insurance company tax giveaway, is pushing the bill. He held a night session tonight to make sure the bill is passed before March 15, when insurance companies would have to pay. The insurance companies are still paying premiums based upon the actuarial tables of the 1930s. Since then, longevity has increased, public health has improved, and insurance companies are coining money hand over fist.

The Russian Embassy today reached me after a roundabout search to tell me that I had been given a visa to go to Moscow. The Embassy didn't seem to know where I lived, sent word to me in New York. If their intelligence on other American matters is that bad, we shouldn't have to worry.

Discovered that Colonel Gordon Moore, Ike's brother-in-law, has a prize stallion and racing horses on his farm in Virginia. Also discovered that the stallion is a gift of the Clint Murchison family, one of the biggest oil operators in Texas. The gifts to the Eisenhower family are unbounded.

March 14: Dined with Chip and Evie Robert in honor of Senator Dick Russell of Georgia. I should not go to these dinners. As I arrived Chip greeted me with "We had nine Senators here but when they heard Drew Pearson was arriving they all left." Chip, of course, was kidding. The Senators had left to vote on the insurance tax giveaway. Afterward, Mike Monroney came back to say they had voted the $124,000,000 for the insurance companies. He voted against them and so did Dick Russell, much to my surprise. But most of the others at the dinner—Knowland of California, Bridges of New Hampshire, McClellan of Arkansas, Stennis of Mississippi—all voted in favor of the giveaway.

I have just finished going over a very critical chapter of the book regarding Under Secretary of Defense Quarles. But at the dinner Quarles came up to exchange pleasantries. I hope I am not tempted to rewrite the book. After dinner, McClellan came up to me slightly tight and proceeded to bawl me out for reporting that he had an interest in his son's law firm in Little Rock. He was so vociferous that Senator Knowland came alongside, together with Stennis of Mississippi, and tried to persuade him to go away. McClellan, while protesting that he had no interest in the law firm, also kept expostulating, "The only reason I kept my name on the door was because of you. If you hadn't written about it I would have taken my name off a long time ago. I'm going to take it off next week."

I had a nice talk with Knowland. He says he's going back to campaign briefly during the Easter recess, then put in an intensive campaign in the fall. Congressman Engle of California had called me up this morning to tell me how Knowland had come out for Pacific Gas and Electric on the Trinity River "partnership" plan and simultaneously how Pacific Gas and Electric had contributed a lot of liquor to the California Society reception. The story, obviously, won't do Knowland any good. Again, I shouldn't come to these dinners. Senator McClellan came back a second time to tell me how wrong I was about his law firm, but how he was now going to take his name off the door.

Skeeter Johnson, the Senate's secretary, got drunk, made passes at Luvie on one side and Evie Gordon on the other. Finally, he fell over backward and had to be taken home.

March 17 [Lexington, Kentucky]: Judge John J. Parker of the Fourth Circuit Court of Appeals, died last night. I remember thirty years ago when the Senate refused by one vote to confirm him. It was a sensational battle with people like George Norris, Bob La Follette, Lud Denny of Scripps-Howard, Dorothy Detzer, Walter White, and William Green of the AFL leading the battle against him. I have written many stories since then trying to correct the record in that fight and urging that Judge Parker be appointed to the Supreme Court by the Democrats—though he is a Republican. The old gentleman never was bitter over his defeat. He used to write me occasionally thanking me for the articles but telling me not to bother because he was quite happy where he was. He wrote many ringing opinions for labor and the Negro —the people who had defeated him for confirmation.

Saw Ed Prichard in Lexington. The people of that city still have not accepted him back into the fold following his conviction for stuffing ballot boxes. I'm afraid he will never stage a comeback now. Fred Wachs, the man who refuses to publish the column in the Lexington *Leader,* is in income tax trouble. He used some due bills on advertising to get tractors and equipment for his farm. Wachs is a man who should have gone to jail, not Ed Prichard, who did what every other Kentucky politician has always done in almost every election since the days of Henry Clay.

March 18 [Washington]:   Al Friendly, of *The Washington Post,* was not so friendly this morning when I called him up regarding the column on Colonel Moore and the Irish stallion he received from Clint Murchison, Texas oil man. *The Post* killed the column, despite the fact that I had sent Larry Berlin all the way to the Moore farm in Virginia, had spent a couple of days of careful checking, and talked to the Murchison people. Friendly claimed it was lack of space, but I'm sure there was a lot more to it than that. Some of the Texas oil men must have put in an emphatic word with *The Post.* When a $65,000 stallion is loaned or given, either one, to the brother-in-law of the President, it's not news. But I remember when I ran the story that Mrs. Roosevelt had received an aquamarine from the President of Brazil, newspapers published it freely. Later she put it in the Hyde Park library.

March 19:   Eisenhower seems to be panic-stricken regarding the depression. He's been striking out in different directions. Last week a tax truce was agreed on with Sam Rayburn whereby neither side would talk about cutting taxes. But yesterday Eisenhower made an almost emotional statement before the Republican women that taxes would be cut if necessary.

March 20:   The first day of spring but there's almost a foot of snow on the ground. I was supposed to have breakfast with ex-Mayor Bill O'Dwyer, who has come up from Mexico City, but couldn't make it. The chief problem is that the electricity has gone out at the farm. We can't milk the cows and they are in real trouble. They kick when they are hand milked. The handicaps of the machine age!

Eisenhower has given up the idea of having Khrushchev come to Washington for the summit conference chiefly because John Foster Dulles told him Khrushchev would be kissing babies, shaking hands, and doing the Harry Truman with the people—so much so that the American people would like him and we would have to make a deal with Russia.

March 24:   Flew to New York and dined with Bill O'Dwyer, Dave Karr, and Art Landa, plus some supernumeraries. A few years ago, if I had dined with the mayor of New York in the Colony, a whole stream of people would have come by to interrupt us and shake hands. But only one person came by. It reminded me of driving with O'Dwyer to

Brooklyn to see the first game in history when the Dodgers won the World Series. We didn't know they were going to win. It was the first game on the home grounds. O'Dwyer had just come back from Mexico and not a ripple stirred through the crowd as we walked through the grandstand. It would never have been that way a few years ago. They have hounded Bill on his income taxes. They even dug up the land around his brother's ranch in El Centro, California. They have threatened to pounce on him when he came back to New York. But they have found nothing against him.

March 25:   Congressman Harris of Arkansas called in Baron Shacklette and fired him. Shacklette is the only member of the Harris committee staff who's been doing any investigation of TV monopoly or anything else. Harris wouldn't even give him one month to find another job. Shacklette walked out, didn't argue, didn't row with him. The next day, at a closed-door meeting of the committee, Harris announced that he was dropping Shacklette and immediately got such a rebellion from committee members, particularly Wolverton of New Jersey, Moss of California, and even Williams of Mississippi, that he had to reverse himself. Shacklette is the only man who has been feeding these Congressmen with material so they could ask intelligent questions. Harris is doing his best to shut up the whole probe. His new counsel, Lishman, is forceful enough to break a soda cracker if he charges head on.

March 26:   The Rumanian Embassy wants me to go to a meeting of the Rumanian Press Union in Bucharest in mid-May. It's a challenging invitation and one which will probably get my head bloody with critics in this country. But since we preach freedom of the press over here we ought to be able to talk freedom of the press over there without being criticized too much. If I can work it in after Italy I shall go.

Had lunch with ex-Governor Sid McMath of Arkansas, who ran against Senator McClellan in 1954, but was licked by only 2,500 votes. McCarthy saved McClellan. McClellan was then sitting on the McCarthy Army committee and although he was always a bosom pal of McCarthy, he proceeded to do a job on him. It made a big hit in Baptist-Methodist Arkansas and won him the primary.

McMath is worried about Governor Faubus being reelected. He has three candidates in the race against him and wants to raise some money to help. He needs at least $50,000.

McMath helped to put Faubus in office. Faubus was on his staff when he was Governor and they integrated the University of Arkansas and they took a lot of other progressive steps. Most of these smaller towns around Little Rock had already been integrated as far as the schools were concerned before the Central High School incident. Faubus's opposition to Central High School integration did not come until after he saw he was going to make a little political hay. I agreed to help McMath raise some money in New York and Washington. If Faubus is reelected it gives us a black eye all over Africa and Asia.

Met the Venezuelan Ambassador. Quite a change from the old days. He was educated at Texas A & M, was arrested three times by Pedro Estrada, the J. Edgar Hoover of Venezuela. He looks like a real friend of the U.S.A. He is going to have a tough time stopping Ike from slapping greater restrictions on Venezuelan oil. He had a session with Ike this morning and came away glowing about Ike's charm and warm personality. He has a lot yet to learn.

March 27: Eisenhower has finally given his O.K. on an attempt to send a rocket to the moon. This is something we have been writing about since last September and the Pentagon has been pushing for since last October. The big question is will the Air Force or the Army get to the moon first. There's as much rivalry between them as there is between the United States and Russia.

Eisenhower made a glowing speech before the Foreign Trade Council advocating free trade and then turned around the same day and slapped down Venezuela, Canada, and other oil-producing countries including the Near East by restricting further oil imports. The new Venezuelan Ambassador now understands that Ike's charm doesn't mean much.

Neither Ike nor Mamie went to the big debutante party given by Perle Mesta for Ruth Eisenhower, Milton's daughter. Ruth is motherless and Perle really outdid herself to give the girl a send-off. But Mamie didn't even drop around. I am beginning to think that Mamie hates Ike's family, and that Ike hates Mamie's family. When Ike went down to the airport to meet Mamie and Mrs. Gordon Moore on their way back from Elizabeth Arden's Maine Chance farm, he did not go over to greet Colonel Moore. Didn't even look at him. Moore, of course, has gotten him into a peck of trouble. Milton Eisenhower comes to breakfast at the White House frequently, but doesn't stick around for lunch or dinner. The report is that Mamie just doesn't like him. Of course, Mamie has had her mother, Mrs. Doud, and her sister, Mrs. Moore, around the White House continually, but Milton isn't there very much—except at breakfast.

March 28:   Breakfasted with Bill O'Dwyer. I guess I was wrong about Bill being ignored in New York. He tells me that he sat in the reviewing stand at the St. Patrick's Day parade and that the crowds went wild over him. They didn't know he was going to be there but spotted him and yelled their heads off. Bill thinks the tide is beginning to turn in his favor. The new president-to-be of Mexico is a close friend and has asked him to help on various plans for Mexico's future.

He showed me a statement that Senator Kefauver had given an Irish newspaperman in London. It said that O'Dwyer was innocent of any wrongdoing. This is what I tried to get Kefauver to say publicly back in 1954, but couldn't quite persuade him. I'll have to tackle him again.

Bill told me how Archbishop Malloy of Brooklyn had gone after him when he was in office because he had championed some of the alleged juvenile delinquents in Brooklyn who were first offenders and hadn't really offended anyway. He got better cooperation from Cardinal Spellman. Spellman is now demanding that an Irish-Catholic run for the Senate against Ives. He wants either Jim Farley or Tom Murray of the AEC. Murray was severely castigated during the Judge Manton trial for taking money. He would not be a good candidate. Jim Farley has been knifing Roosevelt for years but now that the Republicans are on the downgrade he sees the Senate just over the horizon.

Had lunch for Sid McMath and some potential money raisers. He told how Governor Faubus had raised the rates on gas for the Arkansas-Louisiana Gas Company and his friend W. R. Stephens and had generally played in with the big utilities. Having done this and having aroused a lot of opposition, Faubus is trying to cover up with the Negro issue. McMath says a lot of the red-necks are sore at Faubus for raising rates while the plantation owners are sore at him because he's a radical. I remember the day I championed Faubus when he was accused by Governor Cherry of being a Communist because he attended Commonwealth College.

It is indicative of the generosity of the Jews and perhaps also of their worry regarding minority problems that I got my best response at the luncheon from Jewish guests. I think we may have raised about ten or fifteen thousand dollars. The White Citizens Councils have been bombing synagogues in Miami, Nashville, Charlotte, and Gastonia, North Carolina. Bill Kittrell was present and will try to raise some oil money in Texas. There is, after all, some liberal oil money there.

Sheldon Sackett of the Coos Bay *Times* wired me asking for $1,000 to defend the Coos Bay libel suit. He has in mind the very foolish statement I made in the *Saturday Evening Post* that I spent over $250,000 defending libel suits in the past seven years. That, of course, was when I was making $5,000 a week on radio. However, I will have to bail him out.

George Vogel, the new head of the Mutual Broadcasting System, came in to ask that I do a live broadcast five times a week for five minutes daily. I would like to get back on the air live but I can't walk out on the stations which have supported me for so long a time on tape. Ted Scott of the Havana *Post* went over to Miami and telephoned me collect. He says that all hell is going to break in Havana. Batista is not going to budge and is a tough fighter. Some of the people around him are deserting, including, apparently, my old friend Ed Chester. The papal nuncio met with the bishops in Havana last night, but couldn't decide what to do. Batista has about 4,000 men tied up guarding the sugar crop. But it will be over in about two weeks and then he will have more troops at his disposal. Local investors are getting so jittery that they are trying to close up the Seville Biltmore Hotel. Ted didn't know about the report I had heard that the Mafia had placed a $5 million price on Castro's head. He has caused so much turmoil in the islands that the gambling business is practically dead and they want the revolutions stopped. No tourists, no gambling.

April 2:   Mrs. Raymond Carroll, widow of my old friend Ray Carroll of the Philadelphia *Public Ledger,* came to lunch with me at the Mayflower. She is over seventy-five and almost destitute. I agreed to give her a research job so that she could say that she was working for me and thus get a cheaper room at a special women's hotel. She worked for a while with the Export-Import Bank, clipping newspapers, but, after seventy, retired and hasn't any retirement pay.

I remember Ray Carroll as one of the great newspapermen of his day. He went to the Versailles conference with Woodrow Wilson and for years wrote a column almost daily out of Paris. He helped me when

Tyler was kidnapped in London. In fact, it was his young assistant, then working for the UP in London, who was of great advice and counsel.

Mrs. Carroll pulled out of her handbag some programs of the days when she was an opera singer and the toast of Rio de Janeiro, Buenos Aires, and Lima. She sang in Covent Garden, Milan, and Rome. The programs were faded. The clippings still told of her great voice. That was all she had left of a happier day—that and the memory of her husband.

I was glad that the headwaiters at the Mayflower remembered her. It has been years since she used to come with Ray and lunch at the Number One table at the Mayflower. If she had come in unremembered, it would have been a blow. But they were equal to the occasion.

April 4:   Senator Morse called up. It looks as if he and Neuberger had reached the real parting of the ways. He is going to put a candidate into the Democratic primary against Neuberger and is determined to beat him. He says that it was the final straw when Neuberger attacked his integrity.

April 5:   Lamar Caudle and his two boys came for breakfast. I remember when Lamar, Jr., participated in a legal debate at Yale which Justice Hugo Black helped to judge. He gave him the Harlan F. Stone award. But Hugo has just now voted against Lamar, Sr., on his writ of certiorari and in so doing will help to send him to jail in about twenty-five days. The Caudles were working on one more appeal to the Supreme Court for a rehearing. The odds are strong against them. We discussed a mysterious witness, allegedly the former secretary of Brownell, who told of forged papers used in the case against him. We don't know whether she is really bona fide or not. I'm afraid I haven't done as much as I should on this case. Every court in the country has decreed that Lamar is guilty, but I still think he is innocent. When you have reared as fine children as he has, you can't be a crook.

Luvie and I lunched at the Russian Embassy. I started off accepting a vodka, which was probably a mistake. Vodka was served all through lunch, together with two kinds of wines and liqueurs afterward. The Ambassador missed few rounds and didn't appear to show the effects at all. I lagged somewhat behind.

They were interested in my prediction of last July that Russia would send an Ambassador to Washington "who smiles." They wanted to know how I knew that, insomuch as the Ambassador, Mr. Menshikov, said he didn't know himself that he was going to come. He did not add that he didn't know himself whether he was going to smile. They were also interested in my prediction that there would be a summit conference in October. I told them what I had already used on the radio, namely that Eisenhower wanted a summit conference but Dulles didn't, at least not in the United States. When I explained that Eisenhower sincerely wanted peace and felt that he could get along with Khrushchev, the Ambassador remarked: "We are convinced that Mr. Eisenhower is a sincere believer in peace. It would be a great thing for him and Khrushchev to sit down together. I know they would find many things in common." When I pointed out that there was a genuine problem of security and that the FBI was worried over possible attempts on Khrushchev's life by American crackpots, the Ambassador remarked: "What, you mean to say that in this vast country there isn't room for a place to have a summit conference?" He said it with a smile.

I talked about my proposal to produce a film in Russia. They were interested and suggested that I talk with the head of the film department, who is in Washington now. The Ambassador kept urging me to go to Russia and asking me when I was going. I must say that there's an entirely different atmosphere around the Soviet Embassy today. Of course, when you enter the front door, you know that the FBI has a long-distance camera across the street taking a picture of you. And you know that if another McCarthy tries to dominate the United States that picture will probably be used against you.

During one part of the luncheon, the Ambassador was talking about the importance of a summit conference. He said: "Ambassador Thompson comes into the Kremlin. He gets an envelope. I go to the State Department. I get an envelope. We trade envelopes back and forth. It's much better to sit down and talk things over face to face. I am sure that if Khrushchev and Eisenhower sit down face to face we will accomplish many things."

I told the Ambassador I thought it would be a good idea to have two conferences every year—one in Moscow and one in Washington. The two great powers of the world ought to have a continuing series of meetings, just like the boards of directors of corporations. The problems of the world can never be settled at one conference. Menshikov seemed to think this was an excellent idea.

Madame Menshikov was very much interested in Arthur Miller

and *Death of a Salesman.* She said, "Why did he marry Marilyn Monroe?" Luvie replied, "Have you ever seen Marilyn Monroe?" When Luvie mentioned the book *Not for Bread Alone,* the Russian ladies expressed the opinion that it was a terrible book.

The Ambassador was very much interested in Dean Acheson and the fact that he had pretty much the same views as Dulles in regard to Russia. I told him that back in 1945, Henry L. Stimson had proposed that the United States give the secret of the atom bomb to Russia. At that time, Dean Acheson sided with Stimson and believed that there could be cooperation with Russia. Today, he does not feel that way. Menshikov was anxious to know why Dean Acheson had changed. I suppose that I could have given him the answer which Dean once gave some years ago privately: "The Russians are like a thief going down a street trying every latch on the door. If they find one open, they go in." But I didn't. I figured that there was no use disrupting an otherwise pleasant luncheon.

When I asked Menshikov about the idea of interviewing Khrushchev in his kitchen or in his home, he looked a bit dubious. "After all," he said, "that's up to Khrushchev." I also suggested an interview with Zhukov, Bulganin, and some of those who were purged. The Ambassador was deadpan. At least he didn't say no.

April 7:   Lunched with Herb Maletz, who is doing a fine job investigating the telephone monopoly. He swears that Manny Celler will go through with it. I have known Manny to cave in, however, when his law firm got a good client from the people he was investigating.

Dined with the Phil Grahams and Bill Walton. We agreed that one of the most significant pieces of news in yesterday's paper was in the society column, namely that Neil McElroy, the Secretary of Defense, had joined the Episcopalian Church. When a public figure joins the church at the age of fifty plus, it means one thing—he's planning to run for President of the United States.

April 8:   Went to the Russian Embassy to confer with the head of the film bureau regarding my proposed film of Russia. Spent about an hour explaining the plans. What they want is that the film be developed in Russia and that the sound be dubbed in before it leaves Russia. This may make it impossible for an American firm to supply any finances.

April 9:   Hubert Humphrey came for breakfast. He was eloquent and alarmed over the state of the world. If we continue drifting we will be lucky if the country isn't ruined before 1960.

I talked to Hubert about the idea of running for President. I told him that my first allegiance was to Kefauver, but that I was afraid Kefauver was shopworn and that if the Democrats rowed too much among themselves they would lose. I also pointed out that the reactionaries always get together on a candidate and it's time for the liberals to get together on a real candidate. It seemed to me that he was the best qualified. I didn't tell him that I thought some of the others might be better, such as Soapy Williams, but I'm afraid Soapy can never get the nomination. Hubert was noncommittal. He said that he had been a pretty lousy candidate back in 1956 and agreed with me that a lot of spadework would have to be done between now and 1960 if anything could be accomplished.

May 16 [Vienna]:   There are as many sheep on the Vienna airport as there are jack rabbits on the Los Angeles airport. But the sheep on the Vienna airport keep right on grazing when the planes come in. They don't miss a crunch. The jack rabbits in Los Angeles run like crazy. The people in Europe, however, are like the jack rabbits of Los Angeles. They are running like crazy from atomic war. The people of the United States are like the sheep of Vienna—they don't miss a mouthful of free enterprise grass worrying much about war.

It's been twelve years since I was in Vienna. General Mark Clark occupied one part of the city then, the Russians one part, and the British another. They weren't speaking. There was incident after incident.

The opera house at that time was a shambles. Little pieces of rubble were picked up neatly everywhere in an effort to clean up the streets. That was all that could be done then—keep the street free of rubble. No effort was made to repair the gaunt skeletons of bombed and burned-out buildings, their girders rusting in the rain.

As I flew over Austria I could see the scars of the unmerciful bombing, like the marks on the face of a man who has suffered from smallpox. American bombers had made mincemeat of the castles, the towns, the railway stations. Then, rather then carry the bombs home, they had dropped them on the forests and green fields, freely and without favor.

That was how it looked in 1946. Today Vienna is blooming. The opera house is sold out for weeks in advance. We got tickets to *La Bohème* only through the astute know-how of the Hotel Bristol porter.

Today Vienna is prosperous, the people happy—thanks to their own hard work, plus American aid. But as they look back on the aftermath of two world wars and remember the backbreaking sacrifice it took to rebuild their prized opera house, you can realize why they are like the jack rabbits on the airport at Los Angeles.

May 17 [Paris]:   The pigeons are fatter in Paris than any place in the world. Children are rosier, more energetic.

Today France is not apathetic. It is worried. On the surface, life is the same. The *boulevardiers* sit at little café tables drinking their aperitifs. The taxis scuttle up and down the Champs Elysées. Tourists try to blend into the landscape. Americans are polite and circumspect. They don't want to make enemies. But underneath, France is more concerned about the future than at any time since Hitler's Nazis romped around the Maginot Line.

Luvie told me I shouldn't go to Paris and she was right. All my friends were out of town or busy. I stood in the cold waiting for Dave Schoenbrun to film a telecast in front of de Gaulle's house. I looked into the Ritz. The dining room was empty and the bar crowded with Madison Avenueites. I walked down the Rue Danon where I stayed at the Hotel Chatham when I first came to Paris in 1923. The hotel was gone. The Volney Restaurant around the corner where they used to play soulful Russian music was converted to a swank new apartment. A lot can happen in thirty-five years. But the Café de la Paix, known to almost every doughboy in 1917, was still there and still full of Americans from Keokuk or Madison Avenue. They were quiet Americans, however, fading into the landscape as much as possible. The only change was the prostitutes. No one came up to proposition you in the Café de la Paix or anywhere else. Also changed was the guard outside the Embassy. Instead of hurrahs and parades given to Americans in 1917 and to Ike in 1944 and to the Friendship Train in 1947, there was a large police van outside the American Embassy loaded with gendarmes. It was dark inside. But every so often a man would light a cigarette and you could see the line of faces waiting for a move against the Embassy of the nation which had come to the rescue of France in two wars. Man's memory is short.

I went to the airport terminal for the endless hassle over passports, tickets, etc., and got on my plane to come home. (It's impossible to be anonymous any more. Two Americans came up to me out of the clear blue in Paris and asked if I wasn't D.P.)

June 16 [Washington]:   I was supposed to go to the Russian Ballet but stayed home to send out a special column release that Eisenhower himself got a vicuna coat from Boston textile manufacturer Bernard Goldfine. Also included some other activities regarding Goldfine and Sherman Adams, particularly that Goldfine had given Adams several rugs, much of the furniture for his home, and loaned him his airplane credit card. We got the story basically from Senator Cotton of New Hampshire, attorney for Goldfine, whom we got on the telephone at about 9 P.M. to confirm the details. The story moved as a special out of New York at nine and I read it to *The Post* over the telephone.

Went to the Russian Embassy about 11 P.M. and met Al Friendly. He was quite excited about the story; he's using it on page one, had read it to Phil Graham over the telephone, who said, "It's true." Phil has been quite a friend of Sherman Adams, which may explain a lot of things.

During the reception the counselor of the Embassy came up to me and wanted to know when I was going to Moscow. I told him that only when I could spend some time there and I was too rushed right now. I also discussed the motion picture, one done in Russia by me, another done in the United States by them. He thought it had some merit. I told him I was having trouble raising the money for the project.

June 17:   Mailed the last chapter of the book late last night.* Called Jack early this morning to warn him that we would have denials from the White House on our special release, and asked him to see Congressman Moulder of Missouri, Moss of California, together with Mack of Illinois, and have them ask some potent questions of Sherman Adams. Caught the plane to Chicago. Arrived in Chicago at 10 A.M. I was met by a photographer for the Chicago *American.* I was afraid I would run into the same kind of reception I got in Minneapolis two years before, when newspapermen waylaid me on another tough story on Ike, namely his health. At that time, there was hell to pay. This time, the Chicago

---

* *U.S.A.: Second Class Power.*—ED.

American had played the story of Ike's vicuna coat on page one in banner headlines, and wanted a photo of me reading the paper. The minute I got into Chicago, the AP called and I was deluged with other calls for radio and TV interviews. At first, it looked like a repetition of Minneapolis, especially when Jack called from Washington to say that Hagerty had called a press conference at 9:30 A.M. and denied everything in my story except Ike's coat. He fudged on this by saying that Ike had received vicuna cloth but had given it away to someone whom he couldn't remember. This was bad from his point of view because most people remember who they give a present to. Hagerty denied that Adams had used the air travel card, had received any rugs, furniture, etc., from Goldfine. I dictated a statement to the AP which featured the line "A hit dog howls," and went on to enumerate the number of gifts which Eisenhower himself had received from all sorts of people.

Lunched with Jean Beliard, who is now French consul general in Chicago. He thought the reaction to my story was in my favor. Later I called Ed Duffy of the Chicago *American* and he congratulated me on the story, wasn't worried at all about the Hagerty denials. Around midnight, I went on two TV shows where we talked about gifts to Ike, etc., at great length. The interesting reaction about this whole incident is the fact that Ike is now over the crest of popularity and on the way down. Two years ago this would never have happened. Even one year ago I would have been heckled. This time, my statement enumerating Ike's many gifts got tremendous coverage. Hagerty also seems to have lost his cunning with the press.

June 18:   Lamar Caudle was due to go to jail in about four days, his birthday. But last night the Eighth Circuit Court of Appeals gave him a stay of sentence pending the motion for a new trial. It was partly due to some new evidence taken from Harry Schwimmer, the lawyer for Irving Sachs. Schwimmer, who has suffered a stroke and seems to be nearing death, gave a deposition that he had never given anything to Lamar and that the oil royalty placed in his name was placed without Lamar's knowledge. I think the real reason for the stay, however, is all the Adams gifts and some of the stories I have been writing comparing the Adams case with the two suits and one topcoat given to Matt Connolly.

June 19: Tips have been coming in from all sorts of people regarding Ike's gifts. There are several tips that he did not pay for repairs on his house at Gettysburg. He wrote one firm a nice thank-you letter for putting in the intercom system between the house and the barn for $7,000. They sent him a bill, he wrote back a thank-you note. There are also tips that he sold some of his gifts, including a pig and several head of black Angus, together with a mechanical organ.

June 20: Jack went up to New York for a libel session with the publishers. More and more sentiment seems to be building up against Eisenhower on the Goldfine-Adams case. There is a tremendous sentiment on Capitol Hill demanding that Adams resign.

June 21: We went to a charity benefit at Grady Gore's. I saw Mrs. Dawson, ex-wife of Donald Dawson, who said there was no question about Mamie receiving a diamond necklace from King Saud. I had checked with various jewelry stores about an appraisal of the necklace, but got nothing. We had also called Victor Purse in the State Department, who had handled King Saud during his visit, but he clammed up, though he didn't actually deny the story. Mrs. Dawson says that Victor is being kept on by the State Department only because they are afraid he'll talk about the diamond necklace. He himself had received a Pontiac car from King Saud and was almost fired at the time, but still has a State Department job of sorts. A lot of hard-shelled Republicans came up to me at the party to congratulate me on the Sherman Adams stories. This is almost revolutionary.

June 22: Dined with Mike Agron of the Israeli Embassy. Agron thinks that U.S. troops will have to land in Beirut and fairly soon. About 3,000 Marines are with the 6th Fleet just off Lebanon and Agron thinks the United States will have to land them or else show to all the pro-American leaders of the Arab world that we can't be depended upon. Unfortunately, Agron doesn't know John Foster Dulles.
     Finished the book. I hope this will be the end.

June 24: Went to the circus. Mollie Thayer came in before the circus and confirmed that King Saud did give Mamie that diamond necklace. She also told about the gold mesh bag given by Emperor Haile Selassie of Ethiopia. She said the bag was so heavy that Mamie could hardly carry it. The circus was distant and aloof. The old days of the sawdust ring, the clowns, the wild animal tents, the esprit de corps, are gone. Putting a circus in a ball park completely destroys it. The contrast with the Moscow circus in Athens last summer was marked in the extreme. Bigness pays a penalty even in circuses.

June 27:   Had lunch with Tom Hennings at the Senate. Tom was sober and in fine shape. He has been plugging away at some constructive legislation. He was interrupted several times by demands to vote on the Alaska statehood bill. It looks as if Alaskan statehood will finally be voted. Tom can be one of the most effective members of the Senate when he remains sober. We talked about getting a campaign-fund bill passed. It has been stymied for two years.

June 28:   Luvie went to the Eastern Shore and I stayed home and rested. Sam Block came out to see me with a man named Frank V. Connally to say they thought they could solve the Galíndez mystery. John Frank, an ex-FBI agent, who has been convicted of being an unregistered agent for Trujillo, has taken a shine to Connally and seems in a mood to talk. Connally thinks that he can get the story of who murdered Professor Galíndez from Frank. He seems to think that Frank was there when Galíndez's body was brought out to the airplane for transportation to the Dominican Republic. Connally, however, wants some money and I don't think I can afford what he wants.

June 29:   Lamar Caudle and Turner Smith came out for Sunday evening supper. We discussed strategy to make sure that the Eighth Circuit gives him a new trial. Turner told how he was present at a meeting in 1950 when Matt Connelly was determined to get Caudle fired because Caudle was too loudmouthed. They were afraid at the White House that Caudle would talk too much about some of their attempts to fix tax cases. I have always thought that Connelly was guilty as hell but that Caudle, while dumb, was innocent.

Lamar is peculiarly likable and a peculiarly ineffective person. He just doesn't know how to handle his own defense. He has suffered the tortures of the damned, but has kept his sense of humor. His neighbors and his family have been a big help to him. He told how he was raising tomatoes and how he had warned his wife when he went to the penitentiary they must keep on watering those tomatoes.

It was finally decided that I was to talk to Senator John Sherman Cooper of Kentucky, and ask him to talk to Bill Rogers urging that when the petition for a new trial comes up, the Justice Department stand mute. It would seem only fair to give Caudle a new trial in view of the new statement from Schwimmer and this new statement gives the Justice Department a bona-fide reason for going along with a new trial.

June 30: I talked to Senator Cooper. He made a joking remark about bringing influence to bear on the Justice Department, but I pointed out that he wasn't getting a vicuna coat in return. He finally agreed to talk to Rogers about the Connelly-Caudle case. I made my plea not for Connelly but for Caudle. However, the two go hand-in-hand. I would like to see Connelly convicted. I have always thought he was crooked as a dog's hind leg, ever since I found he was bringing influence to bear on the Civil Aeronautics Board on behalf of Pan American Airways and American Airlines and then going back to sleep with the vice president of American Airlines, Corlene Roberts, who used to be called vice-president-in-charge-of-Matt Connelly.

Bernard Goldfine is now at the Carlton with his wife, his secretary Miss Paperman, and a battery of lawyers. His wife is insisting that Miss Paperman keep in the background. There was almost an alienation of affections suit at one time. Mrs. Goldfine got one telephone call from an unidentified lady after which she remarked to her daughter: "I've taken care of him for twenty years, I'm not going to step aside in favor of someone else now."

July 2: Lunched with Senator Neuberger and Tom Corcoran. We discussed the idea of a drive to pass a campaign contributions bill, similar to that proposed by Teddy Roosevelt. Dick Neuberger has some ideas on this, basically sound, partly screwball. He'll never get anywhere if he proposes the bill in the Senate. It would have to come from an older Senator. Lyndon Johnson doesn't want such a bill because he raises plenty of dough from the oil companies. After he raises the dough, he then controls the Senators to whom he contributes the oil money.

Neuberger asked me for advice as to how to get along with his senior colleague, Wayne Morse. I had to tell that I had just received a scathing letter from Wayne myself, bawling me out because I reported there was a deal on the change of filibuster rules in return for passing a moderate labor bill. My only advice to Dick was that Wayne is Wayne Morse. He's a prima donna, but he's too valuable not to get along with.

I talked to Senator Carroll of Colorado regarding a real investigation of the Justice Department showing how case after case against high-placed Republicans had been tossed out or not even considered, while case after case against Democrats had been prosecuted.

July 3:   Talked to Senator Kefauver about an investigation of the Justice Department. He's for it, though he gets bogged down in Tennessee and in antitrust investigations to such an extent that he doesn't get much done.

Goldfine had a pretty good day yesterday on the witness stand before the Harris Committee. Tex McCrary assigned two men to stay with him for about a week to study his mannerisms and his method of speech. The speech they prepared sounded pretty much like Goldfine. They even had Goldfine record the speech on television the night before—which is Madison Avenue to the nth degree. However, McCrary made the mistake of saying he was representing the New York *Herald Tribune* and Roger Robb, Goldfine's attorney, which of course the New York *Herald Tribune* doesn't like at all. They have been doctoring stories on this case to such an extent that Dave Wise refused to let his byline appear on one of them.

I talked to Governor Dewey on the telephone about the report that Frank Bielaski, the famed wire-tapper, was working on the Harris committee members, particularly Morgan Moulder, who has woman trouble. Dewey denied it to high heaven as I knew he would. I suspect he is probably telling me the truth. I then asked them which of the Goldfine companies his law firm represented and he said the Strathmere Woolen Mills. He went on to say that Goldfine had come in quite exercised because the federal grand jury wanted his books and records and that he, Dewey, had arranged for a member of the firm to get the proper books and records to the grand jury. I told Dewey I understood that the question of a $1,000 bribe to a labor leader was involved in this case, and he said he was sure this was not a fact. I am sure he was lying. The real fact is that Bernard Schwartz arranged with the federal grand jury to subpoena Goldfine's books and the Dewey law firm then rushed around to get the case before the Dewey-appointed judge. After trying to get the case dropped, they finally produced some of the books, but not very much.

Dewey asked me about the Goldfine–Sherman Adams case and I said that Adams would have to go. There was too much Republican pressure. Dewey said "Poor old Sherm. He's as honest as the day is long. I wouldn't hesitate to appoint him as a trustee for an estate." But he said the trouble was he'd been just too tough on a lot of people. I told Dewey the remark made by Senator Capehart: that when Adams left, the first fifteen rows of seats on the departing committee should be given to Republican Congressmen who had tried for years to see Adams and could at least see him now. Dewey got a big chuckle out of this.

July 4: Goldfine cracked up on the witness stand yesterday. He refused to answer questions regarding the $700,000 worth of uncashed cashier's checks. The Harris committee thinks that these checks were given to government officials or politicians who could use them for borrowing money without revealing the name of the man who was bribing them. Goldfine pounded the table and flatly refused to produce these checks.

July 5: The Tom Henningses, the McHughs, the Dick Sangers, and several others came for dinner. Tom remained sober until halfway through the evening. Jim McHugh, who was the Marine Corps chief expert on China, says that all the old State Department China hands have been relegated to unimportant jobs in Europe simply because they once served with General George Marshall. Senator Bridges refuses to let them serve in the Far East and Dulles bows to him.

We had a long discussion as to why the State Department came along with the evidence on Galíndez so late. There is still something awfully funny about the whole Galíndez mystery, and particularly how he was able to collect $15,000 to $20,000 a month from Basque refugees. Jim thinks, as Morris Ernst does, that Galíndez was an agent for the CIA. The CIA is the only agency of government which doesn't have to account for its funds. It spends millions. It stirred up a revolution in Indonesia which flopped. It is responsible for the State Department following two divergent policies in the Near East. *Life* magazine is always pulling chestnuts out of the fire for the CIA; and I recall that C. D. Jackson of the Life-Time empire, was the man who arranged for the CIA to finance the Freedom Balloons. C. D. Jackson, Harold

Stassen, and the other boys who went with me to Germany and spent money like money, while I paid my own way. I always was suspicious that a lot of dough was coming from unexplained quarters and didn't learn until sometime later that the CIA was footing the bill.

Congressman Moulder of Missouri, who is being investigated on the q.t. by private detectives for the Goldfine-Adams crowd, seems to be a bit vulnerable regarding his women. One secretary has now got into trouble with the Assistant U.S. Attorney in Arlington. And although the government is cracking down on an abortion ring, the Assistant U.S. Attorney arranged for the young lady to resort to that ring. She has now left for Oklahoma City.

July 7:   I was about to go up to look at the farm early this morning when Jack called me. Jack seldom gets up early so I suspected there was some trouble. There was. He said that he had been in the Carlton Hotel next to the room of Jack Lotto, public relations man for Goldfine, when someone had reached under the door and hooked the microphone which he and Baron Shacklette were using. Lotto had called a press conference and, with Roger Robb present, had staged this for the press. Afterward they banged on Jack's door and he finally persuaded Shacklette to admit them. Goldfine's attorneys were barred, but the press was admitted and Shacklette explained that insomuch as the Goldfine forces were investigating members of the Harris committee, he in turn was watching the Goldfine forces. Obviously, it didn't make many headlines, but it was the best explanation of a very embarrassing situation.

Robb, we found later, had paid a local Washington detective $500 to look for microphones and he, in turn, had been tipped off by someone in the hotel. What makes it particularly bad is that Jack had registered in the room under an assumed name. Actually, Shacklette registered for him but this doesn't look any better.

I rushed a statement to the press associations before leaving the farm, in which I paraphrased Ike's statement on Sherman Adams: "Jack Anderson, of course, has been imprudent. But I need him."

July 8:   Lunched with Marcus Cohn and Leonard Marks. They were quite pessimistic about the general reaction to the incident. What has made it bad is the charge that some of the documents were stolen. Jack assures me that this was not the case and I believe him. However, Miss

Paperman made a hysterical charge that some papers which she had left in her closet were ransacked and looted. Her charge is phony on the surface because she waited a couple of hours before notifying the police. Cigarette ashes and a cigar box were also found in the room. Neither Jack nor Shacklette smokes. Roger Robb has been guilty of using false evidence in the past and this may be another case. However, this does not help us at the moment. The chief detective, Sergeant Edgar Scott, had demanded that Lotto, Miss Paperman, Jack, and Shacklette take lie detector tests. I issued a statement that I would be happy to take one, since Jim Hagerty had called me a liar, but I don't want Jack taking one. Number one, lie detector tests are not court evidence, and, number two, the big question is what questions are asked on such a test.

Leonard and Marcus think I should suspend Jack pending the outcome of the investigation.

They also say that Bob Allen is raising the roof again. He wants $100,000 for his share of the *Merry-Go-Round* trademark. Bob is about to receive $90,000 for his share of the Philadelphia *Bulletin* radio and TV stations. Ruth apparently is sore at Luvie because on one occasion when they were out here Luvie was at the swimming pool instead of being on hand to welcome them at the house.

July 9:   I wrote a letter to Oren Harris regarding the manner in which Sherman Adams had intervened at the Defense Department on behalf of Raylaine Worsteds, a New Hampshire company which had defaulted on Army contracts to the tune of $41,000. Two officials inside the Defense Department wrote memos protesting the unethical conduct of Sherman Adams.

Lunched with Jimmie McHugh. He told how he was in Switzerland when John Carter Vincent, then our Minister to Switzerland, reached into a safe and pulled out three beautiful watches. They were about the most expensive watches it was possible to buy in Switzerland. Vincent told how the Swiss Watchmakers Guild had brought them in as a present to Truman, Mrs. Truman, and Margaret. However, he, Vincent, had warned that he had better consult the State Department and the White House first. He had cabled the Secretary of State and word came back almost immediately that Mr. Truman decided he could not accept them. What a contrast to the present day.

We tried to fathom present events inside of the Kremlin. Jimmie agrees with my theory that the Russians are bound to have increasing trouble with the Chinese. The Chinese have never liked white men and in the past they referred to the Russians in Manchuria with derision. There have been occasions when there was near war in Manchuria as a result of the Chinese Eastern Railroad and its Russian control. Admiral Felix Stump recently told the Joint Chiefs of Staff at Quantico that there were indications that Chinese Communist leaders would be willing to sacrifice half their population in a war because they would still have 300,000,000 people left. Jimmie, who has spent years in China, thinks that the Chinese leaders are having no trouble with their people. The Chinese people have been too docile throughout the centuries. But they are having trouble economically. China has made real progress under the Communists. They have even built a bridge across the Yangtze River at Hankow, which, as I remember the width of the river at this point, is really a superhuman feat. They have built railroads and have shown real evidence of material progress. However, 600,000,000 people are a lot to feed and the Communist regime is ruthless regarding human life. They also regard themselves as the first doctrinaire leaders to pure communism and this is probably why Khrushchev has gotten tough lately regarding both Yugoslavia and the ex-Hungarian leaders.

Jimmie points out that China experiences approximately 1,800 earthquakes every year. This is one reason why inspection of atomic explosions will be so very difficult. Underground explosions cannot be easily differentiated from earthquakes, and it would be impossible to tell whether an explosion in China was an earthquake or an A-bomb, unless inspection teams were on the spot. Jimmie believes this is why Khrushchev has recently changed his position on accepting inspection. Or at least is willing to discuss the matter at Geneva.

July 10:   The Harris committee is really holding Bernard Goldfine's feet to the fire. They have recovered from the Shacklette fumble and are grilling the old boy from Boston unmercifully. They particularly want to know why he had $770,000 worth of uncashed treasurer's checks in his possession or in the possession of his associates for, in some cases, fifteen years, without drawing interest. He has not been willing to explain.

Congressman Harris asked me to come up and see him at noon, which I did. He was courteous. Considering the fact that I had blasted him unmercifully for months, he was amazingly courteous. He was also interested in the facts I had sent him about Sherman Adams's intervention with the Defense Department regarding Raylaine Worsteds and promised to subpoena the papers immediately. He asked me to find out whether Goldfine had any interest in Raylaine. He told me that Perkins Bass, the Congressman from New Hampshire who had defended Adams, was one of the directors of Raylaine, a company which we now find went out of business two or three months ago.

The police are pushing Jack for a lie detector test. It has become evident that this is a public relations game, not a serious hunt for evidence. The police have already handed in their report that there is no evidence and that the case should be dropped. They have been quite suspicious of Miss Paperman. Harris told me also that he thought the Paperman charges were phony. Jack filed an affidavit with the police that he had taken no papers; he has not refused to take a lie detector test, but he wants to know the questions which would be asked, etc.

The man at the Carlton who arranged for Jack to get the room next to Lotto has been hauled in by the police and grilled at length. He seems to be a very unstable witness.

July 11: Lunched with Earle Clements at the Capitol. I reported to him in some detail about the conversation I had with Colonel John Gottlieb in Chicago about two weeks ago. Gottlieb, who raised much of the money for Happy Chandler's gubernatorial campaign in Kentucky and who wants Happy to run for President, suggested that Clements and Chandler might bury the hatchet. I had told Gottlieb I would talk to Earle and I had postponed it for an inexcusably long time, partly because I didn't think there was much use in taking the matter up with Earle. However, he was very much interested in Gottlieb's ideas. I told him that Gottlieb wanted Earle's help in promoting Happy for President and that I had told Gottlieb there wasn't any chance of getting this. Gottlieb replied that the Kentucky delegation would be for Chandler anyway and all Earle would have to do was go along.

Earle finally gave me this reply for Gottlieb: "Tell him that I had thought Chandler wouldn't want to be seen in a dark alley with me. His behavior and his boycott of the Democratic National Committee would certainly indicate that. Though the Senatorial Committee has nothing to do with the National Committee, Happy has boycotted the National Committee simply because of me. However, I bear no grudges and don't believe in hating people. If he wants to talk to me, he can come here and talk any time."

I suggested to Earle that the Democrats had a good way to make up for the fact that they will have very little money during the coming campaign. Number one, they can continue the Harris investigation. Number two, they can start an investigation of the Justice Department and the manner in which it had prosecuted Democrats and given complete immunity to Republicans. Clements liked the general ideas, but shied away from the idea of having Kefauver handle such an investigation. I told him I'd already talked to Kefauver, Carroll of Colorado, and Hennings of Missouri. Earle thinks that Carroll would work harder at the job and also arouse less opposition from the other Senators than if Kefauver were head of the committee.

The President took a bad beating yesterday from the Senate Finance Committee on his reciprocal trade bill. Clements says that Lyndon Johnson did his best and worked hard with Byrd. I talked to Hale Boggs, who won a resounding victory over the President in the House. He says that Senator Kerr of Oklahoma was the chief gutter of the bill in the Senate Finance Committee. Kerr put a few oil companies ahead of the best interests of the United States. Kerr, incidentally, issued a flat denial of my story earlier in the week that he was opposed to the Hennings bill clarifying the release of government information. The story came from Hennings, but Kerr will deny anything.

Oliver Gasch, U.S. Attorney, has been pressured by the White House to go after Jack Anderson. Gasch called in the Carlton Hotel employee and cross-examined him with great enthusiasm. This is a relatively minor case, a very minor witness. Gasch has not bothered with such famous cases as Jimmie Hoffa, Edith Hough, who murdered the Russian Voice of America translator, or the Mallory case. But he has taken off his gloves on this one. The interesting fact is that Gasch was a guest in our home quite recently when Tyler entertained for his fraternity. Gasch was the guest speaker. I was not there. Gasch used to go to dances with Luvie when she was a debutante. Jack tells me that some months ago when I was out of town, he wrote a somewhat critical story about him.

July 23: Wrote a speech for Senator Kefauver on miscarriage of justice in the Justice Department. It highlighted the Caudle case. It was a good speech if I do say so myself.

Eisenhower is getting pulled into a summit conference whether he likes it or not. He spent most of the spring and winter telling Khrushchev that he couldn't attend a summit conference, but now he's on the spot. Prime Minister Macmillan, who was over here on Sunday, had agreed with Dulles that there would be no summit conference. But the minute Macmillan got back to London he reversed himself— thanks to British Labour Party pressure. He has now sent a note to Khrushchev agreeing to meet under the United Nations. I strongly suspect that Dulles had tacitly agreed to this idea but he now claims privately that he didn't. One trouble with our foreign policy is that Ike pays no attention to it whatsoever. Eisenhower was up in Gettysburg playing bridge when Macmillan was spending the weekend with Dulles.

July 26: Lud Denny, who is now married to Dorothy Detzer, came to dinner with Mary Hull. It was very reminiscent of old times. Lud and I covered the State Department back in 1926 and '27. Then he was transferred to Indianapolis, where he was editor of the Indianapolis *Times*, but took his work too seriously for Roy Howard. He wanted to clean up the community. Later he became foreign editor of the Scripps-Howard papers, replacing Phil Simms. I can't really believe it, but he is now retiring. Lud and I have covered all sorts of things but looking back on the news of those days, it was rather unimportant. We used to sit in the old State Department press room in the old State, War, and Navy building, now taken over entirely by the White House, and wait for the news to break. In 1927, there was such momentous news as the landing of U.S. Marines in Nicaragua. There were our notes exchange of Mexico in 1927 over the appropriation of oil lands. There was the Geneva Naval Conference in 1927. I think Lindbergh flew the Atlantic in that year, and later there was the dispute between China and Russia over the Chinese Eastern Railroad. Some of those events seemed to shake the world at the time, but looking back, they were very unimportant.

Mary Hull seems to be looking better and has found herself. She took her mother's death philosophically. She has now weathered four husbands and settled down to a stenographic job at Swarthmore, typing addresses for about $60 or $70 a week. I wonder what would have happened had she decided to marry me.

July 29: General Chennault died yesterday of lung cancer. My old friend Dr. Alton Ochsner took care of him. Dr. Ochsner was the first man to campaign on the evils of cigarettes. There is a lot of whooping and hollering now about what a great man Chennault was, but I can't forget how during the war they discovered he had a strongbox containing about $200,000 in cash. Henry Morgenthau, then Secretary of the Treasury, admitted this to me and said they didn't dare prosecute him for income tax evasion because Chennault was a hero and it would look bad to expose him.

July 30:   Secretary Dulles was really put on the spot in London during the Baghdad Pact conference. The Turkish Ambassador told me about it in some detail. The members threatened to dissolve the Pact and form new separate alliances of their own unless the United States joined. Finally, Dulles did sign Article I, by which the United States agrees to go to the defense of any Pact signatory. This actually puts us in the Pact, though not officially. It would mean that we would have to send an army overseas, however, and this is exactly what the Senate objects to, and why the Constitution of the United States provides that the Senate shall have the right to ratify treaties. However, this new treaty by Dulles will not go to the Senate for ratification. We have completely spurned the Constitution—and have been doing it for a long time.

July 31:   Lunched with Ed Dickinson, who wants to run for the Senate from New York. He's an excellent candidate and a very able young man. However, I suspect that Tom Finletter, former Secretary of the Air Force, might be better qualified. Averell is sitting pretty and being very cagey. I think he would take either Dickinson or Finletter. He doesn't want Farley. Cardinal Spellman wants either Farley or Tom Murray. I asked Dickinson whether he was familiar with the bribe given to Murray during the Judge Manton case. He was. I also asked Ed how the situation was going to stack up from the point of view of religion. Ed is a Catholic and there are three other Catholics in the race. Hitherto, New York has run a Protestant for Governor, a Jew for Attorney General or some other state office, and a Catholic for Lieutenant Governor, etc. Ed thought they ought to get away from religious candidates.

He says that Averell not only has become an excellent politician but knows what he wants. This is quite a change from the old days when he was in Washington, nervous, stuttering, and not knowing exactly what decision he would make next. He always had wonderful instincts but lacked the determination to carry them out. Incidentally, he still wants to be President and if it wasn't for his age, would make an excellent candidate.

Dulles has really got himself in a bind. He promised the British, when he was in London over the weekend, that he would not pull American troops out of Lebanon until the British had agreed to take their troops out of Jordan. Meanwhile, Dulles has been stalling on the summit conference so he could tell Khrushchev that American troops were now out of Lebanon. He's in the position of telling the British one thing, and wanting to tell the Russians another.

Coke Miller came for the weekend. I had a long talk with him about Bob Allen's demands against the column.

August 1: Bill Rogers has a deal with Senator Eastland of Mississippi, which has practically stopped the Civil Rights Commission. The Commission has done nothing about boycotts, discrimination, or other racial developments. It was established by law one year ago this month, yet nothing has happened. Eastland, significantly, asked Bill Rogers no questions whatsoever when he was confirmed. He sailed through like a breeze. Meanwhile, Eastland has held up confirmation of the executive director of the Civil Rights Commission for months.

Coke Miller had a talk with Bob Allen and came back to report that Bob wants $100,000. I now find that I have paid him $163,000 already.

August 4: I talked to Wayne Morse earlier in the day. He is threatening to go after Neuberger publicly. There wasn't much I could say to stop him.

August 6: Robert Harrison, former publisher of *Confidential* magazine, came to lunch. He wants me to publish a Washington edition of *Confidential* which would be called "Drew Pearson's News Beat" and be devoted to cleaning up corruption, rather than cleaning up sex. This is a revival of the old idea I entertained and discussed with George DeLacorte of Dell Publishing back in 1932. In fact, we had plans for a new magazine to be called *Washington Merry-Go-Round* and to be circulated on the day Roosevelt was to be inaugurated in '33. Then two things happened. One was the Depression, which closed the banks. The other was that Bob and I started writing a column. We were too busy. Furthermore, we got the same ideas out in the column that we would have put out in the magazine. Now with more and more newspapers folding and with more and more papers refusing to print the truth, I am sorely tempted by the magazine idea. But it would ruin me to be associated with Harrison.

August 7:   Flew to Chicago to attend the Eagles annual convention where they are giving me an award. Joe Leibowitz met me at the airport. I remember the first time I met Joe. He was trying to clean up racketeering in Chicago. He introduced me to Jack Ragen, who agreed to meet with the FBI. I sold the idea to Tom Clark, then Attorney General, and the FBI interviewed Ragen at great length. They brought back a multitude of tips, leads, and evidence. Tom Clark told me afterward that it led to very high places. J. Edgar Hoover intimated the same thing. He said the people Ragen pointed to had now reformed. I learned later that it pointed to the Hilton hotel chain, Henry Crown, the big Jewish financier in Chicago, and Walter Annenberg, publisher of the Philadelphia *Inquirer*. The investigation never got off even to a start. Ragen was murdered about a month after he gave the information to the FBI and, although I pleaded with J. Edgar Hoover, he wouldn't even give a bodyguard to Joe. He had previously refused a bodyguard to Ragen.

Joe begged me today not to write anything more about Chicago crime. The minute you do, he said, they will be after me again.

August 9:   We came up to Swarthmore last night on the train. This morning I took little Drew through Crumb Creek woods. So many houses have been built up on the edge of the woods that I had trouble finding my way to the paths I knew by heart years ago. It doesn't seem possible that it has been fifty-four years since I first went picnicking with my father and mother and Leon in Crumb Creek woods. I remember how we used to push a wheelbarrow up the steep hill. Or rather, Father pushed it. We were too small. Some years later when I pushed it, I realized how difficult it was.

Drew and I walked along the creek and up the face of Alligator Rock. It was quite a steep climb. There were ashes still in the place between the rocks where we used to cook our suppers. I told Drew that they were probably still our ashes, but he was too smart to believe me.

Drew was impressed by the number of tin cans, old mattresses and other debris which had been washed down the creek and spoiled an otherwise beautiful stream. "If I ever become President," said Drew with some conviction, "I'm going to see that these streams are cleaned up." I told him, though not in full detail, how I had been waging a campaign for sewage disposal to clean up the streams of the United States and how Sherman Adams in the White House had opposed it. Naturally, he couldn't quite understand and he kept very firm in his resolve to clean up the waterways when he becomes President. Thank God the youth of the nation haven't given up that ambition.

Betty Anne's wedding was beautiful. Leon read a poem which made me think he was wasting his time as a radio commentator. The only trouble is that poetry isn't appreciated these days. It was my job to read the certificate. I had rehearsed it a couple of times with Drew's help and as he sat beside me, he looked up to see whether I was going to stumble on one particular "solemnization." I had stumbled on it in rehearsal but I managed to get by in the final reading.

We had a wonderful family reunion both before and after the wedding. I also dropped by to see Vic Shirer who ran the drugstore when I was a boy. He is eighty-six years old and still comes in, with the help of a cane, to visit his old haunts.

Drew had quite a time at the wedding reception. He got into a wrestling match with one of his cousins by marriage. I don't know which one won, but I do know that the knees of Drew's brand new trousers Luvie had painstakingly bought for him were considerably the worse for wear.

August 11:   Eisenhower has still not announced whether he's going to the U.N. Assembly but the hunch is that he will go to either Wednesday's or Thursday's session. I went up on the midnight sleeper.

U.S. policy has definitely changed in the Near East in regard to Russia. Dulles was all for blasting the hell out of Russia the first day, but while he was in Brazil somebody got to Ike and changed this. I have written a column that we will use the soft sell. I think it was C. D. Jackson who switched the President. C.D. is the publisher of *Fortune* magazine who helped me put across the Freedom Balloon launching in Germany in 1951. He had been psychological adviser to the White House back in 1953 but got bored and quit. Now he has come back. God knows they need him.

The White House staff is now pretty well decimated. They

haven't replaced General Cutler or Maxwell Raab or Gabriel Hauge. The smart boys in New York just don't seem to want to work for Ike any more.

August 13:   Eisenhower delivered rather a good speech. C. D. Jackson sat in the wings as nervous as a playwright on opening night. But his star didn't fluff the lines.

Worked until late making final corrections on the page proof for the book and then caught the plane home.

August 14:   The U.N. Assembly meeting really seems to be getting somewhere. Henry Cabot Lodge, I understand, deserves some of the credit though perhaps most of it goes to Dag Hammerskjold.

August 15:   Lunched with Joe Borkin and a Mr. Flurry on Kefauver's antimonopoly subcommittee. Kefauver wanted me to talk to Flurry to see if there was some way his present committee could take over an investigation of political wire-pulling and favoritism in the Justice Department. Flurry agreed with me that the resolution for antitrust investigation was much too narrow. We also agreed that the only man who could do the job is Lyndon Johnson. If he really wants to investigate he can investigate. I suspect he is coasting.

Borkin confided to me afterward that Estes has also muffed up the antitrust probe. I am inclined to agree. If Estes wants to devote his full time to a project, he can really make hay. But he hasn't made much hay in regard either to the cost of living or oil or steel.

Charlie Porter, Congressman from Oregon, called up this morning to say that Wayne Morse and Dick Neuberger had been writing each other more nasty letters. He is trying to get a truce and an agreement that the letters be burned. He asked me to try to talk to Wayne. I doubt if there's much use, but I shall try. Tom Corcoran also called up to beg that something be done regarding Morse and Neuberger. I doubt whether that committee of Kefauver, McNamara, Humphrey has ever even met. Half the trouble with the liberal Senators is they agree to do something and then they get so harassed they never do it. The conservatives are not so busy and have time to follow through.

August 31:   Couldn't sleep last night for worrying about the Florida primary. The Miami *Herald* yesterday refused to publish my column on the doctors' lobby and its opposition to Claude Pepper. I had carefully telephoned Dr. Anderson, head of the doctors' committee, and interviewed him in detail regarding his opposition to Pepper. It was a very carefully written column, but despite this the *Herald* censored it.

Frank Pepper called me last night, very discouraged. Hoodlums have been tearing up Pepper's billboards; two men beat up one of his staff who was putting bumper stickers on cars; only one paper in the entire state has endorsed him—the Daytona Beach paper. The Miami *News*, owned by the Cox family of Dayton, Ohio, which had a fine record under old Jim Cox, criticized Holland for "Palmetto McCarthyism," but in the end endorsed Holland. The reason for the big paper endorsements is Holland's help in trying to get TV stations for them. Nelson Poynter of the St. Petersburg *Times* told me in advance he would support Holland, and almost admitted that Holland had helped him in his battle for a TV channel (which he lost). In Miami, the *News* and the *Herald* ganged up together and secured a TV station, which in the end the U.S. Court of Appeals threw overboard. The *News* and the *Herald* are grateful to Holland.

If we have the only two newspapers in Miami ganging up on one political candidate, when will we ever have a change in administrations or Senators? What difference is this type of press from that in Moscow? I have been considering writing a column recalling the biggest building in Bucharest, Rumania, which housed the monopoly press, dedicated entirely to Communism—which quite rightly has been criticized by the American press. I thought I might compare this with the press monopoly in Florida. But it wouldn't be published anyplace except perhaps Daytona Beach and St. Petersburg. I remember the last time I supported Pepper when he was fighting for his life against George Smathers. John Perry was at my house for dinner on the day before the election and he smilingly had canceled every column I wrote regarding Pepper during that campaign. Yet it was Perry who put Pepper into the Senate race in the first place.

Several people came for dinner, including the Dick Coes. He is drama critic for *The Washington Post* and told me that Tom Donnelly had just been fired by Roy Howard, another great devotee of the free press. Donnelly had gone to New York to work for Roy Howard's

World-Telegram, and one day Howard asked the elevator operator if he could understand one of the words used in Tom Donnelly's column. The elevator operator couldn't. Donnelly was promptly fired. Roy has just fired my column out of Cincinnati after buying the Cincinnati *Times Star,* long owned by the Taft family. There is now no newspaper in Cincinnati except that which expresses the bigoted opinions of the son of the railroad conductor who married into the Scripps family, and has now become one of the most potent chain newspaper operators in the world.

September 3: Wrote a column on the Florida primary. I leaned over backward to try to make it appear impartial, though I don't think there is much grounds for impartiality. If I had not given it some such coloration, however, it would never have gotten into any newspapers in Florida. We did a lot of research on Holland's law firm and the record is pretty clear that the mediocre list of bills he has introduced in the Senate were partly for the benefit of his law clients. In at least two cases, there is a clear conflict of interest.

Dr. Anderson, head of the Florida doctors' lobby, has now issued a statement that I am a liar. I took the trouble to call him and quote his opinions about Pepper, but his opinions as they show up in cold print make him an ignoramus, which of course he is. So he retaliates with the usual name-calling.

Clayton Fritchey came to dinner; has just spent the weekend with Averell Harriman in Albany. He says that Harriman didn't have any alternative but to accept DiSapio's recommendation to take District Attorney Frank Hogan as Senator. Hogan had been endorsed by Republicans and Democrats, and has done an excellent job of keeping New York City clean; the fact that he was opposed by Harriman would have hurt Harriman's election with Catholic voters. So Averell yielded. In retrospect, maybe he was right.

However, the chances of Nelson Rockefeller becoming Governor of New York have increased somewhat. If he makes it, the speculation is that Nixon will fold and not run for President in 1960. In my opinion Nelson, though a nice guy, just doesn't have it. He doesn't know how to fight to kill, and in political battles you have to fight that way. He is a little too much like Eisenhower. He was most unhappy under Mrs. Oveta Culp Hobby, Secretary of Health, Education, and Welfare, when she took a stand against Negro nurses in Texas and refused to push the education bill. But where was Nelson at this time? Meekly sitting at a desk and later meekly resigning.

In my opinion, he will not be elected Governor, nor President.

Arthur Courshon, my radio sponsor, phoned from Miami that the Miami *News* has broken a big story on the Ku Klux Klan. Claude had called me about a week ago to say the Klan was endorsing Holland. I used it on the radio but not in the column because I figured it wouldn't get published. The *News* now features the fact that Bill Hendricks, head of the Knights of the White Camellia branch of the KKK, has publicly endorsed Senator Holland. Holland sputtered and fumed and tried to deny the endorsement. Whereupon Hendricks issued a statement that he had "helped to beat Pepper before and was going to beat him again." He described Holland as "an old man in his dotage who doesn't know what he wants but better than Pepper because he knows what to do with the Jews and the niggers." Hendricks said he was also for Holland because Holland was against the "Jewish Anti-Defamation League."

I talked to Jim Hardee of the Orlando *Sentinel*, who says that the *Sentinel* did not publish the Klan story yesterday, though he sent it to them. He doubts whether many papers in Florida will publish it. They are trying to protect Holland. The Klan is genuinely unpopular in Florida, and this may be the turning point in the campaign. Significantly, the Associated Press also did not carry the quote from Hendricks as to why he was endorsing Holland. The UP did. The AP, of course, is owned by the publishers and caters to the publishers.

I got on the long distance telephone to try to raise some more money for Claude. Finally located Karl Bickel in Canada. I think he may help. But Scott Lucas has taken a runout powder. I can't even get him on the telephone.

September 5:   Dined with George Baker with some young State Department people, not members of the white-spat brigade. Found them most refreshing and independent. Selma Freedman, recently stationed in Rome, now going to Harvard, was amazingly frank regarding the futility of John Foster Dulles. Jack Reinstein, Director of German Affairs and the assistant to Ambassador Murphy, was also quite frank. He remarked that in the days of Dean Acheson the career service got some support against McCarthy and McCarthyism. Now they don't. He belied the general opinion, however, that Dulles never consults his staff. I gather that staff conferences have now been resumed for some time and that Dulles does consult regularly. Reinstein said that the Chinese Reds had given no indication in various talks as to what they wanted and remained something of an enigma. They don't seem to want peace around Quemoy and Matsu.

Mrs. Lakeland, wife of Bill Lakeland who handles the Iraq and Jordanian desk, was alarmed over a recent CBS broadcast saying that the United States might be at war with Red China by next Tuesday. Those present seem to share her alarm, though they were rather vague as to what could be done about it. John Foster Dulles has just been up to Newport conferring with Eisenhower and I learned for the first time that Dulles was the actual high official spokesman who talked to the press after the Eisenhower visit. He had taken a statement with him to Eisenhower which Eisenhower released afterward. The public was given the impression that Eisenhower and Dulles had drafted it in advance. The statement appeared to put the United States firmly on record that it would go to war if Quemoy and Matsu were attacked, yet if you read the statement carefully, it didn't actually say this. In other words, neither we nor the Russians still quite know where the line is going to be drawn around the offshore islands.

We discussed the all-important but unsolved question as to how far Russia wanted to go. There was general agreement that Khrushchev was one of the smartest operators who had ever steered the Russian helm of state. Reinstein said that he had once examined a long interview between Khrushchev and a foreign newspaper man which took an hour and a half to read. He said he studied the interview carefully and that Khrushchev had never deviated from the Soviet line in one single instance. Either the interview had been carefully censored afterward or Khrushchev was extremely clever in answering what appeared to be a give-and-take newspaper interview.

Lakeland seems to think that my idea of a sacred city at Jerusalem guaranteed by the United Nations is impossible. He says the Jews won't buy it. My idea, of course, is to put the old city and Bethlehem under the U.N., not the new and modern parts of the city, which have been developed by Israel and which have less historic significance. Lakeland seems to think that Nasser will let Jordan remain unscathed, at least for a while. He thinks Nasser's smart enough to realize that the fall of King Hussein would mean war with Israel and Nasser isn't ready for war.

September 8:   Jack called early in the morning. Miss Paperman has come down from Boston to testify before a grand jury against the Carlton Hotel clerk and presumably against Jack and Baron Shacklette. It's the old theft-of-papers charge which Roger Robb made such a stew about. I know for a fact that Jack and Shacklette did not take any papers and I strongly suspect that the papers were left in Miss Paperman's closet as a decoy. Had the papers been of any importance they would have been locked up in Robb's safe. The hotel clerk meanwhile has been trying to blackmail Jack for money. Jack has discovered that he has a previous police record for housebreaking.

Went to the movies. Took Luvie and Drew to see *No Time for Sergeants*. During the movie I met Jack in the lobby. We couldn't trust telephones. He has a source inside the police department who reported that the hotel clerk's fingerprints were found all over Miss Paperman's documents. But there were no fingerprints of either Jack or Shacklette. It may well be that this boy either pilfered the papers himself or looked them over. While the fingerprint experts were examining the papers, the chief detective, Scott, rushed in and said, "We've got to get something on Pearson." I have been trying to rack my brain to what I may have done or written regarding Scott. Probably it's the old exposé I published on Joe Shimon and the wire-tapping he did for Pan American Airways, plus the incident where he found the Foreign Minister of Argentina in bed with the granddaughter of Senator White of Maine. At any rate, it appears that the White House has given orders that there's to be some kind of prosecution.

Something like this always happens when I try to take a vacation. I have gone back to writing the column. There are certain things I can write much more appropriately than Jack.

As we drove home from the movies the radio indicated a sweeping Democratic victory in Maine. Governor Muskie has defeated Senator Fred Payne. This ends an interesting chapter which began about six years ago with a drive in Rock Creek Park with Colonel Williamson, assistant to Fred Payne, then Governor of Maine. Williamson wanted $50,000 guarantee before Payne would run for the Senate against Brewster. I put Williamson in touch with Howard Hughes's representative and Payne got a pledge of most of the money. I'm not quite sure how much he actually got in the end, but Hughes came through with a sizable chunk and Brewster was defeated. Brewster was the Senator who masterminded the investigation of Howard Hughes when he chal-

lenged Pan American Airways. Brewster for years had been the kept
Senator of PAA. Campaign contributions counted heavily with
Brewster and he was the bagman for Republican Senators. Campaign
contributions also caused his defeat—this time from Hughes.

Today, however, wrote the end of Senator Payne. He was a less
than mediocre Senator, and deserved to lose—though he was better
than Brewster.

September 9:   Lunched at the Russian Embassy with Ambassador
Menshikov and a new secretary, named Youri Filippov, who is of Greek
origin. I was curious as to why the Russians should invite me to lunch
in the middle of my vacation, and after a two-hour luncheon I am still
curious. We started off with the usual routine of offering vodka. I chose
vodka, the Ambassador took sherry. The Russian maid, however, protected me. She did not automatically refill my vodka glass but asked me
whether I wanted it. Despite the urging of the Ambassador to refill my
glass, she did not do so. For this I was grateful. Maybe she is not a
Communist.

Early in our conversation, the Ambassador brought up the Far
East and asked me what I thought of it. I said that my position was
pretty well known since I had written various columns pointing out that
we occupied an untenable position, due in large part to the China
lobby. The Ambassador then asked what the China lobby was, and I
told him he should read my columns. He apologized profusely and
claimed that he did usually read the column. Filippov obviously had
read the column because he quoted from it frequently. I then gave him
something of an explanation of the China lobby, pointing out, however, that Senator Knowland of California, one of the most vigorous
leaders of the lobby, was not influenced by monetary reward. I mentioned that Chinatown in San Francisco was the chief influence on
Knowland regarding Chiang Kai-shek. The Ambassador did not know
what Chinatown was, but he remarked that he had just received an
invitation from George Christopher, the mayor of San Francisco, to
come there to speak. The Ambassador accepted automatically and then
learned that the State Department would not let him go because San
Francisco was off bounds. Finally, he got word from the State Department that he could go to San Francisco if Ambassador Thompson in
Moscow was given the right to go to any part of Russia at any time.
The Ambassador said he had not bothered to pass this along to his
government.

I tried to draw the Ambassador out regarding some of the others high up in the Soviet and mentioned the fact that I had watched Molotov operate in San Francisco, where he had seemed to be very anti-American and alienated the American people. Again the Ambassador somewhat agreed. He added that Molotov was nice personally, lived very simply. He said he had been in Molotov's apartment, and he was quite a contrast to the stern behavior he presented to the world at large.

I also said that the American people could not understand why Bulganin had been demoted; that they had the impression of Bulganin as a friendly, amiable nice old man who seemed able to get along with the United States. The Ambassador replied that Bulganin's health was bad and that he was not the nice old man that some people thought.

Toward the end of our luncheon, in fact as we were having coffee, the Ambassador came back to the Far East. It was obvious that he was very much concerned about the deadlock there. "What are we going to do about the Far East?" he asked. "If a few convoy ships and a few shots are fired, we would get into a war which nobody wants." He referred to the Khrushchev letter warning that an attack on China would be an attack on Russia. "Khrushchev meant what he said," the Ambassador emphasized.

I maintained that Eisenhower did not want war, but the Ambassador seemed to think this was hard to believe. He wanted to know why Dulles had so much power over Eisenhower. I didn't like to say that it was because we had a lazy President. I explained it was because Eisenhower likes to delegate responsibility.

The Ambassador wanted to know what motivated Dulles and added, "Is it the Rockefellers?"

I said that undoubtedly the Wall Street connections of Dulles's law firm had left a stamp on his whole makeup, but that in my opinion the Rockefellers had no great influence over him. I went on to say that I knew Nelson Rockefeller very well and that he would be inclined to be quite reasonable toward Russia, and he was a man who devoutly wanted peace. I told how Nelson had gone to the Geneva Conference in 1955 and had urged the Good Neighbor policy on Eisenhower. The Ambassador apparently had read the Rockefeller brothers report on the unfortunate lag in American defense and he had this report confused with the Gaither Report, which hints at preventive war.

I have a feeling that the Russians, certainly as represented by the Ambassador, were sincere in wanting to find the way out. I couldn't quite tell whether they were trying to use me. I have been debating whether I should call up some of the leading Democrats, such as Bill Fulbright and Lyndon Johnson, and urge that they put the brakes on Mr. Dulles. I am convinced, and have already written a column to that effect, that Eisenhower is worried sick over the possibility of war, but that Dulles is putting the heat on him in another brinksmanship operation which this time might come too close to the brink for safety.

Late tonight I heard John Sherman Cooper, Republican Senator from Kentucky, state publicly that the United States should persuade Chiang Kai-shek to withdraw from Quemoy and Matsu. Cooper is a Republican moderate and a very staunch Eisenhower man. His statement will probably have more effect on Ike than any statement by Fulbright or Mansfield, though not as much as one by Johnson.

It is difficult to tell whether the Chinese are bluffing in their announced plan to retake Quemoy and Matsu. But I have a hunch that they are not. They have made too many statements about the fact that they could lose three hundred million men and still have three hundred million left. And they have been left out of the world spotlight with Russia playing the big fiddle too long.

September 22:   Went to New York with Luvie—partly business, partly relaxation. Saw Morris Ernst. He has seen the accounts kept by Professor Galíndez which show without question that only about $2,-000 came from the Basques. The rest of his million and half dollars came from Central Intelligence, apparently to undercut or keep an eye on Franco. Frank Hogan has the books. Central Intelligence has sent for them. Wonder if they'll ever come back to Hogan.

Sherman Adams resigned tonight. He went on television and tried to duplicate Nixon's performance six years ago. He wasn't too impressive. Actually, I felt sorry for him. He was so much less guilty than either Nixon or Eisenhower. What people have forgotten is that Nixon was the first big conflict-of-interest case to put across all sorts of favors for those who contributed to him. But Madison Avenue and the free press hushed it up.

With Adams out and Stassen already eased out, Nixon now has a free hand. He is preened for 1960 except for the possibility that Nelson Rockefeller will become Governor of New York. Dave Karr thinks that is a real possibility. He sounds as if he would vote for Rockefeller, says that many liberal Democrats in Manhattan will do likewise. They are fed up with Carmine DiSapio and think that Harriman made a terrible blunder when he yielded to him on Frank Hogan for Senator. I was surprised at the pro-Rockefeller sentiment in New York. Luvie is delighted. She is lunching with Mary Rockefeller and even contributing to his campaign. I am sure he needs it.

September 23: Erna Grunewald called me around midnight last night. Her father is dying. She has been threatening to shoot [Attorney General] Bill Rogers, says that Bill is responsible for prosecuting her father. Her father got word that he would have to appear in court in New York on October 6. An hour or so after getting this news he suffered a stroke and has not recovered. I tried to calm her and get the idea of any incident with Bill Rogers out of her mind, but it was not easy.

I tried to call Bill Rogers during the day, finally reached him late in the afternoon. Erna had already called him and threatened to shoot him. Bill asked me to come in to see him when I got back to Washington. He wants to talk about the school problem in Arkansas and Virginia.

I dictated an ad over the telephone to the office to be inserted in the Star and Post to sell our beans. I suggested that anyone could come out from the city and pick them for $1 a bushel.

September 24: Back in Washington. Grunewald hasn't recovered from his stroke and probably can't last the day. Claude Pepper, for whom I went all out in Florida, didn't get one letter written to the Tallahassee *Democrat*. It has canceled the column. Kefauver's in town talking to his anti-monopoly committee staff. He is spiritless, isn't tackling the real issues, hasn't the personnel to tackle them, is more worried about his own reelection in Tennessee than the high cost of living. He's going back to shake hands with folks

Secretary Dulles says no retreat on Quemoy. Privately Ike is hellbent for retreat. If we get out of this mess without a severe loss of face, we'll be really lucky.

A few people showed up to pick beans at the farm. Melvin [the butler] is in charge.

September 25: Went to see Bill Rogers. He has moved into the big long Attorney General's office that reminds you of a bowling alley or a cathedral. The visit was pleasant but unproductive. I gave him a copy of George Washington's prayer in which he urged tolerance and obedience to the supreme laws of the land. I urged Bill to get Ike to do some public-opinion molding and some leading in the school integration crises, but I don't think I got anywhere.

The books finally arrived. We began working on the book last January and the printed copies came today—for release October 13. I wonder if they will sell. Some of the urgency of the sputnik crisis is now passed.

I called Paul Butler, chairman of the Democratic National Committee, and urged that they shift their attack from Sherman Adams to Nixon and Ike. I pointed out that Nixon had been the first conflict of interest case and that Eisenhower's gifts were far worse than any received by Adams and that he gave even bigger favors in return. Butler was interested, but inconclusive.

I couldn't sell this to Earle Clements either. Had dinner with him at Tyler and Bess's apartment. Took him several copies of the new book for possible use around the country.

September 26:   Flew up to Harrisburg, presumably to meet with Governor Leader on his Senate election campaign. Sat in his cabinet room at the old Harrisburg State Capitol built with such expense and such scandal during the Boise Penrose dictatorship of Pennsylvania. The portraits of some of the great leaders of the United States were lined around the wall, beginning with William Penn and ending with such inconspicuous gentlemen as Ed Martin, now Senator from Pennsylvania. There have been only three Democratic Governors of Pennsylvania since the Civil War—George Leader is one of them.

I met with his brother Henry and Debs Myers, former editor of *Newsweek*, whom I recommended to Leader as his assistant and public relations man. We went over some facts regarding Arthur McGonigle, the Republican candidate for Governor, who is touted as a great and clean businessman, and pretzel manufacturer. Actually, he did not come up the hard way but in a way about as crooked as some of his pretzels.

We decided not to join the Governor at Lancaster. It would make it look as if he had given me the information for the column I'm going to write on McGonigle.

Flew back to Washington in time to go to the farm for dinner. Ike did come across in the school crisis after all. He issued a fairly firm statement to a parent, urging compliance with the Supreme Court and law and order.

September 27:   The farm is being swamped with bean pickers. Melvin has been working until about 8:30 P.M. As we drove out last night
cars were still in the field and people were picking beans by the cars'
headlights. I suppose the field will be pretty well ruined. At least we'll
be able to pay for the ads.

Henry Grunewald died on Thursday. Erna has calmed down. She
vows vengeance against Rogers but is not in the shooting frame of
mind.

The bean picking is still going strong. Jim Reynolds and the
Cuneos came out for late Sunday supper. Jim used to be on the
National Labor Relations Board and is now vice president of American
Locomotive. He talked to NLRB officials yesterday, who told him that
Sherman Adams habitually bombarded the NLRB to demand favora-
ble treatment for Republican manufacturers with labor troubles.

American Locomotive executives will not tangle with General
Motors over the antitrust laws. GM has used unscrupulous cutthroat
methods to monopolize the locomotive market. When American
Locomotive sold thirty diesels to the MK & T railroad, General Motors
came along and said "Look here, we do $14 million worth of business
with you in shipping cars, etc. If you don't buy diesels from us that
freight will be shifted over to the Missouri Pacific." However, the
old-school-tie spirit is too strong between big business moguls. The
American Locomotive people won't go to the Justice Department with
a complaint against GM. Neither will Fairbanks Morse. Fairbanks
Morse is about to be put out of the locomotive business because it
won't tangle with GM.

Caught the midnight sleeper to New York after writing a column
on Senator Theodore Francis Green. I had called him on the telephone
in Providence yesterday and interviewed him for thirty minutes over
the telephone on Presidents he had known. He was quite lucid. His
memory was excellent. If I can do that well at ninety-one, it will be
something.

September 29:   Autographed books in New York. Other book editors
than Simon and Schuster read the book and seem to think it's terrific.
They're putting through another printing of 10,000 copies.

Learned from Washington that Paul plowed up the bean field
with people still in it picking the beans. They were sore as blazes and
naturally wanted their money back.

Autographed books until almost four-thirty when I saw Spruille

Braden, head of the New York Crime Commission. I had known him when he was first made Ambassador to Colombia, later Ambassador to Chile and Argentina and chief of the Latin American division of the State Department. Charlie Taussig, original Roosevelt brain-truster, brought him into the government. Braden told me that the New York Crime Commission was dead. New York businessmen refused to support it after he began going after Republicans. Tom Dewey complained bitterly when they began probing the former Republican Lieutenant Governor of the state; and Standard Oil of New Jersey didn't like it when they found that one of its subsidiaries was paying $17,000 annually to city inspectors to O.K. their installations. Colt Sloan of the Bankers Trust, who was chairman of the money-raising committee, folded up after this. It was the New York Crime Commission which dug up most of the information on Hoffa and turned it over to the Senate rackets committee, where it has just proved a sensation.

Talked to Sam Rosenman, the old Roosevelt brain-truster, who is masterminding Frank Hogan's campaign for the Senate. He says that Hogan is a real New Dealer, not the reactionary he's pictured.

Saw Bill Benton, the ex-Senator from Connecticut, and gave him a copy of the book. He is his usual bubbling self. He tried to buy the New Haven *Register* and also the Hartford *Courant.* He wouldn't run for the House of Representatives as Chet Bowles wants later to become Secretary of State and thinks the House Foreign Relations Committee would be a good buildup.

September 30:   Got back to Washington to learn that Jack has been subpoenaed to go before a grand jury in the Carlton Hotel case. Shacklette is on the West Coast, and therefore hasn't been subpoenaed.

Arthur McGonigle issued a statement to the Republican State Committee in Pennsylvania threatening a suit against me for libel on the column to be published tomorrow. It will be interesting to see whether any newspapers publish it. Two telephoned me today—the Monesson and York papers—a bit worried about libel but they are publishing it.

Dulles reversed himself on Quemoy and Matsu. In his press conference he made public what he has already tried to put across in Warsaw, namely, the willingness to retreat from Quemoy or rather to get Chiang to retreat, in return for a cease-fire. There will be loud noises and protests from Chiang Kai-shek.

The interesting factor in the case is that Nixon had already gone out on a limb and raised Cain about the publication of the fact that the State Department mail was 80 percent against staying in Quemoy. Walter Lippmann now says that Nixon has reverted to type. The old Nixon is back again. Some of the statements he is making in California certainly look like it. But now Dulles has more or less pulled the rug out from under Nixon. Dulles, of course, always reacts to bad political pressure, and Meade Alcorn [RNC Chairman] has been to the White House warning that Quemoy and Matsu could make the November election a landslide for the Democrats.

October 1: Eisenhower in his press conference today supported Dulles regarding a cease-fire and withdrawal from Quemoy. In other words, Ike—who unleashed Chiang Kai-shek in February, 1953, as one of the first official acts of his new administration—has now leashed him again. Chiang, however, is objecting strenuously.

October 2: Admiral Jake Vardaman came in for lunch. He's retiring shortly as Governor of the Federal Reserve Board. He let his hair down on a lot of things, one being big-banker control of the Federal Reserve Board and the fiscal system. All they are interested in, he says, is higher interest rates.

He also talked freely about Ike and Mamie. Ike, he says, is irritated, crusty, and bawling Mamie out more than ever. He even blames Mamie for his running again. I had always heard it was the other way around, that Mamie didn't want him to run, but Vardaman claims that Mamie remarked, "How could I possibly live with him if he wasn't busy in the White House?" Mamie is now the inseparable companion of Mary Allen, wife of George Allen, who, like Vardaman, comes from Mississippi. Vardaman says that Mary and George never make an engagement because they are on call from the White House to play bridge or spend a weekend.

Vardaman claims that Mamie's drinking is due to a leaky heart valve and actually she doesn't overindulge. She simply can't hold her liquor. George Baker has other ideas. During the war he used to see her at the United Nations club sitting alone, noticed, [sic] drinking heavily. Twice he had to boost her into a taxi.

Vardaman told me the origin of the deep-freeze scandal in the White House. He says that as a Navy man he was entrusted with providing the White House with food and had found that the White House was using eighteen pounds of bacon daily, though only the three Trumans, with two servants, were supposed to be fed by the Navy. He put a stop to this. The whole staff had been living off the Navy. In fact, the Navy payroll was covering about three-quarters of the White House staff. When he reported this to Truman it was agreed that George Allen, as a hotel man, should come in and reorganize the White House setup. George had purchased the Wardman Park Hotel for peanuts during the depression and was running it. So George took a small office in the White House and reorganized the setup.

When Truman was about to go to the Potsdam Conference, Mrs. Truman wanted to go back to Independence. She hated the White House. The Navy then had the problem of supplying her with rations and found it would be necessary to send a truck up every day from Fort Riley. They asked if Mrs. Truman had a freezer. Mrs. Truman didn't.

However, Harry Hoffman of Milwaukee, overhearing the conversation, said, "Hell, one of my clients has a lot of those freezers. He'll be glad to send one to the President's home." After looking into it further, Harry Vaughan reported, "Your troubles are over." Stupidly, Vaughan told Hoffman to put all his freezers into a truck and he would distribute them. He gave freezers to Secretary of the Treasury Fred Vinson, John Snyder, two to the Trumans, one to Vaughan, and one to Vardaman. Vardaman said that he never kept his because his apartment on Nineteenth Street was too small. He sent it out to Camp David, got it back only after he moved into a new house.

Vardaman's retirement means the exit of the last Trumanite from Washington. Every other one has been cleaned out by this administration. This marks the end of the chapter of the Missouri cronies. Truman was intensely loyal to his friends. He stood by them through thick and thin, and, in retrospect, a lot of them weren't nearly as bad as I said they were at the time. I remember castigating Admiral Vardaman for borrowing some enlisted men from the Navy to paint his house. He has never forgotten it but is quite gentle when he mentions it. He mentioned it today indirectly, pointing out that he was a combat officer during the war and not a desk admiral as I had insinuated. Actually, he has a fine record—two years as artilleryman in World War I and four years with the Navy, seldom outside of enemy attack in World War II.

October 3: Jack had a long session before the grand jury. They found one of his fingerprints on the documents which Miss Paperman claims were stolen. Jack seemed to have done pretty well in his testimony. Afterward, the district attorney admitted that this was a sort of political case but assured him that there would be no political indictment. Shacklette came back from California, despite warnings, and ran right into a process server. He was subpoenaed and testified yesterday afternoon.

October 29: Wrote story that Rockefeller would win. It's for publication Saturday just before the election. The Harriman camp still insists that their polls show Averell will win but I detect lessening confidence.

October 30: Finished the radio program and left for California at 10:50 P.M. Had to go to dinner given by Colonel Bob Jones at the Anderson House in honor of Marjorie Post Davies May and her new husband, Herbert. Did my best to get out of it but the Colonel insisted it would upset his seating. Marjorie is about seventy-five years old and this is her fourth husband. Joe has been dead less than a year. Herb May looks tired and old. He danced around Peggy Palmer when she had influence, now he's dancing around Marjorie, who has money. It will be interesting to see how long this marriage will last.

General Twining was at the dinner. He was about to leave to Turkey for a meeting of the Baghdad Pact countries. "There's not much left of the Baghdad Pact," the Chairman of the Joint Chiefs confessed.

October 31: I called Billy Graham in North Carolina who agreed to become chairman of the new committee on Americans Against Bigotry. Twenty minutes later he called me back and said "No." Some of his Baptist advisers were against it because it was raising money for Clinton High School.* However, he has agreed to serve on the committee. I also called Governor Hodges in Raleigh, who also agreed to serve. This was a welcome surprise because the other two Governors—Collins of Florida and Coleman of Mississippi—have been getting more aloof. Tom Robinson of the Charlotte *News* and Jim Knight of the Miami

---

*The high school at Clinton, Tennessee, had been dynamited by segregationists, and Pearson had started a fund-raising drive to have it repaired.—ED.

Herald also seemed willing. Bill Graham suggested that we get hold of them. He also suggested that Governor Frank Clement of Tennessee be persuaded to serve on the committee. I had already asked him and he had turned me down when I was in Nashville. I finally got him at the Governor's Mansion on the telephone today. He was helpful but still said no, on the ground that he couldn't be on a committee that was begging money for a Tennessee school. He was going to put an appropriation through the Legislature if the drive failed.

I telephoned Bob Woodruff, head of Coca-Cola in Atlanta, and asked him whether Coca-Cola would help the campaign of "Give up a Coke, buy a brick." He was cordial and he said he was complimented that a Coke should be singled out as the paramount drink of the U.S.A. However, he said his bottlers would probably object if he started a nationwide campaign along this line. He is calling me back.

The representatives of Simon and Schuster in Los Angeles have me scheduled to autograph books at a Communist bookshop just off the University of California campus tomorrow. It's run by a man named Klonsky who was convicted in Philadelphia under the Smith Act for being a Communist, but later was released under a Court of Appeals ruling. A local newspaper in Westwood has raised Cain about Klonsky and the fact that I am autographing books in his store. I talked to Klonsky. He is a rather pathetic type and looks the part of a Communist. I suspect he has left the party only recently. His record is obviously pretty bad. The book autographing party has stirred up quite a lot of discussion and the telephone has been ringing with messages and advice from all sorts of people, both pro and con my autographing books. Klonsky says he has taken out ads with the O.K. of the publisher and he wants to go through with it. Thurman Arnold is emphatic to the contrary. "You will sign books only over my dead body," he reiterated. I don't like to back down, but perhaps that is the wisest thing to do.

November 1:   Got up early in the morning to wrestle with the book autographing deal. I finally decided to go ahead with it. I wrote a statement to be given to the press that if this "so-called Communist bookshop wanted to promote a bristling anti-Communist book," I was going to sign books just the same. I said that I would autograph books "in the Kremlin if they would let me." I read the statement to Ed Murray of the Los Angeles *Mirror* who wanted me not to give it out to other newspapers unless I was asked for it. Since he is primarily concerned in Los Angeles I followed his advice.

The whole incident, however, proved to be a tempest in a teapot and rather unflattering to my vanity. Very few people came in to have the books autographed. I sat in lone splendor in the store while a few people eyed me from the sidewalk and a few people came in to chat. Very few bought books. One gentleman who came in was a rather seedy-looking man of about sixty or sixty-five who asked me point-blank "Do you remember me?" This is a question I hate more than anything under the sun. But I replied, "Isn't your name Collins?" I got his first name wrong, confusing him with his brother Ben. But it was Artie Collins who used to wrestle with Leon, Randolph Ashton, Coates Coleman, and me when we operated the Crum Creek Club at Swarthmore back in the good old days when nobody worried about foreign aid or Russia or bombings of schools and synagogues.

Bill Neel called to say that the American Jewish Congress had gone ahead with a committee to help rebuild the Clinton schoolhouse. Governor Lehman, Mrs. Roosevelt, Nelson Rockefeller, and Averell Harriman are advertised in a letter sent to General Sarnoff as being on the committee. I had previously urged the American Jewish Congress not to get people identified with integration too strongly on the committee. In fact I urged them to keep out of the picture publicly and work from behind the scenes.

I called Julius Edelstein, Assistant to Senator Lehman, who says that the American Jewish Congress are publicity hounds and beyond control. Lehman, he said, would not join the committee, however.

November 2:   I talked to Jimmie Roosevelt, who will urge his mother not to join the other committee.

Mrs. Knowland is going haywire in support of her husband's campaign for Governor. It is rather pathetic—Mrs. Knowland's desperate anxiety to take her husband away from Washington. When there's another woman in the case, the wife will do anything. She has teamed up with some weird rabble-rousing operators, including Joe Kamp, and has lost votes for her husband.

There's quite an anti-Catholic campaign going on in California but I don't believe it's going to hurt Pat Brown, a Catholic. There's also quite an anti-Semitic campaign going on, but again I don't believe it's going to change votes. It may do the opposite.

November 3: Got Charlie Taft on the telephone in Cincinnati, after trying all weekend. He declined to be chairman of the committee but agreed to be vice chairman. This still leaves me without a chairman. Meanwhile, valuable time is passing.

November 4: My plane was supposed to take off at 9:50. It was canceled. I got an American Airlines plane instead which was supposed to leave at 11:15 but which took off about 2:30 A.M. By the time my plane had left it was quite evident that California was going strong for Pat Brown, Clair Engle, and all of the Democratic ticket. It was also evident that the nation generally was going strongly Democratic. All of my predictions seemed to be fulfilled except in Arizona where Barry Goldwater is winning the Senate race and in Pennsylvania where it looks as if George Leader is losing for the Senate.

December 19: Finally managed to write three columns; drove to Baltimore by midnight. The Harlem Globetrotters had finished their game and were already aboard the Air Force plane. We left about one. It was an executive type of plane with too many tables and not enough seats—held only thirty people.

December 20: The Hawaiian basketball team played poker all night in the seats immediately across the aisle from me. I have decided that I am not in favor of statehood for Hawaii.

December 21: We were due at Anchorage last night but finally arrived at 10 A.M. Put on a show at Fort Richardson and at Elmendorf Air Base. I dined with General Necrasin, who is commander of the 10th Air Squadron, and his wife. I am impressed with the type of officer now commanding the Air Force. They are in vivid contrast with the old line officer in the Army and Navy prior to World War II who was just sitting around waiting for promotion.

December 22: We left Kodiak at about four o'clock, arriving in Fairbanks an hour later, where all hell was breaking loose.

Someone in the radio station in Anchorage had sneaked out a garbled version of my radio program and put it on the AP wire. It was on the front page of the Fairbanks *News-Miner*, the paper that I have been suing for libel. It headlined: "Drew Pearson Says Alaska Is Valueless." A prediction I had made which began "Is Alaska Valueless?" had been removed from context and the "is" omitted. I had said that Alaska was more valuable than New York or California. I had to go on a TV program to try to straighten out the mess. My lawyer, Warren Taylor, was much concerned for fear the news account would prejudice a jury —and he was right.

December 23:   I left the Globetrotters to fly north to Unalakleet, an Eskimo village on the Bering Sea. I hated to leave. Ordinarily, I'd have stuck with the entertaining troupe but the Globetrotters were anxious to get home by Christmas and were planning to leave this afternoon.

December 24:   We photographed Eskimos fishing through holes in the ice together with a dog team. It was tough work. We had to run a power line out from the post office with another line from a battery we had borrowed from the Air Force to run our sound-recorder. We wasted an unforgivable amount of time in frittering around.

It was Christmas Eve at the radar station. The men had festooned the mess hall, the NCO Club, and the Officers' quarters with ribbons and evergreens. It was not exactly a jolly Christmas, but it was not a sad one. We worked overtime after dinner to shoot some of the men. I was exhausted from standing on the ice all day and went to bed early.

December 25:   Christmas Day I got up at six but found there was no breakfast until seven-thirty. This was the first sign that it was Christmas. The mess sergeant was slightly oiled and kept telling me what I should write in the column about getting him back to Lowery Field in Colorado. We spent the morning taking some additional shots on the ice.

After we landed I tried to take the crew out to a Christmas dinner but found that all the restaurants were closed. We finally found a Chinese restaurant open. I ate Chinese food. All the others ate steaks. I called on my lawyer Buell Nesbitt, whom I had asked to straighten out the mess regarding the distorted AP dispatch. He had attended a conference at the radio station—together with the opposition publisher Robert Atwood and my publisher Norman Brown, and various others —where they played the tape and chose up sides as to whether Pearson had said Alaska was valueless. I gathered it was quite a hostile group.

December 26: I left at a little after one o'clock on a Northwest Airlines plane to Seattle. The Associated Press manager met me in Seattle to discuss a retraction. He seemed reasonably sympathetic.

December 27: George came in for dinner with all of us. Ellen went out after dinner but George stayed and talked for some time. He and Ellen seem to be getting along fairly well, though separated. They are still talking about a divorce sometime next spring or summer.

December 28: Joe De Silva and George Arnold went on television at noon to explain the pending strike of food stores which probably will be called by the Retail Clerks January 1. The clerks are asking for the equivalent of a 79-cent-an-hour wage increase over a five-year period and the most interesting thing they are asking is psychiatric care. It seemed to me this was rather a poor move from a strategic point of view. Everybody is cracking about the half-cracked clerks. The interesting fact, however, is that the clerks are not going to strike Safeway, which is the biggest store of all. They are going to strike the smaller stores. In other words, the rich get richer and the poor have a harder time. Being five days in Alaska is almost like being five days in jail, as far as news is concerned. I haven't had the ghost of an idea as to what has been happening in the world. We could almost have been at war. Nobody worries much about it in Alaska, and apparently nobody worries very much here in Los Angeles either. I have never seen the American public so generally apathetic about what is going on.

I told about the Clinton schoolhouse and how we were raising the money to rebuild it. The children wanted to know why anyone had blown it up. This made quite an impression on Joe. He has kept asking me whether some bad men are going to come and blow up his house. I lay down with Joe to try to induce him to take a nap but I'm afraid my presence was not too conducive. He remarked: "Pazzy, you don't have enough hair." Again, "Couldn't you let me have more pillow?"

December 29: Lunched with Bart Lytton, owner of a large Los Angeles savings and loan association and the new half-time sponsor for radio. He has been able to make about $40 million in the last ten years. George says the secret of it is easy, that bankers don't pay taxes any more than do oil men. They are permitted 12 percent reserves and all they have to do is siphon their profits into reserves without paying taxes on them. At lunch two supporters of Pat Brown joined us—one being Nat Dumont, head of the Dumont Aviation Company, who says he put up $55,000 for Brown in advance. They are all getting ready for the big inaugural next week when their man becomes Governor of California. It will be interesting to see whether Pat is able to withstand the charms and wiles of his supporters. He has been telling me that he intends to be himself with no obligations to anyone. His backers at lunch have in mind the idea that he will run for Vice President in 1960. They point out, probably with some justice, that Jack Kennedy will run and not make the nomination for President. Then such remorse mingled with Catholic bitterness will set in that it will be necessary to nominate a Catholic for Vice President.

Ellen has been quite nervous with the children. I took them shopping today and I can understand why she gets nervous. Yesterday we went horseback riding. Joe rode in front of me on the saddle and complained toward the end rather plaintively that he was getting squashed. I don't blame him. He then rode behind me and did very well, though the horse bucked a bit. The other two children rode perfectly.

1959

January 3: Dined with Ernest Gruening, the new Senator from Alaska. He is bubbling over with pride and joy—understandably so. He wasn't given a chance to win, but at the age of seventy-one he defeated a thirty-six-year-old ex-Governor. I made a little speech at the dinner recalling how when we first started the column Gruening was the first editor to buy it for the Portland (Maine) *Express*. And later, when he was looking for a job, I helped to get him appointed as chief of the Territories and Insular Affairs Division under Ickes, from which he moved up to be Governor of Alaska. The secret was that he and Ickes used to row constantly and in order to get him out of Washington, Ickes kicked him upstairs to Alaska. This was one of the real reasons for statehood. Gruening has been such an effective lobbyist and in some cases such a bore in buttonholing people for statehood that he finally won out. He deserves to be Senator. However, as I visited Alaska I can understand the reluctance of President Eisenhower and some others to be enthusiastic about statehood.

At the dinner Senator Church of Idaho told a rather revealing story about the occasion when he took the oath as Senator two years ago. As he walked down the aisle, Lyndon Johnson reached out a long arm and said, "We are glad to have you here. We're interested in Rule 22. You'll find a lot of problems where both Idaho and the South will agree." By this time they were blocking traffic but it was obvious that Lyndon wanted support to prevent any change of Rule 22 in continuing the right to filibuster. Church, however, ignored his advice and voted to change the rule and modify filibusters.

"After that," said the young Senator, "I found I was out in the cold. The older Senators were polite but aloof. I didn't get anything.

They just ignored me. Paul Douglas called me the other day asking how I stood on Rule 22 this year. I had to tell him that I wasn't going to go along."

Church didn't mention it, but about a year later he made his peace with Lyndon by proposing trial by jury in the civil rights bill. This is what the South wanted, what the civil rights people didn't want. Shortly thereafter Church was given a very choice assignment to go to Argentina, expenses paid by the government. He was not a member of the Senate Foreign Relations Committee, but Lyndon Johnson was paying off a debt.

January 5: Went to see [Senator] Clinton Anderson of New Mexico regarding a job for Tyler. Anderson is head of a committee to investigate atomic energy. When I mentioned it and the fact that he is going to have $200,000 to spend on the investigation, he replied, "Where did you hear that? There are only four people who know about it and now there are five. Lyndon Johnson has been waving that $200,000 in front of me to get me to give up on the fight to amend the rule on filibusters."

Clint explained that Bob McKinney, my "old friend" from Santa Fe, who had aspired to be an atomic diplomat under Admiral Strauss, had now got bored with Strauss and resigned. So McKinney now wants to investigate Strauss and atomic energy. On the committee will be McKinney and also George Brown, the chief benefactor of Lyndon Johnson, whom Lyndon protected on a scandalous income tax fraud charge back under Roosevelt. I exposed it some years ago, at which time they threatened to sue me. The suit has not been filed and never will be. Brown was too guilty. He continues to get all sorts of concessions from the Eisenhower administration—such as building air bases in Spain—thanks to Lyndon and Sam Rayburn. He is now one of the seventy-six wealthiest men in America. So Lyndon is now going to put him on the atomic energy panel to investigate the peacetime uses of the greatest new source of power. Brown operates a pipeline from Texas. Naturally, he's interested in any type of power that would compete with natural gas.

Clint remarked that he was just sick at having to oppose Lyndon regarding the filibusters. "I have urged Lyndon to agree to continue all the rules except Rule 22 on filibusters. But he's a prisoner of Dick Russell. Dick Russell just won't let him." I asked why, and Clint replied that Russell had got Lyndon his job as Senate Democratic leader when some other people were opposed, and Lyndon couldn't operate on most things without consulting Russell.

"I hate to see Lyndon hurt himself because I consider him my best candidate as President," Clint said. I remarked that Lyndon's health couldn't stand up under the Presidential strain, whereupon Clint went into quite a long story about Lyndon's heart attack. Interestingly, it was the same story he told me about six months after the heart attack. But at that time, Clint was sore at Lyndon and emphasized the fact that Lyndon had had a very serious attack. He said that they just barely got him back to the Naval Hospital in time and that he had been lucky to get there. Now that Clint is rooting for Lyndon for President, he has changed all the emphasis of the story. Here's what he told me today:

"Henrietta and I were driving down to George Brown's at Warrenton and when we got there Mrs. Brown and her daughter met us with some bathing suits on that looked like bikinis. Henrietta and I were asked to go swimming, but Henrietta doesn't like those kind of suits or people wearing them, and turned up her nose. I went in to the downstairs living room where I found Lyndon on a couch. He said he had been driving down and got sick on the way. He stopped at a filling station to stick a couple of fingers down his throat, but couldn't do it. He was still sick, he said, with a bad case of indigestion. I asked him where the pain was and found it was around his neck and shoulders. I told him, 'You've got an arterial occlusion. You haven't got thrombosis.' He was taking bromos but I told him he would have to cut them out and get a doctor. Lyndon pooh-poohed the idea but I finally told George Brown, 'How would you like to have the majority leader of the Senate die in your house—without a doctor. You'd better get a doctor here on the double.'

"So George sent for a doctor who diagnosed Lyndon exactly as I did. They started to send him back in a car but Lyndon couldn't get into the car and finally they summoned an ambulance. However," said Clint, "when they got him back to Bethesda they found that it wasn't anything serious and all he needed was a rest. If you catch those things early the heart heals up and there's no more danger. There's no question in my opinion but that Lyndon could easily stand the strain of the Presidency."

On the other occasion that Anderson told me the story, he emphasized the very dangerous condition in which Lyndon arrived at the hospital and the fact that he was given all of one floor and lorded it around with the nurses and orderlies for some time.

January 6: Joe Martin was kicked out as Republican leader. I had a tip that it was coming but Tom McNamara insisted that I was wrong, so I got scooped on the story. The trouble was that Tom went to see Joe himself, and Joe didn't know about the revolt against him. Martin took it very badly. He almost broke down and wept. He said that the Dewey gang had demanded that some of his old friends vote against him, or otherwise they would never be nominated again. There may have been some truth in this. Congressman John Taber of New York, conservative who sides with Martin, strangely voted to oust him. By and large, however, it was a demand for younger leadership.

Charlie Halleck, who is replacing him, has one of the worst records on Capitol Hill as a friend of big business and for being on the make. I dubbed him "2-Cadillac Charlie" after the war when, strangely, he turned up with two Cadillacs. Cadillacs, in fact any cars at all, were very hard to come by at that time. Halleck came to Washington a young lawyer from a farm district who had hardly a cent. Now he's a wealthy man. I have always been convinced that if anyone did a real check on him, they could send him to the pen. However, he rates very high with Eisenhower, and it was the White House which in large part pulled wires to elevate him to the leadership.

January 7: Congress opened. The Republican liberals lost their battle. Dirksen of Illinois was made their leader. Things are boiling up for a showdown on the filibuster. I published a column today listing the new Senators according to which would wear the LBJ brand and which would not follow the dictate of Lyndon B. Johnson. He isn't going to like the column at all. Neither will some of the new Senators, particularly McGee of Wyoming whom I helped elect. He is a college professor who still has his head up in the clouds.

January 8: Had a cocktail party for some of the new Senators and Congressmen—particularly Senator Philip Hart of Michigan, who looks like a good guy. Governor Williams of Michigan joined the party. In my opinion, he's the ablest Democratic candidate for President, but he will never get it because he has taken too strong a stand on civil rights.

There's something very refreshing about the first-term members of the Senate or the House. They are naive, unspoiled, and act themselves. And they get invited out to dinner too much, are lionized, have to make both ends meet, have to barter for position, or they get ambitious. The result is they lose their freshness and native charm. Nothing can spoil a Senator quicker than Washington. In a few months they take themselves too seriously.

January 9: Went to see Harry Truman at the Mayflower. Gave him a copy of the book. "I read the review of the book in *The New York Times*," he said, "and I was hoping you'd give me a copy." I told him: "There are a lot of things I've written that you didn't approve of, but I think you'll approve of almost every word in that book."

Harry was receiving all sorts of visitors, though most of them were former members of his staff.

"I almost kicked Sherman Adams out of the White House by the seat of his pants," Truman told me. "He was ordering my folks around. 'I let you in here by sufferance,' I told Adams, 'in order to bring about an orderly turnover in government. If you're not going to handle yourself accordingly, I'm going to take you by the seat of the pants and chuck you out.'"

I had told Truman that we pointed out in the book that he had turned over the country to Eisenhower in the strongest position it had ever been. "Yes," he replied, "and in the most orderly turnover."

He talked at some length about the manner in which the White House had increased expenses since he left. He also told how King Saud had given him a dagger with some very expensive pearls and diamonds on the hilt. "We had them appraised and I think they came to about $60,000. Of course, all of those gifts to me as President are now in the Museum, and are the property of the American people.

"I told Bess, however, that if she would trip up Senator Bricker when he came over that shiny White House floor, I'd give her a pearl out of that dagger. One day at a diplomatic reception, along comes Bricker and I told here, 'Here comes Bricker, here's your chance to get a jewel.'

"The madam replied, 'We're in the White House.'" But, continued Harry, "Margaret poked her head out from behind a curtain and said 'Daddy, I'll trip him.'"

As I left, Truman said that he had been out the night before playing poker with some fellows who always took money away from him in the past and last night they did it again. I learned afterward that when I published the first story about him playing poker when he was in the White House, they tried to hush the whole thing up by shifting the poker games around. But today he was quite frank about it.

Harry Vaughan was present and was almost cordial. How times have changed.

January 10:   The liberal Senators lost their fight yesterday to modify the Senate rules at the opening of each session. The margin was very strong on Lyndon's side—surprisingly so. I can't worry too much about changing the filibuster but it does seem to me that the Senate has a right to change its rules at each session by a majority vote. Yet Gruening lined up with Johnson, though he had just given a pledge to the NAACP the other day. Cannon, the new Senator from Nevada who cosponsored the bill, voted to table his own bill.

In other words, Lyndon won the boys right around to his side, though he didn't do too much to elect them. It was Mrs. Roosevelt who raised the money for McGee in Wyoming, and yet he voted against Mrs. Roosevelt.

I was just turning over in my mind some ideas about a story regarding Lyndon's omnipotence and ability to throttle debate when he telephoned me. Luvie was amused. He said in brief: "We've got to do a lot of planning for the coming session. And you've got to help me. We used to have Tom Corcoran and Ben Cohen charting policy back in Roosevelt's day but we've got to do some of our own now. I want to do something about schools. And we've got to have a commission or some expert advisers tell us what is needed. I also want to do something about the old people. Homer Thornberry of Texas, one of my favorite Congressmen, was supporting his mother last year and had to mortgage his house in order to take care of her. We've got to build some old people's homes or else help them somehow. I want to talk to you about foreign affairs. You had some good ideas before. If Ike isn't going to lead, we've got to take the lead. Wayne Morse is working on Latin America. We've got a whole area where we are falling down. I got hold of the people who were arranging that dinner for Mikoyan and insisted that they have some real leaders down there. They invited Sam and Sam went. I got them to invite Mike Mansfield, though Mike wouldn't go. I went down myself. And I wanted Mikoyan to realize that we were willing to sit down with him and talk.

"I want to put a public housing bill on the President's desk by February 1," Johnson continued. "It's hard for the Congress to take the leadership in these things, but if nobody is going to lead in the executive branch, we've got to do it. Did you see what Ike said in his State of the Union message about a TNEC? He popped the idea that I had been talking about. However, we are going ahead with it just the same. I've been talking to Estes Kefauver about an investigation of inflation. He and I aren't going to quarrel over it, but we're going to have an investigation. I want Hennings to take up another investigation of juvenile delinquency. I don't know whether he'll do it or not, but it's got to be done somehow."

Lyndon talked like a machine gun, and kept telling me he wanted me to come up and give him some ideas. Obviously, he was soft-soaping me a bit because I had lined up the freshman Congressmen as being subjected to the LBJ brand. However, you have to admit that the guy has real ideas, and real executive ability.

Talked to Senator [Eugene] McCarthy of Minnesota. He remarked: "There were seven of us who voted against Lyndon on filibusters. It will be interesting to see what happens to the new Senators who voted with him. They are supposed to get the good committee assignments, but he can't put all seven of us on the District of Columbia Committee."

January 13: Went to Cleveland by train. Took along a lot of work, but went to sleep instead. Saw Cyrus Eaton. It was just a few years ago that I was exposing Eaton for welshing on the Kaiser stock flotation, which he had agreed to sell but backed out of at the last minute. I am wondering now which was worse—Kaiser or Eaton. There isn't much honor between any of these big business moguls. At any rate, I had a very interesting hour's talk with Eaton about Mikoyan and also about the former Secretary of the Treasury George Humphrey.

Eaton thinks that Humphrey still controls the Treasury Department; that he picked Bob Anderson to succeed him, having become acquainted with Anderson through Anderson's firm in Canada "Ventures, Limited." He also points to Scribner, now Under Secretary, whom Humphrey appointed and Chapman, who is the Treasury coun-

sel and represents Humphrey's firm in Cleveland. Eaton also points to
the fact that Strauss is now Secretary of Commerce and that Humphrey had picked him first for Atomic Energy, now for Commerce.
Kuhn, Loeb and Company used to float the bonds of Humphrey's
company and this was how he and Strauss became acquainted.

January 14:   Brucan, the Rumanian Minister and his aide Zleneac
came to lunch. The Israeli Ambassador told me the other day that
Brucan is Jewish. Rumania has just started permitting Jews to leave the
country for some mysterious reason which the Israeli government
doesn't understand. I pointed out to Brucan that peace is matter of
mutual trust and that a large number of people in this country don't
trust Russia, while Russia in return doesn't trust us. Yet, the great mass
of the American people want peace and so do the great mass of the
Russian people. I asked him how we could break down this suspicion.
He replied that we could do so by getting an agreement on something
and then working to expand it into broader fields. I asked him what
he thought would be a good start and he replied, "The treaty to
suspend atomic bombing tests." He added we are very near to an
agreement, but "there are some people in your country who do not
want an agreement." I was handicapped by the fact that I had not
followed these negotiations very closely. Later, however, I found that
he was right—we have been very close to an agreement and some of
our atomic experts, plus some members of the Congressional Atomic
Committee appear to be hanging back, particularly regarding underground tests.

January 16:   We tried some preliminary motions to dismiss the
Malaxa case before Judge McLaughlin. He is the judge who gave us
such a rough time in the Littell case. We lost our motion. I will now
have to do hours and hours of work and spend several thousand dollars
preparing to go to trial to defend myself against a man who was the
partner of Hermann Goering's brother and who later teamed up with
the Communists. Now, thanks to the intervention of Nixon and Bill
Rogers, he is permitted to take up permanent residence in the United
States with the help of American courts.

February 6:   Senator Bridges, as per my request, delivered a very nice
critical speech regarding the book on the Senate floor. He pointed out

that it was most unfair to Eisenhower to report as we did that he did not paint his own portraits of Lincoln but had them done by a commercial artist. No one who listened to him would ever have dreamed I had asked him to make the speech.

February 7: Eisenhower is still playing golf and doing some quail shooting in Georgia—believe it or not, with the Secretary of the Treasury, who publicly excoriated him regarding his big budget last year. This year Ike is really trying to balance the budget—so much so that he's probably going to throw the economy out of kilter. Yesterday, however, the Treasury was unable to re-fund about $2 billion of Treasury notes which came due and will have to float a new issue at a much higher interest rate. New York's Governor Nelson Rockefeller is meeting the situation by taxing, but Ike won't tax. Especially he won't plug the loopholes in the oil laws.

Senator and Mrs. Wayne Morse came for supper in the country. He had been working all day on a sick mare and a neighbor's sick heifer. We discussed Presidential possibilities. Wayne thinks that Hubert Humphrey is about the only man who could outcampaign Nelson Rockefeller. He believes that Adlai Stevenson, Lyndon Johnson, and Jack Kennedy would all be defeated. I'm inclined to agree.

February 8: Lunched at the French Embassy. Paul Boncour, nephew of the famous late Minister of Foreign Affairs, was guest of honor. Boncour is now French Minister to Hungary and told me that during the Hungarian revolt of 1956 the Hungarians had gone to Cardinal Mindszenty at the little village where he was living and told him he was now free. Mindszenty, however, did not want to be free. Later, after the death of Pope Pius, Boncour said he went to Mass with his Italian colleague and later they called upon Cardinal Mindszenty at the American Legation, where he is a refugee. He remarked to Mindszenty that probably he would be going back to Rome for the Conclave. Mindszenty replied that he would only go back to Rome if he could return to Hungary. Boncour ascertained that the Hungarians would be delighted to let him go to Rome, but would not let him come back. They are only too anxious to get rid of him.

This coincides with the experience I had when I exchanged letters with Tito for the release of Cardinal Stepinac. All hell broke loose from the Catholic Church because Stepinac had been freed. The Yugoslavs told him he was free to go back to Rome but he didn't want to go back to Rome. They wanted him to stay in Yugoslavia as a symbol of alleged opposition to the Catholic Church by Tito.

Our conversation regarding Mindszenty began when I asked Boncour about former Hungarian Minister Emil Weil, whom I said I had exposed for administering the drug to Cardinal Mindszenty when he was tried. "Are you sure he was drugged?" remarked Boncour. Boncour gave the impression that Mindszenty was up to his ears in plotting inside Hungary and didn't have to be drugged to confess anything.

Went to a cocktail party for Jiggs Donahue. Jiggs said that the Justice Department wanted to appoint Chief Judge Walsh, of the municipal court, to the U.S. District Court but was worried over what I might write about him. Jiggs reminded me that when Walsh was a football coach at Georgetown he became involved in a traffic accident and testified that his brother, not he, was involved. Later the Court of Appeals officially charged Walsh with perjury. I had written this up a good many years ago but, frankly, forgot about it. Jiggs claims that Walsh has been a fine judge and the misdeeds of one's youth should not be held against anyone. I am inclined to agree and told Jiggs to inform Rogers.

February 9:   Over the weekend I had talked to several Senators about making a speech Monday morning regarding the book. Not one press association picked up Senator Bridges's speech on Friday. I figured that if the book was criticized someone would carry it. Praise of Pearson, however, is seldom carried. But anyway, we thought we might get a good debate started on the Senate floor with some praise and perhaps some criticism. Wayne Morse agreed to carry the ball at noon today and Joe Clark of Pennsylvania, Pat McNamara of Michigan, Sparkman of Alabama, also Lister Hill of Alabama, agreed to backstop him. I called Senator Langer and asked him if he wouldn't criticize me. I suggested that if he would demand that I go to jail for criticizing Eisenhower, it would make the first page of all the papers. "Oh, I couldn't do that," replied Langer. "My colleagues wouldn't understand it because they know that you and I have been friends." However, he agreed to be on the floor and try to criticize the book. I also sent word to Senator Cotton of New Hampshire by Larry Fernsworth, to be on hand to criticize.

The show went off very well except for the fact that it was a little late. Our friends did a terrific job and held a very impressive debate.

The Republicans, however, did not criticize. Langer called me up afterward rather plaintively and said he had waited a long time but had to go to a luncheon in honor of the mayor of Berlin. He said he would speak again on Thursday if I wanted him to. Senator Williams of Delaware, whom I had prompted through Glenn Everett, sat and listened to the debate but didn't criticize. Styles Bridges came running in from a committee meeting, having gotten the wrong word that he was being attacked. He listened for a minute and then left. Norris Cotton didn't produce at all. Later, he called me up to thank me for something in the column. But he was too friendly and not critical. In the old days, Senator McKellar would take the floor and really go to town in a six-page speech or over. Sometimes I wish Senator McCarthy was back.

The Rumanian Embassy brought me some very interesting documents regarding Malaxa's tie-up with the Iron Guard. They appear to be conclusive and very incriminating. Malaxa has claimed that he had no connection with the Iron Guard. I read over his secret testimony before the Immigration Service and it's amazing that in view of the fact that he refused to answer so many questions, they admitted him. Obviously, it was a political deal with Nixon and Bill Rogers pulling the strings.

February 14: John Foster Dulles has cancer. When he had his operation a year and a half ago the doctors announced that he could fully recover. I expressed considerable doubt publicly and privately. I am sorry that I was right. Dulles seemed to have been doing a pretty good job toward the end.

Dined with Carlos Perone, counselor of the Italian Embassy, who will leave shortly to become an Ambassador. When I remarked that Dulles was doing a pretty good job recently, Perone said, "Yes, by giving in to everyone." He pointed out that Dulles had agreed with Macmillan in London, with Adenauer in Bonn, and with Mikoyan in Washington. Naturally, everyone praised him.

February 16 [Independence]: Got up fairly early and went to the Truman Library at Independence, where Harry Truman seemed genuinely delighted to see me. He played on both of his pianos for me and gave me a personally conducted tour of the library, which was fascinating. He really knows his history. As I was about to leave, Truman made a little speech about the grave crisis faced by the United States and the question of whether we would go the way of the Roman Empire, the Greek cities, and the Dutch Republic. I didn't like to express my ignorance, but I asked him what happened to the Dutch Republic. He replied, "They got too complacent, too fat, and too prosperous. We are in grave danger of being the same way."

This, incidentally, was almost exactly what John Foster Dulles, in somewhat different words, told the White House meeting of Republican and Democratic leaders right after Christmas.

February 18:   Arrived in Los Angeles about 5 A.M. Ellen was in the kitchen cooking breakfast when I got there about six. Her new fiancé, Dwight Whitney, was also up and helping her cook. He seems like a particularly nice guy though I have become accustomed to George and love him as if he were my own son. Dwight is writing for *TV Guide*, he used to write for *Collier's* and *Time* magazine. He is a brilliant writer and seems easy to get along with.

The children are in good shape, though George has started sucking his thumb again.

Began writing columns on Admiral Strauss, aimed to come out just before he is up for confirmation before the Senate Interstate Commerce Committee.

February 19:   Worked on the radio program all day. It looks as if Eisenhower was determined to keep Dulles on despite the gravity of the Berlin crisis and despite the gravity of Dulles's illness. No other time that I can remember has a nation faced such a serious crisis with the Secretary of State in the hospital, the Under Secretary [Christian Herter] on crutches, and the President himself tired and listless.

February 22:   The main event of the day was that I fell in the Los Angeles River.

Ordinarily, the river has about an inch of water in it, but it was somewhat flooded because of the rain. We went bicycling with the children and started to ford the river over a concrete ford. I took a short cut trying to catch up, went into a hole and up to my hips in rather cold water. We had to go home and I wore my pajamas while I tried to dry off my pants. It was my only pair of pants and I had to sit in the plane that night. We got them dry.

Early in the day I appeared on the Retail Clerks TV show and discussed the book and the state of the nation. Admiral Burke had just announced that the United States was completely ready for any emergency, while Army Chief of Staff Maxwell Taylor had announced that we're ready to deal with the crisis in Berlin. Both statements are as phony as a $3 bill and I said so over TV. General Taylor amended his statement to say that we were ready in Berlin if the American nation mobilized.

Caught the 10 P.M. plane back to Washington.

February 23: Eisenhower continues to insist that Dulles will remain the Secretary of State.

Tyler graduated from George Washington Law School this evening. Since I had been up all night, Luvie insisted that I remain home and not go to the graduation ceremony. However, I sneaked in by myself after she and the others had gone in, and sat in the press room. Tyler looked very tall and handsome. It seems so long ago that he was born at Garfield Hospital, and that I drove him home at the age of one week.

February 24: I have to choose between fighting the battle to defeat Admiral Strauss and getting the narration finished for the Alaskan film. I spent a good part of the day lining up Senators to vote against Strauss —McGee of Wyoming, Hartke of Indiana, Engle of California, Yarborough of Texas, and Mike Monroney of Oklahoma. Kefauver has written a terrific letter to the Attorney General demanding to know whether Strauss was not implicated in the criminal aspects of Dixon-Yates. He has asked that confirmation hearings be held up until this can be considered.

I talked to Magnuson, chairman of the committee, who was slightly miffed at the columns I have been writing, but assured me that the hearing would be very carefully conducted and that he, Maggie, had voted against Strauss for Atomic Energy chairman.

The hearing will be postponed for about two weeks.

February 25: Finally finished the Alaskan narration.

Prime Minister Macmillan in Moscow is having a rough time. The Rumanian Minister had predicted that there would be some give-and-take on both sides, but apparently there is none in Moscow now. I can't figure out exactly what has happened. Khrushchev, of course, figured that Macmillan would be conciliatory since he had to win the British elections. Khrushchev probably figured that Macmillan had to take back some kind of an agreement. I am deducing this from what Brucan told me in advance. Apparently, Macmillan took the same position as Dulles, whereupon Khrushchev got sore and announced that Russia would not consent to sitting in on a Foreign Ministers' conference.

February 26:   The freeze is on in Moscow. Macmillan and Khrushchev attending the Moscow Ballet last night didn't even speak or look at each other.

Senators Hartke, Hart of Michigan, and Estes Kefauver came for dinner. Also the John Perrys. Hartke seems all steamed up about opposing Admiral Strauss and will attempt to link him with Herbert Hoover, Jr., in regard to the unrestricted admission of crude oil to the United States. This is probably the wrong reason for opposing Strauss, but it could be effective.

February 28:   Edward Bennett Williams approached me on the defense of his client Bernard Goldfine. He says he will keep us posted on any inside news regarding Sherman Adams if we will help him on Goldfine's defense. He wants to move that all evidence be thrown out if obtained by electronic devices and wants testimony to that end by Jack and Baron Shacklette. I told him that I was fairly certain that no evidence was thus obtained but he could talk to both men. He says that 200 agents have been working on Goldfine and that, contrary to published reports, Adams has been in frequent touch with his old vicuna coat friend.

March 2:   Talked to Lyndon Johnson. Told him the Republicans were checking into the fact that he had taken eight airplane trips last year at the expense of the Air Force. He denied it except when asked to come to Washington for consultations at the White House; said that he had made $50,000 to $60,000 last year and spent it all on working for the Senate. Unfortunately, though I didn't tell him this, we know of at least one case where he ordered a plane from General Kelly in a hurry to fly back to Texas. It was on purely personal business. I also told Lyndon that he had a lemon named Matthews on the staff of the Senate Campaign Committee. Matthews has been in on a real estate deal on behalf of Batista. When I told Lyndon he should follow Proxmire's advice and hold some Democratic caucuses, Lyndon countered with the question should we have a caucus on the labor bill. "If we do then Harry Byrd and McClellan will hold forth and disrupt the caucus and it will leak out to the press that the Democratic party is torn to shreds. The labor leaders want caucuses on everything except the labor bill."

I talked to Lyndon about Strauss. He is passing the ball back to me to a considerable extent; says to get the top leaders in the committee pledged in the order of their importance from Magnuson down. After you've got the first three senior members, he said, the rest should be fairly easy. Don't go for the young fellows first, he said.

Earle Clements, who has been Executive Director of the Democratic Senate Campaign Committee, came for dinner with Tyler and Bess. When I told him about Matthews he was delighted. Matthews is a Smathers plant inside his committee who double-crosses him on any and every opportunity. Earle has promised to talk to Senator Pastore of Rhode Island to try to block Strauss.

The Rumanian Minister came to lunch. I wanted to find out just what the Russians had up their sleeves regarding Berlin. Brucan claims there will be no showdown over Berlin, that both sides will yield. He pointed out that John Foster Dulles has been all over the map regarding Berlin, and Moscow would like to have him back in a foreign ministers' conference so as to quote his previous statements and hold him to them.

It has been reported from the State Department that the Kremlin has been gleeful over Dulles's illness and wants to take advantage of it to force a harsh showdown over Berlin. Brucan claimed just the opposite. "You will not see any tough position taken by the Kremlin in the long run," he said. "Both sides are sparring." I am never quite sure how far to trust an Iron Curtain diplomat, though Brucan has been amazingly accurate in the past. Some months ago he predicted that this year will be one of diplomatic offensive by the Kremlin. This has certainly been the case. The Kremlin has been making moves all over the face of Europe and Asia.

March 4: Eisenhower at his press conference indicated for the first time that Dulles may not come back. The fact is that cancer has been found all over his body. The doctors naturally are not revealing this, but Ike knows the truth. He dropped a slight hint that Chris Herter might take Dulles's place, though I happen to know that Herter prompted him to say this. Herter explained that it weakened his position with foreign Ambassadors when there was speculation in the press that he would not succeed to Dulles's shoes.

March 6: Made the rounds of three Senators as per instructions from Lyndon to line up votes against Strauss. Pastore of Rhode Island was quite frank. He is going to vote for Strauss. He sides with the private utilities in the Dixon-Yates dispute and says that the Tennessee Valley Authority doesn't deserve to have any more money. It's taking money away from poor New England for the industrial South, which in turn takes more textiles away from New England.

Magnuson, chairman of the committee, was more encouraging. He says that Strauss came in to see him recently and he wanted to make sure that he could leave town to fill a speaking engagement in Houston after two days of hearings. "Oh, you'll be testifying much longer than that," said Maggie. "You'd better fill your speaking engagement in Houston, then come back after Easter."

Maggie says that they have to find something really outstandingly wrong in his character to block the confirmation of a Cabinet officer. He feels the President has a right to appoint his own Cabinet and says that not in a hundred years has a Cabinet officer failed of confirmation.

Clint Anderson has been reported sitting on the sidelines not anxious to get into the battle. I had a long talk with him in which he was eloquent in his opposition to Strauss.

March 16: Had a stag dinner for members of the Senate Interstate Commerce Committee who tomorrow will begin confirmation hearings on Admiral Strauss. Mrs. Pat Brown, as usual, came to dinner. I have come to like her very much. She never talks. We were interrupted somewhat by Eisenhower's telecast in which he straightened out some of the boners he pulled at his press conference regarding the danger of war over Berlin. Aside from this, we had a very fruitful evening.

Clint Anderson held forth eloquently and at length regarding Strauss. He really cut the ground out from under him. He told how Senator Brian McMahon was the real author of the H-bomb, not Strauss, and how Strauss would not permit Brian's widow to declassify the 5,000-word letter Brian wrote to Truman.

Anderson also told how Sir Charles Penny, the British scientist, was the real author of detection of atomic particles in the air, not Strauss, as he claimed. Clint did not go into Strauss's draft dodging during World War I nor the way in which he tried to marry the daughters of the firm's various partners.

Magnuson, who has been wobbly, seemed to have been bolstered somewhat, though I still am worried about him. He has agreed, however, to appoint a subcommittee of about three men to investigate thoroughly. We even discussed who might be on the committee—probably McGee, and Yarborough of Texas. Yarborough was at the dinner and is an eager beaver. Maggie also suggested Morton of Kentucky, Republican, because he is lazy.

March 17: The Strauss hearings began and went off reasonably well. The Senators gave him only a light dusting. They had already agreed to set the hearings over for a couple of weeks after Easter. I telephoned Cyrus Eaton to tip him off that Louis Johnson was going to testify that Strauss had masterminded the hydrogen bomb. Eaton's railroad (the Chesapeake & Ohio) does more business in West Virginia [Johnson's home state] than any other one firm. He called me back later in the day to say that he had talked to Louis and there would be no testimony on behalf of Strauss. I've never quite known first-hand before how big business can operate behind the scenes. I've written about it but never helped to pull the big business wires.

Pat Brown telephoned in the evening to say he was going back to California without doing anything definite regarding the Presidency of the United States. "I'm going to be just as good a Governor of California as I can," he said, "and then see what happens." I think he's wise. Actually, he made a pretty good impression in Washington and it could be that the two nominees will be from opposite ends of the country—Rockefeller of New York and Brown of California.

March 18: Admiral Strauss is complaining over the delay in his confirmation. He says that morale in the Commerce Department is bad. However, the Senators held firm and had agreed among themselves to at least a one month delay. Clint Anderson wants at least two months and I think we'll probably get it.

March 20: Macmillan has arrived and together with Eisenhower went to see Dulles at the hospital. Then he and Ike flew to Camp David, Maryland. It's going to be a cold weekend and Camp David is not particularly enticing. The only reason for going there is to escape the press, but already the press has been able to check on the helicopter loads of experts going up there to know what subjects generally are being discussed.

March 24:   Went to see Senator Joe O'Mahoney of Wyoming. Hadn't talked to him for months. He's now about seventy-three, and beginning to show his age, though vigorous mentally. I took him to lunch with Thurman Arnold. These two trust-busters, both from Wyoming, have had a terrific impact on the economy of the United States. I think Thurman never should have retired from the Justice Department for the Court of Appeals. He was bored stiff with the court. O'Mahoney is now on the new Senate Committee to investigate monopoly. I tried to get Joe to make a speech on the Strauss case warning the Interstate Commerce Committee that one Senate committee must respect another and Strauss's failure to answer questions on the Dixon-Yates case before the Judiciary Committee must be probed thoroughly.

Dined with the Rumanian Minister in his new home. We talked at length about the Macmillan-Eisenhower talks. The Minister apparently had been talking to the British and claimed that Eisenhower and Macmillan agreed on very little, and that Macmillan would have great difficulty explaining his mission to the House of Commons.

"Macmillan was greatly disappointed with the American lack of preparation," he said. "He had expected to find a plan to implement Dulles's statement that there were other ways to bring about German unification than by free elections. But Eisenhower had no plan. He seemed to have taken a negative position as a result of General Norstadt's message that he couldn't keep NATO intact if we yielded to Khrushchev.

"Your greatest problem is going to be to get a united NATO front," the Minister predicted. "The British are much nearer Norway and Denmark, which have formally petitioned against atom arms for Germany. Chancellor Adenauer is determined to go ahead with this and the big problem at your April 4 meetings will be to get a united front in NATO."

March 25:   Wasted an entire morning on Malaxa's deposition. This is the Rumanian multimillionaire who thinks he can buy his way into the United States and has sued me for $5,000,000.

Jim Rowe came to lunch. He explained why he was working for Senator Humphrey though he has always been a Lyndon Johnson man.

He was a bit upset over a column story that Lyndon expected a dead-lock in the 1960 convention, in which case Rowe would be able to swing Humphrey's support to him. Jim said he talked with Lyndon carefully and tried to get him to make up his mind and announce for President but Lyndon refused. He then told Lyndon that he was going to work for Humphrey. Lyndon agreed. He suspects that Lyndon would still like to be the candidate in 1960 and is banking on a deadlock, when the spotlight will focus on him. But Jim thinks these things can't be done at the last minute and cites 1956 as an example when Lyndon thought he could swing the nomination at the very last minute. I didn't mention to Jim the fact that Lyndon had a room opposite me in the Hilton Hotel and I watched his moves carefully.

Jim pointed out that Kefauver got a lot of his support in 1952 from my column and radio broadcasts. He said that wherever he went people were talking about my statements regarding Kefauver. So Jim asked if I wouldn't support Humphrey. I told him that last year I had told Humphrey I would like to talk to him about his candidacy, but that I had never heard from him again and figured that either he didn't take himself seriously or didn't take me seriously. "Oh, that's typically Hubert," said Jim.

We both believe that Hubert's chief trouble is lack of organization and lack of administrative ability. He's a wonderful guy, with wonderful ideas, but not much organization.

March 26: I did a little thinking about Humphrey's campaign and figured that he ought to have a down-to-earth 100 percent investigation of the Agriculture Department showing the tremendous waste under Benson. Benson's expenses have increased from $800 million under Brannan to $7 billion, and a lot of it has not been price supports, just plain inefficiency. I got hold of Hubert on the telephone and he agreed with the idea, though he won't get busy on it until May. Too many speeches in between.

Senator Magnuson is having trouble getting Yarborough of Texas to serve as chairman of the subcommittee to investigate Strauss. I called Yarborough, also got Clinton Anderson and Bob Allen to call him; also called some of his friends in Texas to have them pressure him.

Down in Alabama, Governor John Patterson has let loose a blast against me and Ed Reid, accusing me of starting an investigation of Alabama road scandals in order to elect Humphrey for President. The Governor is a bit psychotic. Actually, Humphrey had nothing to do with the investigation. People from Mobile called me about the road scandals and I called Congressman John Blatnik of Minnesota, who is chairman of the subcommittee on public works. He didn't really want to investigate, but I needled him into it. Now Governor Patterson accuses me and Humphrey—all because Blatnik comes from Minnesota. The tragedy, however, is that Ed Reid, one of the finest public servants in the South, is getting smeared.

Apparently, the Rumanian Minister was right. Macmillan and Eisenhower were a long way from agreement. Eisenhower told the Republican congressional leaders that he agreed to a summit conference only to get Macmillan reelected. He said he would rather face a hostile Khrushchev than a British Labour Government in London. John Foster Dulles, it now turns out, lectured Macmillan both before and after Camp David. This may have been why they called on him at the hospital. Dulles seems determined to block a summit conference. Meanwhile, the medical reports indicate that he won't last too much longer. They are taking him South to keep him away from the NATO Foreign Ministers next week. Yet Mr. Dulles, despite his age, despite his health, insists on keeping his hand in American foreign policy. There never was a time when leadership was so badly needed, yet when there was such a vacuum in leadership.

March 27:   Spent the morning taking the deposition of George Lincoln Rockwell, the young führer, who lives in Arlington and displays a Nazi swastika inside his home with the door open every evening. He's a queer combination. Since I have always wanted to try a case myself, partly to save money, partly because my egotism tells me I can do a better job than the lawyers, I handled this in person. It took several hours of advance work in reading. But I put him through almost every phase of his life. I wasn't very successful in getting any information regarding contributions to him from the Arabs, which was the main point at issue, but I did get him to talk about his love of Hitler and his many meetings with all sorts of people, including one with the head of the Arab secret intelligence, and the fact that the banners used in the demonstration in front of the White House against Marines landing in Lebanon were given to the Egyptian Embassy and turned up in Cairo.

Justice Douglas told me at dinner that Lou Nichols, former Number Two man to J. Edgar Hoover, was the real author of the American Bar Association criticism of the Supreme Court. Peter Brown was chairman of the committee, but Nichols, who was vice chairman, took advantage of Brown's spinelessness to excoriate the Court. Bill also points out that Hoover has $100 million to spend, which is twice as much as the money used to support all the courts of the federal government.

I picked up a report that Tompkins, the man who built Eisenhower's Gettysburg home and didn't charge him for it, was paid off by getting a contract to build the CIA building across the Potomac.

March 28:   I let Melvin and Margaret take the weekend off for Easter. I figured if I did my own cooking I would eat less.

March 29:   Lunched with the Vournases and had supper with Tyler and Bess. The baby is getting fat and looking just like Earle. He is full of smiles and dimples.

April 22:   Eisenhower is insisting on appointing Dulles as special adviser, which means there will be two Secretaries of State. White House staff members urge that Herter carry on alone but Ike wouldn't listen to it. He thinks anyone who detracts from the limelight of Dulles's hospital bed is almost a traitor.

Congressman Porter of Oregon says that Wayne Morse and Neuberger are fighting again. Porter had a showdown with Wayne over the report that Wayne would put somebody in the Democratic primary in Oregon to defeat him. Wayne backed down but insisted he was going to run someone against Neuberger. This is now, I think, inevitable.

April 23:   Went to one of Marjorie Post Davies May's square dances. Sat beside Mrs. Mesta. It was one of the few times when I have seen Gwenn Cafritz and Mrs. Mesta at the same party and reasonably unaloof. Mrs. Mesta said she had some dynamite-laden information which I would love to have but refused to give it to me. I did not press the old bag of wind.

April 24:   Got up early and dictated a speech for Wayne Morse on Clare Luce. I told him if he was going to go all out against her nomination as ambassador to Brazil, he'd better mimeograph his speech and get it out to the press because newspapermen are lazy. He is adopting the suggestion.

Dave Karr came down for lunch. He tells me that next week he will become president of the Fairbanks-Morse Company. Dave is now about forty-one and making around $75,000. He left me in 1948, eleven years ago, when he was making about $7,000.

April 26:   Luvie, Barbara, and I drove out to Mother's grave near Embreeville. The old Quaker meeting house was locked and services are held only once a month. But the old pine trees are just as stately and beautiful as they stand guard over the tombstones of those who lie there. An old barn of the Pennsylvania stone variety is just across the fence with feed bunkers, a tractor, and the accouterments of a dairy farm. Civilization has been encroaching somewhat on the meeting house. It made me remember another spring day when I had just graduated from college in 1919 and was waiting to go to Serbia. I came up to the meeting house with Mary Hull to listen to a lecture by Raymond Robbins, who had been one of the heads of the Red Cross and had just come back from Russia. He told the story of the Russian Revolution and the hopes that he cherished for the new leadership. He felt that if Lenin and Trotsky were given some encouragement they might be friendly to the West. He told of meeting with them behind the lines of 1917 when they were waiting and hoping for some sign of help from their allies. That help never came. He warned that Russia could go one way or the other—as a friend of the United States or an enemy. That was exactly forty years ago. How true was his prediction.

The dates on Mother's tombstone brought back poignant memories. She was born in 1875 and died in 1942, just a few months after Pearl Harbor. How she hated war. I remember how she flinched from the war of 1917–18 and hoped that none of her family would be drawn into it. Although Father was cremated in San Francisco, the dates on Mother's tombstone also gave his life span, 1871 to 1938. He died just before Hitler marched into Czechoslovakia. I am sure he realized that war by that time was almost inevitable. But how he, too, worked to prevent war!

April 27:   I now see what Mrs. Mesta was dangling over me at the square dance. She tipped off George Dixon to a whale of a story, namely that Mrs. Loy Henderson, a White Russian, had bawled out the Russian Ambassador at a recent May dinner. Marjorie [Post Davies] May finally intervened. Loy Henderson is probably the most anti-Russian member of the State Department and one reason, of course, is that he has to live with a woman who is constantly badgering him. If he didn't accept her views, he would have to get a divorce.

I dictated part of a white paper on Admiral Strauss for the confidential use of committee members. The hearings begin tomorrow—or rather the critical phase of them. Hitherto Magnuson has only been sparring with Strauss. But now the committee is supposed to take off the gloves.

Lunched with Al Friendly; he says that Phil Graham is very much impressed by John McCone, who succeeded Strauss as AEC chairman. I can now begin to see why *The Post* has been bucking my column whenever it criticizes Strauss. This afternoon, Russ Wiggins called up to protest against the column for release tomorrow whereby both McCone and Strauss favor General Dynamics and Bechtel, the latter having been McCone's former company. The column was held up and I'm not sure whether it will be used at all.

Wayne Morse delivered his speech on Clare Luce. He mimeographed it in advance and distributed it in the press gallery. It was quite a masterful presentation and took him three hours to deliver. He elaborated on it ad lib on the floor. Significantly, very little of the speech got into the newspapers, even though he distributed copies in advance. It's funny how the Republican newspapers team up with a big Republican publisher like Luce, even though he publishes magazines, not newspapers.

Had a long talk with Senator Fulbright about Ogden Reid, who has been blocked in his confirmation for Ambassador to Israel. Bill explained that back in 1945 when he was a very green freshman he had protested against the appointment of ex-Senator Townsend of Delaware, the strawberry king, and Frank Walker, the former Postmaster General, to be delegates to the United Nations. He felt that he, Fulbright, had had something to do with formation of the UN, as he did, and therefore had a right to demand that there be high quality delegates appointed. He was immediately slapped down by O'Mahoney, who resented the criticism of Frank Walker, and by other Catholic Senators, who in effect, reminded him that he had no right to speak. He was a freshman.

"Hitherto I've not been able to do much about this," Bill said, "but now that I'm chairman of this committee I intend to do something and I'm going to take a firm stand against unqualified, political appointees." I couldn't help but agree with him but I suggested: "Why don't you take on someone your size, such as Mrs. Luce. She has power; Brownie Reid is a young fellow who has now lost his power in the newspaper world. Furthermore, he's been working hard at his new job while Mrs. Luce is temperamental and unstable."

Fulbright was quite frank. "I couldn't defeat her," he confessed. "Look at the speeches made for her by Kennedy, Dodd, and Lausche."

"You know why," I suggested. "It's a matter of religion."

"Yes," replied Fulbright, "but I can't say that publicly."

I pointed out that young Reid had some ideas on getting the oil companies to give up their royalties in order to build public works in the Near East to resettle Arab refugees. Fulbright beat me to it, however, by saying that he had discussed this with the head of Standard Oil and that Eugene Black of the World Bank was working with the oil companies on it. I got nowhere with Fulbright and I confess that in principle I agree with him. However, I do not agree that having voted for Mrs. Luce, a lady with power, the Senate should discriminate against a young fellow without power, who probably would make a better Ambassador.

I called Senator Humphrey and suggested that he explain his position on the Senate floor regarding the magazine article he wrote for *Life* and his vote for Mrs. Luce. It's something I think may cause him trouble in the future. He thanked me and said he would make a statement and abstain from voting for the lady.

April 28: Talked to Mrs. Henry Smythe, wife of the former atomic commissioner, now at Princeton, to urge that her husband testify on the Strauss hearings. She is usually a very warm personality, but she was frigid in this case. The record, she said, would have to wait until her husband can write a book. The things on which she could testify, she said, were not in the public domain. This is pure hogwash. The attitude of these scientists who want other people to get out on the firing line and get wounded while they sit back in their ivory towers is sad but consistent.

Invited several young Congressmen to lunch—Tom Johnson of Maryland, Thompson of New Jersey, Vanick of Ohio, Ashley of Ohio, Quigley of Pennsylvania, Porter of Oregon, and Byron Johnson of Colorado. They opened up on the question of Sam Rayburn's sterile leadership, pointed out that Congress had been elected in a landslide last November to depart from Eisenhower leadership, but that so far the House had done nothing.

There was some very healthy though depressing discussion of Sam Rayburn's bogged-down policies. I brought up the Boykin-Dawson axis which managed to scuttle justice in Mobile, Alabama. They were shocked by it but didn't think they could do anything. To propose a resolution of censure would merely get everybody down on them, and although they want to make an issue of the House leadership they didn't think this was the place to make it. They described, rather graphically, how Congressman O'Hara of Illinois would slip around and talk to John McCormack and how Charlie Halleck of Indiana would line up the Republicans and how they would all go down to defeat faced with the Halleck–Rayburn–John McCormack axis. They suspected that McCormack was the man who induced Blatnik to send his telegram to the grand jury on the final day of the grand jury session. I think they are probably right.

Mrs. Luce, after being confirmed overwhelmingly, made a wisecrack about Wayne Morse having been kicked in the head by a horse. When the remark was read on the Senate floor several Senators got up and said if they had to vote over again, they would now vote against Mrs. Luce.*

May 11: Senator McGee of Wyoming queried Strauss regarding my May 5 column in which I said that a secret document was in front of Strauss when Dr. David Inglis was cross-examined by Senator Scott of Pennsylvania. Strauss called this an unqualified lie. McGee, by prearrangement, then suggested that the author of the column be called upon to testify. Senator Magnuson immediately demurred, apparently in my defense. Senator Monroney also demurred as a former newspaperman. Jack, who was present, went up to Maggie [Magnuson] afterward and said that I would be delighted to testify and so would he. We will try to arrange this shortly.

Phil Graham came for dinner. He had lunched with Strauss recently and Strauss had threatened a libel suit against me. In fact, he has already written the Bell Syndicate with a veiled threat. We have not yet answered him. If he should sue we could bring out his draft-dodging in World War I and his attempts to marry the boss's daughter

*The controversial Mrs. Luce resigned the post shortly thereafter.—ED.

at Kuhn, Loeb, which finally succeeded after various daughters of various partners had turned him down.

Phil seemed very much interested in my statement that Bobby Baker, Lyndon's right-hand man, had taken a nose count and found about fifty votes against Strauss. Phil immediately asked his managing editor to check with Bobby.

May 12: I wrote a letter to Maggie in official language asking that I be permitted to testify at the next hearing. The hearings are in recess for the Quarles funeral. Donald Quarles, Under Secretary of Defense and the man who more than anyone else in the Pentagon had held up appropriations for missiles, died last week in his sleep. It was a blessing all the way around.

Clint Anderson had lunch with Rosemary Silvercruys (Baroness Silvercruys, the widow of Senator Brien McMahon). She told him how Admiral Strauss had telephoned her husband, the Belgian Ambassador, to say: "Rosemary seems very irked with me lately. I don't know why. But I know you're going to retire soon and it occurred to me that you might be interested in an executive position with the American Stude-baker–Packard Company." Strauss knew full well why Rosemary was peeved at him. When she wanted to declassify the 5,000-word letter to Truman which Brien had written urging the building of the hydrogen bomb, Strauss had refused to declassify it. Thus it cannot be published in Brien's memoirs and thus also Strauss, not Brien, gets the credit for building the H-bomb.

The Washington Post used the story that Strauss's chances of confirmation were fifty-fifty.

May 13: I testified before the Senate hearings on Strauss. Before I did so I telephoned the assistant to Chairman McCone of the AEC at 7:30 A.M., catching him at breakfast. He was quite frank in admitting that Strauss had telephoned him to ask about the life and background of David Inglis. Strauss previously had testified that he had never "called anyone" regarding Inglis.*

I also called Chairman Walter of the House Un-American Activi-

---

*One of the issues was whether or not Strauss had, as Drew Pearson reported, conducted a confidential review of one of his critics, David Inglis, Chairman of the Federation of American Scientists.

ties Committee and found that Congressman Gordon Scherer had asked his committee for information on Dr. Inglis on April 30. This was the same day Inglis first testified and one day before Strauss and Senator Scott of Pennsylvania had the dossier on Inglis in front of them during his cross-examination.

The Republicans had a closed door session of the committee this morning in which they voted against my testifying. They were overruled by Maggie. I had telephoned several Democratic Senators to make sure that Maggie had the proxies. The Republicans also demanded that I not be put under oath as requested. Obviously, for me to be put under oath would mean that Strauss would have to be put under oath also.

I testified that if Strauss were put under oath he would have to tell the truth about telephoning the Atomic Energy Commission for information on Dr. Inglis. McGee then asked me where I got this information. I replied that I had telephoned the AEC and that they had answered quite frankly.

Strauss was then called as a witness but not put under oath. He said that he had called the AEC the day after my column appeared in print, May 5. Clint Anderson then read a letter from AEC Chairman McCone that Strauss had telephoned the AEC on April 20 asking for information regarding Dr. Inglis. Obviously, Strauss was alibi-ing and lying.

Jack then got on the witness stand and said that he had seen a piece of paper on Strauss's table marked "confidential" pertaining to Inglis with the words "FBI" in the report. Strauss then testified that he had no such paper. Obviously, he was lying his head off. I don't believe that anyone in the committee believed him.

We went to the Belgian Embassy to a reception in honor of the King. He is twenty-eight years old and looked young and lonely standing all alone in the middle of the floor shaking hands.

Al Friendly called me today to suggest discreetly that I've been writing enough about Strauss.

May 15: Strauss hearings finally ended. Neuberger of Oregon has told Clint that he is going to vote for Strauss because he's a Jew. Frear of Delaware indicated to Clint that he might vote with us if I did not comment on the "Du Pont Amendment." This is a provision which Frear has introduced whereby the Du Ponts would not have to pay a capital gains tax on their stock in General Motors when then sell it as required by the Justice Department. I'm now beginning to see how deals are made in the Senate when important votes are at issue.

I talked to the assistant of Senator Margaret Chase Smith of Maine. She is considering voting against Strauss if she can get some Democratic support in holding up the confirmation of General "Rosy" O'Donnell for promotion. O'Donnell smeared her, was also a great friend of General MacArthur, and advocated using the A-bomb in the Korean War. He made the mistake of passing word to the newspapers that Mrs. Smith was holding up Air Force promotions because she didn't get promoted to be head of the WAFs.

I called the editors of the Atlanta *Journal,* the Raleigh *News & Observer,* and the Tampa *Tribune* to see if they would write some good editorials. We need the votes of Russell of Georgia, Ervin of North Carolina, and Holland of Florida.

Tried to get Lister Hill of Alabama to issue a statement but he seems to be ducking. Joe O'Mahoney issued a fine statement in the form of a letter to *The Post* and will try to reissue another one for Monday morning publication.

May 16:   Spent most of the day working on a statement for Senator Long of Louisiana. He is holding out on Strauss. I think he's going to vote against him but wants to be cagey and demands that I work up a speech for him against Douglas Dillon. Long is the only Senator so far who's going to vote against Dillon's confirmation as Under Secretary of State.

May 17:   Ernest Gruening tells me that Senator Bartlett of Alaska is still doubtful and may vote for Strauss. His vote is essential. If he should vote for Strauss the committee vote would be ten to seven for him. Gruening himself is still flirting around with the idea of supporting Strauss. I think the Jewish issue is at the root of it.

May 18:   The committee votes on Tuesday regarding Strauss. Bob Bartlett is still undecided. We finally got hold of Bobby Baker, who telephoned him. Jack and Clint had previously talked to him separately and after Baker's call Bartlett phoned Jack to say his vote is now firm. The funny thing was that Oscar Chapman had talked to him early in the day and thought he was firm, but two hours after that, when Jack talked to him, he was still wobbling.

I had a long talk with Senator Langer. I had written out a statement for him to issue against Strauss. He asked me to read it out loud. He is thin and his eyes are giving out. His wife is dying of cancer. She has tried Krebiozen and Langer thinks that she would have been dead before this without it.

When I first read the statement to Langer he made no comment. I thought he disapproved of it. Finally he said it isn't strong enough. He put in some good, tough words. He then inserted such words as "insolent," "arrogant," etc. He also put in some statements reminding the public that the Senate is merely the representative of the people. He said he would issue a statement that day.

Talked to Senator Steve Young of Ohio and he is issuing a statement pretty much as I drafted it. Called Governor DiSalle of Ohio to ask him to work on Senator Lausche. He said he had no influence with Lausche whatsoever and I'm sure he was telling the truth.

Clint Anderson showed me a letter he was planning to write to Benson taking his hide off because Benson's men had lied about alleged farm subsidies received by Clint in New Mexico. These subsidies went to Clint's tenant, not to him. When Anderson wrote Benson earlier demanding that the facts be set straight, Benson didn't do so. Yet Clint has been Benson's best Democratic supporter.

May 26:   I suppose I should register as a lobbyist. Talked to Frank Thompson of New Jersey about Senator Harrison Williams, who is thinking of voting for Strauss. Frank says that Governor Meyner has had so much trouble with his Republican legislature that Williams is sympathetic to the problem of an executive getting confirmation. Thompson has just fought to get the education bill out of the Education Committee and blasted John McCormack for trying to sabotage it. "I told John there are two kinds of Catholics—a Roman and an Irish Catholic. I'm a Roman. If Sam Rayburn should die and John would be up for election, he wouldn't get a hundred votes for Speaker." He has outlived his usefulness. He is still coasting along on the reputation of having put across part of Roosevelt's New Deal program, but Frank says that Sam will at least let other people operate and is cooperative regarding New Deal ideas.

Senator McGee called up to say that Nixon had cracked down on him when he started discussing the Strauss issue on the floor of the Senate. He had violated the three-minute rule, though Javits just ahead of him had violated it to praise Strauss.

Talked to George Aiken of Vermont. I wanted to suggest that he issue a statement as a Republican urging Eisenhower to withdraw Strauss's name, on the ground that it wasn't worth trimming administration policies on other fronts such as foreign textiles and appropriations. Aiken remarked: "I haven't voted against an appointee of either Roosevelt or Truman and I don't like to vote against a Republican appointee, but this is a hard vote for me. I am uncommitted."

Talked to Bill Lewis about having Maggie Smith issue a withdrawal statement. She was touched when Senator Byrd came to her and said: "I'll do anything you want on O'Donnell." I reminded Bill that Clint Anderson, without any fanfare or publicity, had got O'Donnell's name held up. Mrs. Smith has written a letter to Senator Russell withdrawing herself from the debate over General O'Donnell. When his name came up last week, she left the room. Russell sent a copy of the letter to all members of the Armed Services Committee. It turns out that "Rosy" O'Donnell is a drunk, as well as a shoot-from-the-hip friend of General Douglas MacArthur. His statements regarding use of the A-bomb in Korea were pretty bad.

Talked to Clint Anderson. Bob Kerr called up irked over my story that he was a pal of Secretary of the Treasury Anderson, and therefore had to vote with Anderson for Admiral Strauss. Mary Dean, cousin of Senator Gore, has been telling Pauline Gore: "You eat with a man, you sleep with him, it's up to you to change his vote." She has threatened to have her father break off his black Angus partnership with Senator Gore if he votes for Strauss.

Clint confirmed the rest of the story of how Strauss had called up Baron Silvercruys to offer him the head of Studebaker. Silvercruys called back later, at which time Strauss was evasive and said it would take a long time to work the deal out.

Clint called Senator "Scoop" Jackson in my presence and asked him not to push the confirmation of General O'Donnell. "Mrs. Smith is very interested in this and she's also interested in something very close to me. We gave you a lot of help on Hanford and I would appreciate your holding this up." Jackson replied: "He's a wild Irishman but Tom White (Chief of Staff of the Air Force) wants a decision soon. I merely brought his name up last week but I'll probably be absent this week." Clint remarked that O'Donnell had been to his office one time so drunk he couldn't hit the floor with his hat.

Bumped into Jack Kennedy and talked to him about Strauss. He weaseled. I finally pointed out: "When I think of the deep freezes and hams I exposed in the Truman administration, I'm ashamed of myself. But you fellows understand the hams and the deep freezes but you don't understand a $200 million Dixon-Yates deal—the worst conflict-of-interest case since Teapot Dome."

Langer called me up and asked for a statement—a good tough one. I dropped it at his office.

I hear that Aiken wants a peacetime reactor built in Burlington, Vermont.

June 2:   Left for Idlewild and London in a terrific rainstorm. There are eighty-seven delegates to the Atlantic Congress on this plane, and most of them have taken part in some form of promotion for European unity.

Before leaving Washington I called Lyndon Johnson on the telephone to ask him about the Strauss fight. He passed the buck to Clint Anderson. Earlier in the day Clint had told me that everything was in Lyndon's hands. Lyndon, as usual, is trying to play the statesman. He claimed not to know what the nose-count was going to be. He was interested in some of the background of General "Rosy" O'Donnell and the fact that he wanted to drop the atom bomb over North Korea during the Korean War. I told him that Margaret Chase Smith might vote with us if we could steam up enough opposition to O'Donnell.

This is a slow plane and it is close to being overloaded. We stopped at Gander for fuel. Spent a pretty packed-in night. These are tourist seats, and every seat is taken.

June 3:   Arrived in London at 11:30 A.M. At 5 P.M. we had a briefing at the American Embassy, where Ambassador Jock Whitney greeted us briefly, and Randolph Burgess, the Under Secretary of the Treasury, who was appointed to that job from the National City Bank in order to hike interest rates on government bonds, talked to us about NATO. Burgess was promoted upstairs to be the American Ambassador in charge of NATO. He talked chiefly on military matters. As he looked down on the audience he may well have thought they were nodding assent. Actually, they were nodding from trying to stay awake.

I have attended all sorts of international conferences in the past, beginning with the Washington Arms Conference of 1921. I was then teaching at the University of Pennsylvania and could only get away a few times. But I managed to squeeze into a couple of plenary sessions. Since then I have covered the Geneva Naval Conference of 1927, the Pan American Conference in Havana in 1928, the London Naval Conference of 1930, the signing of the Kellogg-Briand pact in Paris in 1928, the Foreign Ministers Conference in Rio de Janeiro in 1942, the United Nations Conference in San Francisco in 1945, the Paris Peace Conference in 1946, the Geneva Summit Conference in 1955, plus a lot of other conferences in Washington that I can't remember. However, this is the first conference I've attended as a delegate.

Lest there be a misunderstanding, I hasten to add that it's not a very official conference. There are about a hundred delegates from the United States of America, the same number from England, and a lesser number from each of the other NATO countries. They do include, however, some rather distinguished and important people, including ex-foreign ministers and present members of cabinets and parliaments. Our job is to recommend some moves for the strengthening of NATO and closer unity within Western Europe.

June 5:   The Queen opened our first session at Westminster Hall. I took Mary Roebling, head of the Trenton Trust Company, and we arrived forty-five minutes early as per instructions. There is nothing like kowtowing to royalty unless it be kowtowing to bankers. This banker, who sat beside me, was a little restless about waiting so long for Her Majesty.

But it was worth waiting for. Before the Queen arrived, the yeoman of the Royal Guard in majestic plumes marched up the center aisle, together with the Beefeaters. These are not the manufacturers of gin, but some eminent and distinguished gentlemen of the Court dressed like the jack of diamonds and carrying spears. They looked a little ill at ease and it was obvious that they did not drill regularly as do the professional soldiery of the Court. I would say their average age was sixty, and if the Queen really depended upon them for protection she would be out of luck.

The Queen arrived from a side entrance and stood for a moment or two, shaking hands with members of her Cabinet and chief delegates, which included Senator Kefauver, Eric Johnston, Congressman Wayne Hays of Ohio, and a few others. Then she sat in the same golden throne where I had seen her grandpappy sit twenty-nine years before when he opened the London Naval Conference. He was whiskered and sedate, also a little bored. She was demure and beautiful. She did what is hard to do—at least I find it so before a TV audience— she smiled and bowed. She read her speech well. It had feeling and conviction.

Afterward there were some more trumpets, then salutes, and she stood while the band played, "God Save the Queen." Then she marched out the main aisle with Philip beside her, always careful to stand one pace to the rear. This is difficult to do but he did it. The Duke looked very handsome and royal and as if he enjoyed the ceremony.

Immediately thereafter we had a sherry reception in the House of Lords. I then lunched with General David Sarnoff of RCA and at two-thirty our plenary session was opened at Church House. Church House is actually the headquarters of the Colonial Office, and it is rather paradoxical that we who are supposed to help the under-developed countries of Africa and Asia are meeting there.

The Archbishop of York gave a very dull speech. So did the Foreign Minister of Holland. But Mr. Cahan, who is in charge of economic cooperation under NATO, gave a very stimulating speech, urging more economic trade and warning, "If you don't meet these problems now your children will never forgive you."

We had to rush to get to the American Embassy for a buffet supper given by the Whitneys. The U.S. government, though the richest in the world, never has money enough to buy embassy buildings, and this one was given by Barbara Hutton.

June 6:   London started its usual weekend evacuation, but we worked all day. In the morning there were two rather dull speeches, one by General Norstad, Commander of NATO, and Admiral Wright, head of the Atlantic NATO Fleet, followed by an electrifying speech by the only Negro who spoke, Dr. Mordecai Johnson of Howard University. He introduced himself as the son of an African slave and gave an eloquent plea for more aid for the underdeveloped countries. The British press subsequently criticized him for too much oratory, and one or two Americans walked out on him. However, he got a tremendous hand from the majority of the congress.

In the afternoon our real work began, namely drafting recommen-dations in committee. I am a member of the Subcommittee on Soviet Propaganda. We heard a long report from Mme Suzanne Laban of France, who had made a penetrating study of Soviet propaganda and laid down a comprehensive program to combat it. I proposed that the European Community set up a radio station to be called "The Voice of Unity," for the purpose of welding the free nations closer together. My idea was not so much to try to penetrate the Soviet bloc, but work constructively in Europe—and, for that matter, Canada and the United States—to make people realize there is a NATO and a European Community which is trying to cooperate. Most Americans, and for that matter, most Britishers, don't realize such a thing exists.

June 7: We worked all day. At 11 A.M. there was a briefing at the American Embassy with reports to the American delegation from committee members. Significantly, Eric Johnston, the chairman, was reminded that Senator Kefauver, in reporting on Committee B, had neglected to mention military matters. The military subcommittee comes under B. Johnston replied: "No, Senator Kefauver did not neglect the military report. We previously decided to omit that report. At the last briefing, we felt that too much emphasis was given to military matters."

This, in effect, set the tone for the entire congress. The military are taking a back seat. The emphasis is on other forms of cooperation to bring the free world closer together.

I spent the afternoon arguing in committee over the best means of combating Soviet propaganda. The British took the offensive. They argued that the meat-ax tactics of Mme Laban would accomplish nothing, in fact might do harm. They claim that the way to win friends behind the Iron Curtain is the soft approach; to argue for unity; to show that the West is constructive and friendly. A lot can be said for the British point of view, but they were overwhelmingly voted down.

I couldn't stay for the final argument since, very unwisely, I accepted an invitation to dine with Andrew Roth at his home. Andy is a young newspaperman who got into trouble during the Amerasia case, and I had not seen him since. He has been living abroad, but, I found, has the respect of other American newspapermen in London. He wanted to get some British newspapermen and M.P.'s in for dinner to meet me and I turned up promptly at seven-thirty. Two M.P.'s arrived with their wives, both very interesting and intelligent. We sat and waited. We waited until nine-forty-five. I concluded that this was long enough to wait for a seven-thirty dinner and told them I had to go back to a committee meeting. This was true—except that I had originally planned not to go. In addition to the empty stomach, the room was one of these frigid varieties which has not been heated for years and which creeps into my throat. I could feel a terrible sore throat coming on. When I made excuses to leave they finally brought in a plate of chicken. I ate part of it and departed.

Mrs. Roth, as I left, confessed woefully: "I shouldn't have worked on my garden wall this afternoon. I should have thawed that chicken out instead."

June 8: All morning we haggled in committee over the terms of our recommendation on combating Soviet propaganda. My proposal for a radio station stayed in the final report, but seemed relegated to the sidelines in view of all the verbiage inserted by the aggressive French and Turks. The British once more put up a battle; and having lost it in the subcommittee continued it in the full committee. They moved to strike out all of Section 2, which calls for a Free World Association to undertake propaganda behind the Iron Curtain and also to conduct a radio station. The British lost, though not without making a rather effective argument.

The work of the committee is secret. The discussions in plenary session are public. I have to be careful to remember that as a delegate I cannot report, as a newspaperman, what goes on in secret session. I have been going home every noon to have a sandwich in my hotel room and get off a cabled column. But I have to steer clear of the committee sessions. I suppose no one would object to my reporting on these, because they don't involve matters of life and death, but anyway I am trying to be careful.

I have a chance to fly back tomorrow afternoon in a MATS [Military Air Transport Service] plane carrying the Congressmen direct to Washington. I suppose that I will be criticized for going on a MATS plane inasmuch as I have criticized other people. But my way is being paid round trip across the Atlantic and I don't think it makes much difference whether I go back on the MATS plane, which is military and has a lot of extra seats, or on the chartered plane, which is civilian and crowded.

Mary Roebling gave a dinner. Present, believe it or not, was Armand Erpf, the railroad adviser whom Admiral Strauss had retained to make a study of the railroads and who resigned hurriedly when it was made known that his investment company owns about $20,000,000 worth of railroad stocks. We did not mention Admiral Strauss. Some of the British papers have reported the claim that anti-Semitism is being brought into the Strauss battle. One of the reasons I want to get back is to check on the voting.

As I left, the Royal Guards in scarlet coats and bearskin headdress were still pacing back and forth in front of St. James's Palace, just as they had been twenty-nine years ago when we met for three months trying to settle the relatively unimportant question of 10,000-ton cruisers. Henry L. Stimson wanted to limit their number. The American Admirals did not. Neither did the Japanese. I remember Aristide Briand going to sleep at the council table. He was getting old. I remember how cold it was at St. James's Palace and how the fireplace, although glowing and beautiful, radiated little heat. I remember Dino Grandi, the bearded Foreign Minister under Mussolini, who strutted at the council table. And I remember Premier Wakatsuki of Japan, who, one evening when Will Rogers was entertaining a social gathering and was telling his most hilarious jokes, suddenly got up and announced: "I go now." Will Rogers never had such a cold dishrag thrown in his face.

In those days diplomats really worked at negotiating. They did not fly back and forth across the Atlantic. It took a week to cross the Atlantic; so they stayed in one place. Stimson saw his conference break up mainly on one thing: European nations would not limit their cruisers, unimportant as those cruisers seem today, unless the United States agreed to consult in case war threatened. Stimson agreed to a consultative pact, but back in Washington Herbert Hoover threw him to the wolves.

So Stimson ruefully came home. Today we are not only consulting, but we have our own troops on European soil and air bases in England. We are ready at a moment's notice to go to war in case an enemy strikes. The scarlet-coated Guards in bearskin caps who pace outside St. James's Palace do not change with the passing of years. But American policy does.

June 9:   I did a brief broadcast for BBC at nine-thirty this morning, and much to my surprise they paid me for it. The plenary session began at ten and was, for the first time, intensely interesting. General de Gaulle's representative introduced an amendment to the military resolution stating that the defense of NATO should be based upon global strategy. Actually, he was right. However, there was so much resentment against de Gaulle that morning for having threatened NATO with removal of our 200 H-bomb planes unless the United States gave him the secret of the hydrogen bomb that the French proposal was voted down overwhelmingly. George Brown, a British Labour M.P., then made an impassioned speech against the entire military resolution. He said it had been clarified in committee until it was clarified to death. He moved to substitute the original motion, and although nobody had read the original, almost everybody in the assembly voted for it. Mrs. Edith Green, Congresswoman from Oregon, made another impassioned speech, and a rather effective one, in favor of aiding the underdeveloped countries through the United Nations. She said, first of all, we should not weaken the UN; second, the Asians and Africans were suspicious of aid from NATO; they considered it the kiss of imperialism. Several Britishers supported Mrs. Green, but there was no vote while I was present.

The debate was so hot and heavy that I hated to leave, but in order to catch the MATS plane I had to pull out about 3:00 P.M.

June 10:   It was a reasonably pleasant trip, but I am glad to get home. I doubt whether we have changed the world very much. To read the British newspapers, you would not know that a conference had been taking place. Aside from the London *Times* and the *Telegraph*, the British press goes in for sex, murder, and society. I don't know any newspapers in Washington, New York, or even Chicago which carry as much filth.

June 20:   Got up early, drove to Friendship Airport in Baltimore to meet the children. They came TWA jet from Los Angeles, and thereby beat their grandfather in the new mode of travel. I have flown in an Air Force jet fighter but never in a jet commercial transport.

All three boys looked nonchalant and unconcerned. Drew led little Joe off the plane, his fishing poles clasped in one hand and Joe in the other, as if he were going on a week-end fishing trip. Georgie trailed some distance behind, as usual. They had had breakfast on the plane, but not much sleep.

Went to dinner with Senator John Sparkman. Present were Senator and Mrs. Lausche, whom I had just panned for his Strauss vote; Senator and Mrs. Stennis of Mississippi (she had tried to get me on the telephone some time ago to protest about a story that they used military transportation home); General and Mrs. Omar Bradley, who are good friends; Admiral Arleigh Burke, the Chief of Naval Operations, and his wife (I have panned him consistently and unremittingly regarding his feud with the Air Force); the Fulbrights, and "Scoop" Jackson.

Mrs. Bradley was quite frank—more frank than I've ever heard any other Army wife—regarding the Eisenhowers. She confirmed the fact that in 1948 her husband had warned the Democrats not to nominate Ike because he couldn't "make decisions." She told me something I had never known before—that Ike and Mamie always listened to my broadcasts during and after the war. They started apparently at the time I reported the Patton slapping incident. No matter what was going on, they dropped it to go to the radio at 6 P.M. Sundays.

June 21:   Lunched at the Vournases' to say good-bye to John Tsunis. Everyone is still talking about the Strauss defeat. Ed Foley let drop the remark to Luvie that it all began when Cyrus Eaton contributed to the Democratic campaign deficit and wanted Strauss defeated.

June 22:   Senators McGee and Hartke lunched with me at the Capitol, together with John Moss of California and Leonard Marks. Leonard is worried over the networks' drive to abolish Section 315, which in turn would give them complete control of newscasting. He gave a rather vigorous story of the manner in which the networks are riding roughshod over the FCC. Hartke had introduced an amendment which would remove Section 315 from the Communications Act, but I think we pretty well persuaded him to change his mind. Certainly, McGee was convinced.

I told them the story of my being chucked off the air in Los Angeles and Detroit as the result of my brush with Murray Chotiner and my refusal to take out insurance.* I had hoped to get an investiga-

---

*Drew Pearson refused to buy libel insurance because insurance companies reserved the right to compel a retraction even without the author's concurrence. Instead, he contracted with the papers that carried his column and the radio stations that carried his broadcasts, promising to bear all legal expenses in libel suits and to pay any adverse judgments. He therefore objected to requirements that he take out libel insurance anyway, surmising that the demand was a form of censorship.—ED.

tion started of news suppression but everyone is a bit fatigued after the Strauss investigation, and I don't blame them.

June 28:   Eisenhower, with Admiral Strauss with him, flew up to dedicate the St. Lawrence Seaway with Queen Elizabeth. It was a deliberate slap at the Senate. I have been rather surprised by the mail on Admiral Strauss. It all seems to be against him and some of it has come in from rather intelligent people giving me credit for the battle.

Got hold of Senator Gene McCarthy to urge him to filibuster Monday against the continuation of the Korean excise taxes unless the Senate and House accepted an amendment knocking out the 4 percent tax benefit for stock market manipulators. He seemed just as keen to do battle as I was and discussed plans for getting one man in the House of Representatives to object on Monday, which would automatically throw the debate over until Tuesday, June 30. Then the Senate would only have a few hours in which to filibuster.

The Ways and Means Committee had plenty of time to work up this bill long ago but didn't. Now the Senate has a chance to slap down Wilbur Mills of Arkansas, who is beginning to be another reactionary dictator of taxes as chairman of the Ways and Means Committee— despite the fact that it was only a few years ago that Bob Allen and I helped elect him as a new young liberal Congressman.

Also got hold of Senator Joe Clark of Pennsylvania. He seemed equally enthusiastic about putting up a fight to show that the Senate liberals were not going to take a kicking around on a battle they had already won in the Senate.

June 29:   Ike flew to New York to welcome Deputy Premier Kozlov who arrived nonstop from Moscow yesterday. Ike made the trip only after Ambassador Menshikov made it clear that Nixon would not be welcomed by Khrushchev unless Eisenhower welcomed Kozlov. Ike had refused to go even to the Washington airport to meet the King of the Belgians, the President of Brazil, or the President of Italy, plus many others, but in this case he flew to New York to welcome a man who is not a head of state. Secretary of State Herter had pressured him, mainly because Herter wants Nixon to get the red carpet treatment in Moscow.

Goosed Senator Pat McNamara and Phil Hart, both of Michigan, regarding the fight against the 4 percent tax benefit for stock market investors. Also had Jack Anderson spend the day in the Senate needling the liberals. But the whole strategy flopped, chiefly because of bad footwork. Senator McCarthy got a freshman from Iowa, Wolf, to object in the House and Sam Rayburn outmaneuvered him. Or rather, I should say Sam rode roughshod over him. Wolf's lone objection was simply smothered.

This sent the bill over to the Senate one day earlier than expected. On the Senate floor the liberals figured they couldn't take the lead in the battle because either they were not members of the Finance Committee or because they were freshmen. However, Russell Long did a masterful job. As a member of the Finance Committee he argued with such reactionaries as Kerr of Oklahoma and was effective. McCarthy was also good. Symington, who had been needled by Jack, managed to ask a question helpfully and then seemed very proud of himself that he had asked one lone question.

But there was nothing even remotely resembling a filibuster. I talked later to Wayne Morse, who was ready to filibuster but who said not a single Senator had approached him. In brief, they weren't ready for the kill. The liberals will always talk big but nearly always lose either through faulty footwork or lack of determination. They don't go for the jugular. In the Strauss fight we worked with the conservatives and the moderates. The conservatives are far more efficient with their footwork and they fight to kill—provided they are genuinely on your side.

June 30:   Had a long session with John Carroll of Colorado and Hart of Michigan. They are the two Democratic members of a subcommittee to investigate the FCC and other independent agencies. Hart talked to me early in the session—January—about what a big job his committee could do. However, it has done nothing. I brought Leonard Marks up to tell them of the opportunities in the FCC. They listened but alibied.

July 13:   George Lincoln Rockwell, the so-called führer of Virginia, came to see me. He had sued me for libel some weeks ago, but the judge threw out the case. Rockwell suggested a trade. He wanted something written about the recent convention of hatemongers in Chicago and in return promised to give me inside information regarding the hatemongers. I listened. The guy obviously is a psychopathic case, nevertheless has a very plausible manner and apparently is telling the truth. He told me about a meeting of six top hatemongers, including John Kasper and Joe McWilliams, who planned various strategies for the next year.

I drew him into a conversation regarding the bombing of the temple in Atlanta and the fact that suddenly these church and school bombings have stopped. It has been my opinion that the reason was the vigorous methods of the Atlanta police, plus the fact that the nest inspiring them, namely Rockwell's home in Arlington, had been broken up. Rockwell was quite frank. He said the bombings had been performed by "crackpots." He admitted that they were probably inspired by some of his literature and his operations.

July 17: Dined with Mr. and Mrs. Alfred Strelsin. She went with me to North Africa two Christmases ago to entertain the troops. He is a very wealthy banker and manipulator, an ex-newspaperman who has managed to make money. We got into quite a debate as to whether Dulles was responsible for the withdrawal of British troops from Suez, which Strelsin believes was the most disastrous decision of recent years. I could agree with him on the latter point, but argued that Dulles was ill; that the decision had been made by Eisenhower himself. Strelsin, however, claims that Dulles could have warned the British that if they didn't take Suez in a hurry he would have to demand their withdrawal. Maybe he is right. Certainly the British could have split up their operations and certainly they were terribly, inexcusably slow.

Castro resigned as Premier of Cuba. I was a little flabbergasted even though I had predicted it. As I also predicted, however, he is going to remain the strong man behind the scenes and perhaps resume the premiership again.

Goldfine threw himself on the mercy of the court today. This means that all the involvement of Jack in the bugging case is out.

July 18: Eisenhower has just pulled another amazing boner. Herter announced at a press conference that he was trying to persuade Chip Bohlen to remain on at the State Department as a Russia expert. But at this press conference Eisenhower announced, in reply to questions, that his report on Bohlen was negative and he saw no reason why he should be brought back. What happened was that Eisenhower had been listening to Styles Bridges and Dirksen and hadn't bothered to read the papers. Therefore he didn't know about Herter's statement. Probably also he hadn't read any of Herter's reports. He didn't even know that his own assistant, General Wilton Persons [the White House's congressional liaison man], had been working on Capitol Hill to try to change the Republican Senators.

Result: Doug Dillon came over to theWhite House and forced the President to cable his apologies to Bohlen and also issue a public statement that he hoped Bohlen would remain.

July 19:   Several Senators came for supper: Magnuson of Washington with a very good looking blonde, Bible of Nevada, Engle of California, Hartke of Indiana; also Jimmie Roosevelt, the Bob Allens, and Clayton Fritchey. The chief subject of conversation seemed to be Paul Butler. I didn't hear any defense for him, not even from Bob. Actually, I think Paul has done more to call the turn on Lyndon Johnson than anyone else.

The Venezuelan Ambassador was also there. He got a great kick out of the political discussion.

Jimmie Roosevelt said that he had written to Eisenhower that his three children would like to see the office once occupied by their grandfather. Ike very graciously invited the children to come to the White House and sat back in his chair to talk to them. He wanted to know how much history they were studying in school. He said that his grandchildren who were going to the Friends School were studying a new technique of geography and history at the same time which the President seemed to think was unique and important. He reached into the drawer of his desk and pulled out a bag marked "Chase Manhattan Bank." Then he took three dollars in silver from the bag. He explained that there had only been two issues of silver dollars and one had the word "Peace" marked on it. So he gave the children three dollars, each bearing the word "Peace."

Afterward, Jimmie asked the children what they thought of the President. They said that he looked much older than he appeared in his newspaper photos or on TV. Jimmie said that Ike slumped down in his chair part of the time sitting on his back, and seemed to be thoroughly relaxed and enjoying his talk with the children. This is what Eisenhower loves most.

July 21:   The advertising agent who handled my TV program in Texas came to see me to give the real story of the U.S. Trust and Guaranty Company fiasco. It went into bankruptcy, thereby causing me more headaches and heartaches than I've ever suffered from television or radio. It had persuaded me to start the program with the words "You can put your trust in U.S. Trust."

The story of what happened is that Shumate, the head of U.S. Trust, had been selling savings certificates and using them to float sales of automobiles, thus giving him a 21 percent return on his investment. This is why he was able to offer 5 percent interest to those who bought his savings certificates. The business was quite sound because there was a tremendous demand for automobiles, but some of the big insurance companies became jealous of the business being siphoned away from them to U.S. Trust. Ben Jack Cage, who represented several big insurance companies, particularly wanted to take over U.S. Trust. He has now been convicted and has fled to Brazil. He was caught stealing $1 million.

Cage, in order to take over U.S. Trust, went to the insurance lobbies in Austin; also approached Byron Saunders, the insurance commissioner who is now under indictment for taking bribes from Ben Jack Cage. Saunders told Shumate to sell U.S. Trust to Cage. Shumate told Saunders to go to hell.

A showdown resulted with Shumate being given an ultimatum that either he would sell to Cage or else he would be put out of business. Governor Allan Shivers came to see Shumate two days before the big blowup and told Shumate to sell. Shumate, in turn, told Shivers that he would expose the $70,000 he, Shumate, had paid to Saunders, the insurance commissioner. Governor Shivers replied that if he divulged anything he would be prosecuted for malfeasance.

Shumate was caught betwixt and between. He had been paying off the insurance commissioner, as every other insurance company had. One reason was because he wanted to branch out in Arkansas and wanted to transfer some of his Texas assets to Arkansas. This was contrary to Texas law.

Two days later Shumate shot himself. He is still alive—a mass of human pulp.

After this tragedy, Shivers threw the weight of his prestige and the power of the Texas press against me as a culprit. The receivers for U.S. Trust have now paid off about seventy cents on the dollar. Probably they could have paid eighty or ninety cents off with a little better management. And if the company had been kept operating they would never have lost a cent.

Unfortunately, this is all water over the dam and I can't prove any of it, except that Felix Einsohn, a certified public accountant in Dallas, who was hired by Cage to review the U.S. Trust books, might know the answers.

For a good many years I have not set foot in Texas for fear I might be slapped with a damage suit. Even when I went to San Antonio last December for the commemoration of Colonel Moore's death, I sneaked in very quietly. I have not been on television to any extent since the Texas fiasco.

July 23:   Doris Fleeson is fit to be tied over our book, which takes her new husband Dan Kimball over the hurdles as the lobbyist for General Tire and Rubber and Aero Jet. When she has a couple of drinks, however, she gets a little loquacious about Dan and herself. "When Dan gets too much beer I just lock him up," she says.

Sumner Welles told me that Doris had followed him all over Europe in 1940 covering the Rooseveltian efforts to head off World War II. He got rather fond of her. She came to dinner later and asked, "Where did you get this silverware?" "It came from Mathilde's grandmother." "That's the trouble with you," remarked Doris. "You inherit everything. I work for what I get."

July 28:   Televised all day [in New York], then flew back to Washington for dinner in honor of Tony Biddle and his third wife. Stuart Symington was there. He has washed out as usual on a commitment to stand behind our book in case we got any denials that Eisenhower was really responsible for ditching the first ICBM. Jack tried to get him to make a speech after Ike denied our statement in the book, but as usual Stuart won't stand up.

I sat beside Mrs. John Sparkman of Alabama and Mrs. Alan Bible of Nevada. Joe Martin was at our table and I proposed a toast to a grand old Republican. I think Joe was a little startled to have me propose it because there have been times when I have needled him quite vigorously.

Sam Rayburn was at the dinner and gave me the glassy eye. Jess Larson, the former General Services Administrator, who was there, suggested that I come around and talk to him about war surpluses and stockpiling. He said that the chief beneficiary from stockpiling is George Humphrey, who negotiated that nickel contract with the government just before he, Humphrey, took office in January 1953.

August 1: Nixon is having a very fine reception in Russia and undoubtedly has increased his chances for the Presidential nomination. Rockefeller will have to get started pretty soon if he is going to catch up. Some of the Democratic candidates are talking about going to Russia too.

I learned this week that Eisenhower is really sore at Lyndon Johnson because of the Strauss confirmation battle. Ike used to call him up on the telephone and considered him his secret agent inside the Democratic party. Now he calls him "just another politician." On the whole, I think this will be very healthy for the Democratic party. It's also one reason Lyndon was probably so sore at me after the Strauss fight and told me, "Never get me into a fight like this again." Actually, Lyndon needs a few more good fights. He's too much of a pacifier; a pleaser of both sides.

August 4: Had a party at the farm for Ed Reid, head of the League of Municipalities of Alabama. Several of the Alabama Congressmen came, together with Lister Hill. Lister has been a little aloof ever since he refused to make a speech on Admiral Strauss. He probably has a guilty conscience. After Lister left the dinner party, Ed Reid did a takeoff on him which brought down the house. He mimicked some of Lister's speeches in Alabama where Lister straddled the fence. One of the Congressmen, I think it was Roberts, remarked that whenever Lister's name appeared on a health bill that bill was sure to pass. "But," remarked Ed Reid, "is there anything controversial about health? Have you seen Lister's name on an education bill lately or anything else that's controversial?"

The trouble with Lister according to Ed Reid is that he's inherited a million dollars.

August 5: Nixon returned to Washington. His reception in Poland was even greater than some people realize. My AP friend said that the university students at the University of Warsaw cried, "Give us freedom."

August 7: Lunched with Maurice Rosenblatt, who is secretary for the Committee for an Effective Congress, and helped me put Joe McCarthy out of commission. His committee has probably elected more liberals to the Senate than any other, but I was surprised to hear him say that they had contributed $17,000 to elect Senator Hugh Scott in Pennsylvania against Governor George Leader. Scott has now turned out to be an embryo McCarthy—certainly at least during the Strauss hearings.

Rosenblatt pointed to something which I had forgotten, namely that the liberals had every opportunity to expose labor graft long before Senator McClellan stepped into it. Senator Paul Douglas was chairman of a subcommittee on labor welfare funds but did little about it. When Rosenblatt asked Wayne Morse why the liberals hadn't exposed labor corruption, Wayne replied, "Labor never requested it."

I telephoned Harry Truman in Kansas City to ask him about a conversation he had with DNC Chairman Paul Butler, who had reportedly come to see him. Truman asked me how I was. I replied, "I always feel better when I'm talking to you." He then made quite an unusual statement. "You say that after all I've done to you." He must have had in mind the Littell suit and the recent article in *Time* magazine in which Edward Bennett Williams revealed that he had got secret documents out of the Justice Department against me, thanks to Harry Truman's hatred.

Truman said that he had talked to Butler and had told him the job of the Democratic chairman is "to keep the party together, not stir up trouble.* The party platform is adopted at each convention and it's the job of the chairman to carry it out.

"Butler left in complete agreement," Truman said. "He didn't mean to cause disagreement. I told him that it's up to the chairman to see there is harmony in the party."

"Did you write him a strong letter," I asked.

"No," he replied. "I'm trying not to write letters now."

August 11:   Lyndon telephoned. I figured he was a little irked over my story on housing in the column in which I reported that the Senate liberals wanted a showdown over the housing bill but that Lyndon was opposed. Lyndon told me on the telephone that he had telephoned Sparkman and Fulbright that morning and told them to demand an immediate attempt to override the President's veto of the old housing bill. Lyndon predicted to me that Ike's veto could not be overridden. He said it would fail by about five votes. However, he said that they would now attempt to override it as the result of the column.

---

*Butler had annoyed Democratic Congressional leaders by appointing a committee to advise Congress on policy matters.—ED.

Later Senator Morse called to say that Lyndon had told Senator Proxmire of Wisconsin how he was going to attempt to override the President's veto just to show the liberals what they were up against. "I fixed them," Lyndon told Proximire. "I told John Sparkman and Bill Fulbright to go ahead and call for a showdown in committee." I couldn't help but think that perhaps I had given a bad break to the housing bill and the liberals. Later, when I talked to Joe Clark of Philadelphia he said he didn't think this was true, that it was necessary to have a showdown one way or the other.

Talked to Bob Bicks, acting head of the Antitrust Division, who says that they have 40 percent of their personnel working on the case against General Motors. This is why they haven't been able to do more work on other cases—hence, the criticism by Lyndon Johnson. I told Bicks that I had argued with Lyndon that the Democrats should not be in the position of curtailing the antitrust budget and Bicks said that the Senate subsequently reinstated their cut.

August 12:   There's a rumor that Castro has been shot. He called off a TV cast.

Ike's housing veto was upheld exactly as Lyndon predicted it. Ten Southern Senators voted for him. Eisenhower needed nine. The coalition is functioning perfectly. As a result there will be no civil rights bill this session.

Lunched with Herb Maletz, attorney for the House Judiciary Committee and Congressman Celler. Herb is a dedicated public servant but naive. He claims that Celler is not on the take with his law practice.

I sat in on the Hébert investigation of Western Electric and Donald Douglas, Jr., of Douglas Aircraft. It seems to me that the hearings pulled its punches on Douglas, though Hébert was very good in his cross-examination of Western Electric.

August 13:   Congressman John McCormack has given an ultimatum to Eisenhower that Khrushchev will not be permitted to address a joint session of Congress. I am using this on the radio and attributing it to McCormack as the spokesman for the Catholic Church. I know I will get into a lot of trouble. However, I pointed out that the most prominent Catholic in Congress, Jack Kennedy, does not favor this position.

Lunched with Tom Hennings at the Senate. Tom said that Nixon had held a lunch for Democratic Senators at which he gave a very businesslike and efficient account of his trip to Russia. Nixon has gone out of his way to contact most of the Senators to let them know what he did in Russia. Tom said that Nixon had grown in stature and he could not help but be impressed with him.

Tom summarized the Democratic candidates as only three: Stevenson, Hubert Humphrey, and Lyndon Johnson. Lyndon he described as an operator, Humphrey as a man with real courage and ability, and Stevenson as a statesman.

We agreed that Symington hasn't any courage and that Jack Kennedy won't get anywhere, though he has done a pretty good job on the labor bill.

Tom went to see Lyndon the other day to get some action regarding judges. Wood of Pennsylvania was held up together with a California judge whom Senator Kuchel wants confirmed. Lyndon pulled out a little black book and said no regarding both Wood and the California appointee. He didn't explain why but apparently he is making a trade and wants some action out of the California and Pennsylvania Senators before he confirms their judges.

Bill Rogers bumped into Tom at the Burning Tree Club the other day and told him that if the Senate would confirm Henry Friendly to the Second Circuit Court of Appeals in New York, then the Justice Department would appoint Joe Smith, the Catholic judge in Connecticut, to the same court. Senator Tom Dodd, the Catholic spokesman, has been holding up Friendly's confirmation until Joe Smith is appointed. Friendly is Jewish and is the man Felix Frankfurter is trying to groom as his successor on the Supreme Court. He has told Friendly that if he would get out of Pan American Airways, where he has a chance to be the top dog, and serve for a time on the Circuit Court of Appeals, then he, Felix, would resign and make way for him on the Supreme Court.

August 14: Leonard Shane came for lunch. He advises against any suit against ABC. It would hurt the program with other stations. Leonard had just been to a meeting in Jack Shelly's office last night after the House passed the Landrum-Griffin antilabor bill. Present were Congressmen Jimmie Roosevelt, Chet Holifield, Pucinski of Chicago, and other liberal Democrats. Shelly called it an Irish wake. "Never again will I vote for peanuts, cotton, and the ridding of water hyacinths from southern rivers," said Jimmie Roosevelt. The consensus was that Rayburn had let them down. He didn't speak against the Landrum-Griffin bill and he didn't line up Texas Congressmen. In the battle between Halleck and Rayburn, Sam just didn't fight.

I am wondering whether Halleck may not have outsmarted himself. The real issue in the labor fight is getting a bill tough enough so that unions can't organize the South. If the South remains unorganized Halleck and other Northern Congressmen are going to lose industry to the South. Halleck almost was defeated last November in his Indiana district.

August 16: The Khrushchev visit is beginning to backfire. Senator Bridges is sore at Nixon for initiating it and may turn toward Rockefeller. John McCormack has sent word that he won't permit Khrushchev to speak in the House of Representatives and Senator Dodd of Connecticut has called for a period of mourning.

August 18: Testified before the Hébert committee.* Did reasonably well but couldn't get a rise out of the Republicans. The hearing room was pretty well packed, including Congressman Mendel Rivers of South Carolina, who is a member of the committee and regarding whom I once reported that he had run around the corridor of the Savoy in London in his underpants, chasing gals. He asked no questions.

I testified on the setback to the American satellite program because General Electric's Dr. Richard Porter had switched the rocket launching engine at the last minute; also regarding Dan Kimball's conflict of interest with Aerojet and a number of secret hotel suites kept by the munitions lobby in Washington. Only the satellite setback got any headlines.

It looks as if I would not be going to Moscow. The Russian Embassy has delayed a visa and apparently thinks I don't want one unless I get an interview with Khrushchev. This is probably just as well.

Met Jack Kennedy at the Capitol. He thanked me for noting that he did not agree with John McCormack re Khrushchev's addressing a joint session of Congress.

---

*The Special Investigations Subcommittee of the House Armed Services Committee, chaired by Congressman F. Edward Hébert of Louisiana.—Ed.

August 19:   Went up to see Lyndon Johnson for the first time since the Strauss fight. I think he's been a little irked at my apparent boycott, which was not intentional, but he didn't show it. He looked in wonderful shape considering the beating he's taken.

I asked him whether he was going to get a labor bill passed. I figured this was going to be a tough hurdle; however, he was optimistic; said that of the seven titles in the Kennedy bill, the first six were tougher than the House bill; that the House was interested in preventing union organization rather than stopping racketeering. The Senate bill aimed at racketeering.

He also pointed out that the building trades, which were guilty of the greatest graft, had secured an exemption under the Taft-Hartley Act because Taft was a great friend of Maurice Hutchinson and Dick Gray of the Carpenters Union and the Building Trades Council, both Republicans.

"The mail was heavy when Truman fired MacArthur," Lyndon said, "but I think it's been heavier now on the labor bill. I got 8,000 letters in one week from Texas. Ike did it. That TV speech really got across."

Lyndon pulled out his letters, or rather his summary of them. He had them carefully tabulated. He told me that he thought Wright Patman would be defeated because he had voted with Sam Rayburn against the tough labor bill. "He just couldn't look Sam in the face and vote against him," Lyndon said.

Lyndon pulled a piece of paper out of his pocket which he had typed up in advance and handed it to me. "That's for you," he said. "Cabell Phillips of *The New York Times* came in to see me and asked me about the new Ike. I told him there wasn't any new Ike. Here he is up at Gettysburg golfing while we are working. Does he come down like Franklin Roosevelt to read his veto message? Does he take any interest in legislation other than to say, 'No you can't have housing for old folks,' or 'You can't have housing for college classrooms.' He doesn't want back-door financing for old folk's housing but he asks us to give him $6 billion back-door financing for the International Bank to build homes in Burma and Vietnam. I want you to write a story on the new Ike and show that there ain't no such animal.

"Also I want you to do something on this housing bill. You've got to get Howard Smith to pass it."

"Can't you get Sam to put the heat on Smith?" I asked.

"You can't put the heat on people. It's like putting the heat on Drew Pearson. We've got to get a housing bill. We've got to get a labor bill and we've got to get a civil rights bill," Lyndon summarized.

"They tell me we've got to get out of here by September 15 or Khrushchev will be embarrassed. Styles Bridges will make a speech on the floor just as he threatened to make one against Kozlov when Nixon wanted Kozlov to appear before Congress. Ike gives me the deadline of adjourning Congress and at the same time gives me the job of protecting him from his Republican critics. Yet I've got to get this legislation passed."

Lyndon asked me whether he should bring Congress back in the fall, and I told him that I certainly would, that the young senators and Congressmen were grousing anyway because they couldn't send their children to school. He called attention to an interview Ladybird had given in *The Washington Post* that Congress should come back in the fall and adjourn now. "Ladybird stepped out of turn and I told her so. She doesn't often do that, but she did this time," Lyndon said.

I told him I thought Ladybird was absolutely right. He said that I was wrong if we brought Congress back around November. "The Southerners will filibuster for six weeks against civil rights and that will run us into Christmas. We'd have to come back around October first. They've got six weeks of filibustering in them."

As I was about to go, Lyndon pulled a sheet from his middle drawer and read from a confidential report on Thruston Morton's dinner in which he said that Ike was sore at Johnson because of the Strauss fight. "You wrote about that," said Lyndon, "and you were absolutely right. You caused me a lot of trouble with Mrs. Hobby's paper, the Houston *Post*. You're not in those papers and they've been after me ever since I opposed Strauss. However, we showed Ike that he wasn't able to get a member of his own Cabinet confirmed and that he hasn't got the power up here that he thinks he has. You thought I was too objective but if I had taken a stand on that earlier we might not have won. However, we won, thanks to you and Clint Anderson."

I had a date with Senator Magnuson at twelve and by this time was thirty minutes late. Maggie didn't take up the "watchdog committee" at his committee session this morning. He said they were too irritable. "Sometimes you have to sing hymns to them and sometimes they'll sing 'Hail, Hail the gang's all here,' " said Maggie, "but at the end of a session they are always irritable." He said that he was planning to go down to see Secretary Herter with Senator Cooper to urge that his committee be permitted to go to Red China to study trade. Cooper is going along to use his influence with Nehru to get them into China. Maggie figures that Nixon will go to China next spring and pull off another big publicity stunt to help him get the nomination. He wants to get there with his committee first.

He said that he had already spoken to McGee and Yarborough about serving on the watchdog committee and would try to put Hugh Scott on it too.

August 30:   Dinner for Dwight Whitney, who was introduced to guests by Ellen as "my fiancé." Senator John Carroll of Colorado, Jim Carey of the United Electrical Workers, and Congressman Lud Ashley of Ohio were there. Carey told about his arguments with Meany as to whether the AFL—CIO should invite Khrushchev to speak at their San Francisco convention. The AFL—CIO President was adamant.

Ashley says that there has never been so much disgust with the Democratic leadership. Rayburn, he says, didn't lift a finger to pass the moderate labor bill, McCormack is useless and refused to help out on the public works bill, which means defeat for reelection to many border-line Democrats in marginal districts. When Ashley talked to McCormack about it, he said, "Talk to Bobby Baker," referring of course to Lyndon Johnson's assistant. "I'm not going to talk to Bobby Baker," replied Ashley. "I'm talking to the leader of the House. This is your job, not mine, to talk to Bobby Baker."

Rayburn is now being put in the shade by a younger, more dynamic man on the Republican side—Charlie Halleck.

October 22:   Took my first jet passenger flight—Washington to Los Angeles. Five hours. Quite a difference from the twelve-hour flight in the old days of frequent stops. Also quite a difference from one trip I took by train—eleven days from Montana to Philadelphia by day coach with a stop en route to see the grandparents in Kansas. Also quite a change from the three-week trip by a horse and spring wagon from Columbus, Ohio, to Philadelphia in 1910.

October 23:   Lunched with Jim Geller and Bill Hendricks. I proposed a national friendship committee to promote exchanges of people with Russia. They countered with a proposal of a friendship train to Russia, beginning in Los Angeles, crossing to New York and then resuming in Marseilles across the European continent to Moscow. I doubt if I can get the railroads to cooperate. There is still an awful lot of holding back regarding even people-to-people friendship with Russia.

Went to dinner at Mike Romanoff's. Here is a small-time crook who has really parlayed his past reputation into a lot of fame and money. George Frelinghuysen gave a soiree which must have cost him $10,000. Most of the motion picture stars were too young for me to recognize or remember, but Mary Pickford, looking very fat and unattractive, was there, together with Sonja Henie, who has aged a bit, Debbie Reynolds, who hasn't aged, and a lot of others. I took Ellen, Dan Moore, and Dwight Whitney, none of us in black ties.

I left early—1 A.M.—the others stayed until four.

October 24: Arthur Goldberg put on a terrific argument for the Steelworkers Union in Pittsburgh and again in Philadelphia. He might be able to stop the Taft-Hartley injunction.

Had lunch with Joe De Silva and George. Joe is considering the purchase of a radio station. Since big business has gone in for owning radio I told him I saw no reason why unions shouldn't also.

We had dinner with Mickey Cohen, who is hipped on helping his strip-tease friend, Candy Barr, sentenced to fifteen years in a Texas jail for possession of marijuana. Unquestionably, it was too harsh a sentence but what was in the judge's mind no doubt was the black record of her arrests for prostitution and the pornographic motion picture which is still shown in Tiajuana. I told Mickey that I had taken the matter up carefully with the Governor of Texas but that the Governor was not going to stick his neck out, especially in view of the picture. Mickey put up quite an eloquent plea that a girl has to be forgiven mistakes for youth and that she was only fourteen or fifteen at the time this happened. Of course, I'm inclined to get on my white steed and go charging off for various lost causes, but this is one which I don't enthuse over.

October 25: Took the children to Disneyland. The management had arranged for us to ride on almost everything and do almost everything without standing in line to buy tickets. It was quite a wonderful day even for blasé adults. The children were beside themselves. When it was all over Georgie remarked to one of the men who had taken us through: "We'll come again and you can be our guide." It's amazing how the royal touch goes to one's head when one is treated even briefly like royalty.

October 26:   Talked to a man who manufactures strainers for ballistic missiles. He explained that the strainer is all-important because if small pieces of steel get into the inner workings of the missile it misfires. This is one of the reasons why there have been so many failures, he explained. Yet the Arthur D. Little Company, in Boston, partly backed by Joseph P. Kennedy, will not change its specifications. Went on Goodie Knight's TV program. Goodie has recovered much of his bouncing personality and seemed in excellent form. He had some pretty hot things to say about Senator Bill Knowland and the manner in which Knowland ran against him, Goodie, instead of running against the Democrats. He didn't say much about Nixon. There was a time in San Francisco in 1956 when what he said about Nixon was worse than anything I have ever written. But they patched things up in 1958.

Went to a dinner given by Lytton, my former sponsor, in honor of Senator Gene McCarthy of Minnesota. McCarthy is helping to raise money for a united Democratic "Young Turks" organization in the House of Representatives. This is what has been proposed time after time but Sam Rayburn has always undercut it. McCarthy, now in the Senate, wants to raise about $20,000 to pay for a research staff to operate in the House. About 120 liberal Democrats have already signed an agreement that they will work together next year despite Sam.

If this really goes across, it could be the making of the Democratic party. God knows, neither Lyndon nor Sam has made it in the past six years.

October 27:   Lunched with Matty Fox. He has been plugging away at pay-as-you-go television for years and invested about $5 million of his and other people's money. But he has a deal now with American Telephone and Telegraph and a brokerage firm to put across wired television so as to get around the FCC. It looks as if he might be on the verge of something really big. The tragedy is that Congressman Harris, the man who is now investigating the TV networks, is also the man who has held up pay-as-you-go television. And pay-as-you-go television is probably one of the best means of counteracting the networks series of crime and rape TV programs.

Yesterday Henry Kaiser signed a separate agreement with the Steelworkers Union. This was exactly as I forecast—though with some misgivings.

October 28: Left around noon by jet for Chicago. I suppose that it is hopeless to figure that George and Ellen may be reconciled. But they seemed quite happy when they were with me at dinner. Considering everything, the children are doing remarkably well.

November 23: For approximately one week I have been trying to make up my mind whether to launch on one of the most harebrained trips imaginable—around the world in thirty days, interviewing the heads of state Eisenhower will interview on his trip. Miss Canty has been working with airline schedules; I've been talking to embassies and cabling the Vatican; and now, after about ten days' hectic preparation, I am off.

The first stop is Madrid, where I'm supposed to interview Franco. I have never been fond of Franco, nor he of me. We have never met. But I'm sure he is more than familiar with the campaign I have waged against him. However, the Spanish Ambassador in Washington asked for a set of questions to be put to the Generalissimo and they were cabled to Madrid. It was tentatively agreed that there would be written answers and that Franco and I would then discuss things informally off-the-record.

I departed on Iberia at 5 P.M., relatively on time. It is a decrepit old plane with seedy upholstery. I have a berth.

November 24: About 1 A.M. I was awakened by the steward, who announced that we were going back to New York because we had one engine out of whack. To tell the truth, I hadn't slept much. The mattress was not exactly a mattress. It felt like straw. And the plane was insufferably hot. Also, the flight was bumpy, which probably was due to the conked-out engine. I learned that we were about three and a half to four hours out over the Atlantic when the engine failed.

I finally got back to the Waldorf at about 2:30 A.M., and before I went to bed took stock of the situation. I had lost one day and the interview with Franco was out. However, I had firm appointments in Rome, so I sent telegrams to the Spanish Ambassador that Mr. Franco would miss the pleasure of seeing me, and to the American Ambassador in Madrid to the same effect, and booked on a Pan American jet leaving at 6 P.M. with scheduled arrival in Rome at 11 A.M. This should be in ample time to have my audience with the Pope if Cardinal Cicognani has been able to arrange it.

Pan American Airways has been bragging about its jets, but I got to Idlewild at the stipulated time of one hour in advance only to have to wait three. It was not until forty-five minutes after the plane was scheduled to leave that the crew actually came in for their briefing. No reason was given for the delay. We were just kept waiting. Once we got aloft the captain announced that we would stop in Shannon because the weather was bad in Paris; also because apparently we had taken on a heavy load, though nobody mentioned this fact. The flight is advertised as non-stop to Paris, but Pan American is now milking the cream of the traffic across the Atlantic because it has jets and TWA doesn't. So it overloads and inconveniences its passengers.

November 25:   We stopped in London instead of Shannon and after frittering around for a while, moseyed to Paris. More delays in Paris. Finally we left for Rome. By this time we were five or six hours late, but due in Rome at approximately three o'clock. Instead, we arrived at four-thirty. I scrambled around for my baggage, got through customs, and finally hailed a taxi. While waiting, I managed to call the press relations officer of the Italian Foreign Office, but failed to reach him. Finally I got to the Hotel Excelsior and the reception clerk told me, "There's a very important letter for you with the porter. It's regarding an audience with the Pope." I tore open the letter, and my audience with the Pope was at four-thirty. The clock was now 5 P.M.

I called the Vatican. It was the Pope's birthday and Cardinal Cicognani had arranged for me to see him. Finally I got the Cardinal on the telephone and he said he would arrange for me to attend a special Mass the next day.

Dined that evening with Frank and Catherine Gervasi. He used to cover the State Department for INS when I was a young reporter, working for the *Baltimore Sun.* It was more-or-less a Thanksgiving dinner. Across the dining room seated by herself was Signorina Scarfati, a woman in her sixties and no longer attractive. Frank pointed her out as Mussolini's first mistress. A former Socialist, she had taught Mussolini most of his original social reforms, deserting him when Mussolini took up with Hitler and adopted the Nazi line. Scarfati is Jewish. She lives in the Hotel Ambassador and keeps alive by selling a few portraits now and then from her family's collection.

November 26: Thanksgiving Day. I spent the morning sightseeing at the Vatican and attending the special Mass in honor of the Cardinals who had died during the year. The pomp and ceremony of the Vatican is almost beyond description. I was seated with the diplomatic corps. Its Ambassadors wore ornate uniforms and the women wore black veils. It was terribly crowded.

The Pope seemed to have a tired voice and a tired face. Yet there was a spiritual quality to his voice unlike the litany that I have heard recited by Catholic clergy at home. I had to leave a little early in order to make my appointment with the President of Italy at noon.

President Gronchi is the man whom Ambassador Clare Boothe Luce fought so hard to defeat. She practically elected him because her opposition became known to most members of the Italian Parliament. They took great joy in cracking down on la Luce. Gronchi, though a staunch Catholic and an originator of the Catholic Action Party, is now quarreling with the Pope over his trip to Moscow. I asked him whether this would not increase the prestige of the Communist party in Italy and he replied, to the contrary, and that many other Italian leaders agreed with him on this point. I could find none who did, but then I was in Rome only a short time.

Gronchi spoke quite frankly, but unfortunately I was not permitted to quote him. His most interesting statement was that he planned to tell Eisenhower that the United States and Russia should get together to cooperate in foreign aid. He made the point that Russia was now getting credits from Western nations and that her aid to the underdeveloped countries would merely mean that she was competing with us by using in part borrowed Western funds.

Later, when I talked to Premier Segni and told him of Gronchi's idea, he replied: "The President of the Republic may have told you that, but that doesn't mean it will happen."

Afterward, Segni's press secretary ruled that I could not use this delicious statement. Segni looked tired. He is a little, birdlike man who had to sit all alone listening to the Communists and Socialists castigating his relief program. Italy is relatively prosperous, but still has about a million and a half unemployed.

I left at 8 P.M. on an Italian plane for Athens. It was a relief to be on a plane that started on time.

November 27: Arrived in Athens about 1 A.M. Called first upon Prime Minister Caramanlis, whom I had known before. He spoke quite frankly about the problem of "relaxing" and warned that once you have built up steam against Soviet Russia you can't afford to let it down by talking with Khrushchev. Once you have let down the bars you never can build them up again, he said.

The Prime Minister invited me to lunch down on the Aegean, which I accepted. I told him that I had been invited to lunch by the American Ambassador, so he suggested that I bring the Ambassador along. I hesitated about this because I figured that Caramanlis would not talk very frankly in front of an American official. However, Ellis Briggs, the Ambassador, was an old friend of mine so I invited him. I was right. Caramanlis was not too frank with Briggs present. While waiting for the Prime Minister we heard a crash and discovered later that he had tried to walk through a glass picture-door. He hurt his nose rather severely.

I also had a talk with Foreign Minister Everhoff, who told me in some detail how he had gotten together with the Turkish Foreign Minister in New York at the UN session last year, and they had decided to get sensible and quit this squabbling over the island of Cyprus.

I had requested an audience with the King, who had received me very graciously two years before. However, under the rules of protocol, this had to be referred to the American Embassy and some jerk at the Embassy apparently didn't want me to see the King. This jerk claimed that my name had been misspelled and they had to cable Washington for clearance.

November 29: Ankara reminds me of the old Muslim cities of Yugoslavia. The smell of dried cow dung burned in the stoves and fireplaces hangs over the atmosphere. The days of the fez are gone. Ataturk banned it. The streets are rather dusty. The air was wintry cold. But the Turks have built a tremendous metropolis with opera house and modern buildings in the city up in the hills. I thought to myself and hinted to my Turkish hosts that many of these buildings had been indirectly built with American foreign aid. Meanwhile, the capital of the United States has no opera house.

My interview with President Bayar was slated for 6 P.M. He is a very kindly old gentleman, but not brilliant, and I could understand why he gives no interviews. Mine was the first he has ever given. I had written the questions out in advance and he had carefully answered them. I learned afterward that he had dictated the answers himself.

I had had an interview earlier with Foreign Minister Zorin which was not too productive but which confirmed the story the Greek Foreign Minister told me about the settlement of Cyprus.

November 30: Perhaps I am superstitious, but I find it always pays to shave in airplanes when you have an early morning arrival. I was due to arrive in Tehran at seven-thirty, and so, because I slept a little late, I passed up the delicious breakfast KLM serves in favor of a shave. It was lucky I did.

An emissary from the Shah's palace was waiting at the airport and took me direct to the palace. We did not stop at a hotel. The palace is of green alabaster and sits in a royal park in which are other palaces and residences, amid gardens which at this season featured salvia and calendula. At the palace I was ushered in almost immediately to see the former Iranian Ambassador in Washington who is now Minister of Court, Houssein Ala. He remembered the crisis of 1946 when Russian troops were in northern Iran, ready to march on the entire country, and when I published this fact. Probably what he did not know was that Jimmie Byrnes, then Secretary of State, had not been too concerned over the matter and had not paid much attention to it. But Joe Panuch, one of his assistants, smuggled telegrams to me—telegrams which came from an American consul in northern Iran warning that Russian troops had been marching by in tremendous numbers in the night. When I published this it led to a special session of the United Nations and a demand that Russia withdraw its troops. This was the first indication immediately after the war that Stalin had militaristic designs on some of his neighbors. Caught in the act, he pulled back.

The Shah sat at a small desk inlaid with mother of pearl. He received me, however, at a separate side coffee table with two chairs around it, and offered me tea. Since I'd had no breakfast, I drank the tea. For some reason or other, tea makes me quite sick early in the morning. And on an empty stomach I felt a little worse than usual. However, I was under the compulsion of keeping my mind on the interview, since I've found it is usually disastrous to take notes; you have to make a mental picture of everything the interviewee is saying, then rush out and write it down as soon as possible.

The Shah spoke with fervor and eloquence about the problem of preventing Communism in his country, which he was doing by dividing up his land and forcing others to do likewise. The Shah has about two million acres and has given away approximately 700,000 already.

"Sixteen years ago," he said, "they called me a Communist. But you can't put a lot of wealth in the hands of a few with starvation conditions on the part of the many. Today I will set limitations on the private holdings of the big landowners." "This will get you a lot of criticism," I suggested. "Yes," he said, "but from about twenty people. What do they count as against twenty million?"

In many respects the Shah was the most intelligent man I had talked to so far—or at least the most progressive. He talked about many things, including the curtailment of opium which he said had brought a severe loss of revenue. However, the poppy fields of Iran had now been destroyed by law.

I flew to Karachi on a Pakistani plane. The plane was over an hour late. Why do these little countries insist on having their own airlines running all the way to London, when they neglect their local transportation at home?

The Karachi airport was bedlam. They speak English but have none of the efficiency of the English. A press relations officer from the Pakistani government finally met me with the bad news that President Ayub had gone to Rawalpindi to attend the wedding of his son in a nearby village and would not be able to see me. I said that I would be willing to go to Rawalpindi if they could set up an appointment and arrange for me to go to the nearby village. They seemed wholly frustrated at this idea. However, we went to the office of the airline to get a reservation to Rawalpindi and were told all the planes were booked solid.

December 1: Late last night I learned that an Ariana plane was leaving for Afghanistan at noon today. It was not supposed to leave today. It was supposed to leave one day later. But this is the plane which started out last week and never got to Kabul. So it's going whenever it can get there and prospective passengers are given no notice of departure. I stumbled onto it by accident. I also learned that it would be possible for me to take a Pakistani plane as far as Peshawar, possibly see President Ayub who is in a village nearby, then drive on to Kabul through the Khyber Pass. It's an eight-hour drive, and if it snows you can't get through the pass. On the other hand if the weather's bad you can't fly across the mountains. It's a tough alternative. Finally I decided to take the plane to Afghanistan.

I went to the airport but I never got the plane. We frittered around for a little while, then were told that the weather was bad in the mountains and the plane would not leave. I hurriedly tried to switch my ticket to the Pakistani plane to Peshawar due to leave in about five minutes. But no soap. I could see the plane on the runway but the officials said it was too late. Things don't move fast in this part of the world.

I went back to the hotel, called on the American Ambassador, who used to be Assistant Secretary of State for the Middle East, and who is no great inspiration, and then looked over the city of Karachi.

It is a conglomeration of English colonialism with Muslim backwardism, giving a final product which has none of the charm of Persia and none of the progress of Greece. Huge puddles of filthy water lay in front of the post office and telegraph building. They were more than puddles. They looked as if they had been excavated by pigs.

December 2:   Got up at about five-thirty to catch the 8 A.M. plane to Kabul. It was a DC-3 with no radar and no means of flying by radio beam. We landed at Kandahar, which nestles in a large valley. We had flown through one mountain pass, but still had a very difficult one ahead, and the airline informed us that as the clouds had settled, we would have to stay in Kandahar all night.

It was only about 11:30 A.M. and the prospects of the next twenty-four hours looked bleak. We might not be able to proceed the next day at all. We were told that the weather sometimes stayed this way for a week. It was possible to drive to Kabul, but this meant a twelve-hour trip over very bad roads. At this point a local ICA man, Morgan Holmes, introduced himself. He is building the big airport nearby. He offered to take me and two members of NBC under his wing—if necessary, drive us to Kabul in his Cadillac. Mr. Holmes proved a heaven-sent friend in time of trouble. He put us in the ICA [International Cooperation Administration] guest house where we occupied the suite used by General Quesada, head of the Federal Aviation Authority, the week before. It was a suite, but not a la Waldorf. One kerosene stove heated the sitting room where I slept. Nothing heated the bedroom where the NBC staff slept. The water was cold—very cold—when you tried to shave in the morning.

Holmes took us on a tour of the city and the surroundings.

We passed a big petroleum establishment half hidden under a hill. There were a series of big oil and gasoline tanks. Holmes said that the Russians had come in last summer and established this huge gasoline supply base, so that even though the United States built the airport and Pan American Airways runs the airlines, it must depend upon Russian gasoline. I noted Russian trucks at the airport fueling planes. Holmes took us to see his new airport. He is proud of it and should be. It is one of the most beautiful I have ever seen. He built most of the wartime airports in Alaska, some of those in the Pacific, and redesigned the National Airport in Washington. Airports are his job. He is so in love with this airport and with Afghanistan that he has signed up for another two years. He has one problem at the moment. He wants to build a mud wall around this airport to keep camal caravans and sheep from getting on it. But the local people want a wall made of stone or marble. They say such a beautiful runway should not be protected by a plebeian wall. A stone wall will cost around $120,000, a mud wall $30,000. Congress wants to save money. And because of this impasse there is no wall around the airport at all.

I wrote a column under the dateline "Kandahar" describing the clash of American and Russian forces. One of the NBC men remarked that this is probably the first cable in history written under a Kandahar dateline and actually cabled from the city. When I went to the cable office I found that he was right. Holmes had called up the cable office in advance and established the idea—he thought—that there would be no trouble sending the message as long as it arrived before eight o'clock. We got there about seven. But the telegraph operator, who was barefoot and who ran a very primitive hand Morse key, had no thought of sending the message till morning. It later developed that he had no thought of sending it at all—collect. He wanted to charge me for the entire message in advance and at full rates. He'd never heard of press rates. We argued and explained and cajoled. Finally we persuaded him to send for the director of communications—a rotund Muslim with a heavy girdle, ornate turban, and shoes. He was sympathetic but equally obdurate. Nothing could be done, he said. At this point we started to call on various people. It was 9 P.M. and the city of Kandahar closes down tight after sundown. Only the dogs and a few stragglers are on the streets. Finally I suggested that we go direct to the governor. He proved to be a very intelligent French-speaking bureaucrat sent down from Kabul. Without hesitation he said, "Your cable will be sent. Go back to your home and I will have the Minister of Communications call on you and pick up the cable. Don't worry about it any further."

We went back to Holmes's house, where I had some supper. During the supper, it then being 10 P.M., the telegraph operator, with the Minister of Communications and someone else, called, apologized for the delay, and picked up the cable. They promised it would be sent collect—though not until morning. I didn't argue about the latter point. I was relieved enough just to get the cable sent. It was approximately 800 words. It would have cost me two or three hundred dollars at their rate. And I never could have collected. I couldn't help wondering, however, whether the cable would ever go and ever be received.*

December 3: Up at about 5:30 for an 8 A.M. departure. Holmes was on deck to drive us to the airport, where we waited and waited and waited. In the interim he took us over to a school where thirty Filipino instructors are teaching about 250 Afghans how to be air navigators. They will handle the ground navigation for the airport system of Afghanistan. They were working in a half-finished building with no heat and in many cases no doors or windows. But they were working and working hard. Finally the plane took off at about 10 A.M. and we touched down at the big airport outside of Kabul at around 12 noon. During much of the flight we were in the clouds, but the clouds cleared up enough so that we were able to fly through the mountain pass and you could readily understand why the pilot was worried. To be off course a few hundred yards meant a crackup against one of the mountains.

We landed on a Russian-built airport. It is the airport Ike will have to land on. The chief of communications told me he had arranged for an appointment with the Prime Minister at 4:30 and with the King at 6. Meanwhile, the American Embassy sent word that all airplanes out of Kabul were canceled for tomorrow, but the Embassy has a courier

*It was, but when Drew got back to Washington he found that the State Department had sent a message to his office asking $86.00 in payment for the cable. Despite the effort, it still had not been sent collect, but the State Department had paid.—ED.

going by car at 3 A.M. for Peshawar. I could catch a plane from Peshawar to Lahore—if I can get aboard—and catch a train from Amritsar to New Delhi—if I make it in time. This is the only alternative if I'm going to keep my appointment with Nehru in New Delhi on Saturday at 11 A.M.

Hank Byroade is Ambassador here. I remember dropping in on him in the State Department when he finally decided to leave the Army and become a diplomat. He had been one of General Marshall's top brain-trusters and it was a hard decision for him to make. Later I was quite critical of him when he was Ambassador in Cairo and appeared to be pro-Nasser. When I called on him, he asked: "Have the Zionists in America forgiven me yet?" I asked him about a very famous, but still mysterious, incident when George Allen, an Assistant Secretary of State, had taken a special trip to Cairo to deliver a note to Nasser, serving a semi-ultimatum on Nasser regarding his anti-American policies. It was reported that Kermit Roosevelt, grandson of T.R., had called on Nasser first to explain that he shouldn't really take the Dulles note seriously.

Byroade refused to confirm that Kermit Roosevelt had been the man, but confirmed the fact that somebody had called on Nasser. His explanation was that word of the Dulles note had leaked to the Egyptian government, the Cabinet was up in arms, and there would have been riots against Americans had word of the note been published in the press. The situation was so tense that it had to be smoothed down, otherwise Nasser would not have received George Allen at all.

The interviews with the Prime Minister and the King were rather uneventful. The King of Afghanistan presented me with a prayer rug. It's beautiful, but will be hard to lug home.

The King made one significant statement about Russian relations. Unlike leaders of Turkey, Greece, and Pakistan, he wants to cooperate with Russia and thought the Khrushchev-Eisenhower talks were all to the good. Situated on the firing line, Afghanistan has to get along with its nearest and most powerful neighbor. However, in the rivalry between the U.S.A. and U.S.S.R. for influence in Afghanistan, the King said he thought the United States would be remembered more favorably because of its aid to education. The influence of the schoolroom, he said, is more important than the military.

December 4: We got under way in the Embassy car at about 3:15 A.M.; the American courier has two mailbags locked in the trunk. They contain secret reports of the American Embassy, otherwise known as the diplomatic pouch. I told him that he was in grave jeopardy because my specialty was publishing State Department secret documents.

At the first border outpost between Afghanistan and Pakistan, we stopped for passport inspection and tea. The American courier had to go to the bathroom. He unlocked the trunk, took out the two pouches, and carried them into the men's room. They would have been far safer in the car.

At the Khyber Pass we entered Pakistan officially. You begin to see the landmarks of the British Empire. The British always build well wherever they go. Bodily comfort comes first. The passport control offices are neat. The roads are shaded with trees. There is an efficient watering trough for the camels. I sneaked over to the watering trough to get a shot of about 100 camels, though it is forbidden to take pictures in the Khyber Pass.

We drove up and up through the pass. The road winds between little fortresses placed on every mountaintop. There are cement blocks in the valley to prevent jeeps from crashing through and there are concealed cannon placed behind camouflaged walls in the hillsides. Lone lookouts with rifles slung over their shoulders are along the highways. There should be no reason for these guards, but Afghanistan claims Pakistan has seized part of its territory. So when the United States sent jet fighters to the Pakistan army, the Afghans got MIG-17s from Russia. This in turn alarmed the Shah of Iran, who, fearing Russian MIGs might be aimed at him, in turn demanded more planes from the United States. The motto in foreign aid is, "One good plane deserves another."

We breakfasted on raw almonds which we purchased at a village market along the way. I also produced a couple of cakes of chocolate that Luvie put in my suitcase to be eaten in Formosa when she said Chiang Kai-shek might poison me! I was too hungry to wait for Formosa.

We arrived in Peshawar about noon, in ample time for the plane to Lahore. Peshawar was the chief military base of the British Army and still bears all the earmarks of British rule. There are neat parks, neat roads, neat clubs, and a neat hotel. The hotel, though now run by a Dutchman, serves stodgy British food and is just about as chilly as any hotel in London.

I had taken the precaution three days ago to get the reservation on the plane to Lahore, but there was no record of it at the Peshawar office of the Pakistani Airline. However, they finally let me aboard. The plane was a trifle late, and by the time we got to Lahore it was thirty minutes late. We corralled a taxi, threw the baggage into it, and started at breakneck speed through the crowded streets, dodging oxen and donkeys in a mad race to the Indian border and Amritsar.

The taxi driver did pretty well. We reached the border at 6 P.M. It had been closed since 5:30. This meant no interview with Nehru at 11:30 next morning, for there was no other possible way to get there. I started talking to the Pakistan authorities. They were quite sympathetic and agreed to let me across.

They stamped my passport and baggage and I started walking through that lonesome stretch of no man's land that separates all international boundaries. The Pakistanis and the Indians hate each other, so I hadn't told the Pakistanis that I was going to interview Nehru. I saved this as the trump card to be used on the Indians. But the Indians eyed me with the fishy skepticism of a U.S. immigration official scrutinizing a Chinese Communist who says he wants to interview President Eisenhower.

For half an hour I was kept waiting outside the huge gate that shuts India off from no man's land, while the minutes ticked away. The Frontier Mail, last train to New Delhi, was due to leave at 7:30.

Finally they let me in. Then I got a break. The Frontier Mail, I learned, did not leave at 7:30, but at 8:40. I asked immediately that they call a taxi to come out from Amritsar, supposedly fifteen minutes away.

Then proceeded the most detailed cross-examination and inspection I have ever had. Last year I entered Czechoslovakia, Hungary, and Rumania, all Communist countries. Their border inspection was brief and easy compared with that of friendly India.

I explained that I had an appointment to meet the Prime Minister of India. It made no difference. They still wanted to know why I carried two watches, how much money I had on me, what I was doing with an Afghan prayer rug. It took almost an hour to satisfy the meticulous bureaucrats at the Indian border. Meanwhile I had been asking them about the taxi that was supposed to come out from Amritsar. They assured me it had been ordered, but I suspect it hadn't; because it didn't put in an appearance until 8:25 P.M., with the train due to leave at 8:40.

I got on the phone to the Amritsar stationmaster and asked him to hold the train. He said he would. My baggage was piled into the taxi and we sped off. Down the tree-lined, deserted highway through the tropical night we raced at breakneck speed. The driver did his best. However, the station was not fifteen minutes, but thirty minutes away and we arrived at 9 P.M.

The last train to New Delhi had departed.

December 5: The only way I could keep my appointment with Nehru was to drive all night, and I made inquiries about taxis. It didn't look promising. It was a ten-hour drive and the taxis were old. Finally I started out in what was described as a "good taxi." My suspicions were aroused when I found it cranked by hand. I became more suspicious when I found the driver bought only five gallons of gas for a ten-hour trip, and even more so when I saw our top speed was only thirty miles an hour. I ordered him back to town.

Eventually I learned that two men connected with the U.S. Information Service were planning to drive a truck loaded with USIS equipment to New Delhi the next morning. So at 1:30 A.M. I woke them up and asked if they wouldn't like to get started a little early.

There's a lot of difference between 1:30 A.M. and 7 A.M., but they didn't hesitate. They got dressed and we left for Delhi soon after two.

Mr. Veal Parkash Setti and Mr. Basil A. Martyr had been showing a movie, *Not by Bread Alone,* to Indian audiences all week in the neighborhood of Amritsar. Their truck, loaded with motion picture equipment and other gear, was heavy. But I have never seen more expert or willing drivers, nor did anyone ever have a more grateful passenger.

We went thundering through the Indian night, miraculously avoiding bullock carts, donkeys, and pedestrians; shortly after sunup we arrived in New Delhi. I even had time to shave before going to see Prime Minister Nehru.

I interviewed Nehru at his circular desk in the Ministry of External Affairs. Except for the one photo on it of Mahatma Gandhi, it was the desk of a Madison Avenue executive. The man behind it, however, bore no resemblance to Madison Avenue. His was a gentle face with eyes that had a sad and distant look.

I told the Prime Minister that the many presidents, prime ministers, and potentates I had interviewed in advance of Eisenhower were worried that his talks with Khrushchev would relax the cold war and let down the safeguards of the Free World. What was his opinion, I asked.

"I think you know what my view is, Mr. Pearson," Nehru replied. "Atomic war has become so catastrophic it has made peace a necessity. It may be a blessing. I think the world has reached a turning point. It has reached a turning point in many respects—in human relations, in science, and in regard to war. We have got to go forward to greater and broader horizons. I am sure Mr. Eisenhower senses this too, and that was behind his talks with Premier Khrushchev.

"But to work for better understanding," Nehru added carefully, "does not mean we shut our eyes to the needs of national defense."

I told Nehru many Western diplomats felt the hand of fate had intervened to put Eisenhower in the same position Nehru once had been in, with Ike now a neutralist between India and China.

Nehru smiled, but did not answer directly. He said he had read Eisenhower's recent statement indicating his neutrality between India and China and also Secretary of State Herter's. "I commented at the time," he said, "that Mr. Herter was a friend of ours and we saw no objection to his statement."

"Did you ever get any explanation from Washington as to why Herter made that statement of neutrality?" I asked.

When the Prime Minister replied in the negative, I told him my information was that Khrushchev and Eisenhower had reached an agreement that neither would make any statements calculated to rock the delicate Chinese relations and that Khrushchev in return promised to pacify Red China. "Did you get any information as to what Khrushchev was able to accomplish when he went to Peking?" I asked.

"Our Ambassador to Peking sent us a report that indicated they treated him rather badly," Nehru replied. "At about that time one of the Soviet Cabinet members—I believe he is an Armenian with a very difficult name, Mukhitdinov—came through here on his way to Indonesia and told me that Khrushchev had asked him to give me a full report on his conversations with Eisenhower, which he did. At that time he was most anxious to ascertain what success Khrushchev was having in Peking. Apparently he didn't get very far."

"Was it your impression from that report that Eisenhower and Khrushchev really reached some basis of understanding?" I asked.

"Definitely," the Prime Minister replied.

Discussing Chinese motives in invading northern India, Nehru said, "The Chinese are not easy to understand. They speak few foreign languages, make little effort to know the outside world. But they never forget a claim. They never forgot their claim to Tibet and they waited until the time was propitious to take it.

"If India never forgot its ancient claims we would be moving all over the Middle East. I suppose our reaction to their invasion of Tibet touched them off and they moved on to India."

Nehru will tell Ike that for this winter no developments are likely in the disputed area the Chinese have seized. "Winter has set in and it's a sort of deep-freeze up there. You can't move," he said. "I know," I replied. "I just came from Afghanistan."

"But the mountains the Chinese invaded are far higher than the ones you crossed from Afghanistan," Nehru corrected. "They make it difficult for us to defend the area. At the same time it will be difficult for the Chinese to descend on India."

Nehru doesn't plan to ask Eisenhower for military aid, despite the Indian public's clamor for action. Economic aid is more important, and he intends to wait out the current trouble.

"It's quite understandable the Chinese would pop across our border from time to time," he said philosophically, "but it's highly doubtful that China would invade India proper."

Ordinarily that would be the end of the story. But it isn't. The interview, as most with Nehru, was fully worth the 800-mile drive from Afghanistan. I wrote it up and sent it to the Indian telegraph office. It came back. My press card, hitherto valid in every country of the world, was not good in India. I had to get a special press card. But it was Saturday and I couldn't get one until Monday.

I went to the Minister of Information, O. I. Rahman. He reminded me that I had done India a great favor. He had been in Washington during the war when I had published the secret report of Presidential Envoy William Phillips recommending independence for India.

"You were of great help in getting us independence," he said.

"Then you can be of great help in getting this cable sent," I suggested.

The Minister picked up various telephones, called various people.

We sat almost an hour while he called people regarding the simple matter of reversing charges on a press telegram, which in most countries would take five minutes. In India everyone passed the buck.

Finally I said: "You have just said I was of some help in hastening Indian independence. Now I am trying to send a cable about your Prime Minister. It's a good interview and will help Indian-American relations. Yet your government throws up enough red tape to make me wonder whether you deserved independence. Why don't you have one of your assistants get in the car with me and go to the cable office and we'll send the cable?"

Mr. Rahman complied. But this again does not quite end the story. Americans, I found, can be just as inefficient as Indians. My syndicate in New York had neglected to arrange for the relay of the cable, so the interview with Nehru, despite a long drive from Afghanistan to get it, did not get published until two days later.

A Note to the Index

Considerable thought was given to the best way to treat the problem of identifying the people mentioned in the diary. The editor was aware that for many readers, these names are too familiar to warrant further identification; yet, other younger readers may need some additional information. Consistency was also a problem. Some names are of less than passing interest, while others are quite literally household words. Whether to limit identification only to the period covered in this volume was another question. Also, to be consistent and identify all of the names in the diary would have required a volume approaching *Who's Who* in length.

In the end, Drew Pearson's own work provided the best approach. In most instances, he himself included identification within the entries; as people changed positions, the entries record such changes. Thus, the index that follows offers no identifications. Instead, each name listing is followed by a parenthetical insertion giving the date of the diary entry—or entries in the case of changes—in which the identification occurs.

Finally, there are some cases in which such insertions have been omitted. First, where the person, though prominent, is mentioned only in passing; second, where the person is obscure and does not figure in any significant way in the diary; third, where the person is of such consequence no identification is required; and fourth, where the person, though identified in the text, appears only once in the diary.

INDEX

Tues Feb 7

— went to dinner with Jim Barnes. When I went in I noticed Jim looked glum, But I didn't see anyone in the room I ought to drink. However, pretty soon in came Sam Rayburn. I had just written how Sam had pushed the gas bill through by subsidizing Congressmen, including Geo. Miller to the tune of 2,500 etc. Sam came up to me however & said: "George Miller's going to see you, but I trying to persuade him not to." He was, as usual, as comfortable as an old shoe. Later we talked about Kefauver & Stevenson. He was still bitter against Estes, said the south would never take him. That he wouldn't even consider him for VP. He doesn't like Stevenson too much, thinks he'll probably wash out, & that HST isn't for him — I'm a deadlock his for Symington, never Kefauver.

June 8, 56— Eisenhower was taken sick last night. The White House announced acute indigestion, but then carted him off to Walter Reed, which is not what you do with acute indigestion. I had to re-write a whole column on Noble-to-people friendship or rather junk it. I don't see how the Reps. can possibly run Ike now, though they may try to prop him up and make him last through the campaign.

June 9 — Ike was operated on at 3 AM for suspected malignant Tumor. They didn't announce it as such; rather as partial obstruction of small intestine. Took